The CERN Large Hadron Collider:

Accelerator and Experiments

Volume 2: CMS, LHCb, LHCf, and TOTEM

Edited by Amos Breskin and Rüdiger Voss

CERN
Geneva
2009

First published electronically as 2008 JINST 3 S08001- S08007

http://www.iop.org/EJ/journal/-page=extra.lhc/jinst

Printed in agreement with IOP Publishing Ltd and SISSA Medialab

To cite individual articles from this book, the original JINST reference printed on the right margin of each page should be used

ISBN: 978-92-9083-336-9 (Volumes 1 and 2)
ISBN: 978-92-9083-337-6 (Volume 1)
ISBN: 978-92-9083-338-3 (Volume 2)

Printed and bound in Norway by AIT Otta AS

Printed on 90g/m^2 Tom & Otto Silk Bulk 0,86

1st printing produced in 10.000 copies

Distributed by:
        The Scientific Information Service
        CERN
        1211 Geneva, Switzerland
        library.desk@cern.ch

Preface

The publication of these two volumes coincides with a turning point in the history of CERN. Just days before going to print, the Large Hadron Collider was successfully restarted, established a new world record for laboratory-produced particle energies, and achieved the first proton-proton collisions, which were duly recorded by the experiments. These successes mark the first culmination of a process that started with the historic "ECFA-CERN Workshop on a Large Hadron Collider in the LEP Tunnel" held at Lausanne University and CERN in March 1984. After more than 25 years of brainstorming, design, research, development and construction, the LHC is poised to reap the benefits of a visionary and courageous investment, and to open a new chapter in our understanding of the universe.

The Large Hadron Collider and the six LHC detectors together form a scientific instrument of unprecedented complexity, potential, and promise. In an equally unprecedented move, more than 8000 physicists and engineers have teamed up in a concerted effort to provide the scientific community with a comprehensive documentation of this technological marvel. The seven articles collected in this book will serve as central references for the stream of scientific publications that we expect to emerge from experiments with the LHC over the next 10 – 20 years. They will be equally important to introduce future generations of young scientists to the secrets of conducting physics research with the LHC.

Following extensive peer review, these articles were first published in the *Journal of Instrumentation* (JINST) in August 2008. The focus on electronic publication, and the deliberate choice of a Web-based journal that is free to read for all, reflect CERN's strong commitment to Open Access publishing, and to facilitating the widest possible dissemination of results from the LHC to the scientific and general public. At the same time, it was felt that a print edition would be important both as an appropriate way of marking the completion of accelerator and detector construction, and as a resource for all scientists actively concerned with research at the LHC.

The success of the predecessor project to the LHC, the Large Electron-Positron Collider LEP installed in the same accelerator tunnel, was built on a culture of collaboration that combined elements of friendly competition with a common vision of scientific goals and achievements. The book that we have in front of us today has been prepared in the very same spirit. The success of this unique publication project bodes well for the success of future competition and collaboration at the LHC.

December 2009
Rolf-Dieter Heuer
CERN Director-General

Note by the editors

The articles in this compilation were first published as peer-reviewed papers in electronic form in the *Journal of Instrumentation* (JINST) on August 14, 2008 (http://www.iop.org/EJ/journal/-page=extra.lhc/jinst). They document the status of the accelerator and the experiments as built at the time of the first start-up of the LHC in September 2008. After a few days only, the start-up was disrupted by a major technical incident in the LHC accelerator, which led to a shutdown of more than one year to repair material damage and to upgrade essential diagnostics and safety systems. This shutdown was also used by the experiments to install missing detector components, and for extensive commissioning with cosmic rays. Upgrades and improvements of the accelerator and the detectors carried out between September 2008 and the LHC restart in November 2009 are not covered in this book. Large particle accelerators and detectors are dynamic entities, subject to constant improvement and refinement in order to benefit from technological advances and practical operating experience. Such past and future upgrades may become the subject of separate publications in the scientific literature.

The articles in this book are a testimony to the dedication, perseverance and ingenuity of thousands of scientists and engineers, many of which appear as authors on the following pages. While we cannot thank each of them individually, we should like to acknowledge the hard work of our colleagues who have coordinated this publication project within their respective teams and with the editors in a truly collaborative spirit: Phil Bryant, Lyn Evans and Cecile Noëls (LHC); Hans-Åke Gustafsson and Jürgen Schukraft (ALICE); Daniel Froidevaux and Manuella Vincter (ATLAS); Roberto Tenchini and Jim Virdee (CMS); Elie Aslanides and Clara Matteuzzi (LHCb); Daniela Macina (LHCf); Mario Deile (TOTEM); Gigi Rolandi (CERN Scientific Information Policy Board); Jens Vigen, Salvatore Mele and their team from the CERN

Scientific Information Service; and Enrico Balli and his colleagues from the Editorial Office of JINST at SISSA Medialab in Trieste. We also wish to thank the CERN Management for constant support.

Last but not least, we are grateful to the referees who, faithful to the traditions of scientific publishing, must remain anonymous but who all invested substantial amounts of time in reviewing these complex papers with diligence and in great detail. Their comments and corrections have been extremely valuable, and instrumental in shaping these publications into their final form.

Weizmann Institute, Rehovot, Israel, and CERN, Geneva, Switzerland, December 2009
Amos Breskin and Rüdiger Voss

Contents of Volume 1:

Contents of Volume 2:

PUBLISHED BY INSTITUTE OF PHYSICS PUBLISHING AND SISSA

RECEIVED: *January 9, 2008*
ACCEPTED: *May 18, 2008*
PUBLISHED: *August 14, 2008*

THE CERN LARGE HADRON COLLIDER: ACCELERATOR AND EXPERIMENTS

The CMS experiment at the CERN LHC

CMS Collaboration

ABSTRACT: The Compact Muon Solenoid (CMS) detector is described. The detector operates at the Large Hadron Collider (LHC) at CERN. It was conceived to study proton-proton (and lead-lead) collisions at a centre-of-mass energy of 14 TeV (5.5 TeV nucleon-nucleon) and at luminosities up to 10^{34} cm^{-2}s^{-1} (10^{27} cm^{-2}s^{-1}). At the core of the CMS detector sits a high-magnetic-field and large-bore superconducting solenoid surrounding an all-silicon pixel and strip tracker, a lead-tungstate scintillating-crystals electromagnetic calorimeter, and a brass-scintillator sampling hadron calorimeter. The iron yoke of the flux-return is instrumented with four stations of muon detectors covering most of the 4π solid angle. Forward sampling calorimeters extend the pseudo-rapidity coverage to high values ($|\eta| \leq 5$) assuring very good hermeticity. The overall dimensions of the CMS detector are a length of 21.6 m, a diameter of 14.6 m and a total weight of 12500 t.

KEYWORDS: Instrumentation for particle accelerators and storage rings - high energy; Gaseous detectors; Scintillators, scintillation and light emission processes; Solid state detectors; Calorimeters; Gamma detectors; Large detector systems for particle and astroparticle physics; Particle identification methods; Particle tracking detectors; Spectrometers; Analogue electronic circuits; Control and monitor systems online; Data acquisition circuits; Data acquisition concepts; Detector control systems; Digital electronic circuits; Digital signal processing; Electronic detector readout concepts; Front-end electronics for detector readout; Modular electronics; Online farms and online filtering; Optical detector readout concepts; Trigger concepts and systems; VLSI circuits; Analysis and statistical methods; Computing; Data processing methods; Data reduction methods; Pattern recognition, cluster finding, calibration and fitting methods; Software architectures; Detector alignment and calibration methods; Detector cooling and thermo-stabilization; Detector design and construction technologies and materials; Detector grounding; Manufacturing; Overall mechanics design; Special cables; Voltage distributions.

2008 JINST 3 S08004

CMS Collaboration

Yerevan Physics Institute, Yerevan, Armenia

S. Chatrchyan, G. Hmayakyan, V. Khachatryan, A.M. Sirunyan

Institut für Hochenergiephysik der OeAW, Wien, Austria

W. Adam, T. Bauer, T. Bergauer, H. Bergauer, M. Dragicevic, J. Erö, M. Friedl, R. Frühwirth, V.M. Ghete, P. Glaser, C. Hartl, N. Hoermann, J. Hrubec, S. Hänsel, M. Jeitler, K. Kastner, M. Krammer, I. Magrans de Abril, M. Markytan, I. Mikulec, B. Neuherz, T. Nöbauer, M. Oberegger, M. Padrta, M. Pernicka, P. Porth, H. Rohringer, S. Schmid, T. Schreiner, R. Stark, H. Steininger, J. Strauss, A. Taurok, D. Uhl, W. Waltenberger, G. Walzel, E. Widl, C.-E. Wulz

Byelorussian State University, Minsk, Belarus

V. Petrov, V. Prosolovich

National Centre for Particle and High Energy Physics, Minsk, Belarus

V. Chekhovsky, O. Dvornikov, I. Emeliantchik, A. Litomin, V. Makarenko, I. Marfin, V. Mossolov, N. Shumeiko, A. Solin, R. Stefanovitch, J. Suarez Gonzalez, A. Tikhonov

Research Institute for Nuclear Problems, Minsk, Belarus

A. Fedorov, M. Korzhik, O. Missevitch, R. Zuyeuski

Universiteit Antwerpen, Antwerpen, Belgium

W. Beaumont, M. Cardaci, E. De Langhe, E.A. De Wolf, E. Delmeire, S. Ochesanu, M. Tasevsky, P. Van Mechelen

Vrije Universiteit Brussel, Brussel, Belgium

J. D'Hondt, S. De Weirdt, O. Devroede, R. Goorens, S. Hannaert, J. Heyninck, J. Maes, M.U. Mozer, S. Tavernier, W. Van Doninck,[1] L. Van Lancker, P. Van Mulders, I. Villella, C. Wastiels, C. Yu

Université Libre de Bruxelles, Bruxelles, Belgium

O. Bouhali, O. Charaf, B. Clerbaux, P. De Harenne, G. De Lentdecker, J.P. Dewulf, S. Elgammal, R. Gindroz, G.H. Hammad, T. Mahmoud, L. Neukermans, M. Pins, R. Pins, S. Rugovac, J. Stefanescu, V. Sundararajan, C. Vander Velde, P. Vanlaer, J. Wickens

2008 JINST 3 S08004

Ghent University, Ghent, Belgium
M. Tytgat

Université Catholique de Louvain, Louvain-la-Neuve, Belgium
S. Assouak, J.L. Bonnet, G. Bruno, J. Caudron, B. De Callatay, J. De Favereau De Jeneret, S. De Visscher, P. Demin, D. Favart, C. Felix, B. Florins, E. Forton, A. Giammanco, G. Grégoire, M. Jonckman, D. Kcira, T. Keutgen, V. Lemaitre, D. Michotte, O. Militaru, S. Ovyn, T. Pierzchala, K. Piotrzkowski, V. Roberfroid, X. Rouby, N. Schul, O. Van der Aa

Université de Mons-Hainaut, Mons, Belgium
N. Beliy, E. Daubie, P. Herquet

Centro Brasileiro de Pesquisas Fisicas, Rio de Janeiro, Brazil
G. Alves, M.E. Pol, M.H.G. Souza

Instituto de Fisica - Universidade Federal do Rio de Janeiro, Rio de Janeiro, Brazil
M. Vaz

Universidade do Estado do Rio de Janeiro, Rio de Janeiro, Brazil
D. De Jesus Damiao, V. Oguri, A. Santoro, A. Sznajder

Instituto de Fisica Teorica-Universidade Estadual Paulista, Sao Paulo, Brazil
E. De Moraes Gregores,[2] R.L. Iope, S.F. Novaes, T. Tomei

Institute for Nuclear Research and Nuclear Energy, Sofia, Bulgaria
T. Anguelov, G. Antchev, I. Atanasov, J. Damgov, N. Darmenov,[1] L. Dimitrov, V. Genchev,[1] P. Iaydjiev, A. Marinov, S. Piperov, S. Stoykova, G. Sultanov, R. Trayanov, I. Vankov

University of Sofia, Sofia, Bulgaria
C. Cheshkov, A. Dimitrov, M. Dyulendarova, I. Glushkov, V. Kozhuharov, L. Litov, M. Makariev, E. Marinova, S. Markov, M. Mateev, I. Nasteva, B. Pavlov, P. Petev, P. Petkov, V. Spassov, Z. Toteva,[1] V. Velev, V. Verguilov

Institute of High Energy Physics, Beijing, China
J.G. Bian, G.M. Chen, H.S. Chen, M. Chen, C.H. Jiang, B. Liu, X.Y. Shen, H.S. Sun, J. Tao, J. Wang, M. Yang, Z. Zhang, W.R. Zhao, H.L. Zhuang

Peking University, Beijing, China
Y. Ban, J. Cai, Y.C. Ge, S. Liu, H.T. Liu, L. Liu, S.J. Qian, Q. Wang, Z.H. Xue, Z.C. Yang, Y.L. Ye, J. Ying

2008 JINST 3 S08004

Shanghai Institute of Ceramics, Shanghai, China (Associated Institute)
P.J. Li, J. Liao, Z.L. Xue, D.S. Yan, H. Yuan

Universidad de Los Andes, Bogota, Colombia
C.A. Carrillo Montoya, J.C. Sanabria

Technical University of Split, Split, Croatia
N. Godinovic, I. Puljak, I. Soric

University of Split, Split, Croatia
Z. Antunovic, M. Dzelalija, K. Marasovic

Institute Rudjer Boskovic, Zagreb, Croatia
V. Brigljevic, K. Kadija, S. Morovic

University of Cyprus, Nicosia, Cyprus
R. Fereos, C. Nicolaou, A. Papadakis, F. Ptochos, P.A. Razis, D. Tsiakkouri, Z. Zinonos

National Institute of Chemical Physics and Biophysics, Tallinn, Estonia
A. Hektor, M. Kadastik, K. Kannike, E. Lippmaa, M. Müntel, M. Raidal, L. Rebane

Laboratory of Advanced Energy Systems,
Helsinki University of Technology, Espoo, Finland
P.A. Aarnio

Helsinki Institute of Physics, Helsinki, Finland
E. Anttila, K. Banzuzi, P. Bulteau, S. Czellar, N. Eiden, C. Eklund, P. Engstrom,[1] A. Heikkinen,
A. Honkanen, J. Härkönen, V. Karimäki, H.M. Katajisto, R. Kinnunen, J. Klem, J. Kortesmaa,[1]
M. Kotamäki, A. Kuronen,[1] T. Lampén, K. Lassila-Perini, V. Lefébure, S. Lehti, T. Lindén,
P.R. Luukka, S. Michal,[1] F. Moura Brigido, T. Mäenpää, T. Nyman, J. Nystén, E. Pietarinen,
K. Skog, K. Tammi, E. Tuominen, J. Tuominiemi, D. Ungaro, T.P. Vanhala, L. Wendland,
C. Williams

Lappeenranta University of Technology, Lappeenranta, Finland
M. Iskanius, A. Korpela, G. Polese,[1] T. Tuuva

Laboratoire d'Annecy-le-Vieux de Physique des Particules,
IN2P3-CNRS, Annecy-le-Vieux, France
G. Bassompierre, A. Bazan, P.Y. David, J. Ditta, G. Drobychev, N. Fouque, J.P. Guillaud, V. Hermel, A. Karneyeu, T. Le Flour, S. Lieunard, M. Maire, P. Mendiburu, P. Nedelec, J.P. Peigneux,
M. Schneegans, D. Sillou, J.P. Vialle

2008 JINST 3 S08004

DSM/DAPNIA, CEA/Saclay, Gif-sur-Yvette, France

M. Anfreville, J.P. Bard, P. Besson,* E. Bougamont, M. Boyer, P. Bredy, R. Chipaux, M. Dejardin, D. Denegri, J. Descamps, B. Fabbro, J.L. Faure, S. Ganjour, F.X. Gentit, A. Givernaud, P. Gras, G. Hamel de Monchenault, P. Jarry, C. Jeanney, F. Kircher, M.C. Lemaire, Y. Lemoigne, B. Levesy,[1] E. Locci, J.P. Lottin, I. Mandjavidze, M. Mur, J.P. Pansart, A. Payn, J. Rander, J.M. Reymond, J. Rolquin, F. Rondeaux, A. Rosowsky, J.Y.A. Rousse, Z.H. Sun, J. Tartas, A. Van Lysebetten, P. Venault, P. Verrecchia

Laboratoire Leprince-Ringuet, Ecole Polytechnique, IN2P3-CNRS, Palaiseau, France

M. Anduze, J. Badier, S. Baffioni, M. Bercher, C. Bernet, U. Berthon, J. Bourotte, A. Busata, P. Busson, M. Cerutti, D. Chamont, C. Charlot, C. Collard,[3] A. Debraine, D. Decotigny, L. Dobrzynski, O. Ferreira, Y. Geerebaert, J. Gilly, C. Gregory,* L. Guevara Riveros, M. Haguenauer, A. Karar, B. Koblitz, D. Lecouturier, A. Mathieu, G. Milleret, P. Miné, P. Paganini, P. Poilleux, N. Pukhaeva, N. Regnault, T. Romanteau, I. Semeniouk, Y. Sirois, C. Thiebaux, J.C. Vanel, A. Zabi[4]

Institut Pluridisciplinaire Hubert Curien, IN2P3-CNRS, Université Louis Pasteur Strasbourg, France, and Université de Haute Alsace Mulhouse, Strasbourg, France

J.L. Agram,[5] A. Albert,[5] L. Anckenmann, J. Andrea, F. Anstotz,[6] A.M. Bergdolt, J.D. Berst, R. Blaes,[5] D. Bloch, J.M. Brom, J. Cailleret, F. Charles,* E. Christophel, G. Claus, J. Coffin, C. Colledani, J. Croix, E. Dangelser, N. Dick, F. Didierjean, F. Drouhin[1,5], W. Dulinski, J.P. Ernenwein,[5] R. Fang, J.C. Fontaine,[5] G. Gaudiot, W. Geist, D. Gelé, T. Goeltzenlichter, U. Goerlach,[6] P. Graehling, L. Gross, C. Guo Hu, J.M. Helleboid, T. Henkes, M. Hoffer, C. Hoffmann, J. Hosselet, L. Houchu, Y. Hu,[6] D. Huss,[6] C. Illinger, F. Jeanneau, P. Juillot, T. Kachelhoffer, M.R. Kapp, H. Kettunen, L. Lakehal Ayat, A.C. Le Bihan, A. Lounis,[6] C. Maazouzi, V. Mack, P. Majewski, D. Mangeol, J. Michel,[6] S. Moreau, C. Olivetto, A. Pallarès,[5] Y. Patois, P. Pralavorio, C. Racca, Y. Riahi, I. Ripp-Baudot, P. Schmitt, J.P. Schunck, G. Schuster, B. Schwaller, M.H. Sigward, J.L. Sohler, J. Speck, R. Strub, T. Todorov, R. Turchetta, P. Van Hove, D. Vintache, A. Zghiche

Institut de Physique Nucléaire, IN2P3-CNRS, Université Claude Bernard Lyon 1, Villeurbanne, France

M. Ageron, J.E. Augustin, C. Baty, G. Baulieu, M. Bedjidian, J. Blaha, A. Bonnevaux, G. Boudoul, P. Brunet, E. Chabanat, E.C. Chabert, R. Chierici, V. Chorowicz, C. Combaret, D. Contardo,[1] R. Della Negra, P. Depasse, O. Drapier, M. Dupanloup, T. Dupasquier, H. El Mamouni, N. Estre, J. Fay, S. Gascon, N. Giraud, C. Girerd, G. Guillot, R. Haroutunian, B. Ille, M. Lethuillier, N. Lumb, C. Martin, H. Mathez, G. Maurelli, S. Muanza, P. Pangaud, S. Perries, O. Ravat, E. Schibler, F. Schirra, G. Smadja, S. Tissot, B. Trocme, S. Vanzetto, J.P. Walder

Institute of High Energy Physics and Informatization, Tbilisi State University, Tbilisi, Georgia

Y. Bagaturia, D. Mjavia, A. Mzhavia, Z. Tsamalaidze

Institute of Physics Academy of Science, Tbilisi, Georgia
V. Roinishvili

RWTH Aachen University, I. Physikalisches Institut, Aachen, Germany
R. Adolphi, G. Anagnostou, R. Brauer, W. Braunschweig, H. Esser, L. Feld, W. Karpinski, A. Khomich, K. Klein, C. Kukulies, K. Lübelsmeyer, J. Olzem, A. Ostaptchouk, D. Pandoulas, G. Pierschel, F. Raupach, S. Schael, A. Schultz von Dratzig, G. Schwering, R. Siedling, M. Thomas, M. Weber, B. Wittmer, M. Wlochal

RWTH Aachen University, III. Physikalisches Institut A, Aachen, Germany
F. Adamczyk, A. Adolf, G. Altenhöfer, S. Bechstein, S. Bethke, P. Biallass, O. Biebel, M. Bontenackels, K. Bosseler, A. Böhm, M. Erdmann, H. Faissner,[*] B. Fehr, H. Fesefeldt, G. Fetchenhauer,[1] J. Frangenheim, J.H. Frohn, J. Grooten, T. Hebbeker, S. Hermann, E. Hermens, G. Hilgers, K. Hoepfner, C. Hof, E. Jacobi, S. Kappler, M. Kirsch, P. Kreuzer, R. Kupper, H.R. Lampe, D. Lanske,[*] R. Mameghani, A. Meyer, S. Meyer, T. Moers, E. Müller, R. Pahlke, B. Philipps, D. Rein, H. Reithler, W. Reuter, P. Rütten, S. Schulz, H. Schwarthoff, W. Sobek, M. Sowa, T. Stapelberg, H. Szczesny, H. Teykal, D. Teyssier, H. Tomme, W. Tomme, M. Tonutti, O. Tsigenov, J. Tutas,[*] J. Vandenhirtz, H. Wagner, M. Wegner, C. Zeidler

RWTH Aachen University, III. Physikalisches Institut B, Aachen, Germany
F. Beissel, M. Davids, M. Duda, G. Flügge, M. Giffels, T. Hermanns, D. Heydhausen, S. Kalinin, S. Kasselmann, G. Kaussen, T. Kress, A. Linn, A. Nowack, L. Perchalla, M. Poettgens, O. Pooth, P. Sauerland, A. Stahl, D. Tornier, M.H. Zoeller

Deutsches Elektronen-Synchrotron, Hamburg, Germany
U. Behrens, K. Borras, A. Flossdorf, D. Hatton, B. Hegner, M. Kasemann, R. Mankel, A. Meyer, J. Mnich, C. Rosemann, C. Youngman, W.D. Zeuner[1]

University of Hamburg, Institute for Experimental Physics,
Hamburg, Germany
F. Bechtel, P. Buhmann, E. Butz, G. Flucke, R.H. Hamdorf, U. Holm, R. Klanner, U. Pein, N. Schirm, P. Schleper, G. Steinbrück, R. Van Staa, R. Wolf

Institut für Experimentelle Kernphysik, Karlsruhe, Germany
B. Atz, T. Barvich, P. Blüm, F. Boegelspacher, H. Bol, Z.Y. Chen, S. Chowdhury, W. De Boer, P. Dehm, G. Dirkes, M. Fahrer, U. Felzmann, M. Frey, A. Furgeri, E. Gregoriev, F. Hartmann,[1] F. Hauler, S. Heier, K. Kärcher, B. Ledermann, S. Mueller, Th. Müller, D. Neuberger, C. Piasecki, G. Quast, K. Rabbertz, A. Sabellek, A. Scheurer, F.P. Schilling, H.J. Simonis, A. Skiba, P. Steck, A. Theel, W.H. Thümmel, A. Trunov, A. Vest, T. Weiler, C. Weiser, S. Weseler,[*] V. Zhukov[7]

Institute of Nuclear Physics "Demokritos", Aghia Paraskevi, Greece
M. Barone, G. Daskalakis, N. Dimitriou, G. Fanourakis, C. Filippidis, T. Geralis, C. Kalfas, K. Karafasoulis, A. Koimas, A. Kyriakis, S. Kyriazopoulou, D. Loukas, A. Markou, C. Markou,

2008 JINST 3 S08004

N. Mastroyiannopoulos, C. Mavrommatis, J. Mousa, I. Papadakis, E. Petrakou, I. Siotis, K. Theofilatos, S. Tzamarias, A. Vayaki, G. Vermisoglou, A. Zachariadou

University of Athens, Athens, Greece

L. Gouskos, G. Karapostoli, P. Katsas, A. Panagiotou, C. Papadimitropoulos

University of Ioánnina, Ioánnina, Greece

X. Aslanoglou, I. Evangelou, P. Kokkas, N. Manthos, I. Papadopoulos, F.A. Triantis

KFKI Research Institute for Particle and Nuclear Physics, Budapest, Hungary

G. Bencze,[1] L. Boldizsar, G. Debreczeni, C. Hajdu,[1] P. Hidas, D. Horvath,[8] P. Kovesarki, A. Laszlo, G. Odor, G. Patay, F. Sikler, G. Veres, G. Vesztergombi, P. Zalan

Institute of Nuclear Research ATOMKI, Debrecen, Hungary

A. Fenyvesi, J. Imrek, J. Molnar, D. Novak, J. Palinkas, G. Szekely

University of Debrecen, Debrecen, Hungary

N. Beni, A. Kapusi, G. Marian, B. Radics, P. Raics, Z. Szabo, Z. Szillasi,[1] Z.L. Trocsanyi, G. Zilizi

Panjab University, Chandigarh, India

H.S. Bawa, S.B. Beri, V. Bhandari, V. Bhatnagar, M. Kaur, J.M. Kohli, A. Kumar, B. Singh, J.B. Singh

University of Delhi, Delhi, India

S. Arora, S. Bhattacharya,[9] S. Chatterji, S. Chauhan, B.C. Choudhary, P. Gupta, M. Jha, K. Ranjan, R.K. Shivpuri, A.K. Srivastava

Bhabha Atomic Research Centre, Mumbai, India

R.K. Choudhury, D. Dutta, M. Ghodgaonkar, S. Kailas, S.K. Kataria, A.K. Mohanty, L.M. Pant, P. Shukla, A. Topkar

Tata Institute of Fundamental Research — EHEP, Mumbai, India

T. Aziz, Sunanda Banerjee, S. Bose, S. Chendvankar, P.V. Deshpande, M. Guchait,[10] A. Gurtu, M. Maity,[11] G. Majumder, K. Mazumdar, A. Nayak, M.R. Patil, S. Sharma, K. Sudhakar

Tata Institute of Fundamental Research — HECR, Mumbai, India

B.S. Acharya, Sudeshna Banerjee, S. Bheesette, S. Dugad, S.D. Kalmani, V.R. Lakkireddi, N.K. Mondal, N. Panyam, P. Verma

Institute for Studies in Theoretical Physics & Mathematics (IPM), Tehran, Iran

H. Arfaei, M. Hashemi, M. Mohammadi Najafabadi, A. Moshaii, S. Paktinat Mehdiabadi

University College Dublin, Dublin, Ireland
M. Felcini, M. Grunewald

Università di Bari, Politecnico di Bari e Sezione dell' INFN, Bari, Italy
K. Abadjiev, M. Abbrescia, L. Barbone, P. Cariola, F. Chiumarulo, A. Clemente, A. Colaleo,[1] D. Creanza, N. De Filippis,[25] M. De Palma, G. De Robertis, G. Donvito, R. Ferorelli, L. Fiore, M. Franco, D. Giordano, R. Guida, G. Iaselli, N. Lacalamita, F. Loddo, G. Maggi, M. Maggi, N. Manna, B. Marangelli, M.S. Mennea, S. My, S. Natali, S. Nuzzo, G. Papagni, C. Pinto, A. Pompili, G. Pugliese, A. Ranieri, F. Romano, G. Roselli, G. Sala, G. Selvaggi, L. Silvestris,[1] P. Tempesta, R. Trentadue, S. Tupputi, G. Zito

Università di Bologna e Sezione dell' INFN, Bologna, Italy
G. Abbiendi, W. Bacchi, C. Battilana, A.C. Benvenuti, M. Boldini, D. Bonacorsi, S. Braibant-Giacomelli, V.D. Cafaro, P. Capiluppi, A. Castro, F.R. Cavallo, C. Ciocca, G. Codispoti, M. Cuffiani, I. D'Antone, G.M. Dallavalle, F. Fabbri, A. Fanfani, S. Finelli, P. Giacomelli,[12] V. Giordano, M. Giunta, C. Grandi, M. Guerzoni, L. Guiducci, S. Marcellini, G. Masetti, A. Montanari, F.L. Navarria, F. Odorici, A. Paolucci, G. Pellegrini, A. Perrotta, A.M. Rossi, T. Rovelli, G.P. Siroli, G. Torromeo, R. Travaglini, G.P. Veronese

Università di Catania e Sezione dell' INFN, Catania, Italy
S. Albergo, M. Chiorboli, S. Costa, M. Galanti, G. Gatto Rotondo, N. Giudice, N. Guardone, F. Noto, R. Potenza, M.A. Saizu,[48] G. Salemi, C. Sutera, A. Tricomi, C. Tuve

Università di Firenze e Sezione dell' INFN, Firenze, Italy
L. Bellucci, M. Brianzi, G. Broccolo, E. Catacchini, V. Ciulli, C. Civinini, R. D'Alessandro, E. Focardi, S. Frosali, C. Genta, G. Landi, P. Lenzi, A. Macchiolo, F. Maletta, F. Manolescu, C. Marchettini, L. Masetti,[1] S. Mersi, M. Meschini, C. Minelli, S. Paoletti, G. Parrini, E. Scarlini, G. Sguazzoni

Laboratori Nazionali di Frascati dell' INFN, Frascati, Italy
L. Benussi, M. Bertani, S. Bianco, M. Caponero, D. Colonna,[1] L. Daniello, F. Fabbri, F. Felli, M. Giardoni, A. La Monaca, B. Ortenzi, M. Pallotta, A. Paolozzi, C. Paris, L. Passamonti, D. Pierluigi, B. Ponzio, C. Pucci, A. Russo, G. Saviano

Università di Genova e Sezione dell' INFN, Genova, Italy
P. Fabbricatore, S. Farinon, M. Greco, R. Musenich

**Laboratori Nazionali di Legnaro dell' INFN,
Legnaro, Italy (Associated Institute)**
S. Badoer, L. Berti, M. Biasotto, S. Fantinel, E. Frizziero, U. Gastaldi, M. Gulmini,[1] F. Lelli, G. Maron, S. Squizzato, N. Toniolo, S. Traldi

INFN e Universita Degli Studi Milano-Bicocca, Milano, Italy

S. Banfi, R. Bertoni, M. Bonesini, L. Carbone, G.B. Cerati, F. Chignoli, P. D'Angelo, A. De Min, P. Dini, F.M. Farina,[1] F. Ferri, P. Govoni, S. Magni, M. Malberti, S. Malvezzi, R. Mazza, D. Menasce, V. Miccio, L. Moroni, P. Negri, M. Paganoni, D. Pedrini, A. Pullia, S. Ragazzi, N. Redaelli, M. Rovere, L. Sala, S. Sala, R. Salerno, T. Tabarelli de Fatis, V. Tancini, S. Taroni

Istituto Nazionale di Fisica Nucleare de Napoli (INFN), Napoli, Italy

A. Boiano, F. Cassese, C. Cassese, A. Cimmino, B. D'Aquino, L. Lista, D. Lomidze, P. Noli, P. Paolucci, G. Passeggio, D. Piccolo, L. Roscilli, C. Sciacca, A. Vanzanella

Università di Padova e Sezione dell' INFN, Padova, Italy

P. Azzi, N. Bacchetta,[1] L. Barcellan, M. Bellato, M. Benettoni, D. Bisello, E. Borsato, A. Candelori, R. Carlin, L. Castellani, P. Checchia, L. Ciano, A. Colombo, E. Conti, M. Da Rold, F. Dal Corso, M. De Giorgi, M. De Mattia, T. Dorigo, U. Dosselli, C. Fanin, G. Galet, F. Gasparini, U. Gasparini, A. Giraldo, P. Giubilato, F. Gonella, A. Gresele, A. Griggio, P. Guaita, A. Kaminskiy, S. Karaevskii, V. Khomenkov, D. Kostylev, S. Lacaprara, I. Lazzizzera, I. Lippi, M. Loreti, M. Margoni, R. Martinelli, S. Mattiazzo, M. Mazzucato, A.T. Meneguzzo, L. Modenese, F. Montecassiano,[1] A. Neviani, M. Nigro, A. Paccagnella, D. Pantano, A. Parenti, M. Passaseo,[1] R. Pedrotta, M. Pegoraro, G. Rampazzo, S. Reznikov, P. Ronchese, A. Sancho Daponte, P. Sartori, I. Stavitskiy, M. Tessaro, E. Torassa, A. Triossi, S. Vanini, S. Ventura, L. Ventura, M. Verlato, M. Zago, F. Zatti, P. Zotto, G. Zumerle

Università di Pavia e Sezione dell' INFN, Pavia, Italy

P. Baesso, G. Belli, U. Berzano, S. Bricola, A. Grelli, G. Musitelli, R. Nardò, M.M. Necchi, D. Pagano, S.P. Ratti, C. Riccardi, P. Torre, A. Vicini, P. Vitulo, C. Viviani

Università di Perugia e Sezione dell' INFN, Perugia, Italy

D. Aisa, S. Aisa, F. Ambroglini, M.M. Angarano, E. Babucci, D. Benedetti, M. Biasini, G.M. Bilei,[1] S. Bizzaglia, M.T. Brunetti, B. Caponeri, B. Checcucci, R. Covarelli, N. Dinu, L. Fanò, L. Farnesini, M. Giorgi, P. Lariccia, G. Mantovani, F. Moscatelli, D. Passeri, A. Piluso, P. Placidi, V. Postolache, R. Santinelli, A. Santocchia, L. Servoli, D. Spiga[1]

Università di Pisa, Scuola Normale Superiore e Sezione dell' INFN, Pisa, Italy

P. Azzurri, G. Bagliesi,[1] G. Balestri, A. Basti, R. Bellazzini, L. Benucci, J. Bernardini, L. Berretta, S. Bianucci, T. Boccali, A. Bocci, L. Borrello, F. Bosi, F. Bracci, A. Brez, F. Calzolari, R. Castaldi, U. Cazzola, M. Ceccanti, R. Cecchi, C. Cerri, A.S. Cucoanes, R. Dell'Orso, D. Dobur, S. Dutta, F. Fiori, L. Foà, A. Gaggelli, S. Gennai,[13] A. Giassi, S. Giusti, D. Kartashov, A. Kraan, L. Latronico, F. Ligabue, S. Linari, T. Lomtadze, G.A. Lungu,[48] G. Magazzu, P. Mammini, F. Mariani, G. Martinelli, M. Massa, A. Messineo, A. Moggi, F. Palla, F. Palmonari, G. Petragnani, G. Petrucciani, A. Profeti, F. Raffaelli, D. Rizzi, G. Sanguinetti, S. Sarkar, G. Segneri, D. Sentenac, A.T. Serban, A. Slav, P. Spagnolo, G. Spandre, R. Tenchini, S. Tolaini, G. Tonelli,[1] A. Venturi, P.G. Verdini, M. Vos, L. Zaccarelli

Università di Roma I e Sezione dell' INFN, Roma, Italy

S. Baccaro,[14] L. Barone, A. Bartoloni, B. Borgia, G. Capradossi, F. Cavallari, A. Cecilia,[14] D. D'Angelo, I. Dafinei, D. Del Re, E. Di Marco, M. Diemoz, G. Ferrara,[14] C. Gargiulo, S. Guerra, M. Iannone, E. Longo, M. Montecchi,[14] M. Nuccetelli, G. Organtini, A. Palma, R. Paramatti, F. Pellegrino, S. Rahatlou, C. Rovelli, F. Safai Tehrani, A. Zullo

Università di Torino e Sezione dell' INFN, Torino, Italy

G. Alampi, N. Amapane, R. Arcidiacono, S. Argiro, M. Arneodo,[15] R. Bellan, F. Benotto, C. Bino, S. Bolognesi, M.A. Borgia, C. Botta, A. Brasolin, N. Cartiglia, R. Castello, G. Cerminara, R. Cirio, M. Cordero, M. Costa, D. Dattola, F. Daudo, G. Dellacasa, N. Demaria, G. Dughera, F. Dumitrache, R. Farano, G. Ferrero, E. Filoni, G. Kostyleva, H.E. Larsen, C. Mariotti, M. Marone, S. Maselli, E. Menichetti, P. Mereu, E. Migliore, G. Mila, V. Monaco, M. Musich, M. Nervo, M.M. Obertino,[15] R. Panero, A. Parussa, N. Pastrone, C. Peroni, G. Petrillo, A. Romero, M. Ruspa,[15] R. Sacchi, M. Scalise, A. Solano, A. Staiano, P.P. Trapani,[1] D. Trocino, V. Vaniev, A. Vilela Pereira, A. Zampieri

Università di Trieste e Sezione dell' INFN, Trieste, Italy

S. Belforte, F. Cossutti, G. Della Ricca, B. Gobbo, C. Kavka, A. Penzo

Chungbuk National University, Chongju, Korea

Y.E. Kim

Kangwon National University, Chunchon, Korea

S.K. Nam

Kyungpook National University, Daegu, Korea

D.H. Kim, G.N. Kim, J.C. Kim, D.J. Kong, S.R. Ro, D.C. Son

Wonkwang University, Iksan, Korea

S.Y. Park

Cheju National University, Jeju, Korea

Y.J. Kim

Chonnam National University, Kwangju, Korea

J.Y. Kim, I.T. Lim

Dongshin University, Naju, Korea

M.Y. Pac

Seonam University, Namwon, Korea

S.J. Lee

Konkuk University, Seoul, Korea
S.Y. Jung, J.T. Rhee

Korea University, Seoul, Korea
S.H. Ahn, B.S. Hong, Y.K. Jeng, M.H. Kang, H.C. Kim, J.H. Kim, T.J. Kim, K.S. Lee, J.K. Lim, D.H. Moon, I.C. Park, S.K. Park, M.S. Ryu, K.-S. Sim, K.J. Son

Seoul National University, Seoul, Korea
S.J. Hong

Sungkyunkwan University, Suwon, Korea
Y.I. Choi

Centro de Investigacion y de Estudios Avanzados del IPN, Mexico City, Mexico
H. Castilla Valdez, A. Sanchez Hernandez

Universidad Iberoamericana, Mexico City, Mexico
S. Carrillo Moreno

Universidad Autonoma de San Luis Potosi, San Luis Potosi, Mexico
A. Morelos Pineda

Technische Universiteit Eindhoven, Eindhoven, Netherlands (Associated Institute)
A. Aerts, P. Van der Stok, H. Weffers

University of Auckland, Auckland, New Zealand
P. Allfrey, R.N.C. Gray, M. Hashimoto, D. Krofcheck

University of Canterbury, Christchurch, New Zealand
A.J. Bell, N. Bernardino Rodrigues, P.H. Butler, S. Churchwell, R. Knegjens, S. Whitehead, J.C. Williams

National Centre for Physics, Quaid-I-Azam University, Islamabad, Pakistan
Z. Aftab, U. Ahmad, I. Ahmed, W. Ahmed, M.I. Asghar, S. Asghar, G. Dad, M. Hafeez, H.R. Hoorani, I. Hussain, N. Hussain, M. Iftikhar, M.S. Khan, K. Mehmood, A. Osman, H. Shahzad, A.R. Zafar

National University of Sciences And Technology, Rawalpindi Cantt, Pakistan (Associated Institute)
A. Ali, A. Bashir, A.M. Jan, A. Kamal, F. Khan, M. Saeed, S. Tanwir, M.A. Zafar

Institute of Nuclear Physics, Polish Academy of Sciences, Cracow, Poland
J. Blocki, A. Cyz, E. Gladysz-Dziadus, S. Mikocki, M. Rybczynski, J. Turnau, Z. Wlodarczyk, P. Zychowski

2008 JINST 3 S08004

Institute of Experimental Physics, Warsaw, Poland

K. Bunkowski, M. Cwiok, H. Czyrkowski, R. Dabrowski, W. Dominik, K. Doroba, A. Kalinowski, K. Kierzkowski, M. Konecki, J. Krolikowski, I.M. Kudla, M. Pietrusinski, K. Pozniak,[16] W. Zabolotny,[16] P. Zych

Soltan Institute for Nuclear Studies, Warsaw, Poland

R. Gokieli, L. Goscilo, M. Górski, K. Nawrocki, P. Traczyk, G. Wrochna, P. Zalewski

Warsaw University of Technology, Institute of Electronic Systems, Warsaw, Poland (Associated Institute)

K.T. Pozniak, R. Romaniuk, W.M. Zabolotny

Laboratório de Instrumentação e Física Experimental de Partículas, Lisboa, Portugal

R. Alemany-Fernandez, C. Almeida, N. Almeida, A.S. Araujo Vila Verde, T. Barata Monteiro, M. Bluj, S. Da Mota Silva, A. David Tinoco Mendes, M. Freitas Ferreira, M. Gallinaro, M. Husejko, A. Jain, M. Kazana, P. Musella, R. Nobrega, J. Rasteiro Da Silva, P.Q. Ribeiro, M. Santos, P. Silva, S. Silva, I. Teixeira, J.P. Teixeira, J. Varela,[1] G. Varner, N. Vaz Cardoso

Joint Institute for Nuclear Research, Dubna, Russia

I. Altsybeev, K. Babich, A. Belkov,* I. Belotelov, P. Bunin, S. Chesnevskaya, V. Elsha, Y. Ershov, I. Filozova, M. Finger, M. Finger Jr., A. Golunov, I. Golutvin, N. Gorbounov, I. Gramenitski, V. Kalagin, A. Kamenev, V. Karjavin, S. Khabarov, V. Khabarov, Y. Kiryushin, V. Konoplyanikov, V. Korenkov, G. Kozlov, A. Kurenkov, A. Lanev, V. Lysiakov, A. Malakhov, I. Melnitchenko, V.V. Mitsyn, K. Moisenz, P. Moisenz, S. Movchan, E. Nikonov, D. Oleynik, V. Palichik, V. Perelygin, A. Petrosyan, E. Rogalev, V. Samsonov, M. Savina, R. Semenov, S. Sergeev,[17] S. Shmatov, S. Shulha, V. Smirnov, D. Smolin, A. Tcheremoukhine, O. Teryaev, E. Tikhonenko, A. Urkinbaev, S. Vasil'ev, A. Vishnevskiy, A. Volodko, N. Zamiatin, A. Zarubin, P. Zarubin, E. Zubarev

Petersburg Nuclear Physics Institute, Gatchina (St Petersburg), Russia

N. Bondar, Y. Gavrikov, V. Golovtsov, Y. Ivanov, V. Kim, V. Kozlov, V. Lebedev, G. Makarenkov, F. Moroz, P. Neustroev, G. Obrant, E. Orishchin, A. Petrunin, Y. Shcheglov, A. Shchetkovskiy, V. Sknar, V. Skorobogatov, I. Smirnov, V. Sulimov, V. Tarakanov, L. Uvarov, S. Vavilov, G. Velichko, S. Volkov, A. Vorobyev

High Temperature Technology Center of Research & Development Institute of Power Engineering, (HTTC RDIPE), Moscow, Russia (Associated Institute)

D. Chmelev, D. Druzhkin,[1] A. Ivanov, V. Kudinov, O. Logatchev, S. Onishchenko, A. Orlov, V. Sakharov, V. Smetannikov, A. Tikhomirov, S. Zavodthikov

Institute for Nuclear Research, Moscow, Russia

Yu. Andreev, A. Anisimov, V. Duk, S. Gninenko, N. Golubev, D. Gorbunov, M. Kirsanov, N. Krasnikov, V. Matveev, A. Pashenkov, A. Pastsyak, V.E. Postoev, A. Sadovski, A. Skassyrskaia, Alexander Solovey, Anatoly Solovey, D. Soloviev, A. Toropin, S. Troitsky

Institute for Theoretical and Experimental Physics, Moscow, Russia

A. Alekhin, A. Baldov, V. Epshteyn, V. Gavrilov, N. Ilina, V. Kaftanov,[*] V. Karpishin, I. Kiselevich, V. Kolosov, M. Kossov,[1] A. Krokhotin, S. Kuleshov, A. Oulianov, A. Pozdnyakov, G. Safronov, S. Semenov, N. Stepanov, V. Stolin, E. Vlasov,[1] V. Zaytsev

Moscow State University, Moscow, Russia

E. Boos, M. Dubinin,[18] L. Dudko, A. Ershov, G. Eyyubova, A. Gribushin, V. Ilyin, V. Klyukhin, O. Kodolova, N.A. Kruglov, A. Kryukov, I. Lokhtin, L. Malinina, V. Mikhaylin, S. Petrushanko, L. Sarycheva, V. Savrin, L. Shamardin, A. Sherstnev, A. Snigirev, K. Teplov, I. Vardanyan

P.N. Lebedev Physical Institute, Moscow, Russia

A.M. Fomenko, N. Konovalova, V. Kozlov, A.I. Lebedev, N. Lvova, S.V. Rusakov, A. Terkulov

State Research Center of Russian Federation - Institute for High Energy Physics, Protvino, Russia

V. Abramov, S. Akimenko, A. Artamonov, A. Ashimova, I. Azhgirey, S. Bitioukov, O. Chikilev, K. Datsko, A. Filine, A. Godizov, P. Goncharov, V. Grishin,[1] A. Inyakin,[19] V. Kachanov, A. Kalinin, A. Khmelnikov, D. Konstantinov, A. Korablev, V. Krychkine, A. Krinitsyn, A. Levine, I. Lobov, V. Lukanin, Y. Mel'nik, V. Molchanov, V. Petrov, V. Petukhov, V. Pikalov, A. Ryazanov, R. Ryutin, V. Shelikhov, V. Skvortsov, S. Slabospitsky, A. Sobol, A. Sytine, V. Talov, L. Tourtchanovitch, S. Troshin, N. Tyurin, A. Uzunian, A. Volkov, S. Zelepoukine[20]

Electron National Research Institute, St Petersburg, Russia (Associated Institute)

V. Lukyanov, G. Mamaeva, Z. Prilutskaya, I. Rumyantsev, S. Sokha, S. Tataurschikov, I. Vasilyev

Vinca Institute of Nuclear Sciences, Belgrade, Serbia

P. Adzic, I. Anicin,[21] M. Djordjevic, D. Jovanovic,[21] D. Maletic, J. Puzovic,[21] N. Smiljkovic[1]

Centro de Investigaciones Energeticas Medioambientales y Tecnologicas (CIEMAT), Madrid, Spain

E. Aguayo Navarrete, M. Aguilar-Benitez, J. Ahijado Munoz, J.M. Alarcon Vega, J. Alberdi, J. Alcaraz Maestre, M. Aldaya Martin, P. Arce,[1] J.M. Barcala, J. Berdugo, C.L. Blanco Ramos, C. Burgos Lazaro, J. Caballero Bejar, E. Calvo, M. Cerrada, M. Chamizo Llatas, J.J. Chercoles Catalán, N. Colino, M. Daniel, B. De La Cruz, A. Delgado Peris, C. Fernandez Bedoya, A. Ferrando, M.C. Fouz, D. Francia Ferrero, J. Garcia Romero, P. Garcia-Abia, O. Gonzalez Lopez, J.M. Hernandez, M.I. Josa, J. Marin, G. Merino, A. Molinero, J.J. Navarrete, J.C. Oller, J. Puerta Pelayo, J.C. Puras Sanchez, J. Ramirez, L. Romero, C. Villanueva Munoz, C. Willmott, C. Yuste

2008 JINST 3 S08004

Universidad Autónoma de Madrid, Madrid, Spain
C. Albajar, J.F. de Trocóniz, I. Jimenez, R. Macias, R.F. Teixeira

Universidad de Oviedo, Oviedo, Spain
J. Cuevas, J. Fernández Menéndez, I. Gonzalez Caballero,[22] J. Lopez-Garcia, H. Naves Sordo, J.M. Vizan Garcia

Instituto de Física de Cantabria (IFCA), CSIC-Universidad de Cantabria, Santander, Spain
I.J. Cabrillo, A. Calderon, D. Cano Fernandez, I. Diaz Merino, J. Duarte Campderros, M. Fernandez, J. Fernandez Menendez,[23] C. Figueroa, L.A. Garcia Moral, G. Gomez, F. Gomez Casademunt, J. Gonzalez Sanchez, R. Gonzalez Suarez, C. Jorda, P. Lobelle Pardo, A. Lopez Garcia, A. Lopez Virto, J. Marco, R. Marco, C. Martinez Rivero, P. Martinez Ruiz del Arbol, F. Matorras, P. Orviz Fernandez, A. Patino Revuelta,[1] T. Rodrigo, D. Rodriguez Gonzalez, A. Ruiz Jimeno, L. Scodellaro, M. Sobron Sanudo, I. Vila, R. Vilar Cortabitarte

Universität Basel, Basel, Switzerland
M. Barbero, D. Goldin, B. Henrich, L. Tauscher, S. Vlachos, M. Wadhwa

CERN, European Organization for Nuclear Research, Geneva, Switzerland
D. Abbaneo, S.M. Abbas,[24] I. Ahmed,[24] S. Akhtar, M.I. Akhtar,[24] E. Albert, M. Alidra, S. Ashby, P. Aspell, E. Auffray, P. Baillon, A. Ball, S.L. Bally, N. Bangert, R. Barillère, D. Barney, S. Beauceron, F. Beaudette,[25] G. Benelli, R. Benetta, J.L. Benichou, W. Bialas, A. Bjorkebo, D. Blechschmidt, C. Bloch, P. Bloch, S. Bonacini, J. Bos, M. Bosteels, V. Boyer, A. Branson, H. Breuker, R. Bruneliere, O. Buchmuller, D. Campi, T. Camporesi, A. Caner, E. Cano, E. Carrone, A. Cattai, J.P. Chatelain, M. Chauvey, T. Christiansen, M. Ciganek, S. Cittolin, J. Cogan, A. Conde Garcia, H. Cornet, E. Corrin, M. Corvo, S. Cucciarelli, B. Curé, D. D'Enterria, A. De Roeck, T. de Visser, C. Delaere, M. Delattre, C. Deldicque, D. Delikaris, D. Deyrail, S. Di Vincenzo,[26] A. Domeniconi, S. Dos Santos, G. Duthion, L.M. Edera, A. Elliott-Peisert, M. Eppard, F. Fanzago, M. Favre, H. Foeth, R. Folch, N. Frank, S. Fratianni, M.A. Freire, A. Frey, A. Fucci, W. Funk, A. Gaddi, F. Gagliardi, M. Gastal, M. Gateau, J.C. Gayde, H. Gerwig, A. Ghezzi, D. Gigi, K. Gill, A.S. Giolo-Nicollerat, J.P. Girod, F. Glege, W. Glessing, R. Gomez-Reino Garrido, R. Goudard, R. Grabit, J.P. Grillet, P. Gutierrez Llamas, E. Gutierrez Mlot, J. Gutleber, R. Hall-wilton, R. Hammarstrom, M. Hansen, J. Harvey, A. Hervé, J. Hill, H.F. Hoffmann, A. Holzner, A. Honma, D. Hufnagel, M. Huhtinen, S.D. Ilie, V. Innocente, W. Jank, P. Janot, P. Jarron, M. Jeanrenaud, P. Jouvel, R. Kerkach, K. Kloukinas, L.J. Kottelat, J.C. Labbé, D. Lacroix, X. Lagrue,* C. Lasseur, E. Laure, J.F. Laurens, P. Lazeyras, J.M. Le Goff, M. Lebeau,[28] P. Lecoq, F. Lemeilleur, M. Lenzi, N. Leonardo, C. Leonidopoulos, M. Letheren, M. Liendl, F. Limia-Conde, L. Linssen, C. Ljuslin, B. Lofstedt, R. Loos, J.A. Lopez Perez, C. Lourenco, A. Lyonnet, A. Machard, R. Mackenzie, N. Magini, G. Maire, L. Malgeri, R. Malina, M. Mannelli, A. Marchioro, J. Martin, F. Meijers, P. Meridiani, E. Meschi, T. Meyer, A. Meynet Cordonnier, J.F. Michaud, L. Mirabito, R. Moser, F. Mossiere, J. Muffat-Joly, M. Mulders, J. Mulon, E. Murer, P. Mättig, A. Oh, A. Onnela, M. Oriunno, L. Orsini, J.A. Osborne,

C. Paillard, I. Pal, G. Papotti, G. Passardi, A. Patino-Revuelta, V. Patras, B. Perea Solano, E. Perez, G. Perinic, J.F. Pernot, P. Petagna, P. Petiot, P. Petit, A. Petrilli, A. Pfeiffer, C. Piccut, M. Pimiä, R. Pintus, M. Pioppi, A. Placci, L. Pollet, H. Postema, M.J. Price, R. Principe, A. Racz, E. Radermacher, R. Ranieri, G. Raymond, P. Rebecchi, J. Rehn, S. Reynaud, H. Rezvani Naraghi, D. Ricci, M. Ridel, M. Risoldi, P. Rodrigues Simoes Moreira, A. Rohlev, G. Roiron, G. Rolandi,[27] P. Rumerio, O. Runolfsson, V. Ryjov, H. Sakulin, D. Samyn, L.C. Santos Amaral, H. Sauce, E. Sbrissa, P. Scharff-Hansen, P. Schieferdecker, W.D. Schlatter, B. Schmitt, H.G. Schmuecker, M. Schröder, C. Schwick, C. Schäfer, I. Segoni, P. Sempere Roldán, S. Sgobba, A. Sharma, P. Siegrist, C. Sigaud, N. Sinanis, T. Sobrier, P. Sphicas,[28] M. Spiropulu, G. Stefanini, A. Strandlie, F. Szoncsó, B.G. Taylor, O. Teller, A. Thea, E. Tournefier, D. Treille, P. Tropea, J. Troska, E. Tsesmelis, A. Tsirou, J. Valls, I. Van Vulpen, M. Vander Donckt, F. Vasey, M. Vazquez Acosta, L. Veillet, P. Vichoudis, G. Waurick, J.P. Wellisch, P. Wertelaers, M. Wilhelmsson, I.M. Willers, M. Winkler, M. Zanetti

Paul Scherrer Institut, Villigen, Switzerland
W. Bertl, K. Deiters, P. Dick, W. Erdmann, D. Feichtinger, K. Gabathuler, Z. Hochman, R. Horisberger, Q. Ingram, H.C. Kaestli, D. Kotlinski, S. König, P. Poerschke, D. Renker, T. Rohe, T. Sakhelashvili,[29] A. Starodumov[30]

Institute for Particle Physics, ETH Zurich, Zurich, Switzerland
V. Aleksandrov,[31] F. Behner, I. Beniozef,[31] B. Betev, B. Blau, A.M. Brett, L. Caminada,[32] Z. Chen, N. Chivarov,[31] D. Da Silva Di Calafiori, S. Dambach,[32] G. Davatz, V. Delachenal,[1] R. Della Marina, H. Dimov,[31] G. Dissertori, M. Dittmar, L. Djambazov, M. Dröge, C. Eggel,[32] J. Ehlers, R. Eichler, M. Elmiger, G. Faber, K. Freudenreich, J.F. Fuchs,[1] G.M. Georgiev,[31] C. Grab, C. Haller, J. Herrmann, M. Hilgers, W. Hintz, Hans Hofer, Heinz Hofer, U. Horisberger, I. Horvath, A. Hristov,[31] C. Humbertclaude, B. Iliev,[31] W. Kastli, A. Kruse, J. Kuipers,* U. Langenegger, P. Lecomte, E. Lejeune, G. Leshev, C. Lesmond, B. List, P.D. Luckey, W. Lustermann, J.D. Maillefaud, C. Marchica,[32] A. Maurisset,[1] B. Meier, P. Milenovic,[33] M. Milesi, F. Moortgat, I. Nanov,[31] A. Nardulli, F. Nessi-Tedaldi, B. Panev,[34] L. Pape, F. Pauss, E. Petrov,[31] G. Petrov,[31] M.M. Peynekov,[31] D. Pitzl, T. Punz, P. Riboni, J. Riedlberger, A. Rizzi, F.J. Ronga, P.A. Roykov,[31] U. Röser, D. Schinzel, A. Schöning, A. Sourkov,[35] K. Stanishev,[31] S. Stoenchev,[31] F. Stöckli, H. Suter, P. Trüb,[32] S. Udriot, D.G. Uzunova,[31] I. Veltchev,[31] G. Viertel, H.P. von Gunten, S. Waldmeier-Wicki, R. Weber, M. Weber, J. Weng, M. Wensveen,[1] F. Wittgenstein, K. Zagoursky[31]

Universität Zürich, Zürich, Switzerland
E. Alagoz, C. Amsler, V. Chiochia, C. Hoermann, C. Regenfus, P. Robmann, T. Rommerskirchen, A. Schmidt, S. Steiner, D. Tsirigkas, L. Wilke

National Central University, Chung-Li, Taiwan
S. Blyth, Y.H. Chang, E.A. Chen, A. Go, C.C. Hung, C.M. Kuo, S.W. Li, W. Lin

National Taiwan University (NTU), Taipei, Taiwan

P. Chang, Y. Chao, K.F. Chen, Z. Gao,[1] G.W.S. Hou, Y.B. Hsiung, Y.J. Lei, S.W. Lin, R.S. Lu, J.G. Shiu, Y.M. Tzeng, K. Ueno, Y. Velikzhanin, C.C. Wang, M.-Z. Wang

Cukurova University, Adana, Turkey

S. Aydin, A. Azman, M.N. Bakirci, S. Basegmez, S. Cerci, I. Dumanoglu, S. Erturk,[36] E. Eskut, A. Kayis Topaksu, H. Kisoglu, P. Kurt, K. Ozdemir, N. Ozdes Koca, H. Ozkurt, S. Ozturk, A. Polatöz, K. Sogut,[37] H. Topakli, M. Vergili, G. Önengüt

Middle East Technical University, Physics Department, Ankara, Turkey

H. Gamsizkan, S. Sekmen, M. Serin-Zeyrek, R. Sever, M. Zeyrek

Bogaziçi University, Department of Physics, Istanbul, Turkey

M. Deliomeroglu, E. Gülmez, E. Isiksal,[38] M. Kaya,[39] O. Kaya,[39] S. Ozkorucuklu,[40] N. Sonmez[41]

Institute of Single Crystals of National Academy of Science, Kharkov, Ukraine

B. Grinev, V. Lyubynskiy, V. Senchyshyn

National Scientific Center, Kharkov Institute of Physics and Technology, Kharkov, UKRAINE

L. Levchuk, S. Lukyanenko, D. Soroka, P. Sorokin, S. Zub

Centre for Complex Cooperative Systems, University of the West of England, Bristol, United Kingdom (Associated Institute)

A. Anjum, N. Baker, T. Hauer, R. McClatchey, M. Odeh, D. Rogulin, A. Solomonides

University of Bristol, Bristol, United Kingdom

J.J. Brooke, R. Croft, D. Cussans, D. Evans, R. Frazier, N. Grant, M. Hansen, R.D. Head, G.P. Heath, H.F. Heath, C. Hill, B. Huckvale, J. Jackson,[42] C. Lynch, C.K. Mackay, S. Metson, S.J. Nash, D.M. Newbold,[42] A.D. Presland, M.G. Probert, E.C. Reid, V.J. Smith, R.J. Tapper, R. Walton

Rutherford Appleton Laboratory, Didcot, United Kingdom

E. Bateman, K.W. Bell, R.M. Brown, B. Camanzi, I.T. Church, D.J.A. Cockerill, J.E. Cole, J.F. Connolly,* J.A. Coughlan, P.S. Flower, P. Ford, V.B. Francis, M.J. French, S.B. Galagedera, W. Gannon, A.P.R. Gay, N.I. Geddes, R.J.S. Greenhalgh, R.N.J. Halsall, W.J. Haynes, J.A. Hill, F.R. Jacob, P.W. Jeffreys, L.L. Jones, B.W. Kennedy, A.L. Lintern, A.B. Lodge, A.J. Maddox, Q.R. Morrissey, P. Murray, G.N. Patrick, C.A.X. Pattison, M.R. Pearson, S.P.H. Quinton, G.J. Rogers, J.G. Salisbury, A.A. Shah, C.H. Shepherd-Themistocleous, B.J. Smith, M. Sproston, R. Stephenson, S. Taghavi, I.R. Tomalin, M.J. Torbet, J.H. Williams, W.J. Womersley, S.D. Worm, F. Xing

2008 JINST 3 S08004

Imperial College, University of London, London, United Kingdom

M. Apollonio, F. Arteche, R. Bainbridge, G. Barber, P. Barrillon, J. Batten, R. Beuselinck, P.M. Brambilla Hall, D. Britton, W. Cameron, D.E. Clark, I.W. Clark, D. Colling, N. Cripps, G. Davies, M. Della Negra, G. Dewhirst, S. Dris, C. Foudas, J. Fulcher, D. Futyan, D.J. Graham, S. Greder, S. Greenwood, G. Hall, J.F. Hassard, J. Hays, G. Iles, V. Kasey, M. Khaleeq, J. Leaver, P. Lewis, B.C. MacEvoy, O. Maroney, E.M. McLeod, D.G. Miller, J. Nash, A. Nikitenko,[30] E. Noah Messomo, M. Noy, A. Papageorgiou, M. Pesaresi, K. Petridis, D.R. Price, X. Qu, D.M. Raymond, A. Rose, S. Rutherford, M.J. Ryan, F. Sciacca, C. Seez, P. Sharp,[1] G. Sidiropoulos,[1] M. Stettler,[1] M. Stoye, J. Striebig, M. Takahashi, H. Tallini, A. Tapper, C. Timlin, L. Toudup, T. Virdee,[1] S. Wakefield, P. Walsham, D. Wardrope, M. Wingham, Y. Zhang, O. Zorba

Brunel University, Uxbridge, United Kingdom

C. Da Via, I. Goitom, P.R. Hobson, D.C. Imrie, I. Reid, C. Selby, O. Sharif, L. Teodorescu, S.J. Watts, I. Yaselli

Boston University, Boston, Massachusetts, U.S.A.

E. Hazen, A. Heering, A. Heister, C. Lawlor, D. Lazic, E. Machado, J. Rohlf, L. Sulak, F. Varela Rodriguez, S. X. Wu

Brown University, Providence, Rhode Island, U.S.A.

A. Avetisyan, T. Bose, L. Christofek, D. Cutts, S. Esen, R. Hooper, G. Landsberg, M. Narain, D. Nguyen, T. Speer, K.V. Tsang

University of California, Davis, Davis, California, U.S.A.

R. Breedon, M. Case, M. Chertok, J. Conway, P.T. Cox, J. Dolen, R. Erbacher, Y. Fisyak, E. Friis, G. Grim, B. Holbrook, W. Ko, A. Kopecky, R. Lander, F.C. Lin, A. Lister, S. Maruyama, D. Pellett, J. Rowe, M. Searle, J. Smith, A. Soha, M. Squires, M. Tripathi, R. Vasquez Sierra, C. Veelken

University of California, Los Angeles, Los Angeles, California, U.S.A.

V. Andreev, K. Arisaka, Y. Bonushkin, S. Chandramouly, D. Cline, R. Cousins, S. Erhan,[1] J. Hauser, M. Ignatenko, C. Jarvis, B. Lisowski,* C. Matthey, B. Mohr, J. Mumford, S. Otwinowski, Y. Pischalnikov, G. Rakness, P. Schlein,* Y. Shi, B. Tannenbaum, J. Tucker, V. Valuev, R. Wallny, H.G. Wang, X. Yang, Y. Zheng

University of California, Riverside, Riverside, California, U.S.A.

J. Andreeva, J. Babb, S. Campana, D. Chrisman, R. Clare, J. Ellison, D. Fortin, J.W. Gary, W. Gorn, G. Hanson, G.Y. Jeng, S.C. Kao, J.G. Layter, F. Liu, H. Liu, A. Luthra, G. Pasztor,[43] H. Rick, A. Satpathy, B.C. Shen,* R. Stringer, V. Sytnik, P. Tran, S. Villa, R. Wilken, S. Wimpenny, D. Zer-Zion

University of California, San Diego, La Jolla, California, U.S.A.

J.G. Branson, J.A. Coarasa Perez, E. Dusinberre, R. Kelley, M. Lebourgeois, J. Letts, E. Lipeles,

2008 JINST 3 S08004

B. Mangano, T. Martin, M. Mojaver, J. Muelmenstaedt, M. Norman, H.P. Paar, A. Petrucci, H. Pi, M. Pieri, A. Rana, M. Sani, V. Sharma, S. Simon, A. White, F. Würthwein, A. Yagil

University of California, Santa Barbara, Santa Barbara, California, U.S.A.
A. Affolder, A. Allen, C. Campagnari, M. D'Alfonso, A. Dierlamm,[23] J. Garberson, D. Hale, J. Incandela, P. Kalavase, S.A. Koay, D. Kovalskyi, V. Krutelyov, S. Kyre, J. Lamb, S. Lowette, M. Nikolic, V. Pavlunin, F. Rebassoo, J. Ribnik, J. Richman, R. Rossin, Y.S. Shah, D. Stuart, S. Swain, J.R. Vlimant, D. White, M. Witherell

California Institute of Technology, Pasadena, California, U.S.A.
A. Bornheim, J. Bunn, J. Chen, G. Denis, P. Galvez, M. Gataullin, I. Legrand, V. Litvine, Y. Ma, R. Mao, D. Nae, I. Narsky, H.B. Newman, T. Orimoto, C. Rogan, S. Shevchenko, C. Steenberg, X. Su, M. Thomas, V. Timciuc, F. van Lingen, J. Veverka, B.R. Voicu,[1] A. Weinstein, R. Wilkinson, Y. Xia, Y. Yang, L.Y. Zhang, K. Zhu, R.Y. Zhu

Carnegie Mellon University, Pittsburgh, Pennsylvania, U.S.A.
T. Ferguson, D.W. Jang, S.Y. Jun, M. Paulini, J. Russ, N. Terentyev, H. Vogel, I. Vorobiev

University of Colorado at Boulder, Boulder, Colorado, U.S.A.
M. Bunce, J.P. Cumalat, M.E. Dinardo, B.R. Drell, W.T. Ford, K. Givens, B. Heyburn, D. Johnson, U. Nauenberg, K. Stenson, S.R. Wagner

Cornell University, Ithaca, New York, U.S.A.
L. Agostino, J. Alexander, F. Blekman, D. Cassel, S. Das, J.E. Duboscq, L.K. Gibbons, B. Heltsley, C.D. Jones, V. Kuznetsov, J.R. Patterson, D. Riley, A. Ryd, S. Stroiney, W. Sun, J. Thom, J. Vaughan, P. Wittich

Fairfield University, Fairfield, Connecticut, U.S.A.
C.P. Beetz, G. Cirino, V. Podrasky, C. Sanzeni, D. Winn

Fermi National Accelerator Laboratory, Batavia, Illinois, U.S.A.
S. Abdullin,[1] M.A. Afaq,[1] M. Albrow, J. Amundson, G. Apollinari, M. Atac, W. Badgett, J.A. Bakken, B. Baldin, K. Banicz, L.A.T. Bauerdick, A. Baumbaugh, J. Berryhill, P.C. Bhat, M. Binkley, I. Bloch, F. Borcherding, A. Boubekeur, M. Bowden, K. Burkett, J.N. Butler, H.W.K. Cheung, G. Chevenier,[1] F. Chlebana, I. Churin, S. Cihangir, W. Dagenhart, M. Demarteau, D. Dykstra, D.P. Eartly, J.E. Elias, V.D. Elvira, D. Evans, I. Fisk, J. Freeman, I. Gaines, P. Gartung, F.J.M. Geurts, L. Giacchetti, D.A. Glenzinski, E. Gottschalk, T. Grassi, D. Green, C. Grimm, Y. Guo, O. Gutsche, A. Hahn, J. Hanlon, R.M. Harris, T. Hesselroth, S. Holm, B. Holzman, E. James, H. Jensen, M. Johnson, U. Joshi, B. Klima, S. Kossiakov, K. Kousouris, J. Kowalkowski, T. Kramer, S. Kwan, C.M. Lei, M. Leininger, S. Los, L. Lueking, G. Lukhanin, S. Lusin,[1] K. Maeshima, J.M. Marraffino, D. Mason, P. McBride, T. Miao, S. Moccia, N. Mokhov, S. Mrenna, S.J. Murray, C. Newman-Holmes, C. Noeding, V. O'Dell, M. Paterno, D. Petravick, R. Pordes, O. Prokofyev, N. Ratnikova, A. Ronzhin, V. Sekhri, E. Sexton-Kennedy, I. Sfiligoi,

2008 JINST 3 S08004

T.M. Shaw, E. Skup, R.P. Smith,* W.J. Spalding, L. Spiegel, M. Stavrianakou, G. Stiehr, A.L. Stone, I. Suzuki, P. Tan, W. Tanenbaum, L.E. Temple, S. Tkaczyk,[1] L. Uplegger, E.W. Vaandering, R. Vidal, R. Wands, H. Wenzel, J. Whitmore, E. Wicklund, W.M. Wu, Y. Wu, J. Yarba, V. Yarba, F. Yumiceva, J.C. Yun, T. Zimmerman

University of Florida, Gainesville, Florida, U.S.A.
D. Acosta, P. Avery, V. Barashko, P. Bartalini, D. Bourilkov, R. Cavanaugh, S. Dolinsky, A. Drozdetskiy, R.D. Field, Y. Fu, I.K. Furic, L. Gorn, D. Holmes, B.J. Kim, S. Klimenko, J. Konigsberg, A. Korytov, K. Kotov, P. Levchenko, A. Madorsky, K. Matchev, G. Mitselmakher, Y. Pakhotin, C. Prescott, L. Ramond, P. Ramond, M. Schmitt, B. Scurlock, J. Stasko, H. Stoeck, D. Wang, J. Yelton

Florida International University, Miami, Florida, U.S.A.
V. Gaultney, L. Kramer, L.M. Lebolo, S. Linn, P. Markowitz, G. Martinez, J.L. Rodriguez

Florida State University, Tallahassee, Florida, U.S.A.
T. Adams, A. Askew, O. Atramentov, M. Bertoldi, W.G.D. Dharmaratna,[49] Y. Gershtein, S.V. Gleyzer, S. Hagopian, V. Hagopian, C.J. Jenkins, K.F. Johnson, H. Prosper, D. Simek, J. Thomaston

Florida Institute of Technology, Melbourne, Florida, U.S.A.
M. Baarmand, L. Baksay,[44] S. Guragain, M. Hohlmann, H. Mermerkaya, R. Ralich, I. Vodopiyanov

University of Illinois at Chicago (UIC), Chicago, Illinois, U.S.A.
M.R. Adams, I. M. Anghel, L. Apanasevich, O. Barannikova, V.E. Bazterra, R.R. Betts, C. Dragoiu, E.J. Garcia-Solis, C.E. Gerber, D.J. Hofman, R. Hollis, A. Iordanova, S. Khalatian, C. Mironov, E. Shabalina, A. Smoron, N. Varelas

The University of Iowa, Iowa City, Iowa, U.S.A.
U. Akgun, E.A. Albayrak, A.S. Ayan, R. Briggs, K. Cankocak,[45] W. Clarida, A. Cooper, P. Debbins, F. Duru, M. Fountain, E. McCliment, J.P. Merlo, A. Mestvirishvili, M.J. Miller, A. Moeller, C.R. Newsom, E. Norbeck, J. Olson, Y. Onel, L. Perera, I. Schmidt, S. Wang, T. Yetkin

Iowa State University, Ames, Iowa, U.S.A.
E.W. Anderson, H. Chakir, J.M. Hauptman, J. Lamsa

Johns Hopkins University, Baltimore, Maryland, U.S.A.
B.A. Barnett, B. Blumenfeld, C.Y. Chien, G. Giurgiu, A. Gritsan, D.W. Kim, C.K. Lae, P. Maksimovic, M. Swartz, N. Tran

The University of Kansas, Lawrence, Kansas, U.S.A.
P. Baringer, A. Bean, J. Chen, D. Coppage, O. Grachov, M. Murray, V. Radicci, J.S. Wood, V. Zhukova

2008 JINST 3 S08004

Kansas State University, Manhattan, Kansas, U.S.A.

D. Bandurin, T. Bolton, K. Kaadze, W.E. Kahl, Y. Maravin, D. Onoprienko, R. Sidwell, Z. Wan

Lawrence Livermore National Laboratory, Livermore, California, U.S.A.

B. Dahmes, J. Gronberg, J. Hollar, D. Lange, D. Wright, C.R. Wuest

University of Maryland, College Park, Maryland, U.S.A.

D. Baden, R. Bard, S.C. Eno, D. Ferencek, N.J. Hadley, R.G. Kellogg, M. Kirn, S. Kunori, E. Lockner, F. Ratnikov, F. Santanastasio, A. Skuja, T. Toole, L. Wang, M. Wetstein

Massachusetts Institute of Technology, Cambridge, Massachusetts, U.S.A.

B. Alver, M. Ballintijn, G. Bauer, W. Busza, G. Gomez Ceballos, K.A. Hahn, P. Harris, M. Klute, I. Kravchenko, W. Li, C. Loizides, T. Ma, S. Nahn, C. Paus, S. Pavlon, J. Piedra Gomez, C. Roland, G. Roland, M. Rudolph, G. Stephans, K. Sumorok, S. Vaurynovich, E.A. Wenger, B. Wyslouch

University of Minnesota, Minneapolis, Minnesota, U.S.A.

D. Bailleux, S. Cooper, P. Cushman, A. De Benedetti, A. Dolgopolov, P.R. Dudero, R. Egeland, G. Franzoni, W.J. Gilbert, D. Gong, J. Grahl, J. Haupt, K. Klapoetke, I. Kronkvist, Y. Kubota, J. Mans, R. Rusack, S. Sengupta, B. Sherwood, A. Singovsky, P. Vikas, J. Zhang

University of Mississippi, University, Mississippi, U.S.A.

M. Booke, L.M. Cremaldi, R. Godang, R. Kroeger, M. Reep, J. Reidy, D.A. Sanders, P. Sonnek, D. Summers, S. Watkins

University of Nebraska-Lincoln, Lincoln, Nebraska, U.S.A.

K. Bloom, B. Bockelman, D.R. Claes, A. Dominguez, M. Eads, M. Furukawa, J. Keller, T. Kelly, C. Lundstedt, S. Malik, G.R. Snow, D. Swanson

State University of New York at Buffalo, Buffalo, New York, U.S.A.

K.M. Ecklund, I. Iashvili, A. Kharchilava, A. Kumar, M. Strang

Northeastern University, Boston, Massachusetts, U.S.A.

G. Alverson, E. Barberis, O. Boeriu, G. Eulisse, T. McCauley, Y. Musienko,[46] S. Muzaffar, I. Osborne, S. Reucroft, J. Swain, L. Taylor, L. Tuura

Northwestern University, Evanston, Illinois, U.S.A.

B. Gobbi, M. Kubantsev, A. Kubik, R.A. Ofierzynski, M. Schmitt, E. Spencer, S. Stoynev, M. Szleper, M. Velasco, S. Won

University of Notre Dame, Notre Dame, Indiana, U.S.A.

K. Andert, B. Baumbaugh, B.A. Beiersdorf, L. Castle, J. Chorny, A. Goussiou, M. Hildreth, C. Jessop, D.J. Karmgard, T. Kolberg, J. Marchant, N. Marinelli, M. McKenna, R. Ruchti, M. Vigneault, M. Wayne, D. Wiand

2008 JINST 3 S08004

The Ohio State University, Columbus, Ohio, U.S.A.

B. Bylsma, L.S. Durkin, J. Gilmore, J. Gu, P. Killewald, T.Y. Ling, C.J. Rush, V. Sehgal, G. Williams

Princeton University, Princeton, New Jersey, U.S.A.

N. Adam, S. Chidzik, P. Denes,[47] P. Elmer, A. Garmash, D. Gerbaudo, V. Halyo, J. Jones, D. Marlow, J. Olsen, P. Piroué, D. Stickland, C. Tully, J.S. Werner, T. Wildish, S. Wynhoff,[*] Z. Xie

University of Puerto Rico, Mayaguez, Puerto Rico, U.S.A.

X.T. Huang, A. Lopez, H. Mendez, J.E. Ramirez Vargas, A. Zatserklyaniy

Purdue University, West Lafayette, Indiana, U.S.A.

A. Apresyan, K. Arndt, V.E. Barnes, G. Bolla, D. Bortoletto, A. Bujak, A. Everett, M. Fahling, A.F. Garfinkel, L. Gutay, N. Ippolito, Y. Kozhevnikov,[1] A.T. Laasanen, C. Liu, V. Maroussov, S. Medved, P. Merkel, D.H. Miller, J. Miyamoto, N. Neumeister, A. Pompos, A. Roy, A. Sedov, I. Shipsey

Purdue University Calumet, Hammond, Indiana, U.S.A.

V. Cuplov, N. Parashar

Rice University, Houston, Texas, U.S.A.

P. Bargassa, S.J. Lee, J.H. Liu, D. Maronde, M. Matveev, T. Nussbaum, B.P. Padley, J. Roberts, A. Tumanov

University of Rochester, Rochester, New York, U.S.A.

A. Bodek, H. Budd, J. Cammin, Y.S. Chung, P. De Barbaro,[1] R. Demina, G. Ginther, Y. Gotra, S. Korjenevski, D.C. Miner, W. Sakumoto, P. Slattery, M. Zielinski

The Rockefeller University, New York, New York, U.S.A.

A. Bhatti, L. Demortier, K. Goulianos, K. Hatakeyama, C. Mesropian

Rutgers, the State University of New Jersey, Piscataway, New Jersey, U.S.A.

E. Bartz, S.H. Chuang, J. Doroshenko, E. Halkiadakis, P.F. Jacques, D. Khits, A. Lath, A. Macpherson,[1] R. Plano, K. Rose, S. Schnetzer, S. Somalwar, R. Stone, T.L. Watts

University of Tennessee, Knoxville, Tennessee, U.S.A.

G. Cerizza, M. Hollingsworth, J. Lazoflores, G. Ragghianti, S. Spanier, A. York

Texas A&M University, College Station, Texas, U.S.A.

A. Aurisano, A. Golyash, T. Kamon, C.N. Nguyen, J. Pivarski, A. Safonov, D. Toback, M. Weinberger

Texas Tech University, Lubbock, Texas, U.S.A.

N. Akchurin, L. Berntzon, K.W. Carrell, K. Gumus, C. Jeong, H. Kim, S.W. Lee, B.G. Mc Gonagill, Y. Roh, A. Sill, M. Spezziga, R. Thomas, I. Volobouev, E. Washington, R. Wigmans, E. Yazgan

Vanderbilt University, Nashville, Tennessee, U.S.A.

T. Bapty, D. Engh, C. Florez, W. Johns, T. Keskinpala, E. Luiggi Lopez, S. Neema, S. Nordstrom, S. Pathak, P. Sheldon

University of Virginia, Charlottesville, Virginia, U.S.A.

D. Andelin, M.W. Arenton, M. Balazs, M. Buehler, S. Conetti, B. Cox, R. Hirosky, M. Humphrey, R. Imlay, A. Ledovskoy, D. Phillips II, H. Powell, M. Ronquest, R. Yohay

University of Wisconsin, Madison, Wisconsin, U.S.A.

M. Anderson, Y.W. Baek, J.N. Bellinger, D. Bradley, P. Cannarsa, D. Carlsmith, I. Crotty,[1] S. Dasu, F. Feyzi, T. Gorski, L. Gray, K.S. Grogg, M. Grothe, M. Jaworski, P. Klabbers, J. Klukas, A. Lanaro, C. Lazaridis, J. Leonard, R. Loveless, M. Magrans de Abril, A. Mohapatra, G. Ott, W.H. Smith, M. Weinberg, D. Wenman

Yale University, New Haven, Connecticut, U.S.A.

G.S. Atoian, S. Dhawan, V. Issakov, H. Neal, A. Poblaguev, M.E. Zeller

Institute of Nuclear Physics of the Uzbekistan Academy of Sciences, Ulugbek, Tashkent, Uzbekistan

G. Abdullaeva, A. Avezov, M.I. Fazylov, E.M. Gasanov, A. Khugaev, Y.N. Koblik, M. Nishonov, K. Olimov, A. Umaraliev, B.S. Yuldashev

[1]Also at CERN, European Organization for Nuclear Research, Geneva, Switzerland
[2]Now at Universidade Federal do ABC, Santo Andre, Brazil
[3]Now at Laboratoire de l'Accélérateur Linéaire, Orsay, France
[4]Now at CERN, European Organization for Nuclear Research, Geneva, Switzerland
[5]Also at Université de Haute-Alsace, Mulhouse, France
[6]Also at Université Louis Pasteur, Strasbourg, France
[7]Also at Moscow State University, Moscow, Russia
[8]Also at Institute of Nuclear Research ATOMKI, Debrecen, Hungary
[9]Also at University of California, San Diego, La Jolla, U.S.A.
[10]Also at Tata Institute of Fundamental Research - HECR, Mumbai, India
[11]Also at University of Visva-Bharati, Santiniketan, India
[12]Also at University of California, Riverside, Riverside, U.S.A.
[13]Also at Centro Studi Enrico Fermi, Roma, Italy
[14]Also at ENEA - Casaccia Research Center, S. Maria di Galeria, Italy
[15]Now at Università del Piemonte Orientale, Novara, Italy

[16] Also at Warsaw University of Technology, Institute of Electronic Systems, Warsaw, Poland

[17] Also at Fermi National Accelerator Laboratory, Batavia, U.S.A.

[18] Also at California Institute of Technology, Pasadena, U.S.A.

[19] Also at University of Minnesota, Minneapolis, U.S.A.

[20] Also at Institute for Particle Physics, ETH Zurich, Zurich, Switzerland

[21] Also at Faculty of Physics of University of Belgrade, Belgrade, Serbia

[22] Now at Instituto de Física de Cantabria (IFCA), CSIC-Universidad de Cantabria, Santander, Spain

[23] Also at Institut für Experimentelle Kernphysik, Karlsruhe, Germany

[24] Also at National Centre for Physics, Quaid-I-Azam University, Islamabad, Pakistan

[25] Also at Laboratoire Leprince-Ringuet, Ecole Polytechnique, IN2P3-CNRS, Palaiseau, France

[26] Also at Alstom Contracting, Geneve, Switzerland

[27] Also at Scuola Normale Superiore and Sezione INFN, Pisa, Italy

[28] Also at University of Athens, Athens, Greece

[29] Also at Institute of High Energy Physics and Informatization, Tbilisi State University, Tbilisi, Georgia

[30] Also at Institute for Theoretical and Experimental Physics, Moscow, Russia

[31] Also at Central Laboratory of Mechatronics and Instrumentation, Sofia, Bulgaria

[32] Also at Paul Scherrer Institut, Villigen, Switzerland

[33] Also at Vinca Institute of Nuclear Sciences, Belgrade, Serbia

[34] Also at Institute for Nuclear Research and Nuclear Energy, Sofia, Bulgaria

[35] Also at State Research Center of Russian Federation - Institute for High Energy Physics, Protvino, Russia

[36] Also at Nigde University, Nigde, Turkey

[37] Also at Mersin University, Mersin, Turkey

[38] Also at Marmara University, Istanbul, Turkey

[39] Also at Kafkas University, Kars, Turkey

[40] Also at Suleyman Demirel University, Isparta, Turkey

[41] Also at Ege University, Izmir, Turkey

[42] Also at Rutherford Appleton Laboratory, Didcot, United Kingdom

[43] Also at KFKI Research Institute for Particle and Nuclear Physics, Budapest, Hungary

[44] Also at University of Debrecen, Debrecen, Hungary

[45] Also at Mugla University, Mugla, Turkey

[46] Also at Institute for Nuclear Research, Moscow, Russia

[47] Now at Lawrence Berkeley National Laboratory, Berkeley, U.S.A.

[48] Now at National Institute of Physics and Nuclear Engineering, Bucharest, Romania

[49] Also at University of Ruhuna, Matara, Sri Lanka

*Deceased

Corresponding author: Roberto Tenchini (Roberto.Tenchini@cern.ch)

2008 JINST 3 S08004

Contents

2008 JINST 3 S08004

2008 JINST 3 S08004

Chapter 1

Introduction

The Compact Muon Solenoid (CMS) detector is a multi-purpose apparatus due to operate at the Large Hadron Collider (LHC) at CERN. The LHC is presently being constructed in the already existing 27-km LEP tunnel in the Geneva region. It will yield head-on collisions of two proton (ion) beams of 7 TeV (2.75 TeV per nucleon) each, with a design luminosity of 10^{34} cm^{-2}s^{-1} (10^{27} cm^{-2}s^{-1}). This paper provides a description of the design and construction of the CMS detector. CMS is installed about 100 metres underground close to the French village of Cessy, between Lake Geneva and the Jura mountains.

The prime motivation of the LHC is to elucidate the nature of electroweak symmetry breaking for which the Higgs mechanism is presumed to be responsible. The experimental study of the Higgs mechanism can also shed light on the mathematical consistency of the Standard Model at energy scales above about 1 TeV. Various alternatives to the Standard Model invoke new symmetries, new forces or constituents. Furthermore, there are high hopes for discoveries that could pave the way toward a unified theory. These discoveries could take the form of supersymmetry or extra dimensions, the latter often requiring modification of gravity at the TeV scale. Hence there are many compelling reasons to investigate the TeV energy scale.

The LHC will also provide high-energy heavy-ion beams at energies over 30 times higher than at the previous accelerators, allowing us to further extend the study of QCD matter under extreme conditions of temperature, density, and parton momentum fraction (low-x).

Hadron colliders are well suited to the task of exploring new energy domains, and the region of 1 TeV constituent centre-of-mass energy can be explored if the proton energy and the luminosity are high enough. The beam energy and the design luminosity of the LHC have been chosen in order to study physics at the TeV energy scale. A wide range of physics is potentially possible with the seven-fold increase in energy and a hundred-fold increase in integrated luminosity over the previous hadron collider experiments. These conditions also require a very careful design of the detectors.

The total proton-proton cross-section at $\sqrt{s} = 14$ TeV is expected to be roughly 100 mb. At design luminosity the general-purpose detectors will therefore observe an event rate of approximately 10^9 inelastic events/s. This leads to a number of formidable experimental challenges. The online event selection process (*trigger*) must reduce the huge rate to about 100 events/s for storage and subsequent analysis. The short time between bunch crossings, 25 ns, has major implications for the design of the read-out and trigger systems.

2008 JINST 3 S08004

At the design luminosity, a mean of about 20 inelastic collisions will be superimposed on the event of interest. This implies that around 1000 charged particles will emerge from the interaction region every 25 ns. The products of an interaction under study may be confused with those from other interactions in the same bunch crossing. This problem clearly becomes more severe when the response time of a detector element and its electronic signal is longer than 25 ns. The effect of this pile-up can be reduced by using high-granularity detectors with good time resolution, resulting in low occupancy. This requires a large number of detector channels. The resulting millions of detector electronic channels require very good synchronization.

The large flux of particles coming from the interaction region leads to high radiation levels, requiring radiation-hard detectors and front-end electronics.

The detector requirements for CMS to meet the goals of the LHC physics programme can be summarised as follows:

- Good muon identification and momentum resolution over a wide range of momenta and angles, good dimuon mass resolution ($\approx 1\%$ at 100 GeV), and the ability to determine unambiguously the charge of muons with $p < 1$ TeV;

- Good charged-particle momentum resolution and reconstruction efficiency in the inner tracker. Efficient triggering and offline tagging of τ's and b-jets, requiring pixel detectors close to the interaction region;

- Good electromagnetic energy resolution, good diphoton and dielectron mass resolution ($\approx$ 1% at 100 GeV), wide geometric coverage, π^0 rejection, and efficient photon and lepton isolation at high luminosities;

- Good missing-transverse-energy and dijet-mass resolution, requiring hadron calorimeters with a large hermetic geometric coverage and with fine lateral segmentation.

The design of CMS, detailed in the next section, meets these requirements. The main distinguishing features of CMS are a high-field solenoid, a full-silicon-based inner tracking system, and a homogeneous scintillating-crystals-based electromagnetic calorimeter.

The coordinate system adopted by CMS has the origin centered at the nominal collision point inside the experiment, the y-axis pointing vertically upward, and the x-axis pointing radially inward toward the center of the LHC. Thus, the z-axis points along the beam direction toward the Jura mountains from LHC Point 5. The azimuthal angle ϕ is measured from the x-axis in the x-y plane and the radial coordinate in this plane is denoted by r. The polar angle θ is measured from the z-axis. Pseudorapidity is defined as $\eta = -\ln\tan(\theta/2)$. Thus, the momentum and energy transverse to the beam direction, denoted by p_T and E_T, respectively, are computed from the x and y components. The imbalance of energy measured in the transverse plane is denoted by E_T^{miss}.

1.1 General concept

An important aspect driving the detector design and layout is the choice of the magnetic field configuration for the measurement of the momentum of muons. Large bending power is needed

2008 JINST 3 S08004

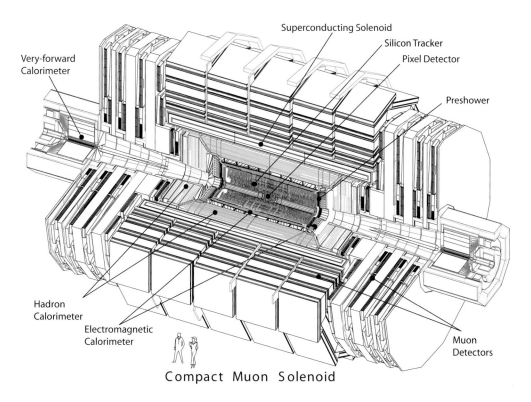

Figure 1.1: A perspective view of the CMS detector.

to measure precisely the momentum of high-energy charged particles. This forces a choice of superconducting technology for the magnets.

The overall layout of CMS [1] is shown in figure 1.1. At the heart of CMS sits a 13-m-long, 6-m-inner-diameter, 4-T superconducting solenoid providing a large bending power (12 Tm) before the muon bending angle is measured by the muon system. The return field is large enough to saturate 1.5 m of iron, allowing 4 muon *stations* to be integrated to ensure robustness and full geometric coverage. Each muon station consists of several layers of aluminium drift tubes (DT) in the barrel region and cathode strip chambers (CSC) in the endcap region, complemented by resistive plate chambers (RPC).

The bore of the magnet coil is large enough to accommodate the inner tracker and the calorimetry inside. The tracking volume is given by a cylinder of 5.8-m length and 2.6-m diameter. In order to deal with high track multiplicities, CMS employs 10 layers of silicon microstrip detectors, which provide the required granularity and precision. In addition, 3 layers of silicon pixel detectors are placed close to the interaction region to improve the measurement of the impact parameter of charged-particle tracks, as well as the position of secondary vertices. The expected muon momentum resolution using only the muon system, using only the inner tracker, and using both sub-detectors is shown in figure 1.2.

The electromagnetic calorimeter (ECAL) uses lead tungstate ($PbWO_4$) crystals with coverage in pseudorapidity up to $|\eta| < 3.0$. The scintillation light is detected by silicon avalanche photodiodes (APDs) in the barrel region and vacuum phototriodes (VPTs) in the endcap region. A preshower system is installed in front of the endcap ECAL for π^0 rejection. The energy resolution

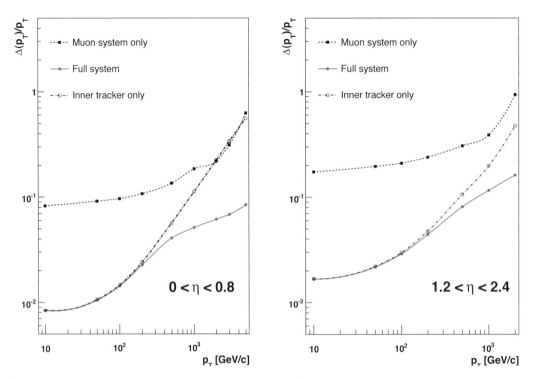

Figure 1.2: The muon transverse-momentum resolution as a function of the transverse-momentum (p_T) using the muon system only, the inner tracking only, and both. Left panel: $|\eta| < 0.8$, right panel: $1.2 < |\eta| < 2.4$.

of the ECAL, for incident electrons as measured in a beam test, is shown in figure 1.3; the stochastic (S), noise (N), and constant (C) terms given in the figure are determined by fitting the measured points to the function

$$\left(\frac{\sigma}{E}\right)^2 = \left(\frac{S}{\sqrt{E}}\right)^2 + \left(\frac{N}{E}\right)^2 + C^2. \tag{1.1}$$

The ECAL is surrounded by a brass/scintillator sampling hadron calorimeter (HCAL) with coverage up to $|\eta| < 3.0$. The scintillation light is converted by wavelength-shifting (WLS) fibres embedded in the scintillator tiles and channeled to photodetectors via clear fibres. This light is detected by photodetectors (hybrid photodiodes, or HPDs) that can provide gain and operate in high axial magnetic fields. This central calorimetry is complemented by a *tail-catcher* in the barrel region (HO) ensuring that hadronic showers are sampled with nearly 11 hadronic interaction lengths. Coverage up to a pseudorapidity of 5.0 is provided by an iron/quartz-fibre calorimeter. The Cerenkov light emitted in the quartz fibres is detected by photomultipliers. The forward calorimeters ensure full geometric coverage for the measurement of the transverse energy in the event. An even higher forward coverage is obtained with additional dedicated calorimeters (CASTOR, ZDC, not shown in figure 1.1) and with the TOTEM [2] tracking detectors. The expected jet transverse-energy resolution in various pseudorapidity regions is shown in figure 1.4.

The CMS detector is 21.6-m long and has a diameter of 14.6 m. It has a total weight of 12 500 t. The ECAL thickness, in radiation lengths, is larger than 25 X_0, while the HCAL thickness, in interaction lengths, varies in the range 7–11 λ_I (10–15 λ_I with the HO included), depending on η.

2008 JINST 3 S08004

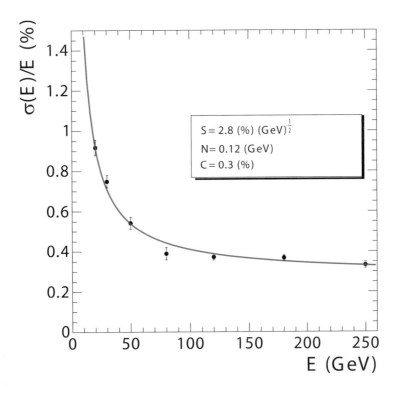

Figure 1.3: ECAL energy resolution, $\sigma(E)/E$, as a function of electron energy as measured from a beam test. The energy was measured in an array of 3×3 crystals with an electron impacting the central crystal. The points correspond to events taken restricting the incident beam to a narrow $(4 \times 4 \text{ mm}^2)$ region. The stochastic (S), noise (N), and constant (C) terms are given.

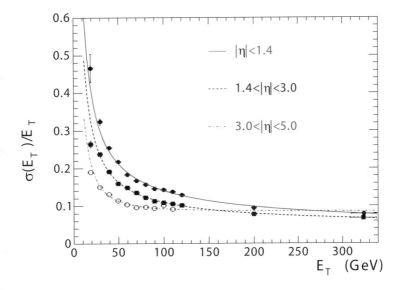

Figure 1.4: The jet transverse-energy resolution as a function of the jet transverse energy for barrel jets ($|\eta| < 1.4$), endcap jets ($1.4 < |\eta| < 3.0$), and very forward jets ($3.0 < |\eta| < 5.0$). The jets are reconstructed with an iterative cone algorithm (cone radius = 0.5).

Chapter 2

Superconducting magnet

2.1 Overview

The superconducting magnet for CMS [3–6] has been designed to reach a 4-T field in a free bore of 6-m diameter and 12.5-m length with a stored energy of 2.6 GJ at full current. The flux is returned through a 10 000-t yoke comprising 5 wheels and 2 endcaps, composed of three disks each (figure 1.1). The distinctive feature of the 220-t cold mass is the 4-layer winding made from a stabilised reinforced NbTi conductor. The ratio between stored energy and cold mass is high (11.6 KJ/kg), causing a large mechanical deformation (0.15%) during energising, well beyond the values of previous solenoidal detector magnets. The parameters of the CMS magnet are summarised in table 2.1. The magnet was designed to be assembled and tested in a surface hall (SX5), prior to being lowered 90 m below ground to its final position in the experimental cavern. After provisional connection to its ancillaries, the CMS Magnet has been fully and successfully tested and commissioned in SX5 during autumn 2006.

2.2 Main features of the magnet components

2.2.1 Superconducting solenoid

The superconducting solenoid (see an artistic view in figure 2.1 and a picture taken during assembly in the vertical position in SX5 in figure 2.2) presents three new features with respect to previous detector magnets:

- Due to the number of ampere-turns required for generating a field of 4 T (41.7 MA-turn), the winding is composed of 4 layers, instead of the usual 1 (as in the Aleph [7] and Delphi [8] coils) or maximum 2 layers (as in the ZEUS [9] and BaBar [10] coils);

- The conductor, made from a Rutherford-type cable co-extruded with pure aluminium (the so-called insert), is mechanically reinforced with an aluminium alloy;

- The dimensions of the solenoid are very large (6.3-m cold bore, 12.5-m length, 220-t mass).

For physics reasons, the radial extent of the coil (ΔR) had to be kept small, and thus the CMS coil is in effect a "thin coil" ($\Delta R/R \sim 0.1$). The hoop strain (ε) is then determined by the

2008 JINST 3 S08004

Figure 2.1: General artistic view of the 5 modules composing the cold mass inside the cryostat, with details of the supporting system (vertical, radial and longitudinal tie rods).

magnetic pressure ($P = \frac{B_0^2}{2\mu_0} = 6.4$ MPa), the elastic modulus of the material (mainly aluminium with $Y = 80$ GPa) and the structural thickness ($\Delta R_s = 170$ mm i.e., about half of the total cold mass thickness), according to $\frac{PR}{\Delta R_s} = Y\varepsilon$, giving $\varepsilon = 1.5 \times 10^{-3}$. This value is high compared to the strain of previous existing detector magnets. This can be better viewed looking at a more significant figure of merit, i.e. the E/M ratio directly proportional to the mechanical hoop strain according to $\frac{E}{M} = \frac{PR}{2\Delta R_s \delta} \frac{\Delta R_s}{\Delta R} = \frac{\Delta R_s}{\Delta R} \frac{Y\varepsilon}{2\delta}$, where δ is the mass density. Figure 2.3 shows the values of E/M as function of stored energy for several detector magnets. The CMS coil is distinguishably far from other detector magnets when combining stored energy and E/M ratio (i.e. mechanical deformation). In order to provide the necessary hoop strength, a large fraction of the CMS coil must have a structural function. To limit the shear stress level inside the winding and prevent cracking the insulation, especially at the border defined by the winding and the external mandrel, the structural material cannot be too far from the current-carrying elements (the turns). On the basis of these considerations, the innovative design of the CMS magnet uses a self-supporting conductor, by including in it the structural material. The magnetic hoop stress (130 MPa) is shared between the layers (70%) and the support cylindrical mandrel (30%) rather than being taken by the outer mandrel only, as was the case in the previous generation of thin detector solenoids. A cross section of the cold mass is shown in figure 2.4.

The construction of a winding using a reinforced conductor required technological developments for both the conductor [11] and the winding. In particular, for the winding many problems had to be faced mainly related to the mandrel construction [12], the winding method [13], and the module-to-module mechanical coupling. The modular concept of the cold mass had to face the problem of the module-to-module mechanical connection. These interfaces (figure 2.5) are critical

2008 JINST 3 S08004

Table 2.1: Main parameters of the CMS magnet.

General parameters	
Magnetic length	12.5 m
Cold bore diameter	6.3 m
Central magnetic induction	4 T
Total Ampere-turns	41.7 MA-turns
Nominal current	19.14 kA
Inductance	14.2 H
Stored energy	2.6 GJ
Cold mass	
Layout	Five modules mechanically and electrically coupled
Radial thickness of cold mass	312 mm
Radiation thickness of cold mass	3.9 X_0
Weight of cold mass	220 t
Maximum induction on conductor	4.6 T
Temperature margin wrt operating temperature	1.8 K
Stored energy/unit cold mass	11.6 kJ/kg
Iron yoke	
Outer diameter of the iron flats	14 m
Length of barrel	13 m
Thickness of the iron layers in barrel	300, 630 and 630 mm
Mass of iron in barrel	6000 t
Thickness of iron disks in endcaps	250, 600 and 600 mm
Mass of iron in each endcap	2000 t
Total mass of iron in return yoke	10 000 t

because they have to transmit the large magnetic axial force corresponding to 14 700 t, without allowing local displacements due to possible gaps. These displacements can be partially converted into heat, causing a premature quench. A construction method which involved the machining of the upper surface of the modules and a local resin impregnation during the mechanical mounting allowed us to get an excellent mechanical coupling between the modules.

2008 JINST 3 S08004

Figure 2.2: The cold mass mounted vertically before integration with thermal shields and insertion in the vacuum chamber.

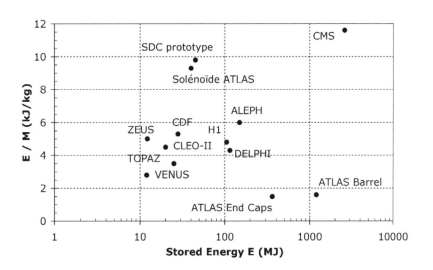

Figure 2.3: The energy-over-mass ratio E/M, for several detector magnets.

2008 JINST 3 S08004

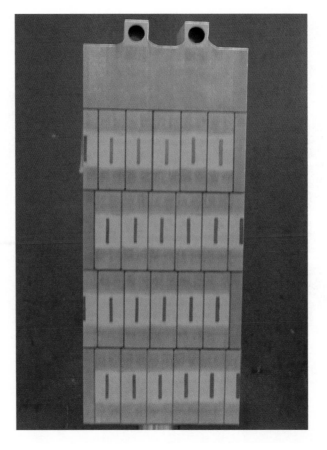

Figure 2.4: Cross section of the cold mass with the details of the 4-layer winding with reinforced conductor.

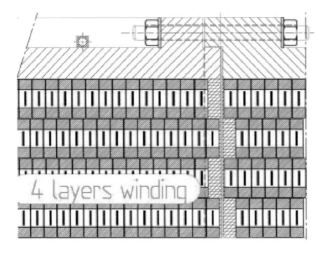

Figure 2.5: Detail of the interface region between 2 modules. In order to guarantee mechanical continuity, false turns are involved. The modules are connected through bolts and pins fixed through the outer mandrels.

2008 JINST 3 S08004

Figure 2.6: A view of the yoke at an early stage of magnet assembly at SX5. The central barrel supports the vacuum chamber of the superconducting coil. At the rear, one of the closing end cap disks is visible.

2.2.2 Yoke

The yoke (figure 2.6) is composed of 11 large elements, 6 endcap disks, and 5 barrel wheels, whose weight goes from 400 t for the lightest up to 1920 t for the central wheel, which includes the coil and its cryostat. The easy relative movement of these elements facilitates the assembly of the sub-detectors. To displace each element a combination of heavy-duty air pads plus grease pads has been chosen. This choice makes the system insensitive to metallic dust on the floor and allows transverse displacements. Two kinds of heavy-duty high-pressure air pads with a capacity of either 250 t (40 bars) or 385 t (60 bars) are used. This is not favourable for the final approach when closing the detector, especially for the YE1 endcap that is protruding into the vacuum tank. A special solution has been adopted: for the last 100 mm of approach, flat grease-pads (working pressure 100 bar) have been developed in order to facilitate the final closing of the detector. Once they touch the axially-installed z-stops, each element is pre-stressed with 100 t to the adjacent element. This assures good contact before switching on the magnet. In the cavern the elements will be moved on the 1.23% inclined floor by a strand jacking hydraulic system that ensures safe operation for uphill pulling as well as for downhill pushing by keeping a retaining force. The maximum movements possible in the cavern are of the order of 11 meters; this will take one hour.

To easily align the yoke elements, a precise reference system of about 70 points was installed in the surface assembly hall. The origin of the reference system is the geometrical center of the coil. The points were made after loading the coil cryostat with the inner detectors, the hadronic barrel in particular which weights 1000 t. A mark on the floor was made showing the position of each foot in order to pre-position each element within a $\pm$ 5 mm tolerance. Finally, all the elements were aligned with an accuracy of 2 mm with respect to the ideal axis of the coil.

2008 JINST 3 S08004

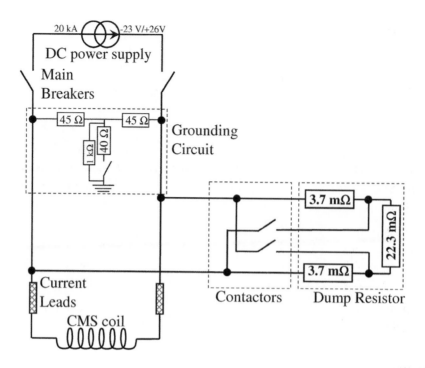

Figure 2.7: The electrical scheme of the magnet with the protection circuit. One of the main components of the protection is the dump resistor, made of three elements.

2.2.3 Electrical scheme

The CMS solenoid can be represented as a 14 H inductance mutually coupled with its external mandrel. This inductive coupling allows for the so-called *quench back* effect, as the eddy currents, induced in the external mandrel at the trigger of a current fast discharge, heat up the whole coil above the superconducting critical temperature. This is the fundamental basis of the protection system, which, in case of a superconducting to resistive transition of the coil, aims at keeping the lowest possible thermal gradients and temperature increase in the superconducting windings, and prevents the occurrence of local overheating, hence reducing the thermal stresses inside the winding. A diagram of the powering circuit with protection is shown in figure 2.7.

A bipolar thyristor power converter rated at 520 kW with passive L-C filters is used to power the CMS solenoid. It covers a range of voltages from +26 V to -23 V, with a nominal DC current of 19.1 kA. In case of a sudden switch off of the power converter, the current decays naturally in the bus-bar resistance and through the free-wheel thyristors until the opening of the main breakers. Inside the power converter, an assembly of free-wheel thyristors, mounted on naturally air-cooled heat sinks, is installed. In case of non-opening of the main switch breakers, the thyristors are rated to support 20 kA DC for 4 minutes. The current discharge is achieved by disconnecting the electrical power source by the use of two redundant 20 kA DC normally-open switch breakers, leaving the solenoid in series with a resistor, in a L-R circuit configuration. The stored magnetic energy is therefore extracted by thermal dissipation in the so-called dump resistor. This resistor is external to the solenoid cryostat and is designed to work without any active device. It is positioned

2008 JINST 3 S08004

outdoors taking advantage of natural air convection cooling. The fast discharge (FD) is automatically triggered by hardwired electronics only in case of a superconductive-to-resistive transition, a so-called quench, and for unrecoverable faults which require fast current dumping. The FD time constant is about 200 s. An emergency FD button is also available to the operator in case of need. As the coil becomes resistive during the FD, energy is dissipated inside the coil, which heats up. As a consequence, this necessitates a post-FD cool-down of the coil. The FD is performed on a 30 mΩ dump resistor, as a compromise to keep the dump voltage lower than 600 V, and to limit the coil warm-up and subsequent cool-down time. For faults involving the 20 kA power source, a slow discharge (SD) is triggered through hardwired electronics on a 2 mΩ dump resistor. The SD current evolution is typically exponential, and its time constant is 7025 s, but the coil stays in the superconducting state as the heat load, about 525 W, is fully absorbed by the cooling refrigerator. For current lower than 4 kA, a FD is performed in any case, as the heat load is small enough for the refrigerator. The same resistor is used in both cases for the FD and the SD, using normally open contactors, leaving the dump resistor modules either in series (FD) or in parallel (SD). For other cases, and depending on the alarms, the coil current can be adjusted by the operator, or ramped down to zero, taking advantage of the two-quadrant converter.

2.2.4 Vacuum system

The vacuum system has been designed to provide a good insulation inside the 40 m^3 vacuum volume of the coil cryostat. It consists of 2 double-primary pumping stations, equipped with 2 rotary pumps and 2 Root's pumps, that provide the fore vacuum to the two oil diffusion pumps located at the top of CMS and connected to the coil cryostat via the current leads chimney and the helium phase separator. The rotary pumps have a capacity of 280 m^3/h while the two Root's pumps have a flow of 1000 m^3/h. The biggest oil diffusion pump, installed via a DN 400 flange on the current leads chimney, has a nominal flow of 8000 l/s at 10^{-4} mbar of fore vacuum. The smallest one delivers 3000 l/s at the phase separator.

2.2.5 Cryogenic plant

The helium refrigeration plant for CMS is specified for a cooling capacity of 800 W at 4.45 K, 4500 W between 60 and 80 K, and simultaneously 4 g/s liquefaction capacity. The primary compressors of the plant have been installed, in their final position, while the cold box, as well as the intermediate cryostat which interfaces the phase separator and the thermo-syphon, were moved underground after the completion of the magnet test. These components were commissioned with the help of a temporary heat load of 6.5 kW that simulated the coil cryostat which was not yet available. The performance of the cold box has been measured in cool-down mode and in nominal and operation mode.

2.2.6 Other ancillaries

- *Current leads.* The two 20-kA current leads are made of a high purity copper braid, having a cross section of 1800 mm^2 and RRR (Residual Resistivity Ratio) of 130, placed inside a conduit and cooled by circulating helium gas. Without cooling, the current leads are able

2008 JINST 3 S08004

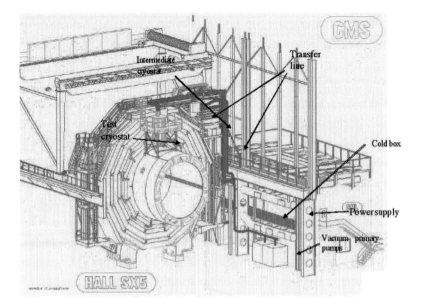

Figure 2.8: The layout for the surface test at SX5, showing only the central barrel. The magnet is connected to the cryoplant (through the proximity cryogenics), the vacuum and the power systems.

to hold a current of 20 kA for 5 minutes, followed by a FD without any damage, as the temperature at the hot spot stays below 400 K [14].

- *Grounding circuit.* The grounding circuit is connected across the solenoid terminals. It fixes the coil circuit potential, through a 1 kΩ resistor, dividing by two the potential to ground. The winding insulation quality is monitored by continuously measuring the leakage current through a 10 Ω grounding resistor.

- *Quench detection system.* The quench detection system is a key element of the Magnet Safety System (MSS). The role of the quench detection system is to detect a resistive voltage between two points of the coil, whose value and duration are compared to adjustable thresholds. The voltage taps are protected by 4.7 kΩ, 6 W resistors. There are 2 redundant systems, with resistor bridge detectors and differential detectors. For each system, there are 5 detectors. Each resistor bridge detector spans two modules and one detector spans the whole solenoid. Each coil module is compared with two other modules through two differential detectors.

2.3   Operating test

The magnet and all its ancillaries were assembled for testing in SX5 and ready for cool-down in January 2006. Figure 2.8 shows the test layout.

2008 JINST 3 S08004

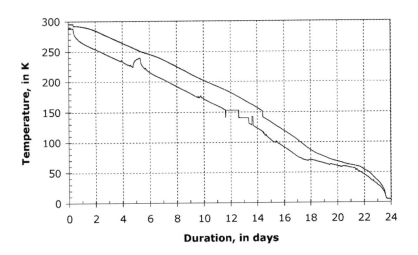

2008 JINST 3 S08004

Figure 2.9: Graph of the coil minimum and maximum temperatures during the cool-down from room temperature to 4.5 K.

2.3.1 Cool-down

The cool-down of the solenoid started on February, the 2nd, 2006 and in a smooth way brought the cold mass to 4.6 K in 24 days. Figure 2.9 shows the cool-down curve. The only glitch was due to an overpressure on a safety release valve that stopped cooling for one night before the system was restarted.

One important aspect monitored during the cool-down was the amount of coil shrinkage. In order to explain this point, we refer to the coil suspension system inside the cryostat (figure 2.1), made of longitudinal, vertical, and axial tie-rods in Ti alloy. The magnet is supported by 2×9 longitudinal tie rods, 4 vertical tie rods, and 8 radial tie rods. The tie rods are equipped with compensated strain gauges to measure the forces on 2×3 longitudinal, plus the vertical and radial tie rods. The tie rods are loaded in tension and flexion. To measure the tension and flexion strain, 3 strain gauges are placed on the tie rods at $0°$, $90°$, and $180°$.

The measured stresses in the tie bars due to the cool-down, causing a shrinkage of the cold mass and putting the tie-bars in tension, are shown in table 2.2. A comparison with the expected values is provided as well. The measured axial and radial shrinkage of the cold mass is shown in figure 2.10.

2.3.2 Charge and discharge cycles

The magnetic tests took place during August 2006, with additional tests during the magnet field mapping campaign in October 2006. The current ramps for the field mapping are detailed in figure 2.11. The tests were carried out through magnet charges to progressively higher currents, setting increasing dI/dt, followed by slow or fast discharges. During these current cycles all the relevant parameters related to electrical, magnetic, thermal, and mechanical behaviours have been

Table 2.2: Calculated and measured cold mass displacements and related stresses on tie-rods due to the cool-down to 4.5 K.

	Expected value	Measured value
Cold Mass Shrinkage		
Longitudinal	26 mm	27 mm
Radial	14 mm	15 mm
Tie rod stress due to cool-down		
Vertical	315 MPa	310±45 MPa
Radial	167 MPa	153±20 MPa
Longitudinal	277 MPa	260±20 MPa

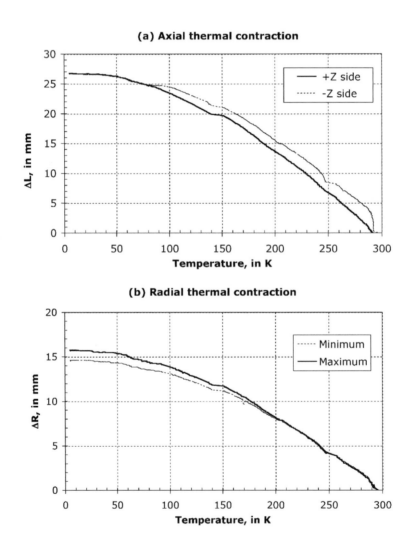

Figure 2.10: Axial (a) and radial (b) shrinkage of the cold mass from 300 K to 4.5 K.

2008 JINST 3 S08004

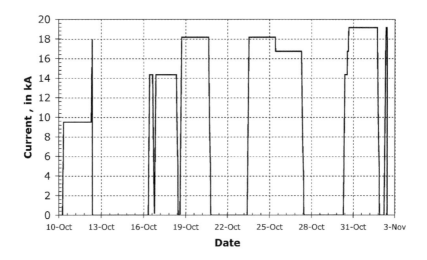

Figure 2.11: Magnet cycles during the CMS magnet tests in October 2006.

recorded. Depending on the level of the current at the trigger of a fast discharge, the time needed for re-cooling the coil can be up to 3 days.

2.3.3 Cold mass misalignment

The support system is designed to withstand the forces created by a 10 mm magnetic misalignment, in any direction of the cold mass with respect to the iron yoke. Geometrical surveys were performed at each step of the magnet assembly to ensure a good positioning. Nevertheless, the monitoring of the coil magnetic misalignment is of prime importance during magnet power test. The misalignment can be calculated either by analysing the displacement of the cold mass or the stresses of the tie rods when the coil is energised. The displacement is measured at several locations and directions at both ends of the coil with respect to the external vacuum tank wall, by the use of rectilinear potentiometers. Results are displayed in figures 2.12 and 2.13. The displacement of the coil's geometric centre is found to be 0.4 mm in z, in the $+z$ direction. According to the computations, such a displacement indicates that the coil centre should be less than 2 mm off the magnetic centre in $+z$. As the coil supporting system is hyper-static, the tie rods are not all initially identically loaded. But the force increase during energising is well distributed, as shown in figure 2.14 and figure 2.15, giving the force measurements on several tie rods. These figures also indicate the forces computed in the case of a 10-mm magnetic misalignment, together with forces calculated for the ideally-centred model, showing there is no noticeable effect of misalignment on the forces.

Using the strain gauges glued on the cold mass (outer mandrel of the central module, CB0), one can determine the Von Mises stress. The cold mass Von Mises stress versus the coil current is given in figure 2.16. The measured value of Von Mises stress at 4.5 K and zero current is 23 MPa. The value at 19.1 kA is 138 MPa. These values are in agreement with computations done during design [3, 6].

2008 JINST 3 S08004

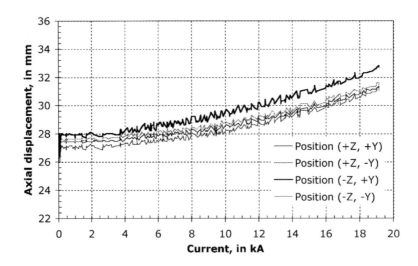

Figure 2.12: Axial displacement in Z at both ends of the coil in different positions during energising.

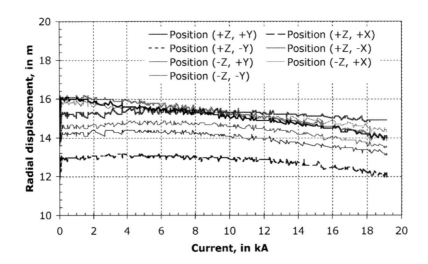

Figure 2.13: Radial displacement at both ends of the coil in different positions during energising.

2.3.4 Electrical measurements

The apparent coil inductance measured through the inductive voltage $V = L\mathrm{d}I/\mathrm{d}t$ is decreasing while increasing the current, as the iron yoke reaches the saturation region. From voltage measurements at the coil ends in the cryostat, while ramping up the coil current at a regulated $\mathrm{d}I/\mathrm{d}t$, the inductance is calculated and results are given in figure 2.17. Initially the apparent inductance of the coil is 14.7 H at zero current, and then it decreases to 13.3 H at 18 kA. The 21 resistive electrical joints, which connect the 5 modules together and, for each module, the 4 layers, are positioned externally to the coil, on the outer radius of the external mandrel, in low magnetic field regions. The

2008 JINST 3 S08004

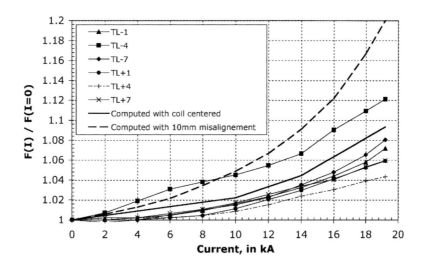

Figure 2.14: Force increase on several axial tie rods; the average force at zero current is 45 t.

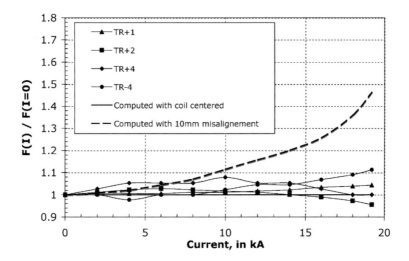

Figure 2.15: Force increase on several radial tie rods; the average force at zero current is 15 tons.

resistance measurements of the joints indicate values ranging from 0.7 nΩ to 1.6 nΩ at 19.1 kA, corresponding to a maximum dissipation in the joint of 0.6 W. The specific joint cooling system is fully efficient to remove this local heat deposit in order to avoid that the resistive joints generate a local quench of the conductor. As mentioned above, the fast discharge causes a quench of the coil, through the quench-back process. The typical current decay at the nominal current of 19.14 kA is given in figure 2.18.

The effect of the mutual coupling of the coil with the external mandrel is clearly visible at the beginning of the current fast discharge as shown in the zoomed detail of figure 2.18. It appears clearly that a high dI/dt of about 500 A/s occurs at the very beginning of the discharge. The

2008 JINST 3 S08004

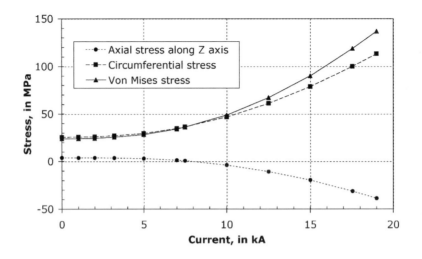

Figure 2.16: Stresses measured on the CB0 module as a function of the current.

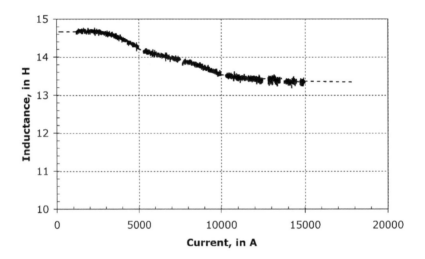

Figure 2.17: Coil inductance as a function of the magnet current.

minimum and maximum temperatures of the coil are displayed in figure 2.19 for a fast discharge at 19.14 kA. A maximum temperature difference of 32 K is measured on the coil between the warmest part, located on the coil central module internal radius, and the coldest part, located on the external radius of the mandrel. It should be noted that the thermal gradient is mainly radial. The temperature tends to equilibrate over the whole coil 2 hours after the trigger of the fast discharge. The average cold mass temperature after a fast discharge at 19 kA is 70 K.

During a magnet discharge, the dump resistor warms up, with a maximum measured temperature increase of 240°C, resulting in an increase of the total dump resistance value by up to 19%. Also the coil internal electrical resistance is increased by up to 0.1 Ω at the end of a FD at 19.14 kA.

2008 JINST 3 S08004

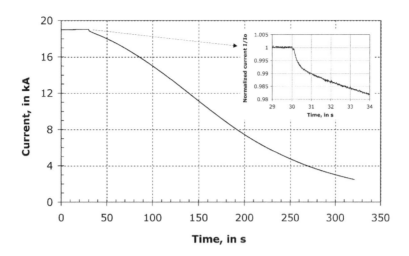

Figure 2.18: Magnet current during fast discharge at the nominal field of 4 T. The insert shows the details at the beginning of the discharge.

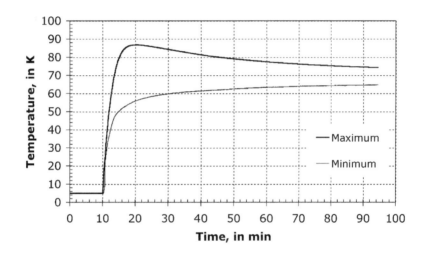

Figure 2.19: Minimum and maximum temperatures detected on the cold mass during the fast discharge from 19.1 kA.

The effect of both the dump resistor and the magnet electrical resistance increasing was revealed through the measurement of the discharge time constant, which was equal to 177 s, 203 s, 263 s, 348 s and 498 s for fast discharges respectively at 19 kA, 17.5 kA, 15 kA, 12.5 kA and 7.5 kA. This is visible in figure 2.20. The temperature recovery of the dump resistor is achieved in less than 2 hours after the trigger of a fast dump. It is 5 hours after the trigger of a slow dump.

In the case of a fast dump at 19.14 kA, typically half of the total energy (1250 MJ) is dissipated as heat in the external dump resistor. The energy dissipated in the dump resistor as a function of the

2008 JINST 3 S08004

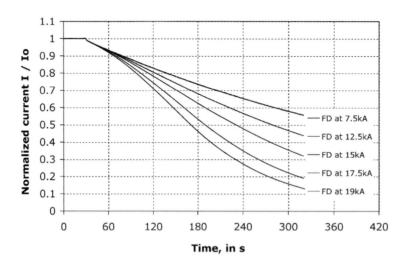

Figure 2.20: The normalised discharge current as a function of time for different initial currents, showing the effect of the increase in magnet and external dump resistance with current.

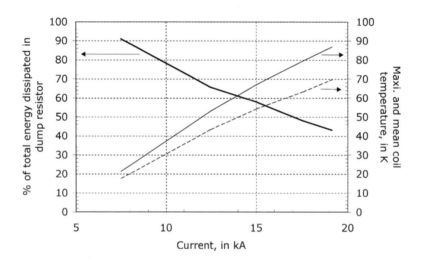

Figure 2.21: Energy dissipated in the external dump resistor and the mean and maximum temperatures of the coil during FD.

magnet current at the trigger of a FD was measured for each FD performed during the magnet tests and is given in figure 2.21. The magnet current is precisely measured by the use of two redundant DCCTs (DC current transformer). The peak-to-peak stability of the current is 7 ppm with a voltage ripple of 2.5% (0.65 V). In order to gain on the operation time, an acceleration of the slow dump has been tested and validated by switching to the fast dump configuration at 4 kA. It has been checked that the cryogenic refrigerator can take the full heat load, and the magnet stays in the superconducting state. This Slow Dump Accelerated (SDA) mode was tested in semi-automatic mode through the cryogenics supervisory system and the magnet control system, and it will be fully automatic for the final installation in the cavern.

2008 JINST 3 S08004

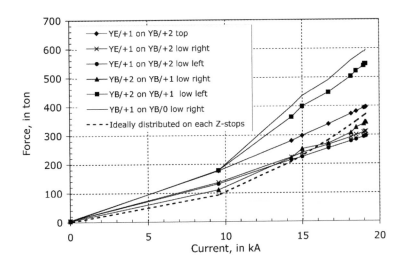

Figure 2.22: Axial forces acting on the yoke Z-stops during the coil energising.

2.3.5 Yoke mechanical measurements

The elements of the return yoke, barrels and endcaps, are attached with several hydraulic locking jacks, which are fixed on each barrel and endcap. They are pre-stressed in order to bring the barrels and endcaps into contact at specific areas using the aluminium-alloy Z-stop blocks. There are 24 Z-stops between each barrel and endcap. A computation of the total axial compressive force gives 8900 tons. The stresses are measured on some Z-stops; the forces on these Z-stops are given in figure 2.22 and compared to the case of a uniformly distributed load on all the Z-stops. To allow for uniform load distribution and distortion during magnet energising, the yoke elements are positioned on grease pads. During magnet energising, the displacement of the barrel yoke elements under the compressive axial force is very limited, while the displacement of the yoke end cap disk YE+1 is clearly noticeable on the outer radius of the disk, due to the axial attraction of the first yoke endcaps towards the interaction point. The measurement of the distance between the barrel elements parallel to the axial axis of the detector is given in figure 2.23. The endcap YE+1 disk is equipped with rosette strain gauges on its inner face, under the muon chambers and near the bolts at the interface between two adjacent segments. The main stresses measured in these regions do not exceed 88 MPa.

2.3.6 Coil stability characteristics

The NbTi superconductor critical temperature is $T_c = 9.25$ K at zero field. At $B = 4.6$ T (peak field on the conductor), $T_c = 7.30$ K. The current-sharing temperature T_g is defined as the maximum temperature for which the current can flow, with no dissipation, in the superconducting part. For CMS the operating current is 19 143 A, while the critical current, according to the measurements done on a short sample extracted from the length used in the inner layer of the central module (the one exposed to the higher field), is I_c (T= 4.5 K, B= 4.6 T) = 62 kA leading to $T_g = 6.44$ K, i.e., the temperature margin is 1.94 K. This margin is a little higher than the designed one (1.83

2008 JINST 3 S08004

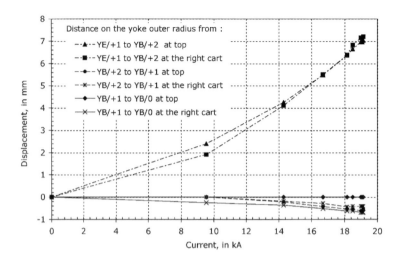

Figure 2.23: Measured displacement of the yoke during the coil energising.

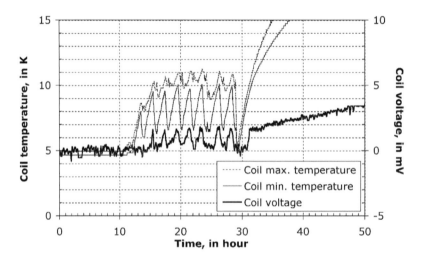

Figure 2.24: The minimum and maximum temperatures and voltage of the coil as a function of time, with only a few amperes of current, showing the superconducting-to-resistive-state transition at around 9.3 K.

K) because the nominal current is less than the one used in this kind of computation (19.5 kA) and the expected conductor critical current was from 7% to 10% lower than the real one obtained through advanced and qualified processes. The T_c value was confirmed at 9.3 K during cryogenic recovery tests (figure 2.24) at zero field. The conductor pure-aluminium stabilizer RRR, deduced from electrical measurements during cool-down, is found to be above 1800.

2008 JINST 3 S08004

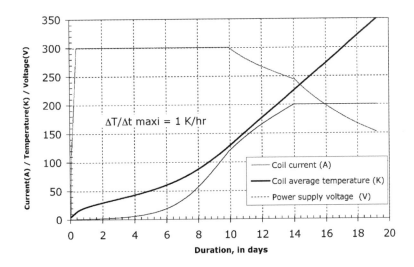

Figure 2.25: Measurements of the coil warm-up behaviour as a function of time; the Y-axis scale is common for all the three curves.

2.3.7 Coil warm-up

Following the test of the magnet on the surface, the cold mass had to be warmed up to room temperature before lowering. The coil, inside its cryostat, was attached to the central barrel YB0 to avoid any risk due to vacuum degradation during the transport operations. The warm-up was performed using a dedicated power supply (200 V-300 A DC) to maintain integrity of the coil/mandrel interface. Knowing the temperature dependence of both the electrical resistivity and the specific heat of the coil materials, the temperature increase for a given electrical power is calculated. Taking into account the capacity of the warm-up supply, and limiting the temperature increase to 1 K/hour, the warm-up was performed as shown in figure 2.25. As the warm-up was done after a fast discharge, the coil temperature was already at 70 K. Nevertheless, the warm-up took place only at night as the yoke was opened to continue integration activities inside the detector. Ultimately, the warm-up lasted only 3 weeks. The maximum temperature gradient across the coil during the warm-up exercise was less than 9 K.

2008 JINST 3 S08004

Chapter 3

Inner tracking system

3.1 Introduction

The inner tracking system of CMS is designed to provide a precise and efficient measurement of the trajectories of charged particles emerging from the LHC collisions, as well as a precise reconstruction of secondary vertices. It surrounds the interaction point and has a length of 5.8 m and a diameter of 2.5 m. The CMS solenoid provides a homogeneous magnetic field of 4 T over the full volume of the tracker. At the LHC design luminosity of $10^{34}\,\mathrm{cm^{-2}\,s^{-1}}$ there will be on average about 1000 particles from more than 20 overlapping proton-proton interactions traversing the tracker for each bunch crossing, i.e. every 25 ns. Therefore a detector technology featuring high granularity and fast response is required, such that the trajectories can be identified reliably and attributed to the correct bunch crossing. However, these features imply a high power density of the on-detector electronics which in turn requires efficient cooling. This is in direct conflict with the aim of keeping to the minimum the amount of material in order to limit multiple scattering, bremsstrahlung, photon conversion and nuclear interactions. A compromise had to be found in this respect. The intense particle flux will also cause severe radiation damage to the tracking system. The main challenge in the design of the tracking system was to develop detector components able to operate in this harsh environment for an expected lifetime of 10 years. These requirements on granularity, speed and radiation hardness lead to a tracker design entirely based on silicon detector technology. The CMS tracker is composed of a pixel detector with three barrel layers at radii between 4.4 cm and 10.2 cm and a silicon strip tracker with 10 barrel detection layers extending outwards to a radius of 1.1 m. Each system is completed by endcaps which consist of 2 disks in the pixel detector and 3 plus 9 disks in the strip tracker on each side of the barrel, extending the acceptance of the tracker up to a pseudorapidity of $|\eta| < 2.5$. With about 200 m^2 of active silicon area the CMS tracker is the largest silicon tracker ever built [15, 16].

The construction of the CMS tracker, composed of 1440 pixel and 15 148 strip detector modules, required the development of production methods and quality control procedures that are new to the field of particle physics detectors. A strong collaboration of 51 institutes with almost 500 physicists and engineers succeeded over a period of 12 to 15 years to design, develop and build this unique device.

3.1.1 Requirements and operating conditions

The expected LHC physics program [17] requires a robust, efficient and precise reconstruction of the trajectories of charged particles with transverse momentum above 1 GeV in the pseudorapidity range $|\eta| < 2.5$. A precise measurement of secondary vertices and impact parameters is necessary for the efficient identification of heavy flavours which are produced in many of the interesting physics channels. Together with the electromagnetic calorimeter and the muon system the tracker has to identify electrons and muons, respectively. Tau leptons are a signature in several discovery channels and need to be reconstructed in one-prong and three-prong decay topologies. In order to reduce the event rate from the LHC bunch crossing rate of 40 MHz to about 100 Hz which can be permanently stored, tracking information is heavily used in the high level trigger of CMS.

The operating conditions for a tracking system at the LHC are very challenging. As already mentioned, each LHC bunch crossing at design luminosity creates on average about 1000 particles hitting the tracker. This leads to a hit rate density of 1 MHz/mm^2 at a radius of 4 cm, falling to 60 kHz/mm^2 at a radius of 22 cm and 3 kHz/mm^2 at a radius of 115 cm. In order to keep the occupancy at or below 1% pixelated detectors have to be used at radii below 10 cm. For a pixel size of $100 \times 150 \, \mu$m^2 in r-ϕ and z, respectively, which is driven by the desired impact parameter resolution, the occupancy is of the order 10^{-4} per pixel and LHC bunch crossing. At intermediate radii ($20 \, \text{cm} < r < 55 \, \text{cm}$) the reduced particle flux allows the use of silicon micro-strip detectors with a typical cell size of 10 cm $\times$ 80 μm, leading to an occupancy of up to 2–3% per strip and LHC bunch crossing. In the outer region ($55 \, \text{cm} < r < 110 \, \text{cm}$) the strip pitch can be further increased. Given the large areas that have to be instrumented in this region, also the strip length has to be increased in order to limit the number of read-out channels. However, the strip capacitance scales with its length and therefore the electronics noise is a linear function of the strip length as well. In order to maintain a good signal to noise ratio of well above 10, CMS uses thicker silicon sensors for the outer tracker region (500 μm thickness as opposed to the 320 μm in the inner tracker) with correspondingly higher signal. These thicker sensors would in principle have a higher depletion voltage. But since the radiation levels in the outer tracker are smaller, a higher initial resistivity can be chosen such that the initial depletion voltages of thick and thin sensors are in the same range of 100 V to 300 V. In this way cell sizes up to about 25 cm $\times$ 180 μm can be used in the outer region of the tracker, with an occupancy of about 1%. These occupancy-driven design choices for the strip tracker also satisfy the requirements on position resolution.

CMS is the first experiment using silicon detectors in this outer tracker region. This novel approach was made possible by three key developments:

- sensor fabrication on 6 inch instead of 4 inch wafers reduced the sensor cost to 5–10 CHF/cm^2 and allowed the coverage of the large required surfaces with silicon sensors,

- implementation of the front-end read-out chip in industry-standard deep sub-micron technology led to large cost savings and to an improved signal-to-noise performance,

- automation of module assembly and use of high throughput wire bonding machines.

The radiation damage introduced by the high particle fluxes at the LHC interaction regions is a severe design constraint. Table 3.1 shows the expected fast hadron fluence and radiation dose

2008 JINST 3 S08004

Table 3.1: Expected hadron fluence and radiation dose in different radial layers of the CMS tracker (barrel part) for an integrated luminosity of $500\,\mathrm{fb}^{-1}$ (≈ 10 years). The fast hadron fluence is a good approximation to the $1\,\mathrm{MeV}$ neutron equivalent fluence [17].

Radius (cm)	Fluence of fast hadrons (10^{14} cm^{-2})	Dose (kGy)	Charged particle flux (cm^{-2}s^{-1})
4	32	840	10^8
11	4.6	190	
22	1.6	70	6×10^6
75	0.3	7	
115	0.2	1.8	3×10^5

in the CMS barrel tracker for an integrated luminosity of $500\,\mathrm{fb}^{-1}$ corresponding to about 10 years of LHC operation [15, 17]. Neutrons generated by hadronic interactions in the ECAL crystals make up a substantial contribution to the fast hadron fluence, which actually dominates in the outer tracker close to the ECAL surface. The uncertainties on these estimates due to the extrapolation error of the inelastic proton proton cross-section, momentum distributions and multiplicities to $\sqrt{s} = 14\,\mathrm{TeV}$ and in the Monte Carlo description of the cascade development lead to a safety factor of 1.5 (2 in regions where the neutron contribution dominates) which was applied to these estimates in order to define the design requirements for the tracker.

Three different effects had to be considered in the design of a radiation tolerant silicon tracker. Surface damage is created when the positively charged holes, generated by the passage of an ionizing particle, get trapped in a silicon oxide layer. This is mostly a concern for the front-end chips where this additional space charge changes for instance the characteristics of MOS structures. Surface damage simply scales with the absorbed dose. The silicon sensors are mainly affected by bulk damage, i.e. modifications to the silicon crystal lattice which are caused by non-ionizing energy loss (NIEL) and lead to additional energy levels in the band gap. NIEL is a complicated process, depending on particle type and energy, but is found to scale approximately with the fast hadron fluence. The consequences are an increase of the leakage current (linear in fluence), a change in the doping from n- to p-type with a corresponding change in depletion voltage by a few hundred volts over the lifetime of the tracker, and the creation of additional trapping centers which will reduce the signal by roughly 10% after 10 years of LHC running [18]. The design of the silicon sensors and the read-out electronics has to take this into account and assure a signal-to-noise ratio of 10:1 or better over the full lifetime of the detector, in order to guarantee a robust hit recognition at an acceptable fake hit rate. Finally, transient phenomena due to the generation of charge by ionizing particles in the electronic circuitry can change for instance the state of memory cells and therefore disturb or even stop the correct functioning of the read-out (single event upset, SEU).

The increased detector leakage current can lead to a dangerous positive feedback of the self heating of the silicon sensor and the exponential dependence of the leakage current on temperature, called thermal runaway. This has to be avoided by efficient coupling of the silicon sensors to the cooling system and by a low operating temperature. For this reason it is foreseen that the whole tracker volume will be operated at or slightly below $-10°\mathrm{C}$. After 10 years of operation it is

2008 JINST 3 S08004

expected that this will require a cooling fluid temperature of about $-27°C$ which in turn means that all structures in the tracker have to survive temperature cycles between room temperature and about $-30°C$. A second effect, called reverse annealing, requires to keep the silicon sensors permanently well below $0°C$ except for short maintenance periods. This effect is caused by the interaction of radiation induced defects in the silicon sensors which can lead to more serious damage and to an even stronger change in depletion voltage with fluence. Experimentally it is found that reverse annealing becomes insignificant for temperatures roughly below $0°C$ [18].

The read-out chips employed in the CMS tracker are fabricated in standard $0.25\ \mu m$ CMOS technology which is inherently radiation hard due to the thin gate oxide (and special design rules). The lifetime of the silicon strip tracker is therefore limited by the radiation damage to the silicon sensors. For efficient charge collection they always need to be over-depleted, requiring bias voltages up to 500 V after 10 years of LHC operation. This reaches the limit of the typical high voltage stability of current sensor layouts. Furthermore, the increased leakage currents of the sensors will at some point lead to thermal runaway. All tests have shown that the silicon strip tracker will remain fully operational for 10 years of LHC running. For the pixel detector on the other hand, which has to survive even higher radiation doses, under-depleted operation is possible due to a different sensor layout. Its lifetime reaches from at least 2 years at full LHC luminosity for the innermost layer to more than 10 years for the third layer.

The ultimate position resolution of the pixel and strip sensors is degraded by multiple scattering in the material that is necessary to precisely hold the sensors, to supply the electrical power (in total about 60 kW for the CMS tracker) and to cool the electronics and the silicon sensors. Nuclear interactions of pions and other hadrons in this material reduce significantly the tracking efficiency for these particles. In addition, this material leads to photon conversion and bremsstrahlung which adversely affect the measurement accuracy of the electromagnetic calorimeter. It was therefore a requirement to keep the amount of this material to a minimum.

3.1.2 Overview of the tracker layout

A schematic drawing of the CMS tracker is shown in figure 3.1. At radii of $4.4, 7.3$ and $10.2\,cm$, three cylindrical layers of hybrid pixel detector modules surround the interaction point. They are complemented by two disks of pixel modules on each side. The pixel detector delivers three high precision space points on each charged particle trajectory. It is described in detail in section 3.2. In total the pixel detector covers an area of about $1\,m^2$ and has 66 million pixels.

The radial region between 20 cm and 116 cm is occupied by the silicon strip tracker, which is described in detail in section 3.3. It is composed of three different subsystems. The Tracker Inner Barrel and Disks (TIB/TID) extend in radius towards 55 cm and are composed of 4 barrel layers, supplemented by 3 disks at each end. TIB/TID delivers up to 4 r-ϕ measurements on a trajectory using $320\,\mu m$ thick silicon micro-strip sensors with their strips parallel to the beam axis in the barrel and radial on the disks. The strip pitch is $80\,\mu m$ on layers 1 and 2 and $120\,\mu m$ on layers 3 and 4 in the TIB, leading to a single point resolution of $23\,\mu m$ and $35\,\mu m$, respectively. In the TID the mean pitch varies between $100\,\mu m$ and $141\,\mu m$. The TIB/TID is surrounded by the Tracker Outer Barrel (TOB). It has an outer radius of 116 cm and consists of 6 barrel layers of $500\,\mu m$ thick micro-strip sensors with strip pitches of $183\,\mu m$ on the first 4 layers and $122\,\mu m$ on

2008 JINST 3 S08004

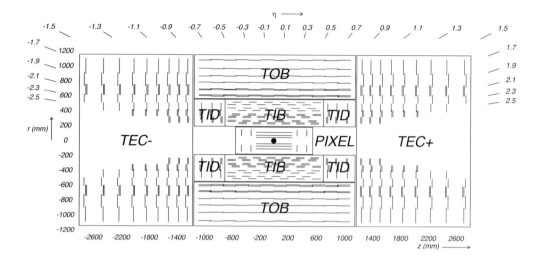

Figure 3.1: Schematic cross section through the CMS tracker. Each line represents a detector module. Double lines indicate back-to-back modules which deliver stereo hits.

layers 5 and 6. It provides another 6 r-ϕ measurements with single point resolution of 53 μm and 35 μm, respectively. The TOB extends in z between $\pm$118 cm. Beyond this z range the Tracker EndCaps (TEC+ and TEC- where the sign indicates the location along the z axis) cover the region 124 cm $< |z| <$ 282 cm and 22.5 cm $< |r| <$ 113.5 cm. Each TEC is composed of 9 disks, carrying up to 7 rings of silicon micro-strip detectors (320 μm thick on the inner 4 rings, 500 μm thick on rings 5-7) with radial strips of 97 μm to 184 μm average pitch. Thus, they provide up to 9 ϕ measurements per trajectory.

In addition, the modules in the first two layers and rings, respectively, of TIB, TID, and TOB as well as rings 1, 2, and 5 of the TECs carry a second micro-strip detector module which is mounted back-to-back with a stereo angle of 100 mrad in order to provide a measurement of the second co-ordinate (z in the barrel and r on the disks). The achieved single point resolution of this measurement is 230 μm and 530 μm in TIB and TOB, respectively, and varies with pitch in TID and TEC. This tracker layout ensures at least $\approx$ 9 hits in the silicon strip tracker in the full range of $|\eta| <$ 2.4 with at least $\approx$ 4 of them being two-dimensional measurements (figure 3.2). The ultimate acceptance of the tracker ends at $|\eta| \approx$ 2.5. The CMS silicon strip tracker has a total of 9.3 million strips and 198 m^2 of active silicon area.

Figure 3.3 shows the material budget of the CMS tracker in units of radiation length. It increases from 0.4 X_0 at $\eta \approx$ 0 to about 1.8 X_0 at $|\eta| \approx$ 1.4, beyond which it falls to about 1 X_0 at $|\eta| \approx$ 2.5.

3.1.3 Expected performance of the CMS tracker

For single muons of transverse momenta of 1, 10 and 100 GeV figure 3.4 shows the expected resolution of transverse momentum, transverse impact parameter and longitudinal impact parameter, as a function of pseudorapidity [17]. For high momentum tracks (100 GeV) the transverse momentum resolution is around $1 - 2$% up to $|\eta| \approx$ 1.6, beyond which it degrades due to the reduced lever arm. At a transverse momentum of 100 GeV multiple scattering in the tracker material accounts for 20 to

2008 JINST 3 S08004

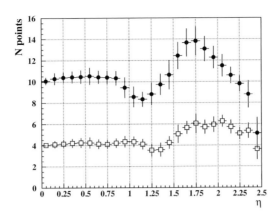

Figure 3.2: Number of measurement points in the strip tracker as a function of pseudorapidity η. Filled circles show the total number (back-to-back modules count as one) while open squares show the number of stereo layers.

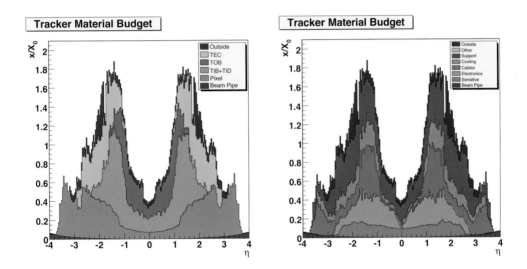

Figure 3.3: Material budget in units of radiation length as a function of pseudorapidity η for the different sub-detectors (left panel) and broken down into the functional contributions (right panel).

30% of the transverse momentum resolution while at lower momentum it is dominated by multiple scattering. The transverse impact parameter resolution reaches $10\,\mu$m for high p_T tracks, dominated by the resolution of the first pixel hit, while at lower momentum it is degraded by multiple scattering (similarly for the longitudinal impact parameter). Figure 3.5 shows the expected track reconstruction efficiency of the CMS tracker for single muons and pions as a function of pseudorapidity. For muons, the efficiency is about 99% over most of the acceptance. For $|\eta| \approx 0$ the efficiency decreases slightly due to gaps between the ladders of the pixel detector at $z \approx 0$. At high η the efficiency drop is mainly due to the reduced coverage by the pixel forward disks. For pions and hadrons in general the efficiency is lower because of interactions with the material in the tracker.

2008 JINST 3 S08004

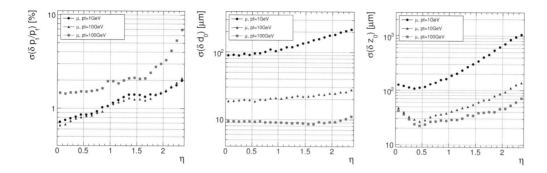

Figure 3.4: Resolution of several track parameters for single muons with transverse momenta of 1, 10 and 100 GeV: transverse momentum (left panel), transverse impact parameter (middle panel), and longitudinal impact parameter (right panel).

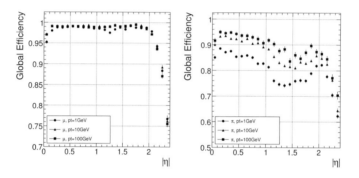

Figure 3.5: Global track reconstruction efficiency for muons (left panel) and pions (right panel) of transverse momenta of 1, 10 and 100 GeV.

3.1.4 Tracker system aspects

All elements of the CMS tracker are housed in the tracker support tube, which is suspended on the HCAL barrel. The tracker support tube is a large cylinder 5.30 m long with an inner diameter of 2.38 m. The 30-mm-thick wall of the cylinder is made by two 950-1/T300 carbon fiber composite skins, 2 mm in thickness, sandwiching a 26-mm-high Nomex core. Over the entire length of the tube's inner surface, two carbon fiber rails are attached on the horizontal plane. The tracker outer barrel (TOB) and both endcaps (TEC+ and TEC-) rest on these rails by means of adjustable sliding pads. The tracker inner barrel and disks (TIB/TID) are in turn supported by the TOB. The angle between the guiding elements of these rails is controlled to better than 0.183 mrad, corresponding to a parallelism between the guides better than ±0.5 mm in all directions over the full length.

An independent support and insertion system for the pixel detectors, the central section of the beam pipe and the inner elements of the radiation monitor system spans the full length of the tracker at its inner radius. This is composed of three long carbon fiber structures, joined together during tracker assembly to form two continuous parallel planes, on which precision tracks for the installation, support and positioning of each element are machined. The central element is a 2266.5-mm-long and 436-mm-wide cylinder which is connected with flanges to the TIB/TID detector. This element provides support and accurate positioning to the pixel detectors. Two 2420-

2008 JINST 3 S08004

mm-long side elements are coupled to it only by very precise pinned connections, bridging the gap between the faces of the TIB/TID and the closing flanges of the tracker without direct contact to the TEC detectors. These side elements are therefore structurally decoupled from the silicon strip detectors and can be installed and removed at any time with no impact on the strip detectors. They serve several purposes: they provide support and alignment features for the central section of the beam pipe, they allow the installation of the inner elements of the radiation monitor system, and they are used for installation and removal of all the components permanently or temporarily housed in the inner region of the tracker: beam pipe, bake-out equipment, pixel barrel, pixel disks and radiation monitor. This system of permanent tracks, light but very stiff and stable, installed in the core of the tracker will allow for the quickest possible intervention in this region during maintenance, inducing no disturbance to the volume occupied by the silicon strip detectors. This feature will be extremely valuable after some years of operation, when activation of components and radiation damage on sensors will start becoming an issue.

The outer surface of the tracker tube faces the electromagnetic calorimeter, which is operated at room temperature and requires good temperature stability. The surface of the electromagnetic calorimeter must be kept at $(18 \pm 4)°C$ while the tracker volume needs to be cooled to below $-10°C$. In order to achieve this thermal gradient over a very limited radial thickness, the inside surface of the tracker support tube is lined with an active thermal screen. It ensures a temperature below $-10°C$ inside the tracker volume even when the sub-detectors and their cooling are switched off, while maintaining a temperature above $+12°C$ on the outer surface of the support tube in order to avoid condensation. It also reduces the thermal stress across the support tube structure. The thermal screen consists of 32 panels. On the inside, cold fluid is circulated in a thin aluminium plate whilst, separated by 8 mm of Rohacell foam, several polyimide-insulated resistive circuits are powered to heat up the outer surface to the required temperature. The system is feed-back controlled, based on 64 temperature sensors.

The total power dissipation inside the tracker volume is expected to be close to 60 kW. Mainly for robustness in operation, the CMS tracker is equipped with a mono-phase liquid cooling system. The liquid used for refrigeration of the silicon strip and pixel detector as well as the thermal screen is C_6F_{14}. It has a sufficiently low viscosity even at the lowest required temperature, excellent behaviour under irradiation and is extremely volatile (with practically no residues) thus minimizing eventual damages from accidental leaks. The cooling system provides up to $77 \, m^3/hour$ of C_6F_{14} liquid to the tracker, at a temperature of down to $-35°C$ and with a pressure drop of up to 8 bar. This corresponds to a cooling capacity of up to 128 kW.

The full tracker volume (about $25 \, m^3$) is flushed with pre-chilled dry nitrogen gas at a rate of up to one volume exchange per hour.

3.2 Pixel detector

3.2.1 Pixel system general

The pixel system is the part of the tracking system that is closest to the interaction region. It contributes precise tracking points in r-ϕ and z and therefore is responsible for a small impact parameter resolution that is important for good secondary vertex reconstruction. With a pixel cell

2008 JINST 3 S08004

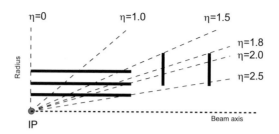

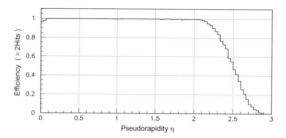

Figure 3.6: Geometrical layout of the pixel detector and hit coverage as a function of pseudorapidity.

size of $100 \times 150 \ \mu m^2$ emphasis has been put on achieving similar track resolution in both r-ϕ and z directions. Through this a 3D vertex reconstruction in space is possible, which will be important for secondary vertices with low track multiplicity. The pixel system has a zero-suppressed read out scheme with analog pulse height read-out. This improves the position resolution due to charge sharing and helps to separate signal and noise hits as well as to identify large hit clusters from overlapping tracks.

The pixel detector covers a pseudorapidity range $-2.5 < \eta < 2.5$, matching the acceptance of the central tracker. The pixel detector is essential for the reconstruction of secondary vertices from b and tau decays, and forming seed tracks for the outer track reconstruction and high level triggering. It consists of three barrel layers (BPix) with two endcap disks (FPix). The 53-cm-long BPix layers will be located at mean radii of 4.4, 7.3 and 10.2 cm. The FPix disks extending from ≈ 6 to 15 cm in radius, will be placed on each side at $z=\pm 34.5$ and $z=\pm 46.5$ cm. BPix (FPix) contain 48 million (18 million) pixels covering a total area of 0.78 (0.28) m^2. The arrangement of the 3 barrel layers and the forward pixel disks on each side gives 3 tracking points over almost the full η-range. Figure 3.6 shows the geometric arrangement and the hit coverage as a function of pseudorapidity η. In the high η region the 2 disk points are combined with the lowest possible radius point from the 4.4 cm barrel layer.

The vicinity to the interaction region also implies a very high track rate and particle fluences that require a radiation tolerant design. For the sensor this led to an n+ pixel on n-substrate detector design that allows partial depleted operation even at very high particle fluences. For the barrel layers the drift of the electrons to the collecting pixel implant is perpendicular to the 4 T magnetic field of CMS. The resulting Lorentz drift leads to charge spreading of the collected signal charge over more than one pixel. With the analog pulse height being read out a charge interpolation allows to achieve a spatial resolution in the range of 15–20 μm. The forward detectors are tilted at 20° in a turbine-like geometry to induce charge-sharing. The charge-sharing is mainly due to the geometric effect of particles entering the detector at an average angle of 20° away from normal incidence [19]; charge-sharing is also enhanced by the $\vec{E} \times \vec{B}$ drift. A position resolution of approximately 15 μm in both directions can be achieved with charge-sharing between neighbouring pixels. The reduction in the depletion depth or the increase in bias voltage will lead to a reduction of charge-sharing and therefore a degradation of the spatial resolution with radiation damage.

In order to allow a replacement of the innermost layers the mechanics and the cabling of the pixel system has been designed to allow a yearly access if needed. At full LHC luminosity we expect the innermost layer to stay operational for at least 2 years. The 3 layer barrel mechanics as well as the forward disks are divided into a left and a right half. This is required to allow installation along the beam pipe and to pass beyond the beam pipe support wires at $z=\pm$ 1632 mm. The 6 individual mechanical pieces are referenced to each other through precisely machined rails inside the TIB cylinder. Power, cooling, the optical controls as well as the optical read-out lines are brought to the detector through supply tube shells. In case of the barrel pixel system the supply tubes have a flexible connection that needs to bend by a few degrees during insertion following the slightly curved rails around the beam pipe support ring.

The pixel system is inserted as the last sub-detector of CMS after the silicon strip tracker has been installed and after the central section of the beam pipe has been installed and baked out.

3.2.2 Sensor description

Technological choices

The sensors for the CMS-pixel detector adopt the so called *n*-on-*n* concept. The pixels consist of high dose n-implants introduced into a high resistance n-substrate. The rectifying pn-junction is placed on the back side of the sensor surrounded by a multi guard ring structure. Despite the higher costs due to the double sided processing this concept was chosen as the collection of electrons ensures a high signal charge at moderate bias voltages (< 600 V) after high hadron fluences. Furthermore the double sided processing allows a guard ring scheme keeping all sensor edges at ground potential.

The isolation technique applied for the regions between the pixel electrodes was developed in close collaboration with the sensor vendors. Open p-stops [20] were chosen for the disks and moderated p-spray [21] for the barrel. Both types of sensors showed sufficient radiation hardness during an extensive qualification procedure including several test beams [22, 23].

Disk sensors

The disk sensors use the p-stop technique for interpixel isolation. To maximize the charge collection efficiency and minimize the pixel capacitance within the design rules of the vendor a width of 8 μm for the p-stop rings and a distance of 12 μm between implants was chosen. Figure 3.7 shows a photograph of 4 pixel cells. The open ring p-stops, the bump-bonding pad and the contact between the aluminium and the implanted collecting electrode are highlighted.

2008 JINST 3 S08004

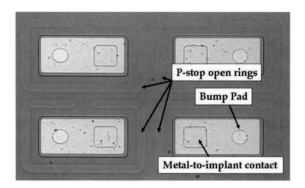

Figure 3.7: Picture of four pixels in the same double column for a pixel disk sensor.

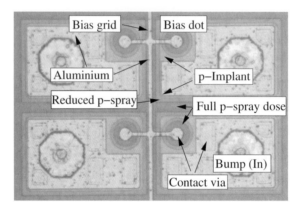

Figure 3.8: Photograph of four pixel cells. The Indium bumps are already deposited but not yet reflown.

The opening on the p-stop rings provides a low resistance path until full depletion is reached to allow IV (current-voltage) characterization of the sensor on wafer and a high resistance path when the sensor is over-depleted (10–20 V over-depletion) to assure interpixel isolation.

The process is completely symmetric with five photolithographic steps on each side to minimize the mechanical stress on the silicon substrate and the potential bowing of the diced sensors.

The sensors were all fabricated in 2005 on 4 inch wafers. The depletion voltage is 45–50 V and the leakage current is less than 10 nA per cm^2. The 7 different sensor tiles needed to populate a disk blade, ranging from 1×2 read-out chips (ROCs) to 2×5 ROCs, are implemented on a single wafer.

A production yield higher than 90% has been achieved and 150 good sensors for each of the seven flavours are available to the project for module assembly.

Barrel sensors

The sensors for the pixel barrel use the moderated p-spray technique for interpixel isolation. A photograph of four pixels in a barrel sensor is shown in figure 3.8. Most area of a pixel is covered with the collecting electrode formed by the n-implant. The gap between the n-implants is kept small ($20 \, \mu$m) to provide a homogeneous drift field which leads to a relatively high capacitance of the order of 80-100 fF per pixel.

2008 JINST 3 S08004

In one corner of each pixel the so called *bias dot* is visible. They provide a high resistance punch-through connection to all pixels which allows on-wafer IV measurements which are important to exclude faulty sensors from the module production.

The dark *frame* around the pixel implants visible in figure 3.8 indicates the opening in the nitride covering the thermal oxide. In this region the p-spray dose reaches the full level. Close to the lateral pn-junction between the pixel implant and the p-sprayed inter-pixel region the boron dose is reduced.

The sensor shown in figure 3.8 has undergone the bump deposition process. The Indium bumps are visible as roughly $50\,\mu$m wide octagons.

The sensors are processed on n-doped DOFZ-silicon [24] with $\langle 111 \rangle$ orientation and a resistivity of about $3.7\,\mathrm{k\Omega cm}$ (after processing). This leads to a full depletion voltage of 50-60 V of the $285\,\mu$m thick sensors. All wafers for the production of the barrel sensors come from the same silicon ingot to provide the best possible homogeneity of all material parameters.

The pixel barrel requires two different sensor geometries, 708 full (2×8 ROCs) and 96 half modules (1×8 ROCs). They were processed in 2005 and 2006 using two different mask sets.

3.2.3 Pixel detector read-out

System overview

The pixel read-out and control system [25] consists of three parts: a read-out data link from the modules/blades to the pixel front end driver (pxFED), a fast control link from the pixel front end controller (pFEC) to the modules/blades and a slow control link from a standard FEC to the supply tube/service cylinder. The latter is used to configure the ASICs on the supply tube/service cylinder through a I^{2}C protocol. Figure 3.9 shows a sketch of the system.

The front end consists of a Token Bit Manager (TBM) chip which controls several read-out chips (ROCs). The pFEC sends the 40MHz clock and fast control signals (e.g. trigger, reset) to the front end and programs all front end devices. The pxFED receives data from the front end, digitizes it, formats it and sends it to the CMS-DAQ event builder. The pFEC, FEC and pxFED are VME modules located in the electronics room and are connected to the front end through 40 MHz optical links. The various components are described in the following sections.

Read-out chip

Sensor signals are read out by ROCs bump bonded to the sensors. A ROC is a full custom ASIC fabricated in a commercial 0.25-μm 5-metal-layer CMOS process and contains 52×80 pixels [26]. Its main purposes are:

- Amplification and buffering of the charge signal from the sensor.

- Zero suppression in the pixel unit cell. Only signals above a certain threshold will be read out. This threshold can be adjusted individually for each pixel by means of four trim bits. The trim bits have a capacitive protection against single event upset (SEU), which has shown to reduce SEUs by 2 orders of magnitude [26]. The mean threshold dispersion after trimming at T$= -10°$C is 90 electrons equivalent with a noise of 170 electrons.

2008 JINST 3 S08004

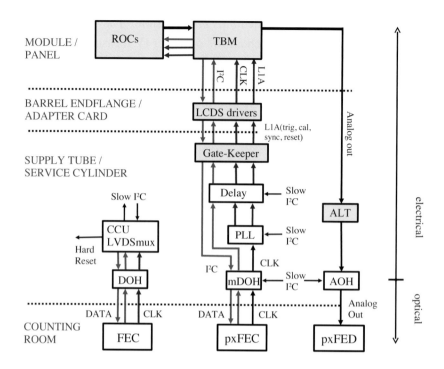

Figure 3.9: Block diagram of the pixel control and read-out system.

- Level 1 trigger verification. Hit information without a corresponding L1 trigger is abandoned.

- Sending hit information and some limited configuration data (analog value of last addressed DAC) to the TBM chip. Pixel addresses are transferred as 6 level analog encoded digital values within 5 clock cycles (125ns) while the pulse height information is truly analog.

- Adjusting various voltage levels, currents and offsets in order to compensate for chip-to-chip variations in the CMOS device parameters. There are a total of 29 DACs on the chip.

The ROC needs two supply voltages of 1.5 V and 2.5 V. There are 6 on chip voltage regulators. They compensate for differences in supply voltage due to voltage drops in module cables of different lengths, improve AC power noise rejection and strongly reduce intermodule cross-talk. An on-chip temperature sensor allows the monitoring of the module temperature online. The ROC is controlled through a modified I^2C interface running at 40 MHz. The configuration data can be downloaded without stopping data acquisition.

There are a few architecture inherent data loss mechanisms. The particle detection inefficiency has been measured in a high-rate pion beam. It is in fairly good agreement with expectations and reaches 0.8%, 1.2% and 3.8% respectively for the three layers at a luminosity of 10^{34} s^{-1}cm^{-2} and 100 kHz L1 trigger rate.

The power consumption depends on the pixel hit rate. At the LHC design luminosity, the ROC contributes with 34 μW per pixel about 88% (62%) to the total pixel detector front end power budget before (after) the detector has received a total fluence of 6×10^{14}/cm^2.

2008 JINST 3 S08004

Token Bit Manager chip

The TBM [27] controls the read-out of a group of pixel ROCs. The TBM is designed to be located on the detector near to the pixel ROCs. In the case of the barrel, they will be mounted on the detector modules and will control the read-out of 8 or 16 ROCs depending upon the layer radius. In the case of the forward disks, they will be mounted on the disk blades and will control the read-out of 21 or 24 ROCs depending on blade side. A TBM and the group of ROCs that it controls will be connected to a single analog optical link over which the data will be sent to the front end driver, a flash ADC module located in the electronics house. The principal functions of the TBM include the following:

- It will control the read-out of the ROCs by initiating a token pass for each incoming Level-1 trigger.

- On each token pass, it will write a header and a trailer word to the data stream.

- The header will contain an 8 bit event number and the trailer will contain 8 bits of error status. These will be transferred as 2 bit analog encoded digital.

- It will distribute the Level-1 triggers, and clock to the ROCs.

Each arriving Level-1 trigger will be placed on a 32-deep stack awaiting its associated token pass. Normally the stack will be empty but is needed to accommodate high burst rates due to noise, high track density events, or trigger bursts. Since there will be two analog data links per module for the inner two layers of the barrel, the TBMs will be configured as pairs in a Dual TBM Chip. In addition to two TBMs, this chip also contains a Control Network. The Hub serves as a port addressing switch for control commands that are sent from the DAQ to the front end TBMs and ROCs. These control commands will be sent over a digital optical link from a front end controller in the electronics house to the front end Hubs. The commands will be sent using a serial protocol, running at a speed of 40 MHz. This high speed is mandated by the need to rapidly cycle through a refreshing of the pixel threshold trim bits that can become corrupted due to single event upsets. There are four external, write only ports on each Hub for communicating with the ROCs and there is one internal read/write port for communicating with the TBMs within the chip. The first byte of each command will contain a 5-bit Hub address and a 3-bit port address. When a Hub is addressed, it selects the addressed port, strips off the byte containing the Hub/port address and passes the remainder of the command stream unmodified onto the addressed port. The outputs of the external ports consist of two low voltage differential lines for sending clock and data.

Analog chain

The hit information is read out serially through analog links in data packets containing all hits belonging to a single trigger. Within such packets a new analog value is transmitted every 25 ns and digitized in the Front End Driver (pxFED) at the same rate. Each pixel hit uses 6 values, or 150 ns. Five values are used to encode the address of a pixel inside a ROC and the sixth value represents the signal charge. Only the charge signals are truly analog while headers and addresses are discrete levels generated by DACs. No ROC IDs are sent but every ROC adds a header, whether

2008 JINST 3 S08004

it has hits or not in order to make the association of hits to ROCs possible. The sequential read-out is controlled by a token bit which is emitted by the TBM, passed from ROC to ROC and back to the TBM. The differential electrical outputs of the ROCs are multiplexed by the TBM onto either one or two output lines. On the same lines the TBM transmits a header before starting the ROC read-out. After receiving the token back from the last ROC in the chain the TBM sends a trailer containing status information. From the TBM to the end ring of the pixel barrel the read-out uses the module Kapton cable. The Kapton cable has a ground mesh on the back side and the differential analog lines are separated by quiet lines from the fast digital signals. Nevertheless, cross-talk from LVDS signals was found to be unacceptable and a low swing digital protocol is being used instead. On the end ring the analog signals are separated from the digital and all analog signals of the sector are sent on a separate Kapton cable to a printed circuit board that houses the Analog Optical Hybrids (AOH). The signal path between TBM and AOH is designed with a constant impedance of 40 Ω and terminated on the AOH. The optical links of the pixel system are identical to those used in the silicon strip tracker. An ASIC that adapts the output levels of the pixel modules to those expected by the laser driver has been added to the AOH of the pixel system. A clean identification of the six levels used for encoding pixel addresses is crucial for the reconstruction of hits. The ratio of RMS width to separation of the digitized levels after the full read-out chain is 1:30. The rise-time at the digitizer input is 3 ns which makes corrections from previously transmitted levels negligible. The full read-out chain adds a noise equivalent to 300 electrons to the analog pulse height, dominated by baseline variations of the laser drivers.

Front End Driver

Optical signals from the pixel front end electronics (ROCs and TBMs) are digitized using the pixel Front End Digitizer (pxFED). A pxFED is a 9U VME module. It has 36 optical inputs each equipped with an optical receiver and an ADC. The ADC converts at LHC frequency supplied by the TTC system which can be adjusted by an individually programmed phase shift (16 steps within 25 ns) for precise timing. A programmable offset voltage to compensate bias shifts can also be set. The output of the 10 bit-ADC is processed by a state machine to deliver pixel event fragments consisting of header, trailer, input channel number, ROC numbers, double column numbers and addresses and amplitudes of hit pixels all at a subject-dependent resolution of 5 to 8 bits. Event fragments are strobed into FIFO-1 (1k deep × 36 bit wide) which can be held on demand to enable read-out via VME. In normal processing mode FIFO-1 is open and data of 4 (5) combined input channels are transmitted to 8 FIFO-2 memories (8k × 72 bits). In order to determine thresholds and levels required for the state machine, FIFO-1 can alternatively be operated in a transparent mode making unprocessed ADC output data available. The output from FIFO-2 is clocked into two FIFO-3 memories (8k × 72 bits) whose outputs are combined to provide the data now at a frequency of 80 MHz (twice the common operating pxFED-frequency) to the S-Link interface acting as a point-to-point link with the CMS-DAQ system. Parallel to the data flow spy FIFOs are implemented (restricted in size) to hold selected event fragments and make them available for checking data integrity. Error detection takes place in the data stream from FIFO-1 to FIFO-2 and corresponding flags are embedded in the event trailer and also accessible from VME. A selected DAC output from each ROC (on default representing the ROC's temperature) is available as well.

2008 JINST 3 S08004

In addition, errors are directly transmitted to the CMS-TTS system using a dedicated connector on the S-Link supplementary card. A histogramming feature has been implemented to monitor the rate of double column hits. This histogram is intended to be read out via VME periodically to check for dead or overloaded columns. The pxFED houses an internal test system which, when enabled, replaces the normal ADC input by a pattern of 256 clocked analog levels simulating a normal pixel event. There are three test DACs (10-bit) available to generate such a pattern meaning that every third input channel receives the same simulated event. This test system allows to test most of the features of the pxFED without the need of external optical input signals. All FIFOs, the state machine with its adjustable parameters, the VME protocol, error detection and histogramming features are integrated into several FPGAs mounted on daughter cards making the pxFED flexible to changes and improvements. The corresponding firmware can be downloaded via VME or using a JTAG bus connector mounted on the mother board. The whole pixel read-out system will consist of 40 pxFED modules (32 for the barrel and 8 for the forward) set up in three 9U VME crates located in the electronics room. Individual modules can be accessed by VME geographical addressing.

Front End Controller

The Pixel Front End Controller (pFEC) supplies clock and trigger information to the front end, and provides a data path to the front end for configuration settings over a fiber optic connection. The pFEC uses the same hardware as the standard CMS FEC-CCS [28]. The firmware which defines the behaviour of the mezzanine FEC (mFEC) module has been replaced by a pixel specific version, converting the FEC into a pFEC. Each mFEC board becomes two command links to the front end. The Trigger Encoder performs all trigger transmission functions, encoding TTC triggers to match the pixel standard, block triggers to a given channel, generate internal triggers, either singly, or continuously, for testing purposes. Within each command link are a one kilobyte output buffer for data transmission, and a two kilobyte input buffer for data receiving. All data, whether write or read operations, are retransmitted back from the front end for possible verification. To minimize the VME data transfer time, the pFEC uses several data transfer modes. When transferring pixel trim values to the front end, the pFEC calculates the row number information for a given column of pixels on the fly. This results in nearly a 50% reduction in the time required to transfer trim values over VME to a given command link buffer. In this way, the entire pixel front end trims can be reloaded in 12 s. Another 2 s are used to load the other configuration registers, for a total of 14 s to reload the front end completely. This column mode is also the reason that the return buffer is twice as big as the transmit buffer. The return buffer receives the row number as well as the trim value for each pixel. Once data is loaded into an output buffer, the transfer may be initiated either by computer control, or by a signal from the TTC system. Since single event upsets are expected to occur in the front end registers, it is anticipated that periodic updates will be necessary. Since updating the front end may disrupt data taking, it is preferable to perform small updates synchronized to orbit gaps or private orbits. This is done through the TTC initiated downloads. For transmission verification purposes, the number of bytes transmitted is compared to the number of bytes returned from the front end. Also, the returning Hub/port address is compared to the transmitted address. Status bits are set with the results of this comparison, and these values are stored, for possible review, should an error condition occur.

2008 JINST 3 S08004

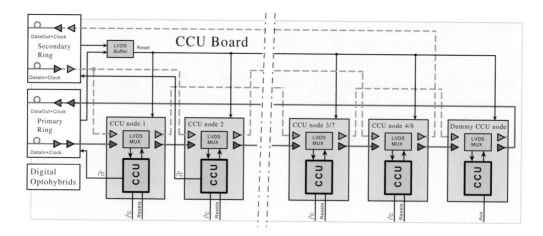

Figure 3.10: Block diagram of the Pixel front end control system. Note that the total number of CCU nodes is 9 for the BPix and 5 for the FPix.

The detector front end control system

The CMS Pixel detector front end control system for both the barrel (BPix) and the forward (FPix) detectors consists of four communication and control unit boards (CCU Boards). Each CCU board controls a quarter of the detector with eight Barrel read-out sectors or twelve Forward port cards. Figure 3.10 shows the block diagram of a CCU Board. The same ring topology configured as a local area network as in the silicon strip tracker is used. The front end controller (FEC) module is the master of the network and uses two optical fibers to send the timing and data signals to a number of slave CCU nodes, and another two fibers to receive return communication traffic. The two receiver channels on the digital optohybrid (DOH) transmit the 40 MHz clock and control data at 40 Mbit/s in the direction from the FEC to the ring of communication and control units (CCUs). The two transmitter channels send clock and data back to the FEC from the ring of CCUs. The CCU is the core component developed for the slow control, monitoring and timing distribution in the tracking system [29]. To improve system reliability against a single component failure a redundant interconnection scheme based on doubling signal paths and bypassing of faulty CCUs is implemented. An additional "dummy" CCU node allows to mitigate a single DOH failure preserving complete functionality. A CCU node failure leads to a loss of communication to all electronics attached to that CCU. The first two CCU nodes in the ring provide also the I^{2}C data channels necessary to control the digital optohybrids on the CCU boards.

In the BPix each read-out sector is controlled by a separate CCU node. Eight active and one dummy CCU node build a single control ring. One I^{2}C data channel is used to access and control the front end read-out electronics and three output channels generate the necessary signals to reset the digital and the analog optohybrids as well as the read-out chips (ROCs) in one read-out sector. The FPix control ring consists of four active and one dummy CCU node. Each of the active CCU nodes control 3 port cards, which constitute a 45° sector in the detector coverage at one end. A connection between a CCU and a port card includes a bi-directional 100 KHz I^{2}C communication channel and two reset signals. One reset signal is for the port card electronics, and the other one goes to the read-out chips on the detector panels.

2008 JINST 3 S08004

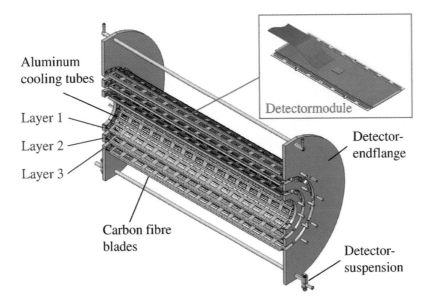

Figure 3.11: Complete support structure half shell with the three detector layers.

3.2.4 The pixel barrel system

The pixel barrel system as installed inside CMS comprises the barrel itself, i.e. detector modules mounted on their cylindrical support structure, as well as supply tubes on both sides. The barrel with its length of 570 mm is much shorter than the Silicon Strip Tracker inside which it is installed. Supply tubes carry services along the beam pipe from patch panels located outside of the tracker volume to the barrel. The supply tubes also house electronics for read-out and control. The length of the full system is 5.60 m. Support structure and supply tubes are split vertically to allow installation in the presence of the beam-pipe and its supports. Electrically the $+z$ and $-z$ sides of the barrel are separated. Each side is divided in 16 sectors which operate almost independently, sharing only the slow control system.

Pixel barrel support structure

The detector support structure for the three layers at the radii of four, seven and eleven centimeters equipped with silicon pixel modules has a length of 570 mm ranging from -285 mm to $+285$ mm closest to the CMS interaction region. Figure 3.11 shows a sketch of a complete support structure half shell.

Aluminium cooling tubes with a wall thickness of 0.3 mm are the backbones of the support structure. Carbon fiber blades with a thickness of 0.24 mm are glued onto the top or bottom of two adjacent cooling tubes in such a way that their normal directions alternate pointing either to the beam or away from it. The tubes have trapezoidal cross sections defined by the azimuthal angles of the ladders they hold.

Four to five of these tubes are laser welded to an aluminium container which distributes the cooling fluid. The resulting manifold provides the necessary cooling of the detector modules to

2008 JINST 3 S08004

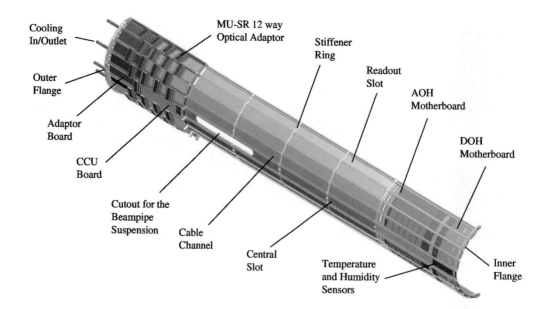

Figure 3.12: Overview of a supply tube half shell.

about $-10\,^{\circ}$C with C_6F_{14}. Support frames on both ends, which connect the single segments, build a complete detector layer half shell. These flanges consist of thin fibreglass frames (FR4) that are filled with foam and covered by carbon fibre blades.

Printed circuit boards mounted on the the flanges hold the connectors for the module cables and provide control signal fan-out and power distribution to the individual modules of a sector.

Pixel detector supply tube. The electrical power lines, the electrical control signal and the optical signals as well as the cooling fluid are transferred across the supply tubes to the pixel barrel. The two supply tube parts of a half shell in $+z$ and $-z$ direction have a length of 2204 mm (figure 3.12).

The supporting elements of the basic structure are the stainless steel tubes with a wall thickness of 0.1 mm running along the z-direction connected to the stiffener rings (FR4) and the inner and outer flanges made out of aluminium. The tubes supply the detector with the cooling fluid. The gaps in between are filled with foamed material with the corresponding shape to guarantee the necessary rigidity. All power and slow control leads are embedded in the supply tube body. This allows a clear layout of the wiring and also makes the system more reliable.

The motherboards, which hold the optical hybrids for the analog and digital control links, are installed in the eight read-out slots near the detector on the integrated supply boards. The corresponding boards at the outer ends carry the power adapter boards, which provide the detector power and the bias voltage for this sector. In the central slot the digital communication and control board (CCU Board) is installed. From here the digital control signals are distributed to the individual read-out boards in each of the eight read-out sectors. Here also all slow control signals like temperatures, pressures and the humidity are brought together and connected by the dedicated slow control adapter board to the cables. The optical fibres are installed in the cable channels. The 36 single fibres for the analog read-out and the eight fibres for the digital control of the detector

2008 JINST 3 S08004

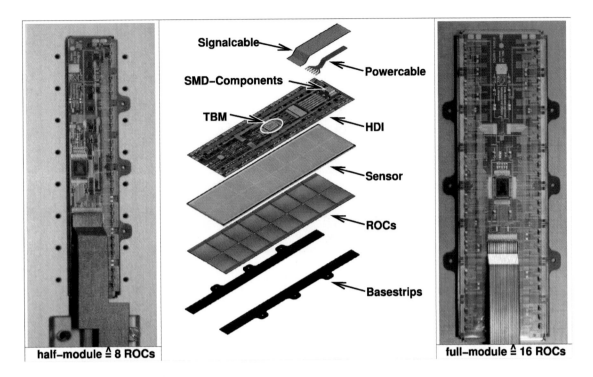

half-module ≙ 8 ROCs **full-module ≙ 16 ROCs**

Signalcable
Powercable
SMD-Components
TBM
HDI
Sensor
ROCs
Basestrips

Figure 3.13: Exploded view (middle panel) of a barrel pixel detector full module (right panel) and picture of an assembled half module (left panel).

modules will then be connected through the MUSR connector to the optical ribbon cable. These adapters are mounted at the circumference in the first part of the supply tube. The length of each supply tube is 2204 mm. Only a flexible mechanical connection is made between the barrel and the supply tube.

Pixel barrel detector modules

The barrel part of the CMS pixel detector consists of about 800 detector modules. While the majority of the modules (672) are full modules as seen in figure 3.13 on the right, the edges of the six half-shells are equipped with 16 half-modules each (96 in total, see figure 3.13 on the left).

Geometry and components. A module is composed of the following components (figure 3.13). One or two basestrips made from 250 μm thick silicon nitride provide the support of the module. The front end electronics consists of 8 to 16 read-out chips with 52×80 pixels of size 100×150 μm^2 each, which are bumpbonded to the sensor. The chips are thinned down to 180 μm . The High Density Interconnect, a flexible low mass 3 layer PCB with a trace thickness of 6 μm equipped with a Token Bit Manager chip that controls the read-out of the ROCs, forms the upper layer of a module and distributes signals and power to the chips. The signals are transferred over an impedance matched 2 layer Kapton/copper compound cable with 21 traces and 300 μm pitch. The module is powered via 6 copper coated aluminium wires of 250 μm diameter.

2008 JINST 3 S08004

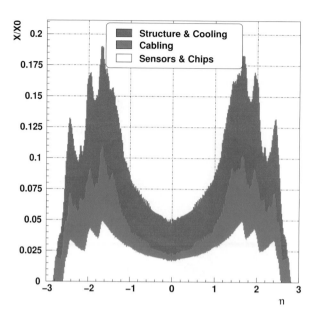

Figure 3.14: Material budget of the pixel barrel in units of radiation length versus rapidity. The plot does not contain contributions from the pixel support cylinder, the supply tube and cabling from the detector end flange to the supply tube.

A completed full-module has the dimensions 66.6×26.0 mm^2, weights 2.2 g plus up to 1.3 g for cables, and consumes 2 W of power. The material of the pixel barrel amounts to 5 percent of a radiation length in the central region. Sensors and read-out chips contribute one third of the material while support structure and cooling fluid contribute about 50 percent. The distribution of material as a function of pseudorapidity is shown in figure 3.14.

3.2.5 The forward pixel detector

The FPix detector consists of two completely separate sections, one on each side of the interaction region. They are located inside the BPix supply tube but are mounted on separate insertion rails. Each section is split vertically down the middle so the detector can be installed around the beam-pipe and its vertical support wire and so it can also be removed for servicing during major maintenance periods without disturbing the beam-pipe. Each of these four sections is called a *half-cylinder*.

Mechanics of a half-cylinder

Each half-cylinder consists of a carbon fiber shell with two half-disks located at its front end, one at 34.5 cm from the IP and the other at 46.5 cm. The half-disks support the actual pixel detectors that extend from 6 cm to 15 cm in radius from the beam.

The half-disk has 12 cooling channels (each in the shape of a "U") assembled between a half ring shown in figure 3.15. The assembly requires three slightly different types of cooling channels. Each channel is made by Al-brazing two blocks of Al with the channel for the cooling fluid already

2008 JINST 3 S08004

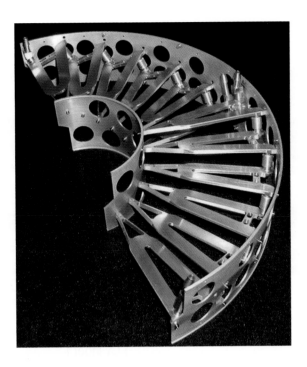

Figure 3.15: The FPix half-disk cooling channels mounted in the outer half-ring structure. The turbine-like geometry is apparent. Panels are mounted on both sides of the cooling channels.

machined in the two parts. The brazed parts are then machined to their final shape. The walls of the channels are 0.5 mm thick. The average weight of the channels is 8.21 g.

All channels passed a Helium leak test at 1.33×10^{-8} mbar-litre/s. The pressure drop of the individual cooling channels for a flow of 2600 sccm of dry N_2 is 0.49 ± 0.02 mbar. Six daisy-chained cooling channels form a *cooling loop*. The pressure drop over a loop (for a flow rate of 1230 sccm) of dry N_2 is 0.96 ± 0.13 mbar. For C_6F_{14} at $-20°C$ with a rate of 12cc-s the pressure drop is 294 mbar.

Each of the twelve cooling channels of a half-disk has trapezoidal beryllium *panels* attached to each side. The panels support the sensors and read-out chips that constitute the actual particle detectors. As explained above, the cooling channels are rotated to form a turbine-like geometry to enhance charge-sharing. The panels are made of 0.5mm beryllium. The beryllium provides a strong, stable and relatively low-mass support for the actual pixel detectors. The cooling channels are supplied with C_6F_{14} at about $-15°C$. A single cooling channel with panels mounted on both sides forms a subassembly called a *blade*. There are 24 panels, forming 12 blades, in each half-disk.

Powering up the electronics on one blade increases the temperature by $\approx 2°C$. The temperature of each ROC is part of the information available for each event. Each panel also has a resistance temperature detection sensor. The pixel sensors have fiducial marks visible with a coordinate measuring machine (CMM). Their position is then related to reference marks mounted on the half-disk units.

After installing the half-disks in the half-cylinder, the disk position is measured relative to the half-cylinder using a CMM and also by photogrammetry. This permits relating the position of the sensors to the CMS detector. The detector is surveyed at room temperature but operated at

2008 JINST 3 S08004

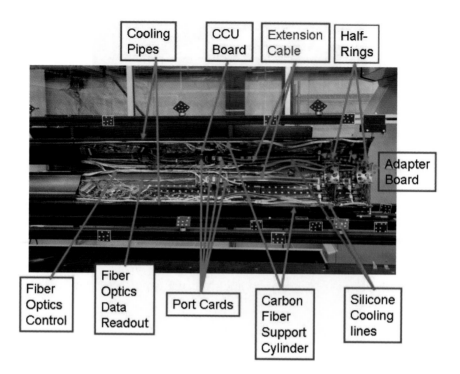

Figure 3.16: Overview of the Forward Pixel half-cylinder. A photograph of the portion of the first production half-cylinder facing the interaction region (IR). The aluminium flange, the filter boards (see below), and the CCU board are not shown. The half-cylinder is mounted in a survey fixture. The carbon fiber cover at the end away from the IR protects the downstream components during insertion of the beam pipe suspension wires that run through a slot in the half-cylinder towards the left end of the picture.

about $-10°$C. The deformation (magnitude and direction) of the panels on a half-disk, when its temperature changes from $20°$C to $-20°$C has been measured to be 150 μm. This result has been reproduced by a finite element analysis of the half-disk and it will be used in the final alignment of the pixels. We anticipate knowing the pixel geometry to a few tens of microns before the final alignment with tracks.

The service half-cylinder also contains all the mechanical and electrical infrastructure needed to support, position, cool, power, control and read out the detector. In particular, it contains electronics for providing bias voltage to the sensors, power to the read-out chips, signals for controlling the read-out chip via optical fibers linking it to the control room, and laser drivers for sending the signals (address and energy deposition) off the detector to the data acquisition system. The service half-cylinder also provides the path for cooling fluid necessary to remove the heat generated by the sensors and read-out chips.

At the end of each service half-cylinder there is an annular aluminium flange that contains holes to pass the power cables, cooling tubes, control and monitoring cables, and fiber optic read-out from intermediate patch panels to the FPix detector. The electronics cards needed for the operation of the detector are mounted on the inner surface of the half-cylinder. A picture of a half-cylinder is shown in figure 3.16.

2008 JINST 3 S08004

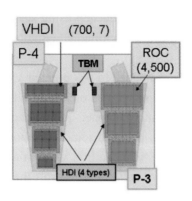

Figure 3.17: Sketches of the two types of FPix panels showing the different sizes and numbers of the plaquettes on each (left side). A photograph of an actual 3-plaquette panel (right side).

Forward pixel detection elements - the plaquettes

The basic unit of construction for the forward pixel detector is the *plaquette*. A plaquette consists of a single pixel sensor bump-bonded to an appropriate number of Read-Out Chips (ROCs) and wire-bonded to a very-high-density-interconnect (VHDI) that provides power, control, and data connections.

In order to cover the trapezoidal or *pie-shaped* panels without leaving cracks, five different sizes of plaquettes are needed. These are respectively 1×2, 2×3, 2×4, 1×5, 2×5, where the first digit refers to the number of rows and the second to the number of columns of read-out chips that are attached to a given sensor. The largest plaquette, the 2×5, has dimensions of 16 mm $\times$ 35 mm. The panels on the side of the cooling channel closest to the IP contain 1×2, 2×3, 2×4, and 1×5 plaquettes or a total of 21 ROCs. The panels on the side of the cooling channels farthest from the IP contain 2×3, 2×4 and 2×5 type plaquettes with a total of 24 ROCs. The sensors are offset on the upstream and downstream panels so that there are no cracks in the coverage due to the ROC read-out periphery. The two types of panels are shown in figure 3.17. A total of 672 plaquettes are needed.

The joining, or *hybridization*, of the pixel sensors and the pixel unit cells of the ROC is achieved by fine-pitch bumping using Pb/Sn solder and then flip-chip mating. The bumping is done on the 8" ROC wafers and the 4" sensor wafers. After bumping, the ROC wafers are thinned by backside grinding to 150 μm and then diced. Finally, each of the 5 different types of sensors are mated to the appropriate number of ROCs. The sensor with its ROCs bump-bonded to it is called a module. For FPix, the hybridization was done in industry. The fraction of broken, bridged, or missing bumps is at the level of a few 10^{-3}.

After delivery from the vendor, the bump-bonded pixel detector module is then installed on a Very High Density Interconnect (VHDI). The VHDI is a two-layer flexible printed circuit, laminated to a 300 μm thick silicon substrate, whose trace geometry and characteristics (impedance, low intrinsic capacitance, and low cross-talk) have been optimized for the intended use of conveying digital control and analog output signals to and from the sensors and ROCs.

2008 JINST 3 S08004

The VHDI is made as follows. A bulk 6" silicon wafer is laminated to a flexible sheet containing several VHDI circuits. Passive components are also attached using surface-mount solder techniques. The wafer of populated circuits is then diced into individual circuits using a diamond saw. The circuits are then electrically tested.

The hybridized pixel module is attached and wire bonded to a populated VHDI to become a *plaquette*. The joining is made using parallel plate fixtures aligned on linear rails. The alignment of components is inspected using a coordinate measuring machine. A flexible plate is used for fine adjustments on the fixtures resulting in alignments between joined components within 100 μm. The adhesive bond between plaquette components is made in a vacuum at 60°C, to soften the adhesive and prevent air entrapment. An air cylinder applies and controls the mating pressure, which is limited by the compression allowed on the bump-bonds.

The effects of thermal cycling and radiation on the assembled plaquettes have been extensively tested. The tests demonstrate that the adhesive and the application method mitigate warping due to temperature changes, and provide reliable strength and thermal conductivity.

Once plaquettes are mechanically joined, they are clamped in cassettes that accommodate all processing steps such as wirebonding which provides electrical connections between the ROCs and the VHDI. After wirebonding we encapsulate the feet of wirebonds. This encapsulation is necessary due to periodic $I\vec{dl} \times \vec{B}$ forces expected to occur during actual CMS operation. The encapsulant acts as a damping force on the wire, preventing large resonant oscillations to work harden the wire and cause eventual breakage [30]. Finally the plaquettes undergo quick testing at room temperature. During this test the quality of the plaquettes is evaluated in terms of the characteristics of the sensor, the read-out chip, the number of bad pixels and missing bonds. The assembly and testing rate is optimized for a rate of six plaquettes per day.

The completed plaquettes are subjected to a quick plug-in test. Then they are loaded into a *Burn-In Box* where they undergo 10 temperature cycles between 20°C and −15°C. These cycles can take up to 2 days to complete, depending upon the thermal load. During these cycles, the plaquettes are monitored for electrical operation. We have seen no failures during the cycling. After the burn-in process is completed, the plaquettes are subjected to a series of electrical tests to ensure their suitability for their eventual mounting on a panel. These tests, at the operating temperature of −15°C, include the functionality of the ROC, the integrity of the bump-bond, and the I-V characteristics of the sensor. Other tests measure the thresholds and noise characteristics of each pixel on the entire plaquette assembly, and the individual pixel thresholds are trimmed via the ROC capability. We have found that the pixel trim values from the plaquette test on each pixel remain valid even after subsequent steps of the assembly process. After testing the plaquette data is loaded into the Pixel Construction Database and the plaquettes are graded. We have three main categories of grades:

- A - the plaquette is available for immediate mounting on a panel;

- B - potential issues have been found during testing and need further analysis;

- C - the plaquettes are unsuitable for mounting.

The data on each B-grade plaquette are examined carefully. In many cases, the plaquettes are found to have missed being classified as A-grade due to very minor deficiencies (e.g. slightly

2008 JINST 3 S08004

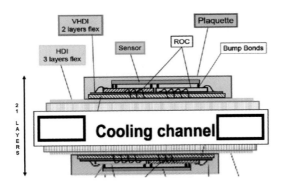

Figure 3.18: Sketch of a plaquette mounted on a panel showing its several layers.

too many noisy pixels) which will not be significant when an entire panel's quality is assessed. These are "promoted" to A-grade and declared usable on panels. Current plaquette yields, based on an original grade of A or a promotion to A-grade from B, are in the 80% range, varying slightly according to plaquette size.

Panel assembly

A panel is formed from three or four plaquettes attached to an assembly of a High Density Interconnect (HDI) laminated to a beryllium plate. The HDI is a three-layer flexible printed circuit whose trace geometry and characteristics (impedance, low cross-talk) have been optimized for the intended use of transferring digital control and analog output signals.

The process by which a panel is assembled is as follows. A single HDI circuit is laminated to a trapezoidal-shaped 0.5 mm thick beryllium plate. Passive components are attached using surface-mount solder techniques. The Token Bit Manager (TBM) is attached to the corner tab of the HDI using a die attach method and wire-bonding. After functional and burn-in tests with only the TBM, the individual plaquettes are attached to the HDI using adhesive for mechanical attachment and wire-bonds for electrical connection.

There are four types of panels, a right and left 3-plaquette version, and a right and left 4-plaquette version. The right and left handed versions have their TBMs on opposite sides of the panel centerline. Both types are required so that no panel part projects past a line in the vertical plane. The reason for the "3" and "4" type panels is that they are eventually mounted on opposite side of a blade, and the gaps between plaquettes on one type are covered by the active area of the other.

A panel is built up out of several layers of components. These are shown in figure 3.18. The total number of panels in all eight half-disks is 192.

Final detector assembly validation

The panels are attached onto the front and back of the half-disk cooling channels. The 4-plaquette panels are mounted on the side closest to the interaction region (IR), and the 3-plaquette versions on the opposite side. The half-disk assembly is mounted onto the half-service cylinder and is again tested.

2008 JINST 3 S08004

Electronics chain

Each HDI is connected to another flexible printed circuit board, the *adapter board*. Each adapter board serves three blades (or 6 panels). One important purpose of the adapter board is to send and receive signals from the panels, which are mounted perpendicular to the axis of the service cylinder to and from the electronics mounted on the inner surface of the service cylinder. This is done by a *pigtail* at the end of each panel that plugs into connectors on the fingers of the adapter board.

The adapter board has three types of ASICs mounted on it. These are used to pass the clock, trigger and control data signals to each panel and return the received control signals back to the pFEC.

The adapter board is connected to another printed circuit board, the *port card*, by a lightweight extension cable. These cables are of two types, a power cable which distributes the power to the ROCs and TBMs, and the HV bias to the sensors. The other cable is to transmit the pixel data and control signals to the panel from the port card. The port card is a low-mass printed circuit board. It houses the electronics needed to interface the front-end chips with the VME electronics (the pFEC and pxFED) and power supplies located in the counting room. The port card transmits the clock signal, L1 trigger and slow control signals to the front end electronics. It distributes the power and bias voltages to the chips and sensors. It also monitors the currents and voltages as well as the temperature on some panels. These functions are done by various ASICs that are common to the CMS tracker. These ASICs include the DCU for monitoring, the TPLL for regenerating the trigger and timing signal, the gatekeeper for keeping the optical up and down links open as needed.

To control and monitor the various ancillary chips and optohybrids, there is a CCU board for each half service cylinder, as described above.

The port card contains the Analog Optohybrid (AOH). Each of the 6 laser diodes of the AOH chip receives data from one panel via its TBM and sends it over its own optical fiber to the Front end Driver (FED).

The control of the ROCs is achieved through the Pixel Front End Controller. Optical signals are sent from it to the Digital Optohybrids on the port card, through the extension cables to the adapter board, then to the TBM on the panel, through the HDI and the VHDI to the ROCs.

Power and monitoring

Power connections are made from CAEN power supplies via cables that run through the flange at the end of the half-cylinder away from the IR into a set of power/filter boards. From these boards, it is sent along wires to the port card, in the case of low voltages, and directly to the adapter board in the case of the sensor bias voltage.

Monitoring points for temperature are distributed throughout the service cylinder. There are also humidity sensors. Additional temperature sensors are mounted on the panels. High and low voltage and detector monitoring are connected to the DCS system described below.

Testing

Testing is a key element of quality assurance in the assembly process. While rework is possible, it is difficult and error prone. At every step, we confirm that we are using only "known good parts".

2008 JINST 3 S08004

Testing must keep up with the driving assembly step, plaquette production. Full characterization of a plaquette requires hundreds of thousands of measurements. To accomplish this, we have developed special read-out hardware and software that can carry out these measurements quickly and efficiently. A software using a USB-based data acquisition scheme is employed when flexibility is needed to develop measurement programs of modest complexity and duration, such as the burn-in procedure. For the most extensive measurements, including plaquette testing and characterization, we use a PCI-based system and a software program called Renaissance [31].

Final testing is performed using the real data-acquisition and control hardware and prototype data-acquisition software and constitutes an end-to-end system test. Detailed testing also establishes an initial set of parameters for the many DACs and thresholds in the system.

3.2.6 Power supply

All needed high and low DC voltages are generated by means of a commercial modular system of the type CAEN-EASY4000 . This system is also employed by the CMS silicon strip tracker for which the main regulating cards (A4601H) were custom designed [32]. Only small changes in hard- and firmware were necessary for adaptation to the pixel project.

The core of this system, accessed through LAN, is located in the detector control room (USC55) and consists of one main controller (SY1527) containing 3 branch controllers (A1676A). The actual power supply cards are placed in two racks of 5 crates in close proximity to the detector thanks to their radiation tolerance and magnetic field resistance. This has been chosen in order to reduce power loss in the cables. The power supply crates are connected by flat cables (≈ 100 m) to the branch controllers. They are fed by local 3-phase $230\,V_{AC}$ to $48\,V_{DC}$ master converters of each $2\,kW$ (A3486H) also suited for operation at hostile environments.

The crates house two types of electronic cards, one of 4 channels of $2.5\,V/7\,A$ (A4602) feeding the service electronics on the supply tubes (auxiliary power), while the other (A4603H) deliver 2 complex channels of each 2 low ($1.75\,V/7\,A$ and $2.5\,V/15\,A$) and 2 high voltage lines ($-600\,V/20\,mA$) for ROC and sensor biasing respectively. Each of these channels contains floating pulse-width-modulated DC/DC switching transformers with a common ground return for the 1.75 and 2.5 V lines. The isolation resistance (ground return versus earth on the racks) is typically $100\,\Omega$ at 5 MHz. Every card is controlled by an optically decoupled microprocessor for setting and measuring voltages, currents, ramp times, trip parameters, interlocks and others.

The DC levels are regulated over sense lines. The reaction time of the sensing circuit (typically 200 μs) is subject to fine tuning to comply with capacitive load, cable impedance and length (typically 50 m). The line drop in the cables amounts to roughly 2 V, while the regulators would allow for a maximum of 6 V. Fourteen A4602 cards, yielding 40 independent channels of auxiliary power, feed the 32 slots of the barrel service tubes with each 2 DOHs and 6 AOHs as well as 4 groups of each 12 port cards of the forward half disks. The main supplies of 112 complex LV and HV channels (56 A4603H cards) feed the 64 barrel groups (192 ROCs, this contains groups with half size modules) of each 12 detector modules, and 48 forward groups (135 ROCs) of each 3 disk blades. Each of these groups draws a typical current of 4.6 A on the analogue (1.75 V) and 9 A on the digital (2.5 V) line respectively. The large current reserve of the supplies is needed to comply with conditions during bootstrapping where the ROCs remain briefly in an undefined state. It was

2008 JINST 3 S08004

verified that the regulators undergo a smooth transition from the constant-voltage to the constant-current regime if the programmed current limits are approached. Beside microprocessor controlled actions (1 s) fast over-current security is guaranteed by various solid state fuses (10 ms) as well as crowbars (100 μs) for over-voltage.

Noise levels are typically 5 mV$_{pp}$ on the LV and 50 mV$_{pp}$ on the HV outputs which can easily be accepted thanks to the LV regulators in the ROCs and the intrinsically small sensor capacitances respectively. Of major concern in the overall design were fast drops in the digital current consumption (2.5 V line) in case of low ROC activity like in orbit gaps. Due to the cable inductance a typical current drop of 2 A per group generates over-voltage spikes at the module level in the order of some Volts depending on local buffer capacitors. The integrity of the cable-module-ROC circuit was therefore checked by a full simulation in SPICE together with measurements on pulsed current loads. This served for the designs of the cables and the electronic layout, e.g. grounding or HV distribution. (In one sector layer-1 modules are fed by one line while layer-2,3 modules are commonly fed by the other.) Finally a 6×4 mm^2 shielded copper cable was chosen for the 40 m from the power supply cards to the patch panel (PP1) located in the HCAL with alternating current directions between adjacent lines. Two twisted pair lines for the senses and a bunch of 10 commonly shielded lines for HV are contained in the same cable complex (0.1 mm^2).

Inductance, capacitance and characteristic impedance between two of the main lines were measured to be 6 μH/m, 0.13 nF/m and 24 Ω respectively. The 4 m connection between PP1 and PP0 (tracker bulkhead) uses Al conductors in the cable. The auxiliary power cable is also shielded and contains 26×0.75 mm^2 and 4 twisted pair copper lines with 0.1 mm^2 for the sense wires.

3.2.7 Cooling

The power consumption per pixel amounts to around 55 μW, including about 13 μW from the sensor leakage current at final fluences of 6×10^{14}/cm^2. For the total of $\approx$ 66 million pixels this adds up to 3.6 kW. The power load on the aluminium cooling tubes is therefore expected to be about 50 W/m. The sensor temperature will be maintained at around -10°C. As for the strip detectors, liquid phase cooling with C$_6$F$_{14}$ is used. To keep the temperature increase of the coolant below 2°C, a total flow rate of 1 litre/s is required.

The pixel system is cooled by a total of 18 cooling loops: 10 for the barrel and 4 for each of the two end disk systems. For the barrel, the coolant enters at $+z$ and exits at $-z$, or vice versa. The coolant for the two disk sets on each side of the interaction region is supplied and reclaimed from the same z side. One barrel loop feeds in parallel 9 thin-walled aluminium pipes, each cooling 8 modules in series. One disk loop cools in parallel one quarter of each of the 2 disks; inside the quarter disks the 6 blade loops are connected serially. The coolant flow at the pixel modules is turbulent. The total lengths of the cooling loops starting from and returning to the pixel cooling rack amount to about 80 m, resulting in pressure drops of below 2 bar.

3.2.8 Slow controls

The safe operation of the barrel and forward pixel detectors is guaranteed by the CMS Pixel slow controls system (DCS). Its tasks are to monitor temperatures and humidities at different locations of the detector and to monitor and control the high and low voltages necessary for operation of the on-detector electronics.

The monitoring of temperatures and humidities is based on a commercial Siemens S7–300 modular mini Programmable Logic Controller (PLC) system. The Siemens S7–300 system monitors a total of 192 temperature and 8 humidity sensors installed in the Pixel barrel and forward endcap disks. For the temperature sensors, platinum resistance temperature detection sensors with a nominal resistance of 1 kΩ (Pt1000 RTD) have been chosen. The measurement of humidity is based on detecting the water vapor induced shear stress in a small polymer element that is connected to a Wheatstone Bridge piezoresistor circuit [33]. This circuit provides a small (mV) output signal that is linearly proportional to relative humidity (RH) between the full range of 0% to 100% RH and is amplified by the same kind of conditioning electronics that is used by the silicon strip tracker. The PLC of the Siemens S7–300 system is programmed in the Statement List (STL) language [34] to convert the currents and voltages of the temperature and humidity sensors into calibrated physical units (i.e. degrees Celsius for temperatures and percentages for humidities). For the purpose of avoiding damage to the detector in case the cooling system (dry air supply) fails, routines are programmed within the PLC to interlock the CAEN power supplies (shut-off the cooling) in that case.

An additional 96 Pt1000 temperature sensors are read out via the data-acquisition (DAQ) system, together with the temperature dependent voltage sources integrated into each one of the pixel read-out chips. The temperatures recorded by the DAQ system are passed to the slow controls system by means of a dedicated software interface [35].

The Barrel and Forward Pixel slow controls system is integrated into the PVSS graphical user interface (chapter 9) of the main CMS DCS.

3.3 Silicon strip tracker

3.3.1 Silicon sensors

The sensor elements in the strip tracker are single sided p-on-n type silicon micro-strip sensors [36, 37]. They have been manufactured on 6 inch wafers in a standard planar process, leading to significant cost reduction per unit area when compared to the more traditional 4 inch wafers. The base material is n doped float zone silicon with $\langle 100 \rangle$ crystal orientation. This crystal orientation was preferred over the more common $\langle 111 \rangle$ orientation because measurements [38] have shown that the built-up of surface charge on $\langle 100 \rangle$ wafers due to irradiation is much smaller and consequently irradiation causes less inter-strip capacitance increase on this material.

In TIB/TID and on the inner 4 rings of the TECs (figure 3.1), thin sensors of $(320 \pm 20)\,\mu$m wafer thickness are used, with substrate resistivity of $\rho = 1.55 - 3.25\,\mathrm{k\Omega\,cm}$. TOB and the outer 3 rings of the TECs are equipped with thicker sensors of $(500 \pm 20)\,\mu$m thickness, with substrate resistivity of $\rho = 4 - 8\,\mathrm{k\Omega\,cm}$. Due to the single sided processing, these sensors show a significant bow, which is required to be less than $100\,\mu$m.

A uniform n^+ implantation on the back side of the wafers, covered by aluminium, forms an ohmic contact which is connected to positive voltage up to about 500 V. Those sensors which are penetrated by the beams of the laser alignment system (section 3.3.7) feature a 10 mm hole in the

2008 JINST 3 S08004

back side metalization, as well as anti-reflective coating in order to achieve transmission through up to four sensors with a sufficient signal on a fifth sensor.

On the front side, strip shaped diodes are formed by p^+ implantation into the n type bulk. Due to the radiation damage to the crystal lattice, the bulk material will undergo type inversion and change to p type. At this point, the pn junction moves from the strip side of the wafer to the rear side contact. Each implanted strip is covered by an aluminium strip from which it is electrically insulated by means of a silicon oxide and nitride multilayer. This integrated capacitor allows for AC coupling of the signals from the strips to the read-out electronics, which is thus protected from the high leakage currents after irradiation. Each metal strip has two bond pads on each end, which are used to make a wire bond connection to the read-out chip and in case of the daisy chained sensors to make a wire bond connection between the two sensors in one detector module. For testing purposes there is also a DC pad connected to the p^+ implant. Each strip implant is connected via a (1.5 ± 0.5) MΩ polysilicon bias resistor to a p^+ bias ring which encloses the strip region and also defines the active area of the sensor.

For all sensors in the CMS strip tracker the ratio of p^+ implant width over strip pitch is $w/p = 0.25$, leading to a uniform total strip capacitance per unit length of about 1.2 pF/cm across all sensor geometries [38]. The actual w/p value was chosen in order to minimize the strip capacitance while still maintaining a good high voltage behaviour of the sensor. The aluminium strips feature a metal overhang of 4 to 8 μm on each side of the strip which pushes the high field region into the silicon oxide where the breakdown voltage is much higher, leading to stable high voltage operation. For the same reason, the bias ring is surrounded by a floating guard ring p^+ implant. It gradually degrades the electric field between the n^+ implant at the cut edge of the sensor and the bias ring, which are at backplane potential (high voltage) and ground, respectively. Figure 3.19 shows the layout of a corner of the active region of a sensor.

In order to equip all regions in the CMS tracker, 15 different sensor geometries are needed [36] (figure 3.19): two rectangular sensor types each for TIB and TOB, and 11 wedge-shaped sensor types for TEC and TID. They have either 512 or 768 strips, reflecting the read-out modularity of 256 channels (two 128-channel front-end chips multiplexed to one read-out channel). Since the sensors are fabricated on 6 inch wafers, they can be made rather large. Typical dimensions are for instance about 6×12 cm^2 and 10×9 cm^2 in the inner and outer barrel, respectively. The total number of silicon sensors in the strip tracker is 24 244, making up a total active area of 198 m^2, with about 9.3 million of strips [36].

3.3.2 Read-out system

The signals from the silicon sensors are amplified, shaped, and stored by a custom integrated circuit, the APV25 [39]. Upon a positive first level trigger decision the analogue signals of all channels are multiplexed and transmitted via optical fibers to Front End Driver (FED) boards in the service cavern where the analogue to digital conversion takes place. This read-out scheme brings the full analogue information to a place where it can be used for accurate pedestal and common mode subtraction as well as data sparsification. Clock, trigger, and control signals are transmitted by optical links as well. A schematic view of the silicon strip tracker read-out scheme is given in figure 3.20. This analogue read-out scheme was chosen for several reasons: optimal spatial reso-

2008 JINST 3 S08004

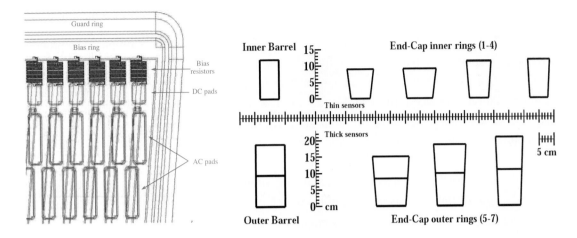

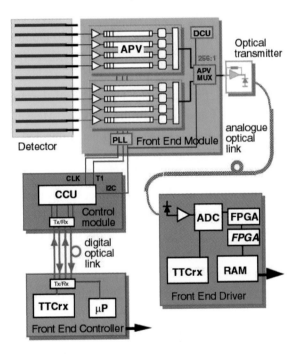

Figure 3.19: Left panel: drawing of one corner of the active region of a wedge-shaped silicon strip sensor for the tracker endcaps. Right panel: silicon sensor geometries utilized in the CMS tracker. In the outer layers the sensors are paired to form a single module, as shown in the figure. The Inner Barrel and Outer Barrel sensors exist in two types, of same area and different pitch. The sensors utilized for the first inner ring exist in two different versions, one for TID and one for TEC, respectively. (Only the TEC version is shown.)

Figure 3.20: Read-out scheme of the CMS tracker.

lution from charge sharing, operational robustness and ease of monitoring due to the availability of the full analogue signal, robustness against possible common mode noise, less custom radiation hard electronics and reduced material budget as the analogue to digital conversion and its power needs are shifted out of the tracker volume.

2008 JINST 3 S08004

Front-end ASICs

The APV25 has been designed in an IBM 0.25 μm bulk CMOS process. Compared to processes with bigger feature sizes, the thin gate oxide inherent to this deep sub-micron process is much less affected by radiation induced charge-up and thereby, in conjunction with special design techniques, ensures radiation tolerance [40]. The APV25 has 128 read-out channels, each consisting of a low noise and power charge sensitive pre-amplifier, a 50 ns CR-RC type shaper and a 192 element deep analogue pipeline which samples the shaped signals at the LHC frequency of 40 MHz. This pipeline is used to store the data for a trigger latency of up to 4 μs and to buffer it. A subsequent stage can either pass the signal as sampled at the maximum of the 50 ns pulse (peak mode) or form a weighted sum of three consecutive samples which effectively reduces the shaping time to 25 ns (deconvolution mode). The latter is needed at high luminosity in order to confine the signals to the correct LHC bunch crossing. The pulse shape depends linearly (linearity better than 5%) on the signal up to a charge corresponding to 5 minimum ionizing particles (MIPs, one MIP is equivalent to 25 000 electrons in this case), with a gradual fall off beyond. When a trigger is received, the analogue data from all 128 channels of the appropriate time slice in the pipeline are multiplexed and output at a rate of 20 MS/s (mega-samples per second) as a differential bi-directional current signal, together with a digital header. Due to the tree structure of the analogue multiplexer the order in which the channels are output is non-consecutive and therefore re-ordering is necessary prior to the actual data processing. An internal calibration circuit allows to inject charge with programmable amplitude and delay into the amplifier inputs in order to be able to monitor the pulse shape.

The APV25 needs supply voltages of 1.25 V and 2.5 V with a typical current consumption of about 65 mA and 90 mA respectively, leading to a total power consumption of typically around 300 mW for one APV25 or 2.3 mW per channel. The noise of the analogue read-out chain is dominated by the front end MOSFET transistor in the APV25. Measurements have shown that the total noise for an APV25 channel depends linearly on the connected detector capacitance C_{det}. The equivalent noise charge is found to be $ENC_{\text{peak}} = 270e + 38e/\text{pF} \cdot C_{\text{det}}$ in peak mode and $ENC_{\text{deconv}} = 430e + 61e/\text{pF} \cdot C_{\text{det}}$ in deconvolution mode, both measured at room temperature [39]. Mainly due to the MOSFET characteristics, the noise reduces with temperature approximately as $ENC \sim \sqrt{T}$. Therefore, the noise at operating temperature is about 10% lower.

More than 100 APV25 chips from all production lots have been irradiated with X-rays to 10 Mrad ionizing dose, in excess of the expectation for 10 years of LHC operation. No significant degradation in pulse shape or noise level has been observed.

The APV25 is fabricated on 8 inch wafers with 360 chips per wafer. More than 600 wafers corresponding to 216 000 chips have been manufactured and probe-tested. After initial yield problems were solved, an average yield of 88% was achieved.

Another custom ASIC, the APVMUX, is used to multiplex the data streams from two APV25 chips onto one optical channel by interleaving the two 20 MS/s streams into one 40 MS/s stream, which is then sent to a laser driver of the optical links. One APVMUX chip contains 4 such multiplexers.

2008 JINST 3 S08004

Optical links

Analogue optical links are used to transmit the data streams from the tracker to the service cavern over a distance of about 100 m at 40 MS/s. Likewise, the digital timing and control signals (see below) are transmitted by digital optical links running at 40 Mb/s [41]. Optical links are superior to an electrical distribution scheme mainly since they have minimal impact on the material budget and are immune to electrical interference. The transmitters are commercially available multi-quantum-well InGaAsP edge-emitting devices, selected for their good linearity, low threshold current and proven reliability. Epitaxially grown planar InGaAs photo-diodes are used as receivers. The optical fiber itself is a standard, single-mode, non dispersion shifted telecommunication fiber. The fibers are grouped in ribbons of 12 fibers which in turn are packaged in a stack of 8 inside a 96-way ribbon cable, which features a small diameter (< 10 mm) and a low bending radius (8 cm). For the analogue data link up to three transmitters are connected to a laser driver ASIC on an Analogue Opto-Hybrid (AOH), one of which sits close to each detector module. The electrical signals from the APVMUX are transmitted differentially over a distance of a few centimeters to the laser driver, which modulates the laser diode current accordingly and provides a programmable bias current to the diode. For the bi-directional digital optical link a set of two receivers and two transmitters is mounted on a Digital Opto-Hybrid (DOH), converting the optical signals to electrical LVDS [42] and vice versa.

Front End Drivers

The strip tracker Front End Driver (FED) is a 9U VME module which receives data from 96 optical fibres, each corresponding to 2 APV25 or 256 detector channels [45]. All 96 fibres are processed in parallel. The optical signals are converted to electrical levels by opto-receivers [43] and then digitized by a 40 MHz, 10 bit ADC. The ADC sampling point for each fibre can be programmed independently in 1 ns steps. After auto-synchronization to the APV data stream, pedestal corrections are applied and the common mode subtracted. The common mode correction is calculated for each trigger and each APV separately. The samples are then re-ordered to restore the physical sequence of detector channels which is essential for the following step of cluster finding. Pedestal values for each detector channel and thresholds for cluster finding are stored in look up tables. The digital functionality of the FED is implemented in FPGAs and can therefore be adjusted with considerable flexibility. In zero suppression mode, which is the standard for normal data taking, the output of the FED is a list of clusters with address information and signal height (8-bit resolution) for each strip in the cluster, thus passing to the central DAQ only those objects which are relevant for track reconstruction and physics analysis. In this way an input data rate per FED of about 3.4 GB/s, at LHC design luminosity, is reduced to roughly 50 MB/s per percent strip occupancy. Other modes are, however, available which suppress one or more steps in the processing chain and therefore transmit additional data to the central DAQ to be used mainly for debugging and system analysis. There are a total of 450 FEDs in the final system.

2008 JINST 3 S08004

Control and monitoring

Clock, trigger and control data are transmitted to the tracker by Front End Controller (FEC) cards [44]. These are VME modules, located in the service cavern, as close as possible to the tracker in order to reduce trigger latency. They receive clock and trigger signals from the global Timing Trigger and Command (TTC) system and distribute those as well as control signals via digital optical links and the digital opto-hybrids to LVDS token ring networks (control rings) inside the tracker volume. Several Communication and Control Units (CCU) [46] participate in one token ring. These are custom ASICs which interface the ring network to the front-end chips. One CCU is mounted on a Communication and Control Unit Module (CCUM) and is dedicated to a set of detector modules. A combined clock and trigger signal is distributed to Phase Locked Loop (PLL) chips [47] on each detector module while the industry standard I^{2}C protocol [48] is used to send control signals to the APV chips as well as to the other ancillary chips. One CCU can control up to 16 units so that one FEC ring typically controls a set of several tens of detector modules. The PLL chips decode the trigger signals and provide a very low jitter, phase adjustable clock signal to the local electronics.

Detector Control Unit (DCU) ASICs [49] on the detector modules are used to monitor the low voltages on the hybrid, the silicon sensor leakage current, and the temperatures of the silicon sensors, the hybrid and the DCU itself. For this purpose, each DCU contains eight 12 bit ADCs. The DCUs are read out through the control rings and digital links so that these readings are only available when the control rings and the detector modules are powered.

Hybrids

The front-end read-out electronics for a detector module is mounted onto a multi chip module called hybrid [50]. Due to the different detector module geometries 12 different types of hybrids are needed in the CMS silicon strip tracker. Each hybrid carries 4 or 6 APV25 read-out chips which are mounted as bare dies, and one APVMUX chip, one PLL chip and one DCU chip which are packaged components. The main features of the hybrid are to distribute and filter the supply voltages to the chips, to route clock, control and data lines between the chips and to remove the heat from the chips into the cooling system. No high voltage is present on the CMS tracker hybrids. The hybrid substrate is fabricated as a four layer polyimide copper multilayer flex circuit (figure 3.21). It is laminated onto a ceramic (Al$_2$O$_3$) carrier plate using double sided acrylic adhesive. A polyimide cable is integrated into the layout of the hybrid. The minimal feature sizes are 120 μm for via diameter and line width. Large metalized through holes under the chips transfer the heat to the underlying ceramic plate, from where it is removed through the frame of the module into the cooling system. Three different flex circuit types (one each for TIB/TID, TOB and TEC) combined with different geometries of the ceramic plates, different connector orientations and different number of APV25 chips (4 or 6) make up the total of 12 different hybrid flavours.

Power supplies

Silicon strip modules are grouped into 1944 detector power groups in order to share the power services. Each group is supplied by a power supply unit (PSU) [32], featuring two low-voltage

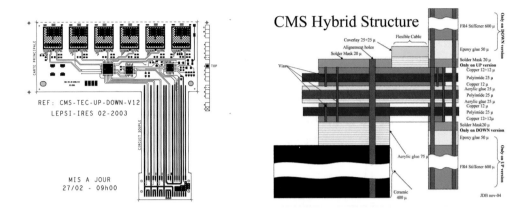

Figure 3.21: Front-end hybrid layout (example for TEC shown on the left) and arrangement of layers.

regulators, respectively 1.25 V (up to 6 A) and 2.5 V (up to 13 A), and two high-voltage regulators (0-600 V, up to 12 mA). All regulators are "floating" (return line isolated from the local earth). The two low-voltage channels share the same return line and use the sensing wire technique to compensate, up to 4 V, the voltage drop along the cables. The two high-voltage regulators are fanned out at the PSU exit into 8 lines; each silicon strip sensor is connected to one of these lines. Two PSU are combined into one power supply module (PSM, A4601H model). In total 984 A4601H boards are needed to power the detector groups; they are located on 129 EASY 4000 crates, disposed on 29 racks, around 10 m away from the beam crossing region, and operate in a "hostile" radiation and magnetic field environment, powering the detector through ≈ 50-m-long low impedance cables [32]. The 356 control rings require a separate power at 2.5 V. This is provided by a different set of 110 control power supply modules (A4602, four 2.5 V channels per module), fully integrated in the same system of the A4601H units and located on the same crates. Both A4601H and A4602 units require two distinct 48V power sources, one source (48Vp) for the regulators, the other (48Vs) for the service electronics. They are both provided by AC-DC converters, CAENs A3486 ("MAO"), disposed on the same racks. Each EASY 4000 crate hosts up to 9 boards (A4601H mixed to A4602) and provides 48Vp and 48Vs rails, interlock and general reset bus lines. The first slot in the crate (*slot 0*) hosts one interlock-card, which interfaces the interlock and reset lines to the control and safety systems (section 3.3.8). The average power consumption of each silicon strip module with 6 (4) APV25 chips is about 2662 mW (1845 mW). The total power supplied by A4601H and A4602 boards is approximately 68 kW, of which nearly 50% is dissipated on power cables. The power consumption is foreseen to increase with the aging of the detector; the power supply system is dimensioned to cope with up to 60% increase of the low-voltage currents, corresponding to a total consumption of nearly 150 kW.

2008 JINST 3 S08004

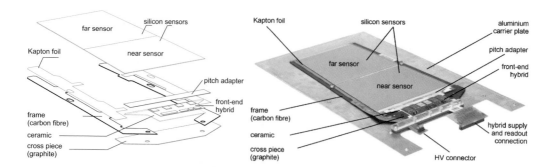

Figure 3.22: Left panel: exploded view of a module housing two sensors. Right panel: photograph of a TEC ring 6 module, mounted on a carrier plate.

3.3.3 Silicon modules

Module design

The silicon strip tracker is composed of 15 148 detector modules distributed among the four different subsystems (TIB, TID, TOB, TEC). Each module carries either one thin (320 μm) or two thick (500 μm) silicon sensors from a total of 24 244 sensors. All modules are supported by a frame made of carbon fiber or graphite, depending on the position in the tracker. A Kapton circuit layer is used to insulate the silicon from the module frame and to provide the electrical connection to the sensor back plane, i.e. bias voltage supply and temperature probe read-out. In addition the module frame carries the front-end hybrid and the pitch adapter. Figure 3.22 shows an exploded view and a photograph of a TEC module.

Modules for the inner barrel, the inner disks and rings 1 to 4 in the endcaps are equipped with one sensor, modules in the outer barrel and rings 5 to 7 in the endcaps have two sensors. In the case of two sensors, their corresponding strips are connected electrically via wire bonds. Depending on the geometry and number of sensors the active area of a module varies between 6243.1 mm^2 (TEC, ring 1) and 17202.4 mm^2 (TOB module). In total 29 different module designs, 15 different sensor designs and twelve different hybrid designs are used in TIB, TOB, TID and TEC. For alignment purposes special modules are prepared with etched holes in the aluminium back plane to allow a laser ray to traverse up to five modules.

The module frame provides the stability, safety and heat removal capability needed in the sensor support and carries the read-out electronics. In addition it has to remove the heat generated in the electronics and the silicon sensor(s) into the cooling points. In the endcaps the frame for the one-sensor modules is U-shaped and made of (780$\pm$5) μm thick graphite (FE779 carbon). For the two-sensor modules a similar U-shaped support structure is obtained by gluing two (640$\pm$40) μm thick carbon fiber legs (K13D2U CFC, 5 $\times$ 125 μm fabric, cyanate ester resin (CE3)) on a 800 μm thick graphite cross-piece (FE779 carbon) which holds the front end electronics. In the inner barrel a 550 μm thick carbon fiber frame that surrounds the silicon sensor on all sides is used . For the TOB, U-shaped module frames are obtained by gluing two carbon fiber legs (K13D2U CFC, 5 $\times$ 125 μm fabric, cyanate ester resin (CE3)) on a carbon fiber cross piece made of the same material.

2008 JINST 3 S08004

Both graphite and carbon fiber fulfil the requirements of high stiffness, low mass, efficient heat removal from the sensors, and radiation hardness. Differences in the expansion coefficients need to be compensated by the glue joint between the frames and the silicon. Several types of glues are used in module construction which all comply with the requirements of radiation hardness, good thermal conductivity and thermal stability. Among them are e. g. Epoxy AW 106 (Araldit, Novartis), silicone glue RTV 3140 (Dow Corning) to compensate for different thermal expansion coefficients and the conductive glue EE 129-4 (Polytec) between the silicon sensor back plane and the HV lines on the Kapton bias strips (see below).

Different types of aluminium inserts and precision bushings in the module frames are used to position and attach the modules to the larger support structures with high precision. TIB/TID and TEC modules are mounted using four points, two being high precision bushings that allow for a mounting precision of better than 20 μm while all four provide thermal contact between the module and the cooling pipes. For TOB modules two Cu-Be springs give the precision positioning and four screws ensure thermal contact.

The high voltage supply to the silicon back plane is provided by Kapton bias circuits running along the legs of the modules between the silicon sensor and the carbon fiber support frame. The connection of the bias voltage to the back plane is done via wire bonds. Thermal probes are placed on the Kapton foil to measure the temperature of the silicon. The glue joint between the temperature sensor and the back plane is done with the silicone glue RTV 3140.

The pitch adapter between the front end hybrid and the silicon sensor adjusts the strip pitch of the sensor (80 μm–205 μm depending on sensor type) to the APV pitch of 44 μm. It also allows placing the heat producing front end electronics farther away from the silicon sensors. A pitch adapter for TOB and TEC consists of a 550 μm thick glass substrate (Schott D263 glass), cut to the correct dimensions, with a pattern of low resistivity aluminium strips. For TIB 300 μm thick glass (Corning 1737F or G glass) is used. The 10 μm narrow lines are etched on a (1.0–1.5) μm thick aluminium layer deposited on a chromium base, resulting in less than 25 mΩ/$\square$.

Module assembly and testing

Sensors and front end hybrids are glued to the frames by high precision gantry robots. The components are aligned by cameras surveying special fiducial marks with a pattern recognition algorithm. In total seven institutes shared the responsibility for the assembly of all modules. The assembly rate was about 20 modules per day per gantry robot. A positioning precision of approximately 10 μm (RMS) has been achieved and one example from the quality control can be seen in figure 3.23.

Thin wire wedge bonding is used in several places on the modules to make electrical connections: APV chip to front-end hybrid, APV chip to pitch adapter, pitch adapter to sensor, sensor to sensor (in case of two-sensor-modules), bias voltage connection to the sensor back plane. In total 15 institutes (*bonding centers*) shared the responsibility for wire bonding all modules. The bonding rate was approximately 1 Hz. Bonding wire (99% aluminium, 1% silicon) with a diameter of 25 μm was used for all connections.

For the TEC and TOB modules the line of bonding wires connecting the hybrid pitch adapter to the silicon strips, and in the case of two sensor modules the strips of the two sensors, can be damaged by vibration during transport. As a protection for the TEC modules the silicon is glued

2008 JINST 3 S08004

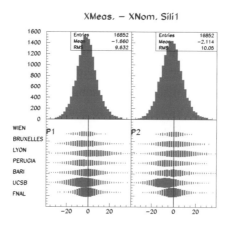

Figure 3.23: A typical residual distribution (in μm) for a reference point on the modules is shown for the different module assembly centers, indicating a precision of 10 μm (RMS) in the module production.

to a supporting strip (400 μm thin ceramic Al_2O_3) which in the case of the pitch adapter-sensor connection is also glued to the graphite cross piece. The reinforcement for the TOB modules was done by dispensing Sylgard 186 glue on the backside of the modules, between the two sensors and between the near sensor and the edge of the hybrid. For the TOB modules the sensor-sensor bonds and the backside APV bondings are encapsulated by Sylgard 186 glue across the bonding wires. For TIB modules no reinforcement was done.

After wire bonding each module was tested and graded, using the ARC system [51]. A detailed description of all tests performed and the acceptance criteria for good channels is given in the reference. Modules were graded A if fewer than 1% of the channels were failing the quality acceptance criteria (due to high noise, open bondings, oxide defects) and B if the failure rate was less than 2%. The remaining modules were graded C and were not used in the experiment. Other reasons to reject modules were imperfect mechanical precision or poor high voltage behaviour. All relevant test results are stored in the central CMS tracker data base. The yield of module production was greater than 97%.

3.3.4 Tracker Inner Barrel and Disks (TIB/TID)

Introduction and mechanics

The Tracker Inner Barrel (TIB) consists of four concentric cylinders placed at radii of 255.0 mm, 339.0 mm, 418.5 mm, and 498.0 mm respectively from the beam axis that extend from -700 mm to $+700$ mm along the z axis. The two innermost layers host double sided modules with a strip pitch of 80 μm, while the outer two layers host single sided modules with a strip pitch of 120 μm. Each cylinder is subdivided into four sub-assemblies ($\pm z$, up/down) for ease of handling and integration. Each of these sub-assemblies (half-shells) hosts an independent array of services from cooling to electronics and thus can be fully equipped and tested before being mechanically coupled to each other during final assembly.

2008 JINST 3 S08004

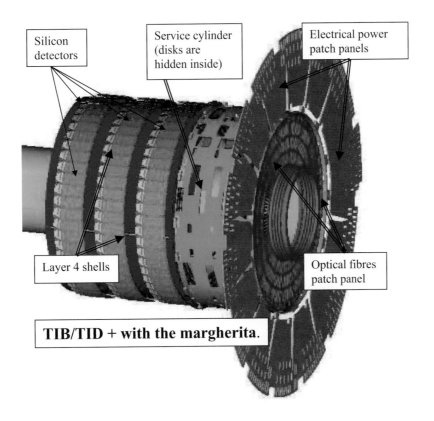

Silicon detectors

Service cylinder (disks are hidden inside)

Electrical power patch panels

Layer 4 shells

Optical fibres patch panel

TIB/TID + with the margherita.

Figure 3.24: Schematic drawing of the TIB/TID+ subassembly. This structure and its twin (TIB/TID-) nest inside the Tracker Outer Barrel (TOB), one for each end. Services routed out from the margherita consist of copper cables for powering and slow controls, optical fibers for signals and controls and also cooling fluid supply lines made of aluminium tubing.

Two service cylinders are coupled to the ends of TIB± (referring to +z or −z) which end in a service distribution disk called the *margherita* (see below). These service cylinders play a dual role: one is to route out services from the shells to the margherita, the other is to support the Tracker Inner Disks (TID) which sit inside them. Figure 3.24 shows a schematic drawing of one half TIB/TID structure together with its corresponding margherita.

The TID± are assemblies of three disks placed in z between ±800 mm and ±900 mm. The disks are identical and each one consists of three rings which span the radius from roughly 200 mm to 500 mm. The two innermost rings host back-to-back modules while the outer one hosts single sided ones. Just like the TIB shells each individual ring can be fully equipped and tested independently of the others before final assembly. Together the full TIB/TID guarantee hermetical coverage up to pseudorapidity $\eta = 2.5$.

All mechanical parts like shells, disks and service cylinders are made of high strength low deformation carbon fiber chosen both for its lightness and its low material budget. The margherita is instead made of conventional G-10 fiber epoxy with $30\,\mu$m copper on both sides.

The silicon detector modules are mounted directly on the structure's shells and rings. Thus, while a large number of modules has to be integrated and tested at any one time, the approach chosen allows for far greater precision of assembly. The individual components of a TIB shell,

2008 JINST 3 S08004

some of which not only service the silicon detector needs but also define its geometric position in space, will be described in some detail in next paragraphs.

Cooling

The cooling circuits must be able to efficiently cool the detectors with a cooling liquid temperature down to about $-25°C$, while keeping the material budget as low as possible. For the TIB/TID the decision was made to use aluminium piping of 6 mm cross section and 0.3 mm wall thickness. These pipes are bent into loops and soldered to inlet/outlet manifolds which connect several loops in parallel. The thermal connection between pipes and silicon modules is made with aluminium ledges which are glued to the pipes. On each ledge there are two threaded M1 holes onto which the modules are tightened. For the TIB each loop hosts three modules placed in straight row (figure 3.25), while in the TID arrangements are more varied even though the number of modules per cooling loop is similar.

Since the position of the ledges defines the position in space of the modules, after the glue has hardened the whole half cylinder is surveyed with a precision measuring machine. Before gluing, the circuits are tested individually for leaks both at cold temperatures ($-30°C$) and at high pressure (20 bars). It is only after the survey that the TIB cylinders (or TID disks) are available for the integration of the electrical parts including the detector modules. The dimensions of the cooling circuit vary from layer to layer and depend on the amount of power dissipated by the modules used for that specific layer. The cooling circuits vary from a minimum of four loops (12 modules equivalent) for the double sided layers to a maximum of 15 loops for the outer single sided ones where individual module heat dissipation is much lower. The TIB/TID uses a total of 70 independent cooling circuits so that in case of an accidental break in one of the circuits only a small part of the tracker is affected. The TIB thus is organized in three module ladders (the cooling loop) which cover the outer and inner surface of the four layers. The same concept applies to the TID with the only difference that the number of modules per cooling loop varies with the ring radius. The electrical grouping which we now describe takes this mechanical distribution into account.

Electrical grouping

The modules have been grouped together electrically. The basic group consists of three modules which sit on any given cooling loop (figure 3.25). The three modules are interconnected through a Kapton circuit (mother cable) through which powering, detector biasing and controls are distributed. At the top of a mother cable sits a CCUM which takes care of clock, trigger and I^2C distribution. These mother cables are then electrically joined in a more complex group called the control ring which distributes trigger, clock and slow control signals to the CCUMs. Control ring groups never straddle two different cooling loops and are dimensioned so that a reasonable compromise between granularity and complexity is achieved. Control rings in the TIB/TID make use of a unit called the DOHM (Digital opto-hybrid module) which receives all the signals from the optical fibers coming from the front end controllers (FEC) and converts them to electrical LVDS signals that are then distributed to up to 45 detector modules (15 mother cables) via CCUs. Given the high number of modules belonging to a Control Ring, TIB/TID has implemented redundancy in its DOHM hardware.

2008 JINST 3 S08004

Figure 3.25: Three TIB modules mounted on a layer 3 shell. The Kapton mother cable runs underneath. A CCUM module at the end of the string interfaces the modules to the control ring. Also visible are the three analog opto-hybrids (see text) and fibers.

Modules have been grouped together to keep the number of power supplies down to a manageable level. The smallest power group consists of three modules (one mother cable) while the largest comprises up to 12 modules (four mother cables). Power groups are contained within a control ring (i.e. there is no straddling across control ring boundaries) and are fed by a specific power supply unit (PSU) developed for the tracker which also supplies HV biasing for the detectors.

Analog signals from the detector front end are converted to optical by analog opto-hybrids which sit next to the silicon modules and are connected directly to the front end hybrids. Thus the system is completely optically decoupled from the DAQ which helps preserve signal integrity while avoiding ground loops.

Grounding of the TIB/TID relies on the cooling circuits which are made of aluminium. The return current wires are connected to the cooling manifolds for all mother cables and DOHMs. The cooling inlet and outlet pipes run along the service cylinder across the margherita, making electrical contact with it. Outside the tracker volume these pipes are then connected to the CMS detector ground. Power cable shields are connected to the margherita which hosts all of the connectors. All detector modules have their own carbon fiber frame directly connected to the front end hybrid local ground. The shells are grounded through the cooling manifolds.

3.3.5 Tracker Outer Barrel (TOB)

Mechanical structure and layout

The Tracker Outer Barrel consists of a single mechanical structure (*wheel*) supporting 688 self-contained sub-assemblies, called *rods*.

The wheel is composed by four identical disks joined by three outer and three inner cylinders (figure 3.26). Disks and cylinders are made of carbon fiber epoxy laminate. The cylinders have a core of aramid-fiber honeycomb. The joints between disks and cylinders are realized with aluminium elements glued to the carbon fiber parts on precision fixtures, and then bolted together. Each of the disks contains 344 openings, in which the rods are inserted. Each rod is supported by two disks, and two rods cover the whole length of the TOB along the z axis. The wheel has a length of 2180 mm, and inner and outer radii of 555 mm and 1160 mm, respectively. With cabling at its two ends the TOB has a total length of 2360 mm. The openings in the disks form six detection layers with average radii of 608, 692, 780, 868, 965, 1080 mm. Within each layer, the centers of gravity of the rods are displaced by ± 16 mm with respect to the average radius of the layer, thus allowing for overlap in ϕ and therefore full coverage within each layer. The rod mechanics are designed in such a way to implement overlap of the silicon sensors at $z = 0$. In each layer, the

2008 JINST 3 S08004

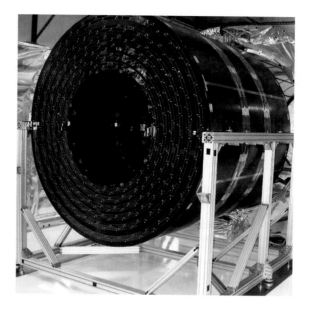

Figure 3.26: Picture of the TOB wheel.

overlap in the r-ϕ view between neighboring rods is always larger than 1.5 mm or 12 strips, while the overlap around $z = 0$ is precisely 1.5 mm. Inside the disk openings, the rod support spheres are held by precision elements made of polyetherimide plastic that are glued to the carbon fiber structure. The four disks have all been assembled in a temperature-controlled room on one single precision table, ensuring a precision on the relative positions of the rod holding elements and the aluminium elements joining disks and cylinder of 100 μm, and a reproducibility between different disks at the 10 μm level.

The wheel is equipped with *targets* for measurements of the geometrical precision of the assembled structure. Photogrammetry, theodolites, and 3D coordinate measurement systems have been used for survey and alignment of the wheel structure. Some of these targets remain visible after insertion of the TOB in the *tracker support tube*, for a precise measurement of the TOB positioning in the tracker reference frame, and even after integration of TIB, to monitor possible movements due to deformations of the loaded structure. The wheel mechanics has been thoroughly measured before starting rod integration, and the relative positioning of the precision elements has been found to be typically within 100 μm of nominal values over the whole TOB dimensions, with maximum deviations observed around 200 μm.

The rod mechanics

The rods are self-contained assemblies providing support and cooling for 6 or 12 silicon detector modules, together with their interconnection and read-out electronics.

The mechanical structure consists of two 1130 mm long carbon fiber C-shaped profiles, joined by several transverse carbon fiber ribs and plates. All rod components are contained in an envelope of $159 \times 1130 \times 22$ mm^3, except the four supporting spheres that stick out laterally in correspondence of the two disks of the wheel, and the *z-stops* that block the rod against the outer disk surface after insertion in the wheel.

2008 JINST 3 S08004

A U-shaped cooling pipe runs around the rod, inside the C-profiles; 24 aluminium inserts are glued through openings along the profiles to the carbon fiber and around the cooling pipe; these inserts provide support and cooling to the detector modules, that are mounted in six positions along the rod, three per side. Each detector is supported by four inserts, two close to the read-out hybrid, and two close to the sensor-to-sensor bonds. The two inserts close to the hybrid implement pins on which the Cu-Be springs on the module frame are clamped, determining the precision of the module positioning; all four inserts have a threaded hole for the fixation of the module to the rod: cup-shaped washers together with a calibrated torque used in tightening the screw ensure efficient cooling contact between the aluminium heat spreader on the module frame and the rod support inserts. On the cooling pipe side, the shape and the size of the inserts is optimized to minimize the thermal impedance of the contact, which in turn allows to minimize the cross section of the cooling pipe.

In single-sided rods, which populate layers 3–6, one detector module is mounted in each of the six positions, with the strips facing the central plane of the rod. In double-sided rods, which populate layers 1 and 2, two detectors are mounted in each position, the inner one as in single-sided rods and the outer one with the backplane facing the backplane of the first module. The distance between the sensor and the middle plane of the rod is ±3.3 mm in single-sided rods, ±3.3 mm and ±7.6 mm in double-sided rods.

The rod cooling pipes, and the manifolds housed on the outer disks of the wheel, are realized in CuNi 70/30 alloy. This material is chosen for its corrosion resistance, and as it allows reliable solder joints to be made relatively easily, avoiding the use of o-rings or ferrules in the pipe connections; the reliability of the cooling circuits is a crucial issue for the tracker, and particularly so for the TOB, which is the most inaccessible subsystem once the detector is fully integrated. The rather high density of the material (its radiation length of about 1.4 cm is 6 times shorter than that of aluminium) is compensated by the reduced thickness of the walls that this technology allows: rod pipes and manifolds have 100 μm and 200 μm wall thickness, respectively. In addition the design of the cooling circuit has been optimized (as already mentioned above), to minimize the cross section of the pipes (the cooling fluid also gives a non-negligible contribution to the material budget), and to maximize the number of rod pipes served by a single manifold (within the constraints of the desired cooling performance). An outer diameter of 2.2 mm is chosen for single-sided rod pipes (providing cooling to 6 detectors), 2.5 mm for double-sided rod pipes (providing cooling to 12 detectors), and 6 mm for the manifolds; one manifold serves on average more than 15 rod pipes, the actual number varying between 8 and 22 depending on the region of the TOB. Overall, the whole TOB is served by 44 cooling lines, giving an average of 118 detectors, or 550 read-out chips, per line.

Rod electrical design

The 6 or 12 modules housed in a rod form a power group, i.e. they are supplied by a single power supply unit. The low voltage lines supplying the front-end hybrids and the Analogue Opto-Hybrids (AOHs) run in the Inter-Connect-Bus (ICB), a 700 mm long printed circuit board sitting in the middle plane of the rod (figure 3.27). The Communication and Control Unit Module (CCUM) is plugged to one end of the ICB. The clock and the control signals issued by the CCUM are also routed to the final destinations through the ICB. The distribution of power, clock and signals to front-end hybrids and AOHs proceeds through four other PCBs, the Inter-Connect-Cards

2008 JINST 3 S08004

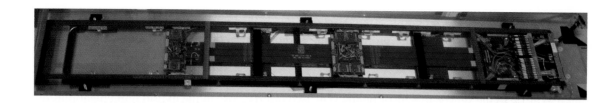

Figure 3.27: Photo of a rod frame equipped with electronics components, ready to receive silicon detector modules.

(ICCs). Two ICCs serve one module position and two other ICCs serve two module positions. ICCs have different design in single-sided rods and double-sided rods, which have one and two modules mounted in each module position, respectively; therefore there are in total four different ICC flavours in the TOB.

The ICB is held in place by small transverse carbon fiber plates; the ICCs and the CCUM are plugged to the ICB and screwed to the aluminium module support inserts (on the opposite side of the module), which also provide a good cooling contact to those boards. The AOHs are supported and cooled only by the connector that plugs to the ICCs. In addition to distributing LV power and CTRL signals, the ICCs receive the data lines from the read-out hybrid and route them to the AOHs (a few cm away) where they are converted to optical signals. The ICCs also receive lines carrying temperature information from the module frame Kapton circuit and route them to the ICB. The optical fibers leaving the AOHs travel inside the carbon fiber profiles, guided by dedicated plastic holders. The only electrical lines not integrated in the ICB/ICCs distribution system are the bias lines for the sensors. These run in dedicated wires (size AWG 26) housed in the carbon fiber profiles, while the line with the return current is integrated in the ICB. There are six lines in single-sided rods (one per module), and 8 lines in double-sided rods (four serving one module each, and four serving two modules each). The LV lines and the HV lines go in separate connectors in the rod end-panel, each of which also hosts some temperature lines, and then run all together to the back-end in one multi-service cable plus low-impedance cable. At the power supply backplane the six or eight bias lines are connected to the two independent high-voltage supply lines in such a way that each line powers one side of the rod. The clock and control lines as well as the LV lines powering the CCUM leave the rod through a short cable which plugs into the next rod of the control ring. The first and the last rod of a control ring are connected to the Digital Opto-Hybrid Module (DOHM). This board houses the digital opto-hybrids optically connected to the remote control system and distributes the clock and the control signals through a token-ring 40 MHz LVDS-based protocol to the connected rods (up to 10). The length of the optical fibers coming from the AOHs is chosen so that all fibers end at the same location near the CCUM, where the connectors of the 12-fiber ribbons are integrated (figure 3.28). The choice of including the optical patch panel inside the rod volume was made to reduce the thickness of the TOB services on the TOB end-flanges, so minimizing the inactive volume between TOB and TEC.

2008 JINST 3 S08004

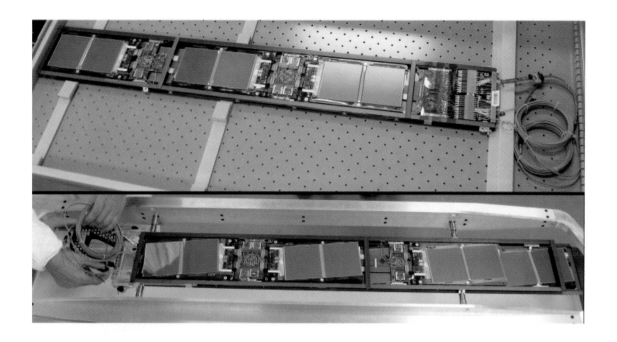

Figure 3.28: Top panel: photo of an assembled double-sided rod, showing the CCUM side, with the 12-way optical ribbons connected to the AOH fibers. Bottom panel: double-sided rod being prepared for insertion in the TOB mechanics; the side opposite to the CCUM is shown.

Electrical and read-out grouping

The grouping of the rods into control rings is designed primarily to avoid having control rings spanning across two different cooling segments, while maximizing the size of a control ring (to reduce cost and material budget) within the recommended limit of 10 CCUMs per ring. This logic results in two or three control rings per cooling segment, with a single exception of a cooling segment containing one control ring only. The average number of CCUMs (i.e. of rods) per ring in the TOB is 7.5. Within a control ring, rods are clustered in groups that are read out by the same FED. Again, a read-out group never spans over two control rings, and the grouping is optimized to minimize the number of unused channels in the FEDs (to reduce cost). The average FED occupancy in the TOB is 94%. In summary, the TOB is made of 688 rods read out by 134 FEDs, controlled by 92 DOHMs, and cooled by 44 independent lines.

Grounding

In each rod the return line of LV and bias is connected inside the CCUM to the return line of the LV power of DOHM and CCUMs, and connected through a short multi-wire cable to the cooling manifold serving the rod: this is the main ground connection of the rod. The grounding is improved by additional ground connections in each ICC, implemented through metalization around the mounting holes.

The DOHMs, mounted on the TOB end-flange (figure 3.29), are protected by alodyned aluminium plates of 0.5 mm thickness, which are locally connected to the power return line.

2008 JINST 3 S08004

Figure 3.29: Photo of the completed z+ side of the TOB. The DOHMs form the outer layer of the services on the TOB end flange. Optical ribbons (green) run out, grouped in 16 channels. Power cables and feeding pipes run parallel to each other on the thermal screen panels.

The cooling circuits of the different segments are then connected electrically through short multi-wire cables soldered to the radial pipes feeding the manifolds (or to the manifolds themselves, for the outer layer) and screwed to the *ground rings*: an alodyned aluminium bar of 10×10 mm^2 square section bent to round shape and equipped all along with threaded holes, which is installed at the outer radius of the TOB, on both sides. Gold-coated copper strips of 30 mm width and 0.2 mm thickness connect the ground ring to the carbon fiber structure of the outer cylinder, in eight locations in ϕ. The connection to the carbon fiber is realized with conductive araldite. The same strip material is used to realize the electrical connections between outer cylinders and disks, and inner cylinders and disks, again in eight locations in ϕ. In addition, copper strips as long as the whole TOB are added on the outer surface of the outer cylinder (visible in figure 3.26); for the inner cylinder instead, which is inside the tracking volume, it was decided to rely on the conductivity of the carbon fiber.

Such design of the grounding scheme ensures good electrical connection of mechanical structures and power return lines making efficient use of the existing conductive materials (cooling pipes and carbon fiber parts), with minimal amount of added metallic elements.

2008 JINST 3 S08004

3.3.6 Tracker EndCaps (TEC)

Mechanical structure

The endcaps extend radially from 220 mm to 1135 mm and from ±1240 mm to ±2800 mm along the z-direction. The two endcaps are called TEC+ and TEC- (according to their location in z in the CMS coordinate system). Each endcap consists of nine disks that carry substructures on which the individual detector modules are mounted plus an additional two disks serving as front/back termination. A sketch of one endcap and a photograph of the completed TEC+ is shown in figures 3.30 and 3.31. Eight U-profiles, referred to as service channels because all services are grouped in their vicinity, join the disks together along their outer periphery, while at its inner diameter each disk is attached at four points to an inner support tube. To preserve the envelope necessary for the insertion of the pixel detector, the last six disks have a larger inner radius (309 mm) as compared to the first three (229 mm).

The disks are Carbon Fiber Composite (CFC) / honeycomb structures. The honeycomb core is 16 mm thick NOMEX, 3.2-92 with a border of epoxy potting. On either side of the core there is a symmetric layup of CFC skins (0.4 mm thickness). The skin material is CF-fabric THENAX HTA 5131,3K (T300) impregnated with EP121 epoxy resin. The same material is used for the service channels and the inner support tube. The latter has a thickness of 3 mm and is azimuthally segmented into four $90°$ segments. Each of these segments is attached to the disks and the gaps at the joints between segments are filled with epoxy glue so that they are gas tight. A thin cylindrical skin made of 0.5 mm thick CFC panels surrounds the endcaps on the outside and serves as a gas envelope for the atmosphere of dry nitrogen. The front plate has the same function and consists of a 5 mm NOMEX core with 0.2 mm CFC skins on each side. The back plate provides an additional thermal shielding for the cold silicon volume and is considerably thicker. The NOMEX core is 45 mm with each CFC skin 1.5 mm thick. The back plate also serves to make the overall structure rigid in the z-direction. The back plate is covered by another carbon fibre disk, the bulkhead, which is, however, mechanically detached from the TEC and supported by the tracker support tube. The bulkhead carries the outer connectors of all TEC cables, thereby forming a patch panel for the electrical connection of the TEC to the external power cables. It is covered by panels with heating foils which close the thermal screen at the end face of the tracker support tube.

Ten different module types are arranged in rings around the beam pipe. For reasons of modularity they are mounted on substructures called *petals*, which in turn are mounted on the disks. Disks 1 to 3 carry seven rings of modules, ring 1 is missing on disks 4 to 6, rings 1 and 2 are missing on disks 7 and 8, and disk 9 carries rings 4 to 7 only. Rings 1, 2 and 5 are built up of so-called double sided modules: two modules are mounted back-to-back with a stereo angle of 100 mrad. This provides space information perpendicular and parallel to the strip orientation.

Petals

To allow easy access to the detector modules they are mounted on modular elements, the petals (figures 3.32 and 3.33). Petals can be individually removed from the endcaps without uncabling and/or disassembling the entire structure. A total of 16 petals are mounted on each of the nine disks of one endcap, eight on the front face of the disk — as seen from the interaction point —

2008 JINST 3 S08004

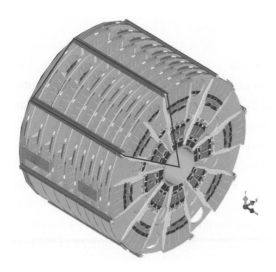

Figure 3.30: Left panel: Sketch of one tracker endcap. Modules are arranged in rings around the beam axis. They are mounted on trapezoidal sub-structures called *petals*. One sector, indicated with a line, consists of nine front petals mounted on the disk sides facing the interaction point (3 FD13, 3 FD46, 2 FD78, 1 FD9) and nine back petals mounted in the opposite side of a disk (3 BD13, 3 BD46, 2 BD78, 1 BD9). Right panel: Photograph of a TEC as seen from the interaction point. The diameter of the TECs is 2.3 m.

Figure 3.31: Side view of a TEC.

(front petals) and eight on the back face (back petals). Mechanically there are two types each of front and back petals, long petals for disks 1–3 and short ones for disks 4–9. As described above, the front and back petals on disks 1–3 carry all seven rings of modules and are labelled FD13 and BD13, respectively. Petals on disks 4–6 carry rings 2 to 7 (FD46/BD46), those on disks 7 and 8 carry rings 3 to 7 (FD78/BD78), and on disk 9 the petals carry rings 4 to 7 (FD9/BD9). The petals have a structure similar to the disks, consisting of a 10 mm NOMEX core sandwiched between

0.4 mm CFC skins. As viewed from the interaction point the modules belonging to rings 1, 3, 5, 7 are mounted on the petal front side (A-side and C-side for the front and back petals, respectively), while modules in rings 2, 4, 6 are mounted on the back side of each petal (B-side and D-side for the front and back petals, respectively). On a given disk the front petals overlap azimuthally with the back petals, as do, for a given petal, detector modules belonging to the same ring. Detectors in adjacent rings are arranged to overlap radially, thus providing full coverage. Each petal is mounted on inserts in the main disks using a three point fixation: one point fixed in x, y and z, one fixed only in phi, and one fixed only in z.

Cooling

The heat generated by all electronic components on a petal must be removed efficiently. In addition the silicon sensors must be operated at a temperature of about $-10°C$ to reduce the effects of radiation damage. The silicon sensors and front end hybrids are cooled via the CFC frames of the detector modules, for which carbon fiber of high thermal conductivity is used (800 W/(m K)). The aluminium inserts for positioning the modules serve at the same time for the coupling to the cooling pipe. The two inserts along the legs of the module frame provide primarily for the cooling of the sensors, while the inserts on the frame base are heat sinks for the front end hybrid. Each petal contains two cooling circuits traversing the petal longitudinally and meandering from one cooling point to the next. The cooling pipes are made of titanium with an outer diameter of 3.9 mm and a wall thickness of 0.25 mm. They are embedded in the petal and serve to cool the components on both back and front side. The tubing is pre-bent into the proper shape. The input/output manifolds are laser welded onto the cooling pipes. After having milled the corresponding grooves and holes into the petals, the tubing is inserted. Gluing jigs are used to position the cooling inserts and to glue them to the pipes and to the petal. To close the grooves and re-establish the integrity of the petal a CFC skin with holes at the location of the inserts is glued onto the petal face. The inserts are then machined to the precision required for module positioning. The maximum heat load from the electronics on a petal is about 87 W, including the heating of the sensors after ten years of LHC operation. In these conditions a mass flow of 2.3 kg/min of the C_6F_{14} coolant gives a temperature difference of $2°C$ between petal inlet and outlet. The connection of the petal circuits to the piping running along z is done at the outer periphery of the petal. These connections can be undone easily in case the petal needs to be removed. A pair of longitudinal pipes serves either 4 or 5 petals, which are connected in parallel. A total of 64 longitudinal stainless steel pipes with 11 mm inner diameter are used per endcap.

Electrical system design

The silicon modules, AOHs and CCUMs on the petals are connected to motherboards, called InterConnect Boards or ICBs, which are mounted on both sides of the petal. In figure 3.32 photos of a bare front petal equipped with ICBs only are shown. There are five individual boards: the main board ICB_46 on side B/D, which carries all the connectors for the cables and two CCUM boards and transmits power and signals to the modules of rings 4 and 6, and four smaller boards, which provide the power and signals for the other rings (ICB_2 on side B/D and ICB_1, ICB_3 and ICB_57 on side A/C, where the numbers correspond to the number of the ring to which the

2008 JINST 3 S08004

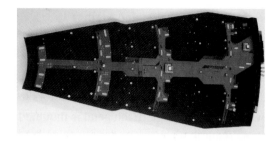
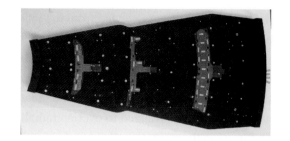

Figure 3.32: The different ICBs on the two sides of a front petal: ICB_2 and ICB_46 on side B, and ICB_1, ICB_3 and ICB_57 on side A (from left to right). On ICB_46, the two CCUMs are plugged.

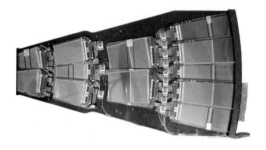

Figure 3.33: Left photograph: front side of a TEC Petal. Right photograph: back side.

connected modules belong). These four boards are connected to the main board. The ICB brings the ground, the various supply voltages and the bias voltage to the electrical devices on the petal, and transmits LVDS and I²C signals. In addition analogue data from the FE hybrids are transmitted differentially to the AOHs over distances of a few centimetres.

To keep the number of low voltage power supplies and connections relatively small while limiting the current that must be provided by one power supply, the modules are organized in three low voltage (LV) groups, which are served by individual power supplies. The LV group 1 consists of rings 1 and 2, group 2 contains rings 3, 4 and 6 and finally rings 5 and 7 belong to group 3. This corresponds to 8/11/9 (4/8/11) modules or 48/44/44 (24/32/56) APVs on front (back) petals in LV group 1/2/3. In total there are eleven power rails on ICB_46, which must carry a current of up to 12 A. Sensing is implemented for the low voltage connections. The sense resistors are located in the electrical centre of each power group. Capacitances are implemented on the ICB near the power input connectors as well as near the front-end connectors to suppress ripples and minimize a possible voltage overshoot caused by switching off the FE-hybrids.

For each low voltage group, two high voltage channels are provided. For each HV channel there are up to four single HV lines, which bias one or two silicon modules.

The ICB_46 and ICB_57 have six copper layers, while the smaller boards have only four layers. To limit the contribution to the material budget, the copper layers are rather narrow and thin.

2008 JINST 3 S08004

The layer thickness amounts to 17 and 25 μm for the inner four and outer two layers, respectively, except for the innermost layer of boards ICB_1, ICB_3 and ICB_57 on front petals and ICB_1, ICB_2 and ICB_3 on back petals, which has a thickness of 35 μm. Digital and data traces are shielded by power and ground layers.

Two petals, one back and one front petal, are connected in a control ring. The front petal is the first in the control loop. Both on back and front petals, rings 1–4 and 5–7 are connected to one CCU, respectively. The Digital Opto-Hybrid (DOH) converts the optical signals to electrical LVDS signals and vice versa. Two DOHs are located on a separate PCB, the Digital Opto-Hybrid Module (DOHM), which is mounted on the back petal. From the DOHM, which also distributes the power for the DOHs, electrical signals are transmitted to the CCUMs on the petal. For the control ring, a redundancy scheme is implemented on the ICB. Each CCU can be bypassed electrically in case of a problem, so that the functionality of the control ring is maintained. The second DOH is needed for redundancy purposes only. To allow also the last CCU on the ring to be bypassed, a fifth CCU is located on the DOHM. It is used only in this special case. However, if two consecutive CCUs are faulty, the complete control ring is lost.

Low-pass filters are implemented for the traces of the temperature signals that are brought out via power cables, to ensure that noise is not coupled in via these lines. In addition to the thermistors located on the Kapton of the silicon modules, several temperature and humidity probes are located on or connected to the ICB. Two 10 kΩ NTC thermistors are located on ICB_46 on front petals and read out via the power cable of low voltage group 2. Both on front and back petals, four 10 kΩ NTC thermistors are glued to the cooling inserts of the ring 6 modules. They are read out via the DCU that is present on each CCUM. On both petal types, a humidity sensor can be connected to ICB_46. For back petals, this sensor is read out via the power cable of LV group 2. On each z-side in total 12 hardwired humidity sensors are distributed over the TEC volume. For front petals, the humidity sensor is read out via the DCU on the CCUM. Front petals of all disks of the top and bottom sectors carry these additional humidity sensors, providing detailed information on the relative humidity along the z-direction.

Kapton cables of about 15 cm length are used to link the petals inside one control ring with each other and with the DOHM, providing the electrical digital signals and the power for the CCUMs. These cables consist of two copper layers with a thickness of 35 μm each, separated by a 100 μm thick polyimide layer.

Each TEC LV group is supplied by one so-called multiservice cable, which transmits the analogue power and the bias voltage and brings out signals from temperature or humidity sensors. Inside the tracker support tube, power cables are arranged around the main TEC cooling pipes that run along the z direction, and end at the bulkhead. These cables implement silver-plated aluminium conductors to minimize the impact on the material budget. Typical currents per cable range from about 5 A to 11 A, depending on the number of APVs connected. Therefore three cable types exist, with wire cross-sections tailored to the differing needs.

The connection from the bulkhead to the so-called patch panel 1, located outside of the tracker volume, is provided by power cables implementing tinned copper conductors. The control power is transmitted via separate cables, which also break at the bulkhead. In this case tinned copper conductors are used both inside and outside the tracker volume.

2008 JINST 3 S08004

The grounding scheme

The so-called TEC common ground is located at the back end of each TEC. It is realized by means of a 5 cm wide and 150 μm thick copper ring, which is glued to the outer radius of each back disk and tied to the brackets that connect the tracker support tube to the hadron calorimeter. The material of the hadron calorimeter represents a very solid ground. The shields of all cables, the reference points of all power groups, the cooling manifolds that are used to connect the cooling pipes of the petals to the main tubes that are mounted on the TEC, the CF skins of the disks and petals and the outer aluminium shields of the TEC are connected to this TEC common ground. On the petal side, one common analogue ground is implemented per petal. This so-called local petal ground is distributed via a 2 cm wide and 20 μm thick copper path along the ICBs as a reference rail. The LV and HV supplies of all power groups are referenced to this local petal ground at the geometrical/electrical centre of each group. The digital ground of a control group is referenced once to the local petal ground. The local petal ground of each petal is connected to the TEC common ground. Copper strips glued to the outer radii of the disks and along the service channels that connect all disks with the back disk provide the electrical connection to the TEC common ground. These copper strips are connected via short copper braids to the ICBs on the petals. The carbon frames of the silicon detectors are connected via a conductive glue spot to the bias Kapton and finally via the ICB to the FE hybrid ground. To avoid ground loops, the frames are electrically insulated from the cooling pipes by an anodized layer between the cooling inserts and the pipe.

3.3.7 Geometry and alignment

The deviation of true position and orientation of tracker modules from their nominal values as specified in the engineering drawings depends on many factors with different origin, some of them time-dependent: the achieved assembly precision, deformation due to tracker cooling, stress from access and magnetic field, out-gassing of components in dry nitrogen. This leads to a degradation of the track parameter resolution (figure 3.4), which needs to be recovered by determining true module position and orientation, called *alignment*.

Alignment of the tracker relies on three key components: the various data about assembly gathered during the integration process, the Laser Alignment System and the alignment with tracks, ordered by increasing precision and availability with time.

For alignment purposes, modules with two sensors are treated as they would have one large sensor with identical active area coverage. This is justified by sensor mask design [36] and achieved sensor placement accuracy (figure 3.23).

The CMS tracker alignment task thus consists of the determination of three translational and three rotational parameters for each of the 15 148 tracker modules. To achieve ultimate precision, it might be necessary to consider additional parameters, e.g. the sensor bow due to single-sided processing.

Geometry

Two methods are mainly used for measuring tracker component assembly precision: survey with coordinate measurement machines with a typical accuracy of a few μm to a few tens of μm, and

2008 JINST 3 S08004

Table 3.2: Estimated assembly precision (RMS, in μm) of tracker components. Values are given with respect to the next level in the hierarchy, e.g. the position accuracy of sensors in modules is $10\,\mu$m.

TIB		TID		TOB		TEC	
Sensor		Sensor		Sensor		Sensor	
	10		10		10		10
Module		Module		Module		Module	
	180		54		30		20
Shell		Ring		Rod		Petal	
	450		185		100		70
Cylinder		Disc		Wheel		Disc	
	750		350		140 ($r\phi$), 500 (z)		150
Tube		Cylinder		Tube		TEC	
			450		1000		600
		Tube		CMS		Tube	

photogrammetry with an accuracy of 150 μm (80 μm) under good (optimal) conditions for relative measurements. The measured and expected mounting precision from those data are summarized in table 3.2. It should be noted that structure deformations due to loading as well as temperature and humidity variations have not been taken into account.

The software description of the position and orientation of the active detector volumes has been validated with survey data and reconstructed tracks from test beams and cosmic muons recorded in various test and integration setups.

Laser Alignment System

The Laser Alignment System (LAS, figure 3.34) uses infrared laser beams with a wavelength $\lambda = 1075$ nm to monitor the position of selected tracker modules. It operates globally on tracker substructures (TIB, TOB and TEC discs) and cannot determine the position of individual modules. The goal of the system is to generate alignment information on a continuous basis, providing geometry reconstruction of the tracker substructures at the level of 100 μm, which is mandatory for track pattern recognition and for the High Level Trigger. In addition, possible tracker structure movements can be monitored at the level of 10 μm, providing additional input for the track based alignment.

In each TEC, laser beams cross all nine TEC discs in ring 6 (ray 2) and ring 4 (ray 3) on back petals, equally distributed in ϕ. Here special silicon sensors with a 10 mm hole in the backside metalization and an anti-reflective coating are mounted. The beams are used for the internal alignment of the TEC discs. The other eight beams (ray 4), distributed in ϕ, are foreseen to align TIB, TOB, and both TECs with respect to each other. Finally, there is a link to the Muon system (ray 1), which is established by 12 laser beams (six on each side) with precise position and orientation in the tracker coordinate system.

The signal induced by the laser beams in the silicon sensors decreases in height as the beams penetrate through subsequent silicon layers in the TECs and through beam splitters in the align-

2008 JINST 3 S08004

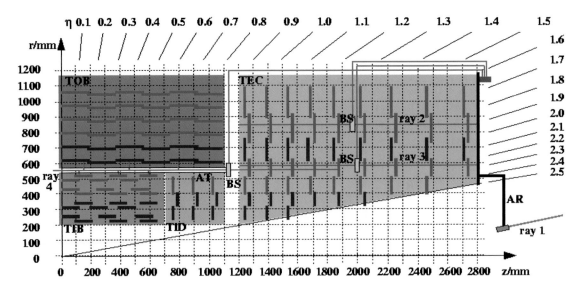

Figure 3.34: Overview of the CMS Laser Alignment System.

ment tubes that partly deflect the beams on TIB and TOB sensors. To obtain optimal signals on all sensors, a sequence of laser pulses with increasing intensities, optimized for each position, is generated. Several triggers per intensity are taken and the signals are averaged. In total, a few hundred triggers are needed to get a full picture of the alignment of the tracker structure. Since the trigger rate for the alignment system is around 100 Hz, this will take only a few seconds. These data will be taken at regular intervals, both in dedicated runs and during physics data taking.

Alignment with tracks

CMS pursues the development of two novel track-based alignment algorithms that allow to quickly solve the system of linear equations of order $\mathscr{O}(100\,000)$. The first is an extension to the well-known global Millepede algorithm [52], that takes all correlations into account and has been shown to successfully align the most sensitive 50 000 parameters. The second is a novel approach using a Kalman Filter [53], which bridges the gap between global and local algorithms by taking into account the most important correlations. In addition the HIP [54] algorithm, which is local in the sense that it takes into account only correlations of parameters within a module, is developed in parallel. In this algorithm, correlations between modules are dealt with implicitly by iterating the alignment many times. All three methods are expected to be able to provide alignment constants for the full silicon pixel and strip tracker.

Experience from other experiments has shown that collision data are not sufficient to constrain certain correlated module movements well enough to obtain a unique set of alignment constants. Therefore complementary data and constraints need to be exploited. Examples are tracks from cosmic muons (with and without magnetic field) that constrain the tracker barrel modules, or beam halo muons for the endcap. Beam gas and minimum bias events are also under consideration. Typical examples of constraints are a vertex constraint for decay particles e.g. from $Z \to \mu^+\mu^-$ or jets, mass constraints, measurements from the Laser Alignment System, and survey constraints. First studies indicate that those data will provide a unique alignment parameter set.

2008 JINST 3 S08004

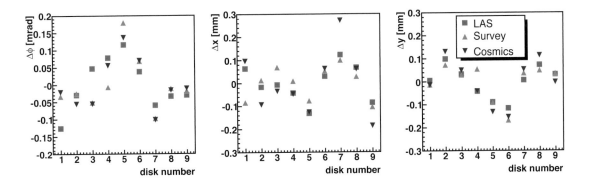

Figure 3.35: TEC+ disk rotation $\Delta\phi$ (around the beam axis) and displacements $\Delta x, \Delta y$ (in the disk plane) as determined from survey, LAS and cosmic muon tracks.

During integration of the TEC+, deviation of disk positions and rotations from nominal values have been determined from survey with photogrammetry, the LAS, and tracks from cosmic muons. Figure 3.35 shows the results from the three complementary methods. The global degrees of freedom (absolute position and orientation, torsion and shear around the symmetry axis) have been fixed by requiring the average displacement and rotation as well as torsion and shear to be zero. The values agree within $60\,\mu$m and $80\,\mu$rad with each other, which can be taken as an upper value on the precision of each method.

3.3.8 Detector control and safety system

The Tracker Detector Safety System (TDSS) and tracker Detector Control System (tracker DCS) is a two pillar system. The TDSS ensures independently the safety, with a large PLC (Programmable Logical Controller) system, occupying 6 LHC racks. A limited set of around 1000 hardwired temperature and humidity sensors are evaluated and out of limit states interlock power supplies. The tracker DCS, as a complementary partner, controls, monitors and archives all important parameters. The heart of the DCS is composed out of an industrial SCADA program (Supervisory Control And Data Acquisition) PVSS (Prozessvisualisierungs- und Steuerungssystem from ETM Austria, chapter 9) together with a Finite State Machine written in SMI++, a derivative of the former DELPHI control software; thus using the standard control software framework for all LHC experiments. The main task of the DCS is to control about 2000 power supplies for silicon module low and high voltage power and about 100 low voltage control power supplies via the OPC (OLE for Process Automation) protocol. Detector interdependencies of control, low and high voltages are handled, as well as fast ramp downs in case of higher than allowed temperatures or currents in the detector, experimental cavern problems, etc. All this is ensured by evaluating 10^4 power supply parameters, 10^3 data points from DSS via a Siemens S7 driver and 10^5 readings from the DCUs situated on all front end hybrids and control units CCUs. Several passive alarms and warning levels are defined for temperature, relative humidity, voltages, currents, etc. and are reported in a global warning panel as well as limits that, if surpassed, would result in automatic shutdown. Information from the tracker cooling plant, the thermal screen, beam conditions and the dry gas system are crucial for safe running and are accessible from the tracker DCS and TDSS.

2008 JINST 3 S08004

All parameters are archived to ORACLE. The TDSS (tracker DCS) system is fully implemented in the global CMS DSS (DCS) and Run Control system.

3.3.9 Operating experience and test results

Performance in test beam experiments

The system performance of integrated structures of the silicon strip tracker and its data acquisition chain as well as the performance of the silicon strip modules themselves has been studied in various test beam experiments at CERN and the Paul Scherrer Institut (PSI), Villigen (CH). In test beam campaigns, performed in May and October 2004 at the X5 test beam complex in the CERN west area, large substructures of TIB, TOB and TEC were exposed to a secondary pion beam with an energy of 120 GeV and a tertiary muon beam with muon energies ranging from 70 to 120 GeV. The TIB setup comprised a prototype half-shell structure of layer 3, equipped with eight single-sided strings, plus four double-sided strings, mounted on a custom support structure. For the TOB, the so-called cosmic rack, a precise mechanical telescope-like structure equipped with four single-sided and two double-sided rods, was used in the beam tests. The TEC setup consisted of one back and one front petal [55]. These setups corresponded to about 1% of the complete TIB, TOB and TEC detectors, respectively. The TOB and TEC setups were operated at a temperature below $-10°C$, while the TIB setup was operated at room temperature. Typical primary trigger rates for the pion beam were 600 000 pions per spill (a 2.2 s long period within a 12 s long SPS cycle during which particles are delivered) corresponding to a mean occupancy of 15 Hz/cm^2.

In the strip-cluster finding the cuts for the signal-to-noise ratio, S/N, of the cluster seed / neighbour strips / total cluster are 4/3/5 for TIB, 5/2/5 for TOB and 3/2/5 for TEC, respectively. The cluster noise is calculated by adding the single strip noise values in quadrature (TIB, TEC) or by taking the seed noise as the cluster noise (TOB). To determine the most probable value for the S/N of a module, a Landau distribution convoluted with a Gaussian is fitted to the signal-to-noise distribution, and the most probable value of the fitted function is quoted as the S/N.

The mean most probable S/N values for all module types, together with their strip length, pitch and abbreviations used in the following, are summarized in table 3.3. For thin (thick) TEC sensors, most probable S/N values of 29–33 (36–42) in peak mode and 19–22 (20–24) in deconvolution mode have been observed [55]. For the thick TOB OB1 (OB2) modules a S/N of typically 36 (38) and 25 (27) was found in peak and deconvolution mode, respectively [17], while the thin TIB IB1 (IB2) modules exhibited a S/N of 26 (30) in peak mode and 18 (20) in deconvolution mode.

Assuming that a MIP creates 24 000 electrons in a 300 μm thick layer of silicon [16], and assuming that the beam particles can be treated as MIPs, the S/N can be used to calculate the equivalent noise charge, ENC. The common mode subtracted noise depends on the capacitance of the sensor, which depends linearly on the strip length and the ratio between strip width and pitch, w/p [16]. Since $w/p = 0.25$ for all sensor types, the ENC varies between different module types according to the strip length. Results for all module types except W1TID are summarized in table 3.3. Measurements performed at low temperature (for the TEC, typically hybrid temperatures of $+10°C$ and $0°C$ were reached for hybrids with six and four APVs, respectively) are plotted versus the strip length in figure 3.36. A linear fit to these data yields the following dependence of the ENC on the strip length L:

$$
\begin{aligned}
\text{ENC}_{\text{peak}} &= (36.6 \pm 1.9)\, e^-/\text{cm} \cdot L + (405 \pm 27)\, e^-, \\
\text{ENC}_{\text{dec}} &= (49.9 \pm 3.2)\, e^-/\text{cm} \cdot L + (590 \pm 47)\, e^-.
\end{aligned}
$$

The common mode noise is the standard deviation of the common mode, calculated per APV from a certain number of events. The mean common mode noise has been evaluated and amounts to (173 ± 38) and (299 ± 76) electrons for TEC (mean from all APVs in the setup) and (265 ± 36) and (300 ± 19) electrons for TIB (mean from all APVs of TIB2 modules) in peak and deconvolution mode, respectively.

Although no dedicated beam telescope was available, efficiency studies have been performed both with the TOB and TEC setups, exploiting the fact that in both cases the beam penetrated several layers of modules. Efficiencies of above 99% have been observed in all such studies.

The uniformity of the module performance along and perpendicular to the strip direction has been studied in 2003 with several TIB modules in a test beam experiment at the X5 complex. Two single-sided strings equipped with IB2 modules were mounted on a structure corresponding to a portion of a layer 3 half-shell, and operated at room temperature. To study the uniformity across the strips, the strips read out by three APVs (on two different modules) were exposed to a pion beam, and between 1000 and 8000 events were collected per strip. A cluster was associated to a strip if the centre of gravity x of the cluster was reconstructed within $(n-0.5) \cdot p < x < (n+0.5) \cdot p$ for strip n and pitch p. The uniformity, defined as the ratio between the RMS and the mean of the respective distribution, was 1.3% for the cluster noise, with an increase close to the APV chip edges. The cluster charge uniformity was of the order of 1.4%, but dropped to 0.5% if calculated separately for groups of 32 adjacent strips. A uniformity of the S/N of 1.6% on average and of 1.0% for groups of 32 strips was measured. To investigate the uniformity along the strips, a muon beam was used for its uniform particle density. The cluster position along the strip could be obtained from the TOB setup that was operated in the same test beam, since the strip direction of the TOB modules was perpendicular to that of the TIB modules. The clusters were binned in 24 intervals according to their centre of gravity, corresponding to length intervals of 5 mm, and about 1500 events were accumulated per bin. Both the uniformity of cluster charge and S/N were found to be 1.4%.

Performance during integration

Testing during integration consisted typically of checks of the control ring functionality, tests of the I^2C communication of all chips, tests of the gain of the optical connections, commissioning (i.e. tuning of chip operation parameters), pedestal runs in peak and deconvolution mode, bias voltage ramping up to 450 V, read-out of currents and module and hybrid temperatures through the DCUs, and a functionality check of the temperature and humidity sensors.

In the following sections the performance of TEC, TIB/TID and TOB during integration is described. Two comments apply to all three sub-detectors:

- Numbers of dead and noisy strips are given below. While dead strips can be identified reliably, the noisiness of strips depends on external conditions such as grounding and the APV read-out mode and the figures given should be regarded as estimates only. APV edge strips

Table 3.3: Pitch, strip length, signal-to-noise ratio and equivalent noise charge after common mode subtraction for different module types. The TEC and TOB measurements are for hybrid temperatures of below 0 °C, the TIB measurements were performed at room temperature. Sensors of type IB1 and IB2 are used in TIB, layers 1 and 2 and layers 3 and 4, respectively. In the TOB, layers 1–4 are equipped with OB2 sensors, layers 5 and 6 with OB1 sensors. The sensor geometries abbreviated with W are wedge-shaped sensors used in TEC and TID, with the number corresponding to the ring. W1 sensors have a slightly different geometry in TID and TEC.

Module type	Pitch [μm]	Strip length [mm]	S/N Peak mode	S/N Dec. mode	ENC [e^-] Peak mode	ENC [e^-] Dec. mode
IB1	80	116.9	25.8 ± 1.3	18.3 ± 0.5	931 ± 48	1315 ± 37
IB2	120	116.9	29.5 ± 1.4	20.3 ± 0.6	815 ± 37	1182 ± 31
OB1	122	183.2	36	25	1110 ± 47	1581 ± 75
OB2	183	183.2	38	27	1057 ± 17	1488 ± 22
W1TEC	81–112	85.2	33.1 ± 0.7	21.9 ± 0.6	714 ± 23	1019 ± 37
W2	113–143	88.2	31.7 ± 0.5	20.7 ± 0.4	741 ± 25	1068 ± 51
W3	123–158	110.7	29.2 ± 0.6	20.0 ± 0.4	802 ± 16	1153 ± 48
W4	113–139	115.2	28.6 ± 0.5	19.2 ± 0.3	819 ± 21	1140 ± 26
W5	126–156	144.4	42.2 ± 1.1	24.1 ± 1.1	971 ± 29	1354 ± 57
W6	163–205	181.0	37.8 ± 0.6	23.0 ± 0.4	1081 ± 26	1517 ± 47
W7	140–172	201.8	35.5 ± 1.0	20.3 ± 1.1	1155 ± 40	1681 ± 107

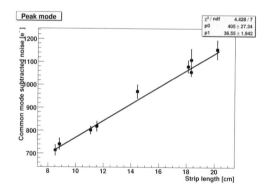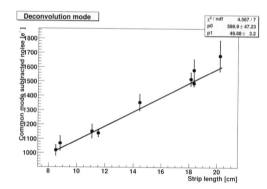

Figure 3.36: Equivalent noise charge after common mode subtraction versus strip length for all TOB and TEC module types, in peak (left panel) and deconvolution mode (right panel).

show typically an increased noise and are frequently flagged as noisy, especially when a fixed noise cut is used for all strips. These edge strips are included in the numbers of flagged strips, although they are usually fully efficient.

- Although all components (petals, rods, single modules in case of the TIB/TID) were tested before insertion and components not fulfilling strict quality criteria were rejected, several defects have been observed during integration. Typical defects are broken optical fibers, bad APVs (i.e. with many noisy or dead strips), and missing or unreliable I²C communication

2008 JINST 3 S08004

of complete modules or single chips. Most of the problems are assumed to be caused by mishandling during insertion or cabling. Since the exchange of components bears a considerable risk, not all defective components have been exchanged. Additional defects could be introduced by any following handling step, such as cabling of the tracker. The numbers given below should thus be regarded as a snapshot reflecting the situation right after integration of the single sub-detectors.

TEC Performance during integration

The TEC petals were integrated sector-wise, where one sector corresponds to one eighth of a TEC in ϕ, and comprises 18 petals that share nine control rings and four cooling circuits. After integration of one sector, a read-out test of the full sector was performed at room temperature, with the coolant at $+15°C$ and mean silicon and hybrid temperatures of about $+23°C$ and $+33°C$, respectively.

During integration a flaw in the crimping of the connectors of the multiservice power cables was found. After all such connectors had been replaced on both TECs, the system performance observed during integration was very robust. In figure 3.37, left side, the common mode subtracted noise of all strips of both TECs is shown for deconvolution mode. Since the measured noise depends on the gain of the optical chain, the noise was normalized to the digital output of the APV (scale on upper x-axis in figure 3.37). In addition, the number of ADC counts in the FED was converted to ENC according to the following method: with a nominal digital APV output of ± 4 mA and a nominal APV gain of 1 MIP/mA for thin sensors, the height of the digital output corresponds to 8 MIPs or 200 000 electrons. This method allows a direct comparison of the measurements from different optical channels and delivers an approximate absolute calibration of the equivalent noise charge. Cross-checks with cosmic muon data performed during TIB/TID integration indicate that this scaling agrees with the real ENC within 10–20%. Furthermore, the noise depends on the strip capacitance and thus on the strip length, i.e. on the module type. For this reason the noise of all strips was normalized to the strip length of modules of ring 1 (8.52 cm). In addition a correction was applied to TEC- data to account for the fact that they were taken with other chip parameter settings than TEC+ data. The common mode subtraction was performed assuming a constant common mode per APV. To extract the mean noise, a gaussian was fitted to the distribution. The resulting mean common mode subtracted noise amounts to 1693 ± 75 electrons in this normalization.

The mean common mode noise, calculated per APV, amounts to $(22 \pm 4)\%$ and $(21 \pm 3)\%$ of the mean intrinsic noise in peak and deconvolution mode, respectively (figure 3.38, left, for all non-defective APVs of TEC+).

The flatness of the noise across the APV is a good indicator for the quality of the grounding. The relative spread of the total noise (before common mode subtraction), i.e. the RMS of the noise divided by the mean noise, both calculated per APV, can be used to quantify the flatness. The relative spread is $(2.5 \pm 0.2)\%$ in both read-out modes, as shown in figure 3.38, right, indicating that the grounding scheme implemented by the TEC works well.

Strips are counted as noisy or dead if their noise is more than five times the RMS of the noise above or below the mean noise of the respective APV. Edge strips are counted as noisy, if

2008 JINST 3 S08004

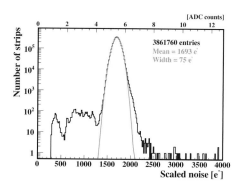
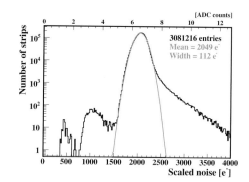

Figure 3.37: Normalized common mode subtracted noise of all strips (scaled to the strip length of ring 1 sensors) of both TECs (left panel) and the TOB (right panel), in deconvolution mode. Details are described in the text.

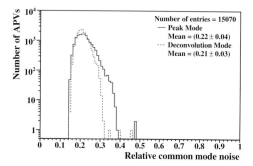
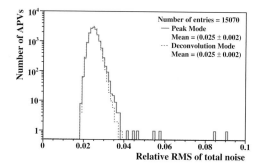

Figure 3.38: Ratio between common mode noise and mean intrinsic noise (left panel) and ratio between the RMS of the total noise and the mean total noise (right panel), calculated per APV, in peak and deconvolution mode for all non-defective APVs of TEC+.

their noise is more than seven sigma above the mean noise. In total, there are 3.0 per mille of bad channels in TEC+, while TEC- has 2.7 per mille of bad channels.

TIB and TID performance during integration

During TIB/TID integration [56], modules and AOHs were assembled onto half layers and disks and tested extensively for functionality, including pedestals, once a mother cable was completed (corresponding to a string in the TIB and three single-sided or five double-sided modules in the TID). Completed disks and half layers were then subjected to a burn-in in a climatic chamber, during which the structures were operated at a silicon sensor temperature of about −15°C. The complete half layers and disks were read out during these tests. Typically, the structures underwent 2–3 cooling cycles during a five day measurement period. After-wards disks and half layers were assembled into the complete TIB/TID+ and TIB/TID- structures and shipped to CERN, where the last integration operations were performed, such as connection of fibers to the final ribbons and cabling of the margherita.

2008 JINST 3 S08004

After optimization of the grounding scheme, the noise performance observed in the TIB and TID structures was very good. For the TIB and TID structures the scaled common mode subtracted noise of all strips, except for two TIB half-shells for which data were taken under non-final running conditions and three half-shells for which the proper grounding scheme was not yet implemented, is shown in figure 3.39 for deconvolution mode. Scaling and common mode subtraction have been implemented as previously described in this section. These data have been taken under nominal CMS conditions, with a mean silicon sensor temperature of about $-15°C$, hybrid temperatures ranging from $-4°C$ (TID double-sided modules) to $-14°C$ (TIB single-sided modules) and APV parameters set as intended for this temperature range. The mean noise, taken from a gaussian fit, amounts to (1233 ± 87) electrons in the TIB and (1246 ± 76) electrons in the TID. Measurements with a silicon sensor temperature of about $+10°C$ and hybrid temperatures of $+10°C$ to $+30°C$ show a mean noise about 20% larger. In contrast to the TEC, a strip is flagged as dead if its noise is below 75% of the average noise of the APV, and APV edge strips are not treated differently. The total number of bad channels is 4.4 per mille in TIB/TID+ and 3.4 per mille in TIB/TID-.

TOB performance during integration

Fully equipped and tested rods were integrated cooling segment-wise. After a first functional test, the cooling connection was soldered and a leak test was performed. Then the cooling segment was cabled, and a full read-out test, including pedestals, was performed at room temperature. During these measurements, the silicon sensor temperature was about $+24°C$ and the hybrid temperature about $+30°C$.

During integration, a sensitivity to pick-up noise has been observed, which leads to non-flat, wing-like common mode subtracted noise distributions. This sensitivity is especially pronounced for layers 3 and 4, which are equipped with single-sided 4 APV modules, and within these layers the effect is worst for modules mounted closest to the CCUM. Defining as a figure of merit the ratio of the highest noise amplitude (taken from a parabola fit to the noise distribution) to the flat noise baseline, and counting all APVs with a ratio above 1.25 as "in the wings", the fraction of APVs in the wings is about 30% in layers 3 and 4 and about 7% and 1% in layers 1/2 and 5/6, respectively. In total, 11.4% of all APVs are found to be in the wings according to this criterion. It has been verified that either with adjusted cluster cuts or with a linear online common mode subtraction the increase in the cluster width and occupancy is negligible.

The normalized noise of all TOB strips is shown in figure 3.37, right. The tail to high noise values comes from the non-flat noise distributions. The mean noise from a gaussian fit amounts to (2049 ± 112) electrons.

Due to this wing-like noise structure, a special algorithm has been adopted to evaluate the number of dead and noisy strips. A parabola is fitted to the noise distribution of each APV in an iterative procedure, and strips are flagged as bad if their noise deviates more than ten times the RMS of the distribution of fit residuals from the fitted function.

Only very few permanent defects, corresponding to 0.6 per mille of lost channels, have been introduced during TOB integration. Including the number of noisy and dead strips, the number of bad channels amounts to 0.6 per mille in TOB+ and 1.9 per mille in TOB-.

2008 JINST 3 S08004

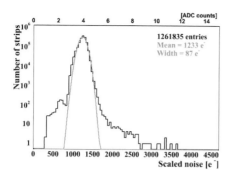 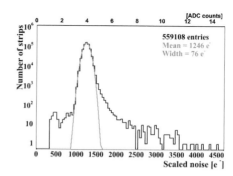

Figure 3.39: Normalized common mode subtracted single strip noise for TIB (left panel) and TID (right panel), in deconvolution mode. Details are described in the text.

Irradiation studies

As already discussed in detail in section 3.1.1, the silicon strip tracker will suffer from a severe level of radiation during its 10 year long lifetime: up to 1.8×10^{14} $n_{eq}cm^{-2}$ for TIB/TID and TEC and up to 0.5×10^{14} $n_{eq}cm^{-2}$ for TOB, assuming an integrated luminosity of $500\,fb^{-1}$. The radial and z dependence of the fluence both for fast hadrons and neutrons is described in detail in [15, 16]. Hadrons are expected to dominate in the inner part of the tracker, up to a radius of about 0.5 m, while neutrons backscattered off the electromagnetic calorimeter dominate further outside. Safety factors of 1.5 and 2.0 on the fluence are typically applied for TIB/TID and TOB/TEC, respectively.

To ensure that both the FE electronics and the silicon sensors can be operated safely and with satisfactory performance after such an irradiation, several irradiation tests with neutrons and protons have been carried out. Neutron irradiation was usually performed at the isochronous cyclotron of the Centre de Recherches du Cyclotron, Louvain-la-Neuve, which delivers neutrons with a mean energy of 20 MeV (hardness factor 1.95 relative to 1 MeV neutrons [58]). Proton irradiation has been carried out e.g. at the compact cyclotron of the Forschungszentrum Karlsruhe, where a 26 MeV proton beam (hardness factor 1.85 relative to 1 MeV neutrons) with a current of $100\,\mu A$ and a beam spot diameter of 1 cm is available.

To study the performance of complete irradiated modules, several OB1 and OB2 modules (table 3.3 for explanation) were irradiated with a proton fluence ranging from 0.1×10^{14} $n_{eq}cm^{-2}$ to 0.7×10^{14} $n_{eq}cm^{-2}$, and one OB2 module was subjected to a neutron fluence of about 1.2×10^{14} $n_{eq}cm^{-2}$ [57]. Two TEC W5 modules were irradiated with a proton fluence of about 1.1×10^{14} $n_{eq}cm^{-2}$, and three TIB IB1 modules were subjected to a proton fluence of 0.5×10^{14} $n_{eq}cm^{-2}$ to 2.1×10^{14} $n_{eq}cm^{-2}$. The effect of annealing was simulated by heating the modules for 80 minutes at 60°C and afterwards storing them at room temperature for at least two hours. To prevent uncontrolled annealing, the modules were stored at -20°C between the irradiation or annealing steps. Measurements were performed at -15°C.

As expected from inversion from n- to p-type doping, the full depletion voltage increased with the fluence, as shown in figure 3.40 (left). However, the required depletion voltage stays below 500 V, which is the maximum depletion voltage for which the sensors are specified. The dependence of the depletion voltage on annealing time was studied as well and found to be in

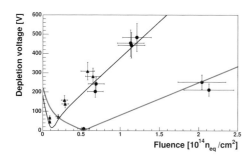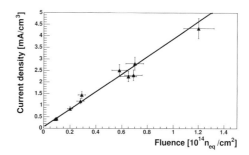

Figure 3.40: Left panel: Variation of depletion voltage with fluence for OB1 (triangles), OB2 and W5 (dots on upper curve) and IB2 (dots on lower curve) modules, after an annealing time of 80 minutes after each irradiation step. The curves correspond to calculations for $500\,\mu$m (upper curve) and $320\,\mu$m (lower curve) sensors for an annealing time of 80 minutes at 60°C. Right panel: Current density, scaled to 20°C, versus fluence after annealing for 80 minutes at 60°C.

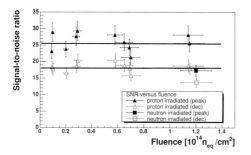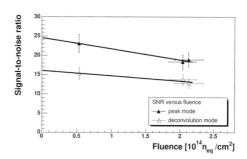

Figure 3.41: Signal-to-noise ratio versus fluence for modules with $500\,\mu$m (left panel) and $320\,\mu$m thick sensors (right panel) in peak (filled symbols) and deconvolution mode (open symbols).

excellent agreement with the Hamburg model [59], with a minimum at 80 minutes annealing time, corresponding to a 10 day shut down period at room temperature.

The leakage current is expected to increase with fluence, leading to a larger heat dissipation and increased noise. In figure 3.40 (right) the dependence of the current density on the fluence is shown. The current related damage rate, defined as the current increase, scaled to 20°C, per sensor volume and equivalent neutron fluence, amounts to $(3.79 \pm 0.27) \times 10^{-17}$ A/cm, which is in good agreement with literature and measurements from test structures.

Measurements of the signal-to-noise ratio, S/N, of irradiated modules have been performed with a ^{90}Sr source. Due to an increase of the noise and a decrease of the charge collection efficiency, the S/N is expected to decrease with fluence. The dependence of the S/N on the accumulated fluence for thick and thin sensors in both read-out modes is shown in figure 3.41. For thick sensors, the S/N decreased from 23 (35) to 15 (21) in deconvolution (peak) mode, while for thin sensors a decrease from 18 (24) to 13 (18) was observed. These figures ensure a hit finding efficiency of above 95% even after 10 years of operation at the LHC [60, 61].

2008 JINST 3 S08004

Chapter 4

Electromagnetic calorimeter

The electromagnetic calorimeter of CMS (ECAL) is a hermetic homogeneous calorimeter made of 61 200 lead tungstate (PbWO$_4$) crystals mounted in the central barrel part, closed by 7 324 crystals in each of the two endcaps. A preshower detector is placed in front of the endcap crystals. Avalanche photodiodes (APDs) are used as photodetectors in the barrel and vacuum phototriodes (VPTs) in the endcaps. The use of high density crystals has allowed the design of a calorimeter which is fast, has fine granularity and is radiation resistant, all important characteristics in the LHC environment. One of the driving criteria in the design was the capability to detect the decay to two photons of the postulated Higgs boson. This capability is enhanced by the good energy resolution provided by a homogeneous crystal calorimeter.

4.1   Lead tungstate crystals

The characteristics [62] of the PbWO$_4$ crystals make them an appropriate choice for operation at LHC. The high density (8.28 g/cm^3), short radiation length (0.89 cm) and small Molière radius (2.2 cm) result in a fine granularity and a compact calorimeter. In recent years, PbWO$_4$ scintillation properties and other qualities have been progressively improved, leading to the mass production of optically clear, fast and radiation-hard crystals [63, 64]. The scintillation decay time of these production crystals is of the same order of magnitude as the LHC bunch crossing time: about 80% of the light is emitted in 25 ns. The light output is relatively low and varies with temperature ($-2.1\%°C^{-1}$ at 18°C [65]): at 18°C about 4.5 photoelectrons per MeV are collected in both APDs and VPTs. The crystals emit blue-green scintillation light with a broad maximum at 420–430 nm [64, 66]. Longitudinal optical transmission and radioluminescence spectra are shown in figure 4.1.

To exploit the total internal reflection for optimum light collection on the photodetector, the crystals are polished after machining. For fully polished crystals, the truncated pyramidal shape makes the light collection non-uniform along the crystal length. The effect is large because of the high refractive index ($n = 2.29$ around the peak wavelength [67]) and the needed uniformity [68] is achieved by depolishing one lateral face. In the endcaps, the light collection is naturally more uniform because the crystal faces are nearly parallel. Pictures of barrel and endcap crystals with the photodetectors attached are shown in figure 4.2.

2008 JINST 3 S08004

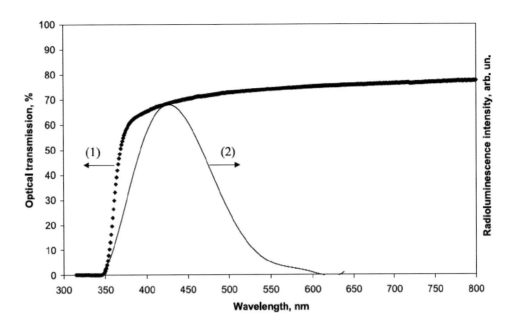

Figure 4.1: Longitudinal optical transmission (1, left scale) and radioluminescence intensity (2, right scale) for production PbWO₄ crystals.

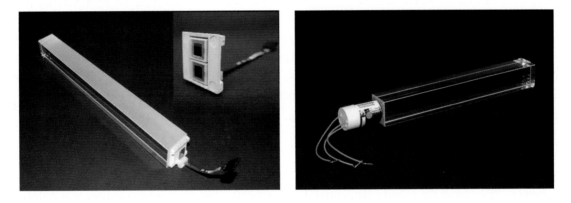

Figure 4.2: PbWO₄ crystals with photodetectors attached. Left panel: A barrel crystal with the upper face depolished and the APD capsule. In the insert, a capsule with the two APDs. Right panel: An endcap crystal and VPT.

The crystals have to withstand the radiation levels and particle fluxes [69] anticipated throughout the duration of the experiment. Ionizing radiation produces absorption bands through the formation of colour centres due to oxygen vacancies and impurities in the lattice. The practical consequence is a wavelength-dependent loss of light transmission without changes to the scintillation mechanism, a damage which can be tracked and corrected for by monitoring the optical transparency with injected laser light (section 4.9). The damage reaches a dose-rate dependent equilibrium level which results from a balance between damage and recovery at 18°C [64, 70].

To ensure an adequate performance throughout LHC operation, the crystals are required to exhibit radiation hardness properties quantified as an induced light attenuation length (at high dose rate) greater than approximately 3 times the crystal length even when the damage is saturated. Hadrons have been measured to induce a specific, cumulative reduction of light transmission, but the extrapolation to LHC conditions indicates that the damage will remain within the limits required for good ECAL performance [71, 72].

4.2   The ECAL layout and mechanics

The barrel part of the ECAL (EB) covers the pseudorapidity range $|\eta| < 1.479$. The barrel granularity is 360-fold in ϕ and (2×85)-fold in η, resulting in a total of 61 200 crystals. The crystals have a tapered shape, slightly varying with position in η. They are mounted in a quasi-projective geometry to avoid cracks aligned with particle trajectories, so that their axes make a small angle (3°) with respect to the vector from the nominal interaction vertex, in both the ϕ and η projections. The crystal cross-section corresponds to approximately 0.0174 × 0.0174 in η-ϕ or 22×22 mm^2 at the front face of crystal, and 26×26 mm^2 at the rear face. The crystal length is 230 mm corresponding to 25.8 X_0. The barrel crystal volume is 8.14 m^3 and the weight is 67.4 t.

The centres of the front faces of the crystals are at a radius 1.29 m. The crystals are contained in a thin-walled alveolar structure (submodule). The alveolar wall is 0.1 mm thick and is made of an aluminium layer, facing the crystal, and two layers of glass fibre-epoxy resin. To avoid oxidation, a special coating is applied to the aluminium surface. The nominal crystal to crystal distance is 0.35 mm inside a submodule, and 0.5 mm between submodules. To reduce the number of different types of crystals, each submodule contains only a pair of shapes, left and right reflections of a single shape. In total, there are 17 such pairs of shapes. The submodules are assembled into modules of different types, according to the position in η, each containing 400 or 500 crystals. Four modules, separated by aluminium conical webs 4-mm thick, are assembled in a supermodule, which contains 1700 crystals (figures 4.3 and 4.4).

In each module, the submodules are held in partial cantilever by an aluminium grid, which supports their weight from the rear. At the front the submodule free ends are connected together by pincers that cancel the relative tangential displacements. The submodule cantilever is reduced by the action of a 4-mm thick cylindrical plate where the front of the submodules are supported by setpins. Not all the submodules are connected to the cylindrical plate but only four rows in ϕ from a total of ten. The portion of the submodule load taken at the front by the cylindrical plate is transmitted to the aluminium grids of the different modules via the conical webs interspaced between the modules [73]. Each module is supported and positioned in the supermodule at the rear end through the grid by a spine beam. The spine is provided with pads which slide into rails housed on the front face of the HCAL barrel, allowing the installation and support of each single supermodule. The cylindrical plate in front of the supermodule also provides the fixation of the monitoring system (see below) and the holes for its optical fibres.

All services, cooling manifolds and cables converge to a patch panel at the external end of the supermodule. Eighteen supermodules, each covering 20° in ϕ, form a half barrel.

The endcaps (EE) cover the rapidity range $1.479 < |\eta| < 3.0$. The longitudinal distance between the interaction point and the endcap envelope is 315.4 cm, taking account of the estimated

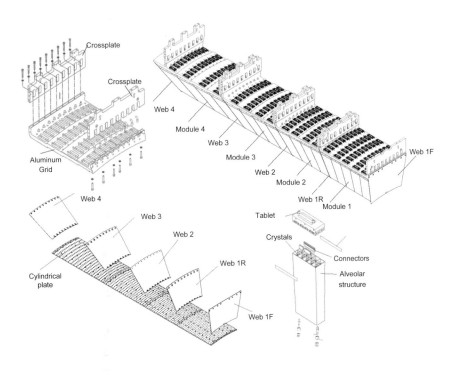

Figure 4.3: Layout of the ECAL barrel mechanics.

shift toward the interaction point by 1.6 cm when the 4-T magnetic field is switched on. The endcap consists of identically shaped crystals grouped in mechanical units of 5×5 crystals (supercrystals, or SCs) consisting of a carbon-fibre alveola structure. Each endcap is divided into 2 halves, or *Dees*. Each Dee holds 3 662 crystals. These are contained in 138 standard SCs and 18 special partial supercrystals on the inner and outer circumference. The crystals and SCs are arranged in a rectangular *x-y* grid, with the crystals pointing at a focus 1 300 mm beyond the interaction point, giving off-pointing angles ranging from 2 to 8 degrees. The crystals have a rear face cross section 30×30 mm^2, a front face cross section 28.62×28.62 mm^2 and a length of 220 mm (24.7 X_0). The endcaps crystal volume is 2.90 m^3 and the weight is 24.0 t. The layout of the calorimeter is shown in figure 4.5. Figure 4.6 shows the barrel already mounted inside the hadron calorimeter, while figure 4.7 shows a picture of a Dee.

The number of scintillation photons emitted by the crystals and the amplification of the APD are both temperature dependent. Both variations are negative with increasing temperature. The overall variation of the response to incident electrons with temperature has been measured in test beam [74] to be $(-3.8 \pm 0.4)\%°\mathrm{C}^{-1}$. The temperature of the system has therefore to be maintained constant to high precision, requiring a cooling system capable of extracting the heat dissipated by the read-out electronics and of keeping the temperature of crystals and photodetectors stable within $\pm 0.05°\mathrm{C}$ to preserve energy resolution. The nominal operating temperature of the CMS ECAL is 18°C. The cooling system has to comply with this severe thermal requirement. The system employs water flow to stabilise the detector. In the barrel, each supermodule is independently supplied

Figure 4.4: Front view of a module equipped with the crystals.

with water at 18°C. The water runs through a thermal screen placed in front of the crystals which thermally decouples them from the silicon tracker, and through pipes embedded in the aluminium grid, connected in parallel. Beyond the grid, a 9 mm thick layer of insulating foam (Armaflex) is placed to minimise the heat flowing from the read-out electronics towards the crystals. Return pipes distribute the water through a manifold to a set of aluminium cooling bars. These bars are in close contact with the very front end electronics (VFE) cards and absorb the heat dissipated by the components mounted on these cards. A thermally conductive paste (gap filler 2000, produced by Bergquist) is used to provide a good contact between the electronic components and a metal plate facing each board. This plate is coupled to the cooling bar by a conductive pad (ultrasoft gap pad, also produced by Bergquist). Both the gap pad and the gap filler have been irradiated with twice the dose expected in the ECAL endcaps after 10 years at the LHC and have shown no change in character or loss of performance.

Extended tests of the cooling system have been performed with good results [74]. Residual effects caused by a possible variation of the power dissipated by the electronics were measured in the extreme case of electronics switched on and off. The conclusion is that contributions to the constant term of the energy resolution due to thermal fluctuations will be negligible, even without temperature corrections.

2008 JINST 3 S08004

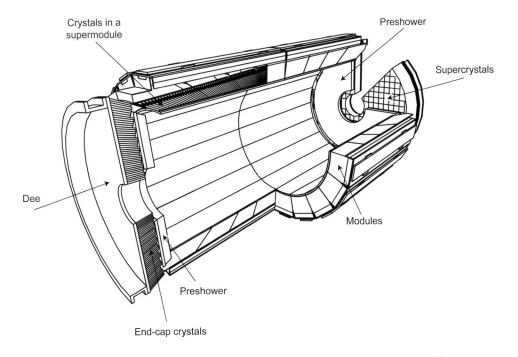

Figure 4.5: Layout of the CMS electromagnetic calorimeter showing the arrangement of crystal modules, supermodules and endcaps, with the preshower in front.

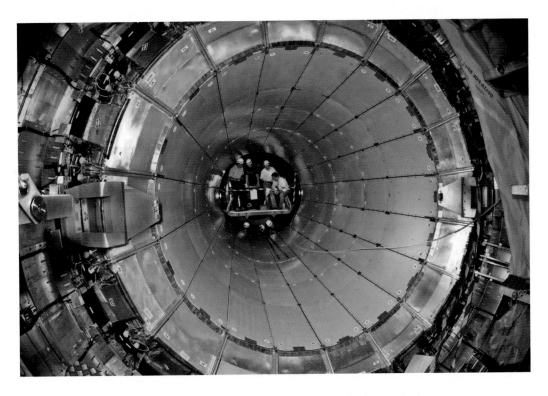

Figure 4.6: The barrel positioned inside the hadron calorimeter.

2008 JINST 3 S08004

Figure 4.7: An endcap Dee, fully equipped with supercrystals.

4.3 Photodetectors

The photodetectors need to be fast, radiation tolerant and be able to operate in the longitudinal 4-T magnetic field. In addition, because of the small light yield of the crystals, they should amplify and be insensitive to particles traversing them (*nuclear counter effect*). The configuration of the magnetic field and the expected level of radiation led to different choices: avalanche photodiodes in the barrel and vacuum phototriodes in the endcaps. The lower quantum efficiency and internal gain of the vacuum phototriodes, compared to the avalanche photodiodes, is offset by their larger surface coverage on the back face of the crystals.

4.3.1 Barrel: avalanche photodiodes

In the barrel, the photodetectors are Hamamatsu type S8148 reverse structure (i.e., with the bulk n-type silicon behind the p-n junction) avalanche photodiodes (APDs) specially developed for the CMS ECAL. Each APD has an active area of $5 \times 5 \, \text{mm}^2$ and a pair is mounted on each crystal. They are operated at gain 50 and read out in parallel. The main properties of the APDs at gain 50 and $18°C$ are listed in table 4.1.

The sensitivity to the nuclear counter effect is given by the effective thickness of 6 μm, which translates into a signal from a minimum ionizing particle traversing an APD equivalent to about 100 MeV deposited in the $PbWO_4$.

2008 JINST 3 S08004

Table 4.1: Properties of the APDs at gain 50 and 18°C.

Sensitive area	5×5 mm^2
Operating voltage	340–430 V
Breakdown voltage - operating voltage	45 ± 5 V
Quantum efficiency (430 nm)	$75 \pm 2\%$
Capacitance	80 ± 2 pF
Excess noise factor	2.1 ± 0.2
Effective thickness	$6 \pm 0.5\ \mu$m
Series resistance	$< 10\ \Omega$
Voltage sensitivity of the gain ($1/M \cdot \mathrm{d}M/\mathrm{d}V$)	$3.1 \pm 0.1\%$/V
Temperature sensitivity of the gain ($1/M \cdot \mathrm{d}M/\mathrm{d}T$)	$-2.4 \pm 0.2\%$/°C
Rise time	< 2 ns
Dark current	< 50 nA
Typical dark current	3 nA
Dark current after 2×10^{13} n/cm^2	$5\ \mu$A

For ECAL acceptance each APD was required to be fully depleted and to pass through a screening procedure involving 5 kGy of ^{60}Co irradiation and 1 month of operation at 80°C. Each APD was tested to breakdown and required to show no significant noise increase up to a gain of 300. The screening and testing aimed to ensure reliable operation for 10 years under high luminosity LHC conditions for over 99% of the APDs installed in the ECAL [75]. Based on tests with hadron irradiations [76] it is expected that the dark current after such operation will have risen to about 5 μA, but that no other properties will have changed. Small samples of APDs were irradiated with a ^{251}Cf source to monitor the effectiveness of the screening procedure in selecting radiation resistant APDs.

The gain stability directly affects the ECAL energy resolution. Since the APD gain has a high dependence on the bias voltage ($\alpha_V = 1/M\mathrm{d}M/\mathrm{d}V \simeq 3.1\%$/V at gain 50), to keep this contribution to the resolution at the level of per mille, the APDs require a very stable power supply system: the stability of the voltage has to be of the order of few tens of mV. This requirement applies to all the electrical system characteristics: noise, ripple, voltage regulation and absolute precision, for short and long term periods. A custom high voltage (HV) power supply system has been designed for the CMS ECAL in collaboration with the CAEN Company [77]. To remain far from high doses of radiation, the HV system is located in the CMS service cavern, some 120 m away from the detector. The HV channels are floating and use sense wires to correct for variations in the voltage drop on the leads. The system is based on a standard control crate (SY1527) hosting 8 boards expressly designed for this application (A1520E). The SY1527 integrate a PC capable of communicating with the board controller via an internal bus and different interfaces are available to integrate the SY1527 on the ECAL detector control system (DCS). The board design is based on a modular concept so that each HV channel is implemented on a separate module and up to 9 channels can be hosted on a single A1520E board. Each channel can give a bias voltage to 50 APD pairs from 0 to 500 V with maximum current of 15 mA. In total, there are 18 crates and 144 boards. Temperature

2008 JINST 3 S08004

drift compensation is possible due to the presence on the crate of temperature probes that can be used to monitor the environment temperature for adjustments of the voltage setting.

The operating gain of 50 requires a voltage between 340 and 430 V. The APDs are sorted according to their operating voltage into bins 5 V wide, and then paired such that each pair has a mean gain of 50. Each pair is mounted in parallel in a *capsule*, a moulded receptacle with foam, which is then glued on the back of each crystal. The capsules are connected to the read-out electronics by Kapton flexible printed circuit boards of variable length, dictated by the capsule's position within the submodule. Each capsule receives the bias voltage through an RC filter network and a protection resistor.

One $100\,\text{k}\Omega$ negative temperature coefficient thermistor from Betatherm, used as temperature sensor, is embedded in every tenth APD capsule. There are twenty-two different types of capsules, differing by the Kapton length and by the presence of the thermistor.

4.3.2 Endcap: vacuum phototriodes

In the endcaps, the photodetectors are vacuum phototriodes (VPTs) (type PMT188 from National Research Institute Electron in St. Petersburg). Vacuum phototriodes are photomultipliers having a single gain stage. These particular devices were developed specially for CMS [78] and have an anode of very fine copper mesh ($10\ \mu$m pitch) allowing them to operate in the 4-T magnetic field. Each VPT is 25 mm in diameter, with an active area of approximately 280 mm^2; one VPT is glued to the back of each crystal. One Betatherm thermistor is embedded into each supercrystal. The VPTs have a mean quantum efficiency of the bialkali photocathode (SbKCs) of 22% at 430 nm, and a mean gain of 10.2 at zero field. When placed in a strong axial magnetic field, the response is slightly reduced and there is a modest variation of response with the angle of the VPT axis with respect to the field over the range of angles relevant to the CMS endcaps (6° to 26°). The mean response in a magnetic field of 4 T, with the VPT axis at 15° to the field direction, is typically > 90% of that in zero field [79].

All VPTs are tested by the manufacturer before delivery, without an applied magnetic field. All VPTs are also tested on receipt by CMS to determine their response as a function of magnetic field up to 1.8 T. Each device is measured at a set of angles with respect to the applied field, spanning the range of angles covered by the endcaps. In addition, at least 10% of the tubes, selected at random, are also tested in a 4-T superconducting magnet, at a fixed angle of 15°, to verify satisfactory operation at the full field of CMS.

The estimated doses and particle fluences for 10 years of LHC operation are 0.5 kGy and 5×10^{13} n/cm^2 at the outer circumference of the endcaps and 20 kGy and 7×10^{14} n/cm^2 at $|\eta| = 2.6$. Sample faceplates from every glass production batch were irradiated with a ^{60}Co source to 20 kGy. The faceplates were required to show a transmission loss, integrated over the wavelength range corresponding to PbWO$_4$ emission, of less than 10%. Irradiation of VPTs in a nuclear reactor to 7×10^{14} n/cm^2 showed a loss in anode sensitivity entirely consistent with discolouration of the faceplate caused by the accompanying gamma dose (100 kGy) [80]. Irradiations of tubes biased to the working voltage, with both gammas and neutrons showed no adverse effects, apart from an increase in anode current, attributable to the production of Cerenkov light in the faceplates.

2008 JINST 3 S08004

The VPTs are operated with the photocathode at ground potential and the dynode and anode biased at +600 V and +800 V respectively. The high voltage system is based (like the APD system) on CAEN SY1527 standard control crates, although for the VPTs, the crates are equipped with standard 12-channel A1735P boards, each channel rated at 1.5 kV and 7 mA. At the operating bias, the VPT gain is close to saturation thus the voltages do not have to be controlled very precisely. However, care must be taken to minimise ripple and noise, since these would feed directly into the input of the sensitive preamplifier that is connected to the anode. Filtering is achieved with RC networks mounted inside the supercrystals (SC), close to the VPTs. An entire endcap is biased using one SY1527 crate equipped with just two A1735P boards. On each board, only eight of the twelve output channels will initially be used, leaving four spare channels. The spare outputs may be used at a later stage, if noisy channels develop which can be recovered by operating at a lower bias voltage. The HV from the CAEN power supplies is transmitted to the SCs via a custom designed HV distribution system which provides hard-wired protection against over-voltage and over-current, and sensitive current monitoring. For each endcap, this system is housed in five crates. Each crate hosts up to five input cards, receiving the HV from the power supplies, and up to six output cards, with each output card serving up to twelve SCs. The HV supplies and distribution system are mounted in two racks (one for each endcap) located in the Service Cavern. Each SC is served by two coaxial cables (one for the anode, one for the dynode) running from the Service Cavern to the detector, via intermediate patch panels. The total cable length is approximately 120 m and the cable capacitance forms part of the filter network. Inside an SC the HV is distributed to the VPTs via five filter cards, each serving five VPTs. The spread in anode sensitivity among the VPTs is 25% (RMS). They are therefore sorted into six groups which are distributed on the endcaps with the highest sensitivities at the outer circumference grading to the lowest sensitivities at the inner circumference. This arrangement provides a roughly constant sensitivity to the transverse energy across the endcaps.

The anode sensitivity of a VPT may show a dependence on count rate (anode current) under certain conditions. For example, in the absence of a magnetic field, if the count rate falls to a few Hz, following a period of high rate operation, the anode sensitivity may rise suddenly and take several hours to return to the nominal value. The magnitude of the effect may vary from a few percent to a few tens of percent. In the presence of a strong magnetic field (as in normal CMS operation), the effect is strongly suppressed or absent. Nevertheless, it has been judged prudent to incorporate a light pulser system on the ECAL endcaps. This delivers a constant background rate of at least 100 Hz of pulses of approximately 50 GeV equivalent energy to all VPTs, thus ensuring that they are kept "active", even in the absence of LHC interactions.

The system consists of a control and trigger unit located in the Service Cavern, and sets of pulsed light sources mounted on the circumference of each Dee. The light is produced by Luxeon III light emitting diodes (type LXHL-PR09), whose peak emission wavelength is 455 nm. The LEDs are driven by high output current op-amps (LT6300 from Linear Technology). The drive pulses have amplitudes of 1.2 A and a widths of 80 ns. A single light source consists of a cluster of seven LEDs and associated drive-circuits. These are configured singly or in pairs, with the drive-circuits and LEDs mounted on double-sided printed circuit boards housed within metal enclosures. There are four such enclosures distributed around the circumference of each Dee, housing 19 light sources. A schematic representation of the system for distributing the light pulses is shown in figure 4.8.

2008 JINST 3 S08004

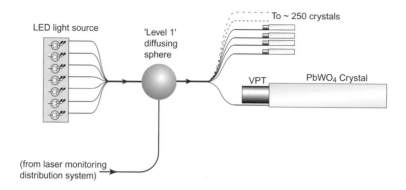

Figure 4.8: Distribution system for VPT stabilisation light pulses.

An all-silica optical fibre (CF01493-43 from OFS (Furukawa)) is inserted into a hole drilled into the lens of each LED and collects light by *proximity focusing*. The seven fibres from a given light source are combined into a single bundle that transports light to a diffusing sphere which has a dual role, acting also as part of the distribution network of the laser monitoring system. Light from each diffusing sphere is distributed to up to 220 individual detector channels through the set of optical fibres that also carry the laser monitoring pulses. Light is injected via the rear face of a crystal, which carries the VPT, and reaches the VPT via reflection from the front of the crystal. The system is synchronized to pulse during a fraction of the 3 μs abort gaps that occur during every 89 μs cycle of the LHC circulating beams.

4.4 On-detector electronics

The ECAL read-out has to acquire the small signals of the photo-detectors with high speed and precision. Every bunch crossing digital sums representing the energy deposit in a trigger tower are generated and sent to the trigger system. The digitized data are stored during the Level-1 trigger latency of $\approx 3\,\mu$s.

The on-detector electronics has been designed to read a complete trigger tower (5×5 crystals in $\eta \times \phi$) or a super-crystal for EB and EE respectively. It consists of five Very Front End (VFE) boards, one Front End (FE) board, two (EB) or six (EE) Gigabit Optical Hybrids (GOH), one Low Voltage Regulator card (LVR) and a motherboard.

The motherboard is located in front of the cooling bars. It connects to 25 photo-detectors and to the temperature sensors using Kapton flexible printed circuit boards and coaxial cables for EB and EE respectively. In the case of the EB the motherboard distributes and filters the APD bias voltage. Two motherboards are connected to one CAEN HV supply located at a distance of about 120 m with remote sensing. In the case of the EE the operating voltages for the VPTs are distributed and filtered by a separate HV filter card, hosting as well the decoupling capacitor for the anode signals. Five of these cards serving five VPTs each are installed into each super-crystal. One LVR and five VFE cards plug into the motherboard.

Each LVR card [81] uses 11 radiation-hard low voltage regulators (LHC4913) developed by ST-microelectronics and the RD49 project at CERN. The regulators have built in over-temperature

2008 JINST 3 S08004

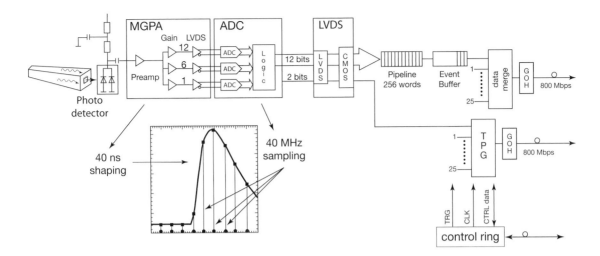

Figure 4.9: Schematic view of the on-detector electronics: the scintillation light is collected by photodetectors (in the figure the case of APD is presented), the signal is shaped by a Multi-Gain Pre-Amplifier and digitized by 40-MHz ADC; a radiation-hard buffer (LVDS) adapts the ADC output to the FE card, where data pipeline and Trigger Primitives Generation (TPG) are performed; trigger words are sent at 25 ns rate, while data are transmitted on receipt of a Level-1 trigger; GOHs provide in both cases the data serializer and the laser diode, sending the signals on a fibre to the off-detector electronics over a distance of about 100 m. A control token ring connects groups of FE cards, providing Level-1 trigger (TRG) and clock (CLK) signals, together with control data in and out (CTRL data).

protection, output current limitation and an inhibit input. The output voltages of 2.5 V are distributed to the FE card and via the motherboard to the VFE cards. Three Detector Control Unit (DCU) ASICs on each LVR card, interfaced to the FE card, monitor all input and output voltages. All regulators, excluding the one providing power to the control interface of the FE card, can be powered down remotely by an external inhibit. Four LVR cards are connected by a passive low voltage distribution (LVD) block to one radiation and magnetic field tolerant Wiener low voltage power supply located about 30 m away in racks attached to the magnet yoke.

The signals are pre-amplified and shaped and then amplified by three amplifiers with nominal gains of 1, 6 and 12. This functionality is built into the Multi Gain Pre-Amplifier (MGPA) [82], an ASIC developed in 0.25 μm technology. The full scale signals of the APDs and VPTs are 60 pC and 12.8 pC corresponding to ≈ 1.5 TeV and 1.6–3.1 TeV for EB and EE respectively. The shaping is done by a CR-RC network with a shaping time of ≈ 40 ns. The MGPA has a power consumption of 580 mW at 2.5 V. The output pulse non-linearity is less than 1%. The noise for gain 12 is about 8000 e$^-$ for the APD configuration and about 4000 e$^-$ for the VPT configuration. The MGPA contains three programmable 8-bit DACs to adjust the baseline to the ADC inputs. An integrated test-pulse generator with an amplitude adjustable by means of an 8-bit DAC allows a test of the read-out electronics over the full dynamic range.

A schematic view of the signal read-out is given in figure 4.9. The 3 analog output signals of the MGPA are digitized in parallel by a multi-channel, 40-MHz, 12-bit ADC, the AD41240 [83], developed in 0.25 μm technology. It has an effective number of bits of 10.9. An integrated logic

2008 JINST 3 S08004

selects the highest non-saturated signal as output and reports the 12 bits of the corresponding ADC together with two bits coding the ADC number.

If the read-out switches to a lower gain as the pulse grows, it is prevented from immediately reverting to the higher gain when the pulse falls: once the pulse has declined to the point where it could be read out at the higher gain again, the read-out is then forced to continue reading out at the lower gain for the next five samples.

A radiation-hard buffer (LVDS_RX) developed in $0.25\,\mu$m technology, adapts the low voltage differential output signals of the AD41240 to the single ended CMOS inputs on the FE card. Five identical read-out channels are integrated into a VFE card, together with a Detector Control Unit (DCU) for the measurement of the APD leakage currents and the read-out of the thermistors. The noise obtained with the VFE cards installed into supermodules is typically 1.1, 0.75 and 0.6 ADC counts for gains 12, 6 and 1 respectively. This corresponds to $\approx 40\,$MeV for gain 12.

The FE card [84] stores the digitized data during the Level-1 trigger latency in 256-word-deep dual-ported memories, so called pipelines. Five such pipelines and the logic to calculate the energy sum of the 5 channels once every bunch crossing are integrated into an ASIC developed in $0.25\,\mu$m technology called FENIX. Each VFE card is serviced by a FENIX chip. Thus the energy is summed in strips of 5 crystals along ϕ. In the case of the EE the five strip sums are transmitted by five GOHs (see below) to the off-detector electronics Trigger Concentrator Card (TCC), while in the case of the EB a sixth FENIX sums the five strip sums and calculates the "fine-grain" electromagnetic bit, set to identify electromagnetic shower candidates on the basis of the energy profile of the trigger tower. The trigger tower energy sum together with the fine-grain bit is transmitted using one GOH to the TCC. On receipt of a Level-1 trigger the corresponding data, ten 40-MHz samples per channel, are transmitted in $\approx 7.5\,\mu$s to the off-detector electronics Data Concentrator Card (DCC) using an identical GOH. The Clock and Control Unit (CCU) ASIC together with the LVDS_MUX ASIC provide the interface to the token rings.

The ECAL serial digital data links are based on the technology developed for the CMS Tracker analog links (section 3.3). The GOH consists of a data serializer and laser driver chip, the GOL, and a laser diode with an attached fibre pigtail. Fibres, fibre interconnections and a 12-channel NGK receiver module complete the optical link system. It uses single mode fibres operating at 1310 nm wavelength over a distance of about 100 m. The fibre attenuation of $\approx 0.04\,$dB is negligible. The optical links are operated at 800 Mbit/s.

The VFE and FE electronics are controlled using a 40-MHz digital optical link system, controlled by the off-detector Clock and Control System (CCS) boards. A 12-fibre ribbon is connected to the token ring link board, generating an electrical control ring, the token ring. Each supermodule has 8 token rings which connect to groups of eight to ten FE cards including the two FE cards of the laser monitoring electronics module (MEM). The system has redundancy, as long as there are no two consecutive FE cards malfunctioning, by means of two independent bi-directional optical links, using 4 fibres each. It provides fast and slow control functions. While the fast control transmits the level one trigger information and the 40-MHz clock, the slow control comprises the configuration of the FE and VFE electronics as well as the read-out of status information, temperatures, voltages and APD leakage currents.

2008 JINST 3 S08004

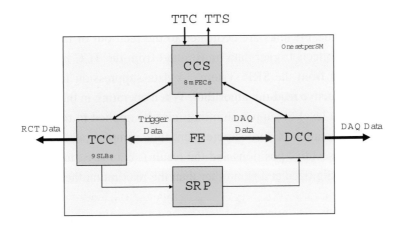

Figure 4.10: Schematic view of ECAL off-detector electronics.

4.5 Off-detector electronics

4.5.1 Global architecture

The ECAL off-detector read-out and trigger architecture [85, 86] is illustrated schematically in figure 4.10. The system is composed of different electronic boards sitting in 18 VME-9U crates (the CCS, TCC and DCC modules) and in 1 VME-6U crate (the selective read-out processor, SRP, system). The system serves both the DAQ and the trigger paths. In the DAQ path, the DCC performs data read-out and data reduction based on the selective read-out flags computed by the SRP system. In the trigger path, at each bunch crossing, trigger primitive generation started in the FE boards is finalized and synchronized in the TCC before transmission to the regional calorimeter trigger.

The clock and control system (CCS) board distributes the system clock, trigger and broadcast commands, configures the FE electronics and provides an interface to the trigger throttling system. The TTC signals are translated and encoded by suppression of clock edges and sent to the *mezzanine* Front End Controller cards (mFEC). The mFEC interfaces optically with a FE token ring. The 8 mFECs of the CCS board control a supermodule.

The trigger concentration card (TCC) [87] main functionalities include the completion of the trigger primitive generation and their transmission to the synchronization and link board (SLB) mezzanines [88] at each bunch crossing, the classification of each trigger tower and its transmission to the Selective Read-out Processor at each Level-1 trigger accept signal, and the storage of the trigger primitives during the Level-1 latency for subsequent reading by the DCC.

Each TCC collects trigger data from 68 FE boards in the barrel, corresponding to a supermodule, and from 48 FE boards in the endcaps corresponding to the inner or outer part of a $20°$ ϕ sector. In the endcaps, trigger primitive computation is completed in the TCCs, which must perform a mapping between the collected pseudo-strips trigger data from the different supercrystals and the associated trigger towers. The encoded trigger primitives (8 bits for the nonlinear representation of the trigger tower E_T plus the fine-grain bit) are time aligned and sent to the regional trigger processors by the SLB. The trigger primitives are stored in the TCC during the Level-1 latency for subsequent reading by the DCC. In the barrel region a single TCC is interfaced with 1 DCC. In the endcap region, a DCC serves 4 TCCs covering a $40°$ sector.

The data concentration card (DCC) [89, 90] is responsible for collecting crystal data from up to 68 FE boards. Two extra FE links are dedicated to the read-out of laser monitoring data (PN diodes). The DCC also collects trigger data transmitted from the TCC modules and the selective read-out flags transmitted from the SRP system. A data suppression factor near 20 is attained using a programmable selective read-out algorithm. When operating in the selective read-out mode the SRP flags indicate the level of suppression that must be applied to the crystal data of a given FE read-out. For the application of zero suppression, time samples pass through a finite impulse response filter with 6 consecutive positions and the result is compared to a threshold. If any time sample of the 6 has been digitized at a gain other than the maximum, then zero suppression is not applied to the channel.

Data integrity is checked, including verification of the event-fragment header, in particular the data synchronization check, verification of the event-fragment word count and verification of the event-fragment parity bits. Identified error conditions, triggered by input event-fragment checks, link errors, data timeouts or buffer memory overflows are flagged in the DCC error registers and incremented in associated error counters. Error conditions are flagged in the DCC event header.

Input and output memory occupancy is monitored to prevent buffer overflows. If a first occupancy level is reached, the Trigger Throttling System (TTS) signal *Warning Overflow* is issued, requesting a reduction of the trigger rate. In a second level a TTS signal *Busy* inhibits new triggers and empty events (events with just the header words and trailer) are stored. DCC events are transmitted to the central CMS DAQ using a S-LINK64 data link interface at a maximum data rate of 528 MB/s, while an average transmission data flow of 200 MB/s is expected after ECAL data reduction. Laser triggers (for crystal transparency monitoring) will occur with a programmable frequency and synchronously with the LHC gap. No data reduction is applied for these events, which are read-out following a TTC test enable command. A VME memory is used for local DAQ, allowing VME access to physics events and laser events in spy mode.

The selective read-out processor (SRP) [91] is responsible for the implementation of the selective read-out algorithm. The system is composed by a single 6U-VME crate with twelve identical algorithm boards (AB). The AB computes the selective read-out flags in different calorimeter partitions. The flags are composed of 3 bits, indicating the suppression level that must be applied to the associated read-out units.

4.5.2 The trigger and read-out paths

The ECAL data, in the form of trigger primitives, are sent to the Level-1 calorimeter trigger processor, for each bunch crossing. The trigger primitives each refer to a single trigger tower and consist of the summed transverse energy deposited in the tower, and the fine-grain bit, which characterizes the lateral profile of the electromagnetic shower. The accept signal, for accepted events, is returned from the global trigger in about $3\mu s$. The selected events are read out through the data acquisition system to the Filter Farm where further rate reduction is performed using the full detector data.

The read-out system is structured in sets of 5×5 crystals. The FE card stores the data, in 256-clock cycles deep memory banks, awaiting a Level-1 trigger decision during at most 128 bunch crossings after the collision occurred. It implements most of the Trigger Primitives Generation (TPG) pipeline (section 4.5.3).

2008 JINST 3 S08004

In the barrel, these 5×5 crystal sets correspond to the trigger towers. Each trigger tower is divided into 5 ϕ-oriented strips, whose energy deposits are summed by the FE board trigger pipeline to give the total transverse energy of the tower, called the main trigger primitive. Each FE is served by two optical links for sending the data and trigger primitives respectively and a third electrical serial link which transmits the clock, control and Level-1 trigger signals.

In the endcaps, the read-out modularity maps onto the 5×5 mechanical units (supercrystals). However the sizes of the trigger towers vary in order to approximately follow the η, ϕ geometry of the HCAL and Level-1 trigger processor. The supercrystals are divided into groups of 5 contiguous crystals. These groups are of variable shape and referred to as pseudo-strips. The trigger towers are composed of several pseudo-strips and may extend over more than one supercrystal. Since the read-out structure does not match the trigger structure, only the pseudo-strip summations are performed on the detector. The total transverse energy of the trigger tower is computed by the off-detector electronics. Hence, each endcap FE board is served by 6 optical links, 5 of them being used to transmit the trigger primitives. As in the barrel an electrical serial link transmits the clock, control and Level-1 trigger signals.

After time alignment the ECAL trigger primitives are sent at 1.2 Gb/s to the regional calorimeter trigger, via 10-m-long electrical cables, where together with HCAL trigger primitives, the electron/photon and jets candidates are computed as well as the total transverse energy.

4.5.3 Algorithms performed by the trigger primitive generation

The TPG logic implemented on the FE boards combines the digitized samples delivered by the VFE boards to determine the trigger primitives and the bunch crossing to which they should be assigned. The logic must reconstruct the signal amplitude to be assigned to each bunchcrossing from the continuous stream of successive digitizations.

The TPG logic is implemented as a pipeline, operated at the LHC bunch crossing frequency. The trigger primitives are delivered to the regional calorimeter trigger after a constant latency of 52 clock cycles, of which 22 are used for transmission over the optical fibres and cables. The signal processing performed in the VFE and FE barrel electronics has a total duration of only 17 clock cycles. The remaining part of the latency is mainly due to formatting and time alignment of the digital signals. Ideally, the output of this processing should be a stream of zeroes, unless there is a signal in the tower resulting from a bunch crossing exactly 17 clock cycles before. In this case the output is a word encoding the summed transverse energy in the tower together with the fine-grain bit. The endcap pipeline is split between the on-detector and off-detector electronics and implements very similar algorithms. The trigger primitives are expected to be delivered to the regional calorimeter trigger in 50 clock cycles in the endcap case.

4.5.4 Classification performed by the selective read-out

About 100 kB per event has been allocated for ECAL data. The full ECAL data for an event, if all channels are read out, exceeds this target by a factor of nearly 20. Reduction of the data volume, *selective read-out*, can be performed by the Selective Read-out Processor [86, 91] so that the suppression applied to a channel takes account of energy deposits in the vicinity. For the measure of the energy in a region, the trigger tower sums are used. In the barrel the read-out

2008 JINST 3 S08004

modularity corresponds exactly to the 5×5-crystal trigger towers. In the endcap, the situation is more complex. The simplified and illustrative description below is given for the barrel case.

The selective read-out algorithm classifies the trigger towers of the ECAL into 3 classes using the Level-1 trigger primitives. The energy deposited in each trigger tower is compared to 2 thresholds. Trigger towers with an energy above the higher threshold are classified as high interest trigger towers, those with an energy between the 2 thresholds as medium interest, and those with an energy below the lower threshold as low interest trigger towers.

These classifications can be used flexibly to implement a range of algorithms by using different thresholds to define the classes, and different suppression levels for the read-out of the channels within each class. The algorithm currently used in the simulation provides adequate data reduction even at high luminosity. The algorithm functions as follows: if a trigger tower belongs to the high interest class ($E_T > 5$ GeV) then the crystals of this trigger tower and of its neighbour trigger towers (225 crystals in total in the barrel case) are read with no zero suppression. If a trigger tower belongs to the medium interest class ($E_T > 2.5$ GeV), then the crystals of this trigger tower (25 crystals in the barrel case) are read with no suppression. If a trigger tower belongs to the low interest class and it is not the neighbour of a high interest trigger tower, then the crystals in it are read with zero suppression at about $3\sigma_{\text{noise}}$.

For debugging purposes, the selective read-out can be deactivated and either a global zero suppression (same threshold for every channel) or no zero suppression applied. Even when the selective read-out is not applied the selective read-out flags are inserted into the data stream and can be used offline for debugging purposes.

4.6   Preshower detector

The principal aim of the CMS Preshower detector is to identify neutral pions in the endcaps within a fiducial region $1.653 < |\eta| < 2.6$. It also helps the identification of electrons against minimum ionizing particles, and improves the position determination of electrons and photons with high granularity.

4.6.1   Geometry

The Preshower is a sampling calorimeter with two layers: lead radiators initiate electromagnetic showers from incoming photons/electrons whilst silicon strip sensors placed after each radiator measure the deposited energy and the transverse shower profiles. The total thickness of the Preshower is 20 cm.

The material thickness of the Preshower traversed at $\eta = 1.653$ before reaching the first sensor plane is $2\,X_0$, followed by a further $1\,X_0$ before reaching the second plane. Thus about 95% of single incident photons start showering before the second sensor plane. The orientation of the strips in the two planes is orthogonal. A major design consideration is that all lead is covered by silicon sensors, including the effects of shower spread, primary vertex spread etc. For optimum Level-1 trigger performance the profile of the outer edge of the lead should follow the shape of the ECAL crystals behind it. For the inner radius the effect of the exact profiling of the lead is far less

2008 JINST 3 S08004

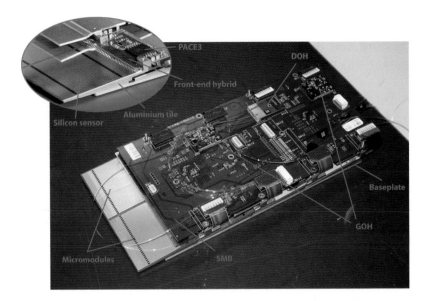

Figure 4.11: Photograph of a complete type-1 ladder, with an inset showing details of a micromodule.

critical, and thus a circular shape has been chosen. The lead planes are arranged in two Dees, one on each side of the beam pipe, with the same orientation as the crystal Dees.

Each silicon sensor measures $63{\times}63\,\mathrm{mm}^2$, with an active area of $61{\times}61\,\mathrm{mm}^2$ divided into 32 strips (1.9 mm pitch). The nominal thickness of the silicon is $320\,\mu\mathrm{m}$; a minimum ionizing particle (MIP) will deposit 3.6 fC of charge in this thickness (at normal incidence). The sensors are precisely glued to ceramic supports, which also support the front-end electronics assembly (see below), and this is in turn glued to an aluminium tile that allows a 2 mm overlap of the active part of the sensors in the direction parallel to the strips. In order to improve noise performance the tile is constructed in two parts, with a glass fibre insulation in between. The combination of sensor + front-end electronics + supports is known as a micromodule.

The micromodules are placed on baseplates in groups of 7, 8 or 10 that, when coupled to an electronics system motherboard (SMB) placed above the micromodules, form a ladder. The spacing between silicon strips (at the edges) in adjacent micromodules within a ladder is 2.4 mm, whilst the spacing between strips in adjacent ladders is normally 2.5 mm. For the region where the two Dees join this spacing is increased to 3.0 mm.

Figure 4.11 shows a complete ladder (*Type-1* for 8 micromodules) and an inset shows the micromodule.

The ladders are attached to the radiators in an *x-y* configuration. Around 500 ladders are required, corresponding to a total of around 4 300 micromodules and 137 000 individual read-out channels. Further details of the layout can be found in [92].

4.6.2 Preshower electronics

Each silicon sensor is DC-coupled to a front-end ASIC (PACE3 [93]) that performs preamplification, signal shaping and voltage sampling. Data is clocked into an on-chip high dynamic range 192-cell deep analogue memory at 40 MHz.

For each Level-1 trigger received, 3 consecutive cells of the memory, corresponding to time samples on the baseline, near the peak and after the peak, are read out for all 32 channels through a 20 MHz multiplexer. The PACE3 has a switchable gain:

- Low gain: For normal physics running with a large dynamic range (0-1600 fC) with a S/N of around 3 for a single MIP;

- High gain: For MIP calibration purposes [94], with a reduced dynamic range (0-200 fC) but with a S/N approaching 10 for a single MIP.

The PACE3 are soldered to front-end hybrids that contain embedded polyimide cables to connect to the SMBs. The SMBs contain AD41240 12-bit ADCs that digitize the data from 1 or 2 PACE3. The digital data are then formatted and packaged by a second Preshower ASIC known as the K-chip [95]. The K-chip also performs synchronization checks on the data, adds bunch/event counter information to the data packets and transmits the data to the Preshower-DCC (see below) via gigabit optical hybrids (GOH). The SMB also contains an implementation of the CMS tracker control system.

Groups of up to 12 ladders are connected via polyimide cables to form control rings. Off-detector CCS cards (identical to those of the ECAL except not all FEC mezzanines are mounted for the Preshower) communicate via digital optical hybrids (DOH) mounted on 2 of the SMBs in each control ring. The full Preshower comprises 4 planes of 12 control rings each.

The Preshower-DCC [96] is based on the DCC of the ECAL except it is a modular design incorporating a VME host board mounted with optoRx12 [97] mezzanines. The modular design has allowed a development collaboration with the TOTEM experiment which uses the same components but in a different manner. The optoRx12 incorporates an NGK 12-way optical receiver and an Altera Stratix GX FPGA that performs data deserialization, pedestal subtraction, common-mode noise reduction, bunch crossing assignment, charge reconstruction and zero suppression [98]. The sparsified data from up to 3 optoRx12 are merged by another FPGA on the host board that then transmits data packets to the event builder via an Slink64 interface. The host board also provides data spying as well as TTC and VME interfaces. A provision has been made on the host board to allow the plug-in of an additional mezzanine board mounted with FPGAs/processors that could provide more data reduction power if necessary in the future.

4.7 ECAL detector control system

The ECAL Detector Control System (DCS) comprises the monitoring of the detector status, in particular various kinds of environmental parameters, as well as the ECAL safety system (ESS), which will generate alarms and hardwired interlocks in case of situations which could lead to damaging the detector hardware. It consists of the following sub-systems: ECAL Safety System (ESS), Precision Temperature Monitoring (PTM), Humidity Monitoring (HM), High Voltage (HV), Low Voltage (LV) and monitoring of the laser operation, the cooling system and of the parameters (temperatures in capsules, temperatures on the printed circuit boards, APD leakage currents) read out by the DCUs on the VFE and LVR boards. Further details on the ECAL DCS are available [99].

The whole DCS software is based on the commercial SCADA package PVSS II (chapter 9). A distributed system is built out of several applications dedicated to the DCS sub-systems. Every application is implemented as a Finite State Machine (FSM) and linked to a supervisory level, which summarizes the overall ECAL DCS status and itself incorporates a FSM. Finally, this ECAL DCS supervisor is linked to the general CMS DCS supervisory node, in order to communicate the status and alarms and to receive commands which are propagated down to the relevant sub-systems.

4.7.1 Safety system

The purpose of the ESS [100] is to monitor the air temperature of the VFE and FE environment (expected to be around 25–30°C) and the water leakage detection cable, which is routed inside the electronics compartment, to control the proper functioning of the cooling system and to automatically perform pre-defined safety actions and generate interlocks in case of any alarm situation. One pair of temperature sensors is placed at the centre of each module. The read-out system, with full built-in redundancy, is independent of the DAQ and control links and based on a Programmable Logic Controller (PLC) situated in the Service Cavern. In case of any critical reading hardwired interlock signals will be routed to the relevant crates in order to switch off the HV and LV and/or the cooling PLC in order to stop the water flow on a certain cooling line. The proper functioning of the ESS PLC itself is monitored by the general CMS detector safety system.

4.7.2 Temperature

The number of scintillation photons emitted by the crystals and the amplification of the APD are both temperature dependent, as described in section 4.2. Therefore a major task for the ECAL DCS is the monitoring of the system's temperature and the verification that the required temperature stability of (18 ± 0.05)°C of the crystal volume and the APDs is achieved. The PTM is designed to read out thermistors, placed on both sides of the crystal volume, with a relative precision better than 0.01°C. In total there are ten sensors per supermodule. Two immersion probes measure the temperature of the incoming and outgoing cooling water, whereas two sensors per module, one on the grid and one on the thermal screen side of the crystal volume, monitor the crystal temperature. The read-out is based on the Embedded Local Monitoring Board (ELMB) developed by ATLAS which functions completely independently of the DAQ and control links. In addition, sensors fixed to the back surface of every tenth crystal in the barrel, and one in 25 crystals in the endcap, are read out by the DCUs placed on the VFE boards. With this temperature monitoring it has been shown that the water cooling system can indeed ensure the required temperature stability [74].

4.7.3 Dark current

The APD dark current will increase during CMS operation due to bulk damage of the silicon structure by neutrons. Part of this damage anneals, but the overall effect will be an increase in electronics noise, due to an increasing dark current, over the lifetime of the detector. The dark current of all APD channels will be continuously monitored.

2008 JINST 3 S08004

4.7.4   HV and LV

The DCS system operates the CAEN HV system via an OPC server. The functionalities include the independent configuration of the HV channels with various set of voltages, the monitor of the voltage and the current delivered by each channel and the database recording of the settings. The ECAL Safety System can switch off the HV via the individual board interlocks.

The ECAL amplification and digitization electronics located on the VFE electronics cards require a very stable low voltage to maintain constant signal amplification. The system uses Low Voltage Regulators that guarantee the required stability of the signal amplification. The Low Voltage Regulator Boards are equipped with DCUs that measure the voltages and these measurements are read via the Token Ring. Overall the power is supplied by MARATON crates (WIENER), which are operated and monitored by the DCS.

4.8   Detector calibration

Calibration is a severe technical challenge for the operation of the CMS ECAL. Many small effects which are negligible at low precision need to be treated with care as the level of precision of a few per mille is approached. ECAL calibration is naturally seen as composed of a global component, giving the absolute energy scale, and a channel-to-channel relative component, which is referred to as intercalibration. The essential issues are uniformity over the whole ECAL and stability, so that showers in different locations in the ECAL in data recorded at different times are accurately related to each other.

The main source of channel-to-channel response variation in the barrel is the crystal-to-crystal variation of scintillation light yield which has an RMS of $\approx 8\%$ within most supermodules, although the total variation among all barrel crystals is $\approx 15\%$. In the endcap the VPT signal yield, the product of the gain, quantum efficiency and photocathode area, has an RMS variation of almost 25%. Preliminary estimates of the intercalibration coefficients are obtained from laboratory measurements of crystal light yield and photodetector/electronics response [101]. Applying this information reduces the channel-to-channel variation to less than 5% in the barrel and less than 10% in the endcaps.

All 36 supermodules were commissioned in turn by operating them on a cosmic ray stand for a period of about one week. A muon traversing the full length of a crystal deposits an energy of approximately 250 MeV, permitting intercalibration information to be obtained for the barrel ECAL [102]. In 2006, nine supermodules were intercalibrated with high energy electrons (90 and 120 GeV), in a geometrical configuration that reproduced the incidence of particles during CMS operation. One of the supermodules was exposed to the beam on two occasions, separated by an interval of one month. The resulting sets of inter-calibration coefficients are in close agreement, the distribution of differences having an RMS spread of 0.27%, indicating a reproducibility within the statistical precision of the individual measurements (figure 4.12).

A comparison of the cosmic ray and high energy electron data demonstrates that the precision of the cosmic ray inter-calibration is better than 1.5% over most of the volume of a supermodule, rising to just above 2% at the outer end (corresponding to $\eta \approx 1.5$). The mean value of the precision

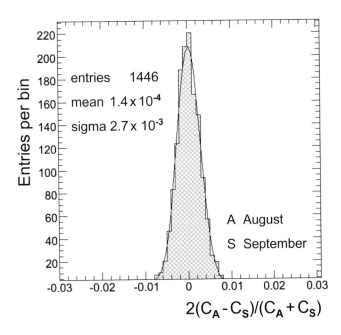

entries   1446

mean 1.4×10^{-4}

sigma 2.7×10^{-3}

A August

S September

Figure 4.12: Distribution of differences of inter-calibration coefficients from a supermodule exposed to a high energy electron beam on two occasions, separated by a period of one month. The reproducibility of the intercalibration coefficients (RMS/$\sqrt{2}$) is measured to be 0.2%.

of the cosmic intercalibration, averaged over all the channels in the nine supermodules for which a comparison with electrons can be made, is 1.5% (figure 4.13).

The ultimate intercalibration precision will be achieved *in situ* with physics events. As a first step, imposing the ϕ-independence of the energy deposited in the calorimeter can be used to rapidly confirm, and possibly improve on, the start-up intercalibration within fixed η regions. The intercalibration method that has been investigated in the most detail uses the momentum of isolated electrons measured in the tracker. These electrons, mainly from $W \rightarrow e\nu$, are abundant ($\sigma \approx 20\,\text{nb}$) and have a similar p_T to the photons of the benchmark channel $H \rightarrow \gamma\gamma$. A complementary method, not relying on the tracker momentum measurement, is based on $\pi^0 \rightarrow \gamma\gamma$ and $\eta \rightarrow \gamma\gamma$ mass reconstruction. Most methods of intercalibration will be local to a region of the ECAL, and a further step intercalibrating these regions to one another will be needed. This is a consequence of the significant systematic variations that occur as a function of pseudorapidity such as (or including): the large variation of the thickness of the tracker material, the variation of the structure of the ECAL (both the major differences between the barrel and endcap, and the small continuous variation of the geometry along the length of the barrel), and the variation of background characteristics for $\pi^0 \rightarrow \gamma\gamma$.

Over the period of time in which the physics events used to provide an intercalibration are taken the response must remain stable to high precision. Where there is a source of significant variation, as in the case of the changes in crystal transparency caused by irradiation and subsequent annealing, the variation must be precisely tracked by an independent measurement. The changes in crystal transparency are tracked and corrected using the laser monitoring system.

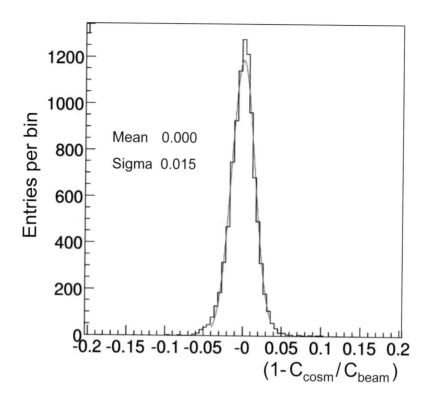

Figure 4.13: Distribution of the relative differences between the inter-calibration coefficients measured with high energy electrons and those obtained from cosmic ray muons.

The final goal of calibration is to achieve the most accurate energy measurements for electrons and photons. Different reconstruction algorithms are used to estimate the energy of different electromagnetic objects, i.e., unconverted photons, electrons and converted photons, each of them having their own correction functions. At present these "algorithmic" corrections are obtained from the simulated data by accessing the generated parameters of the Monte Carlo simulation. For some of the corrections, for example the containment corrections, this is an acceptable procedure provided that test beam data is used to verify the simulation, so that, in effect, the simulation is being used only as a means of interpolating and extrapolating from data taken in the test beam. In other cases, where the test beam provides no useful information, for example in issues related to conversions and bremsstrahlung radiation in the tracker material, it will be important to find ways of using information that can be obtained from data taken in situ with the running detector. Two particularly useful channels which can be used to obtain such information, and also assist in the step of intercalibrating regions of the ECAL to one another, are under investigation: $Z \to e^+e^-$, and $Z \to \mu^+\mu^-\gamma$ (the photon coming from inner bremsstrahlung).

2008 JINST 3 S08004

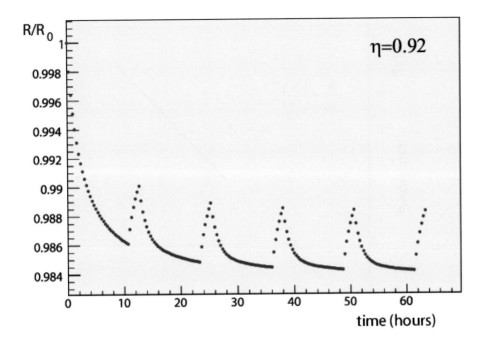

Figure 4.14: Simulation of crystal transparency evolution at LHC based on test-beam results. For this illustrative example a luminosity of $\mathscr{L} = 2 \times 10^{33}$ cm^{-2}s^{-1} was assumed, together with a machine cycle consisting of a 10 hour coast followed by 2 hours filling time. The crystal behaviour under irradiation was modeled on data taken during a crystal irradiation in the test beam.

4.9 Laser monitor system

Although radiation resistant, ECAL PbWO$_4$ crystals show a limited but rapid loss of optical transmission under irradiation due to the production of colour centres which absorb a fraction of the transmitted light. At the ECAL working temperature (18°C) the damage anneals and the balance between damage and annealing results in a dose-rate dependent equilibrium of the optical transmission, if the dose rate is constant. In the varying conditions of LHC running the result is a cyclic transparency behaviour between LHC collision runs and machine refills (figure 4.14). The magnitude of the changes is dose-rate dependent, and is expected to range from 1 or 2 per cent at low luminosity in the barrel, to tens of per cent in the high η regions of the endcap at high luminosity. The performance of the calorimeter would be unacceptably degraded by these radiation induced transparency changes were they not measured and corrected for.

The evolution of the crystal transparency is measured using laser pulses injected into the crystals via optical fibres. The response is normalized by the laser pulse magnitude measured using silicon PN photodiodes. PN type photodiodes were chosen because of their very narrow depletion zone (≈ 7 μm with +4 V reverse bias), making them much less sensitive to type inversion than the faster PIN photodiodes. Thus $R(t) = APD(t)/PN(t)$ is used as the measure of the crystal transparency. The laser monitoring system [69] performing this task is briefly outlined in the next section. Because of the different optical paths and spectra of the injected laser pulses and the scintillation light, the changes in crystal transparency cause a change in response to the laser light which is not necessarily equal to the change in response to scintillation light. For attenuations < 10% the

2008 JINST 3 S08004

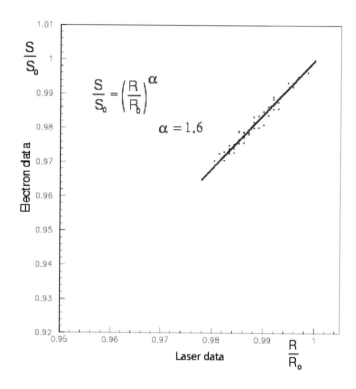

Figure 4.15: Relation between the transmission losses for scintillation light and for laser light for a given crystal. The signals are followed during the irradiation and the recovery.

relationship between the changes can be expressed by a power law,

$$\frac{S(t)}{S(t_0)} = \left[\frac{R(t)}{R(t_0)}\right]^{\alpha} , \tag{4.1}$$

where $S(t)$ represents the response to scintillation light and α is characteristic of the crystal which depends on the production method ($\alpha \approx 1.53$ for BCTP crystals, and $\alpha \approx 1.0$ for SIC crystals). An example of this relationship is given in figure 4.15. This power law describes well the behaviour of all the crystals that have been evaluated in the test beam, and this formula is expected to be valid in the barrel for both low and high luminosity at LHC.

4.9.1 Laser-monitoring system overview

Figure 4.16 shows the basic components of the laser-monitoring system: two laser wavelengths are used for the basic source. One, blue, at λ=440 nm, is very close to the scintillation emission peak, which is used to follow the changes in transparency due to radiation, and the other, near infra-red, at λ=796 nm, is far from the emission peak, and very little affected by changes in transparency, which can be used to verify the stability of other elements in the system. The spectral contamination is less than 10^{-3}. The lasers are operated such that the full width at half maximum of the pulses is ≈ 30 ns. The lasers can be pulsed at a rate of ≈ 80 Hz, and the pulse timing jitter is less than 3 ns which allows adequate trigger synchronization with the LHC bunch train and ECAL ADC clock.

2008 JINST 3 S08004

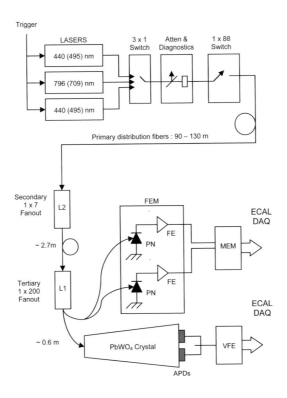

Figure 4.16: The components of the laser monitoring system.

The pulse energy of 1 mJ/pulse at the principal monitoring wavelength corresponds to ≈ 1.3 TeV, and a linear attenuator allows 1% steps down to 13 GeV. The pulse intensity instability is less than 10% which guarantees a monitoring precision of 0.1% by using the PN silicon photodiode normalization.

There are 3 light sources, 2 blue and 1 near infrared. The duplication of the blue source provides fault tolerance and allows maintenance of one while the other is in use, ensuring that a source at the wavelength used to track changes in transparency is always available. Each source consists of an Nd:YLF pump laser, its power supply and cooler unit and corresponding transformer, a Ti:Sapphire laser and its controller, and a NESLAB cooler for an LBO crystal in the Ti:S laser. Each pair of the YLF and Ti:S lasers and their corresponding optics are mounted on an optical table. Each source has its own diagnostics, 2 fibre-optic switches, internal monitors and corresponding PC based controllers. Further details can be found in [103].

The monitoring light pulses are distributed via a system of optical fibres. A fibre optic switch at the laser directs the laser pulses to 1 of 88 calorimeter regions (72 half supermodules in the barrel and 8 regions in each endcap). A two-stage distribution system mounted on each calorimeter region delivers the light to each crystal.

To provide continuous monitoring, about 1% of the 3.17 μs beam gap in every 88.924 μs LHC beam cycle will be used to inject monitoring light pulses into crystals. The time needed to scan the entire ECAL is expected to be about 30 minutes.

The first laser system was installed in the CERN H4 test beam site in August 2001. The other two laser systems were installed at H4 in August, 2003. All three laser systems have been used in

2008 JINST 3 S08004

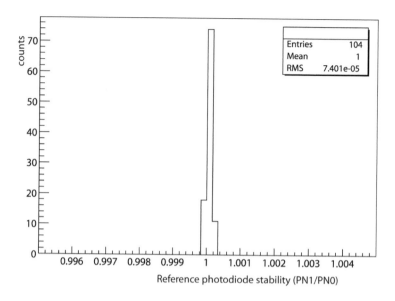

Figure 4.17: Relative stability between a pair of reference PN photodiodes monitoring 200 crystals measured in autumn 2004 at the CERN test beam facility.

the ECAL test beam program since their installation, and more than 10 000 laser hours have been cumulated.

The relative stability between a pair of reference PN photodiodes monitoring the same group of 200 crystals is shown in figure 4.17. The system achieves 0.0074% RMS over 7.5 days operation.

The response to injected laser light (normalized by the reference PN photodiodes) is presented in figure 4.18 for a group of 200 crystals measured for 11.5 days at the wavelength of 440 nm, showing that a stability of 0.068% is achieved at the scintillation wavelength.

The effect of the monitor correction procedure is presented in figure 4.19, showing that electron signals taken during an irradiation test at H4 are effectively corrected using laser monitor runs taken during the same data-taking period, providing an equalisation of the corrected response at the level of few per mille [104] .

4.10   Energy resolution

For energies below about 500 GeV, where shower leakage from the rear of the calorimeter starts to become significant, the energy resolution can be parametrized as in equation (1.1) (chapter 1.1), that is repeated for convenience here:

$$\left(\frac{\sigma}{E}\right)^2 = \left(\frac{S}{\sqrt{E}}\right)^2 + \left(\frac{N}{E}\right)^2 + C^2, \tag{4.2}$$

where S is the stochastic term, N the noise term, and C the constant term. The individual contributions are discussed below.

2008 JINST 3 S08004

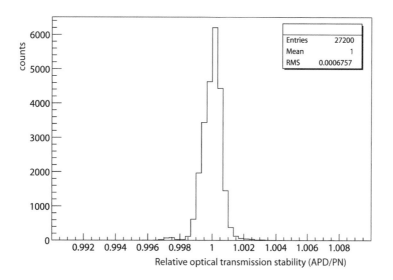

Figure 4.18: Stability of crystal transmission measurements at 440 nm (blue laser) over 11.5 days operation for a module of 200 crystals.

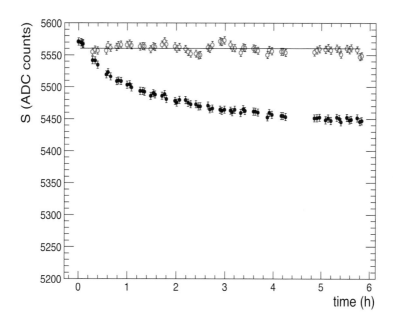

Figure 4.19: Effect of the monitor correction procedure on test beam data: full black points refer to signals measured during test beam irradiation, open red points are the same after the monitor corrections.

The stochastic term

There are three basic contributions to the stochastic term:

1. event-to-event fluctuations in the lateral shower containment,

2008 JINST 3 S08004

2. a photostatistics contribution of 2.1%,

3. fluctuations in the energy deposited in the preshower absorber (where present) with respect to what is measured in the preshower silicon detector.

The contribution to the stochastic term coming from fluctuations in the lateral containment is expected to be about 1.5% when energy is reconstructed by summing an array of 5×5 crystals, and about 2% when using 3×3 crystals.

The photostatistics contribution is given by:

$$a_{\mathrm{pe}} = \sqrt{\frac{F}{N_{\mathrm{pe}}}} \qquad (4.3)$$

where N_{pe} is the number of primary photoelectrons released in the photodetector per GeV, and F is the excess noise factor which parametrizes fluctuations in the gain process. This factor has a value close to 2 for the APDs, and is about 2.5 for the VPTs. A value of $N_{\mathrm{pe}} \approx 4500$ pe/GeV is found for the barrel, giving $\approx 2.1\%$ for the photostatistics contribution to the stochastic term. In the endcap the photostatistics contribution is similar, since the larger collection area of the VPT largely compensates for the reduced quantum efficiency of the photocathode.

The contribution to the energy resolution from the preshower device can be approximately parametrized as a stochastic term with a value of $5\%/\sqrt{E}$, where E is in GeV. But, because it samples only the beginning of the shower, the resolution is, in fact, predicted to vary like $\sigma/E \propto 1/E^{0.75}$. A beam test in 1999 [105] verified this prediction.

The constant term

The most important contributions to the constant term may be listed as follows:

1. non-uniformity of the longitudinal light collection,

2. intercalibration errors,

3. leakage of energy from the back of the crystal.

The effects of the longitudinal light collection curve have been studied in detail. Quite stringent requirements are made on the crystal longitudinal uniformity. Requiring the constant term contribution due to non-uniformity be less than 0.3%, sets a limit on the slope of the longitudinal light collection curve in the region of the shower maximum of $\approx 0.35\%$ per radiation length. A small increase in response towards the rear of the crystal helps to compensate the rear leakage from late developing showers, which would otherwise cause a low energy tail. The required response is achieved in the barrel by depolishing one long face of the crystals to a designated roughness. This surface treatment is incorporated into the crystal production process.

The effect of rear leakage is very small. Charged particles leaking from the back of the crystals can also give a direct signal in the APDs (nuclear counter effect), but test beam data show that this effect is negligible for isolated electromagnetic showers: no tails on the high side of the energy distribution are observed even at the highest electron energy tested (280 GeV).

2008 JINST 3 S08004

The noise term

There are three contributions to the noise term:

1. electronics noise,

2. digitization noise,

3. pileup noise.

The signal amplitude in the test beam is reconstructed using a simple digital filter. The noise measured, after this amplitude reconstruction, for channels in barrel supermodules is $\approx$ 40 MeV/channel in the highest gain range. This noise includes both electronics and digitization noise. The amplitude reconstruction makes use of an event-by-event baseline subtraction using 3 digitization samples taken directly before the signal pulse. This procedure removes the small channel-to-channel correlated noise. Its success is evidenced by the fact that, after this procedure, the noise in the sum of 25 channels is almost exactly 5 times the noise in a single channel [106].

In the endcap it is intended to sort the VPTs in bins of overall signal yield, which includes the photocathode area, the quantum efficiency and the VPT gain. The VPTs with higher overall signal yield are used for the larger radius regions of the endcap. This has the result that the transverse energy equivalent of the noise will be more or less constant, with a value of $\sigma_{ET} \approx 50$ MeV.

Neutron irradiation of the APDs in the barrel induces a leakage current which contributes to the electronics noise. The evolution of the leakage current and induced noise over the lifetime of the experiment has been extensively studied. The expected contribution is equivalent to 8 MeV/channel after one year of operation at $\mathscr{L} = 10^{33}$ cm^{-2}s^{-1}, and 30 MeV/channel at the end of the first year of operation at $\mathscr{L} = 10^{34}$ cm^{-2}s^{-1} [69].

The shaped signals from the preamplifier output will extend over several LHC bunch crossings. When using a multi-weights method to reconstruct the signal amplitude [106], up to 8 time samples are used. Pileup noise will occur if additional particles reaching the calorimeter cause signals which overlap these samples.

The magnitude of pileup noise expected at low luminosity ($\mathscr{L} = 2 \times 10^{33}$ cm^{-2}s^{-1}) has been studied using detailed simulation of minimum bias events generated between -5 and $+3$ bunch crossings before and after the signal. The average number of minimum bias events per bunch crossing was 3.5. Figure 4.20 shows the reconstructed amplitude observed with and without pileup in the absence of any signal. The fraction of events with a signal beyond the Gaussian distribution of the electronics noise is small, showing that at low luminosity the pileup contribution to noise is small.

Energy resolution in the test beam

In 2004 a fully equipped barrel supermodule was tested in the CERN H4 beam. The energy resolution measured with electron beams having momenta between 20 and 250 GeV/c confirmed the expectations described above [107]. Since the electron shower energy contained in a finite crystal matrix depends on the particle impact position with respect to the matrix boundaries, the intrinsic performance of the calorimeter was studied by using events where the electron was limited to a 4×4 mm^2 region around the point of maximum containment (*central impact*). Figure 1.3 shows

2008 JINST 3 S08004

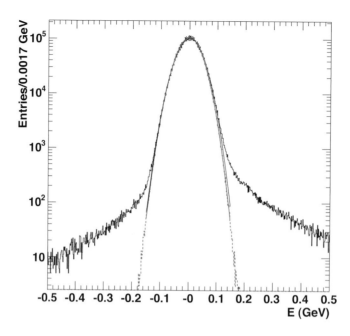

Figure 4.20: Reconstructed amplitude in ECAL barrel channels in the absence of a signal, without pileup (dashed histogram) and with pileup (solid histogram). A Gaussian of width 40 MeV is superimposed on the dashed histogram.

the resolution as a function of energy when the incident electrons were restricted in this way. The energy is reconstructed by summing 3×3 crystals. A typical energy resolution was found to be:

$$\left(\frac{\sigma}{E}\right)^2 = \left(\frac{2.8\%}{\sqrt{E}}\right)^2 + \left(\frac{0.12}{E}\right)^2 + (0.30\%)^2 \,,$$

where E is in GeV. This result is in agreement with the expected contributions detailed in the earlier part of this section. (Results from beam-test runs taken in 2006, using the final VFE card, show a 10% improvement of the noise performance.)

The energy resolution was also measured with no restriction on the lateral position of the incident electrons except that provided by the 20×20 mm^2 trigger. The trigger was roughly centred (±3 mm) on the point of maximum response of a crystals. In this case a shower containment correction was made as a function of incident position, as measured from the distribution of energies in the crystal, to account for the variation of the amount of energy contained in the matrix. For energy reconstruction in either a 3×3 or a 5×5 matrix an energy resolution of better than 0.45% is found for 120 GeV electrons after correction for containment. Figure 4.21 shows an example of the energy distributions before and after correction for the case of reconstruction in a 5×5 matrix, where the correction is smaller than for the 3×3 case.

The energy resolution has also been measured for a series of 25 runs where the beam was directed at locations uniformly covering a 3×3 array of crystals. In this case a resolution of 0.5% was measured for 120 GeV electrons.

2008 JINST 3 S08004

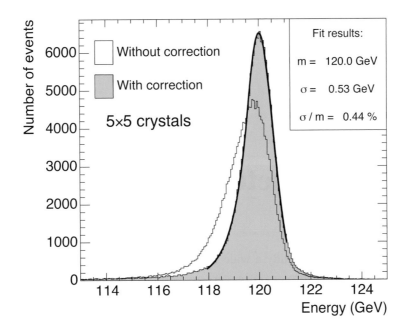

Figure 4.21: Distribution of energy reconstructed in a 5×5 matrix, before and after correction for containment, when $120\,\mathrm{GeV}$ electrons are incident over a $20 \times 20\mathrm{mm}^2$ area.

Chapter 5

Hadron calorimeter

The CMS detector is designed to study a wide range of high-energy processes involving diverse signatures of final states. The hadron calorimeters are particularly important for the measurement of hadron jets and neutrinos or exotic particles resulting in apparent missing transverse energy [1].

Figure 5.1 shows the longitudinal view of the CMS detector. The dashed lines are at fixed η values. The hadron calorimeter barrel and endcaps sit behind the tracker and the electromagnetic calorimeter as seen from the interaction point. The hadron calorimeter barrel is radially restricted between the outer extent of the electromagnetic calorimeter ($R = 1.77$ m) and the inner extent of the magnet coil ($R = 2.95$ m). This constrains the total amount of material which can be put in to absorb the hadronic shower. Therefore, an outer hadron calorimeter or *tail catcher* is placed outside the solenoid complementing the barrel calorimeter. Beyond $|\eta| = 3$, the forward hadron calorimeters placed at 11.2 m from the interaction point extend the pseudorapidity coverage down to $|\eta| = 5.2$ using a Cherenkov-based, radiation-hard technology. The following sections describe these subdetectors in detail.

5.1 Barrel design (HB)

The HB is a sampling calorimeter covering the pseudorapidity range $|\eta| < 1.3$. The HB is divided into two half-barrel sections (figure 5.2), each half-section being inserted from either end of the barrel cryostat of the superconducting solenoid and subsequently hung from rails in the median plane. Since the HB is very rigid compared to the cryostat, great care has been taken to ensure that the barrel load is distributed evenly along the rails [108].

Absorber geometry

The HB consists of 36 identical azimuthal wedges which form the two half-barrels (HB+ and HB−). The wedges are constructed out of flat brass absorber plates (table 5.1) aligned parallel to the beam axis. The numbering scheme of the wedges is shown in figure 5.3. Each wedge is segmented into four azimuthal angle (ϕ) sectors. The plates are bolted together in a staggered geometry resulting in a configuration that contains no projective dead material for the full radial extent of a wedge (figure 5.4). The innermost and outermost plates are made of stainless steel for structural strength. The plastic scintillator is divided into 16 η sectors, resulting in a segmentation

2008 JINST 3 S08004

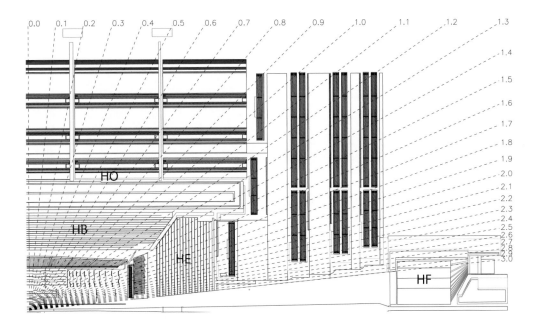

Figure 5.1: Longitudinal view of the CMS detector showing the locations of the hadron barrel (HB), endcap (HE), outer (HO) and forward (HF) calorimeters.

Table 5.1: Physical properties of the HB brass absorber, known as C26000/cartridge brass.

chemical composition	70% Cu, 30% Zn
density	8.53 g/cm^3
radiation length	1.49 cm
interaction length	16.42 cm

$(\Delta\eta, \Delta\phi) = (0.087, 0.087)$. The wedges are themselves bolted together, in such a fashion as to minimize the crack between the wedges to less than 2 mm.

The absorber (table 5.2) consists of a 40-mm-thick front steel plate, followed by eight 50.5-mm-thick brass plates, six 56.5-mm-thick brass plates, and a 75-mm-thick steel back plate. The total absorber thickness at 90° is 5.82 interaction lengths (λ_I). The HB effective thickness increases with polar angle (θ) as $1/\sin\theta$, resulting in 10.6 λ_I at $|\eta| = 1.3$. The electromagnetic crystal calorimeter [69] in front of HB adds about 1.1 λ_I of material.

Scintillator

The active medium uses the well known tile and wavelength shifting fibre concept to bring out the light. The CMS hadron calorimeter consists of about 70 000 tiles. In order to limit the number of individual elements to be handled, the tiles of a given ϕ layer are grouped into a single mechanical scintillator tray unit. Figure 5.5 shows a typical tray. The tray geometry has allowed for construction and testing of the scintillators remote from the experimental installation area. Furthermore,

2008 JINST 3 S08004

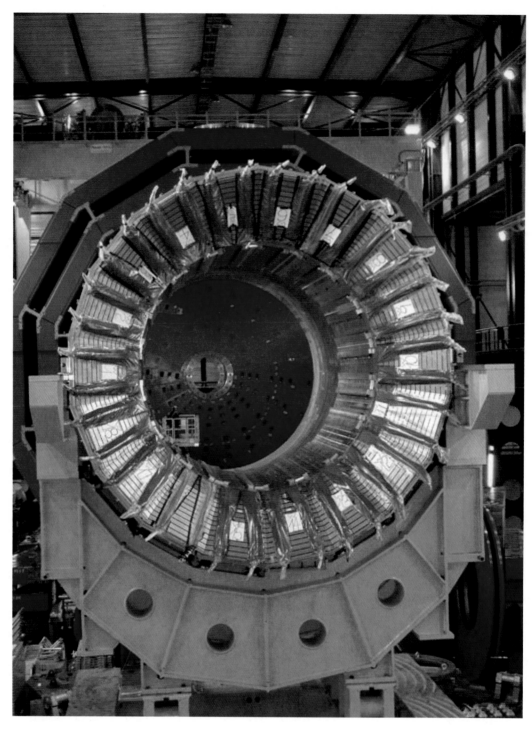

Figure 5.2: Assembled HCAL half-barrel in SX5, the above ground assembly hall.

individual scintillator trays may be replaced without disassembly of the absorber in the event of catastrophic damage. Each HB wedge has four ϕ divisions (ϕ-index = 1–4). Trays with segmentation of ϕ-index 2 and 3 go into the center of a wedge while trays with segmentation of ϕ-index 1 and 4 go into the edge slots in a wedge (figure 5.4). Each layer has 108 trays. Figure 5.6 shows a cross section of the tray.

2008 JINST 3 S08004

Table 5.2: Absorber thickness in the HB wedges.

layer	material	thickness
front plate	steel	40 mm
1-8	brass	50.5 mm
9-14	brass	56.5 mm
back plate	steel	75 mm

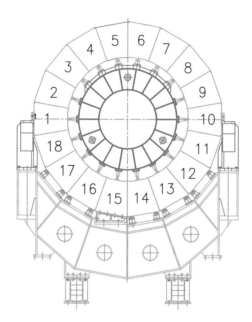

Figure 5.3: Numbering scheme for the HB wedges. Wedge 1 is on the inside ($+x$ direction) of the LHC ring.

The HB baseline active material is 3.7-mm-thick Kuraray SCSN81 plastic scintillator, chosen for its long-term stability and moderate radiation hardness. The first layer of scintillator (layer 0) is located in front of the steel support plate. It was originally foreseen to have a separate read-out [108] and is made of 9-mm-thick Bicron BC408. The scintillators are summarized in table 5.3. The purpose of layer zero is to sample hadronic showers developing in the inert material between the EB and HB. The larger thickness of layer 16 serves to correct for late developing showers leaking out the back of HB.

A tray is made of individual scintillators with edges painted white and wrapped in Tyvek 1073D which are attached to a 0.5-mm-thick plastic substrate with plastic rivets. Light from each tile is collected with a 0.94-mm-diameter green double-cladded wavelength-shifting fibre (Kuraray Y-11) placed in a machined groove in the scintillator. For calibration purposes, each tray has 1-mm-diameter stainless steel tubes, called *source tubes*, that carry Cs^{137} (or optionally Co^{60}) radioactive sources through the center of each tile. An additional quartz fibre is used to inject ultraviolet (337 nm) laser light into the layer 9 tiles. The top of the tray is covered with 2-mm-thick white polystyrene. The cover is grooved to provide routing paths for fibres to the outside of the tray and

2008 JINST 3 S08004

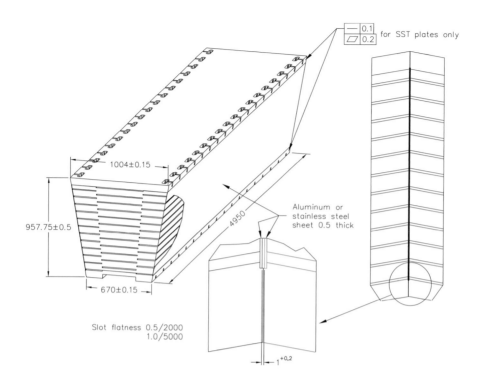

Figure 5.4: Isometric view of the HB wedges, showing the hermetic design of the scintillator sampling.

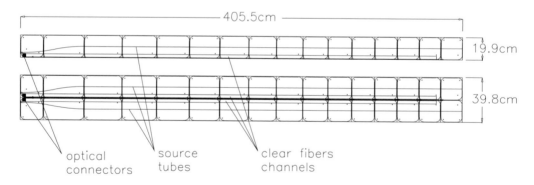

Figure 5.5: Scintillator trays.

also to accommodate the tubes for moving radioactive sources.

After exiting the scintillator, the wavelength shifting fibres (WLS) are spliced to clear fibres (Kuraray double-clad). The clear fibre goes to an optical connector at the end of the tray. An optical cable takes the light to an optical decoding unit (ODU). The ODU arranges the fibres into read-out towers and brings the light to a hybrid photodiode (HPD) [109]. An additional fibre enters each

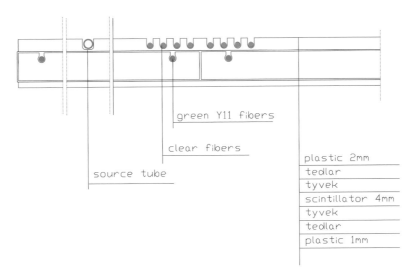

Figure 5.6: Cross-sectional view of a scintillator tray.

Table 5.3: Scintillator in the HB wedges.

layer	material	thickness
0	Bicron BC408	9 mm
1-15	Kuraray SCSN81	3.7 mm
16	Kuraray SCSN81	9 mm

HPD for direct injection of light using either the laser or a light emitting diode (LED). A schematic of the fibre optics is shown in figure 5.7 and the actual cabling is shown in figure 5.8.

The HPD consists of a photocathode held at a HV of -8 kV at a distance of approximately 3.3 mm from a pixelated silicon photodiode. The ionization produced by the accelerated photoelectron in the diode results in a gain of the HPD of approximately 2000. There are 19 hexagonal 20-mm^2 pixels in a single HPD, the centermost of which is not read-out. A cross sectional view of an HPD is shown in figure 5.9.

During the production and assembly process, the WLS fibres are cut, polished, and mirrored. The reflectivity of the mirror is checked by measuring test fibres which are mirrored along with the fibres used in the calorimeter. Measuring the reflectivity of the mirror is done with a computer controlled UV scanner with the fibres read out by photodiodes. Clear fibres are spliced onto WLS fibres with a fusion splicer. The transmission across the splice is checked by splicing a sample of WLS fibres onto WLS fibres. The splice region is measured with the UV scanner. The transmission across the splice is 92.6% with an RMS of 1.8%. Next, the optical fibres are glued into a 10 fibre connector. This configuration is called a pigtail. In order to get the fibre lengths correct, the pigtail is assembled in a template. The connector is diamond polished. The fibres are measured with the

2008 JINST 3 S08004

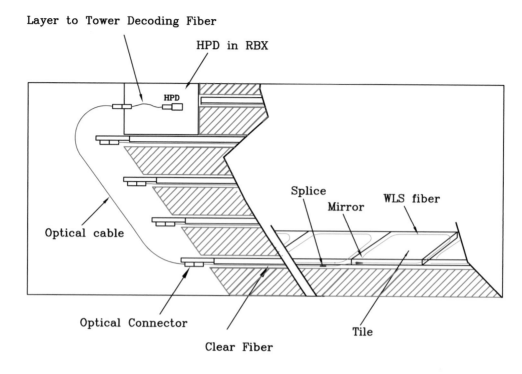

Layer to Tower Decoding Fiber

HPD in RBX

HPD

Splice

Mirror

WLS fiber

Optical cable

Optical Connector

Tile

Clear Fiber

Figure 5.7: Schematic of the HB optics.

UV scanner. The scanner checks the green fibre, clear fibre, splice, and mirror. The RMS of the light from the fibres is 1.9%. After the pigtail is inserted into the tray, the completed tray is checked with an automated source scanner using a Cs^{137} source inside a lead collimator. This yields a 4 cm diameter source spot on the tray. The collimator is moved with a computer controlled x-y motor. From the scanner we determine the relative light yield of each tile and the uniformity of each tray. The light yield of the individual tiles has an RMS of 4.6%, while the transverse uniformity of the tile is 4.5%. A Cs^{137} wire source is run through the 4 source tubes and the light yield is measured. The RMS of the ratio of collimated source to wire source is 1.3%. This means the line sources, which can be used when the calorimeter is completely assembled, can calibrate individual tiles to better than 2%. In addition to the moving wire source, there are laser and LED light injection systems.

Longitudinal segmentation

The η towers 1–14 have a single longitudinal read-out. The η towers closest to the endcap transition region (15 and 16) are segmented in depth. The front segment of tower 15 contains either 12 or 13 scintillators, due to the placement of the read-out box and the staggering of the layers (layers 0–11 for the middle two ϕ sectors and 0–12 layers for the outer two ϕ sectors). The rear segment of tower 15 has three scintillators. Tower 16, which is in front of the endcap (HE) has one scintillators in the front segment and seven in the rear. The front segment of tower 16 does not have a layer-0 scintillator. The tower segmentation is summarized in figure 5.10 and table 5.4.

2008 JINST 3 S08004

Figure 5.8: Close up view of the assembled HB wedges, showing the optical cabling.

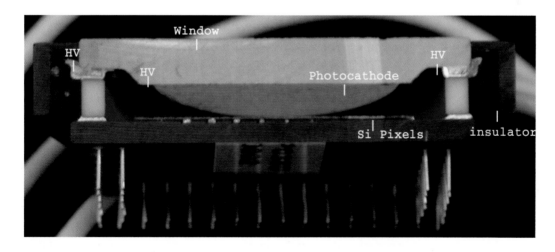

Figure 5.9: Cross sectional view of an HPD.

2008 JINST 3 S08004

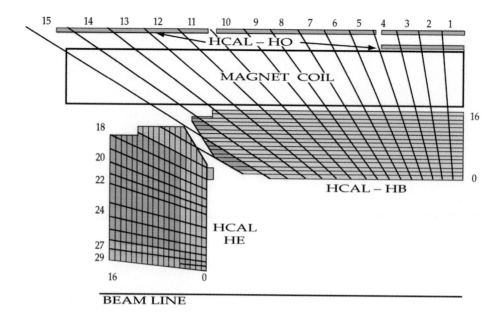

Figure 5.10: The HCAL tower segmentation in the r, z plane for one-fourth of the HB, HO, and HE detectors. The shading represents the optical grouping of scintillator layers into different longitudinal readouts.

Table 5.4: Tower data for HB. The given thicknesses correspond to the center of the tower. Note that tower 16 overlaps with HE.

tower	η range	thickness (λ_I)
1	0.000 – 0.087	5.39
2	0.087 – 0.174	5.43
3	0.174 – 0.261	5.51
4	0.261 – 0.348	5.63
5	0.348 – 0.435	5.80
6	0.435 – 0.522	6.01
7	0.522 – 0.609	6.26
8	0.609 – 0.696	6.57
9	0.696 – 0.783	6.92
10	0.783 – 0.870	7.32
11	0.870 – 0.957	7.79
12	0.957 – 1.044	8.30
13	1.044 – 1.131	8.89
14	1.131 – 1.218	9.54
15	1.218 – 1.305	10.3
16	1.305 – 1.392	overlaps with HE

2008 JINST 3 S08004

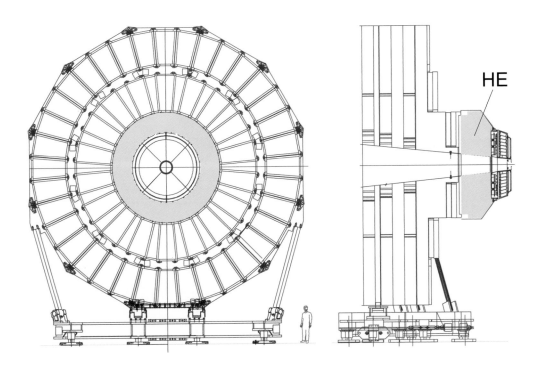

Figure 5.11: Hadron endcap (HE) calorimeter mounted on the endcap iron yoke.

5.2 Endcap design (HE)

The hadron calorimeter endcaps (HE) [108] cover a substantial portion of the rapidity range, $1.3 < |\eta| < 3$ (13.2% of the solid angle), a region containing about 34% of the particles produced in the final state. The high luminosity of the LHC (10^{34} cm^{-2} s^{-1}) requires HE to handle high (MHz) counting rates and have high radiation tolerance (10 MRad after 10 years of operation at design luminosity) at $|\eta| \simeq 3$. Since the calorimeter is inserted into the ends of a 4-T solenoidal magnet, the absorber must be made from a non-magnetic material. It must also have a maximum number of interaction lengths to contain hadronic showers, good mechanical properties and reasonable cost, leading to the choice of C26000 cartridge brass. The endcaps are attached to the muon endcap yoke as shown in figures 5.11 and 5.12. Only a small part of the calorimeter structure can be used for the fixation to the magnet iron, because the majority of the space between HE and muon absorber is occupied with muon cathode strip chambers. A 10-t electromagnetic calorimeter (EE) with a 2-t preshower detector (ES) is attached at the front face of HE. The large weight involved (about 300 t) and a strict requirement to minimize non-instrumented materials along particle trajectories, has made the design of HE a challenge to engineers. An interface kinematic scheme was developed in order to provide precise positioning of the endcap detectors with respect to the adjacent muon station, and to minimize the influence of deformation under magnetic forces. The interface kinematic contains a sliding joint between the interface tube, and HE back-flange and the hinge connection between brackets and the iron disk (YE1). Structural materials used in the interface system are non-magnetic in order not to distort the axial magnetic field of up to 4 T.

2008 JINST 3 S08004

Figure 5.12: Partially assembled HE-minus absorber in the CMS surface hall (SX5). Scintillator trays can be seen to be inserted in some of the outer sectors.

Absorber geometry

The design of the absorber is driven by the need to minimize the cracks between HB and HE, rather than single-particle energy resolution, since the resolution of jets in HE will be limited by pileup, magnetic field effects, and parton fragmentation [110, 111]. The plates are bolted together in a staggered geometry resulting in a configuration that contains no projective "dead" material (figure 5.13). The design provides a self-supporting hermetic construction. The brass plates are 79-mm-thick with 9-mm gaps to accommodate the scintillators. The total length of the calorimeter, including electromagnetic crystals, is about 10 interaction lengths (λ_I).

The outer layers of HE have a cutout region for installation of the photodetectors and front-end electronics. To compensate for the resulting reduction of material, an extra layer (-1) is added to tower 18 [112]. The outer layers are fixed to a 10-cm-thick stainless steel support plate. The optical elements are inserted into the gaps after the absorber is completely assembled; therefore, the optical elements must have a rigid structure to allow insertion from any position.

Scintillator trays

The scintillation light is collected by wavelength shifting (WLS) fibres [113, 114]. The design minimizes dead zones because the absorber can be made as a solid piece without supporting structures while at the same time the light can be easily routed to the photodetectors. Trapezoidal-

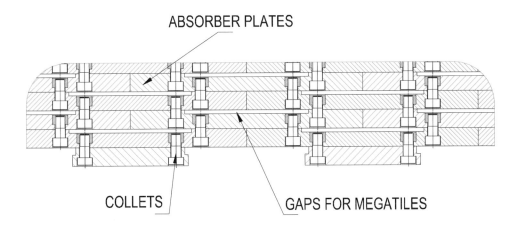

ABSORBER PLATES

COLLETS   GAPS FOR MEGATILES

Figure 5.13: Mechanical structure of the HE absorber. Particles enter the calorimeter from the bottom.

shaped scintillators (figure 5.14), 3.7-mm-thick SCSN81 for layers 1–17 and 9-mm-thick Bicron BC408 for layer 0, have grooves in which the WLS fibres are inserted. The ends of the fibres are machined with a diamond fly cutter and one end is covered with aluminium to increase the light collection. The other end is spliced to a clear fibre, which is terminated in an optical connector. The connector with the glued fibres is also machined by a diamond fly cutter. The scintillator is painted along the narrow edges and put into a frame to form a tray. The total number of tiles for both HE calorimeters is 20 916 and the number of trays is 1368. The design of a tray is presented in figure 5.15. The numbering scheme in η is shown in figure 5.16, and the CMS convention for ϕ as applied to HE is shown in figure 5.17. The scintillators are wrapped with Tyvek and sandwiched between sheets of duraluminum. The stack contains holes for fibres which are terminated with optical connectors. The gap between the duraluminum plates is fixed by brass spacers screwed together. The granularity of the calorimeters is $\Delta\eta \times \Delta\phi = 0.087 \times 0.087$ for $|\eta| < 1.6$ and $\Delta\eta \times \Delta\phi \approx 0.17 \times 0.17$ for $|\eta| \geq 1.6$.

The tray design is very robust and reliable. The trays are relatively stiff which is very important for insertion into the absorber. To control the scintillator tray quality, a UV nitrogen laser was used to excite the scintillators. The light is fed by quartz fibres to the connector and is fanned out as shown in figure 5.15. These fibres are terminated with aluminium reflectors and distribute the light to all tiles. The light signal produced by a UV flash in the scintillator is similar to the signal induced by a charged particle. This allows a performance check of the entire optical route from scintillator to electronics, providing an important technique to track possible degradation of transparency due to radiation damage. For further calibration and monitoring, a radioactive source moving in a stainless steel tube is used to study the time-dependence of calibration coefficients.

The trays are inserted into the gaps in the absorber and fixed by screws. At the back of the calorimeter, boxes with photodetectors and electronics are located in the notch shown in figure 5.18. Optical cables transfer signals from the scintillator trays to the photodetectors. The partially assembled HE is shown in figure 5.12. Multipixel hybrid photodiodes (HPDs) are used as photodetectors due to their low sensitivity to magnetic fields and their large dynamical range.

2008 JINST 3 S08004

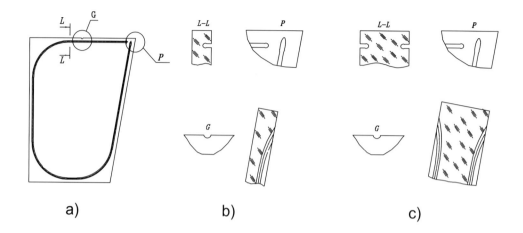

a) b) c)

Figure 5.14: a) Basic structure of a scintillator tile with a groove to fix wavelength shifting fibre, b) cross section of the 3.7-mm-thick scintillator for layers 1–17, and c) cross section of the 9-mm-thick scintillator for layer zero. Two layers of reflecting paint cover the side surfaces of the tile.

Longitudinal segmentation

The longitudinal segmentation of HE (figure 5.10) is, in part, motivated by the radiation environment. Correction of the calibration coefficients after scintillator degradation can be applied, in order to restore the energy resolution. The towers nearest the beam line (27 and 28 plus guard ring "29") have 3 divisions in depth which are read-out separately. The other towers (except 16 and 17 which overlap with the electromagnetic barrel calorimeter) have two longitudinal readouts for potential use during the time period when the electromagnetic endcap calorimeter (EE) may not yet be available. A special scintillator layer of 9 mm BC408 (layer 0) is installed in front of the absorber to partially correct for the different response of EE to electrons and hadrons and for particle absorption in the mechanical structure supporting EE.

2008 JINST 3 S08004

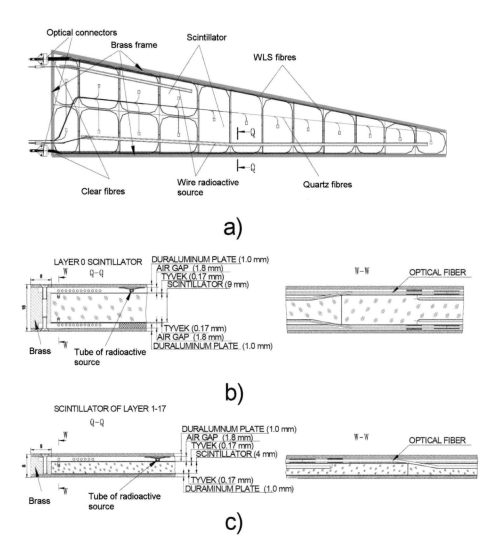

Figure 5.15: The design of the calorimeter scintillator trays: a) front view of a tray without upper aluminium cover, b) cut out view of the layer-0 tray with two fibres from a tile, c) cut out view of a tray for layers 1–17.

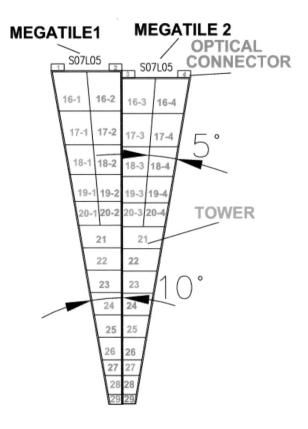

Figure 5.16: Numbering scheme for the tiles in adjacent scintillator trays.

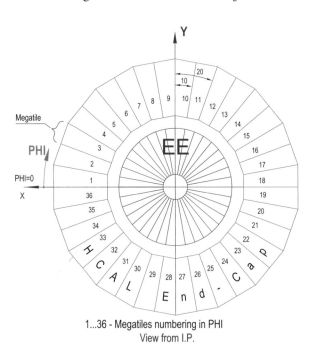

Figure 5.17: Numbering scheme for the HE wedges as viewed from the interaction point. The $+x$ direction points to the center of the LHC ring.

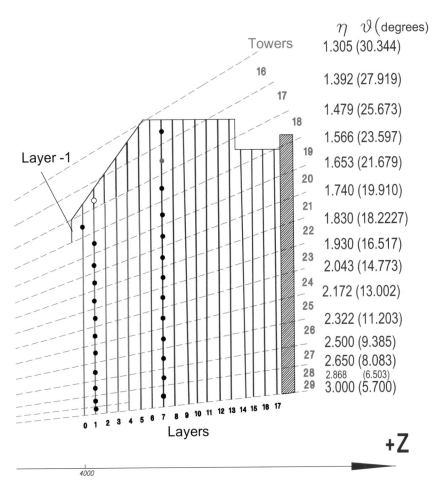

2008 JINST 3 S08004

Figure 5.18: Longitudinal and angular segmentation of the HE calorimeter. The dashed lines point to the interaction point.

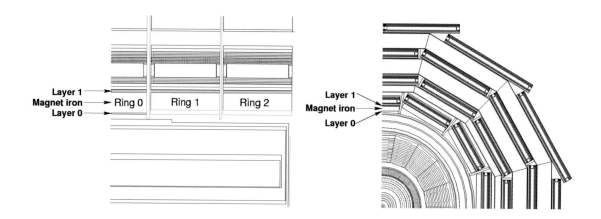

Figure 5.19: Longitudinal and transverse views of the CMS detector showing the position of HO layers.

5.3 Outer calorimeter design (HO)

In the central pseudorapidity region, the combined stopping power of EB plus HB does not provide sufficient containment for hadron showers. To ensure adequate sampling depth for $|\eta| < 1.3$, the hadron calorimeter is extended outside the solenoid with a tail catcher called the HO or outer calorimeter. The HO utilises the solenoid coil as an additional absorber equal to $1.4/\sin\theta$ interaction lengths and is used to identify late starting showers and to measure the shower energy deposited after HB.

Outside the vacuum tank of the solenoid, the magnetic field is returned through an iron yoke designed in the form of five 2.536 m wide (along z-axis) rings. The HO is placed as the first sensitive layer in each of these five rings. The rings are identified by the numbers -2, -1, 0, $+1$, $+2$. The numbering increases with z and the nominal central z positions of the five rings are respectively -5.342 m, -2.686 m, 0, $+2.686$ m and $+5.342$ m. At $\eta = 0$, HB has the minimal absorber depth. Therefore, the central ring (ring 0) has two layers of HO scintillators on either side of a 19.5 cm thick piece of iron (the tail catcher iron) at radial distances of 3.82 m and 4.07 m, respectively. All other rings have a single HO layer at a radial distance of 4.07 m. The total depth of the calorimeter system is thus extended to a minimum of 11.8 λ_I except at the barrel-endcap boundary region.

The HO is constrained by the geometry of the muon system. Figure 5.19 shows the position of HO layers in the rings of the muon stations in the overall CMS setup. The segmentation of these detectors closely follows that of the barrel muon system. Each ring has 12 identical ϕ-sectors. The 12 sectors are separated by 75-mm-thick stainless steel beams which hold successive layers of iron of the return yoke as well as the muon system. The space between successive muon rings in the η direction and also the space occupied by the stainless steel beams in the ϕ direction are not available for HO. In addition, the space occupied by the cryogenic "chimneys" in sector 3 of ring -1, and sector 4 of ring $+1$ are also not available for HO. The chimneys are used for the cryogenic transfer lines and power cables of the magnet system. Finally, the mechanical structures needed to position the scintillator trays further constrain HO along ϕ.

2008 JINST 3 S08004

In the radial direction each HO layer has been allocated a total of 40 mm, of which only 16 mm is available for the detector layer, the rest being used for the aluminium honeycomb support structures. In addition, the HO modules are independently supported from the steel beams located on either side of each ϕ sector. The thickness and position of the iron ribs in the yoke structure further constrain the shape and segmentation of the HO.

The sizes and positions of the tiles in HO are supposed to roughly map the layers of HB to make towers of granularity 0.087×0.087 in η and ϕ. The HO consists of one (rings ± 1 and ± 2) or two (ring 0) layers of scintillator tiles located in front of the first layer of the barrel muon detector. Scintillation light from the tiles is collected using multi-clad Y11 Kuraray wavelength shifting (WLS) fibres of diameter 0.94 mm, and transported to the photo detectors located on the structure of the return yoke by splicing a multi-clad Kuraray clear fibre (also of 0.94 mm diameter) with the WLS fibre. In order to simplify installation of HO, the scintillator tiles are packed into a single unit called a tray. Each tray corresponds to one ϕ slice (5° wide in ϕ). However, along the z (η) direction, a tray covers the entire span of a muon ring. Figure 5.20 shows a schematic view of a HO tray where one tile is mapped to a tower of HB and the optical cable from the tray is connected to the read-out box.

The physics impact of HO has been studied [115] using a simulation of the CMS detector. Single pions of fixed energies are shot at specific η values and the resulting energy deposits in the electromagnetic calorimeter and in the layers of the hadron calorimeter are combined to measure the energy. Figure 5.21 shows distributions of the measured energy scaled to the incident energy for 200 GeV pions at $\eta = 0$ and 225 GeV at $\eta = 0.5$ (pointing towards the middle of ring 1). The solid and dashed lines in the figure indicate measurements without and with HO, respectively. As can be seen in figure 5.21, there is an excess in Energy/$E_{incident} < 1$ for measurements without HO, because of leakage. The measurements with HO are more Gaussian in nature indicating that the addition of HO recovers the effect of leakage. The effect of leakage is visible at $\eta = 0$ (ring 0) from 70 GeV, increasing with energy. The mean fraction of energy in HO increases from 0.38% for 10 GeV pions to 4.3% for 300 GeV pions. There is some evidence of leakage without HO in ring 1 but it is reduced due to the greater HB thickness at larger $|\eta|$. The amount of leakage in ring 2 is found to be negligible at energies below 300 GeV.

The effect of shower leakage has a direct consequence on the measurement of missing transverse energy (E_T^{miss}). Study of QCD events shows that the cross section for those events, where at least one particle has E_T above 500 GeV, is several pb. For these events the HO is useful to decrease the leakage and improve the E_T^{miss} measurement. Figure 5.22 shows the dijet integrated cross section for E_T^{miss} above a certain value. It is clear from the figure that the inclusion of HO reduces the dijet rate by a factor of 1.5 or more for moderate E_T^{miss} values, a region important for searches of supersymmetric particles.

Module specification

HO is physically divided into 5 rings in η conforming to the muon ring structure. The rings are numbered $-2, -1, 0, +1$ and $+2$ with increasing η. Each ring of the HO is divided into 12 identical ϕ sectors and each sector has 6 slices (numbered 1 to 6 counting clockwise) in ϕ. The ϕ slices of a layer are identical in all sectors. The widths of the slices along ϕ are given in table 5.5. In each ϕ

2008 JINST 3 S08004

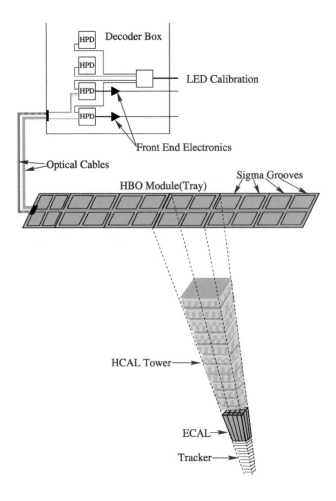

Figure 5.20: Schematic view of a HO tray shown with individual tiles and the corresponding grooves for WLS fibres. Each optically independent (4 WLS fibres) tile is mapped to a tower of HB. Optical fibres from the tray are routed to the decoder box which contains the photodetector and read-out electronics.

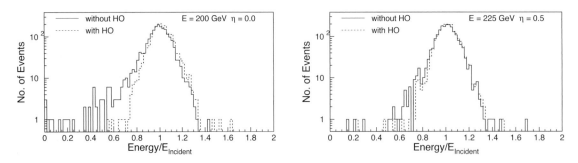

Figure 5.21: A simulation of the distribution of the measured energy scaled to the incident energy for pions with incident energies of (left panel) 200 GeV at $\eta = 0$ and (right panel) 225 GeV at $|\eta| = 0.5$. The solid and dashed histograms are measurements without and with HO, respectively.

2008 JINST 3 S08004

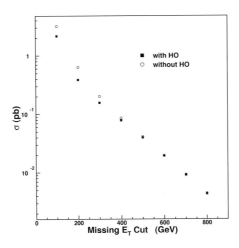

Figure 5.22: Integrated cross section above threshold for intrinsically balanced QCD dijet events as a function of missing E_T with or without HO.

Table 5.5: Dimension of tiles along ϕ for different trays. Each tray corresponds to one ϕ-slice in a ϕ sector.

Ring	Layer	Width along ϕ in mm					
		Tray 1	Tray 2	Tray 3	Tray 4	Tray 5	Tray 6
0	0	274	343	332	327	327	268
0	1	300	364	352	347	347	292
$\pm 1, \pm 2$	1	317	366	354	349	349	406

slice, there is a further division along η. The smallest scintillator unit in HO thus obtained is called a tile. The scintillator tiles in each ϕ sector belong to a plane. The perpendicular distance of this plane from the z-axis is 3.82 m for layer 0 and 4.07 m for layer 1. The tiles in each ϕ slice of a ring are mechanically held together in the form of a tray.

Both layers of ring 0 have 8 η-divisions (i.e. 8 tiles in a tray): $-4, -3, -2, -1, +1, +2, +3, +4$. Ring 1 has 6 divisions: $5 \cdots 10$ and ring 2 has 5 divisions: $11 \cdots 15$. Ring -1 and ring -2 have the same number of divisions as rings 1 and 2 but with $-$ve indices. The η-dimension of any tile with $-$ve tower number is the same as the one with $+$ve number. The tile dimensions along η are shown in table 5.6.

Figure 5.23 shows the final layout of all the HO trays in the CMS detector. The length of a full tray is 2510 mm whereas the shorter trays, the sizes of which are constrained because of the chimney (trays 4 and 5 in sector 4 of ring $+1$ and trays 3, 4, 5 and 6 in sector 3 of ring -1), are 2119-mm long. The shorter trays are constructed without the tile corresponding to tower number ± 5. Because of the constraints imposed by the gap between ring 0 and rings ± 1, the η boundaries of HO tower 4 do not match the barrel η boundaries; therefore, part of HO tower 5 overlaps with tower 4 in the barrel.

2008 JINST 3 S08004

Table 5.6: HO tile dimensions along η for different rings and layers. The tile sizes, which are constrained by muon ring boundaries, are also given.

Tower #	η_{max}	Length (mm)	Tower #	η_{max}	Length (mm)
Ring 0 Layer 0			Ring 0 Layer 1		
1	0.087	331.5	1	0.087	351.2
2	0.174	334.0	2	0.174	353.8
3	0.262	339.0	3	0.262	359.2
4	0.326	248.8	4	0.307	189.1
Ring 1 Layer 1			Ring 2 Layer 1		
5	0.436	391.5	11	0.960	420.1
6	0.524	394.2	12	1.047	545.1
7	0.611	411.0	13	1.135	583.3
8	0.698	430.9	14	1.222	626.0
9	0.785	454.0	15	1.262	333.5
10	0.861	426.0			

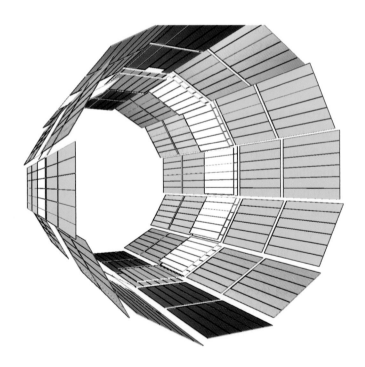

Figure 5.23: Layout of all the HO trays in the CMS detector.

2008 JINST 3 S08004

Figure 5.24: View of a typical tile of HO with WLS fibres inserted in the 4 grooves of the tile.

Tiles

Scintillator tiles are made from Bicron BC408 scintillator plates of thickness 10^{+0}_{-1} mm. Figure 5.24 shows a typical HO scintillator tile. The WLS fibres are held inside the tile in grooves with a key hole cross section. Each groove has a circular part (of diameter 1.35 mm) inside the scintillator and a neck of 0.86 mm width. The grooves are 2.05-mm deep. Each tile has 4 identical grooves, one groove in each quadrant of the tile. The grooves closely follow the quadrant boundary. The corners of the grooves are rounded to prevent damage to the fibre at the bend and to ease fibre insertion. The groove design is slightly different for the tile where the optical connector is placed at the end of the tray. Since the tiles are large, 4 grooves ensure good light collection and less attenuation of light.

The HO has 95 different tile dimensions, 75 for layer 1 and 20 for layer 0. The total number of tiles is 2730 (2154 for layer 1 and 576 for layer 0).

Trays

All tiles in each ϕ slice of a sector are grouped together in the form of a tray. Each tray contains 5 tiles in rings ± 2; 6 tiles in rings ± 1 and 8 tiles in ring 0. The edges of the tiles are painted with Bicron reflecting white paint for better light collection as well as isolating the individual tiles of a tray. Further isolation of tiles is achieved by inserting a piece of black tedler in between the adjacent tiles. The tiles in a tray are covered with a single big piece of white, reflective tyvek paper. Then they are covered with black tedlar paper to prevent light leakage. This package is placed between two black plastic plates for mechanical stability and ease of handling. The top plastic cover is 2-mm-thick and the bottom one is 1-mm-thick. Figure 5.25 shows a cross section of a tray to illustrate the different components. The plastic covers (top and bottom) have holes matching with the holes in the tiles. Specially designed countersunk screws passing through these holes fix the plastic covers firmly on the tiles.

The 2 mm plastic sheet on the top has 1.6 mm deep channels grooved on it (on the outer side) to route the fibres from individual tiles to an optical connector placed in a groove at the edge of the tray. A 1.5-mm-wide straight groove runs along the edge of the top cover to accommodate a stainless steel tube. This is used for the passage of a radioactive source which is employed in calibrating the modules. Each connector has two holes and they are fixed to the scintillator-plastic assembly through matching holes. Each ϕ sector in each ring has 6 trays. There are 360 trays for layer 1 and 72 trays for layer 0.

2008 JINST 3 S08004

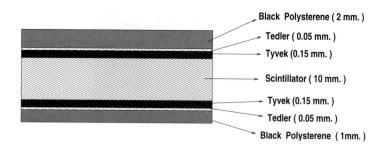

Black Polysterene (2 mm.)
Tedler (0.05 mm.)
Tyvek (0.15 mm.)
Scintillator (10 mm.)
Tyvek (0.15 mm.)
Tedler (0.05 mm.)
Black Polysterene (1mm.)

Figure 5.25: Cross section of a HO tray showing the different components.

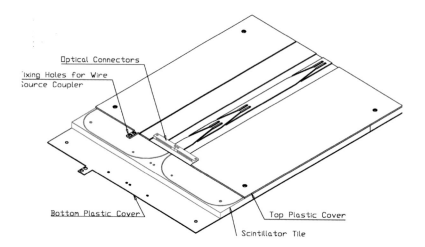

Optical Connectors
Fixing Holes for Wire Source Coupler
Bottom Plastic Cover
Top Plastic Cover
Scintillator Tile

Figure 5.26: The arrangement of scintillation tiles, plastic covers and connectors in a tray. The components are slightly displaced from their true positions to show their matching designs.

Pigtails

The light collected by the WLS fibres inserted in the tiles needs to be transported to photodetectors located far away on the muon rings. The captive ends of the WLS fibres, which reside inside the groove, are polished, aluminized and protected using a thin polymer coating. The other end of the WLS fibre comes out of the tile through a slot made on the 2-mm-thick black plastic cover sheet. To minimise the loss of light in transportation, the WLS fibre (attenuation length of ≈ 1.8 m) is spliced to a clear fibre (attenuation length of ≈ 8.0 m). A fibre is spliced only if the potential WLS light loss is larger than the light loss at a spliced joint. Thus depending on tile length (along η) 2–3 fibres in each pigtail are made only of WLS fibres. The clear fibres from each tile follow the guiding grooves on the top plastic to the optical connector at the end. Each tray has two optical connectors mounted on one end of the tray. In a tray, the grooves of the tiles form two rows along η. The fibres from all grooves on one row terminate on one connector (figure 5.26). The number of fibres from trays in different rings are given in table 5.7.

The bunch of fibres fixed to the optical connector is called a pigtail (figure 5.27). Each tray has 2 pigtails and there are 864 pigtails in total: 720 for layer 1 and 144 for layer 0. Each fibre in a pigtail is cut to the proper length to match the groove length in the scintillator plus the distance from the scintillator to the optical connector at the end of the tray.

2008 JINST 3 S08004

Table 5.7: Tray specifications for different rings of HO.

Ring #	Tiles/tray	Fibres/tray	Fibres/connector
0	8	32	16
±1	6	24	12
±2	5	20	10

Figure 5.27: Illustration of an assembled pigtail (not drawn to scale).

5.4 Forward calorimeter design (HF)

The forward calorimeter will experience unprecedented particle fluxes. On average, 760 GeV per proton-proton interaction is deposited into the two forward calorimeters, compared to only 100 GeV for the rest of the detector. Moreover, this energy is not uniformly distributed but has a pronounced maximum at the highest rapidities. At $|\eta| = 5$ after an integrated luminosity of $5 \times 10^5 \, \text{pb}^{-1}$ (≈ 10 years of LHC operation), the HF will experience $\approx 10 \, \text{MGy}$. The charged hadron rates will also be extremely high. For the same integrated luminosity, inside the HF absorber at 125 cm from the beam-line, the rate will exceed 10^{11} per cm^2 [108]. This hostile environment presents a considerable challenge to calorimetry, and the design of the HF calorimeter was first and foremost guided by the necessity to survive in these harsh conditions, preferably for at least a decade. Successful operation critically depends on the radiation hardness of the active material. This was the principal reason why quartz fibres (fused-silica core and polymer hard-cladding) were chosen as the active medium.

The signal is generated when charged shower particles above the Cherenkov threshold ($E \geq 190 \, \text{keV}$ for electrons) generate Cherenkov light, thereby rendering the calorimeter mostly sensitive to the electromagnetic component of showers [116]. A small fraction of the generated light is captured, $f_{\text{trap}} = \text{NA}/2n_{\text{core}}^2$, where NA is the numerical aperture ($\text{NA} = 0.33 \pm 0.02$) and n_{core} is the refractive index of the quartz core. Only light that hits the core-cladding interface at an angle larger than the critical angle ($71°$) contributes to the calorimeter signal. The half-angle $\theta = 19°$ is determined by the refractive indices of the core (n_{core}) and the cladding (n_{clad}), $\sin\theta = \sqrt{n_{\text{core}}^2 - n_{\text{clad}}^2}$. The fibres measure $600 \pm 10 \, \mu\text{m}$ in diameter for the fused-silica core, $630^{+5}_{-10} \, \mu\text{m}$ with the polymer hard-cladding, and $800 \pm 30 \, \mu\text{m}$ with the protective acrylate buffer. Over 1000 km of fibres are used in the HF calorimeters. The fibres are cleaved at both ends by a diamond cutter. The attenuation length of these fibres is measured to be ≈ 15 m using high energy electrons at $90°$ to the fibres.

2008 JINST 3 S08004

The optical attenuation at a wavelength λ in these types of fibres scales as $a(\lambda)(D/D_0)^{b(\lambda)}$ where D is the accumulated dose, which is normalized to a reference dose ($D_0 = 1$ MGy) for convenience. For example, at a wavelength $\lambda = 450$ nm at the accumulated dose of $D = 1$ MGy, the induced attenuation is ≈ 1.5 dB/m, thus defining a. The a and b parameters characterize the radiation hardness of a given fibre. For high OH$^-$ (300–500 ppm) HF fibres at 450 nm, the measured values are $a \approx 1.5$ and $b \approx 0.3$ [117–119]. An accumulated dose of 10 MGy will result in a loss of optical transmission by a half, which is the worst case for HF after a decade.

The calorimeter consists of a steel absorber structure that is composed of 5 mm thick grooved plates. Fibres are inserted in these grooves. The detector is functionally subdivided into two longitudinal segments. Half of the fibres run over the full depth of the absorber (165 cm $\approx 10\lambda_I$) while the other half starts at a depth of 22 cm from the front of the detector. These two sets of fibres are read out separately. This arrangement makes it possible to distinguish showers generated by electrons and photons, which deposit a large fraction of their energy in the first 22 cm, from those generated by hadrons, which produce nearly equal signals in both calorimeter segments on average. The long fibre section is referred as L (measuring the total signal), and the short fibre section as S (measuring the energy deposition after 22 cm of steel). The absorber has grooves ($0.90^{+0.12}_{-0}$ mm wide and $1.06^{+0.6}_{-0}$ mm in depth) which make a square grid separated by 5.0 ± 0.1 mm center-to-center. Long and short fibres alternate in these grooves. The packing fraction by volume (fibre/total) in the first 22 cm is 0.57% and is twice as large beyond that depth.

The forward calorimeter is essentially a cylindrical steel structure with an outer radius of 130.0 cm. The front face of the calorimeter is located at 11.2 m from the interaction point. The hole for the beam pipe is cylindrical, with radius 12.5 cm from the center of the beam line. This structure is azimuthally subdivided into 20° modular wedges. Thirty-six such wedges (18 on either side of the interaction point) make up the HF calorimeters. A cross sectional view of the HF is shown in figure 5.28. The fibres run parallel to the beam line, and are bundled to form 0.175×0.175 ($\Delta\eta \times \Delta\phi$) towers (figure 5.29 and table 5.8). The detector is housed in a hermetic radiation shielding which consists of layers of 40 cm thick steel, 40 cm of concrete, and 5 cm of polyethylene. A large plug structure in the back of the detector provides additional shielding.

Bundled fibres are held in ferrules which illuminate one end of the air-core light guides that penetrate through 42.5 cm of the shielding matrix (steel, lead, and polyethylene). This shielding is necessary to protect the photomultipliers and the front-end electronics housed in the read-out boxes. The air-core light guide consists of a hollow tube lined on the inside with highly reflective custom-made sheets. These metal-coated reflectors are designed to be very efficient ($> 90\%$) in the visible spectrum at the relevant angles (≈ 70 degrees from normal). Light typically makes five bounces before reaching the photocathode and nearly half the light is lost in this transport. Each light guide is coupled to a standard bialkaline, 8-stage photomultiplier tube with a borosilicate glass window. A read-out box (RBX) houses 24 PMTs and services half of a wedge (10° in ϕ).

The entire calorimeter system, with its shielding components, is mounted on a rigid table which supports more than 240 t with less than 1 mm deflection. The absorber alone weighs 108 t. The table is also designed for horizontal separation of the detector into two sections to clear the beam pipe at installation and removal. It is possible to align the forward calorimeters within ± 1 mm with respect to the rest of the CMS experiment.

2008 JINST 3 S08004

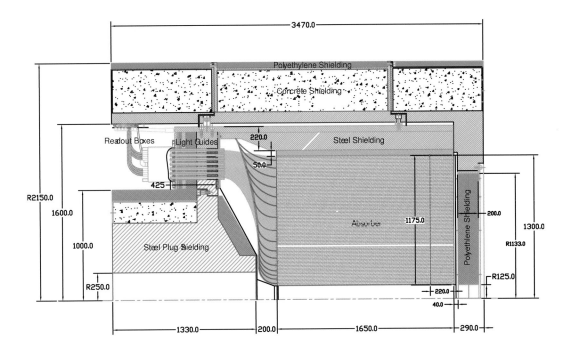

Figure 5.28: The cross sectional view of the HF calorimeter shows that the sensitive area extends from 125 to 1300 mm in the radial direction. The absorber in the beam direction measures 1650 mm. Bundled fibres (shaded area) are routed from the back of the calorimeter to air-core light guides which penetrate through a steel-lead-polyethlene shielding matrix. Light is detected by PMTs housed in the read-out boxes. Stainless steel radioactive source tubes (red lines) are installed for each tower and are accessible from outside the detector for source calibration. The interaction point is at 11.2 meters from the front of the calorimeter to the right. All dimensions are in mm.

The inner part of HF ($4.5 < |\eta| < 5$) will experience radiation doses close to 100 Mrad/year, and large neutron fluxes leading to activation of the absorber material, reaching several mSv/h in the region closest to the beam line after 60 days of running at $10^{34}\,\mathrm{cm}^{-2}\mathrm{s}^{-1}$ luminosity and one day of cooling down. The active elements of HF (quartz fibres) are sufficiently radiation-hard to survive these levels of radiation with limited deterioration. The PMTs are shielded behind 40 cm of steel and borated polyethylene slabs. HF, using Cherenkov light from quartz fibres, is practically insensitive to neutrons and to low energy particles from the decay of activated radionucleids. Further shielding around HF achieves activation levels below 10 μSv/h on the periphery of the detector. A 10-cm-thick lead plate, located in front of HF during operations around the detector, reduces personal exposure to radiation from the absorber. Maintenance of read-out boxes will be performed with the help of semi-automatic extractor tools. HF is equipped with radiation monitors located at the periphery of the detector, and with a system (Raddam) to measure the transmission properties of a few reference quartz fibres embedded in the absorber, as a function of integrated luminosity.

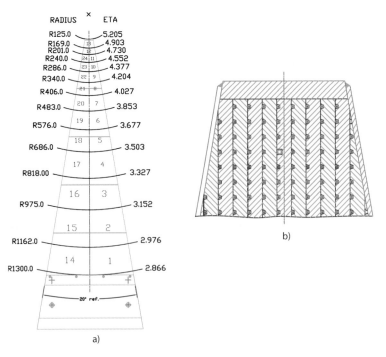

a)

b)

Figure 5.29: a) Transverse segmentation of the HF towers. b) An expanded view of the wedge shows the squared out groove holding the radioactive source tube.

Table 5.8: The tower sizes, number of fibres, bundle sizes and the percentage of photocathode area utilized are listed below for each tower. The air-core light guides are tapered to better match the photocathode area for towers 1, 2 and 3.

Ring No	(r_{in}, r_{out})	$\Delta\eta$	$\Delta\phi$	N_{fib}	A_{bundle}	$\frac{A_{bundle}}{A_{photocathode}}$
	[mm]		[degree]		[mm^2]	
1	(1162–1300)	0.111	10	594	551	1.14
2	(975–1162)	0.175	10	696	652	1.33
3	(818–975)	0.175	10	491	469	0.96
4	(686–818)	0.175	10	346	324	0.66
5	(576–686)	0.175	10	242	231	0.47
6	(483–576)	0.175	10	171	167	0.34
7	(406–483)	0.175	10	120	120	0.25
8	(340–406)	0.175	10	85	88	0.18
9	(286–340)	0.175	10	59	63	0.13
10	(240–286)	0.175	10	41	46	0.94
11	(201–240)	0.175	10	30	35	0.71
12	(169–201)	0.175	20	42	52	0.11
13	(125–169)	0.300	20	45	50	0.10

2008 JINST 3 S08004

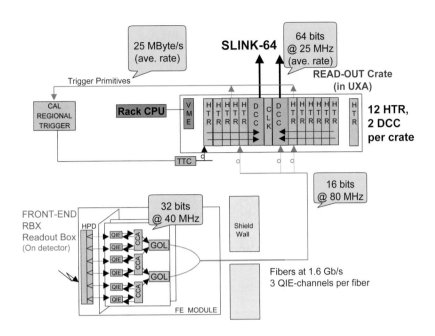

Figure 5.30: Overview of HCAL read-out electronics.

5.5 Read-out electronics and slow control

The overview of the full HCAL read-out chain is shown in figure 5.30. The read-out consists of an optical to electrical transducer followed by a fast charge-integrating ADC. The digital output of the ADC is transmitted for every bunch over a gigabit digital optical fibre to the service cavern, housing the off-detector electronics. In the service cavern, the signal is deserialized and used to construct trigger primitives which are sent to the calorimeter trigger. The data and trigger primitives are also pipelined for transmission to the DAQ upon a Level-1 Accept (L1A) decision.

The optical signals from the scintillator-based detectors (HB/HE/HO) are converted to electrical signals using multichannel hybrid photodiodes (HPDs) which provide a gain of ≈ 2000. A detailed view of the scintillator-based front-end read-out chain is given in figure 5.31. The optical signals from individual sampling layers are brought out on clear fibres. The fibres corresponding to a projective calorimeter tower are mapping via an optical decoding unit (ODU) to a cookie that interfaces to individual pixels on the HPD. In the forward calorimeter, where the magnetic fields are much smaller than in the central detector, conventional photomultiplier tubes (Hamamatsu R7525HA) are used and quartz-fibre bundles are routed directly to the phototube windows.

An overview of the HCAL controls is given in figure 5.32. Several PCs in the CMS control room operated through PVSS are used to control high and low voltages. The control system also downloads pedestal DAC and timing parameters to front-ends and controls many of the calibration and monitoring systems including the source calibration drivers, the LED pulsers, and the laser system. These systems record temperature, humidity and other constants useful for correlation studies of detector/calibration stability.

The configuration database contains the relationships or mapping for all HCAL detector components: wedges, layers, read-out boxes (RBX), cables, HCAL Trigger (HTR) cards, and calibra-

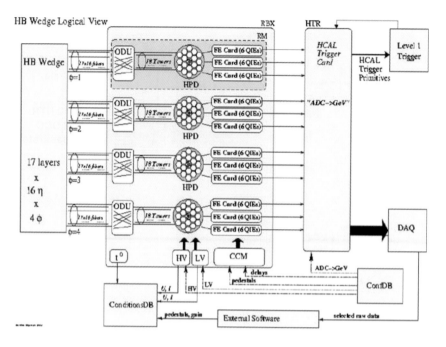

Figure 5.31: Overview of HCAL read-out/trigger chain and connections to database.

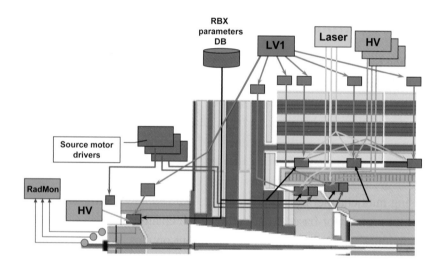

Figure 5.32: Overview of HCAL detector controls.

tion parameters for various components e.g. RBX, QIE, source types and strength. The conditions database has the slow-controls logging, the calibration constants (pedestals, gains, timing information, etc.) and the configuration database downloaded to the read-out system during the initialization.

The analogue signal from the HPD or photomultiplier is converted to a digital signal by a charge-integrating ADC ASIC called the QIE (Charge-Integrator and Encoder). The QIE internally contains four capacitors which are connected in turn to the input, one during each 25 ns period. The integrated charge from the capacitors is converted to a seven-bit non-linear scale to cover the

2008 JINST 3 S08004

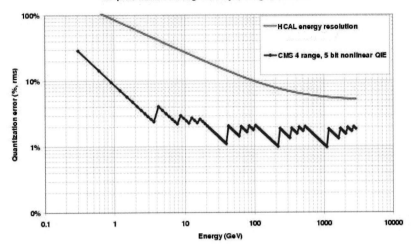

Figure 5.33: Contribution of the FADC quantization error to the resolution, compared with a representative HCAL resolution curve.

large dynamic range of the detector. The ADC is designed so its contribution to the detector energy resolution over its multi-range operation is negligible, as shown in figure 5.33. The QIE input characteristics were chosen from test beam data to optimize speed and noise performance. This resulted in a per channel RMS noise of 4600 electrons (0.7 fC) corresponding to about 180 MeV.

The digital outputs of three QIE channels are combined with some monitoring information to create a 32-bit data word. The 32-bit data, at a rate of 40 MHz, is fed into the Gigabit Optical Link (GOL) chip and transmitted using 8b/10b encoding off the detector to the service cavern. In the service cavern, the data is received by the HCAL Trigger/Read-out (HTR) board. The HTR board contains the Level-1 pipeline and also constructs the trigger primitives for HCAL. These trigger primitives are sent to the Regional Calorimeter trigger via Serial Link Board mezzanine cards. The HTR board receives data for 48 channels (16 data fibres) and may host up to six SLBs.

When a L1A is received by the HTR through the TTC system, it prepares a packet of data for the DAQ including a programmable number of precision read-out values and trigger primitives around the triggered bunch crossing. For normal operations, the HTR will transmit 7 time samples for each non-zero channel and a single trigger primitive for every trigger tower. These packets of data, each covering 24 channels, are transmitted by LVDS to the HCAL Data Concentrator Card (DCC). The DCC is the HCAL Front-End Driver (FED) and concentrates the data from up to 360 channels for transmission into the DAQ.

The Level-1 trigger primitives (TPG) are calculated in the HTR modules. The QIE data are linearized and converted to transverse energy with a single look up table. Two or more consecutive time samples are summed. A sum over depth is made for those towers having longitudinal segmentation. A final look up table is used to compress the data before sending the data across the trigger link to the regional calorimeter trigger. Table 5.9 summarizes the geometry of the trigger towers. The HF towers are summed in η and ϕ before being sent to the trigger.

2008 JINST 3 S08004

Table 5.9: Sizes of the HCAL trigger towers in η and ϕ.

Tower index	$|\eta_{\max}|$	Detector	Size	
			η	ϕ
1–15	$0.087 \times \eta$	HB	0.087	5°
16	1.392	HB, HE	0.087	5°
17–20	$0.087 \times \eta$	HE	0.087	5°
21	1.830	HE	0.090	5°
22	1.930	HE	0.100	5°
23	2.043	HE	0.113	5°
24	2.172	HE	0.129	5°
25	2.322	HE	0.150	5°
26	2.500	HE	0.178	5°
27	2.650	HE	0.150	5°
28	3.000	HE	0.350	5°
29	3.314	HF	0.461	20°
30	3.839	HF	0.525	20°
31	4.363	HF	0.524	20°
32	5.191	HF	0.828	20°

Timing and synchronization

The QIE integration clock is controlled by the Channel Control ASIC (CCA) which allows for fine-skewing of the integration phase of each tower relative to the machine clock. This allows each channel's integration phase to correct for differences in the time-of-flight from the interaction region as well as differences in the optical pathlength within the detector.

Figure 5.34 shows that scintillator tile signals produce relatively fast pulses such that 68% of the pulse is contained within a 25 ns window. Figure 5.35 shows the pulse shape for the forward calorimeter. The Cerenkov process and the phototubes used in the forward calorimeter are extremely fast, so the pulse in HF is only 10 ns wide. The HF is thus subject only to in-time pile-up which is important in the highly active forward region of CMS.

An additional important effect on the HCAL pulse timing in HB/HE/HO comes from the input stage of the QIE. The QIE has an amplitude-dependent impedance which implies a faster pulse shape for large signals than for small ones, as seen in figure 5.36. The amount of time slewing is dependent on the noise characteristics of the QIE, so the final QIE ASICs for the barrel and endcap were chosen to limit the timeslew to the "medium" case in exchange for somewhat increased noise. In the outer calorimeter, the noise level is a critical factor for muon identification and pile-up is much less important so the quieter "slow" characteristics were chosen for the HO QIEs.

The in-situ synchronization of HCAL is performed using the HCAL laser system. The laser system consists of a single UV laser which can illuminate an entire half-barrel of HB or a single endcap at once through a series of optical splitters. The quartz fibres which lead from the laser to the detector have been carefully controlled to equalize the optical path length to each wedge. The laser can be directed either straight onto a scintillator block connected to the HPD or into the

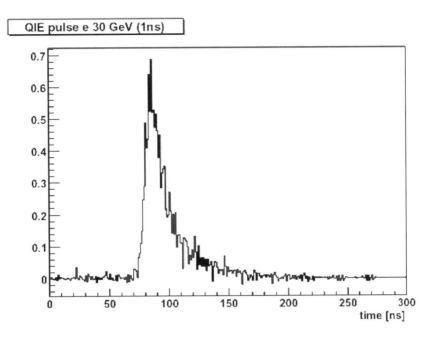

Figure 5.34: Measured single event pulse shape from the scintillator tiles, representative of HB/HE/HO pulse shapes.

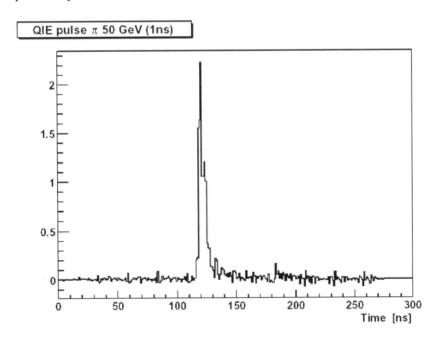

Figure 5.35: Measured pulse shape, energy collected vs. time, for HF.

wedge. Within layer 9 of each wedge is an arrangement of optical fibres which mimic the time-of-flight from the interaction region. This arrangement allows the timing of HCAL to be flattened and monitored, as has been demonstrated in test beam data taking, which verified the timing determined by the laser using the synchronized beam. In the HO and HF detectors, only the photodetector can be illuminated so the alignment will be based on construction and test beam data.

2008 JINST 3 S08004

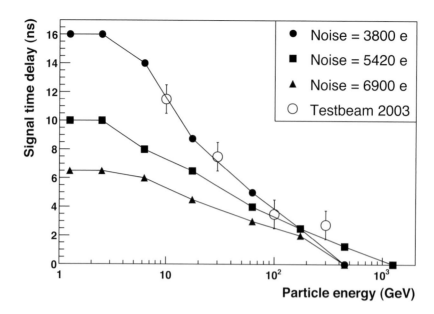

Figure 5.36: Pulse time variation as a function of signal amplitude as measured on the bench (solid points) for several input amplifier configurations compared with test beam measurements from 2003.

The channel-by-channel bunch synchronization of HCAL will be determined using a histogramming procedure in the serial link boards (SLBs) which determine the bunch synchronization using the beam structure of the LHC. The event and bunch synchronization is monitored using fast control signals originating from the TTC system which are transmitted in the data stream between the front-ends and the HTR. On a global scale, the bunch and event synchronization between the HCAL and other detector subsystems is determined using muons and other correlated physics signals.

5.6 HF luminosity monitor

The CMS luminosity measurement will be used to monitor the LHC's performance on a bunch-by-bunch basis in real time and to provide an overall normalization for physics analyses. The design goal for the real-time measurement is to determine the average luminosity with a 1% statistical accuracy with an update rate of 1 Hz. For offline analyses, the design goal is a systematic accuracy of 5%, although every reasonable effort will be made to produce a more accurate result. Both of these requirements must be met over a very large range of luminosities, extending from roughly 10^{28} cm^{-2}s^{-1} to 10^{34} cm^{-2}s^{-1}, and possibly beyond.

A number of techniques capable of providing suitable luminosity information in real time have been identified [17]. One technique employs signals from the forward hadron calorimeter (HF) while another, called the Pixel Luminosity Telescope (PLT), uses a set of purpose-built particle tracking telescopes based on single-crystal diamond pixel detectors. At the time of writing, the PLT has not been formally approved, but is under study. The methods based on signals from the HF are the ones being most vigorously pursued.

Two methods for extracting a real-time relative instantaneous luminosity with the HF have been studied. The first method is based on *zero counting* in which the average fraction of empty towers is used to infer the mean number of interactions per bunch crossing. The second method exploits the linear relationship between the average transverse energy per tower and the luminosity.

Outputs of the QIE chips used to digitize the signals from the HF PMTs on a bunch-by-bunch basis are routed to a set of 36 HCAL Trigger and Read-out (HTR) boards, each of which services 24 HF physical towers. In order to derive a luminosity signal from the HTR, an additional mezzanine board called the HF luminosity transmitter (HLX) is mounted on each of the HTR boards. The HLX taps into the raw HF data stream and collects channel occupancy and E_T-sum data and transmits them to a central collector node over standard 100-Mbps Ethernet. The HLX boards have the same form factor as the Synchronization and Link Boards (SLBs) used to interface the ECAL and HCAL readouts to the Regional Calorimeter Trigger (RCT) system.

Although all HF channels can be read by the HLX, MC studies indicate that the best linearity for occupancy histograms is obtained using just two η rings. Hence two sets of two rings are used for the occupancy histograms. Four rings are combined to form the E_T-sum histogram. The algorithm has been optimized to minimize sensitivity to pedestal drifts, gain changes and other related effects. Each of the two sets of rings sends 12 bits of data to the HLX. There are three occupancy histograms dedicated to each of the following possible states for each tower: enabled-below-threshold, over-threshold-1, over-threshold-2. In addition, a 15-bit E_T sum value is sent to the HLX and a further histogram based on all 13 HF η rings is filled for use by the LHC. As a result, the input to the HLX is used to create eight histograms: two sets of three occupancy histograms, one E_T-sum histogram, and one additional occupancy histogram.

Each histogram has 3564 bins, one for each bunch in the LHC orbit. Each occupancy-histogram bin uses two bytes, and there are four bytes per bin in the E_T sum histogram. The baseline design is to add the results from all desirable channels into a single set of histograms.

The histograms are transmitted as UDP (User Datagram Protocol) packets from the HLX cards once roughly every 0.37 s, which is safely within the 1.45 s (worst case) histogram overflow time. The Ethernet core in the HLX automatically packages the data to make optimal use of network bandwidth. Each histogram spans several Ethernet packets, the precise number depending on the type of histogram. The eight sets of histograms comprise about 70 kB of data, which is transmitted at a rate of approximately 1.6 Mbps to an Ethernet switch that aggregates the data from multiple HLX boards. The switch multi-casts the data to a pair of luminosity server nodes. One of the servers is responsible for publishing the luminosity information to various clients, such as the CMS and LHC control rooms and the Fermilab Remote Operations Center (ROC). The second server archives the data for each luminosity section (one luminosity section corresponds to 2^{20} orbits, or about 93 s). An XDAQ layer on this server makes it possible to communicate with other CMS DAQ systems.

2008 JINST 3 S08004

Chapter 6

Forward detectors

6.1 CASTOR

The CASTOR (Centauro And Strange Object Research) detector is a quartz-tungsten sampling calorimeter [120], designed for the very forward rapidity region in heavy ion and proton-proton collisions at the LHC. Its physics motivation is to complement the nucleus-nucleus physics programme [122], developed essentially in the baryon-free mid-rapidity region, and also the diffractive and low-x physics in pp collisions [123]. CASTOR will be installed at 14.38 m from the interaction point, covering the pseudorapidity range $5.2 < |\eta| < 6.6$. Figure 6.1 shows the location of CASTOR in the CMS forward region. The calorimeter will be constructed in two halves surrounding the beam pipe when closed, as shown in figure 6.2. The calorimeter and its readout are designed in such a way as to permit the observation of the cascade development of the impinging particles as they traverse the calorimeter. The typical total and electromagnetic energies in the CASTOR acceptance range (about 180 TeV and 50 TeV, respectively, according to HIJING [121] Pb-Pb simulations at 5.5 TeV) can be measured with a resolution better than $\approx 1\%$.

The main advantages of quartz calorimeters are radiation hardness, fast response and compact detector dimensions [124], making them suitable for the experimental conditions encountered in the very forward region at the LHC. The typical visible transverse sizes of hadronic and electromagnetic showers in quartz calorimeters are 5–10 cm and about 10 mm respectively (for 95% signal containement), i.e. are a factor 3 to 4 times narrower than those in "standard" (scintillation) calorimeters [124]. A detailed description of the operation principle (including optimal geometrical specifications of the quartz and tungsten plates, and performances of light-guides, reflectors and photodetectors) can be found in references [125, 126].

Tungsten-Quartz plates

The CASTOR detector is a Cerenkov-based calorimeter, similar in concept to the HF. It is constructed from layers of tungsten (W) plates (alloy density ≈ 18.5 g/cm^3) as absorber and fused silica quartz (Q) plates as active medium. For the electromagnetic (EM) section, the W plates have a thickness of 5.0 mm and the Q plates 2.0 mm. For the hadronic (HAD) section, the W and Q plates have thicknesses of 10.0 mm and 4.0 mm, respectively. The W/Q plates are inclined 45° with respect to the direction of the impinging particles, in order to maximize the Cerenkov light

2008 JINST 3 S08004

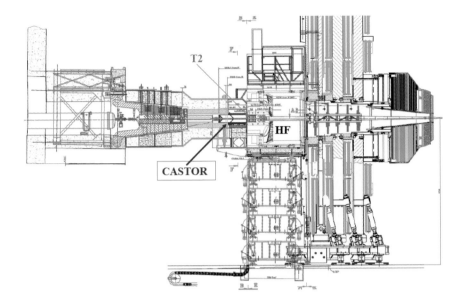

Figure 6.1: Location of CASTOR in the CMS forward region.

output in the quartz. The combination of one W and one Q plate is called a sampling unit (SU). Figure 6.3 shows the complicated geometry of the W/Q plates, due to their 45° inclination.

In the EM section, each sampling unit corresponds to 2.01 X_0 (0.077 λ_I). Each readout unit (RU) consists of 5 SUs and is 10.05 X_0 (0.385 λ_I) deep. The EM section is divided in two successive RUs and has a total of 20.1 X_0 (0.77 λ_I). In the hadronic section, a sampling unit corresponds to 0.154 λ_I. Each readout unit consists of 5 SUs and is 0.77 λ_I deep. The HAD section has 12 RUs, corresponding to 9.24 λ_I. In total, the calorimeter has 10 λ_I. The total number of channels is 224.

Light-guides and photodetectors

The Cerenkov light, produced by the passage of relativistic charged particles through the quartz medium, is collected in sections (RUs) along the length of the calorimeters and focused by air-core light guides onto the photomultiplier (PMT), as shown in figure 6.3. The inside surfaces of the light guides are covered with Dupont [AlO+ SiO_2+TiO_2] reflective foil. The light guide is made out of a 0.8 mm stainless steel sheet. Each light guide subtends 5 SUs in both the EM and HAD sections. The PMT is located in the aluminium housing on the top. Two types of PMTs are currently under consideration: (i) a Hamamatsu R7899 PMT, and (ii) a radiation-hard multi-mesh, small-size PMT FEU-187 produced by Research Institute Electron (RIE, St. Petersburg), with cathode area ≈2 cm^2. Both PMTs allow the muon MIP peak to be separated from the pedestal, an important feature for calibration purposes.

Beam tests results

The energy linearity and resolution as well as the spatial resolution of two CASTOR prototypes have been studied at CERN/SPS tests in 2003 [125] and 2004 [126] (as well as in tests end-of-summer 2007, for the final prototype). The response of the calorimeter to electromagnetic and

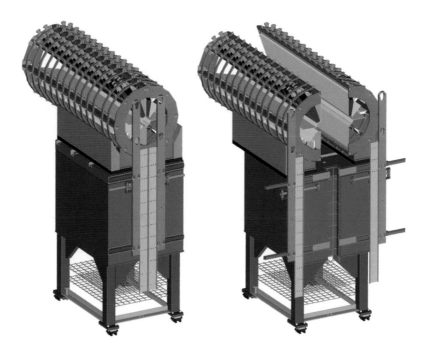

Figure 6.2: CASTOR calorimeter and support.

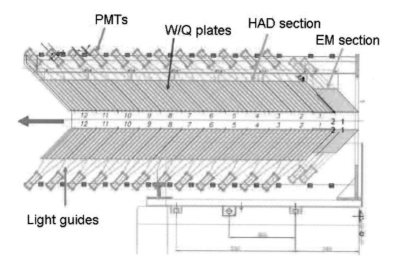

Figure 6.3: Details of the components and geometry of the CASTOR calorimeter.

hadronic showers has been analysed with $E = 20$–$200\,\mathrm{GeV}$ electrons, $E = 20$–$350\,\mathrm{GeV}$ pions, and $E = 50$, $150\,\mathrm{GeV}$ muons. Good energy linearity for electrons and pions in the full range tested is observed. For the EM section, the constant term of the energy resolution, that limits performance at high energies, is less than 1%, whereas the stochastic term is $\approx 50\%$. The measured spatial resolution of the electron (pion) showers is $\sigma_{\mathrm{EM(HAD)}} = 1.7$ (6.4) mm.

2008 JINST 3 S08004

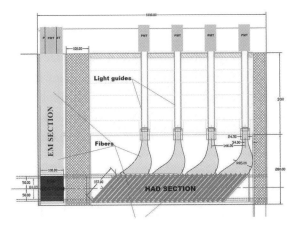 

Figure 6.4: The side view of the ZDC showing the EM and HAD sections.

Figure 6.5: Photograph of the ZDC HAD section.

6.2 Zero degree calorimeter (ZDC)

A set of two zero degree calorimeters [127, 128], with pseudorapidity coverage of $|\eta| \geq 8.3$ for neutral particles, are designed to complement the CMS very forward region, especially for heavy ion and pp diffractive studies. Each ZDC has two independent parts: the electromagnetic (EM) and hadronic (HAD) sections. Two identical ZDCs will be located between the two LHC beam pipes at ≈ 140 m on each side of the CMS interaction region at the detector slot of 1 m length, 96 mm width and 607 mm height inside the neutral particle absorber TAN [129]. The TAN is located in front of the D2 separation dipole. It was designed to protect magnets and detectors against debris generated in the pp collisions, and against beam halo and beam losses. During heavy ion running the combined (EM + HAD) calorimeter should allow the reconstruction of the energy of 2.75 TeV spectator neutrons with a resolution of 10–15%. Sampling calorimeters using tungsten and quartz fibers have been chosen for the detection of the energy in the ZDCs with a design similar to HF and CASTOR. The quartz-quartz fibers [127] can withstand up to 30 GRad with only a few percent loss in transparency in the wavelength range 300–425 nm. During the low-luminosity pp (10^{33} cm^{-2}s^{-1}) and design-luminosity Pb-Pb (10^{27} cm^{-2}s^{-1}) runs, the expected average absorbed radiation doses is about 180 MGy and 300 kGy, respectively, per data-taking year.

Figure 6.4 shows a side view of the ZDC with the EM section in front and the HAD section behind. A photo of the HAD section is shown in figure 6.5. The total depth of the combined system is ≈ 7.5 hadronic interaction lengths (λ_I). The configuration includes 9 mm Cu plates in the front and back of each section. For the TAN's final detector configuration an LHC real-time luminosity monitor (BRAN, Beam RAte of Neutrals [130]) will be mounted in the 120 mm space between the ZDC's calorimetric sections. The HAD section consists of 24 layers of 15.5 mm thick tungsten plates and 24 layers of 0.7 mm diameter quartz fibers (6.5 λ_I). The tungsten plates are tilted by 45° to optimize Cerenkov-light output. The EM section is made of 33 layers of 2-mm-thick tungsten plates and 33 layers of 0.7-mm-diameter quartz fibers (19 X_0). The tungsten plates are oriented vertically. The fibers are laid in ribbons. The hadronic section of each ZDC requires 24 fiber ribbons. After exiting the tungsten plates the fibers from 6 individual ribbons are grouped together to form a readout bundle. This bundle is compressed and glued with epoxy into a tube. From there,

2008 JINST 3 S08004

an optical air-core light guide will carry the light through radiation shielding to the photomultiplier tube. The full hadronic section will consist of four identical towers divided in the longitudinal direction. For the electromagnetic section, fibers from all 33 fiber ribbons will be divided in the horizontal direction into five identical fiber bundles. These 5 bundles will form five horizontal towers and each fiber bundle will be mounted with a 0.5 mm air gap from the photocathode of a phototube. The EM and HAD sections will be instrumented with the same type of phototube as the HF: Hamamatsu R7525 phototubes with a bi-alkali photocathode, resulting in an average quantum efficiency for Cerenkov light of about 10%.

There are a total of 18 readout channels for the two ZDCs. The signals from the ZDCs are transmitted through a long (210 m) coaxial cable to the front-end HCAL VME crates in the underground counting room (USC55). The signal from each channel will be split, with 90% going to the QIE (Charge Integrator and Encoder) while 10% will be used for making trigger signals. An analog sum, proportional to the total energy deposition in each detector, will provide the basic Level 1 trigger in the heavy-ion running mode: the coincidence of (neutron) signals from both sides of the interaction point is sensitive to most of the nuclear and electromagnetic cross section. A left-right timing coincidence will also be used as a fast vertex trigger, to suppress beam-gas events in the heavy ion runs. Information from scalers will be used for tuning the interaction of beams and for defining the real-time luminosity. Finally it may be possible to improve the overall energy resolution of the system by looking at the correlation between the ZDC and the BRAN detector, which sits between the electromagnetic and hadronic sections, near the shower maximum.

The response of the ZDC EM and HAD sections has been studied in beam tests at the CERN/SPS in 2006 [131] and 2007. The calorimeter is found to be linear within 2% in the range from 20 GeV to 100 GeV. The energy resolution obtained for the different positron energies can be parametrized as

$$\left(\frac{\sigma}{E}\right)^2 = \left(\frac{70\%}{\sqrt{E}}\right)^2 + (8\%)^2 \tag{6.1}$$

where E is in GeV. Positive pions with energies of 150 GeV and 300 GeV were used to measure the response of the combined EM+HAD system. The pion energy resolution, obtained by a Landau fit, can be parametrized as

$$\frac{\sigma}{E} = \frac{138\%}{\sqrt{E}} + 13\% \tag{6.2}$$

where E, again, is in GeV. The width of EM showers is $\approx$5 mm. Such a good position resolution will allow measurement of the beam crossing angle with a resolution of $\approx$10 mrad.

The performance of both the left and right ZDCs has been studied with electron, pion and muon beams in 2007. Figure 6.6 shows online plots for positrons entering the electromagnetic section of one calorimeter.

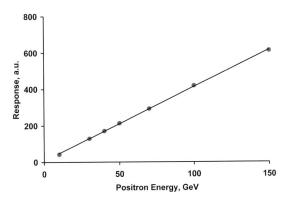

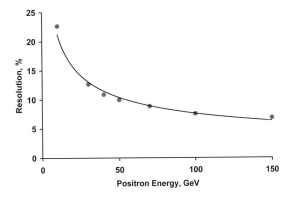

Figure 6.6: Online results for positrons from the 2007 test beam. The top panel shows the response linearity, while the bottom panel gives the energy resolution as a function of the incoming positron beam energy.

2008 JINST 3 S08004

Chapter 7

The muon system

Muon detection is a powerful tool for recognizing signatures of interesting processes over the very high background rate expected at the LHC with full luminosity. For example, the predicted decay of the Standard Model Higgs boson into ZZ or ZZ*, which in turn decay into 4 leptons, has been called "gold plated" for the case in which all the leptons are muons. Besides the relative ease in detecting muons, the best 4-particle mass resolution can be achieved if all the leptons are muons because they are less affected than electrons by radiative losses in the tracker material. This example, and others from SUSY models, emphasize the discovery potential of muon final states and the necessity for wide angular coverage for muon detection.

Therefore, as is implied by the experiment's middle name, the detection of muons is of central importance to CMS: precise and robust muon measurement was a central theme from its earliest design stages. The muon system has 3 functions: muon identification, momentum measurement, and triggering. Good muon momentum resolution and trigger capability are enabled by the high-field solenoidal magnet and its flux-return yoke. The latter also serves as a hadron absorber for the identification of muons. The material thickness crossed by muons, as a function of pseudorapidity, is shown in figure 7.1.

The CMS muon system is designed to have the capability of reconstructing the momentum and charge of muons over the the entire kinematic range of the LHC. CMS uses 3 types of gaseous particle detectors for muon identification [132]. Due to the shape of the solenoid magnet, the muon system was naturally driven to have a cylindrical, barrel section and 2 planar endcap regions. Because the muon system consists of about 25 000 m^2 of detection planes, the muon chambers had to be inexpensive, reliable, and robust.

In the barrel region, where the neutron-induced background is small, the muon rate is low, and the 4-T magnetic field is uniform and mostly contained in the steel yoke, drift chambers with standard rectangular drift cells are used. The barrel drift tube (DT) chambers cover the pseudorapidity region $|\eta| < 1.2$ and are organized into 4 stations interspersed among the layers of the flux return plates. The first 3 stations each contain 8 chambers, in 2 groups of 4, which measure the muon coordinate in the r-ϕ bending plane, and 4 chambers which provide a measurement in the z direction, along the beam line. The fourth station does not contain the z-measuring planes. The 2 sets of 4 chambers in each station are separated as much as possible to achieve the best angular resolution. The drift cells of each chamber are offset by a half-cell width with respect to their

2008 JINST 3 S08004

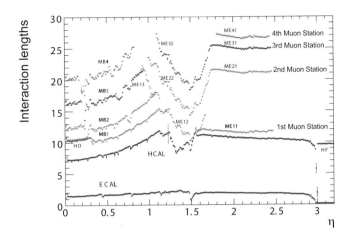

Figure 7.1: Material thickness in interaction lengths at various depths, as a function of pseudora-pidity.

neighbor to eliminate dead spots in the efficiency. This arrangement also provides a convenient way to measure the muon time with excellent time resolution, using simple meantimer circuits, for efficient, standalone bunch crossing identification. The number of chambers in each station and their orientation were chosen to provide good efficiency for linking together muon hits from different stations into a single muon track and for rejecting background hits.

In the 2 endcap regions of CMS, where the muon rates and background levels are high and the magnetic field is large and non-uniform, the muon system uses cathode strip chambers (CSC). With their fast response time, fine segmentation, and radiation resistance, the CSCs identify muons between $|\eta|$ values of 0.9 and 2.4. There are 4 stations of CSCs in each endcap, with chambers positioned perpendicular to the beam line and interspersed between the flux return plates. The cathode strips of each chamber run radially outward and provide a precision measurement in the r-ϕ bending plane. The anode wires run approximately perpendicular to the strips and are also read out in order to provide measurements of η and the beam-crossing time of a muon. Each 6-layer CSC provides robust pattern recognition for rejection of non-muon backgrounds and efficient matching of hits to those in other stations and to the CMS inner tracker.

Because the muon detector elements cover the full pseudorapidity interval $|\eta| < 2.4$ with no acceptance gaps, muon identification is ensured over the range corresponding to $10° < \theta < 170°$. Offline reconstruction efficiency of simulated single-muon samples (figure 7.2) is typically 95–99% except in the regions around $|\eta| = 0.25$ and 0.8 (the regions between 2 DT wheels) and $|\eta| = 1.2$ (the transition region between the DT and CSC systems), where the efficiency drops. Negligible punchthrough reaches the system due to the amount of material in front of the muon system, which exceeds 16 interaction lengths [132].

Due to multiple-scattering in the detector material before the first muon station, the offline muon momentum resolution of the standalone muon system is about 9% for small values of η and p for transverse momenta up to 200 GeV [17]. At 1 TeV the standalone momentum resolution varies between 15% and 40%, depending on $|\eta|$. A global momentum fit using also the inner tracker

2008 JINST 3 S08004

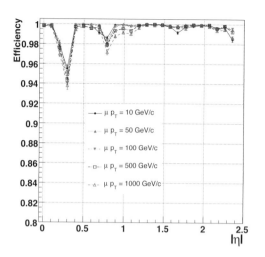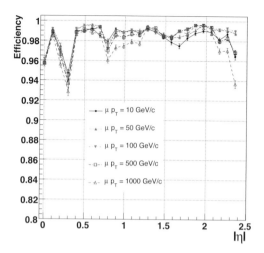

Figure 7.2: Muon reconstruction efficiency as a function of pseudorapidity for selected values of p_T. Left panel: standalone reconstruction (using only hits from the muon system with a vertex constraint). Right panel: global reconstruction (using hits from both the muon system and the tracker).

improves the momentum resolution by an order of magnitude at low momenta. At high momenta (1 TeV) both detector parts together yield a momentum resolution of about 5% (figure 1.2). Note that the muon system and the inner tracker provide independent muon momentum measurements; this redundancy enhances fault finding and permits cross-checking between the systems.

A crucial characteristic of the DT and CSC subsystems is that they can each trigger on the p_T of muons with good efficiency and high background rejection, independent of the rest of the detector. The Level-1 trigger p_T resolution is about 15% in the barrel and 25% in the endcap.

Because of the uncertainty in the eventual background rates and in the ability of the muon system to measure the correct beam-crossing time when the LHC reaches full luminosity, a complementary, dedicated trigger system consisting of resistive plate chambers (RPC) was added in both the barrel and endcap regions. The RPCs provide a fast, independent, and highly-segmented trigger with a sharp p_T threshold over a large portion of the rapidity range ($|\eta| < 1.6$) of the muon system. The RPCs are double-gap chambers, operated in avalanche mode to ensure good operation at high rates. They produce a fast response, with good time resolution but coarser position resolution than the DTs or CSCs. They also help to resolve ambiguities in attempting to make tracks from multiple hits in a chamber.

A total of 6 layers of RPCs are embedded in the barrel muon system, 2 in each of the first 2 stations, and 1 in each of the last 2 stations. The redundancy in the first 2 stations allows the trigger algorithm to work even for low-p_T tracks that may stop before reaching the outer 2 stations. In the endcap region, there is a plane of RPCs in each of the first 3 stations in order for the trigger to use the coincidences between stations to reduce background, to improve the time resolution for bunch crossing identification, and to achieve a good p_T resolution.

Finally, a sophisticated alignment system measures the positions of the muon detectors with respect to each other and to the inner tracker, in order to optimize the muon momentum resolution.

2008 JINST 3 S08004

7.1 Drift tube system

7.1.1 General description

The CMS barrel muon detector consists of 4 stations forming concentric cylinders around the beam line: the 3 inner cylinders have 60 drift chambers each and the outer cylinder has 70. There are about 172 000 sensitive wires. It is possible to use drift chambers as the tracking detectors for the barrel muon system because of the low expected rate and the relatively low strength of the local magnetic field.

The wire length, around 2.4 m in the chambers measured in an r-ϕ projection, is constrained by the longitudinal segmentation of the iron barrel yoke. The transverse dimension of the drift cell, i.e., the maximum path and time of drift, was chosen to be 21 mm (corresponding to a drift time of 380 ns in a gas mixture of 85% Ar + 15% CO_2). This value is small enough to produce a negligible occupancy and to avoid the need for multi-hit electronics, yet the cell is large enough to limit the number of active channels to an affordable value. A tube was chosen as the basic drift unit to obtain protection against damage from a broken wire and to partially decouple contiguous cells from the electromagnetic debris accompanying the muon itself.

The amount of iron in the return yoke was dictated by the decision to have a large and intense solenoidal magnetic field at the core of CMS. Two detector layers, one inside the yoke and the other outside, would be insufficient for reliable identification and measurement of a muon in CMS. Therefore, 2 additional layers are embedded within the yoke iron (figure 7.3). In each of the 12 sectors of the yoke there are 4 muon chambers per wheel, labeled MB1, MB2, MB3, and MB4. The yoke-iron supports that are between the chambers of a station generate 12 unavoidable dead zones in the ϕ coverage, although the supports are placed so as not to overlap in ϕ.

A drift-tube (DT) chamber is made of 3 (or 2) superlayers (SL, see figure 7.4), each made of 4 layers of rectangular drift cells staggered by half a cell. The SL is the smallest independent unit of the design.

The wires in the 2 outer SLs are parallel to the beam line and provide a track measurement in the magnetic bending plane (r-ϕ). In the inner SL, the wires are orthogonal to the beam line and measure the z position along the beam. This third, z-measuring, SL is not present in the fourth station, which therefore measures only the ϕ coordinate. A muon coming from the interaction point first encounters a ϕ-measuring SL, passes through the honeycomb plate, then crosses the z-measuring SL and the second ϕ-measuring SL. In this scenario, there still exist limited regions of η in which the combined effect of the ϕ and z discontinuities limits to only 2 (out of 4), the number of stations crossed by a muon.

At high momenta (≥ 40 GeV), the probability of electromagnetic cascades accompanying the parent muon becomes relevant. A reliable way to cope with this effect in the regions where only 2 stations are available is to have a good tracking efficiency in each station even in the presence of electromagnetic debris. Redundancy is also needed to cope with the uncorrelated background hits generated by neutrons and photons whose rate is much larger than that from prompt muons. Redundancy is obtained by having several layers of separated drift cells per station. The separation, i.e., the thickness of the tube walls, should be large enough to decouple the basic units against low-energy electrons. The relatively thick wall of the DTs, 1.5 mm, gives an effective decoupling among

2008 JINST 3 S08004

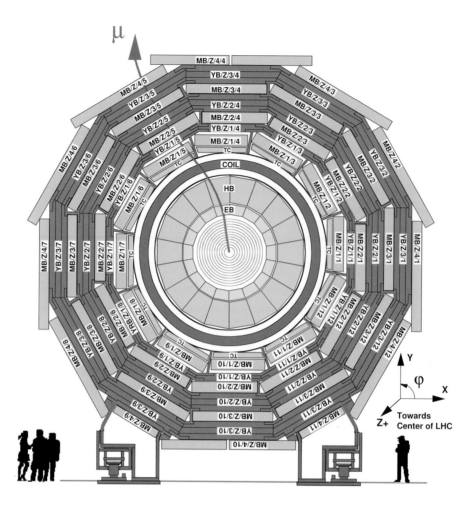

Figure 7.3: Layout of the CMS barrel muon DT chambers in one of the 5 wheels. The chambers in each wheel are identical with the exception of wheels −1 and +1 where the presence of cryogenic chimneys for the magnet shortens the chambers in 2 sectors. Note that in sectors 4 (top) and 10 (bottom) the MB4 chambers are cut in half to simplify the mechanical assembly and the global chamber layout.

the several layers of tubes inside the same station. With this design, the efficiency to reconstruct a high p_T muon track with a momentum measurement delivered by the barrel muon system alone is better than 95% in the pseudorapidity range covered by 4 stations, i.e., $\eta < 0.8$. The constraints of mechanical stability, limited space, and the requirement of redundancy led to the choice of a tube cross section of $13 \times 42 \ mm^2$.

The many layers of heavy tubes require a robust and light mechanical structure to avoid significant deformations due to gravity in the chambers, especially in those that lie nearly horizontal. The chosen structure is basically frameless and for lightness and rigidity uses an aluminium honeycomb plate that separates the outer superlayer(s) from the inner one (figure 7.4). The SLs are glued to the outer faces of the honeycomb. In this design, the honeycomb serves as a very light spacer,

2008 JINST 3 S08004

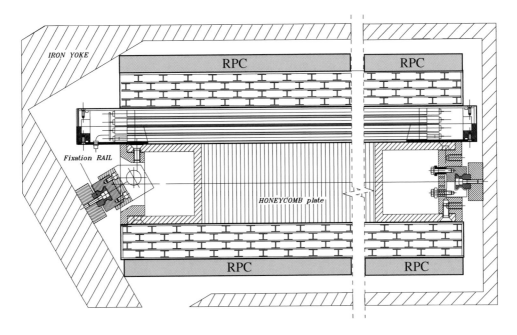

Figure 7.4: A DT chamber in position inside the iron yoke; the view is in the (r-φ) plane. One can see the 2 SLs with wires along the beam direction and the other perpendicular to it. In between is a honeycomb plate with supports attached to the iron yoke. Not shown are the RPCs, which are attached to the DT chambers via support plates glued to the bottom and/or top faces, depending on chamber type.

with rigidity provided by the outer planes of tubes. A thick spacer also helps to improve angular resolution within a station. Table 7.1 provides a summary of the general DT chamber parameters.

One SL, that is, a group of 4 consecutive layers of thin tubes staggered by half a tube, gives excellent time-tagging capability, with a time resolution of a few nanoseconds. This capability provides local, stand-alone, and efficient bunch crossing identification. The time tagging is delayed by a constant amount of time equal to the maximum possible drift-time, which is determined by the size of the tube, the electrical field, and the gas mixture. Within the angular range of interest, the time resolution was shown to be largely independent of the track angle, but this requires the cell optics to maintain a linear relationship between the distance from the wire of the crossing track and the drift-time of the electrons along the entire drift path. bunch crossing tagging is performed independently in each of the 3 SLs by fast pattern-recognition circuitry. Together with the bunch crossing assignment, this circuit delivers the position of the centre of gravity of the track segment and its angle in the SL reference system with precisions of 1.5 mm and 20 mrad, respectively. This information is used by the first-level muon trigger for the time and transverse momentum assignment.

The goal of the mechanical precision of the construction of a chamber was to achieve a global resolution in r-φ of 100 μm. This figure makes the precision of the MB1 chamber (the innermost layer) comparable to the multiple scattering contribution up to $p_T = 200$ GeV. The 100-μm target chamber resolution is achieved by the 8 track points measured in the two φ SLs, since

2008 JINST 3 S08004

Table 7.1: Chambers of the CMS DT system. Notation: MB/wheel/station/sector. W stands for all 5 wheels (numbered –2, –1, 0, 1, and 2) and S means any sector (1 to 12, see figure 7.3). The SLs of type $\Phi(\Theta)$ measure the $\phi(z)$ coordinate in the CMS coordinate system.

chamber type	No. of chambers	No. of SL Φ	No. of SL Θ	No. of ch. SL Φ	No. of ch. SL Θ	Wire length Φ (mm)	Wire length Θ (mm)	Sum of ch.
MB/W/1/S	58	2	1	196	228	2379	2038	35960
MB/1/1/4	1	2	1	196	190	1989	2038	582
MB/-1/1/3	1	2	1	196	190	1989	2038	582
MB/W/2/S	58	2	1	238	228	2379	2501	40832
MB/1/2/4	1	2	1	238	190	1989	2501	666
MB/-1/2/3	1	2	1	238	190	1989	2501	666
MB/W/3/S	58	2	1	286	228	2379	3021	46400
MB/1/3/4	1	2	1	286	190	1989	3021	762
MB/-1/3/3	1	2	1	286	190	1989	3021	762
MB/W/4/S	29	2	0	382	0	2379	0	22156
MB/-1/4/3	1	2	0	382	0	1989	0	764
MB/W/4/4	8	2	0	286	0	2379	0	4576
MB/1/4/4	2	2	0	286	0	1989	0	1144
MB/W/4/8,12	10	2	0	372	0	2379	0	7440
MB/W/4/9,11	10	2	0	190	0	2379	0	3800
MB/W/4/10	10	2	0	238	0	2379	0	4760
total	250							171852

the single wire resolution is better than 250 μm. To avoid corrections to the primary TDC data (section 7.1.3), the deviation from linearity of the space-time relation in each drift cell must be less than 100–150 μm. This figure matches well with the requirements of linearity for the bunch crossing (section 7.1.3) identifier. The cell design includes 5 electrodes, 1 anode wire, 2 field shaping strips, and 2 cathode strips (figure 7.5 and section 7.1.2). The requirements of 250-μm resolution and 150-μm nonlinearity can be obtained by operating the tubes at atmospheric pressure with an Ar/CO$_2$ gas mixture and by keeping the CO$_2$ concentration in the 10–20% range. The multi-electrode design also ensures this performance in the presence of the stray magnetic field present in some regions of the chambers. It is worth noting that to reach this local performance in a single tube, the precision requirement on the position of the field-shaping electrodes, including the wires, is about 300 μm, which is considerably less demanding than the 100 μm required for the mechanical construction.

7.1.2 Technical design

Drift cell

Figure 7.5 shows the drift lines in a cell. The anode is a 50-μm-diameter gold-plated stainless-steel wire. The field electrode is made of a 16-mm-wide, 50-μm thick aluminium tape, glued on a 100-μm thick, 23-mm-wide mylar tape that insulates the electrode with respect to the aluminium plate set to ground. Both the conductive and insulating ribbons are self-adhesive with a pressure-activated glue. Field electrodes are positioned at the top and bottom of the drift cell.   Cathodes

2008 JINST 3 S08004

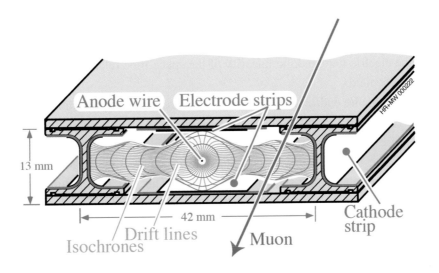

Figure 7.5: Sketch of a cell showing drift lines and isochrones. The plates at the top and bottom of the cell are at ground potential. The voltages applied to the electrodes are +3600V for wires, +1800V for strips, and −1200V for cathodes.

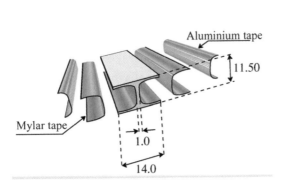

Figure 7.6: Exploded view of the cathode electrodes, glued on the I-beams.

Figure 7.7: Exploded view of the end part of the drift cells showing the different end-plugs and spring contacts for high voltage connections.

are placed on both sides of the I-beams (figure 7.6) following a technique similar to that used for the strip electrodes on the aluminium plates. A cathode consists of a 50-μm-thick, 11.5-mm-wide aluminium tape insulated from the I-beam by 19-mm-wide, 100-μm-thick mylar tape. This design allows for at least 3.5 mm separation of the electrode from the sides of the grounded I-beam. At the extremities the mylar tape is cut flush with respect to the I-beam ends while the aluminium tape is recessed by 5 mm. Special tools were designed and built to glue the electrode strips to both the plates and the I-beams. The only difference between the tapes used for the electrode strips and the

2008 JINST 3 S08004

ones just described is the width: the mylar tape used for the electrode strips is 23-mm wide and the aluminium tape is 16-mm wide. These strips are set to a positive voltage and help to improve the shaping of the electric field and the linearity of the space-time relation, most noticeably in the presence of magnetic fields.

The cathode and wire end-plugs were designed to protect against discharges from the border at the end of the cathode strips and to house the wire holder, which is crucial for the wire position precision. The wire holders protrude inside the cell providing 12 mm of additional protection around the wire. The I-beam and wire end-plug pieces, as well as the springs connecting the electrodes to the high voltage, are shown in figure 7.7. The Ar-CO_2 mixture and the drift-cell optics described above provide a linear relationship between time and drift path. This is an essential requirement for the use of the chamber as a first-level trigger device [133]. A calculation of the drift velocity using GARFIELD [134] showed that drift velocity saturation occurs between 1 and 2 kV/cm (figure 7.8). This may be compared to the the drift velocity as measured with the Drift Velocity Chamber (VdC) (figure 7.9).

The drift cells will operate at a gas gain of 10^5, allowing them to work within an efficiency plateau with a wide threshold range, which is convenient for the operation of large chambers in the environment expected at CMS. A computation of equipotential lines [136] (figure 7.10) is useful for better understanding of the role of each electrode. The position of the 0 V equipotential in the region between the central strips and the cathodes is mainly determined by the size of the electrodes and not by their voltage values. The gas gain is mainly determined by the voltage drop from the wire to the nearest electrode, the strips. The wire/strip voltage difference must be kept between 1.75 and 1.85 kV to achieve a gain not far from the expected value of 10^5. Under the rough assumption of a uniform drift field of 1.5 kV/cm, the distances between the various electrodes imply that the strips should be set to a voltage larger than or equal to 1.7 kV and the cathodes to around −1 kV. As described below, during the chamber commissioning in laboratories and at CERN (with B=0), satisfactory performance was obtained with the voltages of cathodes, strips, and wires set to −1.2, +1.8, and +3.6 kV, respectively.

Chamber mechanics and services

A chamber is assembled by gluing 3 (or 2) SLs to an aluminium honeycomb plate to ensure the required stiffness. Each SL is made of 5 aluminium sheets, 1.5-mm thick, separated by 11.5-mm-high, 1-mm-thick aluminium I-beams, as described in section 7.1.2. The cell pitch is 42 mm, while the layer pitch is 13 mm. For the construction of the SLs, a full layer of cells is built at the same time by gluing together 2 aluminium plates separated by an array of parallel aluminium I-beams. The pitch and height of an I-beam determine the larger and smaller dimensions of a cell, respectively. An SL has an independent gas and electronics enclosure. Each SL is assembled and tested individually before being glued to the honeycomb plate and/or to the other SL to form a chamber.

HV connections to the cells and the front-end electronics are located at opposite ends of the wires. The HV is fed into each SL via two 52-pin custom connectors and distributed to the drift cells via printed-circuit HV boards (HVB). Each HVB is mounted along the edge of the aluminium plate separating 2 layers of drift cells and serves the 8 cells above and the 8 cells below it. One

2008 JINST 3 S08004

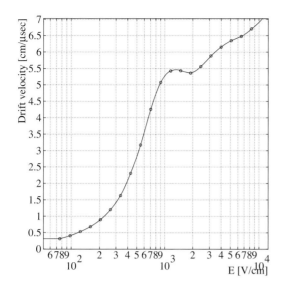 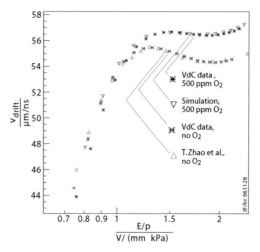

Figure 7.8: Calculated drift velocity (in cm/μs) as a function of the electric field (in V/cm) for a gas mixture Ar/CO_2 (85%/15%). The values obtained are very similar for the 2 different environment pressures, 973 and 1027 hPa.

Figure 7.9: Measured and calculated drift velocities (in μm/ns) as functions of electric field and gas pressure for a pure gas mixture Ar/CO_2 (85%/15%) and for a gas mixture with air impurities corresponding to 500-ppm O_2. The measurements were obtained with the VdC, a dedicated reference drift chamber that will be used for drift-velocity monitoring during CMS running. For comparison, results of measurements from [135] for a pure gas mixture, and a simulation with Magboltz [134] for a mixture with impurities are also shown.

HV channel is dedicated to each group of 8 anode wires, while for the other 2 voltages there is 1 HV channel for 16 cells in the same layer. The strip and the cathode voltages can be daisy chained from an HVB to the next one. On the HVB there is 1 capacitor for filtering for each group. As a current limiter, a 50-MΩ ceramic resistor is used in series. There is 1 resistor for each anode and 1 for each group of 4 strips or cathodes. Due to the restricted space as required to minimise dead space, the size of the HVB is only about 307×37 mm^2 and special care had to be taken to maximise the distance between the printed HV lines and to avoid any embedded gas pocket within the HVB volume.

The gas enclosures are different: on the HV side they contain the HV distribution system and gas connector, whereas on the front-end sides there are the HV decoupling capacitors, the front-end circuitry, the pulse distribution system, the gas distribution, and the necessary cooling for the electronics. Inside the SL, gas is distributed as a "shower", with each cell being fed through a small-diameter (1 mm^2) outlet hole to guarantee that the same amount of gas is circulated to each

2008 JINST 3 S08004

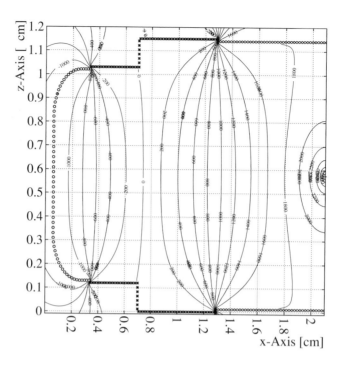

Figure 7.10: Equipotential lines in half of a drift cell. The anode wire is on the right side. The lines are labeled with the potentials in volts (the *x*-axis is perpendicular to the wires on the wire plane, while the *z*-axis is orthogonal to the wire plane).

channel. The distance between the position where the wire enters the end plug and the outer face of the gas enclosure, which determines the SL dead area, corresponds to 60 mm on both the HV and the front-end side (corresponding to ≈10% dead space).

It is very important that the individual SLs of the DT chambers are gas tight because contamination by nitrogen (from air) changes the drift velocity by a sizeable amount, while oxygen reduces the signal efficiency, when its contamination exceeds 2000 ppm. Contamination by air including 1000 ppm of O_2 changes the maximum drift time by about 2% with respect to no contamination, with a sizeable effect on the trigger performance of the detector. In the DT chambers, the gas tightness of the SLs is obtained by gluing profiles to the outer aluminium skins. Along 2 sides of the SL, C-shaped profiles are used and the ends of these profiles are glued to reference blocks (figure 7.11), forming the corners of the SL box. The front and back of the box have L-shaped profiles glued along the plate border to form an open frame, which is then closed with removable long cover plates that contain all necessary gas connectors, HV connectors, and signal outputs, equipped with O-rings that seal the structure. A 3-dimensional computer model of the gas enclosure for one SL, where the outer aluminium plates have been removed to expose all details of the gas enclosure, is shown in figure 7.12. With this type of gas enclosure we can obtain a level of oxygen contamination of 10–20 ppm, downstream of the 3 SLs flushed in parallel with about 1 volume change per day.

During SL assembly, before the fifth aluminium plate is glued closing the structure, reference blocks are glued such that their positions with respect to the wires can be measured precisely. Thus, when the chamber is completed, the wire positions may be determined by measuring the reference

2008 JINST 3 S08004

Figure 7.11: Corner blocks of an SL. These pieces also carry the reference marks with respect to which the wire positions are measured.

Figure 7.12: A 3-dimensional computer model of the gas enclosure of the SLs.

marks on the blocks. Pressure and temperature monitoring probes, ground straps that connect all the aluminium planes to form a unique ground reference, and a Faraday cage for the signals, front-end electronics, and HV distribution complete the equipment that is in the gas enclosures of each SL.

Each SL is fully independent with respect to gas tightness, HV, and front-end electronics; hence an SL can be fully tested before it is glued to form a DT chamber. SLs are glued to a honeycomb panel (figure 7.4) that sustains and gives rigidity to the chamber and provides the fixation points from which it is suspended in the CMS barrel steel yoke (two Φ-type SLs and one Θ-type SL in the case of layers 1, 2, and 3; and two Φ-type SLs for layer 4). The panel thickness varies from 125 mm for the first three stations, to 178 mm for the fourth station. It is delivered with the correct dimensions and equipped with the C-shaped profiles at the periphery that are used for the supports and for part of the electronics.

The space for the chamber supports and attachments, the passages for alignment, and the local read-out and trigger electronics is provided by a channel running around the border of the honeycomb plate. The channel is approximately as wide and deep as the honeycomb plate thickness. The 2 channels parallel to the beam line and to the yoke steel supports house the kinematic fixations to the yoke supports themselves, and the longitudinal alignment passages. One of the 2 remaining sides houses the read-out and trigger electronics that collect the full chamber information (*minicrates*). To ease chamber handling, all services are connected on the same side of the chamber. All the general services for the chambers are located around each barrel wheel on the 4 balconies along the walls of the CMS cavern where there is space for the racks and crates. Each wheel is thus an independent, large subsystem.

2008 JINST 3 S08004

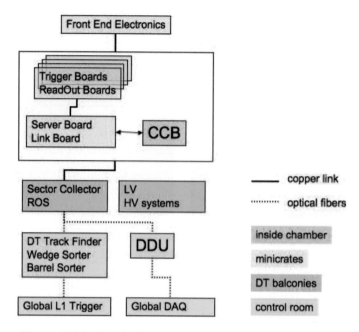

Figure 7.13: Block diagram of the DT electronic system.

7.1.3 Electronics

The DT electronics is a complex, heavily integrated system, which includes L1 trigger logic, read-out data handling, and service electronics, such as the LV and HV systems. A description of the electronic system layout together with the functions associated to each sub-task is shown in figure 7.13 and briefly summarized, whereas detailed information will be described in the following sections.

Front-end electronics and HV distribution are physically embedded in the chamber gas volume. Amplified and shaped signals are directly fed to the *minicrates*. A minicrate, as described previously, is an aluminium structure attached to the honeycomb of the drift tube chambers that houses both the first level of the read-out and of the trigger electronics. The trigger boards located in the minicrates are the Trigger Boards (TRB) and the Server Boards (SB), as described in detail in section 8.2. In each TRB are located the Bunch Crossing and Track Identifier (BTI), which provides independent segments from each chamber SL, and the Track Correlator (TRACO), which correlates ϕ segments in the same chamber by requiring a spatial matching between segments occurring at the same bunch crossing (BX). TRB output signals are fed to the Server Board (SB) which selects the best two tracks from all TRACO candidates and sends the data out of the minicrate. In parallel to the trigger signals, chamber data are fed to the read-out system through the Read Out Boards (ROB), which are in charge of the time digitization of chamber signals related to the Level-1 Accept (L1A) trigger decision and the data merging to the next stages of the data acquisition chain. The Chamber Control Board (CCB) located at the centre of the minicrate, allows ROB and TRB configuration and monitoring. It works together with the CCB link board, on one of the minicrate ends, that receives data from the Slow Control and global experiment Timing and Trigger Control (TTC) system. Among other tasks, the CCB distributes the LHC 40.08 MHz clock and other TTC signals to every board in the minicrate.

2008 JINST 3 S08004

Trigger and data signals coming out of the minicrates are collected by VME electronics installed in the iron balconies attached to the DT wheels, respectively to the Sector Collector (SC, section 8.2) and to the Read Out Server (ROS, section 7.1.3) where data merging is performed. From the wheel balconies, data are sent via optical links, both to the CMS central acquisition system through the Detector Dependent Unit (DDU) (section 7.1.3) and to the CMS L1 system through the Sector Collector (SC) and the Drift Tube Track Finder (DTTF, section 8.2).

Front-end electronics

The front-end electronics for the barrel muon detector must satisfy many stringent requirements. Its functions are to amplify the signals produced by the detector, compare them with a threshold, and send the results to the trigger and read-out chains located on the chamber. Analog signal processing must use a short shaping time to achieve a high spatial resolution while introducing minimal noise; this allows low-gain operation of the drift tubes, thus improving reliability and chamber lifetime. The downstream comparator has to be very fast and precise to allow the use of low threshold values, which reduce the influence of the signal amplitude on the time response. The output driver also must be very fast, and it must deliver differential levels that minimise mutual interferences and can be transmitted through low-cost cables. Besides the above functions, several features that simplify the control and monitoring of the data acquisition have been implemented. The large number of channels and the resulting need for both high reliability and low cost, limited space, and concerns about power consumption led to the necessity to integrate the front-end electronics as much as possible.

The resulting custom front-end application specific integrated circuit chip (ASIC), named MAD, was developed using 0.8 μm BiCMOS technology [138]. This chip integrates signal processing for 4 channels (4 drift tubes) plus some ancillary functions in a 2.5×2.5 mm^2 die and 80 000 pieces were produced with a fabrication yield better than 95%. Figure 7.14 shows the ASIC block diagram and the pinout of the TQFP44 package used for it. Each of the 4 identical analog chains begins with a charge preamplifier that uses a single gain stage, folded/unfolded cascode, having a GBW product in excess of 1 GHz (result from simulation). The feedback time constant is 33 ns while input impedance is $\approx$100 Ω in the range 5–200 MHz.

The shaper that follows is a low-gain integrator with a small time constant. Its output is directly connected to 1 input of a latched discriminator made of 2 differential gain stages, the other input being connected to the external threshold pin V_{th}, common to all channels. Auxiliary circuits allow the masking of individual channels at the shaper input (pins A_ENn in high state) thus stopping the propagation of excessive noise background to the trigger and DAQ electronics. A similar but faster enable/disable function was implemented on the cable-driver stage to select channels that output signals in response to a test input. A temperature probe was also included for monitoring the operating conditions of the detector.

The ASIC operates with 2 distinct supply voltages, 5 V for the analog section and 2.5 V for the output stage, with a total power consumption of 100 mW (25 mW/ch) equally split between the 2 voltages and almost independent of the temperature and signal rate. Several tests have been carried out on the MAD ASIC both on the bench and in the field in various configurations. For the analog section an average gain of about 3.7 mV/fC was found for bare chips with (1370 ± 48)/pF

2008 JINST 3 S08004

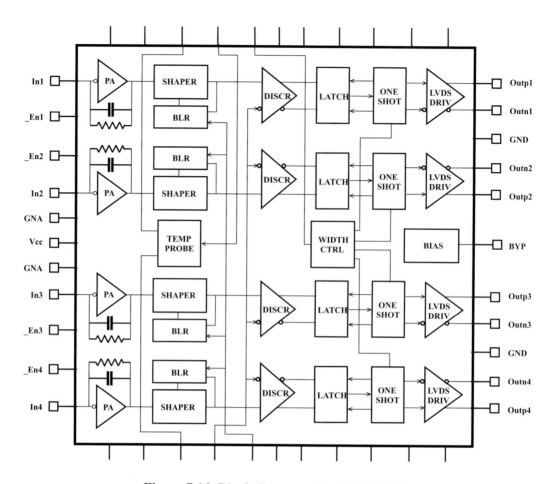

Figure 7.14: Block diagram of the MAD ASIC.

electrons ENC. Another key characteristic for operation with low signals is the crosstalk, which is less than 0.1%; moreover, the baseline restorer and the comparator offsets sum up to less than ± 2 mV total error.

The chip performance is somewhat degraded when it is mounted on a front-end board (figure 7.15): the gain reduces to 3.4 mV/fC and noise and crosstalk increase to (1850 ± 60)/pF electrons and 0.2%, respectively. These effects are caused by the input protection network, which is made of an external resistor and diodes that together with 100 μm gaps included in the PCB are capable of dissipating the energy stored in the 470 pF capacitors that connect the detector wires (biased at 3.6 kV) to the ASIC inputs. This protection is effective even in the case of repeated sparks (ASICs survive >105 sparks at 3.6 kV amplitude with 1 spark/s on all channels).

The above figures enable front-end operation at a threshold well below 10 fC (the value used during test beams was 5 fC) when connected to the detector, which has a maximum capacitance of 40 pF. The propagation delay of the chip is less than 5 ns with little dependence on signal amplitude (time walk is less than 7 ns). The rate capability of the MAD ASIC largely exceeds demand: 800 fC charge pulses (just below saturation) at 2 MHz rate do not affect the efficiency in detecting 5 fC interleaved signals, so there is a wide safety margin with respect to the total rate (about 10 kHz) foreseen per drift tube during CMS operation.

2008 JINST 3 S08004

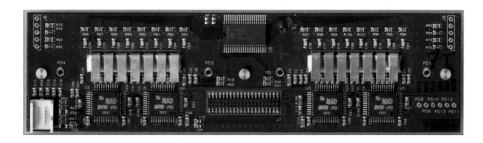

Figure 7.15: Front-end board (FEB).

Finally, the radiation tolerance and overall reliability of the front-end board and associated electronics were investigated [139]. Radiation testing involved a series of tests with thermal and high-energy neutrons, protons, and γ-rays to simulate the behaviour in a CMS-like environment. The results can be summarized in latch-up immunity (undetected SELs even with heavy ions on naked dies), very little sensitivity to SEUs (only a few thousand spurious counts/channel calculated for the whole detector lifetime), and tolerance to total integrated dose orders of magnitude higher than foreseen in 10 years of CMS operation. In addition, accelerated ageing in a climatic chamber at 125°C was carried out for >3000 hours on 20 FEBs and related circuits without revealing any fault.

Read-out electronics

The electronics of the read-out system of the CMS DTs is responsible for the time digitization of the signals generated in the drift chambers and for the data transmission to higher levels of the DAQ system. The time digitization of the signals is performed at the Read-Out Boards (ROB [140]), located in minicrates, as described in section 7.1.3, together with the DT muon trigger electronics. Two FTP cables are used to send digitized data from each minicrate to the rack 30 m away in the towers beside the CMS wheels where the Read-Out Server (ROS) boards are located. Each ROS merges data coming from chambers of one wheel sector through a 70-m optical link to the Detector Dependent Units (DDU) in the USC55 control room, performing the multiplexing of 1500 copper links into 60 optical links. The Read-Out Systems have been developed according to the requirements both of the expected trigger rates (100 kHz) at the high luminosity of LHC, with an average occupancy of 0.76% in the whole detector, a L1 trigger latency of 3.2 μs, and of the need of operating in an environment where the integrated neutron fluence will reach 10^{10}cm^{-2} in 10 years of activity.

Read-Out Boards are built around a 32-channel high performance TDC, the HPTDC, which is the third generation of TDC's developed by the CERN Microelectronics group [141], and it has been implemented in IBM 0.25 μm CMOS technology. This highly programmable TDC is based on the Delay Locked Loop (DLL) principle, providing a time bin of 25/32 ns = 0.78 ns, which corresponds to 265-ps resolution, when it is clocked at the LHC 40.08-MHz frequency. This time resolution is enough to obtain a single wire position resolution of 250 μm.

The number of HPTDCs per ROB has been decided following a compromise between the number of unused channels when the granularity is too small and the multiplication of common components when it is too big. Finally, each ROB has 4 HPTDCs connected in a clock synchronous token ring passing scheme, where one of them is configured as a master to control the token of the

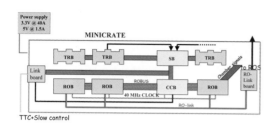

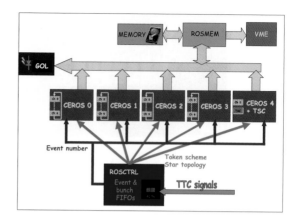

Figure 7.16: Sketch of the read-out and trigger electronics located inside a minicrate.

Figure 7.17: Sketch of the splitting of the 25 channels in four groups.

read-out data chain. The token ring scheme is designed following a failsafe mechanism, which avoids that the failure in one of the TDCs interrupts the whole ROB operation. Both hardware and software bypassing systems have been implemented.

Depending on the chamber type, the number of channels is different and accordingly, the number of ROBs per minicrate. The smallest minicrate has 3 ROBs and the biggest has 7. They are all connected to the Control Board (CCB) that manages, among others, the Timing and Trigger Control (TTC) signals. As can be seen in figure 7.16, Trigger Boards (TRB), located inside the minicrate are connected to the ROBs to receive TTL translated hit signals. As described at the beginning of this section, FTP cables connect the output of the ROBs to the ROS boards [142]. Located in the barrel tower racks there are 60 ROS boards, 12 per wheel, 1 per sector (four to five minicrates), so each ROS receives 25 channels of the LVDS copper ROB-ROS link. These 9U boards have to multiplex data coming from the ROBs, adding necessary information of ROB number, link status and other information, and send them to the DDU through a fast link. Another feature of the ROS board is that it also includes a power supply protection circuitry, current and temperature monitoring, and a 512 kB memory to test and perform data flow snapshots for traceability in case of transmission errors. In Figure 7.17 it can be seen how the 25 channels are split in four groups of six channels each, so-called CEROS, controlled by an FPGA that manages the FIFO read-out performing a pooling search for the next event to be read. These FPGAs also filter the events, discarding headers and trailers of those channels without timing or error information, reducing accordingly the data overhead.

A test performed on 10 prototypes, keeping them in an oven at 125°C for 2000 hours, in order to simulate 10 years of CMS activity, gave no faults. The DT Front-End-Driver (FED, also called DDU [143]) is the last component of the DT read-out electronics. The DT FED system consists of 5 VME64X 9U boards housed in the CMS service cavern; each board collects data through serial optical connections from 12 ROS, corresponding to an entire DT wheel, and transmits a formatted event fragment to the CMS common DAQ through a S-Link transmitter module. The synchronization with the trigger system is guaranteed by the TTC network, providing the LHC timing signal, the L1 trigger accept and fast commands, that are distributed to the different parts of the FED board. The layout of the board is depicted in figure 7.18.

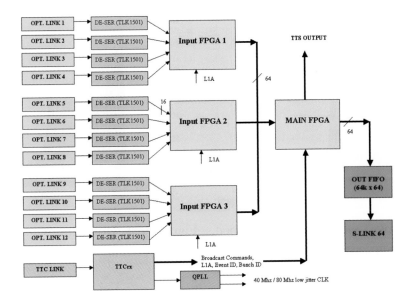

Figure 7.18: Scheme of the DDU architecture.

The data rate in each DT FED board is limited by the maximum rate the CMS DAQ can accept from an S-Link connection (about 200 Mbytes/s). The number of boards has been chosen to deal with the expected DT event size (7 kbytes/event) at 100 kHz trigger rate.

High Voltage and Low Voltage systems

The CAEN SY1527 universal multichannel power supply systems are used to supply high and low voltages (HV and LV) to the muon DT chambers. The basic modules of the DT HV system consist of A876 master boards and A877 remote boards. A maximum of 8 A876 master boards can be housed in the SY1527 mainframe. Each of them supplies high voltages and low voltages, controls and monitoring, to a maximum of 4 independent A877 remote boards, each one powering one DT chamber (two in the case of MB4 of Sectors 4 or 10). The A877 remote boards are located in a separate non-powered mechanical crate sitting in racks on the towers next to the wheels. The A876 delivers to each A877 HV board: a positive HV in the range from 0 to $+4.2$ kV (2.5 mA maximum output current), a negative HV in the range from 0 to -2.2 kV (1 mA maximum output current), a dual LV of ±15V (1.5 A maximum output current). The A877 HV outputs are subdivided into 12 groups (8 for the special A877 boards powering the MB4 chambers) conventionally called macro-channels. Each macro-channel supplies 4 HV channels per layer: 2 anodes (the wires of each layer are divided into 2 groups), 1 strip and 1 cathode. For all HV channels, the maximum output current is hardware limited to 100 μA.

The DT LV system uses three different types of CAEN Easy3000 modules: the A3009 to provide V_{CC} and V_{DD} voltages to the chamber front-end electronics and the V_{CC} voltage to the mini-crates, the A3050 for the mini-crate V_{DD} and the A3100 to power the Sector Collector Crates. The control of the Easy3000 power supply system is done remotely using a branch controller (Mod. A1676A) plugged in a SY1527 mainframe located in the control room. Each A1676A

2008 JINST 3 S08004

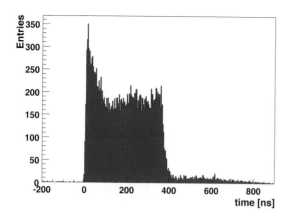

Figure 7.19: Drift Time distribution of a good cell. Wire position corresponds to time 0.

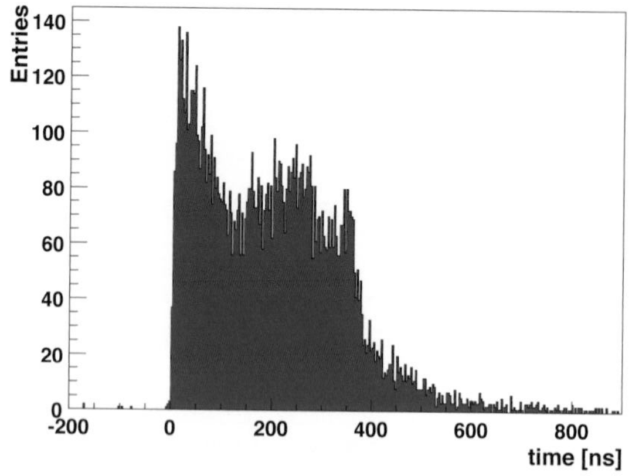

Figure 7.20: Drift Time distribution of a cell with a disconnected cathode.

branch controller can handle up to 6 Easy3000 crates. The Easy3000 crate is powered by external 48 V DC that is provided by the CAEN AC/DC converter A3486S module. The following voltages are delivered:

- VCCMC = 5.8 V, software current limit i_0 = 3 A;

- VDDMC = 4 V, software current limit i_0 = 30 A;

- VCCFE = 5.2 V, software current limit i_0 = 3 A;

- VDDFE = 2.6 V, software current limit i_0 = 4 A;

- VSC = 2.6 V, the current limit depends on the number of SC and ROS boards plugged in the crate.

7.1.4 Chamber assembly, dressing, and installation

Chamber assembly

Mass chamber assembly was started in January 2002 and was fully completed (spares included) in June 2006, with a constant production rate for all the four production sites involved. The collection of a good sample of cosmic muons allowed full testing of a constructed chamber, before sending it to CERN. In each laboratory cosmic-ray events were triggered by an external scintillator system which covered the full acceptance of the chamber. Since final minicrate electronics was not available during chamber assembly, drift times were measured with external TDCs and a custom DAQ. Typical trigger rates were 50–100 Hz, resulting in $\approx 10^6$ events in a few hours. With such a large data sample it was possible to spot and cure problems which could not be detected in previous tests, like disconnected cathodes (figures 7.19 and 7.20) and disconnected strips (figure 7.21).

Beside efficiencies, other relevant working parameters are measured from cosmic-ray data, as calibration stability (drift velocity measured to be stable within ±5%), deviation from linear drift parametrization, measured to be well within 100 μm (figure 7.22), wire positions and comparison with CCD measurements during assembly, relative alignment of layers, and noise (typically below 100 Hz per cell, see figure 7.23).

2008 JINST 3 S08004

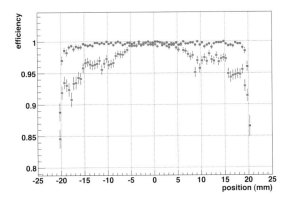

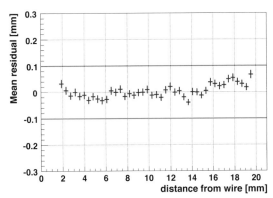

Figure 7.21: Single cell efficiency for a good cell (red dots) and for a cell with a disconnected strip (green dots).

Figure 7.22: Residuals as a function of the distance from the wire, indicating a linear dependence well within ± 100 μm in the full cell range.

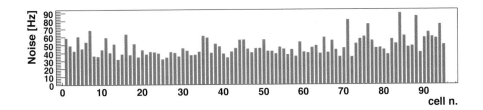

Figure 7.23: Typical hit rate distribution in one layer, as measured during the test of a SuperLayer with cosmic rays. This rate is dominated by noise and is typically below 100 Hz per cell.

Chamber dressing

All chambers, built and fully tested at the production sites, were sent to CERN for final testing and commissioning prior to installation in the experiment. Since the arrival of the first chamber at CERN (an MB2 type chamber arrived in summer 2000, prepared for a test beam [144]), a total of 272 more chambers (including spares) have been received from all four production sites, leading to a continuous workflow of dressing and testing.

At a first stage chambers are assigned to a particular position in CMS, depending on their orientation. Before any test, each chamber undergoes the optical alignment procedure described in section 7.1.4. After going through the alignment procedure, chambers are equipped with gas components (cooling pipes, gas manifolds, PADC pressure meters), HV cables and additional items like stickers, protectors, grounding straps, etc. Basically all components except for the minicrates (section 7.1.3), minicrates-related items and external protections are installed at this stage.

After dressing the chamber the following tests were performed:

- High voltage long term tests;

- Gas tightness tests;

2008 JINST 3 S08004

- Cosmic-muon tests.

The high voltage long term test consists of a continuous monitoring of the high voltage performance (electric current) under the nominal values for all components (3600 V for wires, 1800 V for strips, and -1200 V for cathodes) for a minimum of 6 weeks. The time constant of the chamber with the final gas connections is also computed as a measurement of gas tightness. No significant degradation has been observed with respect to the values measured at the sites.

Finally a cosmic test stand has been set up with trigger scintillators, independent cabling, LV and HV supplies and several HPTDCs, capable of measuring one chamber at a time, and registering several millions of triggers in a few hours. The later analysis of these data allows the recognition of almost all kind of problems related to the chamber itself and its internal electronics.

Once this first certification step is passed, the chamber dressing is completed and the chamber is declared ready for minicrate installation (section 7.1.3). All signal cables from the chamber to the minicrate are installed and tested, and then the minicrate itself is inserted. The performance of the minicrate is tested at this stage for the first time together with a real chamber. All internal connections are checked, as well as configurability and data processing performance of the full local electronics chain.

At this point the chamber has passed all tests and can be considered *ready to install*. Last dressing steps are performed (installation of carters and additional protections) and then DT chambers are coupled together to RPCs, forming an installable barrel muon package.

Chamber survey

To determine the chamber positions in the CMS coordinate system and to follow their movements a position monitoring Alignment System was built (section 7.4). All the 250 DT-chambers positions are recorded by this system via optical connections using LED light sources mounted on the chambers and specially designed video-cameras fixed to the return yoke of the barrel. Four LED-holders called forks are mounted on the side-profile of the honeycomb structure (two per side), using the rectangular 50×65 mm^2 tube as the light-passage. Each fork has 10 LEDs, 6 and 4 respectively, on each side of the fork. The control of the LEDs (on-off, current) is performed via I^{2}C bus system integrated in the minicrate.

The primary aim of the alignment is to give the positions of the anode wires but this is not directly possible. On the other hand all the wire positions are measured with respect to the SL corner during the chamber construction. To establish the connection between the LEDs and the corner blocks a calibration bench was built at the CERN ISR site (figure 7.24). This bench had two functions. The first one was to measure the corner block positions with respect to each other, allowing the full-chamber geometry, including the relative positions of the superlayers in 3D and their planarity, to be measured. The second function was to measure the LED positions in the chamber coordinate system stretched on the corner blocks. The bench contained video-cameras that could observe the LEDs and photogrammetry targets to measure the corner blocks with respect to the LEDs by photogrammetric methods. The bench allowed us to measure all the types of chambers from MB1 to MB4. The full bench was calibrated and recalibrated before each chamber calibration campaign by the CERN survey group. Also, additional LEDs were mounted on the bench to detect any significant deformation of the bench itself. The precision of the bench measurements for the locations of the corner blocks was $\sigma < 40$ μm and the position of the forks relative to the chamber

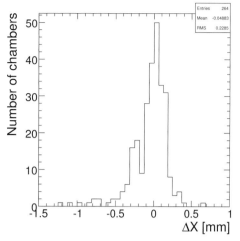

Figure 7.24: The chamber calibration bench in the CERN ISR Lab.

Figure 7.25: Distribution of the ϕ-deviation from the nominal design value for the two Φ-type superlayers.

was $\sigma < 70$ μm. Both values are within the acceptable range defined by physics requirements. Figure 7.25 shows the result of the residual distributions of Φ-type SL corner block positions for all measured chambers.

Gas system

For the DT chambers a safe and inexpensive gas mixture is used, namely Ar/CO_2 in the ratio 85/15 volume. The gas is distributed in parallel to all drift cells in four steps: (1) the main line is split into 5 lines to feed each of the 5 barrel wheels; (2) on the wheel it is split into 50 lines to feed the 50 chambers on the wheel; (3) on the chambers it is split into 3 lines to feed the 3 SuperLayers; (4) within the SL a long tube with small holes distributes the gas over the drift cells. The nominal flow is 50 l/h for each chamber. Due to the large total number of 250 chambers, a closed loop circuit with a cleaning station is used. It is foreseen to add about 10% fresh gas daily. The gas system is run at constant absolute pressure inside the chambers, to avoid any variation of the drift velocity inside the chamber. The pressure is regulated for each wheel. There are flowmeters at the inlet and outlet of each line at the gas distribution rack on the wheel. The gas pressure is also measured with two sensors at the inlet and outlet gas manifolds on the chambers, amounting to 1000 sensors in total. They should ensure a safe and redundant measurement of the pressure at every chamber, as needed for unaccessible chambers. To be able to analyze the gas actually present in every chamber, a return line brings a sample to the gas room. There is one such line per wheel and a remotely controlled multiway valve permits the selection of the desired chamber or the gas arriving at the wheel, for analysis.

The gas is also analysed independently for each of the 5 wheels and consists of a measurement of the oxygen and of the humidity content of the gas, as well as a direct measurement of the main parameter of the DT chambers, the drift velocity. The drift velocity is measured with a small drift chamber (VdC), which features a very homogeneous, constant, known and adjustable electric field in a region where two thin beams of electrons from a beta-source cross the chamber volume and

2008 JINST 3 S08004

Figure 7.26: Installation of MB1 station on Wheel -2. The yellow frame is the *cradle* used to insert the chamber in its location inside the iron slot.

trigger a counter outside the chamber. The distribution of times between the trigger signal and the signal from the anode wire of the chamber is recorded. The distance between the two beams being well known by construction, by measuring the distance in time between the peaks from the two sources, one reads directly the drift velocity. Variations of the drift velocity can be monitored accurately by accumulating data for about 5 min. The data shown in figure 7.8 demonstrate that the absolute values measured with the VdC agree with the expectation. The special merit of a direct monitoring of the drift velocity is that one does not need to know which impurities are affecting the drift velocity to monitor it.

Chamber installation in CMS

The main installation tool is a platform (*cradle*) with the same support rail as in the iron pockets that can be anchored to interface pads mounted on the wheel (figure 7.26). Pneumatic movements allow the precise alignment of the chamber with respect to the iron pockets. Once the rails on the cradle and those in the iron pockets are aligned, the chamber is pushed into position with an electric motor. The installation of the chamber in the MB1 station of Wheel -2 sector 11 is shown in figure 7.26.

The first chambers were installed in the bottom sectors of Wheel +2 in July 2004 and the surface installation was completed in Wheel -2 in December 2006. Installation completion, for sectors 1 and 7, which could not be filled on the surface since these parts of the wheel were reserved for handling during the heavy lowering operation, was made underground.

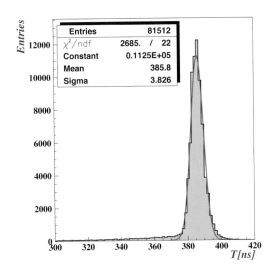

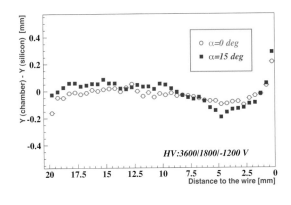

Figure 7.27: Gaussian fitted *MT* distribution with $\sigma_t = 170\ \mu$m. The position of the *MT* peak allows the determination of an average drift velocity of 54.4 μm/ns.

Figure 7.28: Deviation from linearity as a function of the distance to the wire for tracks with angles of incidence $\alpha=0^\circ$ and 15°. The cathode is centred at 21 mm.

7.1.5 Chamber performance

Chamber and trigger performances have been thoroughly analyzed at various stages, on prototypes before mass production (with and without external magnetic field [145]), on final chambers with test beams and with the CERN Gamma Irradiation Facility [144, 146, 147], with cosmic-rays both at production sites and at the commissioning of the installed chambers, and finally with the so-called *Magnet Test and Cosmic Challenge* (MTCC) in 2006, where part of the DT system, completely installed and equipped with final hardware, was tested together with the final CMS DAQ system.

Test beam data: chamber performance

Several dedicated muon test beam runs were set up in order to test chamber performance under different conditions. Single cell spatial resolution could be determined [144] simply by the dispersion of the $MT = (t_1 + t_3)/2 + t_2$ distribution, *MT* being the meantime obtained from the time of the signals (t_1, t_2, t_3) generated by the incoming muon in 3 consecutive, staggered layers. The smoothness of the drift time box and the fast drop of the trailing edge (figure 7.19) are both signs of the saturation of the drift velocity. Under the assumption that the time resolution is the same in all layers $\sigma_t = \sqrt{\frac{2}{3}} \cdot \sigma_{MT}$, one can easily observe an average spatial resolution of 170 μm (figure 7.27). Using a Silicon Beam Telescope, it was possible to measure the deviation from the extrapolated hit on the SL and the reconstructed position. As can be seen in figure 7.28 deviations from linearity are within $\pm$ 100 μm, which corresponds to a trigger jitter smaller than 5 ns.

Silicon Beam Telescope data can also be used to measure precisely the chamber efficiency (figure 7.29). The geometrical acceptance associated with the presence of the I-beam is clearly seen by the drop of efficiency in that region. In the rest of the cell the efficiency is always higher than

2008 JINST 3 S08004

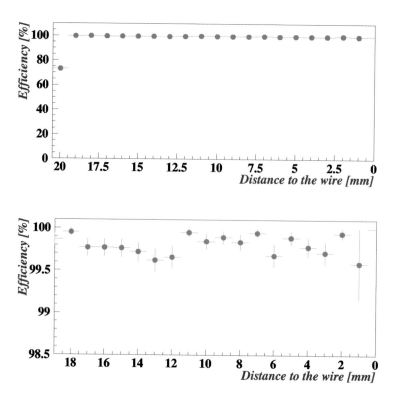

Figure 7.29: Efficiency as a function of the distance to the wire (top), for tracks orthogonal to chamber surface; (bottom) with an expanded scale excluding the I-beam region.

99.5%. The typical intrinsic average noise, as measured during chamber construction or during a test beam in dedicated random trigger runs [146], is shown in figure 7.30. It is reasonably stable, at values of ≈50 Hz, and does not vary much with channel number. Also the effect of higher noise levels, generated at the CERN Irradiation Facility, by photo-conversion in the chamber aluminum walls at chosen rates, both on reconstruction and trigger efficiency, was studied. The SL segment reconstruction efficiency is shown in figure 7.31 for various filter values of the gamma source, showing no significant dependence of the reconstruction algorithm on the gamma irradiation level, even at noise rates higher than the maximum levels expected in any DT chamber during normal LHC operations. Since the chambers are operated in the iron yoke of CMS, where important stray magnetic fields are present, the impact of the radial and longitudinal components of the field were carefully simulated (finite element analysis program ANSYS, figure 7.32), and tested both at dedicated muon test beams where the chambers were operated inside a magnetic field [145, 146], and during the CMS Magnet Test and Cosmic Challenge, with comsic rays. The distortion of the electron drift lines caused by a field of 0.5 T parallel to the wires can be seen in figure 7.33. This distortion can be roughly approximated by a rotation of the drift lines around the wire, simulating a rotation of the drift cell with respect to the direction of the incident particles. A change in the maximum drift path and time is generated, together with a drop of efficiency for inclined tracks which go through the I-beam region where the drift lines do not reach the wire. The staggering of the four layers minimizes the impact on track measurement of this last effect. In the case of

2008 JINST 3 S08004

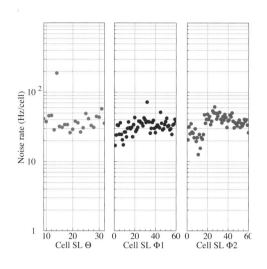

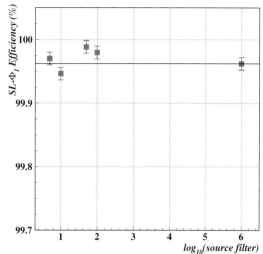

Figure 7.30: The noise cell occupancy as a function of the cell number, for the three SLs.

Figure 7.31: The cell efficiency in superlayer Φ_1 as a function of the irradiation filter value. The smallest filter value provides a background a factor 2 larger than the maximum one to be expected during LHC operation in any of the DT chambers in CMS.

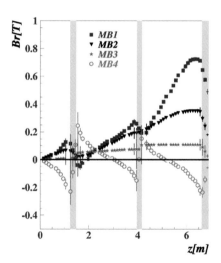

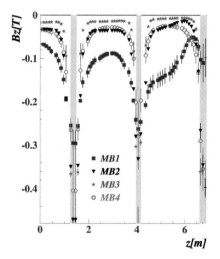

Figure 7.32: Radial (B_r) and longitudinal (B_z) components of the CMS magnetic field in the regions where the barrel chambers are placed as a function of the position along the beam direction (the centre of the detector is at z=0). Vertical bands indicate the separation between chamber wheels (in these particular regions B_z becomes significant). The biggest B_r values (0.7–0.8 T) occur in the MB1 region near the endcaps.

2008 JINST 3 S08004

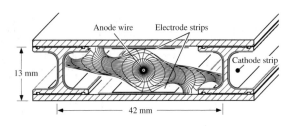

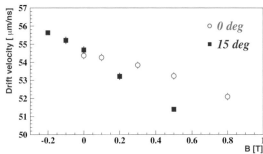

Figure 7.33: Simulation of the distortion produced in the drift lines by a 0.5 T magnetic field parallel to the wires.

Figure 7.34: Drift velocity for several magnetic fields for perpendicular (0°) and inclined (15°) tracks.

a homogeneous magnetic field along the wire, the main consequence would be an effective lower drift velocity, but in CMS the magnetic field is not homogeneous. Figure 7.34 shows the drift velocity values obtained for several magnetic field values in the case of perpendicular tracks. A variation in the drift velocity of around 3% is observed from B=0 to 0.5 T. This corresponds to a change in the maximum drift time of less than 12 ns, which is acceptable both for reconstruction and trigger efficiency. The effects of the magnetic field on linearity are not very important below 0.3 T but increase dramatically for higher fields, mainly near the I-beams. The resolution is also slightly deteriorated by low magnetic fields, but it is still better than 300 μm below 0.3 T. In CMS the magnetic field component parallel to the wires measuring the coordinate in the bending plane is expected to be below 0.1 T, with only very limited regions reaching 0.3 T. In such conditions, the results obtained confirm that the performance of the drift tube chambers fulfil the requirements.

Test beam data: trigger performance

Like the chamber performance, the DT local trigger has also been tested extensively using test beam facilities at CERN [147, 148]. In particular, to fully test the performance of the trigger electronics, bunched beams having the same time structure as the LHC were used at the CERN SPS, producing high momentum muon tracks separated by multiples of 25 ns.

The bunch crossing (BX) identification efficiency is defined as the fraction of selected single muon events for which the local trigger delivered at least one trigger segment at the correct BX. This quantity was measured as a function of the muon momentum, and results are shown in figure 7.35. The measurement was also performed after inserting iron slabs, for a total depth of 15 cm, in front of the muon chamber. The effect of the iron absorber is the enhancement of the probability for a high momentum muon to produce electromagnetic showers. Such a probability also increases as a function of the muon momentum. This has the effect to decrease the BX identification efficiency. Results are also shown in figure 7.35, superimposed on results without iron absorber. Ghosts are copies of the trigger segment at the correct BX, as well as fake triggers at the wrong BX. They may originate from wrong alignment of hits in a DT muon station, due to the presence of extra hits produced by electromagnetic cascades and δ-rays, or from redundancies in the trigger electronics. In the case of single muon events, if two trigger segments are delivered at the same

2008 JINST 3 S08004

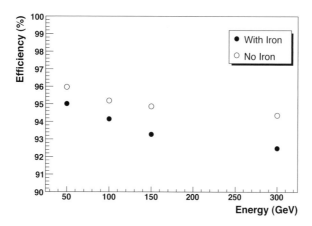

Figure 7.35: BX identification efficiency in a muon station in single muon events, as a function of the incident muon momentum, for events with and without the iron absorber placed in front of the muon station.

BX by the local trigger system in a muon station, the second trigger is considered a ghost copy of the first one. Although generally with a poorer quality, ghosts at the correct BX reproduce the characteristics of the main trigger segment in terms of position and angle. The production of segments associated to a wrong BX, arising from wrong hit alignment, is intrinsic to the BTI algorithm (section 8.2). In addition there are also cases in which the hit alignment is spoiled by δ-ray production or electromagnetic showering. Such fake triggers, which are called out-of-time ghosts, are almost entirely uncorrelated low quality segments, and are distributed over a wide range of BXs. The fraction of ghost triggers at the correct BX as a function of incident muon momentum, and the fraction of out-of-time triggers, as defined above, are shown respectively in figures 7.36 and 7.37 as a function of the incident muon momentum, for events with and without the iron absorber. The performance of the Φ Track Finder (PHTF, section 8.2) was also tested within the same muon test beam at CERN [148]. The PHTF was used to reconstruct muon trigger candidates using both muon stations, using ϕ-view local trigger primitives. Figure 7.38 shows the distribution of the BX assigned to the tracks found by the PHTF. The BX is correctly identified when its value is 24. Superimposed are the distributions of the same quantity determined independently by the local trigger in MB1 and MB3, as well as the distribution of the determined BX when a trigger segment with the same BX was delivered in coincidence in MB1 and MB3. It can be seen that the PHTF is fully efficient to deliver track candidates at the correct BX, whereas for out-of-time triggers the corresponding PHTF trigger rate is suppressed at the level of 1% or less.

A large fraction of the out-of-time triggers is due to real muons crossing the experimental apparatus at a BX different from 24, and which are correctly reconstructed by the PHTF. This is confirmed by the fact that the trigger segments that are matched together to form such tracks, are mainly of the type HH (four hits in both Φ-type SL), thus indicating a real muon track. Figure 7.39 shows the PHTF efficiency to reconstruct a trigger track in events with a MB1 and MB3 coincidence as a function of the BX. Superimposed are the efficiency to reconstruct a trigger track when the two trigger segments are both of HH type, and both of L (three out of four hits in a SL) quality

2008 JINST 3 S08004

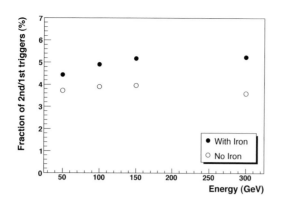 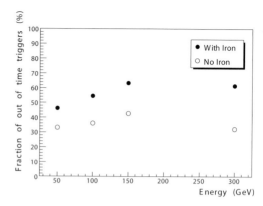

Figure 7.36: Fraction of ghost triggers observed in a muon station in single muon events, defined as the ratio of the number of second tracks over the number of first tracks, delivered by the local trigger at the correct BX, as a function of the muon momentum, for events with and without the iron absorber.

Figure 7.37: The fraction of out-of-time triggers in a muon station in single muon events, defined as the number of out-of-time trigger segments divided by the number of selected single muon events, as a function of the muon momentum, for events with and without the iron absorber.

respectively. The correct BX is 24. The PHTF efficiency for HH coincidences is 99.7±0.1% and is practically constant for any BX. This fits with the expectations, as such tracks are real muons crossing the apparatus. On the other hand, when the trigger segments have a low quality, which is typical for fake triggers, the PHTF ghost suppression is very effective. The rejection power for ghosts (L coincidences at BX ≠ 24) is 9.5±0.4. Therefore, although the out-of-time local trigger rate in a single station is rather high (as shown for example in figure 7.37), the PHTF is very effective in ghost rejection.

Commissioning of installed chambers

After installation in their final positions in the five CMS barrel wheels in the CMS surface hall, the chambers, including read-out and trigger electronics, were tested again with the goal of identifying potential problems before final cabling. Given the previous testing stages, it was mainly a test of the electronics and connections. Possible damage or loose connections as a consequence of installation (where chambers undergo some mechanical movement) could also be detected at this stage. This commissioning step was performed before final cabling (since the cables cover the minicrates and would prevent access for potential repairs) and involved all chambers in the ten sectors (84% of the full system). The commissioning consisted in the following steps:

1. connection to the power supplies and to the test-stand, which handled the trigger and read-out, in order to verify the functionality of the connectors and cabling of the chamber;

2. check of the minicrate performance by testing the internal connections and by monitoring the electronics boards inside the minicrate;

2008 JINST 3 S08004

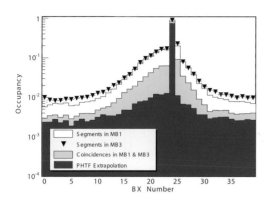 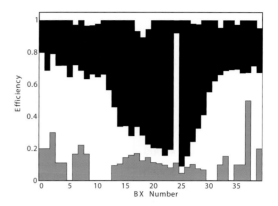

Figure 7.38: Distribution of the BX assigned to the tracks found by the PHTF. The BX is correctly identified when its value is 24. Superimposed are the distributions of the same quantity determined independently by the local trigger in MB1 and MB3, as well as the distribution of the determined BX when a trigger segment at the same BX was delivered in coincidence in MB1 and MB3.

Figure 7.39: Efficiency to reconstruct a trigger track by the PHTF, as a function of the BX (white), in events with a two stations (MB1-MB3) coincidence. The correct BX is 24. Superimposed are the efficiency to reconstruct a trigger track when there is a coincidence of two trigger segments both of HH quality (black), and a coincidence of two trigger segments both of L quality (light green).

3. T0 determination (the starting point) of the drift time spectrum with test pulses. The T0 is specific for every cell, its cell-to-cell variation within a chamber is of the order of ≈ 1–2 ns;

4. cosmics data taking in different trigger configurations;

5. analysis of the cosmics data and verification of the chamber and electronics performance.

Depending on the amount of repairs, between two and five chambers per week were commissioned. Cosmic muon tracks were recorded in auto-trigger mode in different trigger configurations. Trigger rates varied from 80 Hz to 600 Hz per chamber depending on the sector inclination, the trigger configuration, and the chamber type. Higher level trigger components (tower electronics) as well as RPC connections were not tested at this stage since they required full cabling to the tower electronics.

The chamber orientation with respect to incoming cosmic-rays is purely horizontal only in sectors 4 and 10. This yields a reduction in the occupancy near the edges of the Φ-type superlayer for sectors near the vertical. An example comparing the bottom sectors 8, 9, 11 and 12 is shown in figure 7.40, where the occupancy per wire is summed over the four layers of superlayer $\Phi 2$. The reduced geometrical acceptance at the chamber edges is caused by the combination of two effects: i) the direction of cosmic rays, which is mainly vertical, and ii) the shielding of the iron yoke on soft muons.

Data recorded with highly selective trigger condition, 4 hits in both Φ-type superlayers or 3 hits in one and 4 in the other, are used to calculate the efficiency. The cell efficiency is calculated

2008 JINST 3 S08004

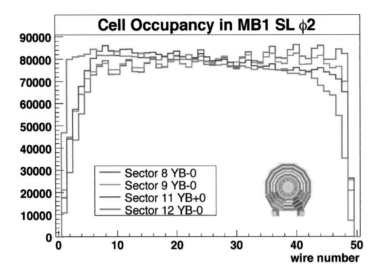

Figure 7.40: Sum of the occupancy of the four layers in MB1 Φ2 superlayer for sectors 8, 9, 11 and 12. The sectors have different inclinations as shown on the right. Material inside the yoke along with the iron yoke itself shield partly the soft cosmic ray muons.

from reconstructed tracks with hits found in the traversed cell or its 2 neighbours (N_h), normalized to the total reconstructed tracks traversing the considered layer (N_{track}):

$$\varepsilon_{Layer} = N_h/N_{track} \tag{7.1}$$

requiring ≥ 5 hits in ϕ and ≥ 3 hits in z. Figure 7.41 (left panel) illustrates the combined track fit in the case of the ϕ projection. Because of the normalization to the number of tracks, the reduced occupancy near the chamber edges does not play a role. The cell efficiency is almost constant across the chamber, usually $\geq 98\%$, as seen, for example, in figure 7.41 (right panel).

Similarly the reconstruction efficiency is determined as the fraction of reconstructed tracks when requiring ≥ 7 hits per track, an example of which can be seen in figure 7.42. Here we should remark that the overall number of dead cells, as measured during chamber commissioning at CERN, amounts to $\approx 0.2\%$ of the total number of channels (298 out of 171 852).

Results from Magnet Test and Cosmic Challenge

A further important test of the muon system with emphasis on integration into the overall CMS DAQ and Trigger system, is the aforementioned Magnet Test and Cosmic Challenge (MTCC), performed at CERN during summer 2006. For the first time, the three muon subsystems were operated together. The DT system made use of the complete read-out and trigger chain with final hardware, and the recorded data allowed the study of cosmic muon tracks in magnetic field. Another important task was the generation of a cosmic-muon trigger for the read-out of all CMS subsystems participating in the MTCC. Several goals were accomplished by the DT system during the MTCC:

1. Check of chamber performance and read-out

2008 JINST 3 S08004

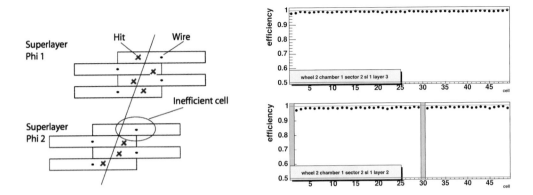

Figure 7.41: Cell efficiencies for two of the four layers of Φ1, MB1 sector 2.

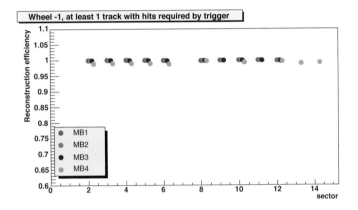

Figure 7.42: Reconstruction efficiency with 7 points in both Φ-type superlayers, according to the trigger condition, requiring either two 4-hit segments in both of the two Φ-type superlayers or one 4-hit and one 3-hit segment.

- check the effect of the fringe field on chamber performance in terms of HV behaviour, drift velocity, position resolution, and efficiency;
- exercise the complete read-out chain from the chamber through the ROS-25 up to the DDU;
- test of HV and LV in the final set-up. Integrate HV and LV control into central CMS services.

2. Trigger

- operate the complete trigger chain with final hardware;
- provide a cosmic-ray trigger to CMS;
- check the effect of magnetic field on trigger timing (i.e. bunch crossing identification), requiring the RPC trigger to set a reference T0.

3. Software

- integration of DAQ and Data Quality Monitoring;

2008 JINST 3 S08004

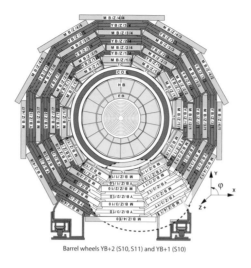

Barrel wheels YB+2 (S10, S11) and YB+1 (S10)

Figure 7.43: The MTCC exploited in the barrel region three sectors in wheels YB+1 (sector 10) and YB+2 (sectors 10, 11) instrumented with DTs and RPCs.

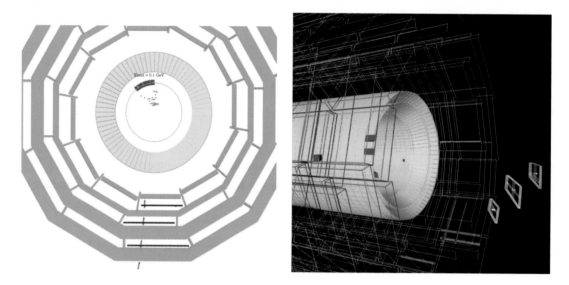

Figure 7.44: Event displays from the MTCC. Left panel: muon reconstructed in a DT sector in conjunction with Tracker activity. Right panel: muon track passing through both DT and CSC chambers.

- exercise the reconstruction software under realistic conditions.

4. Take data with other CMS subsystems.

For the DTs (as well as for the barrel RPCs) three instrumented sectors were read-out, the bottom sector 10 and the adjacent sector 11, both in YB+2, along with sector 10 in YB+1 (figure 7.43). This accounted for 14 DT chambers, corresponding to about 10 000 channels. Beside the cross-check of chamber performance previously carried out in test beams, MTCC data provided a unique opportunity to test the reconstruction algorithms for different magnetic field strengths (figure 7.44(left)) and to observe for the first time tracks combined in different detectors (figure 7.44(right)). As de-

2008 JINST 3 S08004

scribed in section 7.1.5, because of the radial component of the magnetic field between the solenoid and endcap disks, the electron drift direction in the r-ϕ view changes, acquiring a Lorentz angle. The angle is increasingly larger as the B radial component increases along z. Thus signals generated by muon hits in a r-ϕ drift tube at a given distance from the wire but at different z positions will appear at different times. The effect has implications both for the trigger synchronization and for the muon track reconstruction and it should be calibrated out before LHC start-up. During the MTCC a total of 159 million cosmic-muon events (48 million DT triggered) were collected at several values of the B field. Data were collected at 0 T (as a reference), then at 2, 3, 3.5, 3.8, and 4 T (93 million events at 3.8 and 4 T), which allowed a detailed mapping of the Lorentz angle effect in an MB1 and an MB2 chamber. Some 15 million events at 0 T and 3.8 T (1.6 million DT triggered) have been taken with the MB1 local trigger configured to select only muon segments pointing to the centre of the CMS barrel (LHC beam interaction point): this sample is specific for trigger timing studies in the DT-CSC overlap, in particular also the muon time-of-flight is the same as in a LHC run.

While procedures for the synchronization of the DT system in stand-alone were studied in Phase I of the MTCC, in Phase II (during the magnetic field mapping operations) effort was put in tools for fine inter-synchronization of the muon detectors (DT, CSC and RPC). In particular the analysis of the DT trigger data at the chamber output as function of RPC-originated L1A has proven to be sensitive to desynchronization by a few nanoseconds.

To study the efficiency of the DT Local Trigger (DTLT), events were selected by requiring the presence of the RPC triggers RBC1 (for wheel YB+1) or RBC2 (for RPCs in wheel YB+2) triggers. In such events, track segments were reconstructed in each muon station indepedently, whenever possible, using TDC hits. If more than one track segment was reconstructed in a given station, the one with the largest number of associated hits was taken. The efficiency of the DTLT was computed for each muon station separately, by counting events with a reconstructed muon segment, and comparing them with events which also had a trigger segment at any BX in the same muon station. Accepting a trigger regardless of its BX position was dictated by the fact that cosmic rays are likely to generate triggers in nearby BXs, as with non-bunched particles the system is intrinsically not synchronized. Only correlated trigger segments, namely of quality High-High (HH), High-Low (HL) or Low-Low (LL), as defined in section 7.1.5, were released by the trigger sector collector and thus used to compute the DTLT efficiency.

This efficiency was found to be about 65–70% in all stations, independent of the magnetic field. The measurements obtained using 40 MHz bunched muon beams [148] provided a much higher efficiency, of the order of 85% or more, and for which only triggers at the correct BX were considered.

The observed lower efficiency of the DTLT can be explained by the fact that, while the trigger system is clocked every 25 ns, cosmic rays occur at any time. In bunched beams the BTIs can be properly synchronized by choosing the best phase which maximizes the number of HH triggers with respect to higher level triggers. In the case of cosmic rays, this is not possible, due to the random arrival time of the muons thus making the BTI synchronization itself meaningless. In such conditions the rate of Low-quality trigger segments released by the BTIs increases, and also the associated BX can easily fluctuate. As only correlated trigger segments were released by the trigger Sector Collector in each station, we also expect an increase in TRACOs (section 8.2) failing

2008 JINST 3 S08004

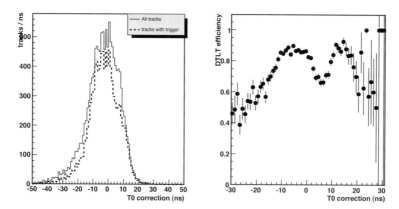

Figure 7.45: Left panel: distribution of t_0 for all track segments in a station, for events triggered by RPC (solid line). The distribution of the same quantity for events also triggered by the DT is superimposed (dashed line). Right panel: DT local trigger efficiency as a function of the quantity t_0, obtained by the ratio of the two histograms shown on the left.

to correlate segments among the two superlayers of a given station, with respect to a perfectly synchronized system, which will turn into a DTLT efficiency loss.

Consequently, one expects that muons crossing the detector at the "correct time" (for which the BTIs behave as perfectly synchronized to the clock) will be detected with the highest efficiency, as such a condition is the same as in the bunched beam tests. On the other hand, muons crossing the detector out of such a "correct time" will be detected with lower efficiency, as for them the synchronization of the system is not optimised.

The quantity t_0 is the time correction to be added to the t_{Trig} of the event to obtain the effective time at which the given muon crossed the detector. It can be computed event-by-event by minimizing the space resolution of the reconstructed track segment in a station. Figure 7.45 (left) shows the distribution of the t_0 correction of the reconstructed track segments in events triggered by the barrel RPC, superimposed to the one for events which also had a DT local trigger. The best trigger efficiency is obtained only at some preferred t_0 values. This can be seen in figure 7.45 (right) which shows the DTLT efficiency as a function of the t_0-correction time, obtained as the ratio of the two distributions previously described. Two peaks at efficiency around 90% are visible. They correspond to the case in which the muon crosses the detector at the "correct time" for which BTIs are synchronized. The two peaks correspond to two adjacent BXs. For other t_0 values, the efficiency can be very low, as in this case the system is not synchronized. The observed DTLT efficiency is therefore explained by the fact that cosmic rays occur at random time with respect to the "correct time" at which the BTIs have maximum efficiency.

The magnetic field modifies the shape of the field lines in the drift cell, thus affecting the effective drift velocity, as discussed in section 7.1.5. The largest effect in the barrel is expected to occur in station MB1 in Wheels +2 and -2. From the point of view of the DTLT, a change of the effective drift velocity, if large enough, could make the BX determination less precise, and shift its value by one unit.

Figure 7.46 shows this effect for the two MB1 stations in Wheel 2, displaying the BX value determined by the DTLT as a function of the z-position of the track in the chamber, with and

2008 JINST 3 S08004

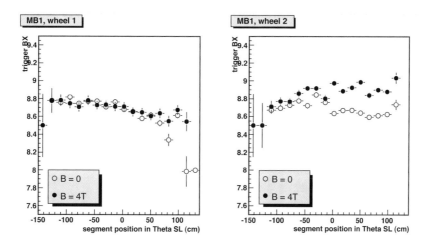

Figure 7.46: BX determined by the DTLT as a function of the track position in the z-direction of the muon station, with and without magnetic field, for MB1 in Wheel 1 on the left, where no effect of the B-field is expected. On the right, the same quantities are shown for MB1 in Wheel 2, where an influence of the magnetic field on the drift velocity is expected.

without magnetic field. While no clear effect is visible in MB1-Wheel 1, in MB1-Wheel 2 there is a slight delay of the average BX value which tends to increase as the track approaches the edge of the wheel, corresponding to larger values of z, where the stray field components are larger. This delay is at most of the order of 0.3 units of BX.

7.2 Cathode strip chambers

At the time of the LHC start-up, the CMS Endcap Muon system will consist of 468 cathode strip chambers (CSC) arranged in groups as follows: 72 ME1/1, 72 ME1/2, 72 ME1/3, 36 ME2/1, 72 ME2/2, 36 ME3/1, 72 ME3/2, and 36 ME4/1 (figures 7.47 and 7.48). The de-scoped 72 ME4/2 chambers will not be available during early years of CMS operation. The chambers are trapezoidal and cover either 10° or 20° in ϕ; all chambers, except for the ME1/3 ring, overlap and provide contiguous ϕ-coverage. A muon in the pseudorapidity range $1.2 < |\eta| < 2.4$ crosses 3 or 4 CSCs. In the endcap-barrel overlap range, $0.9 < |\eta| < 1.2$, muons are detected by both the barrel drift tubes (DT) and endcap CSCs. In the baseline design, muons with $|\eta| < 2.1$ are also detected by resistive plate chambers (RPC); however, in the initial detector this coverage is reduced to $|\eta| < 1.6$.

The CSCs are multiwire proportional chambers comprised of 6 anode wire planes interleaved among 7 cathode panels (figure 7.49). Wires run azimuthally and define a track's radial coordinate. Strips are milled on cathode panels and run lengthwise at constant $\Delta\phi$ width. Following the original CSC idea [149], the muon coordinate along the wires (ϕ in the CMS coordinate system) is obtained by interpolating charges induced on strips (figure 7.50). The largest chambers, ME2/2 and ME3/2, are about 3.4×1.5 m^2 in size. The overall area covered by the sensitive planes of all chambers is about 5000 m^2, the gas volume is >50 m^3, and the number of wires is about 2 million. There are about 9000 high-voltage channels in the system, about 220 000 cathode strip read-out channels with 12-bit signal digitisation, and about 180 000 anode wire read-out channels.

2008 JINST 3 S08004

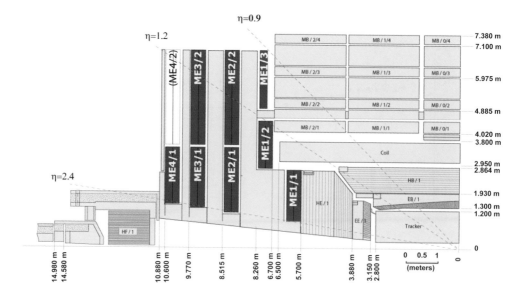

Figure 7.47: Quarter-view of the CMS detector. Cathode strip chambers of the Endcap Muon system are highlighted.

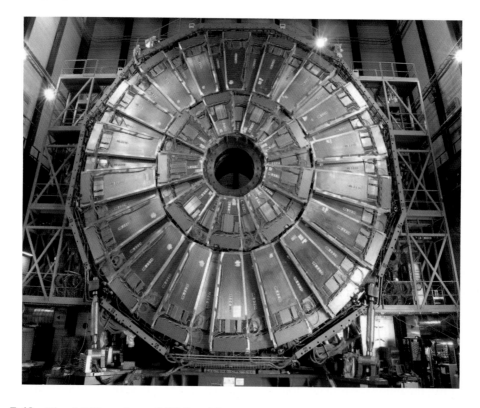

Figure 7.48: The ME2 station of CSCs. The outer ring consists of 36 ME2/2 chambers, each spanning 10° in ϕ, and the inner ring of eighteen 20° ME2/1 chambers. The chambers overlap to provide contiguous coverage in ϕ.

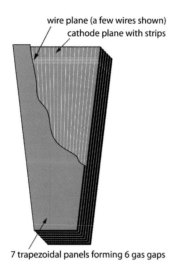

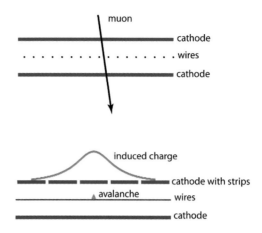

Figure 7.49: Layout of a CSC made of 7 trapezoidal panels. The panels form 6 gas gaps with planes of sensitive anode wires. The cut-out in the top panel reveals anode wires and cathode strips. Only a few wires are shown to indicate their azimuthal direction. Strips of constant $\Delta\phi$ run lengthwise (radially). The 144 largest CSCs are 3.4 m long along the strip direction and up to 1.5 m wide along the wire direction.

Figure 7.50: A schematic view of a single gap illustrating the principle of CSC operation. By interpolating charges induced on cathode strips by avalanche positive ions near a wire, one can obtain a precise localisation of an avalanche along the wire direction.

The CSCs provide the functions of precision muon measurement and muon trigger in one device. They can operate at high rates and in large and non-uniform magnetic fields. They do not require precise gas, temperature, or pressure control. Moreover, a radial fan-shaped strip pattern, natural for measurements in the endcap region, can be easily arranged on the cathode planes.

The performance requirements for the CMS cathode strip chamber system include the following:

- Reliable and low-maintenance operation for at least 10 years at the full LHC luminosity, i.e., at estimated random hit rates up to 1 kHz/cm^2;

- At least 99% efficiency per chamber for finding track stubs by the first-level trigger;

- At least 92% probability per chamber of identifying correct bunch crossings by the first-level trigger. With such an efficiency per chamber and 3–4 CSCs on a muon track path, a simple majority rule ensures that the reconstructed muons will be assigned the correct bunch crossing number in more than 99% of cases;

- About 2 mm resolution in r-ϕ at the first-level trigger.

- About 75 μm off-line spatial resolution in r-ϕ for ME1/1 and ME1/2 chambers and about 150 μm for all others.

2008 JINST 3 S08004

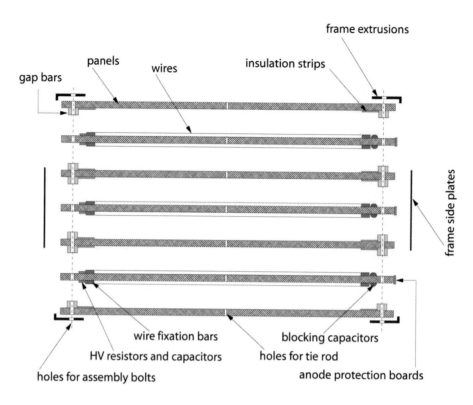

Figure 7.51: Mechanical design of the CMS cathode strip chambers (exploded view).

7.2.1 Chamber mechanical design

The 72 ME1/1 chambers and the larger 396 chambers have somewhat different mechanical designs. Below, we describe the design of the larger chambers using ME2/2 as an example and, then, at the end of this section, summarise the ME1/1-specific features that distinguish them from the other chambers.

The mechanical structure is based on seven 16.2-mm-thick trapezoidal panels (figure 7.51). The panels are made of a 12.7-mm-thick polycarbonate honeycomb core with two 1.6-mm FR4 skins commercially glued on each side. FR4 is a fire-retardant fibreglass/epoxy material widely used for printed circuit boards. The FR4 skins are clad with 36-μm-thick copper on their outer surfaces, forming the cathode planes.

FR4 cathode gap bars are glued to both sides of every other panel (panels 1, 3, 5, 7 in figure 7.51) so that when the panels are stacked together, these cathode bars define 6 gas gaps of 9.5 mm. To provide additional support, there are 4 spacers placed between panels along the chamber centreline. When all 7 panels are put together, the entire stack is tightened down with bolts along the chamber perimeter (through holes in the cathode gap bars) and at 4 points along the chamber centreline (through holes in the spacers). Such an arrangement ensures that no panel has more than 60 cm of unsupported length. Measurements show that most of the panels are flat within the required ± 300 μm on such spans. This specification arises from the desire to keep gas-gain variations within a factor of 2.

Six of the panels have a pattern of 80 strips milled on one side. Strips, being radial, have a pitch that varies from 8.4 mm at the narrow chamber end to 16 mm at the wide end. The gap between strips is about 0.5 mm. The precision of milling was better than 50 μm (rms). Milling was done with a cutter tilted at 45° to make the groove edges smoother (otherwise, sharp edges and burrs might provoke sparking and discharges).

Three of the panels are so-called *anode* panels (panels 2, 4, 6 in figure 7.51) around which anode wires were wound (these panels do not have gap bars). A specially designed winding machine wound wires directly on a panel by rotating it around its long axis at a speed of about 5 turns per minute; one panel could be completed (about 1000 wires on each side) in less than 4 hours. The wire spacing of about 3.2 mm was defined by combs: threaded rods running the full panel length and attached to the panel edges during winding. Gold-plated tungsten wires, 50 μm in diameter, were stretched at 250-g tension (about 70% of the elastic limit) and run their full length up to 1.2 m without any intermediate supports. The electrostatic stability limit for the longest wires is above 6 kV (the nominal operational point is 3.6 kV). Based on measurements during production, the wire tension non-uniformity does not exceed $\pm$10%, while wire spacing variations are less than $\pm$150 μm. Wires found to fall outside of these specifications were replaced.

After winding, the wires were first glued and then soldered to anode bars 4.75 mm in height (half of the gas gap). The anode bars are made of copper-clad FR4 and carry the electric artwork. An automated soldering machine allowed for soldering at a speed of 3.5 s per joint. Groups of 16 wires make 1 anode read-out channel with a width of about 5 cm. High voltage (HV) is distributed to the wire groups on one end and signals are read out on the other end via 1 nF blocking capacitors.

Each wire plane is sub-divided by spacer bars into 5 independent HV segments, which allows us to independently regulate or turn off HV on any of the 5 sections. In places where the spacer bars were inserted (and prior to their installation), 8 wires were removed. Two gold-plated 200-μm guard wires were inserted in place of the first and eighth thin wires that were removed to eliminate edge effects. The very first and last wires in each plane are also thicker. If the edge thin wires were to be left unguarded, the electric field on them would be much larger than for the rest of the wires, which would provoke discharges. Such plane segmentation, because of the intermediate panel supports and the individual HV control over smaller wire-plane sections, makes the overall chamber performance very robust.

After stacking the panels and tightening the bolts (with O-rings), continuous beads of RTV sealant were applied along the outer seams between the panels and gap bars. The O-rings around the bolts and the RTV seal make the chambers hermetic. Should it be necessary, a chamber can be opened, serviced, and resealed. Gas enters into one of the outer gas gaps via an inlet in a cathode gap bar, flows from one plane to another in a zigzag manner via special holes in the panels, then exits from the last gas gap via an outlet in a gap bar. The leak rate, measured during production and after installation of the chambers, was required to be <1% of the chamber volume per day at an over-pressure of 7.5 mbar (e.g., <2 cm^3/min for the largest chambers whose gas volume is about 200 litres).

Side plates made of 3.2-mm-thick Al extrusions were attached around the chamber perimeter. They stiffen the chamber and connect the top and bottom copper skins to form a Faraday cage.

The nominal gas mixture is 40%Ar + 50%CO_2 + 10%CF_4. The CO_2 component is a non-flammable quencher needed to achieve large gas gains, while the main function of the CF_4 is to prevent polymerisation on wires. A detailed discussion of the gas optimisation can be found elsewhere [150].

2008 JINST 3 S08004

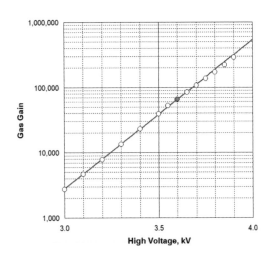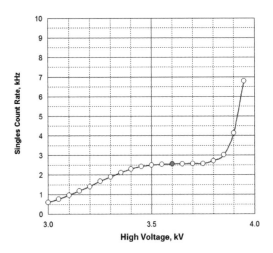

Figure 7.52: Left panel: CSC gas gain vs. high voltage. Right panel: ME2/1 chamber singles rate vs. high voltage (the overall sensitive area of all 6 planes in this chamber is ≈ 9.5 m^2).

Figure 7.52 (left) shows the chamber gas gain vs. high voltage. The nominal operating HV was chosen to be 3.6 kV, which corresponds to a gas gain on the order of 7×10^4. A minimum ionising particle (MIP) produces about 100 electrons in a gas gap, thus the charge per MIP in an avalanche is about 1 pC. As is shown below, at this operational point, the cathode and anode electronics have a very high efficiency and an adequate signal-to-noise ratio. The operational range of the chambers extends to 3.9 kV. Typically, we start seeing a sharp rise in the rate of spurious pulses at about 3.9–4.0 kV (figure 7.52 (right)).

The 72 ME1/1 chambers have differences in their mechanical design with respect to the other CSCs. The gas gap is 7 mm, wire diameter is 30 μm, and wire spacing is 2.5 mm, so the nominal HV for these chambers is somewhat lower: 2.9 kV. Most notably, the ME1/1 anode wires are not azimuthal, but are tilted by an angle $\alpha_L = 29°$ (figure 7.53). Unlike the other CSCs, the ME1/1 chambers are inside the CMS solenoid and see its strong and uniform 4 T axial field. The wire tilt compensates for the Lorentz angle so that electrons drift parallel to the strips, enabling a precise measurement of the r-ϕ-coordinate.

7.2.2 Electronics design

Figure 7.54 shows a schematic layout of the custom-made trigger and read-out electronic boards developed for the CSC system.

An anode front-end board (AFEB) has one 16-channel amplifier-discriminator application-specific integrated circuit (ASIC). The amplifier has a 30-ns shaper (semi-Gaussian with 2-exponent tail cancellation designed to suppress the slow signal component associated with a drift of positive ions away from the anode wires), about 7 mV/fC sensitivity, and 1.4 fC noise at a typical wire group capacitance of 180 pF for the largest chambers. With the 30-ns shaping time, an AFEB sees about 12% of the total avalanche charge, i.e., an average of about 130 fC. A typical chamber signal as seen at the output of this amplifier is shown in figure 7.55 (left). The constant-fraction discriminator has a threshold nominally set at 20 fC (input equivalent charge) and its slewing time is less than 3 ns for the 60–600 fC signal range. Depending on chamber size, there are 12 to 42 AFEBs per chamber. Further details on the AFEB design and performance can be found elsewhere [151].

2008 JINST 3 S08004

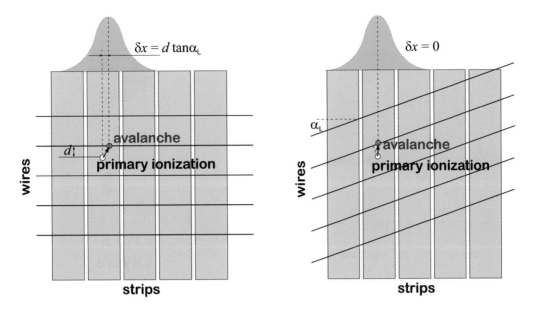

Figure 7.53: Left panel: if the ME1/1 wires were not tilted, ionisation electrons, as they drift toward the anode wires in the strong magnetic field normal to the plane of the drawing, would be carried sideways by the Lorentz force. The direction and size of the shift would depend on whether the electrons drift upwards or downwards and on how far away they were from the wires to begin with. These sideways displacements would spread the charge over the anode wires. Right panel: by tilting the wires at the Lorentz angle α_L, all ionisation electrons arrive near the same point.

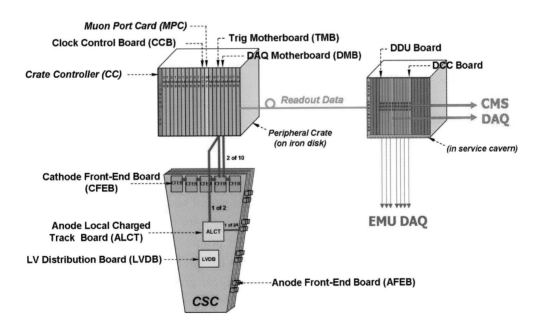

Figure 7.54: Schematic layout of the CSC trigger and read-out electronics.

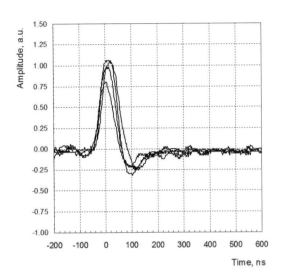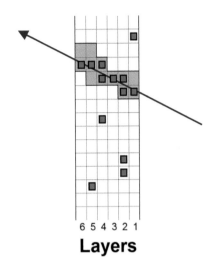

Figure 7.55: Left panel: muon signals as seen at the AFEB amplifier output. Right panel: a schematic event display showing anode signals in the 6 planes of a CSC (small dark squares). The ALCT board FPGA logic is programmed to scan the chamber and search for hits falling inside predefined patterns (grey cells) consistent with muons originating from the interaction point. Hits must be present in at least 4 planes for an ALCT pattern to be found.

Every 25 ns, in synchronization with the LHC collisions, all AFEB outputs, 40-ns-long step pulses, are sampled by an FPGA-based anode local charged track (ALCT) board, 1 board per chamber. The recorded *yes/no* information is stored in a FIFO. Upon receiving a CMS-wide Level-1 Accept (L1A) trigger command, the recorded information within the proper time window is extracted and reported to the DAQ. The latency of the L1A command with respect to the time of a collision is 3.2 μs. The temporal length of the raw-hit record transmitted to the DAQ can be as large as 800 ns.

The ALCT board has another important function. Based on the information from all anode channels, the FPGA code constantly (every 25 ns) searches for patterns of hits among the 6 planes that would be consistent with muon tracks originating from the interaction point. For a pattern to be valid, we require that hits from at least 4 planes be present in the pattern. Figure 7.55 (right) illustrates how patterns are identified in the presence of spurious single-plane hits. Due to a large neutron-induced photon background, a substantial rate of such single-plane hits is expected. However, these hits, being completely uncorrelated, would not typically line up to form track-like patterns. Found patterns, called ALCTs, are trigger primitives. They are transmitted further downstream to the muon Level-1 trigger electronics that builds muon track candidates from these primitives. The time it takes to form an anode track trigger primitive is 225 ns (including drift time). Each ALCT board can find up to 2 such patterns per bunch crossing, which is adequate for the expected chamber track occupancy at the nominal LHC luminosity.

For the cathode strips, 1 cathode front-end board (CFEB) serves (6 planes)×(16 strips) = 96 channels and has 6 parallel chains of the following chips (figure 7.56 (left)): 16-channel amplifier-shaper ASIC, 16-channel switched capacitor array (SCA) ASIC, 12-bit 1-channel ADC, and 16-channel comparator ASIC. There are 4 to 5 CFEBs per chamber.

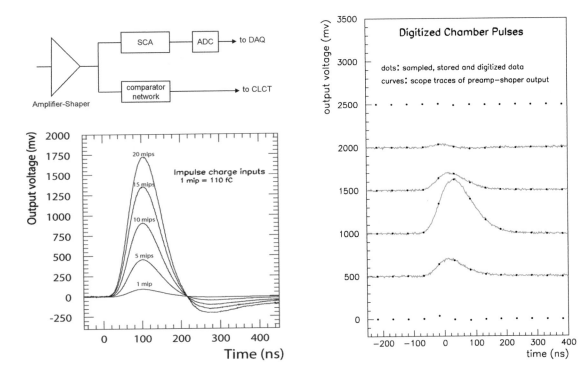

Figure 7.56: Left panel: basic functional diagram of a CFEB and the CFEB amplifier-shaper response to a δ-function input pulse. The undershoot is intended to compensate for the long tail present in muon hit signals resulting from the slow drift of positive ions away from the anode wires. Right panel: signals from a muon track on 6 contiguous strips in a layer. The 4 curves are oscilloscope traces and the 6 lines of dots are digitised outputs. The signals have an arbitrary vertical offset for ease of viewing.

The amplifier-shaper ASIC has 100-ns shaping time and a sensitivity of 0.85 mV/fC over a linear range up to 1 V. The equivalent noise level at ≈300-pF strip capacitance is typically 1.5 fC. The shaping is based on a semi-Gaussian transfer function with an undershoot designed to compensate for the $1/t$ signal tail due to the slow drift of positive ions. After convolution with the current pulse produced in a chamber by a muon, the amplifier-shaper signal peaks around 150 ns and has no tail (figure 7.56 (right)). The CFEB sees about 8% of the total avalanche charge, i.e., about 100 fC on average.

The output from this chip is split into 2 pathways. One leads to the SCA chip [152], which samples the waveform of each strip signal every 50 ns in sync with the LHC clock and stores this analog information on its capacitors. The depth of this analog memory is 96 capacitor cells per channel, or 96×50 ns = 4.8 μs. Upon receiving the L1A command 3.2 μs following a collision, 8 or 16 consecutive samples from the proper time range among the SCA capacitors are retrieved and digitised individually by the 12-bit flash ADCs. The digital information is passed to the DAQ via an intermediate digital data buffer. For the digitisation and subsequent read-out by the DAQ to happen, the L1A signal must be in coincidence with the *cathode local charged track* (CLCT) primitive decision described below.

2008 JINST 3 S08004

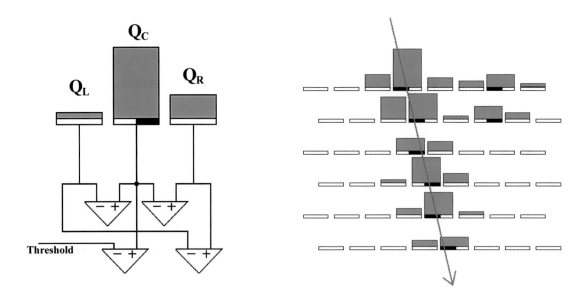

Figure 7.57: Left panel: a simplified schematic of the idea behind the comparator network. For each group of 3 adjacent strips, comparators compare the central strip signal Q_c with a threshold and with the central-to-left $Q_c - Q_l$, central-to-right $Q_c - Q_r$, and right-to-left $Q_r - Q_l$ strip signal differences. If $Q_c >$ threshold, $Q_c - Q_l > 0$, $Q_c - Q_r > 0$, and $Q_r - Q_l > 0$ (as shown here), the hit position is somewhere within the right half of the central strip. Right panel: a *cathode local charged track* is a pattern of half-strip hits consistent with a muon track.

The second amplifier-shaper output goes to the comparator network. This chip compares signals on triplets of adjacent strips at the time when signals reach their maximum amplitude. By means of such comparisons, the comparator network can identify a muon hit location to within one half of a strip width, independent of the signal amplitude, the induced charge shape (as long as it is "bell"-like), and the strip width itself [153] (figure 7.57 (left)).

Comparator half-strip hits are sent to the trigger motherboard (TMB). Like the ALCT board, the TMB searches for patterns of half-strip comparator hits that would be consistent with muon tracks of interest (figure 7.57 (right)). There is 1 TMB per chamber and up to 2 CLCTs per bunch crossing can be found per TMB. As in the ALCT pattern search, for a CLCT pattern to be found, half-strip hits must be present from at least 4 planes. Unlike the ALCT boards, the TMBs are not mounted on the chambers, but are in peripheral VME crates mounted along the outer rim of the endcap steel disks.

The TMB also matches ALCT and CLCT patterns found within a chamber to make correlated 2-dimensional LCTs (2D-LCT = ALCT×CLCT), up to 2 per bunch crossing. These 2D-LCTs are sent to muon port cards (MPC), each of which serves 9 chambers covering either 60°- or 30°-sectors in ϕ. For each bunch crossing, an MPC performs a preliminary sorting of all received correlated 2D-LCTs and finds the 3 best-quality candidates — these are then sent further upstream to the muon L1-trigger electronics.

Raw data are collected by the DAQ motherboards (DMB) located in the peripheral crates. There is one DMB for each chamber. The data consist of anode and comparator hits within a time window up to 32 bunch crossings long, ALCT and CLCT decisions in the same window, and

2008 JINST 3 S08004

digitised strip signal waveforms (eight or sixteen 50-ns time samples). The status of the various electronic boards is also a part of the event record. The data collected by the DMB are passed to a detector-dependent unit (DDU) board, then to a data concentration card (DCC), and finally to the CMS filter farm to be processed by the CMS high-level trigger (HLT) software. The expected event size per chamber is about 5 kBytes.

It is important to note that the CSC read-out is intrinsically zero-suppressed. The anode raw data in a particular chamber are passed downstream only if there is an ALCT pattern in coincidence with the L1A signal. Likewise, the cathode information, comparator hits and digitised strip signal waveforms, are passed downstream to the DAQ only if there was a similar CLCT×L1A coincidence. The coincidence window is programmable, but is nominally set at 75 ns, i.e., ±1 bunch crossing.

At the design LHC luminosity, we expect on average to find track stubs in 2 chambers for each L1A signal. With the maximum CMS L1A rate of 100 kHz, the data flow rate from CSCs to HLT is estimated to be around 1 GB/s.

Operation of the peripheral VME crates is supported by clock-control boards (CCB) and custom crate controllers. As its name implies, the CCB distributes the LHC clock and all CMS control commands (like L1A signals).

The HV system is custom made and provides channel-by-channel regulated voltage up to 4.0 kV with about 10 V precision. Currents of less than 10 μA can be measured with a precision of 100 nA, while the precision for larger currents is about 1%. The system can provide more than 100 μA current for individual channels as long as the average consumption does not exceed 40 μA per channel. The maximum expected current at the design LHC luminosity for the most-loaded HV segment is <10 μA.

7.2.3 Performance

The results presented in this section come from tests conducted with final-design CSCs in high-energy muon beams at CERN, with cosmic-ray muons in a lab or in situ after installation, and at the Gamma Irradiation Facility (GIF).

A high-energy muon beam provides a test environment with maximum control, but it can expose only a small portion of a chamber. We typically used 100–300 GeV beams, which also allowed us to study chamber performance in the presence of bremsstrahlung radiation. To study performance over the entire chamber area, for many years we have tested individual large chambers with cosmic-ray muons at various research laboratories.

During the CMS Magnet Test and Cosmic Challenge (MTCC) in 2006, a substantial part of CMS was operated as a unified system. The CSC subsystem was represented by a 60° sector, or 36 chambers. This allowed us to obtain in situ performance results for a large number of CSCs operating simultaneously with other CMS subsystems. Figure 7.58 shows a muon event as detected by CSCs at the MTCC.

At the design LHC luminosity, we expect a large neutron flux in the underground cavern, which upon thermalization and capture is predicted to result in a substantial flux of $\approx$1 MeV photons. Of the photons that enter a chamber, about 1% will convert to electrons. These electrons will give rise to large rates of random hits up to 1 kHz/cm^2 in the CSCs. The GIF at CERN has a

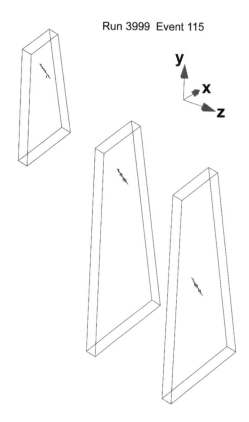

Run 3999 Event 115

Figure 7.58: Part of a CMS event display showing a muon event detected by CSCs during the MTCC. Only those chambers containing muon hits are displayed.

Cs-137 source of 0.7 MeV photons with an intensity of $\approx 0.7 \times 10^{12}$ Bq. Tests at the GIF allowed us to study the chamber performance in an environment of high random-hit rates. We also used these facilities for chamber-ageing studies.

Trigger primitives

It is important to note that the efficiency of finding trigger primitives (LCTs) directly affects not only the muon trigger, but also the DAQ path. As was described earlier, the CSC read-out is driven by an LCT×L1A coincidence. If an LCT is not found, there will not be a coincidence, and no raw hits will be recorded and available for the offline reconstruction.

The anode signal efficiency of a single plane is shown in figure 7.59 (left). The same figure also shows the efficiency for finding ALCTs, patterns of hits in 6 planes consistent with a muon track. The desired ALCT-finding efficiency of 99% is reached above 3.4 kV. At 3.6 kV, the ALCT-finding efficiency is about 99.9%. These results were obtained for test-beam muons going through a small area of a chamber free of dead zones. For CLCT patterns, similar results are achieved at about 50 V higher. This is because the cathode signal is somewhat smaller than the anode signal.

The overall efficiency of finding 2D-LCT patterns (ALCT×CLCT) averaged over the entire area of many chambers was studied with cosmic-ray muons at the MTCC. At the nominal HV of 3.6 kV, the average 2D-LCT efficiency in 6 ME2/2 chambers was found to be (99.93±0.03)%. For the 0.07% of events with missing 2D-LCTs in ME2/2 chambers, the majority of tracks (reconstructed

2008 JINST 3 S08004

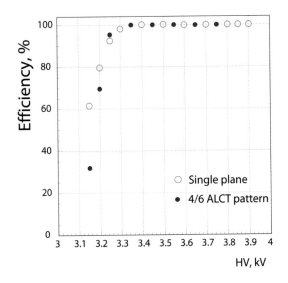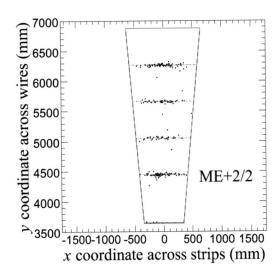

Figure 7.59: Left panel: single-plane anode signal efficiency (open circles) and ALCT pattern finding efficiency (filled circles) vs. high voltage. Right panel: predicted position of muon tracks in ME2/2 chambers for events when no LCT was found in these chambers (superimposed results for 6 chambers). The dashed lines indicate where wire planes of the ME2/2 chambers have inefficient bands separating independent HV segments.

using the ME1 and ME3 LCT stubs) were found to cross ME2/2 chambers in inefficient bands separating the chamber high-voltage segments (figure 7.59 (right)).

To test whether the found LCTs are indeed associated with the muons going through the chambers, we looked at the relative distance between the (x,y) coordinates of 2D-LCTs found in ME2/2 chambers and the muon track (x,y) coordinates in the ME2 station as predicted from the 2D-LCTs in the ME1 and ME3 stations. (Here x and y are the local chamber coordinates across the cathode strips and anode wires, respectively.) The 2D-residuals between the measured and predicted (x,y) coordinates are shown in figure 7.60 (left). The observed spread of ≈ 0.5 cm along the x axis is consistent with the expected multiple scattering of cosmic-ray muons penetrating the endcap steel disks. As is shown below, the intrinsic precision of CLCT localisation is better than that. The distribution along the y axis is noticeably broader due to a much coarser wire group segmentation of 5 cm, which defines the precision of ALCT localisation in these chambers.

For studying the intrinsic CLCT-localisation precision, we used a test chamber in a muon beam and a telescope of Si micro-strip detectors to precisely determine the position of a muon going through the test chamber. To achieve the best results, a given CLCT pattern is assigned an x coordinate corresponding to the average of all muons that can generate such a pattern. Figure 7.60 (right) shows the residuals between the Si-based track coordinate and the CLCT-based coordinate. The distribution is Gaussian and has $\sigma \approx 0.11$ in strip width units, which is better than the desired 2 mm for even the widest 16-mm strips. In the more conservative approach currently implemented in the muon trigger firmware, CLCT patterns are localised within a half-strip. Therefore, in this approach the CLCT spatial resolution is approximately $(w/2)/\sqrt{12} \approx 0.14w$, where w is the strip width.

The time distribution of anode signals from a single chamber plane (figure 7.61 (left, top)) has an RMS of about 11 ns. Clearly this is too wide for a chamber hit to be assigned unambiguously to

2008 JINST 3 S08004

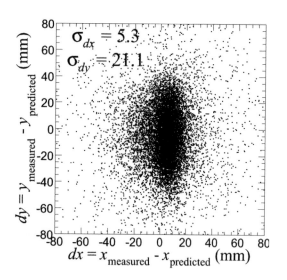
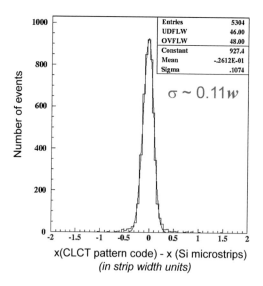

Figure 7.60: Left panel: 2D-coordinate residuals between LCTs found in ME2/2 chambers and muon-track positions. The x axis runs along the wires and the y axis along the strips. The observed spread is consistent with multiple scattering of cosmic-ray muons in the steel disks and the expected CLCT and ALCT spatial resolutions. Right panel: residuals between the CLCT pattern-defined muon coordinate and the coordinate predicted by the Si beam telescope in a 300-GeV muon beam. The residuals are shown in units of strip width.

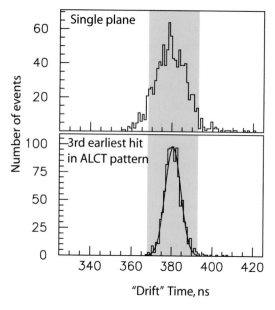
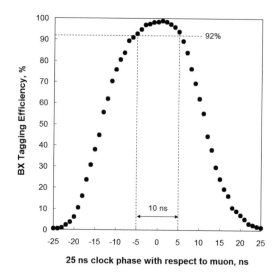

Figure 7.61: Left panel: time distributions of the response of a single plane to a passing muon (top) and for the 3rd earliest hit in an ALCT pattern (bottom). The horizontal scale has an arbitrary offset. The shaded band indicates the 25-ns window, the time between bunch crossings at the LHC. Right panel: probability for correct bunch crossing tagging vs. relative phase shift between the 25-ns clock on an ALCT board and the LHC 25-ns clock.

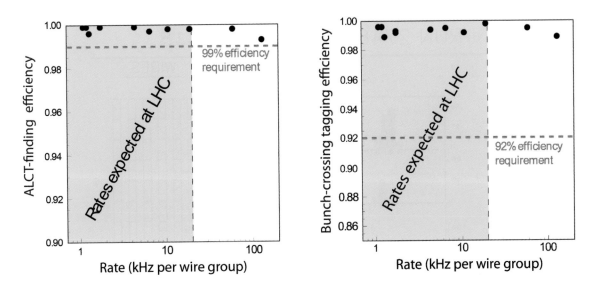

Figure 7.62: Left panel: ALCT-finding efficiency vs. rate of random hits per wire group. Right panel: efficiency of correct bunch tagging vs. rate of random hits per wire group. The shaded areas show the range of rates expected in different chambers at full LHC luminosity.

the correct bunch crossing. We overcome this problem by making use of all 6 planes in a chamber. The time distribution for the 3rd earliest hit in an ALCT pattern (figure 7.61 (left, bottom)) is a much narrower Gaussian with $\sigma < 5$ ns, the use of which results in a bunch-tagging efficiency of 98–99%, well above the desired 92% level. Figure 7.61 (right) shows the accuracy required for aligning the phase of the 25-ns clock on an ALCT board with the LHC clock. The acceptable range of phase misalignment is ± 5 ns. CLCTs tend to have slightly worse timing properties due to the slower CFEB shaping time and smaller amplitude of strip signals, so we assign the time tagged by the ALCT pattern to the matched 2D-LCT.

Results obtained from a CSC irradiated with 0.7 MeV photons in a muon beam at the GIF (figure 7.62) show that the ALCT-finding and bunch-tagging efficiencies remain very robust even at random-hit rates far exceeding those expected at full LHC luminosity.

During 300-GeV muon-beam tests, a 30-cm-thick steel slab was moved in front of the test chamber to study the effect of bremsstrahlung radiation on the reconstruction of muon stubs at the trigger level. In offline analysis of strip data, we classified each muon as either "clean" (multiple charge clusters observed in only 1 plane) or otherwise "contaminated." Without the steel slab, the fraction of "clean" muons was 94% and CLCT patterns were formed from half-strips with a 99.5% efficiency. With the steel slab, the fraction of "clean" muons dropped to 80%, while the CLCT-finding efficiency remained very high (98.9%). Figure 7.63 shows an example of a badly "contaminated" muon where the muon track is nevertheless successfully identified.

2008 JINST 3 S08004

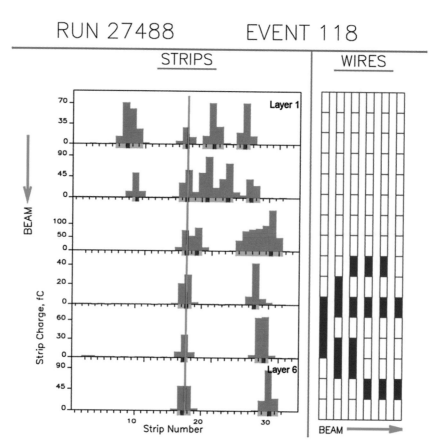

Figure 7.63: A sample CSC event of a muon accompanied by substantial bremsstrahlung radiation. The left side of the plot shows the charge (blocks just above the axes) on each of the 32 strips in each of the 6 chamber layers, while the right side shows the information from the anode wire groups. Strips with charge above the trigger threshold are marked with light shading below the axes, while the half-strip "peaks" are marked with dark squares. The vertical line at $\lambda = 17.56$ shows the track position extrapolated from the Si beam telescope. This event was assigned a 6-layer CLCT code that corresponds to an average track position $\lambda = 17.59$.

Spatial resolution based on digitised strip signals

An avalanche on a wire induces charge on a cathode plane. In a first approximation, the shape of the induced charge can be parameterized by the so-called Gatti function [155]:

$$\frac{1}{Q}\frac{dQ}{d\lambda} = K_1\left[\frac{1 - \tanh^2(K_2\lambda)}{1 + K_3\tanh^2(K_2\lambda)}\right], \tag{7.2}$$

where $\lambda = x/h$, in which x is the coordinate across a strip and h is the cathode-anode spacing, and the coefficients K_1, K_2, and K_3 are defined by the chamber geometry.

Given the geometry of the CSCs, most of the induced charge is shared among 3–4 strips. As described earlier, a strip signal waveform is sampled and digitised every 50 ns. The signal peaks in about 150 ns and comes back very close to the baseline within the next 150 ns so that the

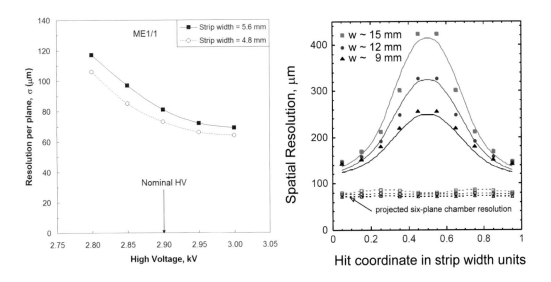

Figure 7.64: Left panel: ME1/1 chamber single-plane resolution vs. HV. Right panel: ultimate large CSC offline resolutions per plane for different muon passage points across a strip for areas with different strip widths for data (closed symbols) and simulation (solid lines). The expected overall 6-plane CSC resolutions are shown by open symbols and dashed lines.

overall pulse duration is roughly 300 ns. Such a 2-dimensional charge cluster can be fit to obtain the spatial coordinate, time, and cluster charge. To achieve the best possible resolution, we take into account empirical corrections for the induced charge shape, the time structure of the signal waveform, strip-to-strip cross-talk, electronic-noise correlations between nearby time samples, and electronic pedestal and gain calibrations.

By design, ME1/1 and ME1/2 chambers have narrower strips and thus deliver better resolution. The ME1/1 single-plane resolution (figure 7.64 (left)) is about 80 μm at nominal HV. The 6-plane chamber resolution is estimated to be $\approx 80/\sqrt{6} = 33$ μm, plus alignment errors. Clearly, the desired resolution of 75 μm per 6-plane chamber is within reach.

The single-plane spatial resolution of the larger CSCs (with very wide strips up to 16 mm) depends very strongly on the muon coordinate across a strip. Muons that pass through a strip centre will be measured poorly (and the wider the strip, the worse the measurement). On the other hand, muons hitting between strips will be measured nearly equally well for any strip width. We took advantage of this feature in our design. In the larger chambers, strips in adjacent planes are staggered by one half of the strip pitch. High-energy muons, for which we need the best chamber resolution, appear as nearly straight-through tracks. If such a muon goes through areas with poor resolution in odd planes, it will have very good measurements in even planes, and vice versa. Therefore, by combining measurements from 6 planes with proper weighting, a muon track segment is accurately localised. Figure 7.64 (right) shows single-plane resolutions, σ_i, for chamber regions with different strip widths and the resulting combined 6-plane resolution, σ_{CSC}, which is estimated by

$$\frac{1}{\sigma_{\text{CSC}}^2(x/w)} = \sum \frac{1}{\sigma_i^2(x/w)}. \tag{7.3}$$

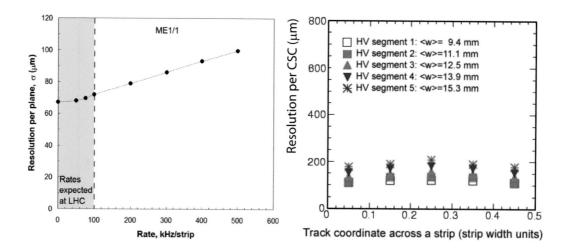

Figure 7.65: Left panel: deterioration of spatial resolution (ME1/1 chambers) with increasing rate of signals. The resolution remains well within the design specs even at rates far exceeding those expected at the LHC. Right panel: expected 6-plane chamber resolution for nearly perpendicular tracks vs. muon coordinate across a strip as evaluated from the single-plane resolution obtained with a simplified and fast reconstruction specifically targeted for the HLT.

The expected combined resolution for a 6-plane chamber is ≈ 80 μm almost independent of the hit position in a chamber, better than the 150-μm goal.

Even at the highest rates expected at the LHC, the CSC resolution will stay well within the design specifications (figure 7.65 (left)). A simplified algorithm for hit-position reconstruction that does not use any fitting, iterative procedures, or chamber- or electronics-specific corrections/calibrations was tested on the 12 largest chambers in the MTCC cosmic-ray runs. Being simple and fast, this algorithm is specifically targeted for the HLT. First, 2D-track segments in the chambers are identified by directly accessing the ALCT- and CLCT-pattern records available in the DAQ. Then, the coordinate is calculated by using a simple analytical function $f_w(r)$ of the ratio r built from the charges Q on 3 adjacent strips (centre, right, and left strips):

$$(x/w)_{\text{measured}} = f_w(r), \quad \text{where } r = \frac{1}{2}\left[\frac{Q_{\text{right}} - Q_{\text{left}}}{Q_{\text{centre}} - min(Q_{\text{right}}, Q_{\text{left}})}\right]. \tag{7.4}$$

This algorithm localises muon stubs in a chamber with a precision of <200 μm (figure 7.65 (right)), which is more than adequate for the HLT. The highest muon p_T threshold used by the HLT is 40 GeV. Due to the muon multiple scattering in the calorimeters and in the steel disks, for muons with transverse momenta $p_T < 40$ GeV, one need not measure muon coordinates with a precision much better than ≈ 0.5 mm. This holds true for a muon momentum measurement in the stand-alone muon system, for associating stand-alone muons with tracks in the central tracker, and for the ultimate muon momentum measurement, which is achieved by means of combining information from the central tracker and the muon system.

Radiation tolerance

The high radiation rates at the LHC could result in devastating problems; thus, the detectors and electronics were designed to be robust. To validate the design, we carried out a series of detailed tests of chamber ageing and electronic board radiation damage.

Ageing studies were conducted [156] by irradiating CSCs at the GIF for several months. The prototype gas system operated in recycling mode as envisioned for full-system operation (2 gas volume exchanges per day with about 5% fresh gas added in each 1-volume cycle). The chambers showed little change in gas gain, dark current, and spurious pulse rate. The total accumulated charge on the wires was about 0.4 C/cm, corresponding to about 50 years of operation at full LHC luminosity in the worst areas closest to the beam line. Upon opening the chambers, we observed a layer of deposits on the cathode surfaces, but not on the anode wires. The deposits on the cathodes, being slightly conductive (established by a small reduction of resistance between strips), did not affect performance (e.g., by the Malter effect [157]).

To test the stability of electronic board performance, we dealt separately with 2 distinct radiation components: total ionisation dose and neutron fluence. The total ionising dose for 10 LHC years is ≈ 20 Gy for on-chamber boards and 2 Gy for peripheral crate electronics. The integrated neutron flux over 10 years ranges from about 10^{10} to 10^{12} cm^{-2}. Analog components of the electronics may suffer a steady and permanent deterioration in performance, while the main danger for digital electronics are Single Event Effects (SEE), including Single Event Upsets (SEU) and Single Event Latching (SEL). Upon an SEE occurrence, the electronics can typically be reset by reloading the FPGAs or cycling the power: SEEs can thus be characterised by the meantime between occurrences.

All electronic chips and components were tested with radiation doses far exceeding the 10 LHC-year equivalent [158]. For final-design boards, no significant deterioration in analog performance was observed (noise, gain, threshold, etc.). All digital-electronic FPGAs were tested for SEEs using typical fluences of $\approx 3 \times 10^{11}$ cm^{-2}. No SEL was observed on any FPGA during testing. SEU rates were dominated by the control logic on the CFEB boards. The SEU rate was lowered significantly by introducing a design with triple-voting logic. The mean time between SEEs on a single CFEB was measured and extrapolated to be 700 h at the LHC neutron fluence. With ≈ 2400 CFEBs in our system, a single CFEB will fail due to an SEU about every 30 min during LHC running, which is an acceptable rate, and will need to be reset.

Reliability

Extensive testing of prototypes has shown that the CMS Endcap Muon System based on CSC technology would meet all performance requirements and could be built within the constraints of the construction budget. There are 468 six-plane CSCs in the system, with CSC planes comprising ≈ 5000 m^2 of sensitive area. The total number of read-out channels is about 400 000. During the years of construction and commissioning, the CMS CSCs have proven to be very reliable in operation (e.g., not a single wire out of about 2 000 000 in the system has ever snapped) and have confirmed the expected performance. As an example, analyses of the first data taken in situ with 36 chambers and cosmic-ray muons showed that chambers had a 99.9% efficiency to detect muon-

2008 JINST 3 S08004

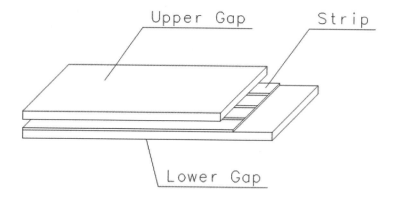

Figure 7.66: Layout of a double-gap RPC.

Table 7.2: Basic construction parameters.

Bakelite thickness	2 mm
Bakelite bulk resistivity	$1\text{–}2 \times 10^{10}$ Ω·cm
Gap width	2 mm

track segments (input to the Level-1 trigger) and the spatial resolution attainable at the high-level trigger and offline was ≈ 150 μm.

7.3 Resistive Plate Chamber system

Resistive Plate Chambers (RPC) are gaseous parallel-plate detectors that combine adequate spatial resolution with a time resolution comparable to that of scintillators [159, 160]. An RPC is capable of tagging the time of an ionising event in a much shorter time than the 25 ns between 2 consecutive LHC bunch crossings (BX). Therefore, a fast dedicated muon trigger device based on RPCs can identify unambiguously the relevant BX to which a muon track is associated even in the presence of the high rate and background expected at the LHC. Signals from such devices directly provide the time and position of a muon hit with the required accuracy. A trigger based on RPCs has to provide the BX assignment to candidate tracks and estimate the transverse momenta with high efficiency in an environment where rates may reach 10^3 Hz/cm^2.

The CMS RPC basic double-gap module consists of 2 gaps, hereafter referred as *up* and *down* gaps, operated in avalanche mode with common pick-up read-out strips in between (figure 7.66) [161, 162]. The total induced signal is the sum of the 2 single-gap signals. This allows the single-gaps to operate at lower gas gain (lower high voltage) with an effective detector efficiency higher than for a single-gap. Table 7.2 lists the basic construction and operating parameters of the CMS double-gap RPCs.

Extensive ageing tests have been performed over the past years with both neutron and gamma sources to verify long term detector performance in the LHC background environment [163, 164]. Results confirm that over a period equivalent to 10 CMS-operation years, no efficiency degradation is expected while all other characteristic parameters stay well within the project specifications. Six layers of RPC chambers are embedded in the barrel iron yoke, 2 located in each of the first and second muon stations and 1 in each of the 2 last stations. The redundancy in the first 2 stations allows the trigger algorithm to perform the reconstruction always on the basis of 4 layers, even for low p_T particles, which may stop inside the iron yoke. In the endcap region, the baseline design foresees the instrumentation of the iron disks with 4 layers of RPCs to cover the region up to $\eta = 2.1$. However, in the first phase, due to budget limitations, only 3 layers up to $\eta = 1.6$ are built. In addition, the background rate in the high η region is significantly higher, well beyond the limit reached during the ageing test. Additional R&D to certify the detector performance under such conditions is ongoing.

7.3.1 Detector layout

Barrel system

In the barrel iron yoke, the RPC chambers form 6 coaxial sensitive cylinders (all around the beam axis) that are approximated with concentric dodecagon arrays arranged into 4 stations (figure 7.67).

In the first and second muon stations there are 2 arrays of RPC chambers located internally and externally with respect to the Drift Tube (DT) chambers: RB1in and RB2in at smaller radius and RB1out and RB2out at larger radius. In the third and fourth stations there are again 2 RPC chambers, both located on the inner side of the DT layer (named RB3+ and RB3−, RB4+ and RB4−). A special case is RB4 in sector 4, which consists of 4 chambers: RB4++, RB4+, RB4−, and RB4−−. Finally, in sectors 9 and 11 there is only 1 RB4 chamber.

In total there are 480 rectangular chambers (table 7.3), each one 2455 mm long in the beam direction. Exceptions are the chambers in sector 3 of wheel −1 and sector 4 of wheel +1, which are 2055 mm long to allow passage of the magnet cooling chimney. Chambers RB1, RB2, and RB3 have widths 2080, 2500, and 1500 mm, respectively. The widths of the RB4 chambers (which depend on location) are given in table 7.4.

Physics requirements demand that the strips always run along the beam direction and are divided into 2 parts for chambers RB1, RB3, and RB4. The RB2 chambers, a special case for the trigger algorithm, have strips divided into 2 parts (RB2in in wheels +2 and −2 and RB2out in wheels +1, 0, and −1) and into 3 parts (RB2out in wheels +2 and −2 and RB2in in wheels +1, 0, and −1). Each chamber therefore consists of either 2 or 3 double-gap modules mounted sequentially in the beam direction to cover the active area. For each double-gap module (up to 96 strips/double-gap), the front-end electronics boards are located at the strip end, which minimises the signal arrival time with respect to the interaction point. The strip widths increase accordingly from the inner stations to the outer ones to preserve projectivity (each strip covers $5/16°$ in ϕ). Figures 7.68 and 7.69 show schematic views of chamber modules with 2 and 3 double-gaps, respectively. Table 7.5 lists some global information regarding the barrel detector.

2008 JINST 3 S08004

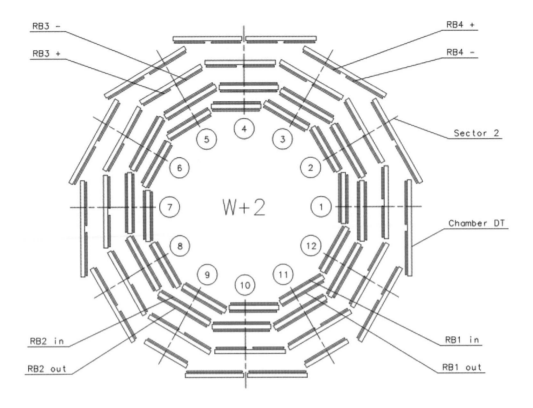

Figure 7.67: Schematic layout of one of the 5 barrel wheels, which are labeled –2, –1, 0, +1, and +2, respectively. Each wheel is divided into 12 sectors that are numbered as shown.

Table 7.3: Number of RPCs for different wheels.

RPC	W+2	W+1	W0	W–1	W–2	Total
RB1in	12	12	12	12	12	60
RB1out	12	12	12	12	12	60
RB2/2in	12	-	-	-	12	24
RB2/2out	-	12	12	12	-	36
RB2/3in	-	12	12	12	-	36
RB2/3out	12	-	-	-	12	24
RB3	24	24	24	24	24	120
RB4	24	24	24	24	24	120
Total	96	96	96	96	96	480

Endcap system

In the forward and backward regions of the CMS detector, 3 iron disks constitute the endcap yokes. Like in the barrel, 2 complementary muon detector systems are deployed for robust muon identifi-

Table 7.4: Widths of the RB4 chambers.

Sector	RB4+	RB4++	RB4−	RB4−−	RB4
S1–S3					
S5–S7	2000 mm		2000 mm		
S8	1500 mm		2000 mm		
S12	2000 mm		1500 mm		
S9, S11					2000 mm
S10	2500 mm		2500 mm		
S4	1500 mm	1500 mm	1500 mm	1500 mm	

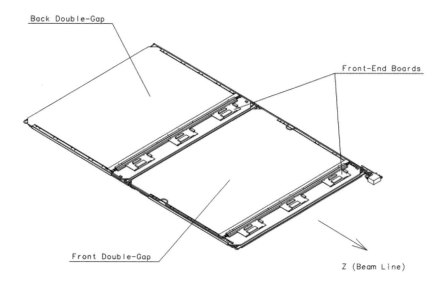

Figure 7.68: Schematic layout of chamber module with 2 double-gaps.

Table 7.5: Barrel RPC system global parameters.

Number of stations	480
Total surface area	2400 m^2
Number of double-gaps	1020
Number of strips	80 640

cation: cathode strip chambers (CSC) and RPCs. They are mounted on both faces of the disks to yield 4 CSC stations (ME1–4) and, for the initial detector, 3 RPC stations (RE1–3). The double-gaps in every station have a trapezoidal shape and are arranged in 3 concentric rings as shown in the r-ϕ view of figure 7.70. They overlap in ϕ as to avoid dead space at chamber edges. Except

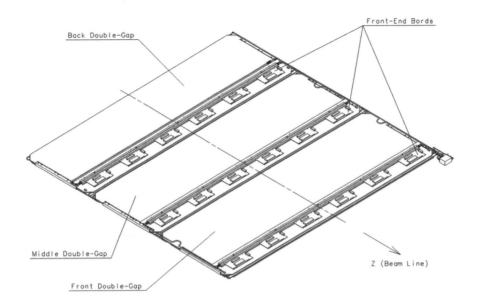

Figure 7.69: Schematic layout of chamber module with 3 double-gaps.

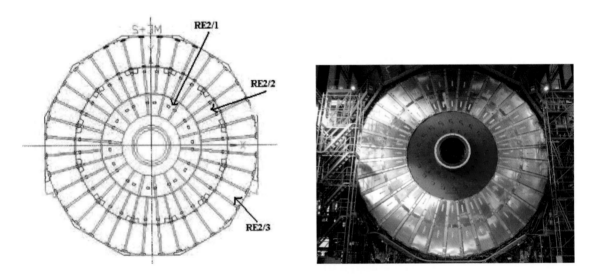

Figure 7.70: Left panel: schematic r-ϕ layout of RPC station RE2 on the back side of the first endcap yoke. Right panel: RPC station RE2 on the back side of the YE-1 yoke. The inner ring has been staged and is absent here.

for station 1, the chambers of the innermost ring span 20° in ϕ, all others span 10°. As mentioned before, the high η part of the RPC system (beyond $\eta \approx 1.6$) has been staged until the LHC is scheduled to deliver its design luminosity of 10^{34} cm^{-2}s^{-1}.

Station RE1 is mounted on the interaction point (IP) side of the first endcap disk (YE1), underneath the CSC chambers of ME1. Stations RE2 and 3 are mounted on the back side of YE1 and on the IP side of YE3, respectively. They remain uncovered since the corresponding CSC stations 2 and 3 are mounted on both faces of YE2. Figure 7.71 shows a schematic layout

2008 JINST 3 S08004

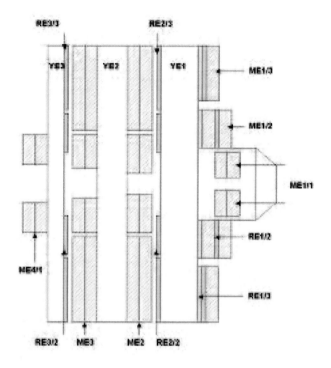

Figure 7.71: Schematic layout of the CMS endcap for the initial muon system.

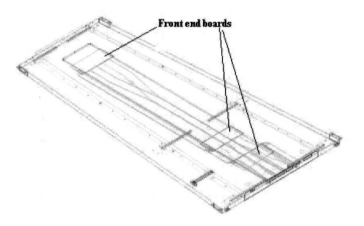

Figure 7.72: A view of an endcap RPC chamber.

of the CMS endcap defining the nomenclature of the muon stations. Each endcap RPC chamber consists of a double-gap structure enclosed in a flat trapezoidal shaped box made of 2 aluminium honeycomb panels of 6 mm thickness each and a 16×16 mm^2 section spacer frame (figure 7.72). The strip panel, sandwiched in between the gas gaps, has copper strip sections on a G10 support. Strips run radially and are radially segmented into 3 trigger sections for the REn/2 and REn/3 chambers (n = 1–3). The 32 strips of the 10° RPC chambers are projective to the beam line, following a homothetic pattern. Besides the different mechanical shape and assembly, the front-end electronics, services, trigger, and read-out schemes of the endcap RPC system are identical to the barrel system. To an operator, the CMS barrel and endcap RPC systems look identical.

2008 JINST 3 S08004

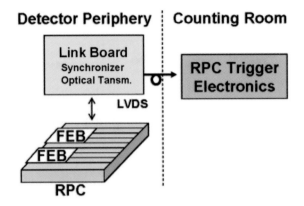

Figure 7.73: Block diagram of RPC read-out electronics.

7.3.2 Readout electronics

Front-end electronics

The read-out strips are connected to Front-End Boards (FEB). After having been amplified and discriminated, signals are sent unsynchronized to Link Boards (LB) placed around the detector. The LBs synchronize the signals with the 40-MHz LHC clock and transmit them to the trigger electronics located in the CMS counting room over a 90-m optical link at 1.6 GHz, as shown in the block diagram of figure 7.73.

The FEBs house two (barrel version) or four (endcap version) front-end chips, which are custom ASICs designed in AMS 0.8 μm CMOS technology [165]. Each chip is made of 8 identical channels, each consisting of an amplifier, zero-crossing discriminator, one-shot, and LVDS driver. The preamplifier is a trans-resistance stage with 15-Ω input impedance to match the characteristic impedance of the strips. It is followed by a gain stage to provide an overall charge sensitivity of 2 mV/fC.

Since accurate RPC timing information is crucial for providing an unambiguous bunch crossing assignment of the event, the zero-crossing discrimination technique was adopted to make the timing response amplitude-independent. In fact, considering that the RPC signals have a wide dynamic range (from few tens of fC to 10 pC), the implemented architecture provides a time walk below 1 ns, while the simpler leading-edge discrimination technique would have provided a time walk of $\approx$10 ns. The discriminator is followed by a one-shot circuit. This produces a pulse shaped at 100 ns to mask possible after-pulses that may follow the avalanche pulse. Finally, an LVDS driver is used to send the signals to the LB in differential mode.

Gamma-irradiation tests showed no performance degradation of either the front-end chip or the control electronics on the FEB [166]. Moreover, tests with thermal and fast reactor neutrons (0.4 eV–10 MeV) and with more energetic neutrons (65 MeV), have certified that the circuit can sustain the expected CMS operational conditions [167].

2008 JINST 3 S08004

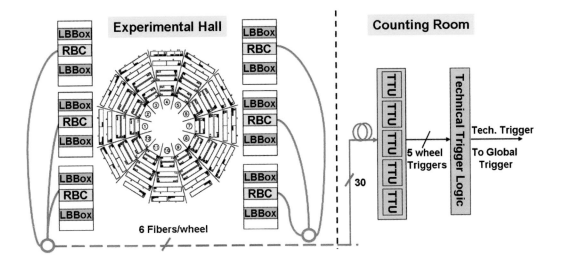

Figure 7.74: Technical Trigger schematic layout.

RPC technical trigger electronics

Study of the detector performance is a crucial aspect during the detector-commissioning phase. The RPC trigger system was designed to identify muon tracks starting from the interaction point. Therefore, all interconnections among the LBs and trigger electronics were optimised to fulfil a projective vertex geometry, not adequate for triggering on cosmic rays. Therefore, an RPC-based trigger (Technical Trigger in the following) has been implemented by means of 2 types of electronic boards: the RPC Balcony Collector (RBC) housed in the cavern and the Technical Trigger Unit (TTU) located in the counting room (figure 7.74) [168].

The RBC collects 96-strip OR signals from the barrel LBs and produces a "local" sector-based cosmic trigger to be used during commissioning or calibration of the detector. The RBC transmits the ORs optically to the TTU boards in the Counting Room (30 fibres in total), where a wheel-level cosmic trigger is produced and sent as a Technical Trigger to the CMS Global Trigger. A proper algorithm for searching for cosmic-muon tracks is implemented in the TTU.

7.3.3 Low voltage and high voltage systems

General requirements

The RPC power systems operate in a hostile environment due to the high magnetic field and high radiation flux. Large portions of the power systems are near the detectors on the balcony racks placed around the barrel wheels and the endcap disks. In these areas the magnetic field can reach 1 T with radiation around $5 \cdot 10^{10}$ protons/cm^2 and $5 \cdot 10^{11}$ neutrons/cm^2. In cooperation with the ATLAS, ALICE, and LHCb groups, the CMS collaboration developed a new design for an RPC power system able to operate in such conditions. The main requirements for the RPC HV and LV power supplies are collected in table 7.6.

The HV and LV systems are both based on a master/slave architecture. The master, called the mainframe, is devoted to controlling and monitoring one or more slaves and is placed in a

2008 JINST 3 S08004

Table 7.6: HV and LV power supply requirements.

	HV	LV
Maximum Voltage	12 kV	7 V
Maximum Current	1 mA	3 A
Ripple	<100 mV pp at load (freq <20 MHz)	<10 mV pp at load (freq <20 MHz)
Programmable Voltage	from 0 to 12 kV	from 0 to 7 V
Current monit. precision	0.1 μA	100 mA
Voltage monit. precision	<10 V	100 mV

safe and accessible area like the control room. The slaves can be located near the detector and are designed to be modular and multi-functional to accept both HV and LV boards. These have to work in a hostile and inaccessible area and are based on radiation-tolerant and magnetic-field-tolerant electronics.

Past experience with RPC detector systems, however, suggested that it is important to have the HV power supplies in an accessible area. In case of unsustainable high current on a detector, the possibility of removing a channel during operation should be available. Therefore, the CMS RPC collaboration decided to keep the master/slave architecture for both the HV and LV systems but to move all HV system components into the control room.

HV and LV system description

The system is based on the EASY (Embedded Assembly SYstem) project. It is made of a master SY1527 (mainframe) which houses up to 16 branch controller boards (A1676A) and of EASY3000 crates (slaves). The EASY3000 crate can house different boards (high and low voltage, ADC, and DAC). Each EASY3000 board operates as a channel of the A1676A and can be accessed through the mainframe. The EASY architecture foresees 2 independent 48-V power supplies to power independently the channel regulators and the control logic. The EASY system is connected to the external world through a serial port and an ETHERNET3 interface that allows the user to monitor and control the whole system with various software from a very easy TELNET interface to a more sophisticated OPC protocol.

HV hardware. The A3512 double-width board is equipped with 6 floating 12 kV/1 mA channels of either positive or negative polarity. The 6 channels have an independent return to avoid ground loops. The board is designed with an output voltage that can be programmed and monitored in the 0–12 kV range with 1 V resolution and with a monitored current resolution of 0.1 μA. This current resolution allows the Detector Control System (DCS) to study the current behaviour of every chamber with an accuracy of at least 1/10 of the measured current (between 10 and 20 μA per chamber). In the barrel there is 1 HV channel per chamber, while in the endcap region 1 channel supplies 2 chambers. In this last case, an upgrade of the system will depend on future budget availability. A summary of the HV systems is given in table 7.7.

2008 JINST 3 S08004

Table 7.7: Summary of HV systems.

	Barrel	Endcap
HV channels	480	216
HV boards	80	36
Easy3000 Crates	14	6

Table 7.8: Summary of LV systems.

	Barrel	Endcap
LV channels	720	432
LV boards	60	36
Easy3000 Crates	20	14

LV hardware. The CAEN A3009 board is a 12-channel 8V/9A power-supply board for the EASY Crate. It was developed for operation in magnetic fields and radioactive environments. The output-voltage range is 1.5–8 V with 5-mV monitor resolution; channel control includes various alarms and protections. The output current is monitored with 10-mA resolution.

Each chamber is supplied by 2 LV lines for the front-end analog (LV_a) and digital (LV_d) parts. To avoid ground loops on the detector, it is important to preserve, when possible, a 1-to-1 correspondence between LV channel and chamber. This is achieved in the barrel system, where there is 1 LV_a and 1 LV_d channel per chamber. However, for the endcap detector, at the start-up 1 LV_a and 1 LV_d are distributed between 2 chambers. A summary of the LV systems is given in table 7.8.

7.3.4 Temperature control system

RPC operation is sensitive to both temperature and atmospheric pressure. Therefore, the chambers are constantly monitored to compensate in real time for the detector operating point (HV value). A network of 420 sensors located inside the barrel chambers is available to monitor the temperature. The AD592BN sensor (Analog Devices) can work in a hostile environment with a resolution of about 0.5°C, better than the CMS requirement (1°C). Sensors are read out by a 128-channel ADC equipped with a 12-V input stage.

Additional sensors are available on each front-end board; they are read out through the LB electronics to monitor the temperature.

7.3.5 Gas system

Test results [169] showed that RPCs are suitably operated with a 3-component non-flammable mixture of 96.2% R134a ($C_2H_2F_4$), 3.5% iC_4H_{10} and 0.3% SF_6. Water vapour is added to the gas mixture to maintain a relative humidity of about 45% and to avoid changes of the bakelite

2008 JINST 3 S08004

Table 7.9: Main gas parameters of the CMS RPC system.

Gas volume	14 m^3
Gas mixture composition	96.2% R134a, 3.5% $i\text{C}_4\text{H}_{10}$, and 0.3% SF_6
Internal chamber pressure above atmosphere	3 mbar
Nominal flow rate	$10 \text{ m}^3/\text{h}$
Fresh gas replenishing rate	$0.2 \text{ m}^3/\text{h}$
Number of gas channels	250 (barrel) + 144 (endcaps)

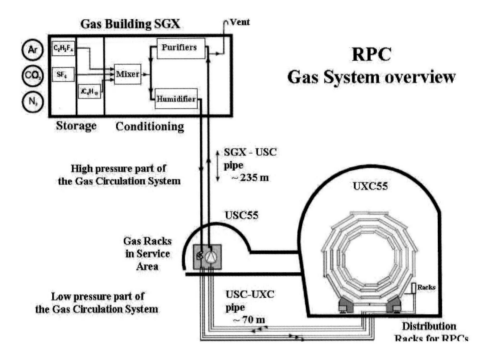

Figure 7.75: Closed-loop circulation system.

resistivity. The basic function of the gas system is to mix the different gas components in the appropriate proportions and to distribute the mixture to the individual chambers. The large detector volume and the use of a relatively expensive gas mixture make a closed-loop circulation system mandatory. The main gas-system parameters are given in table 7.9.

The system consists of several modules: the primary gas supply, mixer and closed-loop circulation system, gas distributors to the chambers, purifier, pump, and gas-analysis station [132]. The full closed-loop circulation system (figure 7.75) extends from the surface gas building SGX to the USC55 service cavern and UXC55 experimental cavern.

Mixer

The primary gas supplies and the mixer are situated in the SGX building. The flow of component gases is controlled by mass-flow meters. Flows are monitored by a computer-controlled process,

Table 7.10: Chamber volumes and gas flow for a single wheel of the barrel detector.

Station	RPCs in that station	Volume per RPC (l)	number of gas channels	Volume per gas channel (l)	Operating channel flow (l/h)	total flow per station type (l/h)
RB1	24	20.6	12	41.2	27.5	330
RB2	24	25.4	12	50.8	33.9	406
RB3	12	31.4	12	31.4	20.9	251
RB4	12	43.4	14	43.4	28.9	347
Total	72		50			1334

which constantly calculates and adjusts the mixture percentages supplied to the system. The gas mixture is maintained non-flammable by permanent monitoring. The gas flow is stopped automatically if the iC_4H_{10} fraction increases beyond the flammability limit. For fast detector filling, parallel rotameters are used, instead of the mass-flow controllers, yielding a complete volume renewal in about 8 hours.

Closed-loop circulation

The mixed gas is circulated in a common closed loop for the barrel and both endcaps. The circulation loop is distributed among 3 locations:

- the purifier, gas input, and exhaust gas connections are located in the SGX building;

- the pressure controllers, separation of barrel and endcaps systems, compressor, and analysis instrumentation are located in the USC (accessible at any time);

- the manifolds for the chamber-gas supplies and channel flow meters are mounted in the distribution racks near the detector.

The high density of the used mixture generates a hydrostatic pressure of about 0.3 mbar/m above atmospheric pressure. Since the total RPC detector height is about 15 m, the barrel detector is split into 2 zones (top and bottom) that have independent pressure regulation systems (figure 7.76). Each barrel muon station has an independent gas line. The 2 RPC chambers located in a station are supplied in parallel from the same patch panel sitting nearby. This configuration leads to 250 gas channels (50 per wheel) for the full barrel detector (table 7.10).

Each endcap detector consists of 3 disks, RE1, RE2, and RE3, with a total of 216 double-gap chambers. Each disk is composed of 2 concentric rings (i.e., for REn: REn/2 and REn/3) of 36 chambers each. In the RE1 rings the chambers are divided in 6 ϕ sections of 60°. A section contains 6 chambers and is supplied with 2 gas lines for the up and down gaps (figure 7.77a). The gas flow in the up gap is in the opposite sense to that in the down gap to improve the average gas quality. In the RE2 and RE3 stations, the chambers are divided into 12 ϕ sections of 30°. Each section contains 3 chambers of the external ring and the corresponding 3 chambers of the internal ring, i.e., an RE2 section includes 3 RE2/2 and 3 RE2/3 chambers (figure 7.77b). In RE2 and RE3

2008 JINST 3 S08004

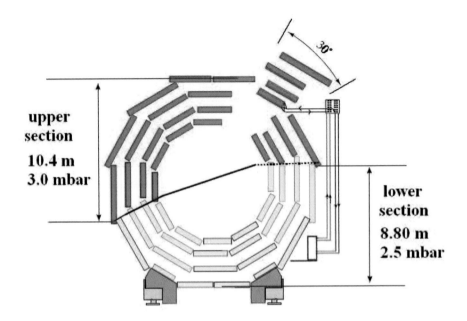

Figure 7.76: The 2 zones into which a wheel is sub-divided. Each station (2 chambers) is supplied by a gas line.

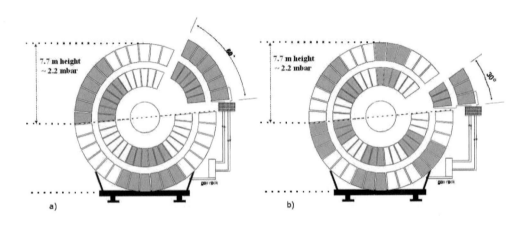

Figure 7.77: In each endcap disk the RPC detectors are divided in 2 rings. RE1 (a) is divided into 60° sectors, while in RE2 and in RE3 (b) sectors are composed of 3 chambers of the internal ring and the corresponding 3 of the external ring. Every sector is supplied by 2 independent gas lines.

as well there are 2 gas lines per section (for the up and down gaps) and the flows are in the opposite sense between the two. The total number of channels and the relative gas flows are summarised in table 7.11.

2008 JINST 3 S08004

Table 7.11: Chamber volumes and gas flows for a single endcap of the CMS RPC system.

Module	RPCs in that module	Volume per RPC (l)	Number of gas channels	Volume per gas channel (l)	Operating channel flow (l/h)	Total flow per module type (l/h)
RE/1/2	36	5.1	12	30.6	20.4	122
RE/1/3	36	7.4	12	44.4	29.6	178
RE/2/2	36	5.1	24	20.3	13.5	324
RE/2/3	36	8.4				
RE/3/2	36	5.1	24	20.3	13.5	324
RE/3/3	36	8.4				
Total	216		72			948

Pressure regulation system and gas distribution in UXC

Pressure regulation is achieved in the USC area for each of the 2 zones. Each height section has its own pressure control and protection system consisting of bubblers located in the distribution racks at the bottom of the wheels/disks. The oil level is adjusted to account for the hydrostatic pressure differences in the 2 zones. The distribution racks are installed at the bottom of each wheel/disk. The supply and return lines for each station are equipped with a mass-flow meter and a needle valve (only at the inlet). The flow measurements allow the detection of possible leaks, while the needle valves are used for the flow adjustment between different stations.

Purifier

Results from long term tests performed by CMS showed that the impurity concentrations produced in the RPC chambers are high enough to influence the detector performance if they are not properly removed from the mixture. Therefore, to achieve a high recycling rate the closed-loop circulation system is equipped with a purifier module containing 3 cleaning agents. In the first running phase the 3 cleaning agents are contained in 2 purifiers. Both the purifiers are 24-l cartridges. The first is filled with a 0.5-nm molecular sieve, while the second is filled with the following combination: 25% Cu-Zn filter (type R12, BASF), 25% Cu filter (type R3-11G, BASF), and 50% Ni-Al2O3 filter (type 6525, Leuna). During the high luminosity running period the second purifier will be split into 2 separate 24-l cartridges, the first containing the R12 and R3-11G cleaning agents and the second containing the 6525 Leuna filter. Each purifier is equipped with an automatic regeneration system: 2 identical cartridges are present allowing the regeneration of a cartridge while the other is in use.

Gas-quality monitoring

Two independent systems are in preparation to continuously monitor the gas quality. The gas-gain monitoring system [170] is based on several small (50×50 cm^2) single-gap RPCs whose working points (gain and efficiency) are continuously monitored online. The system is designed to provide a fast and accurate determination of any shift in the working points. The small single-gap

2008 JINST 3 S08004

RPCs are divided into several sub-groups supplied with gas coming from different parts of the full system (i.e., fresh gas mixture, input to the chambers in closed-loop circulation, and return from the closed-loop circulation). The second gas monitoring system [171] performs both qualitative and quantitative gas chemical analyses with a set-up that includes a gas chromatograph, pH sensors, and specific fluoride electrodes. In the underground service cavern (USC), many sampling points equipped with manual valves allow the analysis of the gas mixtures that return from every half wheel. In the surface gas building (SGX), sampling points are available to monitor the effectiveness as well as the status of each cartridge in the purifier module.

7.3.6 Chamber construction and testing

In view of the extremely large-scale production (a factor of 10 greater than in past experiments), impressive quality control and certification protocols were set along the production chain at many different levels:

- selection of electrodes and resistivity certification;

- certification of single-gaps and double-gaps;

- chamber testing.

Details regarding the quality certification procedures have been reported elsewhere [172]. Only a short summary of the chamber testing results is given below.

Chamber performance at the test sites

Several RPC test stands were in operation. Each telescope consisted of a tower in which several detectors could be placed horizontally and read out in coincidence with the passage of the crossing of cosmic muons. Two sets of scintillators, at the top and the bottom of the telescope, were used for triggering purposes. Atmospheric and environmental conditions were continuously monitored during the tests. These values were used to scale the applied HV for temperature and pressure variations to evaluate the effective high voltage (HV_{eff}) [173] at given reference values ($T_0 = 293$ K and $P_0 = 1010$ mbar).

The final gas mixture (96.2% $C_2H_2F_4$, 3.5% iC_4H_{10}, and 0.3% SF_6) was used and water vapour was added to keep the gas relative humidity at a value of about 45%.

The tracking capabilities of the test telescope provided a full characterisation of the detectors in terms of efficiency, cluster size, and noise rate. Also the chambers' local efficiency and the spatial resolution were studied. Rigourous and automatic protocols were developed and systematically applied at all test sites in order to accept chambers that satisfied the CMS requirements.

First, the chamber efficiency was studied with the "coincidence" method by evaluating the ratio between the number of events in which an RPC module had at least 1 fired strip in the trigger window (100 ns) and the total number of recorded events. In figure 7.78 the distribution of the maximum efficiency for all the barrel RPCs is shown. The mean value of the distribution is 97.2%. In figure 7.79 the efficiency distribution at HV = 9.3 kV for the first 27 endcap chambers is shown.

The chamber response uniformity was also studied by performing track recognition through the telescope. Muon trajectories were reconstructed in 2-dimensional views, where the x coordinate

2008 JINST 3 S08004

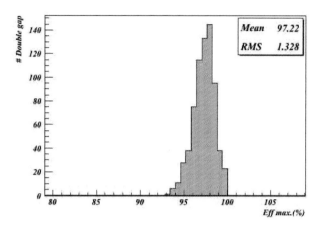

Figure 7.78: Distribution of plateau efficiency for all the barrel chambers.

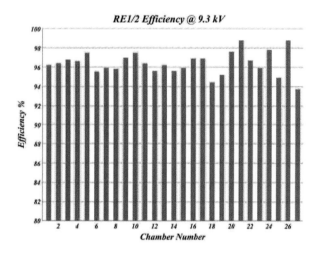

Figure 7.79: Efficiency at HV = 9.3 kV for the first 27 endcap chambers.

is defined by the strip position along the chamber and the y coordinate by the chamber position in the tower. Details about the pattern recognition algorithm have been presented elsewhere [174]. The track-impact point on the chamber under test was also determined and the distance to the nearest cluster centre was evaluated. A chamber was considered efficient if the reconstructed muon trajectory matched the fired strip. A typical strip-by-strip efficiency plot is shown in figure 7.80.

The chamber cluster size is defined as the average value of the cluster-size distribution. In Figure 7.81 the profile histogram of the cluster-size distribution as a function of the HV_{eff} is shown for all the barrel chambers. A chamber was accepted if the cluster size was below 3 strips at the knee of the efficiency plateau.

2008 JINST 3 S08004

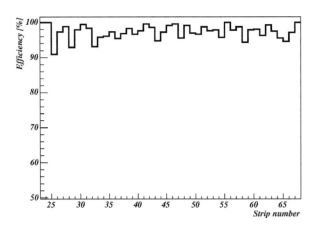

Figure 7.80: Local efficiency at $HV_{eff} = 9.6$ kV for a barrel chamber.

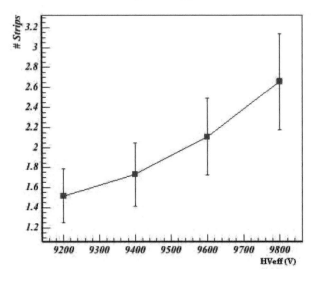

Figure 7.81: Profile histogram of the chambers' cluster-size distribution as a function of HV_{eff}. The dots and bars are the average and the root-mean-square of the cluster-size distributions, respectively.

Magnet Test and Cosmic Challenge (MTCC)

During the summer and fall of 2006 a first integrated test of an entire CMS "slice" was performed in the SX5 experimental surface hall. For the RPC system, 3 barrel sectors and a 60° portion of the first positive endcap disk were involved in the test. The chambers were operated with their final power system configuration, and CMS DAQ software, data quality monitor (DQM), and detector control system (DCS) were implemented for the detector read-out and control.

The RPC Balcony Collector (RBC) board provided a cosmic trigger with a selectable majority level of signals from the 6 RPC barrel chambers. A trigger rate of about 30 Hz/sector for a majority level of 5/6, and 13 Hz/sector for a 6/6 majority was found while operating the detector on the surface. The RBC trigger was well synchronized with the other muon detector (DT and CSC) triggers.

2008 JINST 3 S08004

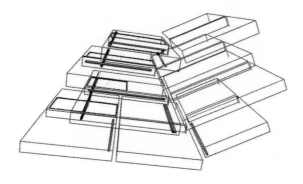

Figure 7.82: Iguana muon reconstruction: RPC-fired strips are in red and DT hits in green.

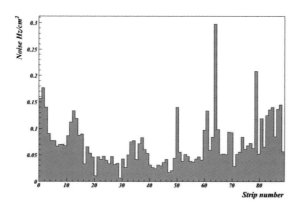

Figure 7.83: Barrel chamber noise profile at HV_{eff} = 9.6 kV.

Several millions of events were collected with different trigger configurations. The DQM was used successfully during the MTCC. It allowed the online checking of the quality of the data and the chamber behaviour in terms of cluster size, number of clusters, etc. Figure 7.82 shows the event display of a typical cosmic muon triggered by the RBC and crossing both RPCs and DTs.

Specific runs were taken before and during the test to evaluate the noise rate. Preliminarily, all the threshold values on the front-end electronic discriminators were set to achieve the best noise configuration with higher efficiency. The chamber noise rate profile for a barrel station is shown in figure 7.83 at HV_{eff} = 9.6 kV, while figure 7.84 shows the overall noise distribution for all the barrel strips involved in the test.

The RPC efficiency can be studied by extrapolating DT segments to the corresponding RPC layer and by requiring matching hits within an appropriate width. In figure 7.85 the chamber efficiency as a function of the HV_{eff} is shown for some RPC stations.

Results are in agreement with those obtained during testing at construction sites and fully meet the design specifications.

2008 JINST 3 S08004

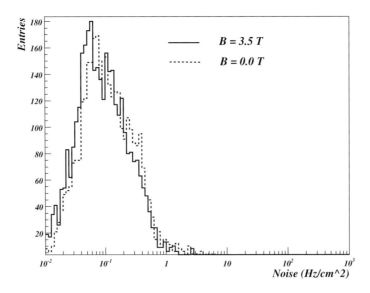

Figure 7.84: Noise distributions in 2 different magnetic fields. All strips of the barrel stations are included in the distribution.

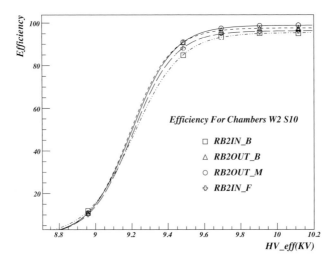

Figure 7.85: Global efficiency vs. HV$_{eff}$, estimated by means of DT segment extrapolation.

7.4 Optical alignment system

For optimal performance of the muon spectrometer [132] over the entire momentum range up to 1 TeV, the different muon chambers must be aligned with respect to each other and to the central tracking system to within a few hundred μm in $r\phi$. The required alignment precision for the endcap chambers is 75–200 μm, while for the barrel the precision varies from 150 μm for the inner chambers of Station 1 to 350 μm for the outer chambers of Station 4. To this end, after following strict chamber construction specifications, CMS combines precise survey and photogrammetry measurements, measurements from an opto-mechanical system, and the results of alignment algorithms based on muon tracks (both from cosmic rays and from pp collisions) crossing the spectrometer.

There are several potential sources of misalignment in the muon spectrometer, from chamber production to final detector operating conditions, including:

- Chamber construction tolerances. These are unavoidable geometrical tolerances in the production of the chamber parts, such as mis-positioning of wires or strips within a layer and relative shifts in the layer-superlayer assembly. The relative positioning of the different internal components of a chamber was measured during construction to be within the required tolerances (section 7.1 and 7.2). After assembly, all chambers were tested with cosmic muon data and showed good correlation between those measurements and the results of muon track fits. Furthermore, the geometry of the DT chambers was measured at the CERN ISR assembly hall using optical and survey techniques. These data are compared with construction drawings and cosmic data to provide corrections to the nominal chamber geometry when necessary.

- Detector assembly, closing tolerances. Gravitational distortions of the return yoke lead to static deformations of the steel support. This effect, together with the installation tolerances, results in displacements of the chambers in the different barrel wheels and endcap disks of up to several millimetres with respect to their nominal detector positions. After chamber installation, survey and photogrammetry measurements were performed for each wheel and disk. These measurements provide an initial geometry — position and orientation of each muon chamber in the different yoke structures — which absorbs installation tolerances and static steel deformations [175].

- Solenoid effects. Magnetic field distortions lead to almost perfect elastic deformations of the return yoke, at the level of a few centimetres. They result in further displacement of the chambers. The new detector geometry resulting from the magnetic forces is accessed with measurements of the optical system and track-based alignment techniques.

- Time-dependent effects. During operation, thermal instabilities and other time-dependent factors can cause dynamic misalignments at the sub-millimetre level.

The Muon Alignment (MA) system was designed to provide continuous and accurate monitoring of the barrel and endcap muon detectors among themselves as well as alignment between them and the inner tracker detector. To fulfil these tasks the system is organized in separate blocks:

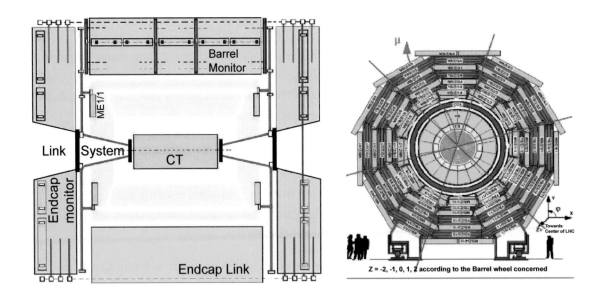

Figure 7.86: Schematic view of the alignment system. Left panel: longitudinal view of CMS. The continuous and dotted lines show different optical light paths. Right panel: transverse view of the barrel muon detector. The crossing lines indicate the r-z alignment planes with 60° staggering in ϕ.

local systems for barrel and endcap muon detectors to monitor the relative positions of the chambers, and a link system that relates the muon and central tracker systems and allows simultaneous monitoring of the detectors.

The system must generate alignment information for the detector geometry with or without collisions in the accelerator. The dynamic range of the system allows it to work in the solenoidal magnetic field between 0 and 4 T. Its goal is to provide independent monitoring of the CMS tracking detector geometry with respect to an internal light-based reference system. This will help to disentangle geometrical errors from sources of uncertainty present in the track-based alignment approach, e.g., knowledge of the magnetic field, material description, and drift velocity.

The basic geometrical segmentation consists of 3 r-z alignment planes with 60° staggering in ϕ. This segmentation is based on the 12-fold geometry of the barrel muon detector. Within each plane, the 3 tracking sub-detectors of CMS (central tracker, barrel and endcap muon detectors) are linked together. Figure 7.86 shows schematic longitudinal and transverse views of CMS, with the light paths indicated. Furthermore, the barrel and endcap monitoring systems can work in stand-alone mode, in which they provide reconstruction of the full geometry of each independent sub-detector. The layout of the optical paths allows the monitoring of each of the 250 DT chambers, while only one sixth of selected CSCs in the 4 endcap stations are directly monitored. Alignment sensors located in the region between the muon barrel wheels and endcap disks allow the tracker and muon detectors to be aligned with respect to each other.

7.4.1 System layout and calibration procedures

The optical network uses two types of light sources: LEDs and laser beams. It is composed of 10 000 LEDs and 150 laser beams together with precise measuring devices: $\approx$ 900 photo-detectors and ≈ 600 analog sensors (distance sensors and inclinometers), complemented by temperature, humidity and Hall probes. The system is structured into three basic blocks whose main features are described below.

Muon barrel alignment

The monitoring of the barrel muon detector (figure 7.87) is based on the measurement of all the 250 DT chamber positions with respect to a floating network of 36 rigid reference structures, called MABs (Module for the Alignment of Barrel). The MAB design was optimised to achieve adequate mechanical rigidity of the structures under load and in thermal and humidity gradients. Long term measurements showed deviations below 100 μm and 50 μrad [176]. The MABs are fixed to the barrel yoke forming 12 r-z planes parallel to the beam line and distributed in ϕ every 60°. Each structure contains 8 specially designed video cameras that observe LED sources mounted on the DT chambers. Extra light sources and video-cameras in specific MABs serve to connect MABs in different planes forming a closed optical network (called diagonal connections). The MAB positions in the z coordinate are measured with respect to 6 calibrated carbon-fibre bars (z-bars) sitting on the outer surface of the vacuum tank of the solenoid. The MABs in the external wheels, YB$\pm$2, are equipped with extra alignment sensors and light sources that connect the barrel monitoring system with the endcap and tracker detectors.

The 4 corners of the DTs are equipped with LED light sources. Four LED-holders, or forks, are rigidly mounted on the side-profile of the honeycomb structure (2 per side) and use the rectangular 50×65 mm^2 tube as a light passage. Each fork contains 10 LEDs, 6 and 4, respectively, on each side. There are 10 000 light sources mounted on the DT chambers. The position of the forks with respect to the chamber geometry was measured on a dedicated bench with a precision of < 70 μm. As an important by-product, the calibration also provides the full geometry, including the planarity, trapezoidity, and the relative positions of superlayers for each DT chamber with < 40 μm precision, as described in section 7.1.4. Each LED-holder and video-sensor was individually calibrated before its assembly on the DT chambers or MABs and z-bars. LED-holders were measured and the position of the light centroid was determined with respect to the holder mechanics with an accuracy of 10 μm. Long term measurements showed good stability of the centroids and light intensity distributions. CMOS miniature video sensors, containing 384×288 pixels with 12×12 μm^2 pixel size, were calibrated to absorb residual response non-uniformities and the intensity nonlinearities. The video cameras, consisting of a video sensor and a single-element lens assembled in an aluminium box, were also calibrated to determine their inner geometrical parameters. Fully instrumented MABs containing the necessary number of survey fiducials were calibrated on a special bench, where the whole geometry of the structure, positions, and orientations of elements were determined with overall accuracies of 70 μm and 50 μrad.

Once MABs were installed (figure 7.88), the initial MAB positions on the barrel wheels were determined by photogrammetry measurements.

The control, read-out, and data preprocessing [177] are performed by a network of local minicomputers (1 per MAB, 36 in total) that makes it possible to run the full system in parallel. The minicomputers are connected to the main control PC via an Ethernet network capable of working in magnetic fields. The main control PC synchronizes the operation of the light sources mounted on

2008 JINST 3 S08004

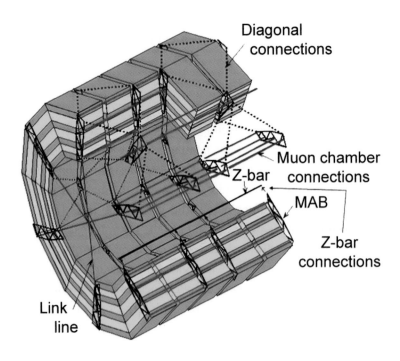

Figure 7.87: Schematic view of the barrel monitoring system showing the optical network among the MAB structures.

Figure 7.88: Installation of the MABs on wheel YB+2.

2008 JINST 3 S08004

the DT chambers and the read-out of the images taken by the cameras. The minicomputers control the light sources mounted on the MABs and the z-bars, read out the temperature and humidity sensors, perform the image read-out and digitisation, and calculate the image centroids of the light sources. The results are transferred to the main control PC, which is connected to the corresponding central CMS units.

Based on simulation, the barrel monitoring system should provide a stand-alone measurement of the barrel chambers with an average r-ϕ position accuracy of 100 μm for chambers in the same sector and about 250 μm between barrel sectors. The current understanding of its performance is discussed in section 7.4.3.

Muon endcap alignment

The muon endcap alignment system [178] is designed to continuously and accurately monitor the actual positions of the 486 CSCs relative to each other, relative to the tracking system, and ultimately within the absolute coordinates of CMS. Due to the large magnetic field, the chambers mounted on the endcap yoke undergo substantial motion and deformation, on the order of a few centimetres, when the field is switched on and off. The alignment system must measure the disk deformation and monitor the absolute positions of the CSCs in the r-ϕ plane and in z. From simulations, the required absolute alignment accuracies were found to run from 75 to 200 μm in r-ϕ. Because the r and r-ϕ accuracies are directly coupled, the required accuracy in the r-position is $\approx$400 μm. The z displacement due to the deformation of the iron yoke disks caused by the strong and non-uniform magnetic field in the endcaps requires the alignment sensors to be able to accommodate a dynamic range of $\approx$2 cm with an accuracy of $\approx$1 mm.

The system uses a complex arrangement of 5 types of sensors for the transferring and monitoring of ϕ, r, and z coordinates (figure 7.89). The system measures one sixth of all endcap chambers. The main monitoring tools within the r-ϕ plane are the Straight Line Monitors (SLM). Each SLM consist of 2 cross-hair lasers, which emit a nearly radial laser beam across 4 chambers from each end, and provide straight reference lines that are picked up by 2 optical sensors (Digital CCD Optical Position Sensors, DCOPS [179]). This arrangement provides references for the chamber positions relative to the laser lines. Figure 7.90 shows a photograph of a complete SLM on station ME+2. The figure also indicates r-sensors for monitoring radial chamber positions, z-sensors for axial distance measurements between stations, and a clinometer for monitoring the tilt of the mechanical support assembly (transfer plate) onto which lasers, reference DCOPS, and z-sensors are mounted. The inset in figure 7.90 shows the location of proximity sensors on the outer ring of the ME+1 station, which monitor the azimuthal distance between neighbouring chambers. These are necessary because the outer ring of ME1 chambers is the only ring for which the CSCs do not overlap in ϕ. Furthermore, every CSC and alignment device is equipped with photogrammetry targets to allow absolute magnet-off measurements.

The ϕ coordinate alignment is handled by optical SLMs and transfer lines. Transfer laser lines run parallel to the CMS z-axis along the outer cylindrical envelope of CMS at 6 points separated by 60° in ϕ. The SLMs run across the surface of one sixth of all the CSCs, along radial directions, and link transfer lines on opposite sides of a disk. Both laser lines have a similar basic configuration: a laser beam defines a direction in space that is picked up by several DCOPS precisely mounted

2008 JINST 3 S08004

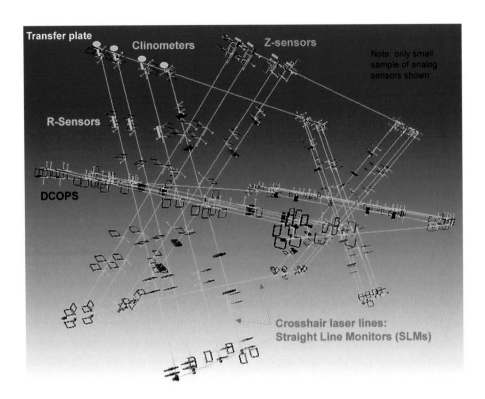

Figure 7.89: Visualisation of the geometry and components of the muon endcap alignment system. The square objects represent optical sensors (DCOPS) for monitoring 3 straight laser lines across each endcap station.

on CSCs or transfer plates to reference their own positions. Mounting accuracies due to tolerances of dowel pins and dowel holes are ≈ 50 μm. Every DCOPS comprises 4 linear CCDs, each with 2048 pixels and 14 μm pixel pitch. The CCDs are basically arranged in the shape of a square and can be illuminated by cross-hair lasers from either side. The r and z coordinate measurements are performed by analog linear potentiometers and optical distance devices in contact with aluminium tubes of calibrated length.

All analog sensors were calibrated with a 1D precision linear mover with 6.4 μm step size. The uncertainty in the absolute distance calibration is 100 μm for r sensors and 53 μm for z sensors [180]. Calibration for optical DCOPS consisted in determining the distance from the surface of the mount hole for a reference dowel pin to the first active CCD pixel and measuring the projected pixel pitch of each of the 4 CCDs. This was done on a calibration bench where a fibre-bundle variable light source at the focus of a parabolic mirror illuminated a mask with 8 optical slits. A simple geometry reconstruction, based on coordinate-measuring-machine data for the calibration mask and sensor mounts, determined the physical pixel positions. Calibration errors were typically 30 to 50 μm.

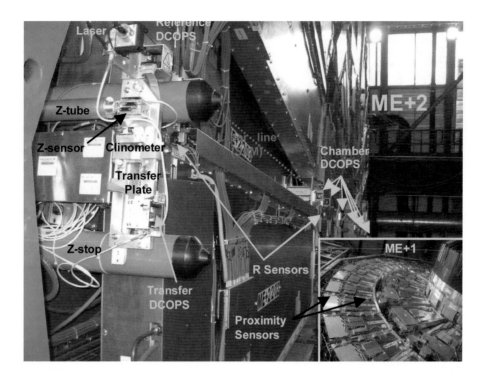

Figure 7.90: Close-up of one of the 3 Straight Line Monitors (SLM) on the ME+2 station with cross-hair laser, DCOPS, and analog sensors (r, z, and Tiltmeter). The insert indicates the location of proximity sensors on ME+1.

Link system

The purpose of the link alignment system is to measure the relative position of the muon spectrometer and the tracker in a common CMS coordinate system. It is designed to work in a challenging environment of very high radiation and magnetic field, meet tight space constraints, and provide high precision measurements over long distances. A distributed network of opto-electronic position sensors, ASPDs (amorphous-silicon position detectors) [181], placed around the muon spectrometer and tracker volumes are connected by laser lines. The entire system is divided into 3 ϕ-planes 60° apart; this segmentation allows a direct reference of each muon barrel sector with the tracker detector and provides a direct reference also to the endcap alignment lines in the first endcap station, ME1. Each plane consists of 4 quadrants (figure 7.86) resulting in 12 laser paths: 6 on each z-side of the CMS detector, and generated by 36 laser sources. The system uses 3 types of reference structures: rigid carbon-fibre annular structures placed at both ends of the tracker (alignment rings, AR) and at the YE±1 wheels of the endcap muon spectrometer (link disks, LD); and the MAB structures attached at the external barrel wheels, YB±2. Figure 7.91 (left) shows the LD and AR carbon fibre structures installed in the inner $\eta = 3$ cone. The link measurement network is complemented by electrolytic tiltmeters, proximity sensors in contact with aluminium tubes of calibrated length, magnetic probes, and temperature sensors.

The ARs are rigidly attached to the endcap tracker detectors, TECs, through a purely mechanical connection with the instrumented silicon volume (section 3.3.7). Three pillars, acting as support fixations, connect the last instrumented disk of each TEC with the corresponding AR, at

Figure 7.91: Left panel: Link Disk and Alignment Ring installed in the inner $\eta = 3$ cone during the first closing of the detector in summer 2006, MTCC period. Right panel: Alignment Ring mounted in the TEC end flange.

both ends of the tracker volume, see figure 7.91 (right). The position and orientation of the ARs with respect to the TEC disks 9 and 10 were measured with a coordinate-measurement machine using the external survey fiducials prior to the TEC assembly and instrumentation. Changes in angular orientations are monitored by high precision tiltmeters placed at the AR and TEC disk 10. Laser sources originating at the AR and running along the inner detector boundary reach ASPD sensors on the first endcap disk, ME1, and on the external barrel wheel.

The ASPDs are 2D semitransparent photo-sensors, which consist of 2 groups of 64 silicon micro-strips with a pitch of 430 μm oriented perpendicularly. With $\geq 80\%$ transmittance for the 685 nm wavelength used in the system, they allow multi-point measurements along the light path without significant distortions in the beam direction. The intrinsic position resolution is about 2 μm. The location, centre position, and orientation of the ASPD with respect to reference pins in their mechanical mount are measured with a non-contact CMM (Coordinate Measuring Machine) with an overall accuracy of 15 μm. Distance measurement devices (optical distance sensors and linear potentiometers) already mounted in their final mechanics were calibrated using 2 μm resolution linear movers and pre-measured calibration fixtures. The uncertainties in absolute and relative calibration [182] are below 50 μm and 20 μm, respectively, for the different sensor types. The intrinsic accuracy of the tiltmeters sensors, after calibration, is about 2 μrad; mechanical offsets inherent to the mechanical mounts and assembly tolerances are determined by survey and photogrammetry techniques.

The light sources (collimators) and specific optical devices housed on the alignment reference structures (AR, LD, and MABs) create the laser beam paths with the layout described above. Each collimator is focused to its working distance to ensure Gaussian beam profiles along the propagation path to avoid beam-shape-induced bias in the position reconstruction. The adjustment and calibration [183] of the laser rays for the AR and LD structures were done on a dedicated bench instrumented with a precise survey network that mimics the nominal detector geometry. Beams were adjusted to their nominal geometry with a precision better than 100 μrad. Long term measurements were performed after beam adjustments. Beam pointing stability, including temperature

2008 JINST 3 S08004

effects, was found to be better than 30 μrad. The adjustment and calibration accuracy was limited to 30–100 μrad due to the finite dimension of the structures combined with the intrinsic accuracy of the survey and photogrammetry measurement techniques of 70 μm.

Survey and photogrammetry measurements are also performed during the installation of the alignment structures in the detector. An installation accuracy of the order of a few millimetres and milliradians is needed to ensure correct functionality of the system, taking into account the standard CMS assembly tolerances of the big endcap disks and barrel wheels.

The control, read-out, and data preprocessing are performed by two types of electronic boards. Analog sensors read-out and laser control use standard ELMB (embedded local monitor board) cards [184]. For the read-out of ASPD sensors, custom made LEB (local electronic board) cards were developed. LEBs are intelligent imaging acquisition boards made to read and control up to 4 ASPD sensors. They are based on Hitachi micro-controllers. ELMB and LEB boards use the CAN communication protocol to connect the front-end electronics and the main control PC unit.

7.4.2 Geometry reconstruction

The DAQ, monitoring, and control software are integrated into the DCS (detector control system) environment. Data are recorded in an online Oracle database and subsequently converted into ntuples by specialised programs that perform database queries and apply calibrations to convert raw values into meaningful physical quantities. This provides the necessary information for global geometry reconstruction, which is handled by COCOA (CMS Object-Oriented Code for Optical Alignment) [185], an offline program to simulate and reconstruct the complex optical alignment system. Due to the unknown movements of different CMS structures, the sensors of the optical alignment systems will not measure the expected nominal values. The aim of COCOA is to analyse the observed changes in these measurements to determine which are the displacements and/or rotations that caused them. The approach adopted by COCOA to tackle this problem is to solve the system of equations that relate the measurement values to all the positions, rotations, and internal parameters of all the objects that make up the system. In fact, to solve the system of equations, one does not need to know the explicit form of the equations, but only the derivatives of each measurement value with respect to each object parameter. COCOA uses a geometrical approximation of the propagation of light to calculate numerically these derivatives and then solves the system of equations through a nonlinear least squares method. Due to the large number of parameters in CMS (about 30 000), big matrices are needed. COCOA matrix manipulations are based on the Meschach Library [186].

COCOA has proved its robustness through its extensive use in CMS for several design studies, as well as for the analysis of several test benches and magnet test results. Its output, the aligned geometry, will be used as input geometry for track reconstruction as well as for further alignment studies based on muon tracks from cosmic rays and from pp collisions.

7.4.3 System commissioning and operating performance

A first test of the large superconducting solenoid magnet in the CMS detector was successfully performed between June and November 2006, during which stable operation at full field (4 T) was achieved (section 3.3). The alignment sensors, read-out, and DAQ software were commissioned

2008 JINST 3 S08004

during this test period for about one third of the system, instrumented at the +z side of the detector. This allowed the first full-scale dynamic test of the system. The performance of the system as well as the main features of the yoke displacement and deformation were studied. The relevant results are summarised below:

- Measurement of relative movements due to thermal changes.

  The effects of thermal changes (day-night variations) for DT and CSC chambers were recorded for the conditions present during the test, with the detector in the surface assembly hall and power on only ≈5% of the muon spectrometer. The measured relative movement did not exceed 50 μm over the entire test period, with changes in position showing a good correlation with temperature. Although a movement of this magnitude is not relevant from the physics analysis point of view, its measurement illustrates the good resolution of the alignment system.

- Measurement of the displacements and deformations of the yoke structures.

  Two effects were observed. The first is the change in the original positions of the structures (the positions before any magnet operation). The displacements of the structures along the z direction towards the solenoid seem to stabilise after the first 2.5–3 T are reached. This compression is permanent, meaning it is not reversed/recovered in subsequent magnet off states, and it is interpreted as the final closing of the structures due to the magnetic forces acting on the iron. These measured displacements are specific to the first CMS closing experience and cannot be extrapolated to other scenarios.

  The second effect is the almost perfectly elastic deformations between magnet-on and magnet-off states, as illustrated in figure 7.92. At 4 T, the elastic deformation of the barrel yoke, measured at the end of the +z side with respect of the plane of the interaction point, is about 2.5 mm. Figure 7.92 shows the elastic compression of the barrel wheels versus the magnet current as recorded in the second phase of the Magnet Test period. Despite the large overall compression of the barrel spectrometer, an important measurement was the stability of the barrel chambers during the whole data-taking period. The relative movements in the r-ϕ direction did not exceed 60 μm.

  The behaviour of the endcap disk is more complicated. Due to the strong gradient in the magnetic field near the end of the solenoid, strong magnetic forces pull the central portions of the endcap disks towards the center of the detector. As shown in figure 7.92, the nose is pulled towards the interaction point, the magnitude of the compression is perfectly correlated with the magnet current, reaching up to ≈16 mm at 4 T. The various z-stops, which prevent the disks from getting pushed into each other and onto the barrel wheels, cause the endcap disks to bend into a cone shape. The z-stops between endcap and barrel, positioned at nearly half the disk radius, cause the side of the YE1 disk facing the barrel to compress radially around them by ≈600 μm, while expanding azimuthally by ≈800 μm. This explains the radial compression of the face of ME+1 and the larger bending angles at mid-radius than at the outer edge (figure 7.93). Endcap disk deformations are predicted by finite element analysis (FEA) using the ANSYS program [3]. The measurements are in reasonable quantitative agreement for all displacements and deformations, as shown in figure 7.93. Note that the

2008 JINST 3 S08004

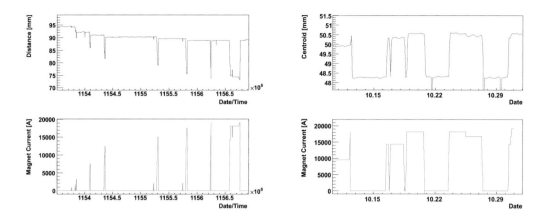

Figure 7.92: Deformations of endcap disks and barrel wheels vs magnet current cycling. Left panel: The bottom plot shows the magnet powering cycle exercised during the first phase of the Magnet Test period. The top plot shows the measured YE+1 nose compression towards the interaction point. Right panel: The bottom plot shows the magnet powering cycle exercised during the second phase of the Magnet Test period. The top plot shows the calculated approximate YB+2 compression towards the interaction point.

front z-stops, between the ME1 and barrel wheels, were not included in the FEA, which explains the difference. The difference between top and bottom is also explained by the presence of the carts that support the disks.

The rest of the endcap stations on YE+2 and YE+3 experience a maximum bending angle of $\approx$2.5 mrad relative to the vertical, as sketched in figure 7.94. As in the case of the barrel chambers, with stable 4 T field, the observed relative movements were very small.

• Detector closing tolerances and reproducibility.
The test of the magnet was divided into 2 phases, separated by a short period during which the yoke was open to extract the inner detectors, tracker, and ECAL modules. This allowed a test of the reproducibility in the closing procedure and tolerances, as well as the study of the compatibility of measurements between the two phases. Reproducibility in the closing was at the level of a few millimetres for the barrel wheels and about an order of magnitude higher for the endcap disks. The particular conditions of the test did not allow the establishment of a solid understanding of reproducibility for the process of closing the different structures. Instead, the system was able to reproduce the same magnetic-force-induced effects as measured in the first period.

From this test we conclude that the system operates adequately under magnetic fields both in terms of dynamic range and measurement performance. The system precision achieved is $\leq$ 300 μm and the measurement accuracy has been validated against results from photogrammetry and cosmic ray tracks.

2008 JINST 3 S08004

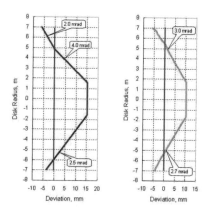 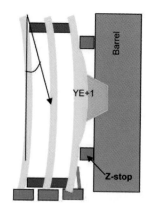

Figure 7.93: Comparison of the YE+1 disk deformations in the *r-z* plane at full magnetic field (4 T) measured by the alignment system (left panel) and predictions from finite element analysis (right panel). The vertical lines correspond to 0 magnetic field.

Figure 7.94: Current understanding of disk deformation due to magnetic forces based on alignment system measurements. The *z*-stops (red) prevent the disks from getting pushed into each other. Note that the indicated bending angle is exaggerated for illustrative purposes. Its measured magnitude is 2.5 mrad.

Chapter 8

Trigger

2008 JINST 3 S08004

The LHC provides proton-proton and heavy-ion collisions at high interaction rates. For protons the beam crossing interval is 25 ns, corresponding to a crossing frequency of 40 MHz. Depending on luminosity, several collisions occur at each crossing of the proton bunches (approximately 20 simultaneous pp collisions at the nominal design luminosity of 10^{34} cm^{-2}s^{-1}). Since it is impossible to store and process the large amount of data associated with the resulting high number of events, a drastic rate reduction has to be achieved. This task is performed by the trigger system, which is the start of the physics event selection process. The rate is reduced in two steps called Level-1 (L1) Trigger [187] and High-Level Trigger (HLT) [188], respectively. The Level-1 Trigger consists of custom-designed, largely programmable electronics, whereas the HLT is a software system implemented in a filter farm of about one thousand commercial processors. The rate reduction capability is designed to be at least a factor of 10^6 for the combined L1 Trigger and HLT. The design output rate limit of the L1 Trigger is 100 kHz, which translates in practice to a calculated maximal output rate of 30 kHz, assuming an approximate safety factor of three. The L1 Trigger uses coarsely segmented data from the calorimeters and the muon system, while holding the high-resolution data in pipelined memories in the front-end electronics. The HLT has access to the complete read-out data and can therefore perform complex calculations similar to those made in the the analysis off-line software if required for specially interesting events. Since HLT algorithms will evolve with time and experience they are not described here. More information may be found in [189]. For reasons of flexibility the L1 Trigger hardware is implemented in FPGA technology where possible, but ASICs and programmable memory lookup tables (LUT) are also widely used where speed, density and radiation resistance requirements are important. A software system, the Trigger Supervisor [190], controls the configuration and operation of the trigger components.

The L1 Trigger has local, regional and global components. At the bottom end, the Local Triggers, also called Trigger Primitive Generators (TPG), are based on energy deposits in calorimeter trigger towers and track segments or hit patterns in muon chambers, respectively. Regional Triggers combine their information and use pattern logic to determine ranked and sorted trigger objects such as electron or muon candidates in limited spatial regions. The rank is determined as a function of energy or momentum and quality, which reflects the level of confidence attributed to the L1 parameter measurements, based on detailed knowledge of the detectors and trigger electronics and on the amount of information available. The Global Calorimeter and Global Muon Triggers

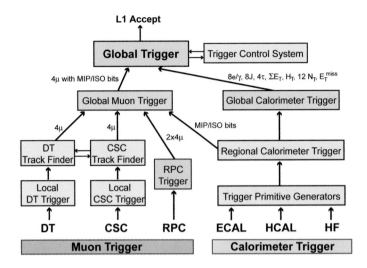

Figure 8.1: Architecture of the Level-1 Trigger.

determine the highest-rank calorimeter and muon objects across the entire experiment and transfer them to the Global Trigger, the top entity of the Level-1 hierarchy. The latter takes the decision to reject an event or to accept it for further evaluation by the HLT. The decision is based on algorithm calculations and on the readiness of the sub-detectors and the DAQ, which is determined by the Trigger Control System (TCS). The Level-1 Accept (L1A) decision is communicated to the sub-detectors through the Timing, Trigger and Control (TTC) system. The architecture of the L1 Trigger is depicted in figure 8.1. The L1 Trigger has to analyze every bunch crossing. The allowed L1 Trigger latency, between a given bunch crossing and the distribution of the trigger decision to the detector front-end electronics, is 3.2 μs. The processing must therefore be pipelined in order to enable a quasi-deadtime-free operation. The L1 Trigger electronics is housed partly on the detectors, partly in the underground control room located at a distance of approximately 90 m from the experimental cavern.

8.1 Calorimeter trigger

The Trigger Primitive Generators (TPG) make up the first or local step of the Calorimeter Trigger pipeline. For triggering purposes the calorimeters are subdivided in trigger towers. The TPGs sum the transverse energies measured in ECAL crystals or HCAL read-out towers to obtain the trigger tower E_T and attach the correct bunch crossing number. In the region up to $|\eta| = 1.74$ each trigger tower has an (η, ϕ)-coverage of 0.087×0.087. Beyond that boundary the towers are larger. The TPG electronics is integrated with the calorimeter read-out. The TPGs are transmitted through high-speed serial links to the Regional Calorimeter Trigger, which determines regional candidate electrons/photons, transverse energy sums, τ-veto bits and information relevant for muons in the form of minimum-ionizing particle (MIP) and isolation (ISO) bits. The Global Calorimeter Trigger determines the highest-rank calorimeter trigger objects across the entire detector.

Calorimeter trigger primitive generators

The ECAL on-detector front-end electronics boards, each serving 25 crystals, receive the ADC signals from the very front-end electronics located at the rear of the detector modules. They contain most of the TPG pipeline in six radiation-hard 0.25 μm CMOS ASIC chips named FENIX. An off-detector Trigger Concentrator Card (TCC) collects the primitives from 68 front-end boards in the barrel and 48 boards in the endcaps through optical links. The TCCs finalize the TPG generation and encoding, store the trigger primitives during the L1 latency time and transmit them to the RCT by dedicated daughter boards, the Synchronization and Link Boards (SLB), upon reception of a L1A signal. The SLBs synchronize the trigger data through circuits that histogram the LHC bunch crossing structure. Each trigger tower is aligned with the bunch crossing zero signal. A Data Concentrator Card (DCC) performs the opto-electronic conversion and deserialization of the serial input data streams and sends the read-out data collected from the front-end boards to the DAQ. Clock and Control System (CCS) boards distribute the clock, the L1A and control signals to the TCC, the DCC and the on-detector electronics. The ECAL TPG hardware is contained in twelve 9U VME crates for the barrel and six for the endcaps.

The front-end modules of the hadron calorimeter contain Charge Integrator and Encoder (QIE) ADC chips to digitize the signals from the photo detectors. Optical links transmit the data to the HCAL Trigger and Readout (HTR) boards. Each HTR board processes 48 channels. It linearizes, filters and converts the input data to generate the HCAL trigger primitives. The energy values of front and back towers are added and the bunch crossing number is assigned by a peak filtering algorithm. As for the ECAL, the primitives are sent to the RCT by SLBs, and read-out data are collected by a DCC. The HCAL trigger electronics is contained in 26 9U VME crates. Each crate houses 18 HTR boards and one DCC.

Regional Calorimeter Trigger

The Regional Calorimeter Trigger [191] determines electron/photon candidates and transverse energy sums per calorimeter region. Information relevant for muons about isolation and compatibility with minimally ionizing particles is also calculated. A region consists of 4×4 trigger towers except in HF where a region is one trigger tower. Electromagnetic and hadronic transverse energies are summed in each tower.

The e/γ trigger algorithm (figure 8.2) starts by determining the tower with the largest energy deposit and is applied across the entire ECAL region. The energy of the tower with the next-highest deposit in one of the four broad side neighbours is then added. Isolated and non-isolated e/γ within $|\eta| \leq 2.5$ are determined by the trigger. A non-isolated e/γ requires passing of two shower profile vetoes. The first one is based on a fine-grain crystal energy profile reflecting the lateral extension of a shower. The fine-grain bit is set by the TPG if the shower is contained in a matrix of 2×5 crystals. The matrix is dimensioned such that it also allows for the detection of bremsstrahlung due to the magnetic field. The second one is based on the ratio of the deposited energies in the hadronic and in the electromagnetic sections. A typical maximal value of 5% is allowed for that ratio. An isolated electron/photon candidate has to pass the previous vetoes for all eight neighbouring towers. In addition, at least one quiet corner made of four groups of five electromagnetic towers surrounding the hit tower is required. Four isolated and four non-isolated e/γ per region are forwarded to the GCT.

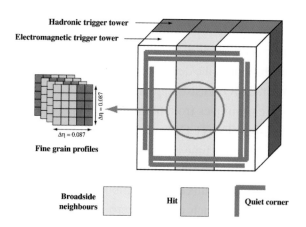

Figure 8.2: Electron/photon algorithm. **Figure 8.3**: Electron Isolation Card.

The RCT also sums the transverse energy in a given region of the central calorimeter (HF is not included) and determines τ-veto bits for the identification of jets from one- and three-prong τ-decays, which are narrower than ordinary quark/gluon jets. A τ-veto bit is set unless the pattern of active towers corresponds to at most 2×2 contiguous trigger towers within a 4×4 tower region. Jets can be classified as τ-jet only at $|\eta| < 3.0$ (not in HF).

The RCT hardware consists of 18 regional 9U VME crates and one 6U clock distribution crate located in the underground control room. Each crate covers a region of $\Delta\eta \times \Delta\phi = 5.0 \times 0.7$. Receiver cards are plugged into the rear of the regional crates. Seven cards per crate receive the ECAL and HCAL primitives. The HF primitives are directly received on a Jet/Summary card. The serial input data are converted to 120 MHz parallel data, deskewed, linearized and summed before transmission on a 160 MHz custom monolithic backplane to seven Electron Isolation Cards (EIC) and one Jet/Summary Card (JSC) mounted at the front side of the crate. Different ASICs perform the algorithm calculations. An EIC is shown in figure 8.3.

Global Calorimeter Trigger

The Global Calorimeter Trigger determines jets, the total transverse energy, the missing transverse energy, jet counts, and H_T (the scalar transverse energy sum of all jets above a programmable threshold). It also provides the highest-rank isolated and non-isolated e/γ candidates.

Jets are found by a four-stage clustering technique based on jet finders operating in 2×12 cells in ϕ and η, spanning $40°$ and half the detector, respectively, in these directions. The cell at $\eta=0$ is duplicated. In the first stage mini-clusters are created by summing energies within 2×3 cells if a central cell has more energy than neighbouring cells. In the second stage the three largest mini-clusters in each of the two ϕ-strips are transferred in opposite ϕ-directions. These are compared against the existing mini-clusters on the receiving ϕ-strip. Mini-clusters adjacent or diagonally adjacent to a larger mini-cluster are removed. In the third and fourth stages the received mini-clusters that survive have their three adjacent cells in the receiving ϕ-strip combined to make a 3×3 cell. A jet is classified as a τ jet if none of the corresponding RCT regions had a τ-veto bit set. After sorting, up to four jets and four τ jets from the central HCAL and four jets from HF are forwarded to the GT. The magnitude and direction of the missing energy and the total transverse energy are computed from the regional transverse energy sums in the two coordinates transverse to the beam within $|\eta| < 5$. Twelve jet counts for different programmable E_T-thresholds and optionally also different (η, ϕ)-regions are computed. Muon MIP/ISO bits are received from the RCT along with the e/γ data and are forwarded to the GMT through a dedicated muon processing system. Apart from triggering, the GCT also acts as the read-out system for the RCT. The GCT has in addition the capability to monitor rates for certain trigger algorithms and from those deduce information about the LHC luminosity as seen by the CMS trigger system.

All GCT electronics is located in the underground control room. The large amount of data from the RCT crates are transmitted electronically to 63 Source Cards, which reorder the data onto 252 optical fibres. The core of the GCT processing is performed by Leaf Cards, which can be configured as electron or jet cards. Several Leaf Cards can be connected with each other in order to perform complex tasks such as the jet finding. There are two Leaf Cards for electrons and six for jets. Each electron leaf card receives the e/γ data from one half of the RCT crates on 27 fibres and sorts them. Each jet card receives 30 regional sum fibres from three RCT crates via the source cards. They perform the jet clustering and transmit the jet candidates to two Wheel Cards for sorting and data compression. They also calculate partial energy sums and jet counts and forward them to the Wheel Cards. A Concentrator Card finally collects the data from all Electron Leaf and Wheel Cards and performs the final sorting for electrons/photons, completes the jet finding in the boundaries between groups of three Leaf Cards, sorts all jets, calculates the global energy and jet count quantities and sends the final results to the GT and the DAQ. In addition to the tasks involving e/γ's, jets and energy sums, the GCT also handles MIP/ISO bits for muons. They are processed by three muon processing cards, which receive 6 muon fibres each from Source Cards. The processor design is built on an evolution of the leaf concept and uses a modular, low-latency architecture based on the μTCA industry standard [193]. An active custom backplane based on the principle of a crosspoint switch allows a programmable routing of the 504 MIP/ISO bits, which are then transmitted to the GMT on 24 links.

8.2 Muon trigger

All three muon systems – the DT, the CSC and the RPC – take part in the trigger. The barrel DT chambers provide local trigger information in the form of track segments in the ϕ-projection and hit patterns in the η-projection. The endcap CSCs deliver 3-dimensional track segments. All chamber types also identify the bunch crossing from which an event originated. The Regional Muon Trigger consists of the DT and CSC Track Finders, which join segments to complete tracks and assign physical parameters to them. In addition, the RPC trigger chambers, which have excellent timing resolution, deliver their own track candidates based on regional hit patterns. The Global Muon Trigger then combines the information from the three sub-detectors, achieving an improved momentum resolution and efficiency compared to the stand-alone systems. The initial rapidity coverage of the muon trigger is $|\eta| \leq 2.1$ at the startup of LHC. The design coverage is $|\eta| \leq 2.4$.

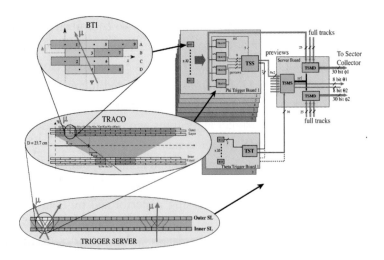

Figure 8.4: Drift Tube Local Trigger.

Drift Tube local trigger

The electronics of the DT local trigger consists of four basic components (figure 8.4): Bunch and Track Identifiers (BTI), Track Correlators (TRACO), Trigger Servers (TS) and Sector Collectors (SC). While the SCs are placed on the sides of the experimental cavern, all other trigger and read-out electronics is housed in minicrates on the front side of each chamber. All devices are implemented in custom-built integrated circuits. The BTIs are interfaced to the front-end electronics of the chambers. Using the signals from the wires they generate a trigger at a fixed time after the passage of the muon. Each BTI searches for coincident, aligned hits in the four equidistant planes of staggered drift tubes in each chamber superlayer. The association of hits is based on a mean-timer technique [194], which uses the fact that there is a fixed relation between the drift times of any three adjacent planes. From the associated hits, track segments defined by position and angular direction are determined. The spatial resolution of one BTI is better than 1.4 mm, the angular resolution better than 60 mrad. The BTI algorithm is implemented in a 64-pin ASIC with CMOS 0.5 μm Standard Cell technology. There are a few hundred BTIs per chamber.

The DT chambers have two Φ-type superlayers, measuring ϕ coordinates. The TRACO attempts to correlate the track segments measured in each of them. If a correlation can be found, the TRACO defines a new segment, enhancing the angular resolution and producing a quality hierarchy. Four BTIs in the inner Φ-type superlayer and 12 BTIs in the outer Φ-type superlayer are connected to one TRACO. The number of TRACOs is 25 for the largest muon chamber type. The TRACO is implemented in a 240-pin ASIC with CMOS 0.35 μm Gate Array technology. The trigger data of at most two track segments per bunch crossing reconstructed by each TRACO are transmitted to the TS, whose purpose is to perform a track selection in a multitrack environment.

The TS has two components, one for the transverse projection (TSϕ) and the other for the longitudinal projection (TSθ). The first one processes the output from the TRACO, whilst the second uses directly the output of the BTIs of the θ view delivered by the Θ-type superlayers present in the three innermost muon stations. The TSϕ consists itself of two components, the

2008 JINST 3 S08004

Track Sorter Slave (TSS) and the Track Sorter Master (TSM). The TSS preselects the tracks with the best quality and the smallest bending angle based on a reduced preview data set coming from the TRACOs in order to save processing time. A select line in the TRACO with the best track is then activated and the TRACO is allowed to send the full data to the TSM. The corresponding preview data are also sent to the TSM for a second stage processing. The TSM analyzes up to seven preview words from the TSSs. The output consists of the two tracks with the highest transverse momentum. There is one TSM per muon station. In the longitudinal view the TSθ groups the information from the 64 BTIs per chamber. From each BTI two bits are received, a trigger bit and a quality bit. A logic OR of groups of eight bits is applied. The output data consist of 8 bits indicating the position of the muon and 8 quality bits.

The requirement of robustness implies redundancy, which introduces, however, a certain amount of noise or duplicate tracks giving rise to false triggers. Therefore the BTIs, the TRACOs and the different parts of the TS contain complex noise and ghost reduction mechanisms. The trigger and also the read-out data from each of the sixty 30°-sectors of CMS are sent to Sector Collector (SC) units, where the trigger information — the position, transverse momentum and track quality — is coded and transmitted to the DT regional trigger, called the Drift Tube Trigger Track Finder (DTTF), through high-speed optical links.

Cathode Strip Chamber local trigger

The endcap regions are challenging for the trigger since many particles are present and muons at a given p_T have a higher momentum than in the barrel, which gives rise to more bremsstrahlung photons. In addition, photon conversions in a high-radiation (neutron-induced) environment occur frequently. Therefore the CSCs consist of six layers equipped with anode wires and cathode strips, which can be correlated. Muon track segments, also called Local Charged Tracks (LCT), consisting of positions, angles and bunch crossing information are first determined separately in the nearly orthogonal anode and cathode views. They are then correlated in time and in the number of layers hit. The cathode electronics is optimized to measure the ϕ-coordinate, the anode electronics to identify the bunch crossing with high efficiency.

An electric charge collected by the anode wires induces a charge of opposite sign in the cathode strips nearby. The trigger electronics determines the centre of gravity of the charge with a resolution of half a strip width, between 1.5 and 8 mm, depending on the radius. By demanding that at least four layers are hit, the position of a muon can be determined with a resolution of 0.15 strip widths. Due to the finite drift time the anode signals in the six chamber layers are spread out over an interval of more than two bunch crossings. As for the cathodes, at least four coincident hits are required, since in contrast to neutron-induced background a real muon leaves coincident signals in at least four layers with a probability that exceeds 99%. Actually a coincidence of two signals (pre-trigger) is used to identify the crossing, in order to allow for long drift time hits to arrive. A validation of the track occurs if in the following two bunch crossings at least four coincident signals are found. In order to reduce the number of trigger channels 10 to 15 anode wires are ORed. Figure 8.5 shows the principles of the cathode and anode trigger electronics and the bunch crossing assignment.

2008 JINST 3 S08004

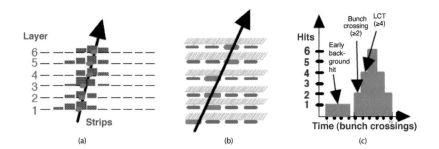

Figure 8.5: Cathode Strip Chamber Local Trigger: (a) Cathode LCT formation from strips, (b) Anode LCT formation from wire group hits, (c) Bunch crossing assignment.

The track segments from the cathode and anode electronics are finally combined into three-dimensional LCTs. They are characterized by the high-precision ϕ-coordinate in the bending plane, the bending angle ϕ_b, a rough η-value and the bunch crossing number. The best two LCTs of each chamber are transmitted to the regional CSC trigger, called the CSC Track Finder (CSCTF), which joins segments to complete tracks.

The hardware of the CSC local trigger consists of seven types of electronics boards. Cathode and anode front-end boards (CFEB and AFEB) amplify and digitize the signals. Anode LCT-finding boards (ALCT) latch the anode hits at 40 MHz, find hit patterns in the six chamber layers that are consistent with having originated at the vertex, and determine the bunch crossing. They send the anode information to the Cathode LCT-finding plus Trigger Motherboard (CLTC/TMB) cards. The CLCT circuits look for strip hit patterns consistent with high-momentum tracks. The TMB circuits perform a time coincidence of cathode and anode LCT information. If a coincidence is found, they send the information to the Muon Port Cards (MPC). The TMB selects up to two LCTs based on quality cuts. In order to cancel out ghosts a coincidence with RPC hits is established if two or more LCTs are found. A MPC receives the LCTs from the CLTC/TMBs of one endcap muon station sector, selects the best two or three LCTs depending on the station number and sends them over optical links to the CSC Track Finder. The anode and cathode LCTs and the raw hits are recorded by DAQ motherboards (DAQMB) and transmitted to the CSC detector-dependent units (DDU) belonging to the DAQ system upon reception of a L1A signal. The LHC timing reference, the L1A decision, the bunch crossing number and bunch counter reset signals are distributed by the Clock and Control Boards (CCB). The front-end boards and the ALCTs are mounted directly on the chambers. The rest of the local trigger electronics is housed in 48 peripheral crates on the endcap disks. The optical fibres to the control room depart from there. Except for the comparator-network ASIC implemented in the CLCT module, the CSC trigger electronics is built in FPGA technology.

Resistive Plate Chamber trigger

The RPCs are dedicated trigger detectors. Several layers of double-gap RPCs are mounted on the DT and CSC tracking chambers, six in the central region (two layers on the inside and outside of the two innermost muon stations, one on the inside of the two outermost stations) and four in the forward parts (one layer on the inside of each station). Their main advantage is their excellent

2008 JINST 3 S08004

timing resolution of about 1 ns, which ensures an unambiguous bunch crossing identification. For triggering purposes the measurement of the momentum of a particle is also important. In the magnetic field, muons are bent in the plane transverse to the LHC beams. It is sufficient to measure the azimuthal coordinate ϕ at several points along the track to determine the bending and thus the p_T. Therefore the RPC strips run parallel to the beam pipe in the barrel, and radially in the endcaps. There are about 165 000 strips in total, which are connected to front-end boards (FEB) handling 16 channels each.

The RPC trigger is based on the spatial and temporal coincidence of hits in several layers. It is segmented in 33 trigger towers in η, which are each subdivided in 144 segments in ϕ. As opposed to the DT/CSC, there is no local processing on a chamber apart from synchronization and cluster reduction. The Pattern Comparator Trigger (PACT) logic [195] compares strip signals of all four muon stations to predefined patterns in order to assign p_T and electric charge, after having established at least three coincident hits in time in four planes. Spatially the PACT algorithm requires a minimum number of hit planes, which varies depending on the trigger tower and on the p_T of the muon. Either 4/6 (four out of six), 4/5, 3/4 or 3/3 hit layers are minimally required. A quality parameter reflects the numbers of hit layers. For six planes there are typically 14 000 possible patterns. The outer section of the hadron calorimeter (HO) consists of scintillators placed after the magnet coil up to $|\eta| < 1.24$. Their signals can also be taken into account by the RPC trigger in order to reduce rates and suppress background [196]. The algorithm requires HO confirmation for low-quality RPC triggers. The optical links from the four HO HTR boards are received by the RPC trigger boards, and the signals are treated and incorporated in the PACT logic like an additional RPC plane, with the required number of planes hit increased by one.

The RPC signals are transmitted from the FEBs, which contain ASICs manufactured in 0.8 μm BiCMOS technology, to the Link Boards (LB), where they are synchronized, multiplexed, serialized and then sent via 1732 optical links to 108 Trigger Boards in 12 trigger crates in the control room. The 1640 LBs are housed in 136 Link Board Boxes. The Trigger Boards contain the complex PACT logic which fits into a large FPGA. There are 396 PACT chips in the system. Since duplicate tracks may be found due to the algorithm concept and the geometry, a *ghost busting* logic is also necessary. The RPC muon candidates are sorted separately in the barrel and forward regions. The best four barrel and the best four forward muons are sent to the Global Muon Trigger. The RPC data record is generated on the Data Concentrator Card, which receives data from the individual trigger boards.

Drift Tube and Cathode Strip Chamber track finders

The regional muon trigger based on the precision tracking chambers consists of the Drift Tube Track Finder (DTTF) in the barrel [197] and the CSC Track Finder (CSCTF) in the endcaps [198]. They identify muon candidates, determine their transverse momenta, locations and quality. The candidates are sorted by rank, which is a function of p_T and quality. The DTTF and the CSCTF each deliver up to four muons to the Global Muon Trigger.

The track finding principle relies on extrapolation from a source track segment in one muon station to a possible target segment in another station according to a pre-calculated trajectory originating at the vertex. If a compatible target segment with respect to location and bending angle is

2008 JINST 3 S08004

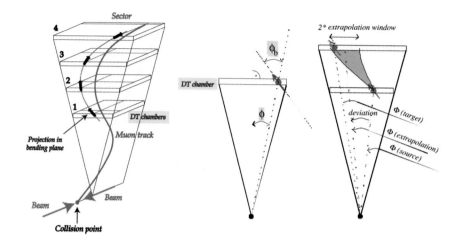

Figure 8.6: Track Finder extrapolation scheme.

found, it is linked to the source segment. A maximum number of compatible track segments in up to four muon stations is joined to form a complete track, to which parameters are then assigned. The extrapolation principle is shown in figure 8.6. While the CSCTF incorporates 3-dimensional spatial information from the CSC chambers in the track finding procedure, the DTTF operates 2-dimensionally in the ϕ-projection. A coarse assignment of η is nevertheless possible by determining which chambers were crossed by the track. In most cases an even more refined η-value can be assigned using the information from the θ-superlayers. Both for the DTTF and the CSCTF, the track finder logic fits into high-density FPGAs. For the regional trigger the DT chambers are organized in sectors and wedges. There are twelve horizontal wedges parallel to the beams. Each wedge has six 30°-sectors in ϕ. The central wheel has 2×12 half-width sectors, whereas the four outer wheels are subdivided in 12 full-width sectors each. In the two endcaps the track finding is partitioned in 2×6 60°-sectors. In the overlap region between the DT and CSC chambers, around $|\eta| \approx 1$, information from both devices is used.

In the DTTF the track finding in ϕ is performed by 72 sector processors, also called Phi Track Finders (PHTF). Per chamber they receive at most two track segments from the DT local trigger through optical links. The segment information is composed of the relative position of the segments inside a sector, its bending angle and a quality code. If there are two segments present in a chamber, the second one is sent not at the bunch crossing from which it originated but at the subsequent one, provided that in that crossing no other segment occured. A tag bit to indicate this *second track segment* status is therefore necessary. The sector processors attempt to join track segments to form complete tracks. The parameters of all compatible segments are pre-calculated. Extrapolation windows, which are adjustable, are stored in look-up tables. Muon tracks can cross sector boundaries, therefore data are exchanged between sector processors and a cancellation scheme to avoid duplicated tracks has to be incorporated.

The track finding in η, with the goal to refine η-values, is performed by 12 η assignment units, also called Eta Track Finders (ETTF). A pattern matching rather than an extrapolation method is used, since for muon stations 1, 2 and 3 the η-information coming from the DT local trigger is contained in a bit pattern representing adjacent chamber areas. The tracks in η are matched with those of the ϕ-projection, if possible. For each wedge, the combined output of the PHTFs and the ETTFs, which consists of the transverse momentum including the electric charge, the ϕ- and η-values and quality for at most 12 muon candidates corresponding to a maximum of two track candidates per 30°-sector, is delivered to a first sorting stage, the Wedge Sorter (WS). There are twelve of these sorters, which have to sort at most 144 candidates in total by p_T and quality. Suppression of remaining duplicate candidates found by adjacent sector processors and track quality filtering is also performed by these units. The two highest-rank muons found in each WS, at most 24 in total, are then transmitted to the final Barrel Sorter (BS). The latter selects the best four candidates in the entire central region, which are then delivered to the Global Muon Trigger for matching with the RPC and CSC candidates.

The DTTF data are recorded by the data acquisition system. A special read-out unit, the DAQ Concentrator Card (DCC) has been developed. It gathers the data from each wedge, through six Data Link Interface Boards (DLI). Each DLI serves two wedges. The DTTF electronics is contained in three racks in the control room. Two racks contain six track finder crates, which each house the electronics for two wedges as well as a crate controller. There is also one Timing Module (TIM) in each of these crates to distribute the clock and other timing signals. The third rack houses the central crate containing the BS, the DCC, a TIM module and boards for interfacing with the LHC machine clock and the Trigger Control System.

As for the DTTF, the core components of the CSCTF are the sector processors. They receive, through optical links, the LCT data from the Muon Port Cards in the peripheral crates. Each sector processor receives up to six LCTs from ME1 and three LCTs each from stations ME2, ME3 and ME4. Up to four track segments are also transmitted from DT station MB2. First the data are latched and synchronized, and the original LCT information is converted to reflect global (η, ϕ)-coordinates. Then nearly all possible pairwise combinations of track segments are tested for consistency with a single track in the processors' extrapolation units. In contrast to the DTTF, no data exchange between neighbour processors is performed. Complete tracks are assembled from the extrapolation results and redundant tracks canceled as in the DTTF. The best three muons per processor are selected and assigned kinematic and quality parameters. The p_T assignment, through SRAM look-up tables, is based on the ϕ-information from up to three muon stations. The data are collected in a detector-dependent unit (DDU) for the read-out. The twelve sector processors are housed in a single crate in the counting room. This crate also contains a Clock and Control Board (CCB) similar to the ones in the local CSC trigger electronics, which distributes the clock, bunch crossing reset, bunch crossing zero and other timing signals. Over the custom-developed GTL+ backplane a maximum of 36 candidate tracks is transmitted to the forward Muon Sorter board, which determines the best four muons in the two endcaps and sends them to the GMT.

Global Muon Trigger

The purpose of the Global Muon Trigger [199] is to improve trigger efficiency, reduce trigger rates and suppress background by making use of the complementarity and redundancy of the three muon systems. It receives for every bunch crossing up to four muon candidates each from the DTs and barrel RPCs, and up to four each from the CSCs and endcap RPCs. The candidate information

2008 JINST 3 S08004

consists of p_T and charge, η, ϕ and a quality code. From the GCT it also receives isolation and minimally ionizing particle bits for each calorimeter region sized $\Delta\eta \times \Delta\phi = 0.35 \times 0.35$. A muon is considered isolated if its energy deposit in the calorimeter region from which it emerged is below a defined threshold. DT and CSC candidates are first matched with barrel and forward RPC candidates based on their spatial coordinates. If a match is possible, the kinematic parameters are merged. Several merging options are possible and can be selected individually for all of these parameters, taking into account the strengths of the individual muon systems. Unmatched candidates are optionally suppressed based on η and quality. Cancel-out units reduce duplication of muons in the overlap region between the barrel and the endcaps, where the same muon may be reported by both the DT and CSC triggers. Muons are back-extrapolated through the calorimeter regions to the vertex, in order to retrieve the corresponding MIP and ISO bits, which are then added to the GMT output and can be taken into account by the Global Trigger. Finally, the muons are sorted by transverse momentum and quality, first separately in the barrel and forward regions, and then together to deliver four final candidates to the GT. A read-out processor collects the input muon data and the output record. The GMT electronics is housed in the same crate as the GT (figure 8.7). The 16 muon cables are directly connected to the GMT logic board, which has a special four VME slot wide front panel. The logic itself, which is contained in FPGA chips, only occupies one slot. The MIP/ISO bits from the GCT are received and synchronized by three Pipeline Synchronizing Buffer (PSB) input modules, which are also used in the GT. The PSB boards receive the bits via 1.4 Gbit/s serial links and are mounted at the back of the crate, behind the wide logic front panel. The MIP/ISO bits are transmitted from the PSBs to the logic board by GTL+ point-to-point links on the GT backplane.

8.3 Global Trigger

The Global Trigger [200] takes the decision to accept or reject an event at L1 based on trigger objects delivered by the GCT and GMT. These objects consist in candidate-particle, such as e/γ (isolated and non-isolated), muons, central and forward hadronic jets, τ jets, as well as global quantities: total and missing transverse energies, the scalar sum (H_T) of the transverse energies of jets above a programmable threshold, and twelve threshold-dependent jet multiplicities. Objects representing particles and jets are ranked and sorted. Up to four objects are available. They are characterized by their p_T or E_T, (η, ϕ)-coordinates, and quality. For muons, charge, MIP and ISO bits are also available.

The GT has five basic stages: input, logic, decision, distribution and read-out. The corresponding electronics boards use FPGA technology [201]. All of them, as well as the boards of the GMT, are housed in one central 9U high crate, which is shown in figure 8.7. Three Pipeline Synchronizing Buffer (PSB) input boards receive the calorimeter trigger objects from the GCT and align them in time. The muons are received from the GMT through the backplane. An additional PSB board can receive direct trigger signals from sub-detectors or the TOTEM experiment for special purposes such as calibration. These signals are called *technical triggers*. The core of the GT is the Global Trigger Logic (GTL) stage, in which algorithm calculations are performed. The most basic algorithms consist of applying p_T or E_T thresholds to single objects, or of requiring the jet multiplicities to exceed defined values. Since location and quality information is available, more

2008 JINST 3 S08004

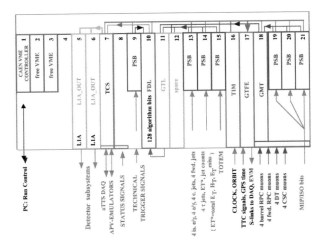

Figure 8.7: Global Trigger central crate.

complex algorithms based on topological conditions can also be programmed into the logic. A graphical interface [202] is used to set up the trigger algorithm menu. The results of the algorithm calculations are sent to the Final Decision Logic (FDL) in the form of one bit per algorithm. The number of algorithms that can be executed in parallel is 128. Up to 64 technical trigger bits may in addition be received directly from the dedicated PSB board. For normal physics data taking a single trigger mask is applied, and the L1A decision is taken accordingly. For commissioning, calibration and tests of individual subsystems up to eight final ORs can be applied and correspondingly eight L1A signals can be issued. The distribution of the L1A decision to the subsystems is performed by two L1A_OUT output boards, provided that it is authorized by the Trigger Control System described in section 8.4. A Timing Module (TIM) is also necessary to receive the LHC machine clock and to distribute it to the boards. Finally, the Global Trigger Frontend (GTFE) board collects the GT data records, appends the GPS event time received from the machine, and sends them to the data acquisition for read-out.

8.4   Trigger Control System

The Trigger Control System (TCS) [203] controls the delivery of the L1A signals, depending on the status of the sub-detector read-out systems and the data acquisition. The status is derived from signals provided by the Trigger Throttle System (TTS). The TCS also issues synchronization and reset commands, and controls the delivery of test and calibration triggers. It uses the Timing, Trigger and Control distribution network [204], which is interfaced to the LHC machine.

The TCS architecture is represented in figure 8.8. Different subsystems may be operated independently if required. For this purpose the experiment is divided into 32 partitions, each representing a subsystem or a major component of it. Each partition is assigned to a partition group, also called a TCS partition. Within such a TCS partition all connected partitions operate concurrently. For commissioning and testing up to eight TCS partitions are available, with their own L1A signals distributed in different time slots allocated by a priority scheme or in round robin mode.

2008 JINST 3 S08004

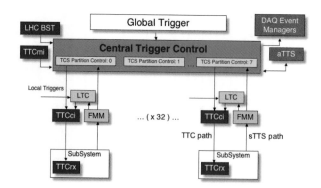

Figure 8.8: Trigger Control System architecture.

During normal physics data taking there is only one single TCS partition. Subsystems may either be operated centrally as members of a partition or privately through a Local Trigger Controller (LTC). Switching between central and local mode is performed by the TTCci (TTC CMS interface) module, which provides the interface between the respective trigger control module and the destinations for the transmission of the L1A signal and other fast commands for synchronization and control. The TTC Encoder and Transmitter (TTCex) module encodes the signals received from the TTCci and drives optical splitters with a laser transmitter. The LHC clock is received from the TTC machine interface (TTCmi). At the destinations the TTC signals are received by TTC receivers (TTCrx) containing low-jitter quartz PLLs. The Beam Synchronous Timing (BST) system of the LHC sends the GPS time.

The central TCS module, which resides in the Global Trigger crate, is connected to the LHC machine through the TIM module, to the FDL through the GT backplane, and to 32 TTCci modules through the LA1_OUT boards. The TTS, to which it is also connected, has a synchronous (sTTS) and an asynchronous (aTTS) branch. The sTTS collects status information from the front-end electronics of 24 sub-detector partitions and up to eight tracker and preshower front-end buffer emulators. The status signals, coded in four bits, denote the conditions *disconnected, overflow warning, synchronization loss, busy, ready* and *error*. The signals are generated by the Fast Merging Modules (FMM) through logical operations on up to 32 groups of four sTTS binary signals and are received by four conversion boards located in a 6U crate next to the GT central crate. The aTTS runs under control of the DAQ software and monitors the behaviour of the read-out and trigger electronics. It receives and sends status information concerning the 8 DAQ partitions, which match the TCS partitions. It is coded in a similar way as the sTTS. Depending on the meaning of the status signals different protocols are executed. For example, in case of warning on the use of resources due to excessive trigger rates, prescale factors may be applied in the FDL to algorithms causing them. A loss of synchronization would initiate a reset procedure. General trigger rules for minimal spacing of L1As are also implemented in the TCS. The total deadtime estimated at the maximum L1 output rate of 100 kHz is estimated to be below 1%. Deadtime and monitoring counters are provided in the TCS. The central board sends to the DAQ Event Manager (EVM) located in the surface control room the total L1A count, the bunch crossing number in the range from 1 to 3564, the orbit number, the event number for each TCS/DAQ partition, all FDL algorithm bits and other information.

Chapter 9

Data Acquisition

The architecture of the CMS Data Acquisition (DAQ) system is shown schematically in figure 9.1. The CMS Trigger and DAQ system is designed to collect and analyse the detector information at the LHC bunch crossing frequency of 40 MHz. The rate of events to be recorded for offline processing and analysis is on the order of a few 10^2 Hz. At the design luminosity of $10^{34}\,\mathrm{cm}^{-2}\mathrm{s}^{-1}$, the LHC rate of proton collisions will be around 20 per bunch crossing, producing approximately 1 MByte of zero-suppressed data in the CMS read-out systems. The first level trigger is designed to reduce the incoming average data rate to a maximum of 100 kHz, by processing fast trigger information coming from the calorimeters and the muon chambers, and selecting events with interesting signatures. Therefore, the DAQ system must sustain a maximum input rate of 100 kHz, for a data flow of $\approx$ 100 GByte/s coming from approximately 650 data sources, and must provide enough computing power for a software filter system, the High Level Trigger (HLT), to reduce the rate of stored events by a factor of 1000. In CMS all events that pass the Level-1 (L1) trigger are sent to a computer farm (Event Filter) that performs physics selections, using faster versions of the offline reconstruction software, to filter events and achieve the required output rate. The design of the CMS Data Acquisition System and of the High Level Trigger is described in detail in the respective Technical Design Report [188].

The read-out parameters of all sub-detectors are summarized in table 9.1. Each data source to the DAQ system is expected to deliver an average event fragment size of $\approx$2 kByte (for pp

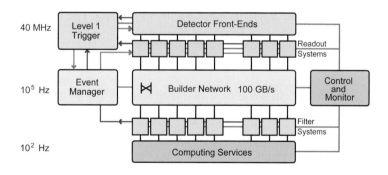

Figure 9.1: Architecture of the CMS DAQ system.

Table 9.1: Sub-detector read-out parameters.

sub-detector	number of channels	number of FE chips	number of detector data links	number of data sources (FEDs)	number of DAQ links (FRLs)
Tracker pixel	≈ 66 M	15840	≈ 1500	40	40
Tracker strips	≈ 9.3 M	≈ 72 k	≈ 36 k	440	250 (merged)
Preshower	144384	4512	1128	56	56
ECAL	75848	≈ 21 k	≈ 9 k	54	54
HCAL	9072	9072	3072	32	32
Muons CSC	≈ 500 k	≈ 76 k	540	8	8
Muons RPC	192 k	≈ 8.6 k	732	3	3
Muons DT	195 k	48820	60	10	10
Global Trigger	n/a	n/a	n/a	3	3
CSC, DT Track Finder	n/a	n/a	n/a	2	2
Total	≈ 55 M			626	458

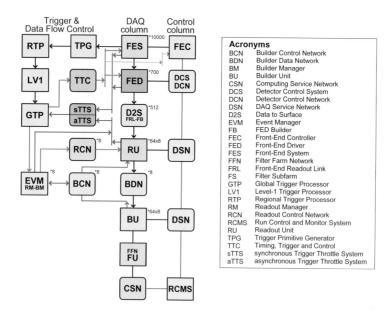

Figure 9.2: Schematic of the functional decomposition of the DAQ. The multiplicity of each entity is not shown for clarity.

collisions at design luminosity). In some case two data sources are merged in order to reach this nominal size.

A schematic view of the components of the CMS DAQ system is shown in figure 9.2. The various sub-detector front-end systems (FES) store data continuously in 40-MHz pipelined buffers. Upon arrival of a synchronous L1 trigger (3.2 μs latency) via the Timing, Trigger and Control (TTC) system [204, 207], the corresponding data are extracted from the front-end buffers and pushed into the DAQ system by the Front-End Drivers (FEDs). The data from the FEDs are read into the Front-end Read-out Links (FRLs) that are able to merge data from two FEDs. The number of FRLs corresponding to the CMS read-out parameters of table 9.1 is 458. In the "baseline" configuration, there are 512 FRLs. These additional inputs are used for combined operation with the TOTEM experiment [2], and for inputs from local trigger units, among others. The sub-detector read-out and FRL electronics are located in the underground electronics room (USC).

The event builder assembles the event fragments belonging to the same L1 from all FEDs into a complete event and transmits it to one Filter Unit (FU) in the Event Filter for further processing. The event builder is implemented in two stages (referred to as FED-builder and RU-builder) and comprises a number of components, which are described below (section 9.4). The DAQ system can be deployed in up to 8 *slices*, each of which is a nearly autonomous system, capable of handling a 12.5 kHz event rate. The event builder is also in charge of transporting the data from the underground to the surface building (SCX), where the filter farm is located.

The DAQ system includes back-pressure all the way from the filter farm through the event builder to the FEDs. Back-pressure from the down-stream event-processing, or variations in the size and rate of events, may give rise to buffer overflows in the sub-detector's front-end electronics, which would result in data corruption and loss of synchronization. The Trigger-Throttling System (TTS) protects against these buffer overflows. It provides fast feedback from any of the sub-detector front-ends to the Global Trigger Processor (GTP) so that the trigger can be throttled before buffers overflow. During operation, trigger thresholds and pre-scales will be optimized in order to fully utilize the available DAQ and HLT throughput capacity. However, instantaneous fluctuations might lead to L1 trigger throttling and introduce dead-time. CMS has defined a *luminosity section* as a fixed period of time (set to 2^{20} LHC orbits, corresponding to 93 s), during which trigger thresholds and pre-scales are not changed. The GTP counts the live-time (in numbers of bunch crossings) for each luminosity section and records them in the Conditions Database for later analysis.

The required computing power of the filter farm to allow the HLT algorithms to achieve the design rejection factor of 1000 is substantial and corresponds to O(1000) processing nodes. At the LHC luminosity of $2 \times 10^{33}\,\mathrm{cm^{-2}s^{-1}}$ it is foreseen to operate at a maximum L1 rate of 50 kHz, corresponding to 4 installed DAQ slices. It has been estimated [189] that under these conditions the HLT algorithms will demand a mean processing time of around 50 ms on a 3-GHz Xeon CPU-core. This implies for the 50-kHz DAQ system that an equivalent of about 2500 CPU-cores must be deployed for the HLT. After optimising the trigger selection for the LHC design luminosity, the estimated required computing power is expected to be roughly twice as much for 8 DAQ slices operating at a 100 kHz L1 rate.

For the first LHC run, the Event Filter is foreseen to comprise 720 PC-nodes (with two quad-core processors) for 50 kHz operation. Based on initial experience and evaluation of candidate hardware, the additional filter farm nodes for 100 kHz operation at design luminosity will be procured. The design of the DAQ system allows for this gradual expansion in event building rate and processing.

9.1 Sub-detector read-out interface

The design of the FED is sub-detector specific, however, a common interface from the FED to the central DAQ system has been implemented. The hardware of this interface is based on S-

2008 JINST 3 S08004

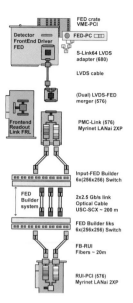

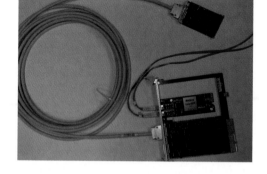

Figure 9.3: Diagram of a generic sub-detector read-out into the FED builder.

Figure 9.4: Photograph of S-link64 sender card, LVDS cable and compact-PCI FRL card with embedded LANai2XP NIC. Connected to the NIC are fibres that go to the FED Builder input switch.

Link64 [208]. The FED encapsulates the data received from the front-end electronics in a common data structure by adding a header and a trailer that mark the beginning and the end of an event fragment. The header and trailer partially consists of event information used in the event building process, such as the event number derived from the TTC L1A signals. The trailer includes a CRC (Cyclic Redundancy Check) of the data record. The payload of the event fragments is only inspected in the Event Filter.

The physical implementation of one element of the sub-detector read-out interface and its FED builder port is shown in figures 9.3 and 9.4.

The S-Link64 Sender card

The S-Link64 Sender card is a custom developed Common Mezzanine Card (CMC), directly plugged into the sub-detector FED. It receives data from the FED via an S-Link64 port and checks the CRC in order to check transmission errors over the S-Link. The card is able to buffer up to 1.6 kByte of data before generating back-pressure to the FED. The CMC has an LVDS converter to interface with a copper cable which can have a maximum length of 11 m. This cable (Multi-conductor round cable v98 manufactured by 3M) comprises 14 twisted pairs, which are individually shielded. The link provides feedback lines in order to signal back-pressure and to initiate an automatic self test. The nominal data transfer rate over the LVDS cable is 400 MByte/s (50 MHz clock, 64 bits), which is twice the maximum sustained design throughput of the DAQ system.

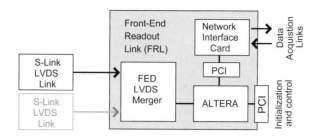

Figure 9.5: FRL layout.

The Front-end Read-out Link

The FRL is a custom 6U Compact-PCI card (figure 9.5). It has three interfaces: an input interface which handles up to two LVDS cables; an output interface to the FED Builder implemented as a 64-bit/66-MHz PCI connector for a Network Interface Card (NIC); and a configuration and control interface which is a PCI bus interface connected to the Compact-PCI backplane. The function of the FRL board is performed by two FPGAs (Altera EP20K100EFC324-1 for the PCI bridge and EP1S10F672C6 for the main logic).

The FRL receives event fragments and checks the CRC in order to check transmission errors over the LVDS cable. In the case where the FRL receives data from two FEDs, the two data records are merged. Data are buffered in memories of 64 kByte size and pushed into the NIC in fixed size blocks via the onboard PCI bus.

The FRL card also provides monitoring features, such as the ability to spy on a fraction of events via the Compact-PCI bus, and to accumulate histograms of quantities such as fragment size.

Up to 16 FRL cards are placed in a crate with a Compact-PCI backplane. Each crate is connected to a PC via a compact PCI bridge (StarFabric CPCI/PCI system expansion board from Hartmann Elektronik), which is used for configuration, control and monitoring. There are 50 FRL crates in total.

9.2 The Trigger Throttling System and sub-detector fast-control interface

The TTS provides the feedback from all FEDs and their associated front-end systems to the GTP. It is a hardwired system, acting on the dataflow with a reaction time of less than 1 μs. Each FED provides fast signals indicating the state of the read-out. The states *Ready, Warning, Busy, Out-Of-Sync* and *Error* are defined (listed in order of increasing priority). Ready, Warning and Busy are generated according to the amount of internal data buffering available and are used to indicate if more triggers can be accepted. Given the trigger rules (section 8.4) and a TTS latency of 1 μs, a FED has to be able to accept 2 more triggers after asserting Busy state. Out-Of-Sync and Error indicate that synchronization was lost or an error occurred in the front-end electronics. The GTP attempts to recover automatically from these states by issuing a L1-Resync or L1-Reset command

2008 JINST 3 S08004

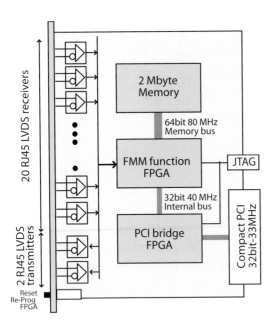

Figure 9.6: Block diagram of the FMM. **Figure 9.7**: Photograph of a FMM module.

via the TTC system. These fast TTS signals are transmitted over shielded RJ-45 cables with four twisted pairs using the LVDS signaling standard.

The Fast Merging Module

For flexibility, FEDs are grouped into 32 TTC partitions which may be operated independently of each other. The Level-1 Trigger Control System separately distributes triggers to these 32 TTC partitions and separately receives trigger throttling signals for each TTC partition. TTS signals from all FEDs in a TTC partition thus need to be merged with low latency. Dedicated Fast Merging Modules (FMMs), have been designed for this task. These modules can merge and monitor up to 20 inputs and have quad outputs. Optionally, FMMs can be configured to merge two independent groups of 10 inputs with two independent twin outputs. For partitions with more than 20 FEDs, FMMs are cascaded in two layers.

The FMM is a custom-built 6U compact-PCI card (figures 9.6 and 9.7). It has three main components: a PCI Interface FPGA, a main logic FPGA and an on-board memory block. The 80 MHz internal clock of the FMM is not synchronized to the LHC clock. Input signals are synchronized to the internal clock by requiring two successive samples in the same state. The input signals are then merged by selecting the highest priority input signal from the enabled inputs according to the signal priorities listed above. Optionally, Out-of-Sync input signals are only taken into account if the number of inputs in Out-of-Sync state exceeds a programmable threshold.

The FMM also provides extensive monitoring capabilities in order to diagnose the causes for dead-times. Each state transition at the inputs is detected and stored with a time-stamp (25 ns resolution) in a circular buffer memory that can hold up to 128 k transitions. The times spent in the states Warning and Busy are counted with 25 ns resolution for each input channel and for the output(s).

FMM cards are configured, controlled and monitored by a PC via a compact-PCI interface (StarFabric CPCI/PCI system expansion board from Hartmann Elektronik). The total system comprises 8 FMM crates with up to 9 FMMs in each crate. A total of 60 FMM modules are needed in order to merge the TTS signals of all TTC partitions of CMS.

9.3 Testing

In order to test and commission the central DAQ system independently of the GTP and of the sub-detector DAQ systems, a number of additional components have been developed. These are not used in standard data taking.

The Global Trigger Processor emulator (GTPe) [205] emulates the functionality of the GTP (see figure 9.2). It reproduces the LHC beam structure, generates random or clocked triggers up to 4 MHz, respects the trigger rules, applies partitioning, transmits the GTPe data fragment over S-Link64 and receives and handles sTTS and aTTS backpressure signals. The hardware implementation is based on the Generic-III PCI card [206] and an interface module GTPe-IO.

In normal data taking mode, triggers from the global trigger are distributed to the FEDs via the TTC. When using the GTPe, special test triggers are sent directly to the FRL crates via a lemo cable to a trigger distributer card which distributes the trigger over the backplane to all the FRLs in the crate. Because the FEDs are not being used in this mode, busy signals from the FRLs are collected by the trigger distributer card and sent to a dedicated set of FMM modules for fast merging of this subset of sTTS signals. A dedicated mode of the FRL firmware handles the GTPe test triggers and instead of reading out the FEDs, the FRL generates data fragments with sizes according to a predefined table. In this way, the full central DAQ system can be tested.

9.4 The Event Builder

A schematic view of the Event Builder system is shown in figure 9.8. The event builder is composed of two stages: the FED-builder and the RU-builder. Each of the $\approx$512 FRLs generate event fragments with an average size of $\approx$2 kByte and the FED-builder is in charge of transporting these fragments to the surface building (SCX) and assembling them into 72 super-fragments with an average size of $\approx$16 kByte. The super-fragments are then stored in large buffers in Read-out Units (RU), waiting for the second stage of event building (RU-builder), which is implemented with multiple 72×72 networks. There can be up to 8 RU-builders, or DAQ slices, connected to the FED-builder layer. Each FED-builder is in charge of distributing the super-fragments, on an event by event basis, to the RU-builders and ensures that all super-fragments corresponding to one event go to one and only one DAQ slice, and are read by one Builder Unit (BU) of the RU-builder network. The complete event is then transferred to a single unit of the Event Filter. By utilising an architecture with two-stage event building, the full size system can be progressively deployed slice by slice while the traffic load to the second stage is optimized. The event builder is implemented with commodity equipment, including processing nodes, network switches and network interfaces. The processing nodes are server PC's with PCI busses to host the NICs. They run the Linux operating system.

2008 JINST 3 S08004

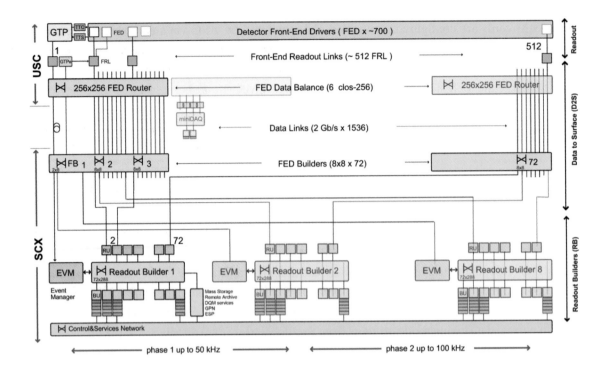

Figure 9.8: Schematic view of the Event Builder.

The event builder is lossless and when necessary back-pressure is propagated up to the FRL and subsequently to the FED, which can throttle the trigger via the TTS.

The FED-Builder stage

The FED Builder is based on Myrinet [209], an interconnect technology for clusters, composed of crossbar switches and NICs, connected by point to point bi-directional links. It employs wormhole routing and flow control at the link level. The LANai ASIC on the NIC contains an embedded RISC processor.

The FED-builder stage is implemented using multiple $N \times M$ FED-builders. In the baseline configuration, $N \leq 8$ and M equals the number of DAQ slices, which is 8 for the full system. In general, one $N \times M$ FED-builder comprises N input NICs hosted by the FRL, M output NICs hosted by the RU PCs, and two independent $N \times M$ switches to form 2 rails (figure 9.9). The NIC (M3F2-PCIXE-2 based on the LANai2XP) has two bi-directional fibre optic ports, with 2 Gbit/s data rate each. Each rail of one NIC is connected to an independent switch. In practice, instead of a large amount of small physical switches, a single large switching fabric is used per rail (see below). This 2-rail configuration doubles the bandwidth to 4 Gbit/s per FRL and provides redundancy.

The software running on the NICs has been custom developed in the C language. The FED-builder input NICs are programmed to read fragments from the FRL and to send them to the switch fabric, with a destination assigned on the basis of the fragment event number and a predefined look-up table. The FED-builder output NICs are hosted by the RU-builder PCs. They are programmed to concatenate fragments with the same event number from all the connected input cards,

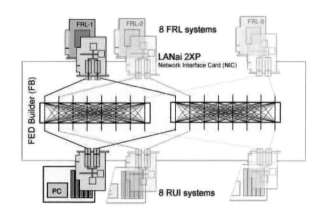

Figure 9.9: 8×8 FED builder with a two-rail network.

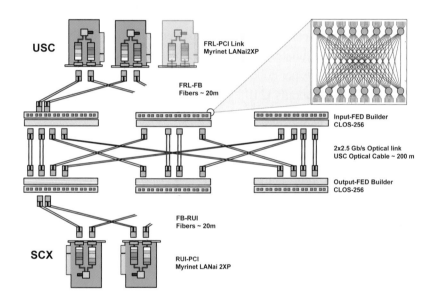

Figure 9.10: The FED builder stage switching fabric (only 1 rail is shown).

in order to build the super-fragments. The FED-builder is lossless due to a basic flow control and retransmission protocol, implemented on the RISC processor on the NIC.

The physical switching fabric is composed of six Clos-256 enclosures per rail (figure 9.10). A Clos-256 enclosure is internally composed of two layers of 16×16 (Xbar32) cross-bars. Three Clos-256 enclosures are located in the underground electronics room (USC), while the other three are in the surface DAQ building (SCX). They are connected by 768 200 m optical fiber pairs per rail, bundled in 12 cables. The Clos-256 enclosures are partly populated with linecards. Currently, the system has ports to accommodate a total of 576 FRLs and 576 RU PCs. In the baseline it is configured as 72 times 8×8 FED-builders. The use of a large switching fabric allows for a high

2008 JINST 3 S08004

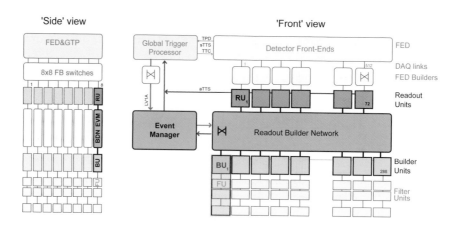

'Side' view   'Front' view

Figure 9.11: A Read-out Builder slice.

re-configurability of the FED-builders in software, which enables traffic balancing by redefining the super-fragment composition and traffic rerouting in case of a hardware failure.

The Myrinet NIC can transfer 4.0 Gbit/s data rate over the two optical rails. For random traffic the network efficiency is approximately 60%, due to head-of-line blocking. An event building throughput of about 300 MBbyte/s per node is achieved for variable sized fragments with a nominal average of 2 kBytes by using two rails [210]. Hence, the sustained aggregate throughput through the FED-builder stage is $\approx$1.4 Tbit/s, satisfying the CMS DAQ requirements. A maximum peak throughput of $\approx$2 Tbit/s is possible, if fully exploiting the FRL and Myrinet bandwidth, and using traffic shaping in the FED-builders.

The RU-builder stage

The RU-builder stage assembles super-fragments into complete events. Each RU-builder must collect event superfragments of average size $\approx$16 kByte from 72 data sources and build them into complete events at a rate of 12.5 kHz. A diagram of one slice of the RU-builder, indicating its various components is shown in figure 9.11. A RU-builder is made up of a number of Read-out Units (RU), Builder Units (BU) and a single Event Manager (EVM) connected together by a switching network. The EVM supervises the data flow in the RU-builder and receives a data record from the GTP via a dedicated FED-builder. The EVM allocates events on request to a BU, which subsequently collects the super-fragments from all RUs. From the BUs the complete events are sent to the Filter Units (FU).

In the baseline configuration the number of RUs per RU-builder is 72 and there is a factor of 4 more FU nodes. The RU, BU and EVM software components can be distributed in various ways on the PC nodes. In the baseline, there are two layers of PCs: RUs and BU-FUs. Here, the events are built by the BU software component in the same PC that runs the filter unit (FU) software, referred to as BU-FU. The RU nodes are server PCs with two 2 GHz dual-core Xeon processors (e5120) and 4 GByte of main memory (Dell PowerEdge 2950). They host a Myrinet NIC (M3F2-PCIXE-2) for the input from the FED-builder and a 4-port GbE NIC (PEG4I-ROHS Quad port copper Gigabit

Ethernet PCI Express Server Adapter from Silicom Ltd.). In the baseline, two links of the 4-port NIC are cabled to the network switch, which is sufficient to satisfy the throughput requirement of at least 200 MByte/s per RU node. A single ethernet link for each BU-FU node is sufficient, as the required throughput is 50 MByte/s. The EVB switching network is implemented with eight E-1200 switches (Terascale E-1200 router from Force10), one per DAQ-slice.

The RU-builder is based on TCP/IP over Gigabit Ethernet. The design choice of TCP/IP over Gigabit Ethernet has the advantage of using standard hardware and software. When operating an event builder over Ethernet close to wire speed, typically packet loss occurs because hardware flow control is not propagated from end-point to end-point through the switches. TCP/IP provides a reliable transport service that removes the need for the event building application to detect and deal with lost packets. It also provides flow control and congestion control. TCP/IP uses a substantial amount of host resources. Roughly 20% of a 2 GHz Xeon CPU core is required to transmit 1 Gbit/s, when using jumbo-frames (MTU=9000 Bytes).

For the event builder with 2 Ethernet links per RU node, a throughput of $\approx$240 MByte/s per RU node has been achieved at the nominal super-fragment size of 16 kBytes [211]. This can be increased, if needed for higher trigger rate or larger event sizes, to $\approx$360 MByte/s per RU node by installing a third Ethernet link per RU node. At a nominal throughput of 60 MByte/s, corresponding to 1/4 of the RU throughput, the event building tasks consume roughly 10% of the CPU resources on the BU-FU event filter nodes.

9.5   The Event Filter

The primary goal of the Event Filter complex is to reduce the nominal Level-1 Trigger accept rate of 100 kHz to a manageable level for the mass storage and offline processing systems while preserving interesting physics events and not introducing additional experiment dead-time.

The Event Filter complex:

- collects events accepted by the Level-1 Trigger system from the Event Builder and distributes them to worker nodes for further processing;

- performs basic consistency checks on the event data;

- runs offline-quality reconstruction modules and filters to process and select events for storage (High Level Trigger, "HLT");

- generates, collects, and distributes Data Quality Monitoring (DQM) information resulting from online event processing in the HLT;

- serves a subset of the events to local and remote online consumers (EventServer, ES) for calibration and DQM;

- routes selected events to local storage in several online streams according to their trigger configuration;

- transfers data from local storage at the CMS site to mass storage in the CERN data centre at the Meyrin site.

2008 JINST 3 S08004

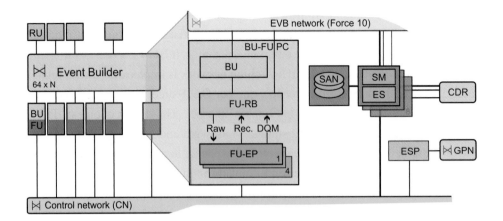

Figure 9.12: Architecture and data flow of the Filter Farm.

Architecture and data flow

The architecture of the CMS Event Filter is schematically illustrated in figure 9.12. The Event Filter hardware consists of a large farm of processors (on the order of 1000), running the HLT selection (Filter Farm), and a data logging system connected to a Storage Area Network (SAN). The Builder Unit (BU), belonging to the event builder, delivers complete events to one of multiple copies of the Filter Unit Event Processors (FU-EP) via the Filter Unit Resource Broker (FU-RB). A logically separate switch fabric provides the connectivity from the Filter Units to the data logging nodes. These data logging nodes are connected to a Fibre-Channel SAN, that is capable of a peak bandwidth of 1 GByte/s and has a capacity of several hundred TBytes.

The filter farm is logically subdivided into groups of processing nodes (Builder/Filter Unit, BU-FU). Each BU-FU hosts an identical set of software modules in a distributed environment based on the XDAQ online framework (section 9.7). As mentioned above, there are three separate applications, the Builder Unit (BU), the Filter Unit "Resource Broker" (RB) and the Event Processor (EP). The RB is responsible for managing memory resources for input and output to/from the HLT processes, and the communication with the Event Builder and the data logger. A complete event is handed by the RB, upon request, to the Event Processor (EP). The EP process uses the CMS reconstruction framework (CMSSW) [212] to steer the execution of reconstruction and selection code forming the HLT selection. Multiple EP processes can coexist in a single processor to provide concurrent execution and thus saturate the processing CPU resources.

Event processing

The EP reconstruction and selection algorithms are configured at the start of each data-taking run, by a configuration management system based on Oracle and working under run control supervision. The reconstruction, selection, and analysis modules specified in the configuration are instructed to obtain calibration constants and other time-dependent information from an Oracle database using standard access methods supported by the reconstruction framework.

2008 JINST 3 S08004

Each reconstruction or selection algorithm runs in a predefined sequence, starting from raw data unpacking modules, which deal with sub-detector specific raw-data formats. The binary raw-data is formatted into C++ objects associated with sub-detector channels through a channel map using the FED block identifiers. Reconstruction modules can attach reconstructed objects to the event data structure. A full history of the execution of the HLT is attached to each accepted event. In addition, bookkeeping information is maintained by each EP process, and periodically collected by a supervising system to provide full accounting of events accepted and rejected by each HLT path. When a decision is reached, accepted events, comprising raw data and event reconstruction information produced by the HLT, are handed back to the RB for transfer to the data logging process.

Monitoring

The operation of unpacking and reconstruction modules running in the Event Processors is monitored using the Physics and Data Quality Monitoring infrastructure (DQM). Additional analysis modules may be executed in the process, outside the normal selection sequences, to provide fast feedback about the quality of the data using the same infrastructure. Information collected by the DQM on the individual FU nodes is periodically forwarded to the data logging system via the RB, providing a DQM Collector functionality (DQMC).

Data logging and Event Server

Events accepted for storage by one of the EP processes are transmitted to the RB, which forwards them to the Storage Manager (SM) process running in the data logger nodes via the data logging network. The SM is responsible of managing the various online streams to provide an appropriate granularity of event data for transfer, processing and bookkeeping. The data logger supports both disk streams for physics or calibration data, and network streams for the usage of consumer processes carrying out calibration or monitoring tasks. The network streams are created "on demand" by a consumer process connecting to the EventServer (ES) function of each SM. In normal operation with multiple SMs, the ES is multiplexed across the various sub-farm SMs by a caching Event Server Proxy (ESP). File and network streams can deal transparently with event data or DQM data.

Each data logger node hosting a SM is responsible for direct management of its disk pool in the storage area network. This includes correct interleaving of write transactions of the SM and data transfer, via the Central Data Recording (CDR) network to the offline systems for analysis and distribution to remote sites.

9.6   Networking and Computing Infrastructure

Networking Infrastructure

The general networking infrastructure of the experiment is based on Ethernet and is separated into:

- CMS Technical Network (CMS-TN);

- CERN general purpose network (CERN-GPN);

2008 JINST 3 S08004

- Connection to the Central Data Recording (CDR);

- LHC technical network (LHC-TN).

These four networks are interconnected. In addition there are the dedicated DAQ event building networks (Myrinet and Ethernet) and dedicated networks for equipment control which have no connection to any of those four.

The CMS-TN is a general purpose network connecting all machines directly related to the operation of the experiment. It is used for system administration of all computers and for configuration, control and monitoring of all online applications. This network is not accessible directly from outside, but can be reached through dual-homed Application Gateway (AG) machines, which have one connection to CMS-TN and one to CERN-GPN switches. The CMS-TN is implemented as a distributed backbone with two routers located in SCX, and two in USC. Typically all computers in a rack are served by a switch in that rack. Each switch has two Gigabit Ethernet uplinks to the backbone routers. The desktop computers in the control room are also connected to the CMS-TN.

The CERN-GPN is the CERN-site network. The GPN will be used at all places to connect visitors (wired or wireless), who will use the application gateways to connect to the CMS-TN. This network will typically provide 1 Gbit/s connections to the GPN backbone.

The CDR connects to the Tier0 (chapter 11) system at the CERN Meyrin site using a minimum of 10 Gbit/s. A set of 8 triple-homed servers (one connection on the DAQ, one to CERN-TN, one on the CDR switches) are dedicated to this task. These are the Storage Manager nodes.

The LHC-TN allows data exchange between some of the CMS equipment and the LHC controls. The CMS-TN interconnects with the CERN-GPN and the LHC-TN using a filter implemented in the backbone routers.

Computing infrastructure

As previously discussed, the DAQ system comprises thousands of computing nodes. These are all rack mounted PCs. All PCs are Intel x86 based, running the CERN distribution of the Redhat Linux OS. The PC cluster includes a global file server and other services to be able to operate independently from the CERN-GPN. System installation is done with the Quattor toolkit [213]. In addition around a hundred PCs are used for DCS, running Microsoft Windows.

Database services are provided by a 6-node Oracle Real Application Cluster.

9.7 DAQ software, control and monitor

As stated previously, the CMS DAQ is designed in a way such that its hardware implementation can be staged as the LHC accelerator luminosity increases as well as the experiment's need for higher throughput. Thus the CMS DAQ online software must be highly scalable and must also support a diverse hardware base. The online software encompasses a distributed processing environment, data acquisition components, the run control and the detector control system. All subsystems of the DAQ have adopted the central online software frameworks with the philosophy of using common and standardized software technologies in order to reduce the effort associated with the maintenance and evolution of the detector read-out system over the long lifetime of the experiment.

2008 JINST 3 S08004

XDAQ Framework

The XDAQ (Cross-Platform DAQ Framework) framework [214] is designed for the development of distributed data acquisition systems. XDAQ includes a distributed processing environment called the "executive" that provides applications with the necessary functions for communication, configuration control and monitoring. Written entirely in C++, it provides applications with efficient, asynchronous communication in a platform independent way, including the use of memory pools for fast and predictable buffer allocation, support for zero-copy operation and a dispatching mechanism for an event-driven processing scheme. A copy of the executive process runs on every processing node in the data acquisition network.

XDAQ Applications are modeled according to a software component model [216] and follow a prescribed interface. They are compiled and the object code is loaded and configured dynamically at run-time into a running executive using the XML schema [221]. Multiple application components, even of the same application class, may coexist in a single executive process.

All configuration, control and monitoring can be performed through the SOAP/http [217] protocol, widely used in Web enabled applications. A rich set of data structures, including lists, vectors and histograms are exportable and can be inspected by clients through the executive SOAP services. Additional utility components provide support for hardware and database access.

XDAQ Applications and Libraries

XDAQ components [219] developed for CMS include applications such as the distributed Event Builder (EVB), sub-detector electronics configuration and monitoring components (FEC and FED), and central DAQ applications.

The generic event builder application consists of the main XDAQ components: a read-out unit (RU), a builder unit (BU) and an event manager (EVM). Data that are recorded by custom read-out devices are forwarded to the read-out unit application. A RU buffers data from subsequent single events until it receives a control message to forward a specific event fragment to a BU. A BU collects the event fragments belonging to a single event from all the RUs and combines them into a complete event. The BU provides an interface to the event data processors that apply event-filtering algorithms and provide data persistency (section 9.5). The EVM interfaces to the trigger read-out electronics and so controls the event building process by mediating control messages between RUs and BUs. For efficient transmission of binary (i.e. event) data the I2O specification [218] is followed. The event builder is a generic application that can run on a wide range of underlying hardware and is also used in local data acquisition systems, such as sub-detector test beams [215].

Data transmission in the XDAQ programming environment is carried out by special application components named peer transports. Peer transports register themselves with the XDAQ executive as being capable of resolving addresses as well as transmitting and receiving data. Communication between XDAQ applications is then accomplished by using an executive function that, when invoked, redirects the outgoing message to the proper peer-transport that in turn delivers the data over the associated medium. In this way the framework is independent of any transport protocol or network and can be extended at any time to accommodate newly appearing communication technologies. Baseline peer transports have been implemented for efficient binary data transmission using an asynchronous TCP/IP protocol and for simple message handling using the

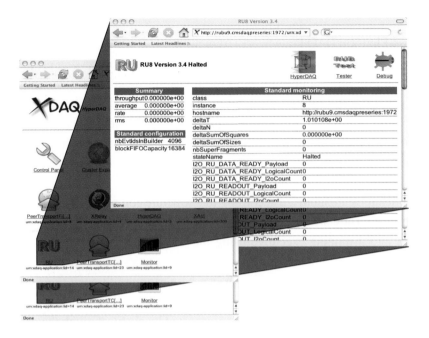

Figure 9.13: Example HyperDAQ page. Clicking on the RU application in the HyperDAQ page brings up monitoring information for the Read-out Unit application.

SOAP XML message format, however the framework is independent of the peer transport used, so optimisation of this layer is transparent to the rest of the XDAQ applications.

Libraries and device drivers have been developed that provide generic user access to VME and PCI modules and support Myrinet. Additional XDAQ components include support for the CMS custom front end devices, persistent monitoring message support and a gateway application to interface the XDAQ SOAP environment to the Detector Control System (section 9.8).

HyperDAQ

An extension to the XDAQ framework, HyperDAQ [220], exploits the http protocol which creates an entry point into XDAQ executives. A combination of HyperDAQ and Peer-to-Peer technology, used to discover new XDAQ applications providing data content, presents to the user links to the data content providers as they become available (figure 9.13). In this way, any node in the distributed online cluster can become an access point from which the entire distributed system can be explored by navigating from one application to another as the links become available. The HyperDAQ system has proved to be invaluable in debugging and monitoring the DAQ during full system integration tests.

Run Control System

The Run Control System configures and controls the online applications of the DAQ components and interfaces to the Detector Control Systems. It is an interactive system furnishing diagnostic

2008 JINST 3 S08004

and status information and providing the entry point for control. There are O(10000) applications to manage, running on O(1000) PCs.

The Run Control structure is organized into eleven different sub-systems, with each sub-system corresponding to a sub-detector or self-contained component, e.g. the Hadron Calorimeter, central DAQ or global trigger. The Run Control and Monitoring System (RCMS) framework, provides a uniform API to common tasks like storage and retrieval of process configuration data, state-machine models for process control and access to the online monitoring system.

Run Control applications and services are implemented in Java as components of a common web application "RCMS" provided by the framework. The Run Control is designed as a scalable and distributed system to run on multiple machines, thus the system can be easily expanded by adding additional hardware.

In RCMS the basic unit is the Function Manager (section 9.7). The interfaces are specified with the Web Service Description Language (WSDL) using the Axis [222] implementation of Web Services (WS). Various Web Service clients including Java, LabView and Perl have been implemented to provide access to the Run Control services. The publicly available official reference implementation of the Java Servlet technology Tomcat [223], by the Apache Software Foundation, has been chosen as the platform to run the Run Control web-applications. For persistency both Oracle and MySQL are supported by the RCMS framework.

For the baseline DAQ system, ten PCs running Linux are sufficient to control the experiment. A special copy of the XDAQ executive, the job control, is always running on each online node to accept SOAP commands from the run control to start and configure additional XDAQ executives. One common database (Oracle) is shared by all online processes and RCMS installations. Configuration management across sub-systems is achieved using global configuration keys (section 9.7).

The services and tools provided by RCMS comprise:

- Function Manager Framework;

- Resource and Account Management Services;

- Configurator;

- Log Message Collector.

In the following a few key components of Run Control are discussed.

Function Manager

A hierarchical control tree, with a central controller on the top and one or more controllers for each sub-system, structures the flow of commands and state information. The controllers are written using a common design paradigm, the so-called "Function Manager" (FM).

The FM has available a finite state machine, an interface for remote invocation, and a set of services to start, configure and control remote processes and to access configuration information from a DBMS. The FM is the basic element in the control tree. A standardized state machine model has been adopted by the sub-system for the first level of FMs which are directly steered by the central controller in the control tree (figure 9.14).

2008 JINST 3 S08004

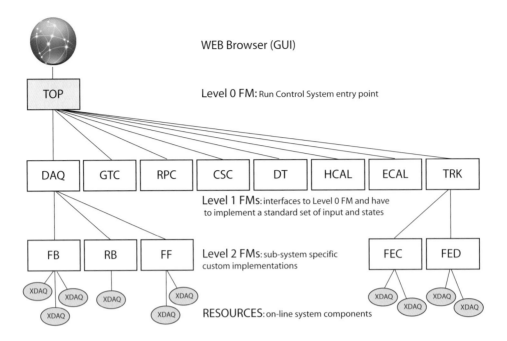

Figure 9.14: The RC hierarchy showing the full DAQ system. The Top Function Manager controls the next layer (Level 1) of Function Managers who in turn control the Level 2 (sub-detector level) Function Managers. The sub-detector Function Managers are responsible for managing the online system component resources.

Resource and Account Management Services

The Resource Service (RS) stores all information necessary to start and configure the online processes of the DAQ and sub-detectors. The data is represented as Java objects which are made persistent in the DBMS both as blobs and optionally as relational tables. RCS views the experiment as a collection of configurations, where a configuration is one or more groups of resources and one or more function manager implementations for control. The configuration is specific to each sub-system. Each sub-system has its own schema instance of the RS in the DBMS. The resource definition of a run is then the set of configurations of all participating sub-systems. The configuration of a given sub-system is resolved via a key mechanism. The sub-systems register a "configuration key" to a given global key identifying the configuration of the global run. All changes to configurations and global keys are versioned and trackable.

Users have to be authenticated to get access to the RCS resources. The resource service manages the configurations based on RCMS user accounts. Multiple configurations by multiple users can be run simultaneously in the same instance of the RCMS web-application.

Configurator

In order to create central DAQ configurations for different data taking scenarios, the CMS DAQ configurator application has been developed. The configurations can be tailored for reading out specific sub-sets of FEDs with specific throughput requirements, using different FED-Builder configurations and different sub-sets of the available event builder hardware. The configurations can be adapted to different versions and parameter settings of the online software components. The process of parametrising tens of thousands applications on thousands of hosts is largely simplified by factorizing the structure of the DAQ system and of the software settings. The structural representations of the DAQ configurations are stored in the CMS DAQ hardware and configuration database which also holds a representation of the available hardware components and their connectivity. Templates of software parameters for all software components are stored in a separate software template database. The CMS DAQ configurator application reads from both databases. It automatically calculates application parameters such as those depending on the connectivity information of the underlying hardware and creates the Java objects of the Resource Service. XML configuration files for the XDAQ executive processes are generated from these Java objects and stored in the Resource Service database. The CMS DAQ configurator application can also be used to generate configurations for test-bed hardware.

Log Message Collector

The Log Message Collector (LMC) is a web application to collect logging information from log4j and log4c compliant applications. The LMC has receiver modules for log4c messages used with C++ applications and log4j messages used with Java applications in XML and in binary format. Appender modules are implemented for TCP socket, TCP socket hub and JMS connections. Log messages can be stored on files with a File Appender, or in a DBMS with a DB Appender. Appenders can be active concurrently. Log messages are filtered by severity in the appender modules.

Each subsystem has its own instance of a LMC. A central LMC concentrates the messages of the subsystems and forms the entry point for the visualization client of messages, e.g. the Apache Chainsaw log message viewer.

9.8 Detector Control System

Function

The main purpose of the Detector Control System (DCS) is to ensure the correct operation of the CMS experiment, so that high quality data is taken with the apparatus. The scope of DCS includes all subsystems involved in the control and monitor of the detector, its active elements, the electronics on and off the detector and the overall environment.

The Detector Control Systems of individual sub-detectors are connected to the central DCS Supervisor (figure 9.15) for combined operation. These sub-detector DCS subsystems handle all the individual detector electronics such as the CAEN high-voltage power supplies and other electronics both commercial and custom made. The low-voltage system and the gas system are common for all sub-detectors whereas the cooling systems are built individually by each sub-detector. Additional components such as front-end detector read-out links are also monitored by the DCS.

The DCS provides both bookkeeping of detector parameters (table 9.2) and safety-related functions, including alarm handling and limiting the control of critical components via a software

2008 JINST 3 S08004

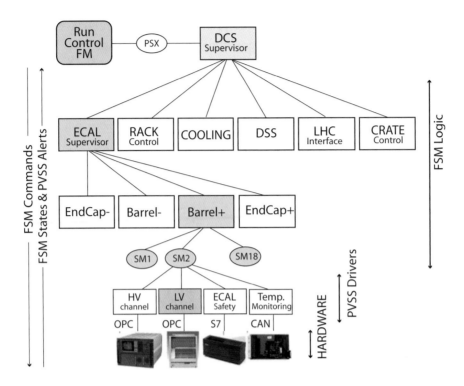

Figure 9.15: Outline of the Detector Control System hierarchy. Shown are all global services and ECAL as an example of a sub-detector control.

access control. The alarm handling and automated actions are designed in a way to anticipate major problems that would otherwise initiate Detector Safety System (DSS) actions, and warn the operator in advance that some action is needed. The alarm handling includes an SMS (mobile "text messaging") system that warns DCS users (for example a sub-detector expert) about abnormal system parameters. These SMS messages may require an acknowledgment by replying to the received alert SMS, and the status of both the alerts and acknowledgment's is displayed in the control room so that the operators in the control room are aware that experts are investigating the alarms. The DCS also collects relevant information from DSS. Monitoring of DCS parameters is possible via the Oracle Portal web pages that allow users to analyse both real time and archived data.

The DCS has to communicate with external entities as well, in particular the DAQ run control, and serves as the interface between the CMS experiment and the LHC accelerator. Many of the features provided by the DCS are needed at all times, and as a result selected parts of the DCS must function continually on a 24-hour basis during the entire year. To ensure this continuity UPS and redundant software and hardware systems are implemented in critical areas, however even non-critical nodes can be recovered in the order of minutes thanks to a CMS specific automated software recovery system.

2008 JINST 3 S08004

Table 9.2: Summary of detector parameters that are specific to each sub-detector.

Sub-detector	Monitored Parameters	Drivers	PCs / PLCs
muon CSCs	HV: 11 k channels, 218 k params LV: 8 k params Peripheral crate controller: 24 k params	Wiener and CAEN OPC custom: HV controller, Peripheral crate ctr CANopen-ELMB OPC	16
muon DTs	HV: 15 k channels - 110 k params LV: 1100 channels - 10 k parameters trigger: ≈12 k params	CAEN OPC CAEN OPC custom	7 5
muon RPCs	HV: 1200 channels LV: 1400 channels sensors: 500 channels Front end: 50 k params	CAEN OPC CAEN OPC same as LV custom	2 2
HCAL	HV: 450 channels, 3500 params LV: 270 channels, ≈1600 params HSS: 220 params Front end: 21 k params	custom CAEN OPC custom	
ECAL	LV: ≈4500 params HV: ≈2600 params Cooling: ≈200 params FE monitoring: ≈80 k params ESS: ≈600 params PTM/HM: ≈1 k params	CAN (Wiener) CAEN OPC Simatic S7, PSX custom: PSX Simatic S7 CANopen-ELMB OPC	3 4 2 / 1 1 1 / 2 2
Strip tracker	HV: 4 k channels LV: 4 k channels + 365 ctrl ch, 160 k params Temperature: 1100 sensors DCUs: 18 k channels, ≈ 100 k params	CAEN OPC, Siemens S7 custom: PSX	10 / 9
Pixel tracker	HV: 192 channels, 384 params LV: 192 channels, 384 params Temperature: 200 sensors	CAEN OPC, Siemens S7 custom: PSX	2 / 1
Alignment	LV: 200 channels 10 k LEDs, 150 lasers ≈2 k sensors	CAEN OPC ELMB, custom	5
Central DCS Services	rack control: 10 k params LHC interface: 1 k params cooling and ventilation DSS	Wiener OPC, CAN, SNMP custom: PSX	15

Implementation

The DCS software is based on the Siemens commercial SCADA package PVSS-II and the CERN Joint Controls Project (JCOP) framework [224]. Industrial controls hardware is interfaced by PVSS-II via various supported drivers OPC (OLE for Process Automation) [225] protocol, Siemens S7, SNMP, or Modbus. The JCOP framework provides common solutions to similar problems across all LHC experiments. This framework includes PVSS-II components to control and monitor the most commonly used commercial hardware (CAEN and Wiener) as well as control for additional hardware devices designed at CERN like the widely used ELMB (Embedded Local

2008 JINST 3 S08004

Monitoring Board). It also provides a Data Interchange Protocol (DIP). For hardware not covered by JCOP, PVSS-II offers the possibility of implementing new drivers and components, and CMS has developed sub-detector specific software.

The control application behaviour of all sub-detectors and support services are modeled as Finite State Machine (FSM) nodes, using the FSM toolkit provided by the JCOP framework. The detector controls are organized in a tree-like FSM node hierarchy representing the logical structure of the detector, where commands flow down and states and alarms are propagated up (figure 9.15). The different control systems of the experiment have been integrated into a single control tree, whose top node is referred to as the CMS DCS Supervisor. CMS has put policies into place to ensure a homogeneous and coherent use of the DCS [226].

The DCS is a distributed system and comprises all control applications dedicated to subsystems, communicating via the PVSS proprietary network protocol. In total there will be around 100 PCs with the majority of them running Microsoft Windows, although Linux is also supported.

PVSS-II includes a proprietary database that is used to store in real time the values of all the parameters defining the current state of the system (e.g. high-voltage settings, alarms, etc.). The configuration of PVSS-II itself is also stored in this database. For static and large amounts of data, an external Oracle database is used to store configuration data, and to archive measured values of parameters from PVSS to Oracle tables. Selected data from DCS is exported to the CMS conditions database, which contains all the data describing the detector environment needed for the offline reconstruction. The DCS access control system uses the LDAP and Oracle identity management tools which has web support for account management.

During normal physics data taking the DCS will act as a slave to run control and will therefore have to receive commands and send back status information. A communication mechanism between DCS and external entities is provided by the CMS specific PVSS SOAP interface (PSX). The PSX is a SOAP server implemented with XDAQ (section 9.7) using the PVSS native interface and JCOP framework, and allows access to the entire PVSS-II system via SOAP.

2008 JINST 3 S08004

Chapter 10

Detector infrastructures and safety systems

2008 JINST 3 S08004

The common term *infrastructures* includes very different systems, ranging from basic site facilities to more detector-specific and safety-related services. In this section, the main general systems are described.

10.1 Detector powering

CMS, like any other modern particle physics detector, needs considerable electrical power for its front-end electronics (FEE), for electronics racks in counting rooms and in site control centres, and finally for auxiliary services (cranes, ventilation and cooling stations, lifts and access facilities, etc.). Different power sources are available on site. Uninterruptible Power Systems (UPS), for valuable equipment that must stay on in case of power disruption, secure power for specific users for a short period, before being backed-up by a diesel engine. Common users are connected to standard network power. Table 10.1 gives an overview of the power requirements for CMS.

With the exception of the cooling stations, the racks system is the most important client in

Table 10.1: Power requirements for CMS.

System	Power (kW)
General site services	2200
Electronics racks	2300
Low voltage to front-end electronics	1000
Magnet and cryogenics	1250
Ventilation stations	1250
Surface cooling stations	4000
Underground cooling stations	1500
Total steady-state consumption	9000

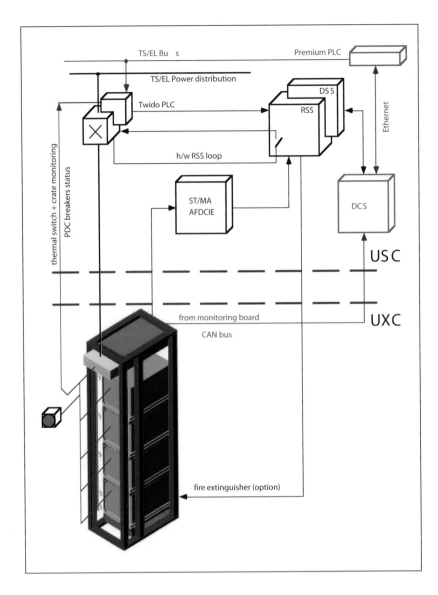

Figure 10.1: Control loops for rack powering.

terms of power. Rows of racks are fed by power bus-bars. Each single rack has a main breaker piloted by a dedicated PLC, the whole system being located in a box attached to the bus-bar. A power and a control cable run from this box to the power distributor cabinet inside each rack. Cabinets provide single-phase, three-phase or three-phase + neutral current distribution. The breaker PLC is controlled by the Detector Control System (DCS) via a network connection. Single racks can be switched on-off upon DCS request and the status of each breaker is known by DCS as well. Moreover, a hardwired connection to the Detector Safety System (DSS) secures the system in case of smoke or a high temperature is detected inside a rack. Figure 10.1 describes the logic behind the power controls.

Table 10.2: Cooling power for different sub-systems.

System	Power (kW)
Muon Endcaps	100
Muon Barrel	50
HCAL and Yoke Barrel	60
ECAL	300
Rack system	1600
Tracker, Pixel, Preshower	150

10.2   Detector cooling

10.2.1   Front-end electronics cooling

The CMS front-end electronics dissipates some 800 kW in the experimental cavern. This huge amount of heat is intercepted by cooling water at 18°C for the ECAL, HCAL and Muon systems, and by C_6F_{14} fluid at temperature ranging from -15°C to -25°C for the Preshower, Pixel and Tracker systems. In addition, some 1600 kW are dissipated by the rack system. Table 10.2 shows the power dissipated by each system.

Chilled water at 14°C is produced at the surface in the SU5 building and then transferred to the USC55 cooling plant, where five independent water circuits, each one with its own heat-exchangers, pumps and controls, produce and distribute water at 18°C to the experiment cavern. The Tracker, Pixel, and Preshower systems have on their primary side chilled water at 6°C, and they have their own cooling cabinets in UXC55 to shorten the transfer lines. Cooling status is monitored by the central DCS via ethernet connection to TS/CV control units. The DSS monitors crucial parameters such as flow rate, temperature, and dew point, in order to take actions in case of need. Loss of coolant is detected by measuring the fluid level in the expansion tanks of every cooling loop.

10.2.2   Cryogenics

The cryogenic plant at the CMS site has the function to cool down and keep at 4.7 K the 230 t of the CMS superconducting coil. The refrigerator system can deliver a cooling power of 800 W at 4.7 K, plus 4500 W at 60 K to cool the coil's thermal screens, in addition to the 4 g/s of liquid helium used to cool the 20 kA coil current leads. Cooling the coil down from room temperature takes 3 weeks, with a maximum thermal gradient inside the cold mass of 30 K. In case of a quench, the temperature rises to 70 K and 3 days are necessary to bring the cold mass down to 4.7 K. A 6000 l liquid helium storage tank sits close to the coil cryostat to allow a slow discharge from full current without warming up the coil.

2008 JINST 3 S08004

Figure 10.2: YB+2 and YE+1 cable-chains in UXC55 basement trenches.

10.3 Detector cabling

Due to the specific CMS design, with one central element (YB0) that is fixed and 6 mobile elements for each side moving on the cavern floor during shut-down periods, power cables, coolant, gas and optical fibres have to run through huge cable-chains in order to open and close the detector without disconnecting everything (figure 10.2).

Cables are labeled and stored in a database with web interface, that allows identification of each cable by sub-system, type, length, starting point, endpoint and routing. The main cable types can be summarised as follows:

- HV cables;

- LV cables for DC power to FEE;

- FEE read-out cables;

- optical fibres read-out;

- monitoring and control (DCS) cables;

- general pourpose power cables (230-400 V AC);

- safety system cables (DSS) for hard-wired signals and interlocks.

The cable-trays include also the gas-sniffer soft-pipes. Some 30 000 cables are referenced in the data-base.

2008 JINST 3 S08004

10.4 Detector moving system

The CMS moving system has been designed according to the following criteria: affordability, robustness, preciseness, easyness in handling and compactness. The boundary conditions have been determined on the one hand by the weight and dimensions of the assemblies and on the other hand by the friction, the slope and the size of the cavern.

10.4.1 Sliding system

In order to limit friction and thus the power of the pulling system, CMS has chosen a heavy duty air pad system for the long movements (10 cm to 10 m) and a flat grease pad system for the final approach (up to 10 cm). In addition, these systems allow, without any additional structure, movement perpendicular to the beam. The air pads (figure 10.3) have rubber sealing rings that prevent air losses. The system can be used with compressed air bottles only. At the same time, this sealing increases somewhat the friction factor, which lies around 0.8% before moving and goes down to around 0.4% once moving has begun. The grease pad system produces a final approach with practically no friction.

10.4.2 Pulling system

The pulling system consists of a hydraulic strand jack system and includes 6 jacks with strands (of which the two in the center are pivotable) and a strand storage mandrel. Taking into account the slope of the cavern (1.234%) and the friction of the airpads and cable chain, the system must be capable of safely pulling uphill 2.5% of the maximum load, which is 2600 t (3 endcaps together). Whereas going uphill is a pure pulling, going downhill needs a retaining force in order to produce a smooth, constant movement of the load. This was integrated into the design of the hydraulic control unit.

10.5 The Detector Safety System

The Detector Safety System (DSS) is a common development carried out by the 4 large LHC experiments together with the CERN IT department. The purpose of the DSS is to protect the detector and the experimental equipment from hazards. The DSS works complementary to the Detector Control System (DCS) and the CERN Safety System (CSS) (figure 10.4).

Normal operation of the experiments proceeds with the DCS which monitors and controls any deviation from normal operation or the occurrence of anomalies. In this respect, the DCS is ensuring a safe operation of the experiment. The DCS is designed such as to monitor and react up to a very detailed level and in a highly granular way, a necessary feature which on the other hand makes the system quite complex and thus vulnerable.

For emergency situations though, the LHC experiments are equipped with the CERN Safety System. The CSS is designed to reliably detect the main hazards, like smoke, flammable gas, oxygen deficiency, etc. that could endanger the human life, and will transmit a corresponding alarm to the CERN fire brigade. The CSS, however, does not foresee immediate actions for the protection of the equipment.

2008 JINST 3 S08004

Figure 10.3: A transport beam for barrel rings with 4 air pads fixed on it.

Equipment protection is the purpose of the DSS which triggers automatic actions in order to avoid or to reduce eventual damage to the experimental equipment when it detects abnormal and potentially dangerous situations. The DSS is designed to be simple and reliable and consequently the DSS actions have to be fast and quite coarse, e.g., cutting the power to the entire cavern in the case that smoke is detected. In order to do so, the DSS partially recuperates signals from the CSS (e.g., smoke detection) and triggers actions on the main infrastructure, as cutting the 18 kV supply. DSS actions thus will in general disrupt the data taking, but in the long run, by avoiding damage to experimental equipment, will increase the overall data taking efficiency of the experiment.

10.5.1 DSS Requirements

In order to fulfill its purpose, the DSS has the following characteristics:

- high reliability and availability to make the system simple and robust;

2008 JINST 3 S08004

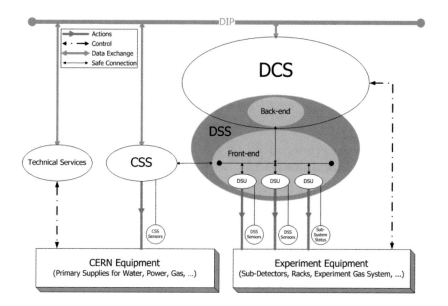

Figure 10.4: Context diagram of the DSS system, showing its rôle with respect to the CERN Safety System (CSS), the Detector Control System (DCS) and other technical services. The interconnection network is provided by the Data Interchange Protocol (DIP).

- operational independence of all other systems, running in stand alone system mode;

- autonomy from outside services, especially power supply and computer network;

- input from its own sensors and actuators (nevertheless some are owned by the CSS);

- capability of immediate and automatic actions;

- flexibility to be adopted and configured in order to adapt to the evolving needs of the experiments;

- full integration into the DCS.

10.5.2 DSS Architecture

The DSS consists of two main pillars: the front-end and the back-end.

The front-end is a redundant array of two Siemens S7-400 H PLCs. These PLCs interpret the signals coming from the connected sensors according to a programmable alarm-action matrix. Actuators, attached to the output of the PLCs trigger actions. The PLCs are scanning all input channels, processing the alarm-action matrix and modifying the state of the outputs accordingly. Such a cycle will take about 500 ms, allowing the DSS to react to any hazardous situation with a response time below one second. Different type of sensors can be connected to the DSS that are digital inputs, analogue inputs (4–20 mA) and PT100 temperature probes. The front-end can operate completely independent from the back-end and is thus the safety relevant part of the DSS. It is also connected to an uninterruptible power supply which gives the DSS autonomy of several hours.

2008 JINST 3 S08004

The back-end of the DSS consists of a standard PC running the PVSS software. It serves as interface between the front end and the operator. The back-end provides tools for post mortem and data analysis, e.g. the possibility to retrieve and display data based on user-defined selection criteria, trending tools and the possibility to filter alarms according to criteria such as time, origin, alarm priority. However, it is not necessary for the user to initiate any DSS actions, as these are all performed as automated actions in the DSS front-end.

10.5.3 CMS Implementation of DSS

Due to the rather large number of input channels for the CMS experiment, the DSS is split into two completely separate entities. One entity collects input channels from the equipment housed in the USC cavern and the surface buildings and one entity for the UXC cavern. Both systems, each equipped with a set of redundant PLCs, are stand alone and communicate only via hard wired input and output. The USC/surface system consists of 6 Detector Safety Units (DSU) each housed in a rack, where the UXC system consists of 10 DSU's. A typical DSU is made of 224 digital input channels, 64 analogue or PT100 input channels and a few digital output channels. The bulk amount of signals originates form the 230 V rack power distribution system and from the low voltage system. The about 200 racks in the USC cavern produce each an individual smoke detection alarm and an alarm from the power distribution box (TWIDO). The about 200 racks in the UXC cavern will give as additional signals the status of the electrical breaker inside the TWIDO box and a signal in case of an electrical fault since the racks in the UXC cavern are not accessible during the LHC operation. Concerning the low voltage supply for the UXC racks, the DSS receives about 180 status- and electrical-fault bits, and it is able to cut the low voltage power supply to each rack individually.

In addition to the protection of the racks, the DSS also directly safeguards the sub-detectors via a number of sensors. These are temperature sensors placed directly on the sub-detector or in the vicinity of them, flow meters measuring their cooling circuit, water leak detectors inside the vacuum tank of the solenoid, etc. Since the functioning of the DCS is mandatory for the operation of the DSS, every sub-detector shall send a status bit to DSS, such that DSS can take appropriate actions in case the DCS of a sub-detector or the central DCS is not functioning. The typical DSS action is to cut the power to part of the detector equipment, but other actions can be taken as, for example, triggering the CO_2 rack extinguishing system, as well as the water mist system.

10.6 Beam and Radiation Monitoring systems

10.6.1 Introduction

The Beam and Radiation Monitoring systems (BRM) [227] perform both a monitoring and a protection function for CMS. To this end, multiple and redundant systems have been installed, some of which can be used to initiate LHC beam aborts and/or CMS equipment control, others of which can be used for fast beam/detector optimisations. All systems will provide long term monitoring of the received radiation dose in various regions of the CMS detector.

2008 JINST 3 S08004

The CMS experiment sits in an unprecedentedly high radiation field for a HEP experiment and much effort has gone into the design and construction of systems with very high radiation tolerance. Nevertheless, the LHC is designed to run with 362 MJ of stored energy in one beam and with proton intensities in excess of 10^{14} per beam. Even very small fractional losses of this beam risk causing serious damage to detector elements. Whilst the LHC itself has extensive instrumentation designed for machine protection, CMS requirements dictate that CMS must be able to detect beam-related problems as they develop and to assert beam aborts if required. In addition, CMS must be able to log data and perform post-mortem analyses in the case of accidents and understand the accumulated dosage and potential longer term damage to the detector elements. To this end CMS has implemented the BRM systems.

While radiation damage can lead to long term effects, the most likely damage scenarios involve very fast bursts of radiation/energy-dissipation in detector elements. Thus the protection systems must be sensitive to very fast changes in beam conditions; the BRM systems can detect changes at the 25 ns level, though the initially deployed protection systems will react in times of order 3–40 μs. Additionally, the BRM systems provide monitoring and tuning data to permit operator intervention to diagnose and improve beam conditions. In addition, all BRM systems can be used to monitor integrated dose and detector component aging over the years of LHC operation.

In designing the BRM, CMS imposed several design constraints; namely to implement systems which can stay alive at any time when beam may be in the LHC independently of the state of CMS operations; that have readout and post-mortem capabilities extremely close to those of the LHC machine protection systems; and that offer a high degree of redundancy and a wide dynamic range for protection and monitoring scenarios. Given these constraints, the BRM protection system, summarised in table 10.3, has been implemented. The BRM system, its nomenclature and sub-system locations in CMS are also represented in figure 10.5.

10.6.2 Protection systems

The protection systems are based on chemical vapour deposition diamond detectors [228] similar to those that have been widely used in recent collider experiments [229, 230] where they have proven to be radiation hard [231], fast enough to match beam abort scenarios, and small enough to be inserted into areas close to key detector components without adding substantial material or services.

In CMS there are two protection systems foreseen for initial LHC operation. The first is the BCM1L made of four polycrystalline diamonds, each $10 \times 10 \times 0.4$ mm^3, positioned on either side of the IP at z values of $\pm$ 1.8 m, close to the beam pipe and the inner-tracker pixel detectors (chapter 3) at a radius of 4.5 cm. The second protection system is the BCM2L. This is a set of twelve polycrystalline diamonds, each $10 \times 10 \times 0.4$ mm^3, on either side of the IP behind the TOTEM T2 detector at a z position of $\pm$ 14.4 m. On each side of the IP, a set of eight sensors are deployed at an outer radius of 29 cm and an additional four at an inner radius of 5 cm. Here BCM refers to Beam Conditions Monitor, the index 1 or 2 refers to the two locations in z and L indicates that these detectors are used in a leakage current measurement mode as relative flux monitors, typically integrating the leakage current over μs time scales. The BCM1L diamonds are arranged on the x and y axes. The BCM2L comprise eight diamonds at 45° intervals at large radius

2008 JINST 3 S08004

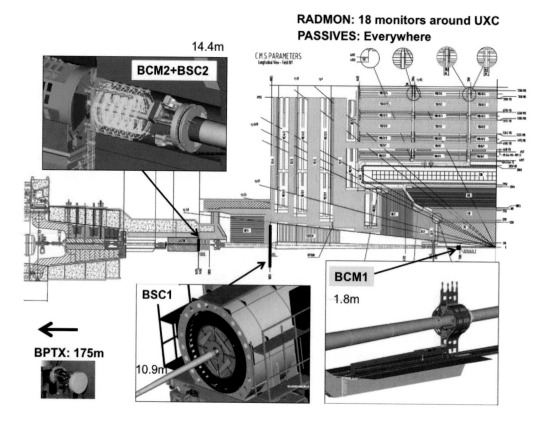

Figure 10.5: Layout of CMS BRM sub-systems.

and four on the x, y axes at small radius. The BCM1L and inner BCM2L diamonds measure a rate which is dominated by pp interactions at the IP. The outer BCM2L diamonds are hidden from the beam-spot and are expected to be largely sensitive to beam-halo rates.

The diamonds used for BCM1L and BCM2L are essentially identical, but the two systems differ in the readout methods adopted. The BCM2L uses a standard LHC Beam Loss Monitor (BLM) electronics and data processing [232, 233] that is read out asynchronously with respect to the LHC machine with 40 μs sampling. The BCM1L readout uses the same LHC BLM back-end electronics, but uses an additional mezzanine card to provide sub-orbit sampling. The readout is synchronized with the 89-μs LHC orbit, allowing user-configurable sampling, so that the sampling can be matched to the LHC bunch trains. In addition the BCM1L allows sampling of the LHC abort gap, which must be kept empty to avoid a spray of particles being directed at CMS during a beam dump.

Using a set of thresholds in the readout systems and a combinatorial logic to reduce sensitivity to individual noise events, a hardware beam abort signal can be generated and transmitted to the LHC machine via the Beam Interlock System [234], leading to the dumping of the beams within 3 orbits. A lower threshold value can be used to send hardware signals to CMS sub-detector clients to initiate high and/or low voltage ramp-downs.

In the event of a beam abort initiated by CMS, or by any of the other LHC (or experiment) protection systems, a full history of the BCM1L and BCM2L signals is produced and transmitted to the LHC control room.

Table 10.3: The sub-systems to be deployed as part of the initial BRM. The table is ordered from top to bottom in increasing time resolution.

sub-system (Sensor type)	Location Distance from IP (m)	Sampling Time	Function	Readout + Interface LHC or CMS type	Number of Sensors
Passives (TLD+Alanine)	CMS and UXC	~ months	Monitoring	N/A	Many
RADMON (RadFets+SRAM)	CMS and UXC	1 s	Monitoring	Standard LHC	18
BCM2L (Polycrystalline Diamond)	Behind TOTEM T2 z=±14.4 m	40 μs	Protection	Standard LHC	24
BCM1L (Polycrystalline Diamond)	Pixel Volume z=±1.8 m	5 μs	Protection	Standard LHC	8
BCM2F (Polycrystalline Diamond)	Behind TOTEM T2 z=±14.4 m	~ns	Monitoring	CMS Standalone	8
BSC (Scintillator Tiles)	Front of HF z=±10.9 m	~ns	Monitoring	CMS Standalone	32
BCM1F (Single Crystal Diamond)	Pixel Volume z=±1.8 m	~ns	Monitoring	CMS Standalone	8
BPTX (Button Beam Pickup)	Upstream of IP5 z=±175 m	200 ps	Monitoring	CMS Standalone	2

10.6.3 Monitoring systems

Several monitoring systems are listed in table 10.3: the BCM1F and BCM2F are also based upon diamond sensors, but with readouts able to resolve the sub-bunch structure, the Beam Scintillator Counters (BSC) are a series of scintillator tiles designed to provide hit and coincidence rates, the Button Beam Pickup (BPTX) is designed to provide precise information on the bunch structure and timing of the beam, and the RADMON and Passives systems give calibrated information on the radiation field within the CMS cavern.

The BCM1F, BSC and BPTX are sensitive to time structure below the 25-ns level; as such they also provide technical trigger inputs into the global CMS trigger. In particular, the inputs from the BPTX and BSC provide zero- and minimum-bias triggers, respectively. Additionally, all three of these systems are sensitive to all foreseen beam intensities including the LHC pilot beam, where a single low intensity bunch is injected for studies or to confirm parameter settings prior to full intensity injection.

The BCM1F consists of four single crystal diamonds, each 5×5×0.5 mm^3, positioned on either side of the IP at z values of ± 1.8 m at a radius of 4.5 cm, in close proximity to the BCM1L detectors. The BCM1F is used as a diagnostic tool to flag problematic beam conditions resulting in "bursts" of beam loss over very short periods of time. Such beam losses are expected to be one of the principle damage scenarios for the CMS detector systems. The location of the BCM1F is close to the optimal position in terms of timing separation between ingoing and outgoing particles from the IP (i.e. 6.25 ns from the IP). The gated rate information from the BCM1F should therefore give a very good handle on the comparative rate of background from beam halo to that from lumonisity products. The sensor is connected to the JK16 radiation hard amplifier [235], after which the

2008 JINST 3 S08004

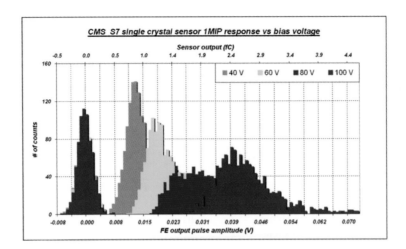

Figure 10.6: MIP response of BCM1F single-crystal diamond with front-end electronics, as a function of bias voltage of the sensor. The superposition of histograms around 0-V output amplitude indicates the noise.

signal is transmitted to the counting room over an analog optical link built from the tracker optical components [236].

The detector is sensitive to one MIP and has a timing resolution for single hits of a few ns. The performance of the front end electronics is shown in figure 10.6. Good separation can be seen between the signal and the noise. The pulse height was found to saturate at 100 V bias voltage across the sensor. The back-end readout produces rate, multiplicity, timing and coincidence information independently of the CMS DAQ. However, there is the possibility to feed information into the event stream via a standard CMS SLINK.

In a similar vein to the BCM1F, the BCM2F is composed of four diamonds at the BCM2L location, read out by a fast digitiser. The aim of this system is to provide additional diagnostic information at this location, as the digitiser can sample at 1 GHz, giving information on the sub-bunch level [237]. Whilst this will not be MIP-sensitive, it will help resolve the timing structure of periods of enhanced background.

The Beam Scintillator Counters (BSC) are a series of scintillator tiles designed to provide hit and coincidence rates, with a design similar to those used at previous experiments [238]. The scintillators and PMTs used for the BSC are recycled from OPAL [239]. The layout and geometry of the scintillator tiles are shown in figure 10.7. The BSC1 is located on the front of the HF, at ±10.9 m from the IP, and consists of two types of tiles. Next to the beampipe are the disks, segmented into 8 independent slices in ϕ, with an inner radius of 22 cm and an outer radius of 45 cm. The primary function of the disks is to provide the rate information corresponding to the beam conditions. In addition, there are four large area "paddles" further out, at a radial distance of between ≈ 55 cm and ≈ 80 cm, which in addition to providing rate information, will also provide coincidence information which can be used to tag halo muons passing through the detector, for calibration purposes. The area covered by the BSC is about 25% of the tracker; therefore these tiles can be indicative of activity within this bunch crossing, and can be used to provide a minimum-

2008 JINST 3 S08004

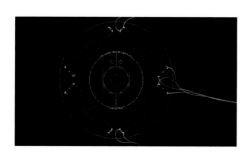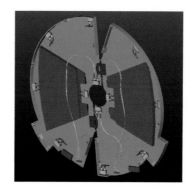

Figure 10.7: Layout of the Beam Scintillator Counters tiles. The left-hand panel shows the layout for BSC1, the right-hand panel for BSC2. The locations of the BCM2 sensors can also be seen in the right-hand panel.

bias trigger for commissioning and systematic studies. The BSC2 is located behind TOTEM T2 at ±14.4 m from the IP. The BSC2 consists of two tiles on each side of the IP, with a minimum inner radius of 5 cm and a maximum outer radius of 29 cm. The primary function of the BSC2 is to distinguish between ingoing and outgoing particles along the beamline, as there is a 4-ns timing difference between them. The rates at this location can therefore be tagged as to whether they are incoming (beam halo only) or outgoing (collision products and beam halo).

The Beam Timing for the experiments (BPTX) is a beam pickup device specifically installed to provide the experiments with the timing structure of the LHC beam. This beam pickup is a standard button monitor used everywhere around the LHC ring for the beam position monitors. Two are installed for CMS: 175 m left and right upstream of the IP. At this location there are two beampipes, and therefore the timing measurement is only of the incoming beam. To optimise the timing measurement, the four buttons (left, right, up, down) of the pickup have been electrically connected together. This is done to maximise the signal strength and hence the resolution on the timing, at the price of loosing the position information.

An oscilloscope-based read-out was chosen for the BPTX and developed in common with ATLAS [240]. The BPTX will provide accurate information on the timing and phase of each bunch and its intensity. The phases of all the experimental clocks can be compared to the measured phase of each bunch with a precision better than 200 ps. This will also allow the interaction-point z position to be calculated from the relative phases of the BPTX measurements on opposite sides of the IP. The BPTX can also detect problems with the bunch structure, and measure the proportion of beam which has drifted into the neighbouring RF bucket.

In parallel to the oscilloscope based read-out, the signals from the BPTX will also be discriminated and sent as three technical trigger inputs to the CMS global trigger. This will provide three flags on each bunch crossing as to whether: a) bunch in beam 1 is occupied; b) bunch in beam 2 is occupied; c) both beams are occupied. The flag where both beams are occupied is indicative of whether collisions can occur in this bunch crossing, and therefore provides a zero-bias trigger for commissioning of the trigger system.

At 18 locations around the CMS cavern, RADMON [241] detectors are installed. The RAD-MON detectors each provide well calibrated measurements of: a) the dose and dose rate using

2008 JINST 3 S08004

RadFETs; b) the hadron flux with energies above 20 MeV and the single event upset rate using SRAM; c) the 1-MeV-equivalent neutron fluence using pin diodes. RADMON detectors are installed all around the LHC ring, and in the experimental insertions. The RADMON detectors at CMS will be integrated into and read out via the accelerator-wide RADMON system.

The integrated radiation dose throughout the CMS cavern will be measured during each run period with passive dosimetry. This allows to map the radiation field throughout the cavern and will be used to validate the simulations of the anticipated doses. This gives an absolute scale to the other measurements. The dosimeters chosen are TLDs and Alanine.

2008 JINST 3 S08004

Chapter 11

Computing

11.1 Overview

The CMS offline computing system must support the storage, transfer and manipulation of the recorded data for the lifetime of the experiment. The system accepts real-time detector information from the data acquisition system at the experimental site; ensures safe curation of the raw data; performs pattern recognition, event filtering, and data reduction; supports the physics analysis activities of the collaboration. The system also supports production and distribution of simulated data, and access to conditions and calibration information and other non-event data.

The users of the system, and the physical computer centres it comprises, are distributed worldwide, interconnected by high-speed international networks. Unlike previous generations of experiments, the majority of data storage and processing resources available to CMS lie outside the host laboratory. A fully distributed computing model has therefore been designed from the outset. The system is based upon Grid middleware, with the common Grid services at centres defined and managed through the Worldwide LHC Computing Grid (WLCG) project [242], a collaboration between LHC experiments, computing centres, and middleware providers.

The nature of the CMS experimental programme poses several challenges for the offline computing system:

- The requirement to analyse very large statistics datasets in pursuit of rare signals, coupled with the fine granularity of the CMS detector, implies a volume of data unprecedented in scientific computing. This requires a system of *large scale*, supporting efficient approaches to data reduction and pattern recognition.

- The system is required to be *highly flexible*, allowing any user access to any data item recorded or calculated during the lifetime of the experiment. A software framework is required which supports a wide variety of data processing tasks in a consistent way, and which must evolve along with the goals of the experiment. Since the CMS programme centres on discovery of new phenomena, under new experimental conditions, analysis requirements cannot be wholly defined in advance.

- A complex distributed system of such large scale must be designed from the outset for *manageability*, both in the operation of computing resources for physics, and in terms of software

2008 JINST 3 S08004

construction and maintenance. The *longevity* of the system, of 15 years or more, implies several generations of underlying hardware and software, and many changes of personnel, during the lifetime of the system.

Key components of the computing system include:

- An event data model and corresponding application framework;

- Distributed database systems allowing access to non-event data;

- A set of computing services, providing tools to transfer, locate, and process large collections of events;

- Underlying generic Grid services giving access to distributed computing resources;

- Computer centres, managing and providing access to storage and CPU at a local level.

At each level, the design challenges have been addressed through construction of a modular system of loosely coupled components with well-defined interfaces, and with emphasis on scalability to very large event samples [243].

11.2   Application framework

The CMS application software must perform a variety of event processing, selection and analysis tasks, and is used in both offline and online contexts. The software must be sufficiently modular that it can be developed and maintained by a large group of geographically dispersed collaborators. The chosen architecture consists of a common framework which is adaptable for each type of computing environment, physics modules which plug into the framework via a well-defined interface, and a service and utility toolkit which decouples the physics modules from details of event I/O, user interface, and other environmental constraints [212].

The central concept of the CMS data model is the *Event*. The Event provides access to the recorded data from a single triggered bunch crossing, and to new data derived from it. This may include raw digitised data, reconstructed products, or high-level analysis objects, for real or simulated crossings. The Event also contains information describing the origin of the raw data, and the provenance of all derived data products. The inclusion of provenance information allows users to unambiguously identify how each event contributing to a final analysis was produced; it includes a record of the software configuration and conditions / calibration setup used to produce each new data product. Events are physically stored as persistent ROOT files [244].

The Event is used by a variety of *physics modules*, which may read data from it, or add new data, with provenance information automatically included. Each module performs a well-defined function relating to the selection, reconstruction or analysis of the Event. Several module types exist, each with a specialised interface. These include: *event data producers*, which add new data products into the event; *filters* used in online triggering and selection; *analysers*, producing summary information from an event collection; and *input and output modules* for both disk storage and DAQ.

2008 JINST 3 S08004

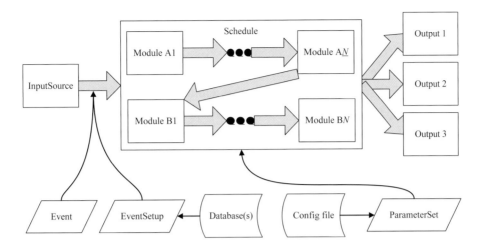

Figure 11.1: Modules within the CMS Application Framework.

Modules are insulated from the computing environment, execute independently from one another, and communicate only though the Event; this allows modules to be developed and verified independently. A complete CMS application is constructed by specifying to the Framework one or more ordered sequences of modules through which each Event must flow, along with the configuration for each. The Framework configures the modules, schedules their execution, and provides access to global services and utilities (figure 11.1).

11.3 Data formats and processing

In order to achieve the required level of data reduction, whilst maintaining flexibility, CMS makes use of several event formats with differing levels of detail and precision. Other specialised event formats are used for heavy-ion data. The process of data reduction and analysis takes place in several steps, typically carried out at different computer centres.

RAW format

RAW events contain the full recorded information from the detector, plus a record of the trigger decision and other metadata. RAW data is accepted into the offline system at the HLT output rate (nominally 300 Hz for pp collisions). An extension of the RAW data format is used to store the output of CMS Monte Carlo simulation tools. The RAW data is permanently archived in safe storage, and is designed to occupy around 1.5 MB/event (2 MB/event for simulated data, due to additional Monte Carlo truth information).

The RAW data will be classified by the online system into several distinct *primary datasets*, based upon the trigger signature. Event classification at the earliest possible stage has several advantages, including the possibility of assigning priorities for data reconstruction and transfer in the case of backlog, and balancing of data placement at centres outside CERN. CMS will also define one or more flexible "express streams" used for prompt calibration and rapid access to interesting or anomalous events.

2008 JINST 3 S08004

RECO format

Reconstructed (RECO) data is produced by applying several levels of pattern recognition and compression algorithms to the RAW data. These algorithms include: detector-specific filtering and correction of the the digitised data; cluster- and track-finding; primary and secondary vertex reconstruction; and particle ID, using a variety of algorithms operating on cross-detector information.

Reconstruction is the most CPU-intensive activity in the CMS data processing chain. The resulting RECO events contain high-level *physics objects*, plus a full record of the reconstructed hits and clusters used to produce them. Sufficient information is retained to allow subsequent application of new calibrations or algorithms without recourse to RAW data, though basic improvements in pattern recognition or event formats will probably require re-production of the RECO data at least once per year. RECO events are foreseen to occupy around 0.5 MB/event.

AOD format

AOD (Analysis Object Data) is the compact analysis format, designed to allow a wide range of physics analyses whilst occupying sufficiently small storage so that very large event samples may be held at many centres. AOD events contain the parameters of high-level physics objects, plus sufficient additional information to allow kinematic refitting. This format will require around 100 kB/event, small enough to allow a complete copy of the experimental data in AOD format to be held at computing centres outside CERN. AOD data is produced by filtering of RECO data, either in bulk production, or in a skimming process which may also filter a primary dataset into several analysis datasets.

Non-Event data

In addition to event data recorded from the detector, a variety of *non-event data* is required in order to interpret and reconstruct events. CMS makes use of four types of non-event data: construction data, generated during the construction of the detector; equipment management data; configuration data, comprising programmable parameters related to detector operation; and conditions data, including calibrations, alignments and detector status information. We concentrate here on the lattermost category.

Conditions data are produced and required by both online and offline applications, and have a well-defined interval of validity (IOV). For instance, calibration constants for a given run may be derived from prompt reconstruction of a subset of recorded events, and then used both by the HLT system and for subsequent reconstruction and analysis at computing centres around the world. Non-event data are held in a number of central Oracle databases, for access by online and offline applications. New conditions data, including calibration and alignment constants produced offline, may be replicated between the databases as required. Conditions data access at remote sites takes place via the FroNTier system [245] which uses a distributed network of caching http proxy servers.

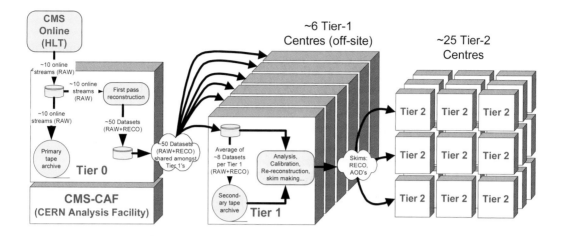

Figure 11.2: Dataflow between CMS Computing Centres.

11.4 Computing centres

The scale of the computing system is such that it could not, even in principle, be hosted entirely at one site. The system is built using computing resources at a range of scales, provided by collaborating institutes around the world. CMS proposes to use a hierarchical architecture of Tiered centres, similar to that originally devised in the MONARC working group [246], with a single Tier-0 centre at CERN, a few Tier-1 centres at national computing facilities, and several Tier-2 centres at institutes. A representation of the dataflow between centres is shown in figure 11.2.

The CMS computing model depends upon reliable and performant network links between sites. In the case of transfers between Tier-0 and Tier-1 centres, these network links are implemented as an optical private network (LHC-OPN) [247]. Data transfers between Tier-1 and Tier-2 centres typically takes place over general-purpose national and international research networks.

Tier-0 centre

A single Tier-0 centre is hosted at CERN. Its primary functions are to:

- Accept data from the online system with guaranteed integrity and latency, and copy it to permanent mass storage;

- Carry out prompt reconstruction of the RAW data to produce first-pass RECO datasets. The centre must keep pace with the average rate of data recording, and must provide sufficient input buffering to absorb fluctuations in data rate;

- Reliably export a copy of RAW and RECO data to Tier-1 centres. Data is not considered "safe" for deletion from Tier-0 buffers until it is held at at least two independent sites. (One of these is CERN computing centre, playing the role of a Tier-1.)

During the LHC low-luminosity phase, the Tier-0 is intended to be available outside data-taking periods for second-pass reconstruction and other scheduled processing activities. High-luminosity running will require the use of the Tier-0 for most of the year. The Tier-0 is a common CMS facility used only for well-controlled batch work; it is not accessible for analysis use.

Tier-1 centres

A few large Tier-1 centres are hosted at collaborating national labs and computing centres around the world. These centres are operated by a professional staff on a 24/365 basis, with the emphasis on extremely reliable delivery of data-intensive processing services. Each site provides large batch CPU facilities, a mass storage system including a robotic tape archive, and very high speed international network links including a dedicated link to the LHC-OPN. The primary functions of a Tier-1 are to:

- Provide long-term safe storage of RAW data from CMS, providing a second complete copy outside CERN distributed across the centres. Each Tier-1 takes long-term custodial responsibility for a fraction of the CMS dataset;

- Store and serve to Tier-2 centres simulated and derived data. Each Tier-1 holds a fraction of the CMS simulated and RECO data, and a complete copy of the AOD data. It can rapidly transfers these data to any Tier-2 centre which requires them for analysis;

- Carry out second-pass reconstruction: a Tier-1 provides access to its archive of RAW data to allow reproduction of RECO datasets using improved algorithms or calibrations;

- Provide rapid access to very large data samples for skimming and data-intensive analysis: a Tier-1 can support high-statistics analysis projects which would be infeasible at a Tier-2 centre.

Since each Tier-1 centre holds unique RAW and RECO datasets, it must be capable of serving data to any CMS Tier-2. However, for the purposes of Monte Carlo data receipt and AOD data serving, the Tier-1 serves a defined set of a few "associated" Tier-2 centres, usually defined by geographical proximity.

Tier-2 centres

Several Tier-2 centres of varying sizes are hosted at CMS institutes. A Tier-2 centre typically divides its resources between the local user community and CMS as a whole. Tier-2 centres are subject to less stringent requirements on availability and data security than a Tier-1 centre, making them feasible to manage with the resources available to a typical University group. The functions of a Tier-2 centre may include:

- Support of analysis activities, including local storage of data samples transferred from Tier-1 centres, and access to a flexible CPU farm; in particular, the Tier-2 centres are designed to support final-stage analysis requiring repeated passes over a reduced dataset;

- Support of specialised activities such as offline calibration and alignment tasks, and detector studies;

- Production of Monte Carlo data, and its transfer to an associated Tier-1 centre for long term storage.

2008 JINST 3 S08004

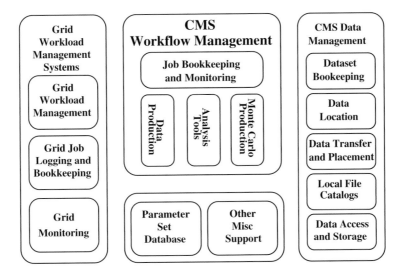

Figure 11.3: Overview of the CMS Computing Services.

CERN Analysis Facility

In addition to the Tier-0 centre, CERN also hosts an Analysis Facility which combines flexible CPU resources with rapid access to the entire CMS dataset. This centre supports fast turn-around analysis when required, and a variety of other specialised functions (calibration, performance monitoring) related to the operation of the CMS detector. The centre effectively combines the rapid data access capabilities of a Tier-1 with the flexibility of a very large Tier-2.

11.5   Computing services

Grid computing

The integration of the resources at CMS computing centres into a single coherent system relies upon Grid middleware which presents a standardised interface to storage and CPU facilities at each WLCG (Worldwide LHC Computing Grid) site. The Grid allows remote job submission and data access with robust security and accounting. The detailed architecture of the Grid is described in the WLCG Technical Design Report [242].

A number of CMS-specific distributed computing services operate above the generic Grid layer, facilitating higher-level data and workload management functions. These services require CMS-specific software agents to run at some sites, in addition to generic Grid services. CMS also provides specialised user-intelligible interfaces to the Grid for analysis job submission and monitoring, and tools for automated steering and monitoring of large-scale data production and processing. An overview of the CMS Computing Services components is shown in figure 11.3.

2008 JINST 3 S08004

Data management

CMS requires tools to catalogue the data which exist, to track the location of the corresponding physical data files on site storage systems, and to manage and monitor the flow of data between sites. In order to simplify the data management problem, the data management system therefore defines higher-level concepts including: *dataset*, a logical collection of data grouped by physical-meaningful criteria; *event collection*, roughly corresponding to an experiment "run" for a given dataset definition; and *file block*, an aggregation of a few TB of data files, representing the smallest unit of operation of the data transfer system.

To provide the connection between abstract datasets and physical files, a multi-tiered catalogue system is used. The *Dataset Bookkeeping System* provides a standardised and queryable means of cataloguing and describing event data [249]. It is the principle means of data discovery for the end user, answering the question "which data of this type exists in the system?" A second catalogue system, the *Data Location Service* provides the mapping between file blocks to the particular sites at which they are located, taking into account the possibility of replicas at multiple sites. *Local File Catalogues* at each site map logical files onto physical files in local storage.

The *data transfer and placement system* is responsible for the physical movement of file-blocks between sites on demand; it is currently implemented by the PhEDEx system [248]. This system must schedule, monitor and verify the movement of data in conjunction with the storage interfaces at CMS sites, ensuring optimal use of the available bandwidth. The baseline mode of operation for the data management system is that the collaboration will explicitly place datasets at defined sites, where they will remain for access by CMS applications until removed.

Workload management

Processing and analysis of data at sites is typically performed by submission of batch jobs to a remote site via the Grid workload management system. A standard job wrapper performs the necessary setup, executes a CMSSW application upon data present on local storage at the site, arranges for any produced data to be made accessible via Grid data management tools, and provides logging information. This process is supported by several CMS-specific services.

A *parameter set management system*, implemented with either global or local scope according to the application, allows the storage and tracking of the configuration of CMSSW applications submitted to the Grid. A lightweight *job bookkeeping and monitoring system* allows users to track, monitor, and retrieve output from jobs currently submitted to and executing at remote sites [250]. The system also provides a uniform interface to a variety of Grid-based and local batch-system based submission tools. In addition, a suite of software distribution tools provide facilities for automated installation of standard CMS applications and libraries at remote sites.

Bulk workflow management

For very large-scale data processing (including Monte Carlo production, skimming and event reconstruction), a specialised bulk workflow management tool has been developed. The ProdAgent system comprises a collaborative distributed network of automated job managers, operating at Tier-0, Tier-1 and Tier-2 sites [250]. The system provides facilities for large-scale Grid job submission, interface to the CMS data catalogues and data management system, and handling of large flows of logging and status information. A highly automated system such as ProdAgent is essential in order to allow the CMS data processing system to be controlled and monitored by a moderately-sized data operations team.

User workflow management

For a generic CMS physicist, a dedicated tool (CRAB) for workflow management is available [250]. It allows to submit user-specific jobs to a remote computing element which can access data previously transferred to a close storage element. CRAB takes care of interfacing with the user environment, it provides data-discovery and data-location services, and Grid infrastructure. It also manages status reporting, monitoring, and user job output which can be put on a user-selected storage element. Via a simple configuration file, a physicist can thus access data available on remote sites as easily as he can access local data: all infrastructure complexities are hidden to him as much as possible. There is also a client-server architecture available, so the job is not directly submitted to the Grid but to a dedicated CRAB server, which, in turn, handles the job on behalf of the user, interacting with the Grid services.

11.6 System commissioning and tests

It has been recognised since the very start of preparations for LHC that the construction and organisation of the experiment computing systems would be a key challenge. Each component of the system must be designed with attention to both scalability and flexibility, and rigorously tested at realistic scale. The reliance on distributed computing, using the relatively new Grid approach, has many advantages, but adds further complexity in controlled deployment and testing compared to a system located primarily at a single site.

The relatively large cost of the computing system dictates that centres must build up their resources in a carefully controlled way; the rapidly falling price of hardware dictates that full-scale resources will only become available shortly before they are required, and that efficient use of resources is a strong requirement. The emphasis in CMS has been on a series of increasing scale full-system tests ("data challenges") over the last three years, exercising all available components in a realistic way.

In 2006 and 2007, CMS carried out large-scale Computing, Software and Analysis challenges (CSA06, CSA07). The scale of the two tests was set at 25% and 50% of the nominal 2008 performance, respectively, with the computing system operated continuously at this level for more than four weeks. The challenges were carried out using realistic application software and computing tools. Typical targets for the tests were:

- Preparation of large Monte Carlo datasets ($\approx$ 100 million events) at around twenty CMS Tier-1 and Tier-2 centres in the weeks preceding the challenge, and upload to CERN;

- Playback of the MC dataset for prompt Tier-0 reconstruction at around 100 Hz, including the application of calibration constants from the offline database, and splitting the event sample into around ten datasets;

2008 JINST 3 S08004

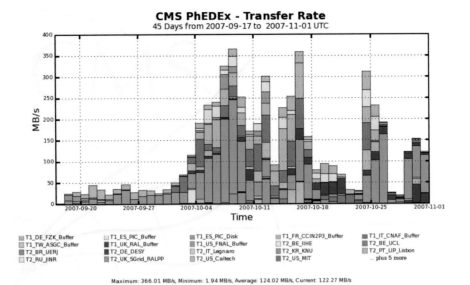

Figure 11.4: Dataflow from CERN during the CSA07 Data Challenge.

• Distribution of AOD and RAW to all Tier-1 centres, and subsequent alignment / calibration, reconstruction and skimming operations at several sites;

• Transfer of skimmed data to Tier-2 centres and running of physics analysis jobs.

Overall, many of the key metrics for success in the challenges were met: the reconstruction rate at the Tier-0 exceeded 100 Hz for periods of time; an export rate of over 350 MB/s was achieved from CERN (figure 11.4). CMS will finalise its data challenge programme with additional scale tests during 2008, which are in the final stages of preparation at the time of writing. In parallel with data challenges, continuous programmes are under way to deploy, commission and test the increasing hardware resources at the computing centres, and to debug and demonstrate reliable and high-speed data network links between them. The CMS computing model itself is also under ungoing review, with many new lessons expected to be learnt as detector data begins to flow.

Chapter 12

Conclusions

The Compact Muon Solenoid detector has been described in detail. The expected physics performance of the apparatus has been described elsewhere [17].

At the time of this paper, the apparatus is essentially completed and installed.

After more than 10 years of design and construction, the CMS magnet has been constructed and successfully tested. Most of the magnetic, electrical, mechanical, and cryogenics parameters measured during the tests are in good agreement with calculated values. The CMS magnet is the largest superconducting solenoid ever built for a physics experiment in terms of bending power for physics, total stored energy, and stored energy per unit of cold mass.

The silicon-strip inner tracker, with about 200 m^2 of active silicon, has been integrated into its support tube, commissioned, and thoroughly tested with cosmic rays. Its performance is excellent, fulfilling the design specifications. The silicon tracker was installed into CMS in december 2007. All the pixel modules are completed; it is planned to install the Pixel detector into CMS in mid-2008.

The ECAL, comprising over 75 000 lead tungstate crystals, is the largest crystal calorimeter ever built. The crystals in the barrel part, comprising over 60 000 crystals, have been inter-calibrated using cosmic rays and about a third in particle beams, demonstrating the ability to measure the energies ranging from those deposited by minimum ionising particles to high-energy electrons. An energy resolution of 0.5% for 120 GeV electrons has been attained. The ECAL barrel has been installed in the experiment and is being commissioned. The endcaps are foreseen to be inserted into the experiment in 2008.

The entire HCAL has been completed and commissioned on the surface. The HCAL modules are currently being commissioned in the experiment proper.

The various components of the Muon System (drift tubes, cathode strip chambers, resistive plate chambers) have been completed. A significant fraction of the Muon System has been commissioned and tested on surface with cosmic rays, and it is now being integrated into the experiment and being commissioned in-situ.

In the very forward region, the Zero Degree Calorimeter has been completed and CASTOR is expected to be completed in 2008.

The off-detector electronics are currently being installed and operations for trigger commissioning are taking place.

Common data-acquisition runs with various sub-detectors, sometimes using cosmic rays, are regularly taking place at the experiment and will continue into spring 2008 in anticipation of collisions at LHC in mid-2008.

2008 JINST 3 S08004

Acknowledgements

The design, construction, installation and commissioning of CMS would have been impossible without the devoted efforts of our numerous technical colleagues from the CERN departments and from all the CMS Institutes. The cost of the detectors, computing infrastructure, data acquisition and all other systems without which CMS would not be able to operate, was generously supported by the financing agencies involved in the experiment. We are particularly indebted to: Austrian Federal Ministry of Science and Research; FNRS and FWO (Belgium); CNPq and FAPERJ (Brazil); Bulgarian Ministry of Education and Science; CERN; CAS and NSFC (China); Croatian Ministry of Science and Technology; University of Cyprus; Estonian Academy of Sciences and NICPB; Academy of Finland, Finish Ministry of Education and Helsinki Institute of Physics; CEA and CNRS/IN2P3 (France); BMBF and DESY (Germany); General Secretariat for Research and Technology (Greece); NKTH (Hungary); DAE and DST (India); IPM (Iran); UCD (Ireland); INFN (Italy); KICOS (Korea); CINVESTAV (Mexico); PAEC (Pakistan); State Commission for Scientific Research (Poland); FCT (Portugal); JINR (Armenia, Belarus, Georgia, Ukraine, Uzbekistan), Ministry of Education and Science of the Russian Federation, Russian Federal Agency of Atomic Energy; Ministry of Science and Environmental Protection of the Republic of Serbia; Oficina de Ciencia y Tecnologia (Spain); ETHZ, PSI, University of Zurich (Switzerland); National Science Council (Taipei); TUBITAK and TAEK (Turkey); STFC (United Kingdom); DOE and NSF (USA).

We also acknowledge the important contributions provided by the following institutes: Research Institute of Applied Physical Problems, Minsk, Belarus; University for Science and Technology of China, Hefei, Anhui, China; Digital and Computer Systems Laboratory, Tampere University of Technology, Tampere, Finland; Seoul National University of Education, Seoul, Korea; Benemerita Universidad Autonoma de Puebla, Puebla, Mexico; Myasishchev Design Bureau, Zhukovsky, Russia; Russian Federal Nuclear Centre, Scientific Research Institute for Technical Physics, Snezhinsk, Russia; Kharkov State University, Kharkov, Ukraine; University of Strathclyde, Glasgow, United Kingdom; Virginia Polytechnic Institute and State University, Blacksburg, Virginia, USA.

CMS acronym list

AB	Algorithm Board
AC	Alternating Current
ADC	Analog to Digital Converter
AFEB	Anode Front-End Board, CSC system
AG	Application Gateway
ALCT	Anode Local Charged Track trigger primitive, CSC system
AOD	Analysis Object Data - a compact event format for physics analysis
AOH	Analog Opto-Hybrid
APD	Avalanche Photo-Diode
API	Application Programming Interface
APV	Analogue Pipeline (Voltage mode), front-end read-out chip of Tracker
ASIC	Application Specific Integrated Circuit
ATLAS	A Toroidal LHC ApparatuS experiment
aTTS	Asynchronous Trigger Throttle System
AWG	American Wire Gauge
BMU	Barrel Muon system
BD	Back Disk
BP	Back Petal
BPix	Barrel Pixel
BR	Branching Ratio
BRAN	Beam RAte of Neutrals
BST	Beam Synchronous Timing
BTI	Bunch and Track Identifier trigger primitive, DT system
BU	Builder Unit
BX	Bunch Crossing
BXN	Bunch Crossing Number
CASTOR	Centauro And Strange Object Research
CC	Cosmic Challenge
CCS	Clock and Control System
CCU	Communication and Control Unit
CCUM	Communication and Control Unit Module
CDR	Central Data Recording
CFC	Carbon Fiber Composite

2008 JINST 3 S08004

CFEB	Cathode Front-End Board of the CSC system
CLCT	Cathode Local Charged Track trigger primitive, CSC system
CMM	Coordinate Measuring Machine
CMN	Common Mode Noise
CMOS	Complementary Metal Oxide Semiconductor
CMS	Compact Muon Solenoid experiment
CMSSW	CMS SoftWare framework
COSINE	Consistent Online Software INtegration Environment, project integrating online with offline software
CPU	Central Processing Unit
COCOA	CMS Object-oriented Code for optical Alignment
CRAB	CMS Remote Analysis Builder
CRack	Cosmic Rack, a set of TOB rods
CRC	Cyclic Redundancy Check error detection
CSC	Cathode Strip Chamber muon system
CSCTF	Cathode Strip Chamber Trigger Track Finder
D2S	Data to Surface
DAC	Digital to Analog Converter
DAQ	Data Acquisition
DAQMB	Data Acquisition Motherboard, CSC L1 trigger
DBMS	Database Management System
DC	Direct Current
DCC	Data Concentrator Card
DCCT	DC Current Transformer
DCS	Detector Control System
DCU	Detector Control Unit
DDD	Detector Description Database
DDL	Data Description Language
DDU	Detector Dependent Unit in DAQ system
DIP	Data Interchange Protocol (CERN)
DMB	DAQ MotherBoard of CSC system
DOFZ	Diffusion Oxygenated Float Zone
DOH	Digital Opto-Hybrid
DOHM	Digital Opto-Hybrid Module
DQM	Data Quality Monitoring
DQMC	Data Quality Monitoring Collector
DSS	Detector Safety System
DT	Drift Tube muon system
DTTF	Drift Tube Trigger Track Finder, DT L1 trigger
EB	Electromagnetic Calorimeter (Barrel)
ECAL	Electromagnetic Calorimeter
EDM	Event Data Model
EDMS	Engineering Database Management System

2008 JINST 3 S08004

EE	Electromagnetic Calorimeter (Endcap)
EIC	Electromagnetic Isolation Card, regional calorimeter trigger
ELMB	Embedded Local Monitoring Board (ECAL)
EMDB	Equipment Management DataBase
EMU	Endcap Muon system
ENC	Equivalent Noise Charge
EP	Event Processor
ES	Endcap preShower detector, also Event Server
ESP	Event Server Proxy
ESS	ECAL Safety System
ETTF	Eta Track Finder, DT regional muon trigger
EVB	EVent Builder
EVF	Event Filter Farm
EVM	Event Manager
FB	FED builder
FD	Front Disk
FDL	Final Decision Logic, L1 Global Trigger
FE	Front-End
FEB	Front-End Board
FEC	Front-End Card, Front End Controller
FED	Front-End Driver
FEE	Front-End Electronics
FES	Front-End System
FENIX	ECAL front-end read-out ASIC
FEVT	Event format comprising the union of RAW and RECO data
FF	Filter Farm
FMM	Fast Merging Module
FIFO	First In First Out buffer
FP	Front Petal
FPGA	Field Programmable Gate Array
FPix	Forward Pixel
FRL	Front-End Read-out Link
FSM	Finite State Machine
FTP	Foil screened Twisted Pair cables
FU	Filter Unit
Gb	Gigabit (10^9 bits)
GB	Gigabyte (10^9 bytes)
GBW	Gain BandWidth product
GCALOR	Computer program for hadron shower calculations
GCT	Global Calorimeter Trigger (L1)
GIF	Gamma Irradiation Facility
GMR	Global Muon Reconstructor
GMT	Global Muon Trigger (L1)

GOH	Giga Optical Hybrid
GOL	Gigabit Optical Link
GPN	General Purpose Network (CERN campus)
GT	Global Trigger (L1)
GTFE	Global Trigger Front-end board (L1)
GTL	Global Trigger Logic board (L1)
GTL+	Gunning Transceiver Logic, upgraded version, developed by Fairchild Semiconductor
GTP	Global Trigger Processor
GTPe	Global Trigger Processor emulator
GUI	Graphical User Interface
H2	Beamline at CERN
HCAL	Hadron Calorimeter
HB	Hadron Calorimeter (Barrel)
HDI	High Density Interconnect
HE	Hadron Calorimeter (Endcap)
HF	Hadron Calorimeter (Forward)
HG	High Gain
HI	Heavy Ion(s)
HIJING	Heavy Ion Jet INteraction Generator, Monte Carlo event generator for heavy-ion collisions
HIP	Hits and Impact Point alignment method, also Highly Ionizing Particle
HLT	High-Level Trigger
HM	Humidity Monitoring
HO	Hadron Calorimeter (Outer Barrel)
HPD	Hybrid Photo-Diode
HTML	HyperText Mark-up Language
HTR	HCAL Trigger and Read-out
HV	High Voltage
IGUANA	Interactive Graphics for User ANAlysis
I^{2}C	Inter-Integrated Circuit
ICB	InterConnect Board (TEC), InterConnect Bus (TOB)
ICC	InterConnect Card
I/O	Input/Output
IOV	Interval Of Validity
IP	Interaction Point or Internet Protocol
ISO	Isolation bit in muon trigger
ISR	Intersecting Storage Ring collider at CERN
JCOP	Joint controls Project at CERN
JSC	Jet Summary Card, in Regional Calorimeter Trigger
JTAG	Joint Test Action Group
kb	kilobit (10^3 bits)
kB	kilobytes (10^3 bytes)

2008 JINST 3 S08004

L1	Level-1 hardware-based trigger
L1A	Level-1 Accept
LAN	Local Area Network
LAS	Laser Alignment System
LCG	LHC Computing Grid (a common computing project)
LCT	Local Charged Track trigger primitive of CSC system
LDAP	Lightweight Directory Access Protocol
LED	Light Emitting Diode
LEP	Large Electron Positron collider at CERN
LG	Low Gain
LHC	Large Hadron Collider
LSB	Least Significant Bit
LUT	Lookup table
LTC	Local Trigger Controller
LV	Low Voltage
LVD	Low Voltage Distribution
LVDS	Low Voltage Differential Signaling
LVR	Low Voltage Regulator
MA	Module Alignment
MAB	Module Alignment of Barrel
Mb	Megabit (10^6 bits)
MB	Muon system (Barrel), also Mother Board or Megabyte (10^6 bytes)
MC	Monte Carlo simulation program/technique, also Mini-Crate of DT system
ME	Muon system (Endcap) or Monitoring Element
MEM	Monitoring Electronics Module
mFEC	mezzanine Front End Controller
MGPA	Multiple Gain Pre-Amplifier chip, ECAL
MILLEPEDE	Algorithm for tracker alignment
MIP	Minimum Ionizing Particle
MOS	Metal Oxide Semiconductor
MOSFET	Metal Oxide Semiconductor Field Effect Transistor
MPC	Muon Port Card, CSC L1 trigger
MSS	Magnet Safety System
MT	Mean Time
MTCC	Magnet Test Cosmic Challenge
MTU	Maximum Transfer Unit
NIC	Network Interface Card
NIEL	Non-Ionizing Energy Loss
O2O	Online to Offline
ODBMS	Object Database Management System
OMDS	Online Master Data Storage
OPC	OLE for Process Automation
ORCOF	Offline ReConstruction OFfline subset, conditions database

2008 JINST 3 S08004

ORCON	Offline ReConstruction ONline subset, conditions database
OS	Operating System
P5	Point 5 collision area of LHC
PACE	Preshower front end ASIC
PACT	PAttern Comparator Trigger, RPC system
PB	Petabyte (10^{15} bytes)
PC	Personal Computer
PCB	Printed Circuit Board
PCI	Peripheral Component Interconnect
PD	Pixel Detector
PDF	Parton Density Function, also Probability Distribution Function
PHTF	Phi Track Finder, DT regional muon trigger
PLC	Programmable Logic Controller
PLD	Programmable Logic Device
PLL	Phase-Locked Loop
PP	Patch Panel
PLT	Pixel Luminosity Telescope
PS	Proton Synchrotron
PSB	Pipeline Synchronizing Buffer, L1 Global Trigger and Global Muon Trigger
PSX	PVSS SOAP Interface
PTM	Precision Temperature Monitoring, ECAL
PV	Primary Vertex
PVSS	Prozessvisualisierungs- und Steuerungs-System
QIE	Charge Integrator and Decoder, ECAL frontend electronics
QPLL	Quartz Phase-Locked Loop
RAW	Event format from the online containing full detector and trigger data
RB	Read-out Unit Builder, also Resource Broker
RCT	Regional Calorimeter Trigger (L1)
RCS	Run Control System
RECO	Event format for reconstructed objects such as tracks, vertices, jets, etc.
RH	Relative Humidity
RISC	Reduced Instruction Set Computer
RMS	Root Mean Square
ROB	ReadOut Board, DT system
ROC	ReadOut Chip, pixels
ROS	ReadOut Server board, DT system
RPC	Resistive Plate Chamber muon system
RS	Resource Service
RU	Read-out Unit
SAN	Storage Area Network
SC	Sector Collector, DT muon L1 trigger or Super Crystal, ECAL
SCA	Switched Capacitor Array buffer, CSC system
SCADA	Supervisory Control And Data Acquisition

SCX	Surface Control eXperimental building at P5
SDA	Slow Dump Accelerated
SEL	Single Event Lathcup
SEU	Single Event Upset
SFM	SubFarm Manager
Skim	Subset of events selected from a larger set
SLB	Sychronization and Link Board
SM	SuperModule (ECAL) or Storage Manager (DAQ)
SMB	System Mother Board
SMD	Surface Mounted Device
SMS	Short Message Service (mobile phones)
S/N	Signal to Noise ratio
SNMP	Simple Network Management Protocol
SOAP	Simple Object Access Protocol
SPS	Super Proton Synchrotron
SRP	Selective Read-out Processor
SST	Silicon Strip Tracker
STL	Standard Template Library
sTTS	Synchronous Trigger Throttle System
SV	Secondary Vertex
SX5	Surface hall at Point 5 for CMS
T1, T2	Tracking telescopes of TOTEM
TAG	Event index information such as run/event number, trigger bits, etc.
Tb	Terabit (10^{12} bits)
TB	Terabyte (10^{12} bytes)
TBM	Token Bit Manager
TCA	Telecom Computing Architecture
TCC	Trigger Concentrator Card
TCP	Transmission Control Protocol
TCS	Trigger Control System
TDC	Time to Digital Converter
TDR	Technical Design Report
TDSS	Tracker Detector Safety System
TEC	Tracker EndCap
TF	Track-Finder, muon L1 trigger
TIB	Tracker Inner Barrel
TID	Tracker Inner Disks
TIM	Timing Module, Global Trigger and Drift Tube Trigger Track Finder
TMB	Trigger MotherBoard, CSC L1 trigger
TN	Technical Network
TOB	Tracker Outer Barrel
TOTEM	TOTal Elastic and diffractive cross section Measurement
TPD	Tracker Pixel Detector

TPG	Trigger Primitive Generator
TRACO	Track Correlator, DT L1 trigger
TriDAS	Trigger and Data Acquisition project
TRLB	Token Ring Link Board
TS	Trigger Server, DT L1 trigger
TSM	Track Sorter Master, DT L1 trigger
TSS	Track Sorter Slave, DT L1 trigger
TTC	Trigger Timing and Control
TTCex	TTC Encoder and Transmitter
TTCmi	TTC Machine Interface
TTCrx	TTC Receiver
TTS	Trigger Throttling System
UDP	User Datagram Protocol
USC55	Underground Service Cavern at Point 5 for CMS
UXC55	Underground eXperimental Cavern at Point 5 for CMS
VFE	Very Front End
VHDI	Very High Density Interconnect
VME	Versa Module Eurocard
VPT	Vacuum PhotoTriode
WAN	Wide Area Network
WLCG	Worldwide LHC Computing Grid
WLS	WaveLength Shifting
XDAQ	Software framework for CMS Data Acquisition
XML	eXtensible Markup Language
YB	Yoke (Barrel)
YE	Yoke (Endcap)
ZDC	Zero Degree Calorimeter

2008 JINST 3 S08004

Bibliography

[1] CMS collaboration, *The Compact Muon Solenoid technical proposal*, CERN-LHCC-94-38, http://cdsweb.cern.ch/record/290969.

[2] TOTEM collaboration, *The TOTEM Experiment at the LHC*, 2008 *JINST* **3** S08007.

[3] CMS collaboration, *The CMS magnet project: technical design report*, CERN-LHCC-97-010, http://cdsweb.cern.ch/record/331056.

[4] A. Hervé et al., *Status of the construction of the CMS magnet, IEEE Trans. Appl. Supercond.* **14** (2004) 524.

[5] A. Hervé, *The CMS detector magnet, IEEE Trans. Appl. Supercond.* **10** (2000) 389.

[6] F. Kircher et al., *Final design of the CMS solenoid cold mass, IEEE Trans. Appl. Supercond.*. **10** (2000) 407.

[7] ALEPH collaboration, *ALEPH: a detector for electron-positron annihilation at LEP, Nucl. Instrum. Meth.* **A 294** (1990) 121.

[8] DELPHI collaboration, *The DELPHI detector at LEP, Nucl. Instrum. Meth.* **A 303** (1991) 233.

[9] ZEUS collaboration, *The ZEUS detector*, unpublished, available at http://www-zeus.desy.de/bluebook/bluebook.html.

[10] BABAR collaboration, *The BABAR detector, Nucl. Instrum. Meth.* **A 479** (2000) 1.

[11] I. Horvath et al., *The CMS conductor, IEEE Trans. Appl. Supercond.* **12** (2002) 345.

[12] S. Sgobba et al., *Mechanical performance at cryogenic temperature of the modules of the external cylinder of CMS and quality controls applied during their fabrication, IEEE Trans. Appl. Supercond.* **14** (2004) 556.

[13] P. Fabbricatore et al., *The construction of the modules composing the CMS superconducting coil, IEEE Trans. Appl. Supercond.* **14** (2004) 552.

[14] P. Fazilleau et al., *Design, construction and tests of the 20kA current leads for the CMS solenoid, IEEE Trans. Appl. Supercond.* **14** (2004) 1766.

2008 JINST 3 S08004

[15] CMS collaboration, *The CMS tracker system project: technical design report*, CERN-LHCC-98-006, http://cdsweb.cern.ch/record/368412.

[16] CMS collaboration, *The CMS tracker: addendum to the technical design report*, CERN-LHCC-2000-016, http://cdsweb.cern.ch/record/490194.

[17] CMS collaboration, *CMS Physics Technical Design Report Volume 1: Detector Performance and Software*, CERN-LHCC-2006-001, http://cdsweb.cern.ch/record/922757; CMS collaboration, *CMS Physics Technical Design Report Volume 2: Physics Performance*, J. Phys. **G 34** (2006) 995, CERN-LHCC-2006-021, http://cdsweb.cern.ch/record/942733.

[18] ROSE collaboration, 2nd *RD48 status report: R & D on silicon for future experiments*, CERN-LHCC-98-039, http://cdsweb.cern.ch/record/376432.

[19] M. Atac et al., *Beam test results of the US-CMS forward pixel detector*, Nucl. Instrum. Meth. **A 488** (2002) 271.

[20] G. Bolla et al., *Design and test of pixel sensors for the CMS experiment*, Nucl. Instrum. Meth. **A 461** (2001) 182.

[21] J. Kemmer et al., *Streifendetektor*, Patentoffenlegungsschrift DE 19620081 A1, Munich, Germany, 21 October 1997.

[22] K. Arndt et al., *Silicon sensors development for the CMS pixel system*, Nucl. Instrum. Meth. **A 511** (2003) 106.

[23] Y. Allkofer et al., *Design and performance of the silicon sensors for the CMS barrel pixel detector*, Nucl. Instrum. Meth. **584** (2008) 25.

[24] G. Lindström et al., *Radiation hard silicon detectors — Developments by the RD48 (ROSE) collaboration*, Nucl. Instrum. Meth. **A 466** (2001) 308.

[25] D. Kotlinski, *The control and readout system of the CMS pixel barrel detector*, Nucl. Instrum. Meth. **A 565** (2006) 73.

[26] H.C. Kästli, *Design and performance of the CMS pixel detector readout chip*, Nucl. Instrum. Meth. **A 565** (2006) 188.

[27] E. Bartz, *The 0.25μm token bit manager chip for the CMS pixel readout*, in *Proceedings of the 11th Workshop on Electronics for LHC and Future Experiments*, Heidelberg Germany (2005).

[28] K. Kloukinas et al., *FEC-CCS: a common front-end controller card for the CMS detector electronics*, in *Proceedings of the 12th Workshop on Electronics for LHC and Future Experiments*, Valencia Spain (2006), http://cdsweb.cern.ch/record/1027434.

[29] CERN ASICs manuals, online at http://cmstrackercontrol.web.cern.ch/cmstrackercontrol/manuals.htm.

2008 JINST 3 S08004

[30] G. Bolla et al., *Wire-bond failures induced by resonant vibrations in the CDF silicon detector, IEEE Nucl. Sci. Symp. Conf. Rec.* **3** (2003) 1641.

[31] D. Menasce, M. Turqueti and L. Uplegger, *The renaissance: a test-stand for the forward CMS pixel tracker assembly, Nucl. Instrum. Meth.* **A 579** (2007) 1141.

[32] S. Paoletti et al., *The powering scheme of the CMS silicon strip tracker*, in 10th *Workshop on Electronics for LHC and future experiments*, CERN-2004-010, CERN-LHCC-2004-030, http://cdsweb.cern.ch/record/814088.

[33] R. Fenner and E. Zdankiewicz, *Micromachined water vapor sensors: a review of sensing technologies, IEEE Sens. J.* **1** (2001) 309.

[34] SIEMENS, SIMATIC, *Statement List (STL) for S7-300 and S7-400 programming*, reference manual, Siemens ag automation and drives, http://www.fer.hr/_download/repository/S7_300_STL_programming_manual.pdf.

[35] *Interface for accessing the PVSS system through SOAP XML protocol*, online at http://xdaqwiki.cern.ch/index.php/PSX.

[36] L. Borrello et al., *Sensor design for the CMS silicon strip tracker*, CMS-NOTE-2003-020, http://cdsweb.cern.ch/record/687861.

[37] J.L. Agram et al., *The silicon sensors for the Compact Muon Solenoid tracker: design and qualification procedure, Nucl. Instrum. Meth.* **A 517** (2004) 77.

[38] S. Braibant et al., *Investigation of design parameters for radiation hard silicon microstrip detectors, Nucl. Instrum. Meth.* **A 485** (2002) 343.

[39] M. Raymond et al., *The CMS Tracker APV25 0.25 μm CMOS readout chip*, in *Proceedings of the* 6th *Workshop on Electronics for LHC Experiments*, Cracow Poland (2000).

[40] A. Marchioro, *Deep submicron technologies for HEP*, in *Proceedings of the* 4th *Workshop on Electronics for LHC Experiments*, Rome Italy, CERN-LHCC-98-36, CERN-LHCC-40-46, http://cdsweb.cern.ch/record/405093.

[41] J. Troska et al., *Optical readout and control systems for the CMS tracker, IEEE Trans. Nucl. Sci.* **50** (2003) 1067.

[42] Telecommunications Industry Association, *Electrical characteristics of Low Voltage Differential Signaling (LVDS) interface circuits*, ANSI/TIA/EIA-644-A-2001.

[43] F. Vasey, C. Biber, M. Sugiyama and J. Troska, *A 12-channel analog optical-receiver module, J. Lightwave Technol.* **23** (2005) 4270.

[44] K. Gill et al., *Progress on the CMS tracker control system*, in *Proceedings of the* 11th *Workshop on Electronics for LHC and Future Experiments*, Heidelberg Germany (2005), http://cdsweb.cern.ch/record/921198.

2008 JINST 3 S08004

[45] J. Coughlan et al., *The CMS tracker front-end driver*, in *Proceedings of the 9th Workshop on Electronics for LHC Experiments*, Amsterdam, The Netherlands (2003), http://cdsweb.cern.ch/record/722058.

[46] C. Ljuslin, A. Marchioro and C. Paillard, *The CCU25: a network oriented communication and control unit integrated circuit in a* 0.25 *$\mu mCMOS$ technology*, in *Proceedings of the 8th Workshop on Electronics for LHC Experiments*, Colmar France (2002), http://cdsweb.cern.ch/record/593914.

[47] K. Kloukinas, A. Marchioro, P. Moreira and P. Placidi, *A 40 MHz clock and trigger recovery circuit for the CMS tracker fabricated in a* 0.25 *$\mu mCMOS$ technology and using a self calibration technique*, in *Proceedings of the 5th Workshop on Electronics for LHC Experiments*, Snowmass U.S.A. (1999).

[48] Philips Semiconductors, *The I^2C-bus specification, version* 2.1, document order number 9398 393 40011, January (2001), http://www.semiconductors.philips.com/i2c.

[49] G. Magazzu, A. Marchioro and P. Moreira, *The detector control unit: an ASIC for the monitoring of the CMS silicon tracker*, *IEEE Trans. Nucl. Sci.* **51** (2004) 1333.

[50] U. Goerlach, *Industrial production of front-end hybrids for the CMS silicon tracker*, in *Proceedings of the 9th Workshop on Electronics for LHC Experiments*, Amsterdam, The Netherlands (2003), http://cdsweb.cern.ch/record/720615.

[51] M. Axer et al., *The qualification of silicon microstrip detector modules for the CMS inner tracking detector*, CMS-NOTE-2006-141, http://cdsweb.cern.ch/record/1000390.

[52] P. Schleper, G. Steinbrück and M. Stoye, *Software alignment of the CMS tracker using MILLEPEDE II*, CMS-NOTE-2006-011, http://cdsweb.cern.ch/record/926543.

[53] E. Widl, R. Frühwirth and W. Adam, *A Kalman filter for track-based alignment*, CMS-NOTE-2006-022, http://cdsweb.cern.ch/record/927376.

[54] V. Karimäki, A. Heikkinen, T. Lampén and T. Lindén, *Sensor alignment by tracks*, in *Proceedings of the CHEP2003 - International Conference on Computing in High Energy and Nuclear Physics*, La Jolla U.S.A. (2003), CMS-CR-2003-022, http://cdsweb.cern.ch/record/619975.

[55] R. Brauer et al., *Design and test beam performance of substructures of the CMS tracker end caps*, CMS-NOTE-2005-025, http://cdsweb.cern.ch/record/927381.

[56] CMS TIB collaboration, *Validation tests of CMS TIB/TID structures*, in preparation.

[57] W. deBoer et al., *The performance of irradiated CMS silicon micro-strip detector modules*, CMS-NOTE-2006-049, http://cdsweb.cern.ch/record/951391.

[58] A. Chilingarov et al., *Radiation studies and operational projections for silicon in the ATLAS inner detector*, *Nucl. Instrum. Meth.* **A 360** (1995) 432.

2008 JINST 3 S08004

[59] CERN DETECTOR R&D collaboration RD2, E. Fretwurst et al., *Reverse annealing of the effective impurity concentration and long term operational scenario for silicon detectors in future collider experiments*, *Nucl. Instrum. Meth.* **A 342** (1994) 119.

[60] M.M. Angarano et al., *Study of radiation damage and substrate resistivity effects from beam test of silicon microstrip detectors using LHC readout electronics*, CMS-NOTE-2000-053, http://cdsweb.cern.ch/record/593000.

[61] H.W. Gu et al., *High voltage operation of heavily irradiated silicon microstrip detectors*, CMS-CR-1999-010, http://cdsweb.cern.ch/record/687105.

[62] PARTICLE DATA GROUP collaboration, S. Eidelman et al., *Review of particle physics*, *Phys. Lett.* **B 592** (2004) 1.

[63] P. Lecoq et al, *Lead tungstate (PbWO$_4$) scintillators for LHC EM calorimetry*, *Nucl. Instrum. Meth.* **A 365** (1995) 291;
S. Baccaro et al., *Influence of La^{3+}-doping on radiation hardness and thermoluminescence characteristics of PbWO$_4$*, *Phys. Status Solidi* **A 160** (1997) R5;
E. Auffray et al., *Improvement of several properties of lead tungstate crystals with different doping ions*, *Nucl. Instrum. Meth.* **A 402** (1998) 75;
M. Kobayashi et al., *Improvement of radiation hardness of PbWO$_4$ scintillating crystals by La-doping*, *Nucl. Instrum. Meth.* **A 404** (1998) 149;
H.F. Chen et al., *Radiation damage measurements of undoped lead tungstate crystals for the CMS electromagnetic calorimeter at LHC*, *Nucl. Instrum. Meth.* **A 414** (1998) 149;
H. Hofer et al., *Afterglow measurements of lead tungstate crystals*, *Nucl. Instrum. Meth.* **A 433** (1999) 630;
M. Kobayashi et al., *Significant improvement of PbWO$_4$ scintillating crystals by doping with trivalent ions*, *Nucl. Instrum. Meth.* **A 434** (1999) 412.

[64] A.A. Annenkov, M.V. Korzhik and P. Lecoq, *Lead tungstate scintillation material*, *Nucl. Instrum. Meth.* **A 490** (2002) 30.

[65] I. Dafinei, E. Auffray, P. Lecoq M. Schneegans, *Lead tungstate for high energy calorimetry*, *Mat. Res. Soc. Symp. Proc.* **348** (1994) 99, also in *Proceedings of Scintillator and Phosphor Materials Symposium*, San Francisco U.S.A. (1994).

[66] X.D. Qu, L.Y. Zhang and R.Y. Zhu, *Radiation induced color centers and light monitoring for lead tungstate crystals*, *IEEE Trans. Nucl. Sci.* **47** (2000) 1741.

[67] S. Baccaro et al., *Ordinary and extraordinary complex refractive index of the lead tungstate (PbWO$_4$) crystals*, *Nucl. Instrum. Meth.* **A 385** (1997) 209.

[68] D. Graham and C. Seez, *Simulation of Longitudinal Light Collection Uniformity in PbWO4 crystals*, CMS-NOTE-1996-002, http://cdsweb.cern.ch/record/687541.

[69] CMS collaboration, *The electromagnetic calorimeter project: technical design report*, CERN-LHCC-97-033, http://cdsweb.cern.ch/record/349375; *Changes to CMS ECAL*

electronics: addendum to the technical design report, CERN-LHCC-2002-027, http://cdsweb.cern.ch/record/581342.

[70] R.Y. Zhu, *Radiation damage in scintillating crystals*, Nucl. Instrum. Meth. **A 413** (1998) 297.

[71] M. Huhtinen et al., *High-energy proton induced damage in PbWO$_4$ calorimeter crystals*, Nucl. Instrum. Meth. **A 545** (2005) 63.

[72] P. Lecomte et al., *High-energy proton induced damage study of scintillation light output from PbWO$_4$ calorimeter crystals*, Nucl. Instrum. Meth. **A 564** (2006) 164.

[73] M. Lebeau, F. Mossire and H. Rezvani Naraghi, *The super-basket: incorporation of conical reinforcements in the CMS ECAL EB support structure*, CMS-NOTE-2003-010, http://cdsweb.cern.ch/record/687869.

[74] THE CMS ELECTROMAGNETIC CALORIMETER group, P. Adzic et al., *Results of the first performance tests of the CMS electromagnetic calorimeter*, Eur. Phys. J. **C44** (2006) S1.1

[75] K. Deiters et al., *Double screening tests of the CMS ECAL avalanche photodiodes*, Nucl. Instrum. Meth. **A 543** (2005) 549.

[76] S. Baccaro et al., *Radiation damage effect on avalanche photo diodes*, Nucl. Instrum. Meth. **A 426** (1999) 206.

[77] A. Bartoloni, *The power supply system for CMS-ECAL APDs*, in *Proceedings of the* 7th *Workshop on Electronics for LHC Experiments*, Stockholm Sweden (2001), http://cdsweb.cern.ch/record/530694;
A. Bartoloni et al., *High voltage system for the CMS electromagnetic calorimeter*, Nucl. Instrum. Meth. **A 582** (2007) 462.

[78] K.W. Bell et al., *Vacuum phototriodes for the CMS electromagnetic calorimeter endcap*, IEEE Trans. Nucl. Sci. **51** (2004) 2284;
N.A. Bajanov et al., *Fine-mesh photodetectors for CMS endcap electromagnetic calorimeter*, Nucl. Instrum. Meth. **A 442** (2000) 146;
Yu. Blinnikov et al., *Radiation hardness, excess noise factor and short-term gain instability of vacuum phototriodes for the operation in pseudorapidity range* $1.5 \leq \eta \leq 3.0$ *at CMS ECAL*, Nucl. Instrum. Meth. **A 504** (2003) 228.

[79] K.W. Bell et al., *The response to high magnetic fields of the vacuum photriodes for the Compact Muon Solenoid endcap electromagnetic calorimeter*, Nucl. Instrum. Meth. **A 504** (2003) 255.

[80] Yu. I. Gusev et al., *Super radiation hard vacuum phototriodes for the CMS endcap ECAL*, Nucl. Instrum. Meth. **A 535** (2004) 511.

[81] B. Betev et al., *Low voltage supply system for the very front end readout electronics of the CMS electromagnetic calorimeter*, in 9th *Workshop on Electronics for LHC Experiments*,

Amsterdam The Netherlands (2003), CERN-LHCC-2003-055 page 353,
http://cdsweb.cern.ch/record/744282.

[82] M. Raymond et al., *The MGPA electromagnetic calorimeter readout chip for CMS*, in 9th *Workshop on Electronics for LHC Experiments*, Amsterdam The Netherlands (2003), CERN-LHCC-2003-055 page 83, http://cdsweb.cern.ch/record/712053.

[83] G. Minderico et al., *A CMOS low power, quad channel, 12 bit, 40 MS/s pipelined ADC for applications in particle physics calorimetry*, in 9th *Workshop on Electronics for LHC Experiments*, Amsterdam The Netherlands (2003), CERN-LHCC-2003-055 page 88, http://cdsweb.cern.ch/record/712054.

[84] M. Hansen, *The new readout architecture for the CMS ECAL*, in 9th *Workshop on Electronics for LHC Experiments*, Amsterdam The Netherlands (2003), CERN-LHCC-2003-055 page 78, http://cdsweb.cern.ch/record/712052.

[85] R. Alemany et al., *CMS ECAL off-detector electronics*, in *Proceedings of the 11th International Conference on Calorimetry in High Energy Physics (CALOR2004)*, Perugia Italy (2004), CMS-CR-2004-022, http://cdsweb.cern.ch/record/787474.

[86] R. Alemany et al., *Overview of the ECAL off-detector electronics of the CMS experiment*, *IEEE Nucl. Sci. Symp. Conf. Rec.* **2** (2004) 1053.

[87] P. Paganini et al., *Tests of the boards generating the CMS ECAL trigger primitives: from the on-detector electronics to the off-detector electronics system*, in *Proceedings of the 10th Workshop on Electronics for LHC Experiments*, Boston U.S.A. (2004), CMS-CR-2004-066, http://cdsweb.cern.ch/record/814461.

[88] N. Almeida et al., *Calorimeter trigger synchronization in CMS, implementation and test system*, in *Proceedings of the 10th Workshop on Electronics for LHC Experiments*, Boston U.S.A. (2004), CMS-CR-2004-068, http://cdsweb.cern.ch/record/823745.

[89] N. Almeida et al., *Data concentrator card and test system for the CMS ECAL readout*, in *Proceedings of the 9th Workshop on Electronics for the LHC Experiments*, Amsterdam The Netherlands (2003), CMS-CR-2003-056, http://cdsweb.cern.ch/record/692739.

[90] R. Alemany et al., *Test results of the data concentrator card of the CMS electromagnetic calorimeter readout system*, in *Proceedings of the* 10th *Workshop on Electronics for LHC Experiments*, Boston U.S.A. (2004), http://cdsweb.cern.ch/record/814237.

[91] N. Almeida et al., *The selective read-out processor for the CMS electromagnetic calorimeter*, *IEEE Nucl. Sci. Symp. Conf. Rec.* **3** (2004) 1721.

[92] R. Loos et al., *CMS ECAL Preshower and Endcap Engineering Design Review. v.2 - Preshower*, CMS-2000-054-MEETING, CERN-ECAL-EDR-4, http://cdsweb.cern.ch/record/539819.

[93] P. Aspell et al., *PACE3: A large dynamic range analogue memory ASIC assembly designed for the readout of silicon sensors in the LHC CMS preshower*, in *Proceedings of the 10th Workshop on Electronics for LHC Experiments*, Boston U.S.A. (2004), http://cdsweb.cern.ch/record/814076.

[94] I. Evangelou, *CMS Preshower in-situ absolute calibration*, in *Proceedings of the 9th ICATPP conference*, Villa-Olmo, Como Italy (2005), http://cdsweb.cern.ch/record/981557.

[95] K. Kloukinas et al., *Kchip: a radiation tolerent digital data concentrator chip for the CMS Preshower detector*, in *Proceedings of the 9th Workshop on Electronics for LHC Experiments*, Amsterdam The Netherlands (2003), CERN-LHCC-2003-055 page 66, http://cdsweb.cern.ch/record/712049.

[96] G. Antchev et al., *A VME-based readout system for the CMS preshower sub-detector*, *IEEE Trans. Nucl. Sci.* **54** (2007) 623.

[97] S. Reynaud and P. Vichoudis, *A multi-channel optical plug-in module for gigabit data reception*, in *Proceedings of the 12th Workshop on Electronics for LHC and Future Experiments*, Valencia Spain (2006), CERN-LHCC-2007-006, http://cdsweb.cern.ch/record/1027469.

[98] D. Barney et al., *Implementation of on-line data reduction algorithms in the CMS endcap preshower data concentrator card*, 2007 *JINST* **2** P03001.

[99] P. Adzic et al., *The detector control system for the electromagnetic calorimeter of the CMS experiment at the LHC*, in *Proceedings of the 10th International Conference on Accelerator and Large Experimental Physics Control Systems (ICALEPS2005)*, Geneva Switzerland, CMS-CR-2005-028, http://cdsweb.cern.ch/record/904796.

[100] P. Milenovic et al., *Performance of the CMS ECAL safety system for Super Modules SM0 and SM1*, *Nucl. Instrum. Meth.* **A 554** (2005) 427.

[101] F. Cavallari et al., *CMS ECAL intercalibration of ECAL crystals using laboratory measurements*, CMS-NOTE-2006-073, http://cdsweb.cern.ch/record/962038.

[102] W. Bertl et al., *Feasibility of intercalibration of CMS ECAL supermodules with cosmic rays*, *Eur. Phys. J.* **C 41** (2005) S2.11;
F. Ferri and P. Govoni, *The CMS electromagnetic calorimeter pre-calibration with cosmic rays and test beam electrons*, in *Proceedings of VCI2007*, Vienna Austria, CMS-CR-2007-012, http://cdsweb.cern.ch/record/1027034.

[103] L. Zhang et al., *Performance of the monitoring light source for the CMS lead tungstate crystal calorimeter*, *IEEE Trans. Nucl. Sci.* **52** (2005) 1123;
M. Anfreville et al., *Laser monitoring system for the CMS lead tungstate crystal calorimeter*, CMS-NOTE-2007-028, http://cdsweb.cern.ch/record/1073694.

[104] A. Ghezzi et al., *Analysis of the response evolution of the CMS electromagnetic calorimeter under electron and pion irradiation*, CMS-NOTE-2006-038, http://cdsweb.cern.ch/record/934066.

[105] P. Aspell et al., *Results from the 1999 beam test of a preshower prototype*, CMS-NOTE-2000-001, http://cdsweb.cern.ch/record/687210.

[106] P. Adzic et al., *Reconstruction of the signal amplitude of the CMS electromagnetic calorimeter*, Eur. Phys. J. **C 46** (2006) S1.23.

[107] P. Adzic et al., *Energy resolution of the barrel of the CMS electromagnetic calorimeter*, 2007 *JINST* **2** P04004.

[108] CMS collaboration, *The hadron calorimeter project: technical design report*, CERN-LHCC-97-031, http://cdsweb.cern.ch/record/357153.

[109] P. Cushman, A. Heering and A. Ronzhin, *Custom HPD readout for the CMS HCAL*, Nucl. Instrum. Meth. **A 442** (2000) 289.

[110] A. Heister et al., *Measurement of jets with the CMS detector at the LHC*, CMS-NOTE-2006-036, http://cdsweb.cern.ch/record/933705.

[111] H. Pi et al., *Measurement of missing transverse energy with the CMS detector at the LHC*, Eur. Phys. J. **C 46** (2006) 45, CMS-NOTE-2006-035, http://cdsweb.cern.ch/record/933706.

[112] S. Abdullin et al., *Design, performance, and calibration of CMS hadron-barrel calorimeter wedges*, Eur. Phys. J. **55** (2008) 159, CMS-NOTE-2006-138, http://cdsweb.cern.ch/record/1049915.

[113] V.I. Kryshkin and A.I. Ronzhin, *An optical fiber readout for scintillator calorimeters* Nucl. Instrum. Meth. **A 247** (1986) 583.

[114] M.G. Albrow et al., *A uranium scintillator calorimeter with plastic-fibre readout*, Nucl. Instrum. Meth. **A 256** (1987) 23.

[115] S. Banerjee and S. Banerjee, *Performance of hadron calorimeter with and without HO*, CMS-NOTE-1999-063, http://cdsweb.cern.ch/record/687178.

[116] N. Akchurin and R. Wigmans, *Quartz fibers as active elements in detectors for particle physics*, Rev. Sci. Instrum. **74** (2002) 2955.

[117] I. Dumanoglu et al., *Radiation-hardness studies of high OH^- content quartz fibers irradiated with 500 MeV electrons*, Nucl. Instrum. Meth. **A 490** (2002) 444.

[118] N. Akchurin et al., *Effects of radiation damage and their consequences for the performance of the forward calorimeters in the CMS experiment*, Nucl. Instrum. Meth. **B 187** (2002) 66.

[119] R. Thomas, *Study of radiation hardness of optical fibers*, M.Sc. Thesis, Texas Tech University, U.S.A. (2004).

2008 JINST 3 S08004

[120] A. Panagiotou et al., *CASTOR engineering design report*, CMS Note in preparation (2008).

[121] X.N. Wang and M. Gyulassy, *HIJING: a Monte Carlo model for multiple jet production in pp, pA and AA collisions*, *Phys. Rev.* **D 44** (1991) 3501;
X.N. Wang, *A pQCD-based approach to parton production and equilibration in high-energy nuclear collisions*, *Phys. Rept.* **280** (1997) 287.

[122] D. D'Enterria et al., *CMS physics technical design report: addendum on high density QCD with heavy ions*, *J. Phys.* **G 34** (2007) 2307, CERN-LHCC-2007-009, http://cdsweb.cern.ch/record/1019832.

[123] M. Albrow et al., *Prospects for diffractive and forward physics at the LHC*, CMS-NOTE-2007-002, CERN-LHCC-2006-039, http://cdsweb.cern.ch/record/1005180.

[124] G. Mavromanolakis, *Quartz fiber calorimetry and calorimeters*, physics/0412123v1.

[125] X. Aslanoglou et al., *First performance studies of a prototype for the CASTOR forward calorimeter at the CMS experiment*, arXiv:0706.2576v3.

[126] X. Aslanoglou et al., *Performance studies of prototype II for the CASTOR forward calorimeter at the CMS experiment*, *Eur. Phys. J.* **C 52** (2007) 495 [arXiv:0706.2641v2].

[127] A.S. Ayan et al., *CMS Zero-Degree-Calorimeter (ZDC). Technical design report*, in preparation.

[128] O.A. Grachov et al., *Status of zero degree calorimeter for CMS experiment*, *AIP Conf. Proc.* **867** (2006) 258 [nucl-ex/0608052].

[129] E.H. Hoyer, W.C. Turner and N.V. Mokhov, *Absorbers for the high luminosity insertions of the LHC*, in *Proceedings of the 6th European Particle Accelerator Conference*, Stockholm Sweden (1998), http://accelconf.web.cern.ch/AccelConf/e98/PAPERS/MOP13C.PDF.

[130] J.-F. Beche et al., *An ionization chamber shower detector for the LHC luminosity monitor*, *IEEE Nucl. Sci. Symp. Conf. Rec.* **1** (2000) 5.

[131] O.A. Grachov et al., *Measuring photons and neutrons at zero degrees in CMS*, nucl-ex/0703001.

[132] CMS collaboration, *The CMS muon project, technical design report*, CERN-LHCC-97-032, http://cdsweb.cern.ch/record/343814.

[133] M. De Giorgi et al., *Design and simulations of the trigger electronics for the CMS muon barrel chambers*, *Proceedings of the first Workshop on Electronics for LHC Experiments*, Lisbon Portugal (1995), CERN-LHCC-95-56, http://cdsweb.cern.ch/record/1062706.

[134] R. Veenhof, *Garfield. A drift chamber simulation program user's guide*, CERN Program Library W5050 (1994).

[135] T. Zhao et al., *A study of electron drift velocity in Ar-CO_2 and Ar-CO_2-CF_4 gas mixtures*, *Nucl. Instrum. Meth.* **A 340** (1994) 485.

[136] A. Benvenuti et al., *Simulations in the development of the barrel muon chambers for the CMS detector at LHC*, *Nucl. Instrum. Meth.* **A 405** (1998) 20.

[137] CMS MUON group, G. Alampi et al., *Electrode strip deposition for the CMS barrel drift tube system*, CMS-NOTE-2006-144, http://cdsweb.cern.ch/record/1000408.

[138] F. Gonella and M. Pegoraro, *A prototype frontend ASIC for the readout of the drift tubes of CMS barrel muon chambers*, in 4th *Workshop on Electronics for LHC Experiments*, CERN-LHCC-98-036 page 257, http://cdsweb.cern.ch/record/1062709.

[139] L. Barcellan et al., *Single events effects induced by heavy ions on the frontend ASIC developed for the muon DT chambers*, LNL Annual Report (2000) page 247, http://cdsweb.cern.ch/record/1062712.

[140] C. Fernandez Bedoya et al., *Electronics for the CMS muon drift tube chambers: the read-out minicrate*, *IEEE Trans. Nucl. Sci.* **52** (2005) 944.

[141] J. Christiansen et al., *A data driven high performance time to digital converter*, *Proceedings of the* 6th *Workshop on Electronics for LHC Experiments*, Cracow Poland (2000), CERN-2000-010 page 169, http://cdsweb.cern.ch/record/478865.

[142] P. Moreira et al., *A radiation tolerant gigabit serializer for LHC data transmission*, *Proceedings of the* 7th *workshop on electronics for LHC experiments*, Stockholm Sweden (2001), CERN-2001-005 page 145, http://cdsweb.cern.ch/record/588665.

[143] G. Dellacasa, V. Monaco and A. Staiano, *DDU: the front end driver system (FED) of the CMS drifttube detector*, *Nucl. Phys.* **B 177-178** *(Proc. Suppl.)* (2008) 281, also in *Proceedings of hadron collider physics*, La Biodola, Isola d'Elba Italy (2007).

[144] C. Albajar et al., *Test beam analysis of the first CMS drift tube muon chamber*, *Nucl. Instrum. Meth.* **A 525** (2004) 465.

[145] M. Aguilar-Benitez et al., *Study of magnetic field effects in drift tubes for the barrel muon chambers of the CMS detector at the LHC*, *Nucl. Instrum. Meth.* **A 416** (1998) 243.

[146] M. Aguilar-Benitez et al., *Construction and test of the final CMS barrel drift tube muon chamber prototype*, *Nucl. Instrum. Meth.* **A 480** (2002) 658.

[147] P. Arce et al., *Bunched beam test of the CMS drift tubes local muon trigger*, *Nucl. Instrum. Meth.* **A 534** (2004) 441.

[148] M. Aldaya et al., *Results of the first integration test of the CMS drift tubes muon trigger*, *Nucl. Instrum. Meth.* **A 579** (2007) 951.

[149] G. Charpak and F. Sauli, *High-accuracy, two-dimensional read-out in multiwire proportional chambers*, *Nucl. Instrum. Meth.* **113** (1973) 381.

2008 JINST 3 S08004

[150] C. Anderson et al., *Effect of gas composition on the performance of cathode strip chambers for the CMS endcap muon system*, CMS-NOTE-2004-033, http://cdsweb.cern.ch/record/837542.

[151] T. Ferguson et al., *Anode front-end electronics for the cathode strip chambers of the CMS endcap muon detector*, Nucl. Instrum. Meth. **A 539** (2005) 386.

[152] R. Breedon et al., *Performance and radiation testing of a low-noise switched capacitor array for the CMS endcap muon system*, in *Proceedings of the 6th Workshop on Electronics for LHC Experiments*, CMS-CR-2000-013, http://cdsweb.cern.ch/record/478866.

[153] M.M. Baarmand et al., *Spatial resolution attainable with cathode strip chambers at the trigger level*, Nucl. Instrum. Meth. **A 425** (1999) 92.

[154] V. Barashko, *Performance validation tests of the cathode strip chambers for CMS muon system*, IEEE Nucl. Sci. Symp. Conf. Rec. **2** (2005) 827.

[155] E. Gatti et al., *Optimum geometry for strip cathodes on grids in MWPC for avalanche localization along the anode wires*, Nucl. Instrum. Meth. **163** (1979) 83.

[156] D. Acosta et al., *Aging tests of full scale CMS muon cathode strip chambers*, Nucl. Instrum. Meth. **A 515** (2003) 226.

[157] L. Malter, *Thin film field emission*, Phys. Rev. **50** (1936) 48.

[158] R. Breedon et al., *Results of radiation test of the cathode front-end board for CMS endcap muon chambers*, Nucl. Instrum. Meth. **A 471** (2001) 340.

[159] R. Santonico and R. Cardarelli, *Development of resistive plate counters*, Nucl. Instrum. Meth. **187** (1981) 377.

[160] R. Cardarelli, A. Di Ciaccioa and R. Santonico, *Performance of a resistive plate chamber operating with pure CF_3Br*, Nucl. Instrum. Meth. **A 333** (1993) 399.

[161] M. Abbrescia et al., *The simulation of resistive plate chambers in avalanche mode: charge spectra and efficiency*, Nucl. Instrum. Meth. **A 431** (1999) 413.

[162] M. Abbrescia et al., *Local and global performance of double-gap resistive plate chambers operated in avalanche mode*, Nucl. Instrum. Meth. **A 434** (1999) 244.

[163] M. Abbrescia et al., *Study of long term performance of CMS RPC under irradiation at the CERN GIF*, Nucl. Instrum. Meth. **A 533** (2004) 102.

[164] M. Abbrescia et al., *Neutron irradiation of the RPCs for the CMS experiment*, Nucl. Instrum. Meth. **A 508** (2003) 120.

[165] M. Abbrescia et al., *New developments on front-end electronics for the CMS resistive plate chambers*, Nucl. Instrum. Meth. **A 456** (2000) 143.

[166] M. Abbrescia et al., *Long term perfomance of double gap resistive plate chamber under gamma irradiation*, *Nucl. Instrum. Meth.* **A 477** (2002) 293.

[167] M. Abbrescia et al., *Neutron induced single event upset on the RPC front-end chips for the CMS experiment*, *Nucl. Instrum. Meth.* **A 484** (2002) 494.

[168] M. Abbrescia et al., *An RPC-based technical trigger for the CMS experiment*, in *Proceedings of the 12th Workshop on Electronics for LHC and Future Experiments*, Valencia Spain (2006), http://cdsweb.cern.ch/record/1000404.

[169] G. Iaselli et al., *Properties of $C_2H_2F_4$-based gas mixture for avalanche mode operation of Resistive Plate Chambers*, *Nucl. Instrum. Meth.* **A 398** (1997) 173.

[170] M. Abbrescia et al., *Gas analysis and monitoring systems for the RPC detector of CMS at LHC*, *IEEE Nucl. Sci. Symp. Conf. Rec.* **2** (2006) 891 [Frascati preprint LNF-06-34(P)].

[171] M. Abbrescia et al., *HF production in CMS-resistive plate chambers*, *Nucl. Phys.* **B 158** *(Proc. Suppl.)* (2006) 30.

[172] M. Abbrescia et al., *The bakelite for the RPCs of the experiment CMS*, *Nucl. Instrum. Meth.* **A 456** (2000) 132;
M. Abbrescia et al., *Production and quality control of the Barrel RPC chambers of the CMS experiment*, *Nucl. Phys.* **B 150** *(Proc. Suppl.)* (2006) 290;
M. Abbrescia et al., *Quality control tests for the CMS barrel RPCs*, *Nucl. Phys.* **B 158** *(Proc. Suppl.)* (2006) 73;
A. Ball et al., *Cosmic ray certification of the first 100 CMS endcap RPCs and the corresponding construction database*, *Nucl. Phys.* **B 158** *(Proc. Suppl.)* (2006) 99;
Z. Aftab et al., *Production and quality control for the CMS endcap RPCs*, *Nucl. Phys.* **B 158** *(Proc. Suppl.)* (2006) 16;
Z. Aftab et al., *Assembly and quality certification for the first station of the endcap RPCs (RE1)*, *Nucl. Phys.* **B 158** *(Proc. Suppl.)* (2006) 103.

[173] M. Abbrescia et al., *Resistive plate chambers performances at cosmic rays fluxes*, *Nucl. Instrum. Meth.* **A 359** (1995) 603.

[174] M. Abbrescia et al., *Cosmic ray tests of double-gap resistive plate chambers for the CMS experiment*, *Nucl. Instrum. Meth.* **A 550** (2005) 116.

[175] CMS, *CMS muon detector survey documents*, EDMS document CMS-00000083880, https://edms.cern.ch/cedar/plsql/cms.

[176] C. Carneiro, R. Goudard and C. Humbertclaude, *CMS MAB prototype-deformation test under load and humidity-measurements from July to October* 2002, EDMS Doc. CMS-MA-UR-0001, http://cdsweb.cern.ch/record/1062715, also https://edms.cern.ch/cedar/plsql/cms.

2008 JINST 3 S08004

[177] G. Szekely et al., *Muon barrel alignment system based on a net of PC/104 board computers*, in *Proceedings of the 9th workshop on electronics for LHC experiments*, Amsterdam The Netherlands (2003), CERN-2003-006, http://cdsweb.cern.ch/record/722098.

[178] M. Hohlmann et al., *Design and performance of the alignment system for the CMS muon endcaps*, *IEEE Nucl. Sci. Symp. Conf. Rec.* **1** (2006) 489;
R.H. Lee, *Simulation and study of the CMS Endcap Muon alignment scheme*, Ph.D. Thesis, Purdue University, U.S.A (2002).

[179] J. Moromisato et al., *The development of totally transparent position sensors*, *Nucl. Instrum. Meth.* **A 538** (2005) 234.

[180] M. Ripert, *Calibration of analog sensors for the alignment of muon chambers in the CMS experiment*, M.Sc. thesis, Florida Institute of Technology, U.S.A. (2005).

[181] A. Calderón et al., *Large size high performance transparent amorphous silicon sensors for laser beam position detection*, *Nucl. Instrum. Meth.* **A 565** (2006) 603.

[182] A. Lopez Virto, *Caracterizacion y pruebas de validacion del sistema link de alineamiento de CMS*, Ph.D. Thesis, Universidad de Cantabria, Spain (2003).

[183] A. Calderón, *Construccion, calibracion y evaluacion del sistema link de alineamiento del espectrometro de muones del experimento CMS*, PhD Thesis, Universidad de Cantabria, Spain (2006).

[184] *ELMB Boards*, http://elmb.web.cern.ch/ELMB/elmb128.html.

[185] P. Arce, *Object oriented software for simulation and reconstruction of big alignment systems*, *Nucl. Instrum. Meth.* **A 502** (2003) 696.

[186] D.E. Stewart and Z. Leyk, *Meschach library*, http://www.netlib.org/c/meschach/readme.

[187] CMS collaboration, *The TriDAS project, technical design report. Volume 1: The level-1 trigger*, CERN-LHCC-2000-038, http://cdsweb.cern.ch/record/706847.

[188] CMS collaboration, *The TriDAS project, technical design report. Volume 2: Data acquisition and high-level trigger technical design report*, CERN-LHCC-2002-026, http://cdsweb.cern.ch/record/578006.

[189] CMS COLLABORATION group, W. Adam et al., *The CMS high level trigger*, *Eur. Phys. J.* **C 46** (2005) 605 [hep-ex/0512077].

[190] I. Magrans de Arbril, C.-E. Wulz and J. Varela, *Conceptual design of the CMS trigger supervisor*, *IEEE Trans. Nucl. Sci.* **53** (2006) 474.

[191] P. Chumney et al., *Level-1 regional calorimeter trigger system for CMS*, in *Proceedings of Computing in High Energy Physics and Nuclear Physics*, La Jolla (2003), hep-ex/0305047.

[192] See http://www.hep.ph.ic.ac.uk/cms/gct.

[193] See http://www.picmg.org/v2internal/microTCA.htm.

[194] RD5 collaboration, F. Gasparini et al., *Bunch crossing identification at LHC using a mean-timer technique*, *Nucl. Instrum. Meth.* **A 336** (1993) 91.

[195] M. Andlinger et al., *Pattern Comparator Trigger (PACT) for the muon system of the CMS experiment*, *Nucl. Instrum. Meth.* **A 370** (1996) 389.

[196] C. Albajar et al., *Conceptual design of an improved CMS RPC muon trigger using the hadron outer scintillators*, *Nucl. Instrum. Meth.* **A 545** (2005) 97.

[197] J. Erö et al., *The CMS drift tube trigger track finder*, CMS-NOTE-2008-009, http://cdsweb.cern.ch/record/1103001.

[198] D. Acosta et al., *Performance of a pre-production track-finding processor for the level-1 trigger of the CMS endcap muon system*, in *Proceedings of the 10th Workshop on Electronics for LHC and Future Experiments*, Boston U.S.A. (2004), http://cdsweb.cern.ch/record/814321.

[199] H. Sakulin et al., *Implementation and test of the first-level global muon trigger of the CMS experiment*, in *Proceedings of the 11th Workshop on Electronics for LHC and Future Experiments*, Heidelberg Germany (2005), http://cdsweb.cern.ch/record/921035.

[200] C.-E. Wulz, *Concept of the first level global trigger for the CMS experiment at LHC*, *Nucl. Instrum. Meth.* **A 473** (2001) 231.

[201] A. Taurok, H. Bergauer and M. Padrta, *Implementation and synchronisation of the first level global trigger for the CMS experiment at LHC*, *Nucl. Instrum. Meth.* **A 473** (2001) 243.

[202] P. Glaser et al., *Design and development of a graphical setup software for the CMS global trigger*, *IEEE Trans. Nucl. Sci.* **53** (2006) 1282.

[203] CMS TRIGGER and DATA ACQUISITION GROUP, *CMS L1 trigger control system*, CMS-NOTE-2002-033, http://cdsweb.cern.ch/record/687458.

[204] B.G. Taylor, *Timing distribution at the LHC*, in *Proceedings of the 8th Workshop on Electronics for LHC and Future Experiments*, Colmar France (2002), http://cdsweb.cern.ch/record/592719.

[205] T. Geralis et al., *The global trigger processor emulator system for the CMS experiment*, *IEEE Trans. Nucl. Sci.* **52** (2005) 1679.

[206] E. Cano et al., *FED-kit design for CMS DAQ system*, *Proceedings of the 8th Workshop on Electronics for LHC Experiments*, Colmar France (2002), http://cdsweb.cern.ch/record/594312.

[207] B.G. Taylor, *TTC distribution for LHC detectors*, *IEEE Trans. Nucl. Sci.* **45** (1998) 82, see, http://www.cern.ch/TTC/intro.html.

2008 JINST 3 S08004

[208] A. Racz, R. McLaren and E. van der Bij, *The S-Link64 bit extension specification: S-Link64*, http://hsi.web.cern.ch/HSI/s-link.

[209] N.J. Boden et al., *Myrinet — A gigabit per second local area network*, *IEEE Micro* **15** (1995) 29.

[210] G. Bauer et al., *The Tera-bit/s super-fragment builder and trigger throttling system for the Compact Muon Solenoid experiment at CERN*, *IEEE Trans. Nucl. Sci.* **55** (2008) 190, also in 15th *IEEE Real Time Conference* 2007, Batavia U.S.A., CMS-CR-2007-020, http://cdsweb.cern.ch/record/1046342.

[211] G. Bauer et al., *CMS DAQ event builder based on gigabit ethernet*, *IEEE Trans. Nucl. Sci.* **55** (2008) 198, also in 15th *IEEE real time conference* 2007, Batavia U.S.A., CMS-CR-2007-016, http://cdsweb.cern.ch/record/1046338.

[212] C.-D. Jones et al., *The new CMS data model and framework*, in *Proocedings of the Conference on Computing in High Energy Physics*, Mumbai India (2006).

[213] QUATTOR is a system administration toolkit, http://www.quattor.org or http://quattor.web.cern.ch.

[214] J. Gutleber and L. Orsini, *Software architecture for processing clusters based on I2O*, *Cluster Comput.* **5** (2002) 55.

[215] V. Briglijevic et al., *Using XDAQ in application scenarios of the CMS experiment*, in *Proocedings of Computing in High Energy Physics*, La Jolla U.S.A. (2003), CMS-CR-2003-007, http://cdsweb.cern.ch/record/687845.

[216] O. Nierstrasz, S. Gibbs and D. Tsichritzis, *Component-oriented software development*, *Comm. ACM* **35** (1992) 160.

[217] D. Box et al., *Simple Object Access Protocol (SOAP)* 1.1, W3C Note 08, http://www.w3.org/TR/SOAP.

[218] For the I2O standard, http://developer.osdl.org/dev/opendoc/Online/Local/I20/index.html.

[219] See http://xdaqwiki.cern.ch, and references therein.

[220] R. Arcidiacono et al., *HyperDAQ — Where data acquisition meets the web*, in 10th *ICALEPCS International Conference on Accelerator and Large Experimental Physics Control Systems*, Geneva Switzerland (2005), http://accelconf.web.cern.ch/AccelConf/ica05/proceedings/pdf/O5_004.pdf.

[221] J. Boyer, *Canonical XML version* 1.0, W3C Recommendation, 16 August 2006, http://www.w3c.org/XML.

[222] Apache Axis is an XML based Web service framework, http://ws.apache.org/axis/.

[223] The Apache Tomcat servlet container, http://tomcat.apache.org.

[224] *JCOP framework*, http://itcobe.web.cern.ch/itcobe/Projects/Framework/welcome.html.

[225] OLE for Process Control (OPC), http://www.opcfoundation.org/.

[226] R. Arcidiacono et al., *CMS DCS design concepts*, in *Proceedings of the 10th International Conference on Accelerator and Large Experimental Physics Control Systems (ICALEPCS2005)*, Geneva Switzerland (2005).

[227] L. Fernandez-Hernando et al., *Development of a CVD diamond beam condition monitor for CMS at the Large Hadron Collider*, *Nucl. Instrum. Meth.* **A 552** (2005) 183;
A. Macpherson, *Beam condition monitoring and radiation damage concerns of the experiment*, in *Proceedings of the XV LHC Project Chamonix Workshop*, Divonne Switzerland (2006);
D. Chong et al., *Validation of synthetic diamond for a beam condition monitor for the Compact Muon solenoid experiment*, *IEEE Trans. Nucl. Sci.* **54** (2007) 182.

[228] R.J. Tapper, *Diamond detectors in particle physics*, *Rept. Prog. Phys.* **63** (2000) 1273.

[229] R. Eusebi et al., *A diamond-based beam condition monitor for the CDF experiment*, *IEEE Trans. Nucl. Sci.* **2** (2006) 709.

[230] M. Brunisma et al., *CVD diamonds in the BaBar radiation monitoring system*, *Nucl. Phys.* **B 150** *(Proc. Suppl.)* (2006) 164.

[231] W. de Boer et al., *Radiation hardness of diamond and silicon sensors compared*, *Phys. Status Solidi* **A 204** (2007) 3004.

[232] B. Dehning et al., *The beam loss monitoring system*, in *Proceedings of the XIII LHC Project Chamonix Workshop*, Chamonix France (2004), http://cdsweb.cern.ch/record/726322;
E. Effinger et al., *The LHC beam loss monitoring system's data acquisition card*, in *Proceedings of LECC*, Valencia Spain (2006), http://cdsweb.cern.ch/record/1027422;
C. Zamantzas et al., *The LHC beam loss monitoring system's surface building installation*, in *Proceedings of LECC*, Valencia Spain (2006), http://cdsweb.cern.ch/record/1020105.

[233] C. Zamantzas, *The real-time data analysis and decision system for particle flux detection in the LHC accelerator at CERN*, Ph.D. Thesis, Brunel University, U.K., CERN-THESIS-2006-037, http://cdsweb.cern.ch/record/976628.

[234] R. Schmidt et al., *Beam interlocks for LHC and SPS*, in *Proceedings of the International Conference on Accelerator and Large Experimental Physics Control Systems (ICALEPCS)*, Gyeongju South Korea (2003), CERN-AB-2003-106-CO, http://cdsweb.cern.ch/record/693161;
B. Todd, *A beam interlock system for CERN high energy accelerators*, Ph.D. Thesis, Brunel University, U.K., CERN-THESIS-2007-019, http://cdsweb.cern.ch/record/1019495.

[235] J. Kaplon and W. Dabrowski, *Fast CMOS binary front end for silicon strip detectors at LHC experiments*, *IEEE Trans. Nucl. Sci.* **52** (2005) 2713.

2008 JINST 3 S08004

[236] J. Troska et al., *Optical readout and control systems for the CMS tracker, IEEE Trans. Nucl. Sci.* **50** (2003) 1067.

[237] J. Bol, *Strahlmonitore aus Diamant für primäre Teilchenstrahlen hoher Intensität*, Ph.D. Thesis, Karlsruhe University, Germany (2006), IEKP-KA-2006-8.

[238] J. Furletova, *Search for exotic processes in events with large missing transverse momentum in ZEUS at HERA*, Ph.D. thesis, Hamburg University, Germany, DESY-THESIS-2004-046, http://cdsweb.cern.ch/record/824243.

[239] G. Aguillion et al., *Thin scintillating tiles with high light yield for the OPAL endcaps, Nucl. Instrum. Meth.* **A 417** (1998) 266.

[240] C. Ohm, *Phase and intensity monitoring of the particle beams at the ATLAS experiment*, M.Sc. thesis, Linköping University, Sweden, http://www.ep.liu.se/abstract.xsql?dbid=9614.

[241] T. Wijnands, *Radiation monitoring for equipment in the LHC tunnel, functional specification*, 2005 EDMS Document 565013, https://edms.cern.ch/file/565013/0.2/LHC-PM-ES-0006-00-10.pdf; C. Pignard and T. Wijnands, *Radiation tolerant commercial of the shelf components for the remote readout of PIN diodes and Radfets*, in *Proceedings of the RADECS Conference*, Cap d'Agde France (2005).

[242] J. Knobloch et al., *LHC computing grid: technical design report*, CERN-LHCC-2005-024, http://cdsweb.cern.ch/record/840543.

[243] CMS collaboration, *CMS computing: technical design report*, CERN-LHCC-2005-023, http://cdsweb.cern.ch/record/838359.

[244] R. Brun and F. Rademakers, *ROOT — An object oriented data analysis framework, Nucl. Instrum. Meth.* **A 389** (1997) 81, see also http://root.cern.ch.

[245] S. Kosyakov et al., *FroNtier: high performance database access using standard web components in a scalable multi-tier architecture*, in *Proceedings of the Conference on Computing in High Energy Physics*, Interlaken Switzerland (2004), http://cdsweb.cern.ch/record/865676.

[246] M. Aderholz et al., *Models of networked analysis at regional centres for LHC experiments (MONARC) — Phase 2 report*, 24th March 2000, CERN-LCB-2000-001, http://cdsweb.cern.ch/record/510694.

[247] http://lhcopn.cern.ch.

[248] J. Rehn et al., *PhEDEx high-throughput data transfer management system*, in *Proocedings of the conference on computing in high energy physics*, Mumbai India (2006).

[249] A. Fanfani et al., *Distributed Data Management in CMS*, in *Proocedings of the conference on computing in high energy physics*, Mumbai India (2006), CMS-CR-2006-013, http://cdsweb.cern.ch/record/933704.

[250] D. Spiga et al., *CMS workload management, Nucl. Phys.* **B 172** *(Proc. Suppl.)* (2007) 141.

PUBLISHED BY INSTITUTE OF PHYSICS PUBLISHING AND SISSA

RECEIVED: *February 19, 2008*
ACCEPTED: *June 14, 2008*
PUBLISHED: *August 14, 2008*

THE CERN LARGE HADRON COLLIDER: ACCELERATOR AND EXPERIMENTS

The LHCb Detector at the LHC

The LHCb Collaboration

ABSTRACT: The LHCb experiment is dedicated to precision measurements of CP violation and rare decays of B hadrons at the Large Hadron Collider (LHC) at CERN (Geneva). The initial configuration and expected performance of the detector and associated systems, as established by test beam measurements and simulation studies, is described.

KEYWORDS: Large detector systems for particle and astroparticle physics; Particle tracking detectors; Gaseous detectors; Calorimeters; Cherenkov detectors; Particle identification methods; Photon detectors for UV, visible and IR photons; Detector alignment and calibration methods; Detector cooling and thermo-stabilization; Detector design and construction technologies and materials.

2008 JINST 3 S08005

The LHCb Collaboration

2008 JINST 3 S08005

Centro Brasileiro de Pesquisas Físicas (CBPF), Rio de Janeiro, Brazil
A. Augusto Alves Jr., L.M. Andrade Filho,[1] A.F. Barbosa, I. Bediaga, G. Cernicchiaro, G. Guerrer,
H.P. Lima Jr, A.A. Machado, J. Magnin, F. Marujo, J.M. de Miranda, A. Reis, A. Santos, A. Toledo

Instituto de Física - Universidade Federal do Rio de Janeiro (IF-UFRJ), Rio de Janeiro, Brazil
K. Akiba, S. Amato, B. de Paula, L. de Paula, T. da Silva,[2] M. Gandelman, J.H. Lopes,
B. Maréchal, D. Moraes,[3] E. Polycarpo, F. Rodrigues

Laboratoire d'Annecy-le-Vieux de Physique des Particules (LAPP), Université de Savoie, CNRS/IN2P3, Annecy-le-Vieux, France
J. Ballansat, Y. Bastian, D. Boget, I. De Bonis, V. Coco, P.Y. David, D. Decamp, P. Delebecque,
C. Drancourt, N. Dumont-Dayot, C. Girard, B. Lieunard, M.N. Minard, B. Pietrzyk, T. Rambure,
G. Rospabe, S. T'Jampens

Laboratoire de Physique Corpusculaire Université Blaise Pascal (LPC), CNRS/IN2P3, Aubière, France
Z. Ajaltouni, G. Bohner, R. Bonnefoy, D. Borras,[||] C. Carloganu, H. Chanal, E. Conte, R. Cornat,
M. Crouau, E. Delage, O. Deschamps,[49] P. Henrard, P. Jacquet, C. Lacan, J. Laubser, J. Lecoq,
R. Lefèvre, M. Magne, M. Martemiyanov,[51] M.-L. Mercier, S. Monteil, V. Niess, P. Perret,
G. Reinmuth, A. Robert ,[4] S. Suchorski

Centre de Physique des Particules de Marseille, Aix-Marseille Université (CPPM) CNRS/IN2P3, Marseille, France
K. Arnaud, E. Aslanides, J. Babel,[5] C. Benchouk,[6] J.-P. Cachemiche, J. Cogan, F. Derue,[7]
B. Dinkespiler, P.-Y. Duval, V. Garonne,[8] S. Favard,[9] R. Le Gac, F. Leon, O. Leroy, P.-L. Liotard,[**]
F. Marin, M. Menouni, P. Ollive, S. Poss, A. Roche, M. Sapunov, L. Tocco,[||] B. Viaud,[10]
A. Tsaregorodtsev

Laboratoire de l'Accélérateur Linéaire (LAL), Université Paris-Sud, CNRS/IN2P3, Orsay, France
Y. Amhis, G. Barrand, S. Barsuk, C. Beigbeder, R. Beneyton, D. Breton, O. Callot, D. Charlet,
B. DŠ'Almagne, O. Duarte, F. Fulda-Quenzer, A. Jacholkowska,[11] B. Jean-Marie, J. Lefrancois,
F. Machefert, P. Robbe, M.-H. Schune, V. Tocut, I. Videau

Laboratoire de Physique Nucléaire et des Hautes Energies(LPNHE), Universités Paris VI et VII, CNRS/IN2P3, Paris, France
M. Benayoun, P. David, L. Del Buono, G. Gilles

Fakultät Physik, Technische Universität Dortmund, Dortmund, Germany
M. Domke, H. Futterschneider,[12] Ch. Ilgner, P. Kapusta,[12,52] M. Kolander, R. Krause,[12] M. Lieng, M. Nedos, K. Rudloff, S. Schleich, R. Schwierz,[12] B. Spaan, K. Wacker, K. Warda

Max-Planck-Institute for Nuclear Physics, Heidelberg, Germany
M. Agari,[||] C. Bauer, D. Baumeister,[||] N. Bulian,[**] H.P. Fuchs, W. Fallot-Burghardt,[||] T. Glebe,[||] W. Hofmann, K.T. Knöpfle, S. Löchner,[13] A. Ludwig, F. Maciuc, F. Sanchez Nieto,[14] M. Schmelling, B. Schwingenheuer, E. Sexauer,[||] N.J. Smale,[15] U. Trunk, H. Voss

Physikalisches Institut der Universität Heidelberg, Heidelberg, Germany J. Albrecht, S. Bachmann, J. Blouw, M. Deissenroth, H. Deppe,[13] H.B. Dreis, F. Eisele, T. Haas, S. Hansmann-Menzemer,[‡] S. Hennenberger, J. Knopf, M. Moch,[‡] A. Perieanu,[‡] S. Rabenecker, A. Rausch, C. Rummel, R. Rusnyak, M. Schiller,[‡] U. Stange, U. Uwer, M. Walter, R. Ziegler

Università di Bologna and Sezione INFN, Bologna, Italy
G. Avoni, G. Balbi,[53] F. Bonifazi, D. Bortolotti, A. Carbone, I. D'Antone, D. Galli,[53] D. Gregori,[53] I. Lax, U. Marconi, G. Peco, V. Vagnoni, G. Valenti, S. Vecchi

Università di Cagliari and Sezione INFN, Cagliari, Italy
W. Bonivento, A. Cardini, S. Cadeddu, V. DeLeo,[||] C. Deplano, S. Furcas, A. Lai, R. Oldeman, D. Raspino, B. Saitta, N. Serra

Università di Ferrara and Sezione INFN, Ferrara, Italy
W. Baldini, S. Brusa, S. Chiozzi, A. Cotta Ramusino, F. Evangelisti, A. Franconieri, S. Germani,[16] A. Gianoli, L. Guoming, L. Landi, R. Malaguti, C. Padoan, C. Pennini, M. Savriè, S. Squerzanti, T. Zhao,[17] M. Zhu

Università di Firenze and Sezione INFN, Firenze, Italy
A. Bizzeti,[54] G. Graziani, M. Lenti, M. Lenzi, F. Maletta, S. Pennazzi, G. Passaleva, M. Veltri,[56]

Laboratori Nazionali di Frascati dell'INFN, Frascati, Italy
M. Alfonsi, M. Anelli, A. Balla, A. Battisti, G. Bencivenni, P. Campana, M. Carletti, P. Ciambrone, G. Corradi, E. Dané,[57] A. DiVirgilio, P. DeSimone, G. Felici, C. Forti,[49] M. Gatta, G. Lanfranchi, F. Murtas, M. Pistilli, M. Poli Lener, R. Rosellini, M. Santoni, A. Saputi, A. Sarti, A. Sciubba,[57] A. Zossi

Università di Genova and Sezione INFN, Genova, Italy
M. Ameri, S. Cuneo, F. Fontanelli, V. Gracco, G. Miní, M. Parodi, A. Petrolini, M. Sannino, A. Vinci

Università di Milano-Bicocca and Sezione INFN, Milano, Italy
M. Alemi, C. Arnaboldi, T. Bellunato, M. Calvi, F. Chignoli, A. De Lucia, G. Galotta, R. Mazza, C. Matteuzzi, M. Musy, P. Negri, D. Perego,[§] G. Pessina

Università di Roma "La Sapienza" and Sezione INFN, Roma, Italy
G. Auriemma,[58] V. Bocci, A. Buccheri, G. Chiodi, S. Di Marco, F. Iacoangeli, G. Martellotti, R. Nobrega,[59] A. Pelosi, G. Penso,[59] D. Pinci, W. Rinaldi, A. Rossi, R. Santacesaria, C. Satriano,[58]

Università di Roma "Tor Vergata" and Sezione INFN, Roma, Italy
G. Carboni, M. Iannilli, A. Massafferri Rodrigues,[18] R. Messi, G. Paoluzzi, G. Sabatino,[60] E. Santovetti, A. Satta

National Institute for Subatomic Physics, Nikhef, Amsterdam, Netherlands
J. Amoraal, G. van Apeldoorn,[**] R. Arink,[**] N. van Bakel,[19] H. Band, Th. Bauer, A. Berkien, M. van Beuzekom, E. Bos, Ch. Bron,[**] L. Ceelie, M. Doets, R. van der Eijk,[∥] J.-P. Fransen, P. de Groen, V. Gromov, R. Hierck,[∥] J. Homma, B. Hommels,[20] W. Hoogland,[**] E. Jans, F. Jansen, L. Jansen, M. Jaspers, B. Kaan,[**] B. Koene,[**] J. Koopstra, F. Kroes,[**] M. Kraan, J. Langedijk,[**] M. Merk, S. Mos, B. Munneke, J. Palacios, A. Papadelis, A. Pellegrino,[49] O. van Petten, T. du Pree, E. Roeland, W. Ruckstuhl,[†] A. Schimmel, H. Schuijlenburg, T. Sluijk, J. Spelt, J. Stolte, H. Terrier, N. Tuning, A. Van Lysebetten, P. Vankov, J. Verkooijen, B. Verlaat, W. Vink, H. de Vries, L. Wiggers, G. Ybeles Smit, N. Zaitsev,[∥] M. Zupan,[∥] A. Zwart

Vrije Universiteit, Amsterdam, Netherlands
J. van den Brand, H.J. Bulten, M. de Jong, T. Ketel, S. Klous, J. Kos, B. M'charek, F. Mul, G. Raven, E. Simioni

Center for High Energy Physics, Tsinghua University (TUHEP), Beijing, People's Republic of China
J. Cheng, G. Dai, Z. Deng, Y. Gao, G. Gong, H. Gong, J. He, L. Hou, J. Li, W. Qian, B. Shao, T. Xue, Z. Yang, M. Zeng

AGH-University of Science and Technology, Cracow, Poland
B. Muryn, K. Ciba, A. Oblakowska-Mucha

Henryk Niewodniczanski Institute of Nuclear Physics Polish Academy of Sciences, Cracow, Poland
J. Blocki, K. Galuszka, L. Hajduk, J. Michalowski, Z. Natkaniec, G. Polok, M. Stodulski, M. Witek

Soltan Institute for Nuclear Studies (SINS), Warsaw, Poland
K. Brzozowski, A. Chlopik, P. Gawor, Z. Guzik, A. Nawrot, A. Srednicki, K. Syryczynski, M. Szczekowski

Horia Hulubei National Institute for Physics and Nuclear Engineering, IFIN-HH, Magurele-Bucharest, Romania

D.V. Anghel, A. Cimpean, C. Coca, F. Constantin, P. Cristian, D.D. Dumitru, D.T. Dumitru, G. Giolu, C. Kusko, C. Magureanu, Gh. Mihon, M. Orlandea, C. Pavel, R. Petrescu, S. Popescu, T. Preda, A. Rosca, V.L. Rusu, R. Stoica, S. Stoica, P.D. Tarta

Institute for Nuclear Research (INR), Russian Academy of Science, Moscow, Russia

S. Filippov, Yu. Gavrilov, L. Golyshkin, E. Gushchin, O. Karavichev, V. Klubakov, L. Kravchuk, V. Kutuzov, S. Laptev, S. Popov

Institute for Theoretical and Experimental Physics (ITEP), Moscow, Russia

A. Aref'ev, B. Bobchenko, V. Dolgoshein, V. Egorychev, A. Golutvin, O. Gushchin, A. Konoplyannikov,[49] I. Korolko, T. Kvaratskheliya, I. Machikhiliyan,[49] S. Malyshev, E. Mayatskaya, M. Prokudin, D. Rusinov, V. Rusinov, P. Shatalov, L. Shchutska, E. Tarkovskiy, A. Tayduganov, K. Voronchev, O. Zhiryakova

Budker Institute for Nuclear Physics (INP), Novosibirsk, Russia

A. BobrovA. Bondar, S. Eidelman, A. Kozlinsky, L. Shekhtman

Institute for High Energy Physics (IHEP), Protvino, Russia

K.S. Beloous, R.I. Dzhelyadin,[49] Yu.V. Gelitsky, Yu.P. Gouz, K.G. Kachnov, A.S. Kobelev, V.D. Matveev, V.P. Novikov, V.F. Obraztsov, A.P. Ostankov, V.I. Romanovsky, V.I. Rykalin, A.P. Soldatov, M.M. Soldatov, E.N. Tchernov, O.P. Yushchenko

Petersburg Nuclear Physics Institute, Gatchina, St-Petersburg, Russia

B. Bochin, N. Bondar, O. Fedorov, V. Golovtsov, S. Guets, A. Kashchuk,[49]V. Lazarev, O. Maev, P. Neustroev, N. Sagidova, E. Spiridenkov, S. Volkov, An. Vorobyev, A. Vorobyov

University of Barcelona, Barcelona, Spain

E. Aguilo, S. Bota, M. Calvo, A. Comerma, X. Cano, A. Dieguez, A. Herms, E. Lopez, S. Luengo,[61] J. Garra, Ll. Garrido, D. Gascon, A. Gaspar de Valenzuela,[61] C. Gonzalez, R. Graciani, E. Grauges, A. Perez Calero, E. Picatoste, J. Riera,[61] M. Rosello,[61] H. Ruiz, X. Vilasis,[61] X. Xirgu

University of Santiago de Compostela (USC), Santiago de Compostela, Spain

B. Adeva, X. Cid Vidal, D. Martĩnez Santos, D. Esperante Pereira, J.L. Fungueiriño Pazos, A. Gallas Torreira, C. Lois Gómez, A. Pazos Alvarez, E. Pérez Trigo, M. Pló Casasús, C. Rodriguez Cobo, P. Rodríguez Pérez, J.J. Saborido, M. Seco P. Vazquez Regueiro

Ecole Polytechnique Fédérale de Lausanne (EPFL), Lausanne, Switzerland

P. Bartalini,[21] A. Bay, M.-O. Bettler, F. Blanc, J. Borel, B. Carron,[||] C. Currat, G. Conti, O. Dormond,[||]Y. Ermoline,[22] P. Fauland, L. Fernandez,[||] R. Frei, G. Gagliardi,[23] N. Gueissaz, G. Haefeli, A. Hicheur, C. Jacoby,[||] P. Jalocha,[||] S. Jimenez-Otero, J.-P. Hertig, M. Knecht, F. Legger, L. Locatelli, J.-R. Moser, M. Needham, L. Nicolas, A. Perrin-Giacomin, J.-P. Perroud,[**] C. Potterat, F. Ronga,[24] O. Schneider, T. Schietinger,[25] D. Steele, L. Studer,[||] M. Tareb, M.T. Tran, J. van Hunen,[||] K. Vervink, S. Villa,[||] N. Zwahlen

University of Zürich, Zürich, Switzerland
R. Bernet, A. Büchler, J. Gassner, F. Lehner, T. Sakhelashvili, C. Salzmann, P. Sievers, S. Steiner, O. Steinkamp, U. Straumann, J. van Tilburg, A. Vollhardt, D. Volyanskyy, M. Ziegler

Institute of Physics and Technologies, Kharkiv, Ukraine
A. Dovbnya, Yu. Ranyuk, I. Shapoval

Institute for Nuclear Research, National Academy of Sciences of Ukraine, KINR, Kiev, Ukraine
M. Borisova, V. Iakovenko, V. Kyva, O. Kovalchuk O. Okhrimenko, V. Pugatch, Yu. Pylypchenko,[26]

H.H. Wills Physics Laboratory, University of Bristol, Bristol, United Kingdom
M. Adinolfi, N.H. Brook, R.D. Head, J.P. Imong, K.A. Lessnoff, F.C.D. Metlica, A.J. Muir, J.H. Rademacker, A. Solomin, P.M. Szczypka

Cavendish Laboratory, University of Cambridge, Cambridge, United Kingdom
C. Barham, C. Buszello, J. Dickens, V. Gibson, S. Haines, K. Harrison, C.R. Jones, S. Katvars, U. Kerzel, C. Lazzeroni,[27] Y.Y. Li ,[§] G. Rogers, J. Storey,[28] H. Skottowe, S.A. Wotton

Science and Technology Facilities Council: Rutherford-Appleton Laboratory (RAL), Didcot, United Kingdom
T.J. Adye, C.J. Densham, S. Easo, B. Franek, P. Loveridge, D. Morrow, J.V. Morris, R. Nandakumar, J. Nardulli, A. Papanestis, G.N. Patrick, S. Ricciardi, M.L. Woodward, Z. Zhang

University of Edinburgh, Edinburgh, United Kingdom
R.J.U. Chamonal, P.J. Clark, P. Clarke, S. Eisenhardt, N. Gilardi, A. Khan,[29] Y.M. Kim, R. Lambert, J. Lawrence, A. Main, J. McCarron, C. Mclean, F. Muheim, A.F. Osorio-Oliveros, S. Playfer, N. Styles, Y. Xie

University of Glasgow, Glasgow, United Kingdom
A. Bates, L. Carson, F. da Cunha Marinho, F. Doherty, L. Eklund, M. Gersabeck, L. Haddad, A.A. Macgregor, J. Melone, F. McEwan, D.M. Petrie, S.K. Paterson,[49,§] C. Parkes, A. Pickford, B. Rakotomiaramanana, E. Rodrigues, A.F. Saavedra,[30] F.J.P. Soler,[62] T. Szumlak, S. Viret

Imperial College London, London, United Kingdom
L. Allebone, O. Awunor, J. Back,[31] G. Barber, C. Barnes, B. Cameron, D. Clark, I. Clark, P. Dornan, A. Duane, C. Eames, U. Egede, M. Girone,[49] S. Greenwood, R. Hallam, R. Hare, A. Howard,[32] S. Jolly, V. Kasey, M. Khaleeq, P. Koppenburg, D. Miller, R. Plackett, D. Price, W. Reece, P. Savage, T. Savidge, B. Simmons,[3] G. Vidal-Sitjes, D. Websdale

University of Liverpool, Liverpool, United Kingdom

A. Affolder, J.S. Anderson,* S.F. Biagi, T.J.V. Bowcock, J.L. Carroll, G. Casse, P. Cooke, S. Donleavy, L. Dwyer, K. Hennessy,* T. Huse, D. Hutchcroft, D. Jones, M. Lockwood, M. McCubbin, R. McNulty,* D. Muskett, A. Noor, G.D. Patel, K. Rinnert, T. Shears, N.A. Smith, G. Southern, I. Stavitski, P. Sutcliffe, M. Tobin, S.M. Traynor,* P. Turner, M. Whitley, M. Wormald, V. Wright

University of Oxford, Oxford, United Kingdom

J.H. Bibby, S. Brisbane, M. Brock, M. Charles, C. Cioffi, V.V. Gligorov, T. Handford, N. Harnew, F. Harris, M.J.J. John, M. Jones, J. Libby, L. Martin, I.A. McArthur, R. Muresan, C. Newby, B. Ottewell, A. Powell, N. Rotolo, R.S. Senanayake, L. Somerville, A. Soroko, P. Spradlin, P. Sullivan, I. Stokes-Rees,||,§ S. Topp-Jorgensen, F. Xing, G. Wilkinson

Physics Department, Syracuse University, Syracuse, N.Y, United States of America

M. Artuso, I. Belyaev, S. Blusk, G. Lefeuvre, N. Menaa, R. Menaa-Sia, R. Mountain, T. Skwarnicki, S. Stone, J.C. Wang

European Organisation for Nuclear Research (CERN), Geneva, Switzerland

L. Abadie, G. Aglieri-Rinella, E. Albrecht, J. André,** G. Anelli,|| N. Arnaud, A. Augustinus, F. Bal, M.C. Barandela Pazos,¶ A. Barczyk ,[33] M. Bargiotti, J. Batista Lopes, O. Behrendt, S. Berni, P. Binko,|| V. Bobillier, A. Braem, L. Brarda, J. Buytaert, L. Camilleri, M. Cambpell, G. Castellani, F. Cataneo,** M. Cattaneo, B. Chadaj, P. Charpentier, S. Cherukuwada,¶ E. Chesi,** J. Christiansen, R. Chytracek,[34] M. Clemencic, J. Closier, P. Collins, P. Colrain,|| O. Cooke,|| B. Corajod, G. Corti, C. D'Ambrosio, B. Damodaran,¶ C. David, S. de Capua, G. Decreuse, H. Degaudenzi, H. Dijkstra, J.-P. Droulez,** D. Duarte Ramos, J.P. Dufey,** R. Dumps, D. Eckstein,[35] M. Ferro-Luzzi, F. Fiedler ,[36] F. Filthaut,[37] W. Flegel,** R. Forty, C. Fournier, M. Frank, C. Frei, B. Gaidioz, C. Gaspar, J.-C. Gayde, P. Gavillet,** A. Go,[38] G. Gracia Abril,|| J.-S. Graulich,[39] P.-A. Giudici, A. Guirao Elias, P. Guglielmini, T. Gys, F. Hahn, S. Haider, J. Harvey, B. Hay,|| J.-A. Hernando Morata, J. Herranz Alvarez, E. van Herwijnen, H.J. Hilke,** G. von Holtey,** W. Hulsbergen, R. Jacobsson, O. Jamet, C. Joram, B. Jost, N. Kanaya, J. Knaster Refolio, S. Koestner, M. Koratzinos,[40] R. Kristic, D. Lacarrère, C. Lasseur, T. Lastovicka,[41] M. Laub, D. Liko,[42] C. Lippmann,[43] R. Lindner, M. Losasso, A. Maier, K. Mair, P. Maley,|| P. Mato Vila, G. Moine, J. Morant, M. Moritz,|| J. Moscicki, M. Muecke,[44] H. Mueller, T. Nakada,[63] N. Neufeld, J. Ocariz,[45] C. Padilla Aranda, U. Parzefall,[46] M. Patel, M. Pepe-Altarelli, D. Piedigrossi, M. Pivk,|| W. Pokorski, S. Ponce,[34] F. Ranjard, W. Riegler, J. Renaud,** S. Roiser, A. Rossi, L. Roy, T. Ruf, D. Ruffinoni,** S. Saladino,|| A. Sambade Varela, R. Santinelli, S. Schmelling, B. Schmidt, T. Schneider, A. Schöning,[24] A. Schopper, J. Seguinot,[47] W. Snoeys, A. Smith, A.C. Smith,¶ P. Somogyi, R. Stoica,¶ W. Tejessy,** F. Teubert, E. Thomas, J. Toledo Alarcon,[48] O. Ullaland, A. Valassi,[34] P. Vannerem,** R. Veness, P. Wicht,** D. Wiedner, W. Witzeling, A. Wright,|| K. Wyllie, T. Ypsilantis,†

[1] now at COPPE - Universidade Federal do Rio de Janeiro, COPPE-UFRJ, Rio de Janeiro, Brazil
[2] now at Universidade Federal de Santa Catarina, Florianopolis, Brazil
[3] now at European Organisation for Nuclear Research (CERN), Geneva, Switzerland

[4]now at LPNHE, Université Pierre et Marie Curie, Paris, France

[5]now at Faculté de Sciences Sociales de Toulouse, Toulouse, France

[6]now at Université des Sciences et de la Technologie, Houari Boumediéne, Alger,Algérie

[7]now at Laboratoire de Physique Nucléaire et de Hautes Energies, Paris, France

[8]now at Laboratoire de l'Accélérateur Linéaire, Orsay, France

[9]now at Observatoire de Haute Provence, Saint-Michel de l'Observatoire, France

[10]now at Université de Montréal, Montréal, Canada

[11]now at Laboratoire de Physique Théorique et Astroparticule, Université de Montpellier, Montpellier, France

[12]now at Institut für Kern- und Teilchenphysik, Technische Universität Dresden, Dresden, Germany

[13]now at Gesellschaft für Schwerionenforschung (GSI) Darmstadt, Germany

[14]now at Universitat Autonoma de Barcelona/IFAE, Barcelona, Spain

[15]now at Forschungszentrum Karlsruhe, Eggenstein-Leopoldshafen, Germany

[16]now at Università di Perugia, Perugia, Italy

[17]now at Institute of High Energy Physics (IHEP), Beijing, People's Republic of China

[18]now at Universidade do Estado do Rio de Janeiro (UERJ), Rio de Janeiro, Brazil

[19]now at Stanford University, Palo Alto,United States of America

[20]now at Cavendish Laboratory, University of Cambridge, Cambridge, United Kingdom

[21]now at University of Florida, Gainesville, United States of America

[22]now at Michigan State University, Lansing, United States of America

[23]now at University of Genova and INFN sez. Genova, Genova, Italy

[24]now at Eidgenössische Technische Hochshule Zürich, Zürich, Switzerland

[25]now at Paul Scherrer Institute, Villigen, Switzerland

[26]now at the University of Oslo, Oslo, Norway

[27]now at University of Birmingham, Birmingham, United Kingdom

[28]now at TRIUMF, Vancouver, Canada

[29]now at Brunel University, Uxbridge, United Kingdom

[30]now at University of Sydney, Sydney, Australia

[31]now at University of Warwick, Warwick, United Kingdom

[32]now at University College, London, United Kingdom

[33]now at California Institute of Technology (Caltech),Pasadena, United States of America

[34]now at IT Department, CERN, Geneva, Switzerland

[35]now at Deustches Elektronen-Synchrotron (DESY), Hamburg, Germany

[36]now at Ludwigs-Maximilians University, Munich, Germany

[37]now at Radboud University Nijmegen, Nijmegen, The Netherlands

[38]now at National Center University, Taiwan, Taiwan

[39]now at University of Geneva, Geneva, Switzerland

[40]now at AB Department, CERN, Geneva, Switzerland

[41]now at Oxford University, Oxford, United Kingdom

[42]on leave from Institute of High Energy Physics, Vienna, Austria

[43]now at Gesellschaft für Schwerionenforschung (GSI), Darmstadt, Germany

[44]now at University of Technology, Graz, Austria

[45]now at Université de Paris VI et VII (LPNHE), Paris, France

2008 JINST 3 S08005

[46]now at Albert-Ludwigs-University, Freiburg, Germany

[47]Emeritus, Collège de France, Paris, France

[48]now at Polytechnical University of Valencia, Valencia, Spain

[49]also at CERN, Geneva, Switzerland

[51]also at Institute for Theoretical and Experimental Physics(ITEP), Moscow, Russia

[52]also at Henryk Niewodniczanski Institute of Nuclear Physics, Polish Academy of Sciences, Cracow, Poland

[53]also at Alma Mater Studiorum, Università di Bologna, Bologna, Italy

[54]also at University of Modena, Modena, Italy

[55]also at University of Florence, Florence, Italy

[56]also at University of Urbino, Urbino, Italy

[57]also at Dipartimento di Energetica, Università di Roma La Sapienza, Roma, Italy

[58]also at University of Basilicata, Potenza, Italy

[59]also at University of Roma "La Sapienza", Rome, Italy

[60]also at LNF, Frascati, Italy

[61]also at Enginyeria i Arquitectura La Salle, Universitat Ramon Llull, Barcelona, Spain

[62]also at Rutherford Appleton Laboratory, Chilton, Didcot, United Kingdom

[63]also at Ecole Polytechnique Fédérale de Lausanne, Lausanne, Switzerland

[*]from University College Dublin (UCD), Dublin, Ireland

[‡]supported by the Emmy Noether Programme of the Deutsche Forschungsgemeinschaft

[§]partially supported by the European Community's 5th PCRDT Marie Curie Training Site Programme, at the Centre de Physique des Particules de Marseille, under the Host Fellowship contract HPMT-CT-2001-00339

[¶]supported by Marie Curie Early Stage Research Training Fellowship of the European Community's Sixth Framework Programme under contract numbers MEST-CT-2004-007307-MITELCO and MEST-CT-2005-020216-ELACCO

[‖]currently not working in HEP

[**]retired

[†]deceased

Corresponding author: Clara Matteuzzi (cxm@mail.cern.ch)

Contents

2008 JINST 3 S08005

Chapter 1

Physics motivations and requirements

LHCb is an experiment dedicated to heavy flavour physics at the LHC [1, 2]. Its primary goal is to look for indirect evidence of new physics in CP violation and rare decays of beauty and charm hadrons.

The current results in heavy flavour physics obtained at the B factories and at the Tevatron are, so far, fully consistent with the CKM mechanism. On the other hand, the level of CP violation in the Standard Model weak interactions cannot explain the amount of matter in the universe. A new source of CP violation beyond the Standard Model is therefore needed to solve this puzzle. With much improved precision, the effect of such a new source might be seen in heavy flavour physics. Many models of new physics indeed produce contributions that change the expectations of the CP violating phases, rare decay branching fractions, and may generate decay modes which are forbidden in the Standard Model. To examine such possibilities, CP violation and rare decays of B_d, B_s and D mesons must be studied with much higher statistics and using many different decay modes.

With the large $b\bar{b}$ production cross section of $\sim 500\,\mu$b expected at an energy of 14 TeV, the LHC will be the most copious source of B mesons in the world. Also B_c and b-baryons such as Λ_b will be produced in large quantities. With a modest luminosity of 2×10^{32} cm^{-2}s^{-1} for LHCb, 10^{12} $b\bar{b}$ pairs would be produced in 10^7 s, corresponding to the canonical one year of data taking. Running at the lower luminosity has some advantages: events are dominated by a single pp interaction per bunch crossing (simpler to analyse than those with multiple primary pp interactions), the occupancy in the detector remains low and radiation damage is reduced. The luminosity for the LHCb experiment can be tuned by changing the beam focus at its interaction point independently from the other interaction points. This will allow LHCb to maintain the optimal luminosity for the experiment for many years from the LHC start-up.

The LHCb detector must be able to exploit this large number of b hadrons. This requires an efficient, robust and flexible trigger in order to cope with the harsh hadronic environment. The trigger must be sensitive to many different final states. Excellent vertex and momentum resolution are essential prerequisites for the good proper-time resolution necessary to study the rapidly oscillating B_s-$\overline{B}_s$ meson system and also for the good invariant mass resolution, needed to reduce combinatorial background. In addition to electron, muon, γ, π^0 and η detection, identification of protons, kaons and pions is crucial in order to cleanly reconstruct many hadronic B meson decay final states such as $B^0 \rightarrow \pi^+\pi^-$, $B \rightarrow DK^{(*)}$ and $B_s \rightarrow D_s^{\pm}K^{\mp}$. These are key channels for the physics goals of the experiment. Finally, a data acquisition system with high bandwidth and powerful online data processing capability is needed to optimise the data taking.

2008 JINST 3 S08005

Chapter 2

The LHCb Detector

2.1 Detector layout

LHCb is a single-arm spectrometer with a forward angular coverage from approximately 10 mrad to 300 (250) mrad in the bending (non-bending) plane. The choice of the detector geometry is justified by the fact that at high energies both the b- and $\bar{\mathrm{b}}$-hadrons are predominantly produced in the same forward or backward cone.

The layout of the LHCb spectrometer is shown in figure 2.1. The right-handed coordinate system adopted has the z axis along the beam, and the y axis along the vertical.

Intersection Point 8 of the LHC, previously used by the DELPHI experiment during the LEP

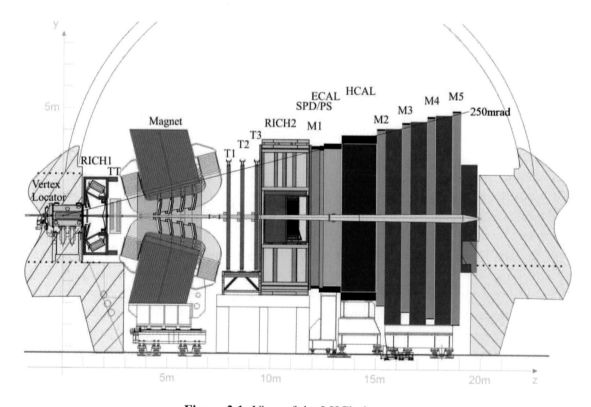

Figure 2.1: View of the LHCb detector.

time, has been allocated to the LHCb detector. A modification to the LHC optics, displacing the interaction point by 11.25 m from the centre, has permitted maximum use to be made of the existing cavern for the LHCb detector components.

The present paper describes the LHCb experiment, its interface to the machine, the spectrometer magnet, the tracking and the particle identification, as well as the trigger and online systems, including front-end electronics, the data acquisition and the experiment control system. Finally, taking into account the performance of the detectors as deduced from test beam studies, the expected global performance of LHCb, based on detailed MonteCarlo simulations, is summarized.

The interface with the LHC machine is described in section 3. The description of the detector components is made in the following sequence: the spectrometer magnet, a warm dipole magnet providing an integrated field of 4 Tm, is described in section 4; the vertex locator system (including a pile-up veto counter), called the VELO, is described in section 5.1; the tracking system made of a Trigger Tracker (a silicon microstrip detector, TT) in front of the spectrometer magnet, and three tracking stations behind the magnet, made of silicon microstrips in the inner parts (IT) and of Kapton/Al straws for the outer parts (OT) is described in sections 5.2 and 5.3; two Ring Imaging Cherencov counters (RICH1 and RICH2) using Aerogel, C_4F_{10} and CF_4 as radiators, to achieve excellent π-K separation in the momentum range from 2 to 100 GeV/c, and Hybrid Photon Detectors are described in section 6.1; the calorimeter system composed of a Scintillator Pad Detector and Preshower (SPD/PS), an electromagnetic (shashlik type) calorimeter (ECAL) and a hadronic (Fe and scintillator tiles) calorimeter (HCAL) is described in section 6.2; the muon detection system composed of MWPC (except in the highest rate region, where triple-GEM's are used) is described in section 6.3. The trigger, the online system, the computing resources and the expected performance of the detector are described in sections 7, 8, 9, and 10, respectively.

Most detector subsystems are assembled in two halves, which can be moved out separately horizontally for assembly and maintenance, as well as to provide access to the beampipe.

Interactions in the detector material reduce the detection efficiency for electrons and photons; multiple scattering of pions and kaons complicates the pattern recognition and degrades the momentum resolution. Therefore special attention was paid to the material budget up to the end of the tracking system. Estimations of the material budget of the detector [3] using realistic geometries for the vacuum chamber and all the sub-detectors show that at the end of the tracking, just before entering RICH2, a particle has seen, on average, about 60% of a radiation length and about 20% of an absorption length.

2.2 Architecture of the front-end electronics

The front-end architecture chosen for LHCb [4, 5] has to a very large extent been determined by the requirement of making a hardware-based short latency trigger, with an efficient event selection, for complicated B events. A fast first level trigger has been found capable of making an event rate reduction of the order of 1 in 10. This has for the chosen LHCb luminosity enforced the use of a front-end architecture with a first level trigger rate of up to 1 MHz. This was considered to be the highest rate affordable for the data acquisition system (DAQ) and required readout links. The general front-end electronics architecture and data flow in the DAQ interface are shown in figure 2.2. All sub-detectors store sampled detector signals at the 40 MHz bunch crossing rate in

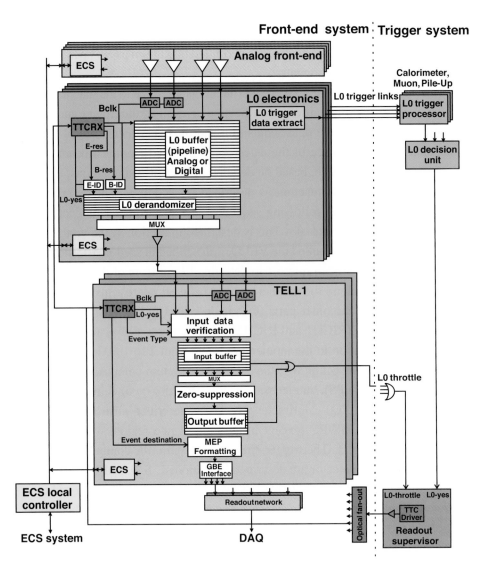

Figure 2.2: General front-end electronics architecture and data flow in the DAQ interface.

$4\,\mu$s deep pipeline buffers, while the hardware-based first level trigger (hereafter called Level-0 or L0) makes the required trigger selection. The speed of the analog detector signal shaping is in general such that only a single sample from one bunch crossing within 25 ns is extracted from each detector channel when a positive trigger is given (with an exception for the OT with a drift time of up to two bunch crossings). After the first level trigger acceptance, event data are transferred to 16 event deep first level derandomizing buffers to enable a nearly constant data readout rate to the DAQ interface modules located in the counting house. The 16-deep derandomizer allows the front-end to handle closely spaced triggers efficiently. At the output of the derandomizer, data from 32 channels are transferred at a rate of 40MHz, giving a maximum rate of 1.1 MHz, and multiplexed into constant data rate links.

All sub-detectors, except the VELO, use optical links (6000 in LHCb) based on the radiation hard GOL (Gigabit Optical Link) serializer chip [6]. A centralized scheme, implemented in the readout supervisor module (see section 8.3), imposes global restrictions on the trigger accept rate to prevent overflows of the derandomizer buffers and the following readout and data processing stages. Specific test and monitoring features are integrated into the different front-end systems to assure that thorough testing and monitoring can be made [7] as indicated in figure 2.2.

The Trigger, Timing and Control system (TTC) developed for the LHC experiments [8] is used to distribute clock and sampling phase, timing control (reset and synchronization signals), trigger (trigger accept and trigger types) and a set of dedicated test and calibration commands to all front-end and DAQ interface modules. Control and monitoring of the front-end electronics are based on either the LHCb specific *SPECS* control interface or the *ELMB* CAN bus module developed by ATLAS [9].

The reception of accepted event data from the sub-detectors is handled by 350 9U VME sized DAQ interface modules in the counting house. These *Field Programmable Gate Array* (FPGA) based modules receive front-end data, perform data and event synchronization verifications, appropriate zero-suppression and/or data compression, data buffering and finally send the event information to the DAQ system over up to four Gigabit-Ethernet links per module, as indicated in the lower part of figure 2. The DAQ interface module is in general based on a highly flexible and programmable module named TELL1 [10] with the exception of the RICH detector that has chosen to use a dedicated module[1] (c.f. section 6.1).

The electronics equipment is located in two different areas. Front-end electronics are installed on the subdetectors or in their close vicinity. Readout and trigger electronics as well as the Experiment Control System and the Data Acquisition system are located in a radiation protected *counting house*, composed of three levels of *electronic barracks* separated by a concrete shielding from the experimental area. The *control room* of the experiment in located on the ground floor.

The present paper does not contain a dedicated chapter with the detailed description of the electronics. The implementation of the specific front-end electronics is described in more detail in the chapters on the individual sub-detectors. Details of the readout supervisor, the Experiment Control System (ECS) and the DAQ system are described as part of the online system (section 8).

Radiation tolerance of the electronics

All detector components need to tolerate significant radiation doses. Parts of the trigger outside of the counting house are no exception.

The front-end electronics of each sub-detector are located either within the sub-detector itself or on its periphery. Sub-detector specific ASIC's and modules have been custom developed to handle the signal processing needed for the large channel counts in an environment with significant radiation levels. Radiation resistance requirements for all locations with electronics have been defined based on FLUKA simulations with appropriate safety factors [11] (e.g. 10 MRad and 10^{14} 1 MeV-neutron equivalent (n_{eq}) per cm^2 for the front-end chip used for the VELO and the Silicon Tracker; 4 kRad and 10^{12} n_{eq}/cm^2 for the ECAL/HCAL electronics, over 10 years of running). Extensive radiation tests have been made for all electronics components used in the front-end electronics, to verify their correct behaviour, after radiation (total dose and displacement damage), and during radiation exposure (single event upsets).

---

[1]Called UKL1 board.

Chapter 3

The interface to the LHC machine

3.1 Beampipe

The beampipe design is particularly delicate since the LHCb experiment is focussed on the high rapidity region, where the particle density is high. The number of secondary particles depends on the amount of material seen by incident primary particles. The mass of the beampipe and the presence of flanges and bellows have a direct influence on the occupancy, in particular for the tracking chambers and the RICH detectors. Optimisation of the design and selection of materials were therefore performed in order to maximize transparency in these critical regions [12, 13].

3.1.1 Layout

The beampipe, schematically represented in figure 3.1, includes the forward window of the VELO covering the full LHCb acceptance and four main conical sections, the three closer to the interaction point being made of beryllium and the one further away of stainless steel.

Beryllium was chosen as the material for 12 m out of the 19 m long beampipe, for its high transparency to the particles resulting from the collisions. It is the best available material for this application given its high radiation length combined with a modulus of elasticity higher than that of stainless steel. However, its toxicity [14], fragility and cost are drawbacks which had to be taken into account in the design, installation and operation phases. Flanges, bellows and the VELO exit window are made of high strength aluminium alloys which provide a suitable compromise between performance and feasibility. The remaining length, situated outside the critical zone in terms of transparency, is made of stainless steel, a material widely used in vacuum chambers because of its good mechanical and vacuum properties. The VELO window, a spherically shaped thin shell made of aluminium 6061-T6, is 800 mm in diameter and was machined from a specially forged block down to the final thickness of 2 mm. The machining of the block included a four convolution bellows at its smallest radius. The first beampipe section (UX85/1), that traverses RICH1 and TT (see figure 3.2), is made of 1 mm thick Be, includes a 25 mrad half-angle cone and the transition to the 10 mrad half-angle cone of the three following beampipe sections. In order to avoid having a flange between the VELO window and UX85/1, the two pieces were electron beam welded before installation. Sections UX85/2 (inside the dipole magnet) and UX85/3 (that traverses the Tracker, RICH2, M1 and part of ECAL) are 10 mrad beryllium cones of wall thickness varying from 1

2008 JINST 3 S08005

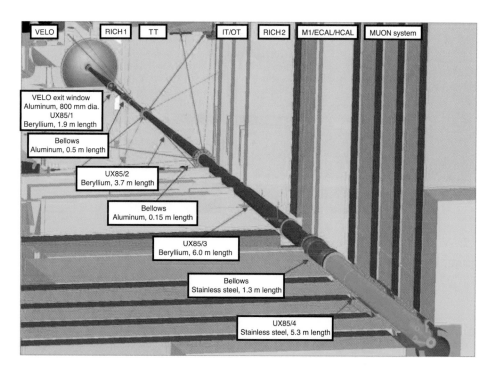

Figure 3.1: The 19 m long vacuum chamber inside the LHCb experiment is divided into four main sections. The first three are made of machined beryllium cones assembled by welding and the fourth of stainless steel. Bellows expansion joints provide interconnect flexibility in order to compensate for thermal expansions and mechanical tolerances.

to 2.4 mm as the diameter increases from 65 up to 262 mm. UX85/3 is connected to a stainless steel bellows through a Conflat seal on the larger diameter. The transition between aluminium and stainless steel is formed using an explosion bonded connection. The three Be beampipes were machined from billets up to 450 mm long and assembled by arc welding with a non-consumable electrode under inert gas protection (TIG) to achieve the required length. TIG welding was also used to connect the aluminium flanges at the extremities of the tubes.

The UX85/4 section completes the 10 mrad cone and includes a 15° half-angle conical extremity that provides a smooth transition down to the 60 mm final aperture. It was manufactured from rolled and welded stainless steel sheet of 4 mm thickness. A copper coating of 100 μm was deposited before assembly on the downstream side end cone to minimise the impedance seen by the beam. The aluminium and stainless steel bellows compensate for thermal expansion during bakeout and provide the necessary flexibility to allow beampipe alignment. Optimised Ultra High Vacuum (UHV) flanges were developed in order to minimise the background contribution from the various connections in the high transparency region [15]. The resulting flange design is based on all-metal Helicoflex seals and high strength AA 2219 aluminium alloy flanges to ensure reliable leak tightness and baking temperatures up to 250°C. A relatively low sealing force allows the use of aluminium and a significant reduction of the overall mass compared to a standard Conflat flange.

Another important source of background is the beampipe support system [16]. Each beampipe section must be supported at two points, with one fixed, i.e. with displacements restrained in all directions, and the other movable, the latter allowing free displacements along the

2008 JINST 3 S08005

Figure 3.2: View of the VELO exit window and UX85/1 beampipe as installed inside the RICH1 gas enclosure.

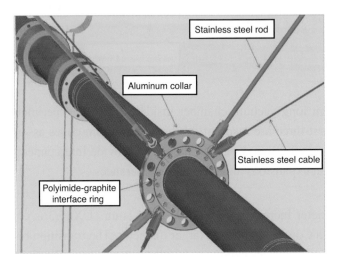

Figure 3.3: Optimised beampipe support inside the acceptance region. A system of eight high resistance cables and rods provide the required rigidity in all directions. A polyimide-graphite ring split in several parts, which are bolted together between the collar and the beampipe, prevents scratches on the beryllium and reduces local stresses at the contact surfaces.

beampipe axis. The fixed supports, which must compensate the unbalanced vacuum forces due to the conical shape of the beampipe, are each constructed using a combination of eight stainless steel cables or rods mounted under tension, pulling in both upstream and downstream directions with an angle to the beam axis (figure 3.3). Where a movable support is required to allow thermal expansion, four stainless steel cables are mounted in the plane perpendicular to the beampipe, blocking all movements except along the beam axis. The support cables and rods are connected to the beampipe through aluminium alloy collars with minimised mass, and an intermediate polyimide-graphite ring to avoid scratching the beryllium and to reduce stresses on contacting surfaces.

The experiment beam vacuum is isolated from the LHC with two sector valves, installed at the cavern entrances, which allow interventions and commissioning independently of the machine vacuum system.

2008 JINST 3 S08005

3.1.2 Vacuum chamber

In order to achieve an average total dynamic pressure of 10^{-8} to 10^{-9} mbar with beam passing through, the LHCb beampipe and the VELO RF-boxes are coated with sputtered non-evaporable getter (NEG) [17]. This works as a distributed pump, providing simultaneously low outgassing and desorption from particle interactions with the walls. Another purpose of the NEG coating is to prevent electron multipacting [18] inside the chamber, since the secondary electron emission yield is much lower than for the chamber material. The UHV pumping system is completed by sputter-ion pumps in the VELO vessel and at the opposite end of the beampipe in order to pump non-getterable gases. Once the NEG coating has been saturated, the chamber must be heated periodically (baked out) to 200°C, for 24 hours, in order to recover the NEG pumping capacity. The temperature will have to be gradually increased with the number of activation cycles, however it is limited to 250°C in the optimised flange assemblies for mechanical reasons. Before NEG activation, the vacuum commissioning procedure also includes the bakeout of the non-coated surfaces inside the VELO vacuum vessel to a temperature of 150°C. Removable heating jackets are installed during shutdowns covering the VELO window and the beampipe up to the end of RICH2. From there to the end of the muon chambers, a permanent system is installed. As there are no transparency constraints, the insulation of the beampipe inside the muon filters is made from a mixture of silica, metal oxides and glass fiber, whilst the heating is provided by standard resistive tapes.

Such an optimised vacuum chamber must not be submitted to any additional external pressure or shocks while under vacuum, due to the risk of implosion. Hence, it must be vented to atmospheric pressure before certain interventions in the surrounding detectors. Saturation of the NEG coating and consequent reactivation after the venting will be avoided by injecting an inert gas not pumped by the NEG. Neon was found to be the most suitable gas for this purpose because of its low mass and the fact that it is not used as a tracer for leak detection, such as helium or argon. However, commercially available Ne must first be purified before injection. A gas injection system installed in the cavern will provide the clean neon to be injected simultaneously into both VELO beam vacuum and detector vacuum volumes, as the pressure difference between the two volumes must be kept lower than 5 mbar to prevent damage to the VELO RF-boxes (c.f. section 5.1).

3.2 The Beam Conditions Monitor

In order to cope with possible adverse LHC beam conditions, particularly with hadronic showers caused by misaligned beams or components performance failures upon particle injection into the LHC, the LHCb experiment is equipped with a Beam Conditions Monitor (BCM) [19]. This system continuously monitors the particle flux at two locations in the close vicinity of the vacuum chamber in order to protect the sensitive LHCb tracking devices. In the case of problems, the BCM system will be the first to respond and will request a dump of the LHC beams. The BCM connects to both the LHCb experiment control system and to the beam interlock controller of the LHC [20]. As a safety system, the BCM is equipped with an uninterruptable power supply and continuously reports its operability also to the vertex locator control system through a hardwired link.

The BCM detectors consist of chemical-vapor deposition (CVD) diamond sensors, which have been proven to withstand radiation doses as high as those that may occur in LHC accident

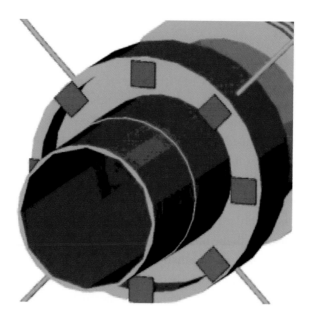

Figure 3.4: Schematic view of the eight CVD-diamond sensors surrounding the beampipe at the downstream BCM station.

scenarios. In order to assure compatibility of the signals with those from other LHC experiments, the dimensions of the sensors are the same as those of the ATLAS and CMS experiments, i.e. their thickness is $500 \,\mu$m, the lateral dimensions are $10 \,$mm $\times 10 \,$mm, with a centered $8 \,$mm $\times 8 \,$mm metallized area. The metallization is made of a $500 \,$Å thick gold layer on a $500 \,$Å thick layer of titanium. The radiation resistance of the metallization has been studied with the exposure of a $4 \,$mm^2 surface to 4×10^{15} protons of an energy of $25 \,$MeV over 18 hours. No sign of degradation was observed.

The two BCM stations are placed at $2131 \,$mm upstream and $2765 \,$mm downstream from the interaction point. Each station consists of eight diamond sensors, symmetrically distributed around the vacuum chamber with the sensitive area starting at a radial distance of $50.5 \,$mm (upstream) and $37.0 \,$mm (downstream). Figure 3.4 shows the downstream BCM station around the beampipe. The sensors are read out by a current-to-frequency converter card [21] with an integration time of $40 \,\mu$s, developed for the Beam Loss Monitors of the LHC.

Simulations were carried out with the GAUSS package [22] to study the expected performance of the BCM. Unstable beam situations are described in a simplified way in generating $7 \,$GeV protons at $3000 \,$mm upstream of the interaction point in a direction parallel to the beam and in calculating the energy deposited in the BCM sensors caused by these protons. All sensors experience an increase of their signals due to hadronic showers produced by the protons in intermediate material layers. Assuming that during unstable LHC beam condition, the beam comes as close as $475 \,\mu$m (approximately 6 times its RMS) to the RF foil of the VELO (see section 5.1), it would take 40–$80 \,\mu$s of integration time (or about 20 LHC turns) for the BCM to detect the critical situation and request a beam dump.

2008 JINST 3 S08005

Chapter 4

Magnet

4.1 General description

A dipole magnet is used in the LHCb experiment to measure the momentum of charged particles. The measurement covers the forward acceptance of ±250 mrad vertically and of ±300 mrad horizontally. The super-conducting magnet originally proposed in the Technical Proposal [1], would have required unacceptably high investment costs and very long construction time. It was replaced by a warm magnet design with saddle-shaped coils in a window-frame yoke with sloping poles in order to match the required detector acceptance. Details on the design of the magnet are given in the Magnet Technical Design Report [23] and in [24, 25]. The design of the magnet with an integrated magnetic field of 4 Tm for tracks of 10 m length had to accommodate the contrasting needs for a field level inside the RICHs envelope less than 2 mT and a field as high as possible in the regions between the vertex locator, and the Trigger Tracker tracking station [26]. The design was also driven by the boundary conditions in the experimental hall previously occupied by the DELPHI detector. This implied that the magnet had to be assembled in a temporary position and to be subdivided into two relatively light elements. The DELPHI rail systems and parts of the magnet carriages have been reused as the platform for the LHCb magnet for economic reasons. Plates, 100 mm thick, of laminated low carbon steel, having a maximum weight of 25 tons, were used to form the identical horizontal bottom and top parts and the two mirror-symmetrical vertical parts (uprights) of the magnet yoke.[1] The total weight of the yoke is 1500 tons and of the two coils is 54 tons.

The two identical coils are of conical saddle shape and are placed mirror-symmetrically to each other in the magnet yoke. Each coil consists of fifteen pancakes arranged in five triplets and produced of pure Al-99.7 hollow conductor in an annealed state which has a central cooling channel of 25 mm diameter. The conductor has a specific ohmic resistance below $28 \, \Omega \cdot$ m at 20°C. It is produced in single-length of about 320 m by rotary extrusion[2] and tested for leaks with water up to 50 bars and for extrusion imperfections before being wound. The coils were produced in industry[3] with some equipment and technical support from CERN. Cast Aluminum clamps are used to hold together the triplets making up the coils, and to support and centre the

---

[1] Jebens, Germany.
[2] Holton Machinery, Bournemouth, UK.
[3] SigmaPhi, Vannes, France.

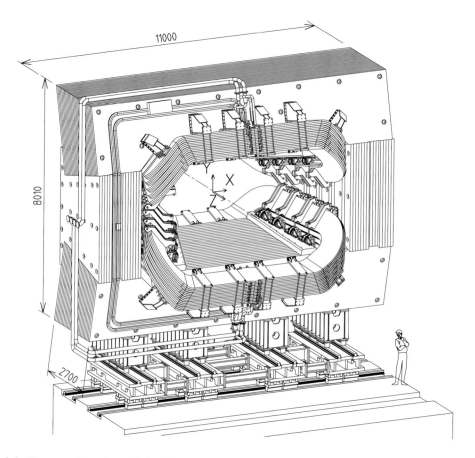

Figure 4.1: Perspective view of the LHCb dipole magnet with its current and water connections (units in mm). The interaction point lies behind the magnet.

coils with respect to the measured mechanical axis of the iron poles with tolerances of several millimeters. As the main stress on the conductor is of thermal origin, the design choice was to leave the pancakes of the coils free to slide upon their supports, with only one coil extremity kept fixed on the symmetry axis, against the iron yoke, where electrical and hydraulic terminations are located. Finite element models (TOSCA, ANSYS) have been extensively used to investigate the coils support system with respect to the effect of the electromagnetic and thermal stresses on the conductor, and the measured displacement of the coils during magnet operation matches the predicted value quite well. After rolling the magnet into its nominal position, final precise alignment of the yoke was carried out in order to follow the 3.6 mrad slope of the LHC machine and its beam. The resolution of the alignment measurements was about 0.2 mm while the magnet could be aligned to its nominal position with a precision of ±2 mm. Details of the measurements of the dipole parameters are given in table 4.1. A perspective view of the magnet is given in figure 4.1.

The magnet is operated via the Magnet Control System that controls the power supply and monitors a number of operational parameters (e.g. temperatures, voltages, water flow, mechanical movements, etc.). A second, fully independent system, the Magnet Safety System (MSS), ensures the safe operation and acts autonomously by enforcing a discharge of the magnet if critical parameters are outside the operating range. The magnet was put into operation and reached its nominal

Table 4.1: Measured main parameters of the LHCb magnet.

Non-uniformity of $|B|$	$\pm 1\%$ in planes xy of $1\,m^2$ from z=3m to z=8 m
$\int Bdl$ upstream TT region (0–2.5 m)	0.1159 Tm
$\int Bdl$ downstream TT region (2.5 - 7.95 m)	3.615 Tm
Max field at HPD's of RICH1	20×10^{-4} T (14×10^{-4} T with mu-metal)
Max field at HPD's of RICH2	9×10^{-4} T
Electric power dissipation	4.2 MW
Inductance L	1.3 H
Nominal / maximum current in conductor	5.85 kA / 6.6 kA
Total resistance (two coils + bus bars)	R = $130\,m\Omega$ @ 20° C
Total voltage drop (two coils)	730 V
Total number of turns	2 x 225
Total water flow	$150\,m^3$/h
Water Pressure drop	11 bar @ ΔT = 25°C
Overall dimensions H x V x L	11m x 8 m x 5 m
Total weight	1600 tons

current of 5.85 kA in November 2004, thereby being the first magnet of the LHC experiments operational in the underground experimental areas. Several magnetic field measurement campaigns have been carried out during which the magnet has shown stable and reliable performance.

4.2 Field mapping

In order to achieve the required momentum resolution for charged particles, the magnetic field integral $\int Bdl$ must be measured with a relative precision of a few times 10^{-4} and the position of the B-field peak with a precision of a few millimetres. A semi-automatic measuring device was constructed which allowed remotely controlled scanning along the longitudinal axis of the dipole by means of an array of Hall probes. The measuring machine was aligned with a precision of 1 mm with respect to the experiment reference frame. The support carrying the Hall probes could be manually positioned in the horizontal and vertical direction such as to cover the magnetic field volume of interest. The Hall probe array consisted of 60 sensor cards mounted on a G10 support covering a grid of 80 mm x 80 mm. Each sensor card contained three Hall probes mounted orthogonally on a cube together with a temperature sensor and the electronics required for remote readout. These 3D sensor cards[4] have been calibrated to a precision of 10^{-4} using a rotating setup in an homogeneous field together with an NMR for absolute field calibration [27]. The calibration process allowed correcting for non-linearity, temperature dependence and non-orthogonal mounting of the Hall probes.

The goal of the field mapping campaigns was to measure the three components of the magnetic field inside the tracking volume of the detector for both magnet polarities and to compare it to the magnetic field calculations obtained with TOSCA.[5] For the measurement of CP asymmetries it

---

[4]Developed in collaboration between CERN and NIKHEF for the ATLAS muon system.
[5]Vector Field TM.

2008 JINST 3 S08005

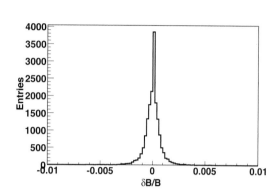

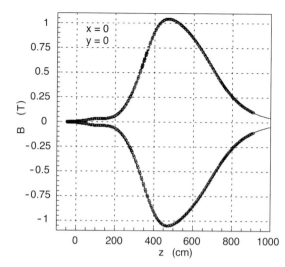

Figure 4.2: Relative difference between the measurements of B using different Hall probes at the same position in the magnet. The resolution is completely dominated by the precision of the calibration of the Hall probes.

Figure 4.3: Magnetic field along the z axis.

is important to control the systematic effects of the detector, by changing periodically the direction of the magnetic field. To this purpose, the impact of hysteresis effects on the reproducibility of the magnetic field has to be taken into account.

The magnetic field has been measured in the complete tracking volume inside the magnet and in the region of the VELO and the tracking stations, and also inside the magnetic shielding for the RICH1 and RICH2 photon detectors. The precision of the measurement obtained for the field mapping in the tracking volume is about 4×10^{-4}, as shown in figure 4.2. The main component, B_y, is shown in figure 4.3 for both polarities, together with the result of the model calculation. The overall agreement is excellent; however, in the upstream region of the detector (VELO, RICH1) a discrepancy of about 3.5% for the field integral has been found which can be attributed both to the precision of the TOSCA model computation and to the vicinity of the massive iron reinforcement embedded in the concrete of the hall. In all other regions the agreement between measurement and calculation is better than 1%.

In conclusion, the three components of the magnetic field have been measured with a fine grid of 8 x 8 x 10 cm^3 spanning from the interaction point to the RICH2 detector (i.e. over distance of about 9 m) and covering most of the LHCb acceptance region. The precision of the field map obtained is about 4×10^{-4} and the absolute field value is reproducible for both polarities to better than this value, provided the right procedure for the demagnetization of the iron yoke is applied.

Chapter 5

Tracking

The LHCb tracking system consists of the vertex locator system (VELO) and four planar tracking stations: the Tracker Turicensis (TT) upstream of the dipole magnet and T1-T3 downstream of the magnet. VELO and TT use silicon microstrip detectors. In T1-T3, silicon microstrips are used in the region close to the beam pipe (Inner Tracker, IT) whereas straw-tubes are employed in the outer region of the stations (Outer Tracker, OT). The TT and the IT were developed in a common project called the Silicon Tracker (ST).

The VELO is described in section 5.1 the ST in section 5.2 and the OT in section 5.3.

5.1 Vertex locator

The VErtex LOcator (VELO) provides precise measurements of track coordinates close to the interaction region, which are used to identify the displaced secondary vertices which are a distinctive feature of b and c-hadron decays [28]. The VELO consists of a series of silicon modules, each providing a measure of the r and ϕ coordinates, arranged along the beam direction (figure 5.1). Two planes perpendicular to the beam line and located upstream of the VELO sensors are called the *pile-up veto system* and are described in section 7.1. The VELO sensors are placed at a radial distance from the beam which is smaller than the aperture required by the LHC during injection and must therefore be retractable. The detectors are mounted in a vessel that maintains vacuum around the sensors and is separated from the machine vacuum by a thin walled corrugated aluminum sheet. This is done to minimize the material traversed by a charged particle before it crosses the sensors and the geometry is such that it allows the two halves of the VELO to overlap when in the closed position. Figure 5.2 shows a cross section of the VELO vessel, illustrating the separation between the primary (beam) vacuum and the secondary (detector) vacuum enclosed by the VELO boxes. Figure 5.3 shows an expanded view from inside one of the boxes, with the sides cut away to show the staggered and overlapping modules of the opposite detector half. The corrugated foils, hereafter referred to as *RF-foils*, form the inner faces of the boxes (*RF-boxes*) within which the modules are housed. They provide a number of functions which are discussed in the following sections.

2008 JINST 3 S08005

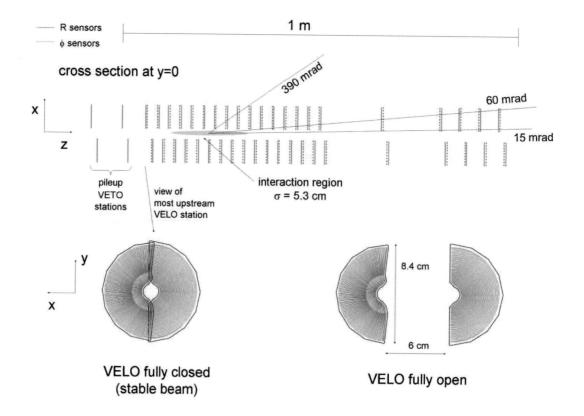

Figure 5.1: Cross section in the (x,z) plane of the VELO silicon sensors, at $y = 0$, with the detector in the fully closed position. The front face of the first modules is also illustrated in both the closed and open positions. The two pile-up veto stations are located upstream of the VELO sensors.

5.1.1 Requirements and constraints

The ability to reconstruct vertices is fundamental for the LHCb experiment. The track coordinates provided by the VELO are used to reconstruct production and decay vertices of beauty- and charm-hadrons, to provide an accurate measurement of their decay lifetimes and to measure the impact parameter of particles used to tag their flavour. Detached vertices play a vital role in the High Level Trigger (HLT, see section 7.2), and are used to enrich the b-hadron content of the data written to tape, as well as in the LHCb off-line analysis. The global performance requirements of the detector can be characterised with the following interrelated criteria:

- Signal to noise[1] ratio (S/N): in order to ensure efficient trigger performance, the VELO aimed for an initial signal to noise ratio of greater than 14 [29].

- Efficiency: the overall channel efficiency was required to be at least 99% for a signal to noise cut S/N> 5 (giving about 200 noise hits per event in the whole VELO detector).

---

[1] Signal S is defined as the most probable value of a cluster due to a minimum-ionizing particle and noise N as the RMS value of an individual channel.

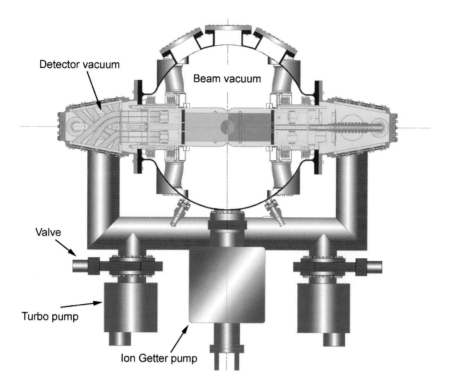

Figure 5.2: Cross section of the VELO vacuum vessel, with the detectors in the fully closed position. The routing of the signals via kapton cables to vacuum feedthroughs are illustrated. The separation between the beam and detector vacua is achieved with thin walled aluminium boxes enclosing each half.

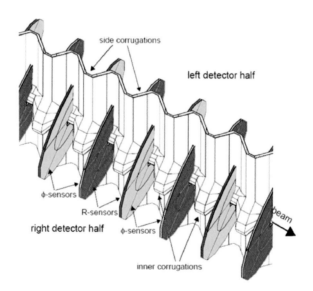

Figure 5.3: Zoom on the inside of an RF-foil, as modelled in GEANT, with the detector halves in the fully closed position. The edges of the box are cut away to show the overlap with the staggered opposing half. The R- and ϕ-sensors are illustrated with alternate shading.

- Resolution: a spatial cluster resolution of about 4 μm was aimed at for 100 mrad tracks in the smallest strip pitch region (about 40 μm), in order to achieve the impact parameter resolution performance described in section 10. Furthermore, it was required that the resolution not be degraded by irradiation nor by any aspect of the sensor design.

Another important consideration is the *spillover probability*, which is defined as the fraction of the peak signal remaining after 25 ns. An additional requirement imposed on the system, affecting the readout electronics, is that the spillover probability be less than 0.3, in order to keep the number of remnant hits at a level acceptable for the HLT [30].

The construction of the VELO followed a number of requirements and constraints, which are briefly described in this section.

Geometrical

The VELO has to cover the angular acceptance of the downstream detectors, i.e. detect particles with a pseudorapidity in the range[2] $1.6 < \eta < 4.9$ and emerging from primary vertices in the range $|z| < 10.6$ cm. The detector setup was further constrained by the following considerations:

- Polar angle coverage down to 15 mrad for a track emerging at $z=10.6$ cm downstream from the nominal interaction point (IP), together with the minimum distance of the sensitive area to the beam axis (8 mm, see below), and the requirement that a track should cross at least three VELO stations, defined the position z_{N-2} of the first of the three most downstream stations: $z_{N-2} \simeq 65$ cm.

- A track in the LHCb spectrometer angular acceptance of 300 mrad should cross at least three VELO stations. Given a maximum[3] outer radius of the sensors of about 42 mm, the distance between stations in the central region needed to be smaller than 5 cm. Requiring four stations to be traversed (or allowing for missing hits in one of four stations), imposed a module pitch of at most 3.5 cm. Dense packing of stations near the IP also reduces the average extrapolation distance from the first measured hit to the vertex.

- For covering the full azimuthal acceptance and for alignment issues, the two detector halves were required to overlap. This was achieved by shifting along z the positions of sensors in one half by 1.5 cm relative to sensors in the opposite half.

The use of cylindrical geometry ($r\phi$ coordinates), rather than a simpler rectilinear scheme, was chosen in order to enable fast reconstruction of tracks and vertices in the LHCb trigger. Indeed, simulations showed that 2D (rz) tracking allows a fast reconstruction in the HLT with sufficient impact parameter resolution to efficiently select events with b-hadrons. For this reason, an $r\phi$ geometry was selected for the design. Each VELO module was designed to provide the necessary 3D spatial information to reconstruct the tracks and vertices. One of the two sensors of the module, called the ϕ-measuring sensor, or ϕ-sensor, provides information on the azimuthal coordinate

---

[2]Some coverage of negative pseudorapidity is used to improve the primary vertex reconstruction and, using two special stations, to reduce the number of multiple-interaction events passing the Level-0 trigger (L0, see section 7.1).

[3]This allowed the use of 10 cm Si wafers for sensor production.

around the beam. The other sensor, called the *r*-measuring sensor, or R-sensor, provides information on the radial distance from the beam axis. The third coordinate is provided by knowledge of the position of each sensor plane within the experiment. The *rz* tracking requirement imposes the additional constraint that the VELO circular strips should be centered as perfectly as possible around the beam axis. The result of simulation studies showing how the trigger performance would degrade as a function of various VELO R-sensor misalignments [31] indicate that the R-sensors should be mounted with a mechanical accuracy of better than 20 μm in *x* and *y* relative to each other within each half, and the two halves should be aligned to better than 100 μm relative to each other in these coordinates. The number of strips for both sensor types needed to satisfy the competing requirements of the LHCb environment, physics and a budgetary limit, is about 180000 channels.

Environmental

The VELO detector will be operated in an extreme radiation environment with strongly non-uniform fluences. The damage to silicon in the most irradiated area for one nominal year of running, i.e. an accumulated luminosity of 2 fb^{-1}, is equivalent to that of 1 MeV neutrons with a flux of 1.3×10^{14} n$_{eq}$/cm^2, whereas the irradiation in the outer regions does not exceed a flux of 5×10^{12} n$_{eq}$/cm^2. The detector is required to sustain 3 years of nominal LHCb operation. In order to evacuate the heat generated in the sensor electronics (in vacuum) and to minimize radiation-induced effects, the VELO cooling system was required to be capable of maintaining the sensors at a temperature between -10 and 0°C with a heat dissipation of about 24 W per sensor and hybrid. To increase the sensor lifetime, continuous cooling after irradiation was also requested (with the aim to expose the irradiated sensors to room temperature for periods shorter than 1 week per year).

The sensor full depletion voltage is expected to increase with fluence. The ability to increase the operational bias voltage to ensure full depletion during the 3 years lifetime of the sensors was imposed as a further requirement.

Machine integration constraints

The required performance demands positioning of the sensitive area of the detectors as close as possible to the beams and with a minimum amount of material in the detector acceptance. This is best accomplished by operating the silicon sensors in vacuum. As a consequence, integration into the LHC machine became a central issue in the design of the VELO, imposing a number of special constraints which are briefly discussed here.

- The amount of material in front of the silicon detector is mainly determined by the necessity to shield against RF pickup and the mechanical constraint of building a sufficiently rigid foil. The detectors operate in a secondary vacuum and hence the foils are not required to withstand atmospheric pressure. However, the design of the vacuum system had to ensure that the pressure difference between detector and beam vacuum never be so large as to cause inelastic deformations of the detector box. The VELO surfaces exposed to beam-induced bombardment (secondary electrons, ions, synchrotron radiation) needed to be coated with suitable material in order to maintain beam-induced effects, such as electron multipacting and gas desorption, at acceptable levels for efficient LHC and LHCb operation. The LHC

2008 JINST 3 S08005

beam vacuum chamber, and therefore also the VELO vacuum vessel, were required to be bakeable (to 160°C in the case of the VELO).

- A short track extrapolation distance leads to a better impact parameter measurement. Therefore, the innermost radius of the sensors should be as small as possible. In practice, this is limited by the aperture required by the LHC machine. During physics running conditions, the RMS spread of the beams will be less than 100 μm, but for safety reasons, the closest approach allowed to the nominal beam axis is 5 mm. This value is dominated by the yet unknown closed-orbit variations of the LHC and could be reduced in an upgraded detector. To this must be added the thickness of the RF-foil, the clearance between the RF-foil and the sensors, and the design of about 1 mm of guard-ring structures on the silicon. Taking everything into account, the sensitive area can only start at a radius of about 8 mm.

- During injection, the aperture required by the LHC machine increases, necessitating retraction of the two detector halves by 3 cm, which brings the movable parts into the shadow of the LHCb beampipe (54 mm diameter). Furthermore, the repeatability of the beam positions could not be guaranteed, initially, to be better than a few mm. This imposed that the VELO detectors be mounted on a remote-controllable positioning system, allowing fine adjustment in the x and y directions.

- The need for shielding against RF pickup from the LHC beams, and the need to protect the LHC vacuum from outgassing of the detector modules, required a protection to be placed around the detector modules. This function is carried out by the RF-foils, which represent a major fraction of the VELO material budget in the LHCb acceptance. In addition, the beam bunches passing through the VELO structures will generate wake fields which can affect the LHC beams. The RF foils, together with wake field suppressors which provide the connection to the rest of the beampipe, also provide the function of suppressing wake fields by providing continuous conductive surfaces which guide the mirror charges from one end of the VELO vessel to the other. These issues have been addressed in detail [32] and are further discussed in section 5.1.3.

5.1.2 Sensors and modules

Sensors

The severe radiation environment at 8mm from the LHC beam axis required the adoption of a radiation tolerant technology. The choice was n-implants in n-bulk technology with strip isolation achieved through the use of a p-spray. The minimum pitch achievable[4] using this technology was approximately 32 μm, depending on the precise structure of the readout strips. For both the R and ϕ-sensors the minimum pitch is designed to be at the inner radius to optimize the vertex resolution.

The conceptual layout of the strips on the sensors is illustrated in figure 5.4. For the R-sensor the diode implants are concentric semi-circles with their centre at the nominal LHC beam position. In order to minimize the occupancy each strip is subdivided into four 45° regions. This also has the beneficial effect of reducing the strip capacitance. The minimum pitch at the innermost radius

---

[4]The company chosen to fabricate the LHCb sensors was Micron Semiconductor Ltd.

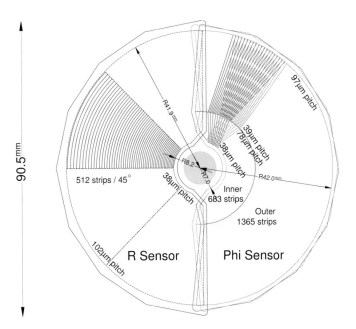

Figure 5.4: Sketch illustrating the $r\phi$ geometry of the VELO sensors. For clarity, only a portion of the strips are illustrated. In the ϕ-sensor, the strips on two adjacent modules are indicated, to highlight the stereo angle. The different arrangement of the bonding pads leads to the slightly larger radius of the R-sensor; the sensitive area is identical.

is 38 μm, increasing linearly to 101.6 μm at the outer radius of 41.9 mm. This ensures that measurements along the track contribute to the impact parameter precision with roughly equal weight.

The ϕ-sensor is designed to readout the orthogonal coordinate to the R-sensor. In the simplest possible design these strips would run radially from the inner to the outer radius and point at the nominal LHC beam position with the pitch increasing linearly with radius starting with a pitch of 35.5 μm. However, this would result in unacceptably high strip occupancies and too large a strip pitch at the outer edge of the sensor. Hence, the ϕ-sensor is subdivided into two regions, inner and outer. The outer region starts at a radius of 17.25 mm and its pitch is set to be roughly half (39.3 μm) that of the inner region (78.3 μm), which ends at the same radius. The design of the strips in the ϕ-sensor is complicated by the introduction of a skew to improve pattern recognition. At 8 mm from the beam the inner strips have an angle of approximately 20° to the radial whereas the outer strips make an angle of approximately 10° to the radial at 17 mm. The skew of inner and outer sections is reversed giving the strips a distinctive *dog-leg* design. The modules are placed so that adjacent ϕ-sensors have the opposite skew with respect to the each other. This ensures that adjacent stations are able to distinguish ghost hits from true hits through the use of a traditional stereo view. The principal characteristics of the VELO sensors are summarized in table 5.1.

The technology utilized in both the R- and ϕ-sensors is otherwise identical. Both sets of sensors are 300 μm thick. Readout of both R- and ϕ-sensors is at the outer radius and requires the use of a second layer of metal (a routing layer or *double metal*) isolated from the AC-coupled diode strips by approximately 3 μm of chemically vapour deposited (CVD) SiO_2. The second metal layer is connected to the first metal layer by wet etched *vias*. The strips are biased using

2008 JINST 3 S08005

Table 5.1: Principal characteristics of VELO sensors.

	R sensor	ϕ-sensor
number of sensors	42 + 4 (VETO)	42
readout channels per sensor	2048	2048
sensor thickness	300 μm	300 μm
smallest pitch	40 μm	38 μm
largest pitch	102 μm	97 μm
length of shortest strip	3.8 mm	5.9 mm
length of longest strip	33.8 mm	24.9 mm
inner radius of active area	8.2 mm	8.2 mm
outer radius of active area	42 mm	42 mm
angular coverage	182 deg	≈ 182 deg
stereo angle	-	10–20 deg
double metal layer	yes	yes
average occupancy	1.1%	1.1/0.7% inner/outer

polysilicon 1 MΩ resistors and both detectors are protected by an implanted guard ring structure.

The pitch as a function of the radius r in μm increases linearly and is given by the following expressions:

$$\mathrm{R-sensor}: \quad 40 + (101.6 - 40) \times \frac{r - 8190}{41949 - 8190}$$

$$\phi-\mathrm{sensor}: \quad 37.7 + (79.5 - 37.7) \times \frac{r - 8170}{17250 - 8170} \quad (r < 17250)$$

$$\phi-\mathrm{sensor}: \quad 39.8 + (96.9 - 39.8) \times \frac{r - 17250}{42000 - 17250} \quad (r > 17250)$$

The sensors were developed for high radiation tolerance. Early prototype detectors used p-stop isolation. This was later replaced by p-spray isolated detectors which showed much higher resistance to micro-discharges. The n$^+$n design was compared with an almost geometrically identical p$^+$n design and was shown to have much better radiation characteristics as measured by charge collection as a function of voltage.

Prototype sensors were also irradiated with non-uniform fluence in order to study the effects of cluster bias due to inhomogeneous irradiation. It was shown that the transverse electric fields produce less than 2 μm effects on the cluster centroid.

A subset of the production sensors were exposed to a high neutron fluence (1.3×10^{14} n$_{\mathrm{eq}}$/cm^2) representing 1 year of operation at nominal luminosity. A strong suppression of surface breakdown effects was demonstrated. The evolution of the depletion voltage was found to correspond to the expectation over LHC operation: with an integrated luminosity of 2 fb^{-1} per year, the maximum deliverable full depletion voltage (500 V) is reached after approximately 3 years. During production the possibility arose of manufacturing full size n$^+$p sensors. These are expected to have similar long term radiation resistance characteristics to the n$^+$n technology, but feature some advantages, principally in cost of manufacture due to the fact that double sided processing is not needed. One full size module was produced in this technology and installed in one of the most upstream slots. It is forseen to replace all the VELO modules after damage due to accumulated radiation or beam accidents. The replacement modules will be constructed in the n$^+$p technology [33].

2008 JINST 3 S08005

Modules

The module has three basic functions. Firstly it must hold the sensors in a fixed position relative to the module support. Secondly it provides and connects the electrical readout to the sensors. Finally it must enable thermal management of the modules which are operating in vacuum.

Each module is designed to hold the sensors in place to better than $50\,\mu$m in the plane perpendicular to the beam and within $800\,\mu$m along the direction of the beam. Sensor-to-sensor alignment (within a module) is designed to be better than $20\,\mu$m.

The module is comprised of a substrate, for thermal management and stability, onto which two circuits are laminated. This forms the hybrid. The substrate is fabricated *in-house* and is approximately $120\times170\times1$ mm. It has a core of $400\,\mu$m thick thermal pyrolytic graphite (TPG), and is encapsulated, on each side, with $250\,\mu$m of carbon fibre (CF). A CF frame of about 7 mm thickness surrounds the TPG and is bonded directly to the CF encapsulation to prevent delamination. The TPG is designed to carry a maximum load of 32 W away from the front-end chips. A semicircular hole is cut into the substrate under the region where the detectors are glued. Particular attention in the design and fabrication process is given to producing almost planar hybrids, to simplify the subsequent module production. Typical non-planarities of order $250\,\mu$m were achieved.

The circuits[5] were commercially hand populated to minimize exposure of the hybrid to high temperature and hence the possibility of delamination. The sensor front-end ASICs (Beetle 1.5 [34]) were then glued to the circuits. A total of 32 Beetle chips are used in each module. Kapton pitch adaptors,[6] were glued to the circuits in order to facilitate the wire bonding of the sensors to the Beetle chips. Sensors were glued to the double-sided hybrid with a sensor-to-sensor accuracy of better than $10\,\mu$m. The sensors were bonded to the electronics using a combination of H&K 710 and K&S 8090 bonding machines with $25\,\mu$m thick Al wire. After bonding and final testing 99.4% of all strips were operational, with no sensor having more than 30/2048 faulty channels.

The final mechanical mounting of the hybrid was to the module pedestal and base. The pedestal is a low mass CF fibre construction designed to hold the hybrid stably. It is a hollow rigid structure approximately $140\times150\times10$ mm. Holes are drilled where appropriate to reduce the possibility of outgassing. One end was glued to the hybrid and the other to a CF base which contains two precisely manufactured invar feet. The design of the base allows repeatable mounting of the module to the module support with a precision a better than $10\,\mu$m. The accuracy of the final assembled modules satisfied the design criteria. The complete module, in schematic and after final assembly, is illustrated in figure 5.5.

The thermal performance of the modules was required to be such that the silicon could be operated below zero degrees, for a minimum cooling liquid temperature of -30°C. The performance of each module was monitored individually in a vacuum tank during construction with a thermal camera, as illustrated in figure 5.6. After the final cooling connections had been made on the module bases, all modules were rechecked for their thermal performance in vacuum. The temperature difference between the cooling blocks and the silicon is estimated to be about (21.4 ± 1)°C for individually cooled modules, and an improvement of up to 2°C is expected when the modules are

---

[5]The circuits were fabricated and laminated to the substrates by Stevenage Circuits, Ltd.
[6]The pitch adapters were manufactured at CERN.

2008 JINST 3 S08005

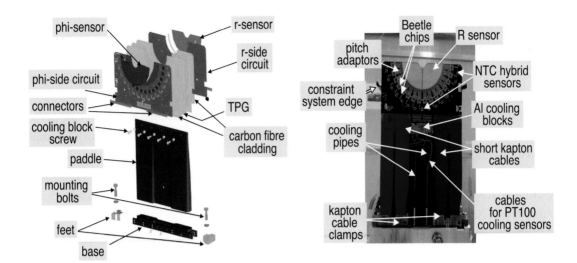

Figure 5.5: The left part of the figure illustrates the principal components of the VELO module. The right part of the figure is a photograph of the module as finally mounted. The short kapton cables are visible, along with the clamps at the base which prevent any long kapton cable movement coupling to the module itself. The aluminium blocks encasing the stainless steel CO_2 cooling tubes are also partially visible.

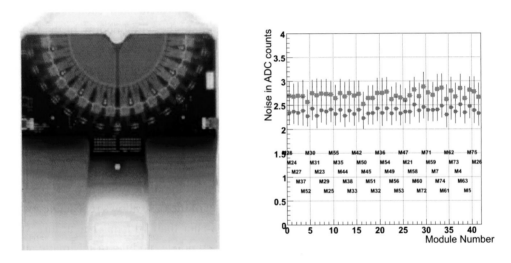

Figure 5.6: Quality control of the VELO modules. The left part of the figure shows an example of a thermograph which was routinely taken on both sides of the module during the construction. The right plot shows an example of a noise uniformity measurement for all the ϕ-sensors. The green squares are before common mode correction, and the red circles after the common mode correction. The error bars show the noise spread which is due to varying strip capacitances on the sensor.

cooled simultaneously. At the same time, the noise uniformity of the modules was checked, as shown in figure 5.6.

Each module was transported to CERN in a dedicated transport box [35] and submitted to a visual inspection with a high resolution microscope, including the survey of all bond wires, on

2008 JINST 3 S08005

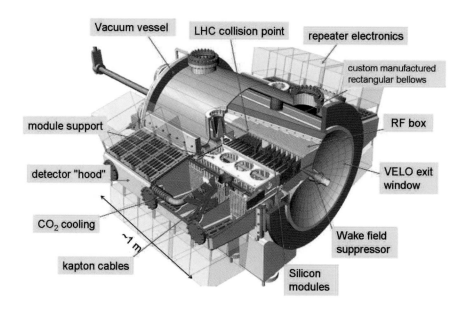

Figure 5.7: Overview of the VELO vacuum vessel.

reception. After this it underwent a 16 hour burn-in [36] consisting of a sequence of powering, cooling and data taking cycles, in vacuum. This was designed to uncover any inherent weaknesses introduced to the modules during manufacturing. Of all the modules transported, one was finally taken as a reserve as a result of the burn-in procedure, and a second was rejected after assembly due to a slightly worse thermal performance.

5.1.3 Mechanics

Introduction

The ultra high vacuum requirements of the LHC ring, the necessity for wake field suppression, the need to shield the detectors from electromagnetic effects induced by the high frequency beam structure, and the necessity to retract the detectors by 30 mm from the interaction region during injection of a new LHC fill, make the VELO mechanical design demanding. To meet all these constraints, a design with two detector halves was chosen, each placed inside a thin-walled aluminum box, as introduced in the previous sections. Aluminum was chosen since it has a relatively low Z (resulting in a small radiation length), good electrical conductivity, and can be machined quite easily. The side walls of these boxes are 0.5 mm thick. In order to allow for overlap in the two detector halves, the top surfaces of these vacuum boxes have a corrugated shape and are made from 0.3 mm thick AlMg3 foil (an aluminum alloy with 3% magnesium). The two detector boxes are placed in a 1.4 m long vacuum vessel with a diameter of 1.1 m. The whole assembly is shown in figure 5.7. Two rectangular bellows allow for the movement of the detector boxes inside the vacuum system. Each detector support is connected via three spheres on holders placed within circular bellows to

2008 JINST 3 S08005

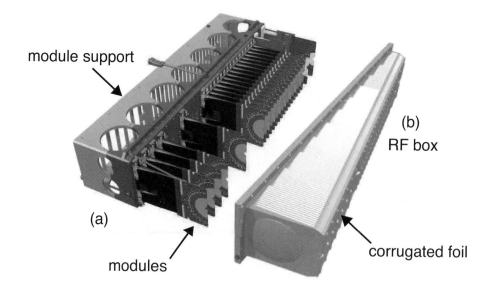

module support

(b)
RF box

(a)

corrugated foil

modules

Figure 5.8: Exploded view of the module support and the modules (a), and the RF box (b). The corrugated foil on the front face of the box, which forms a beam passage can be seen. Its form allows the two halves to overlap when in the closed position.

the movement mechanism that is located outside the vacuum vessel. The module support, illustrated in figure 5.8, is mounted on bearings which lie in precisely machined slots inside the detector support and is bolted into position against three precision surfaces. The positioning of the modules on the module support is fully constrained with a combination of a slot and a dowel pin. The positioning of the modules relative to one another is determined by the precision of the machining of the module support. The positioning of the two halves relative to each other is determined by the precision of the module support, together with its positioning inside the detector support, which is adjustable. To suppress wake field effects, the dimension of the beampipe as seen by the proton beams has to vary very gradually. To match the beampipe upstream and downstream from the VELO, wake field suppressors made of $50\,\mu$m thick copper-beryllium have been constructed, so a good electrical match is provided in both the open and closed positions.

The durability of the wake field suppressors has been tested by performing an opening and closing movement 30,000 times, after which no damage was observed. A photograph of the downstream wake field suppressors is shown in figure 5.9. The exit foil of the vessel consists of a 2 mm thick aluminum window (see section 3).

Movement system

Before the LHC ring is filled, the detectors have to move away from the interaction region by 30 mm in order to allow for beam excursions during injection and ramping. After stable beam conditions have been obtained, the detectors should be placed into an optimized position centered in x and y around the interaction region. This position is not exactly known beforehand; it may vary over ± 5 mm in both x and y, even from fill to fill. Therefore, a procedure has been developed to determine the beam position with the detectors not completely moved in, and then move to

2008 JINST 3 S08005

Figure 5.9: Photograph of the downstream wakefield suppressor.

the optimal position. This is performed with a motion mechanism that can bring the detectors to their position with an accuracy of the order of $10\,\mu$m by means of a stepping motor with resolver readout. Additional potentiometers have been used to verify independently the proper functioning. The motion procedures are controlled by a Programmable Logic Controller (PLC). The boxes can move together in y and independently in x, and a series of stops prevents mechanical interference.

Vacuum system

In the LHC ring, Ultra High Vacuum conditions of better than 10^{-8} mbar are required, compatible with reduced beam-induced effects. To maintain these conditions, the beampipes are equipped with a Non-Evaporable Getter (NEG) layer. To maintain the low desorption yield of the NEG coating, the vacuum system will be vented during maintenance with ultra-pure neon. The thin walled detector boxes are expected to plastically deform at a pressure difference of 20 mbar (and to rupture above 50 mbar). Therefore, the detectors also have to be operated under vacuum. Due to outgassing of detectors, hybrids, cables and connectors, a vacuum around 10^{-4} mbar is expected. Hence a good separation between the beam and detector vacuum is necessary as exposure to the detector vacuum would saturate and contaminate the NEG material on the inside of the beampipe.

A procedure has been implemented to make sure that during venting and evacuation of the VELO vacuum system the pressure difference between beam and detector vacuum will never exceed 5 mbar overpressure in the detector vacuum and 2 mbar overpressure in the beam vacuum. This asymmetry is designed to maximise the protection of the modules. This is achieved by using dedicated valves and restrictions, that are activated by membrane switches that react at the desired pressure difference. The complete vacuum system between the two sector valves around LHCb is controlled by a PLC.

2008 JINST 3 S08005

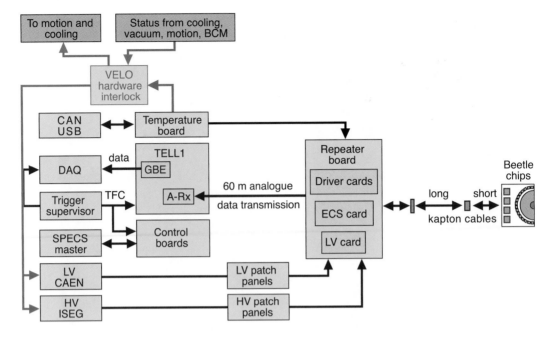

Figure 5.10: VELO readout chain for one side of one module.

Cooling system

Since the detectors and read-out electronics are operated inside the vacuum system, active cooling is required. Furthermore, in order to limit the effects of radiation damage of the silicon sensors, the irradiated sensors should be operated and kept at temperatures below -5°C at all times. The radiation hard refrigerant in the system is two-phase CO_2 cooled by a conventional freon cooler. The liquid CO_2 is transported via a 60 m long transfer line to the VELO, where it is distributed over 27 capillaries per detector half. Each capillary is thermally connected to five cooling blocks that are attached to each detector module. A redundant pumping system is incorporated, so that also during maintenance periods cooling capacity is available. The complete cooling system is controlled by a PLC.

5.1.4 Electronics chain

The electronics layout is summarised in figure 5.10, which shows the readout chain for one side of one module. The individual components are discussed in this section.

Beetle chip

The VELO uses the Beetle, a custom designed radiation hard ASIC based on 0.12 µm CMOS technology[7] with an analog front-end, as the FE chip [34]. The chip was designed with a peaking time and sampling frequency to match the LHC bunch crossing rate of 40 MHz, and to be able to readout at a speed which can match the L0 accept rate of 1 MHz. For a full discussion of the design requirements see [28, 37]. Each of the 128 channels consists of a charge sensitive

---

[7]IBM, USA.

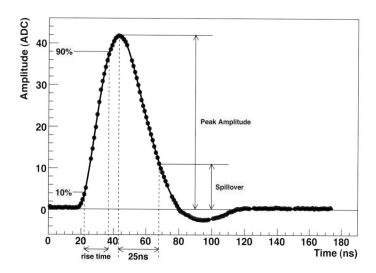

Figure 5.11: Beetle pulse shape as measured for a VELO sensor using test-pulses.

preamplifier/shaper and an analog pipeline of 160 stages designed to match the L0 4 μs latency. The data are brought off chip at a clock frequency of 40 MHz, with 32 channels multiplexed on each of 4 output lines. This allows the readout of one event to be achieved in 900 ns. The chip specifications required a survival more than 5 years of nominal operation at a dose of 2 MRad per year. In fact the chip is radiation hard against total dose effects of more than 100 MRad. Robustness against single event upset is achieved with redundant logic. It is programmable via a standard I2C interface, which controls the bias settings and various other parameters. The circuit can be tested via a charge injector (test-pulse circuit) with adjustable pulse height. In the case of the pile-up readout, where the data are used in the L0 trigger, a fast binary signal is required. This is achieved by routing the output of the front-end amplifier to a comparator stage with extra output pads on the chip.

For the VELO, the spillover value, or the remnant signal remaining after 25 ns, is of particular importance, and must be below 0.3 of its peak value for reliable HLT performance. Figure 5.11 shows the measured pulse shape on a Beetle fully mounted on a VELO module and bonded to the sensor, using a test-pulse corresponding to a minimum ionising particle in 300 μm of silicon, for the bias settings expected for LHCb operation. The rise time is measured to be 14.7 ± 0.5 ns and the spillover $(26.0 \pm 0.6)\%$. For more details on the measurement see [38].

Kapton cables

During injection of the proton beams in the ring, the detectors have to be retracted by 30 mm. The total number of data and control signals that run between the hybrids and the feed-through flanges at the vessel exceeds 18000. Kapton cables were chosen as they are thin, flexible and radiation hard. The central part of the cable consists of a 17 μm thick copper layer with 150 μm wide strips. This layer is covered on each side with a 100 μm thick kapton foil, a 17 μm thick rolled annealed (RA) copper foil which is used to supply power to the Beetle chips, and a 25 μm thick cover kapton foil.

Each cable consists of two parts: a short tail from the hybrid to a fixed connector, and a long cable from this connector to the vacuum feed through on the vessel.

2008 JINST 3 S08005

Repeater boards

The repeater board (RPT) is located directly outside of the VELO tank inside repeater crates. The RPT function is mainly a repeater for the differential signals arriving at the board, including data signals, Time and Fast Control (TFC, see section 8.3) and FE chips configuration signals. Also, monitoring signals are sent out via the board to the detector slow control system. The RPT carries the voltage regulators required by the FE and the L0 electronics service system. For flexibility in design and mainly for maintenance, the RPT is built as a motherboard hosting several mezzanine cards:

- Four Driver Cards: four driver cards are mounted in the RPT board as mezzanine cards. Each card contains 16 fully differential analog drivers. Because the data streams are sent to the digitizer card via a 60 m individual shielded twisted-pair cable, the drivers include a line equalizer to compensate distortions introduced by the cable.

- One LV card: the low voltage card provides the power for the FE hybrid, the analog driver cards and the ECS card (c.f. 8.4). Eight radiation hard voltage regulators are mounted on the board. Each voltage is monitored through an amplifier. The card is supplied by three power supplies located at 60 m cable distance. Sense-lines are used to compensate the voltage drop through the long supply cable.

- One ECS card: the ECS repeats the signals for the I2C configuration bus and controls and monitors the LV regulators. The applied voltage and the current limit signals are multiplexed and sent on differential lines. The ECS card communicates with the control boards located in intermediate crates 15 m away from the VELO.

Another part implemented on the board is the TFC functionality. These fast LVDS signals are signals required by the FE chips and are sent through a LVDS repeater mounted on the board. The boards and their components underwent radiation tests to confirm that they could tolerate more than ten times the expected level of 73 kRad during 10 years of operation [39].

Control board

The control board [40] is the heart of the control system of the L0 electronics. The timing signals and fast commands from the Readout Supervisor are distributed to the L0 electronics via the control board. Moreover the configuration data is received by the SPECS slave [41] on the control board and distributed to the configurable components via I2C. The monitored voltages are digitized on the control board and the values are propagated to the ECS system via the SPECS bus. Each control board supports six VELO electronics hybrids or two PU electronics hybrids and four PU optical boards.

Temperature board

The temperatures of the electronics hybrids and voltage regulators are monitored by the temperature boards. The temperature boards also generate signals to the VELO interlock board, which is the last safety mechanism in case of failure (see below). Each temperature board hosts one ELMB (Embedded Local Monitoring Board [9]) and four Interlock Boxes (IBox [42]) , which together serve 16 repeater boards. The ELMB has an embedded Atmel ATMega128 processor and communicates with the supervisory system via a CAN bus. It has digital I/O ports, 64 16-bit ADC channels and a voltage reference circuit. This provides a stand-alone system for temperature monitoring read out via a CAN bus. The IBox supplies a voltage across the NTC resistor and a precision resistor in series. The voltage drop across the NTC resistor is compared to a reference on the IBox and two bits per temperature channel are generated signalling the states *OK*, *too warm*, *too cold* or *error*. The ELMB is in this configuration connected in parallel with the IBox, passively monitoring the voltage drop and hence the temperature. The interlock states of the 64 temperature sensors are read out by one temperature board and combined into a common interlock state of the board. This interlock matrix is implemented in an FPGA and provides the facility to monitor the interlock status and mask faulty channels.

VELO specific TELL1 features

The TELL1 boards of LHCb are described in section 8.2. Specific to the VELO is the digitization of the data on the TELL1 and the complex pre-processing of the data.

Due to the high radiation levels and space constraints, the digitization of the data and the use of optical drivers close to the detector were discarded as solutions for the VELO. As a consequence, the analog data are directly transmitted to the TELL1 board and digitized on *plug-in* cards. Each TELL1 board deals with the data from one sensor, i.e. 64 analog links, and features 4 A-Rx cards. One A-Rx card provides 16 channels of 10-bit ADC's to sample the analog data from 4 Beetle chips at 40 MHz. In order to compensate for the time skew of the signals resulting from different cable lengths the sampling time can be chosen by phase adjustable programmable clocks, individually for each ADC channel.

After digitization, the TELL1 performs data processing in the ppFPGAs (pre-processing FPGAs, of which there are four per TELL1) before sending the zero-suppressed data to the trigger farm [43]. The first stages are implemented in 10-bits and the precision is then reduced to 8 bits. The steps in this data processing include pedestal subtraction, cross-talk removal, channel re-ordering, common mode suppression, and clustering. Pedestal subtraction is implemented with a running average pedestal following algorithm available, if required, to calculate the value for each channel. Although most of the signal distortion in the long data cable is removed already through frequency compensation, a Finite Impulse Response Filter is used to correct for cross-talk and further improve the system performance. In both the R- and the ϕ-sensors, adjacent physical strips are scrambled in the readout chain. For the clustering it is essential to bring them back into order by implementing a channel reordering step. Common mode suppression algorithms may be performed in both the readout chip channel ordering and in the physical strip ordering. This allows correlated noise pickup or other baseline level shifts on the sensors or in the front-end chips and readout chain to be corrected. A mean common mode algorithm that corrects for a constant shift and a linear common mode algorithm that corrects for both a constant and a slope are implemented over appropriate groupings of channels. The last processing step is the clustering [44]. Strips are selected as seeding strips if the signal passes a certain seeding threshold. Strips next to the seeding strips are included in the cluster if their signals are above the inclusion threshold cut. A cluster can be formed by a maximum of four strips. The cluster centre is calculated with a 3-bit precision.

2008 JINST 3 S08005

The VELO raw data are sent in a format that allows a fast access of the cluster information by the trigger by sending the calculated 14-bit cluster position. For more refined calculations of the cluster centre and offline analyses, the ADC information of all strips is added in another data block [45].

The VELO hardware interlock system

The VELO is protected with a simple and failsafe hardware interlock system. An overview of its functionality is given in [46]. Switching on the low voltage when the VELO is not properly cooled is for instance prevented by this system. The status of the cooling, vacuum, motion and detector front-end systems and the BCM (cf. section 3) are combined in an interlock logic unit and fed back to high and low voltage systems and to the motion and cooling system. The interlock unit is based on a FPGA to provide flexibility and possible future interfacing to PVSS (see section 8.4) for monitoring. All input signals are continuously monitored and their status shown on the front panel LED's. The inputs are fail safe such that any disconnection or power loss will result in a bad status and the interlocks will fire. Any of the inputs may additionally be forced to a good status by internal switches for debugging or override purposes, and this is also indicated on the front panel. The interlock outputs are also fail safe such that cable removal or power failure will result in module power and cooling being removed. The status of the outputs is shown on the front panel and all individual outputs can be overidden by internal switches. Hardware signals are also exchanged between motion, cooling and vacuum PLCs to prevent, for example, cooling when there is no vacuum. As the VELO cannot be allowed to move in while the LHC beam is not stable, beam inhibit and beam status signals are exchanged with the BCM and the LHC beam interlock system [20]. Direct signals from the LHC sector valves and the neon injection system are given to the VELO vacuum system to prevent venting, evacuating or neon injection when one of these systems is not ready.

LV system

The VELO and pile-up low voltage system is based on a multi-channel power supply system.[8] All the power supplies are installed in the detector counting house. Each module has 12 fully floating channels and can supply 4 repeater boards. Each channel has its own voltage sense-line to permit a correction to be made for any voltage drop over the long distance cable. Each repeater board requires three voltages which are supplied over shielded twisted-pairs. The LV power supplies interface to the hardware interlock system.

HV system

The silicon sensors will be operated under a reverse bias ranging from 100–500 V, with the operating voltage being increased as the sensors undergo radiation damage. The biasing scheme ties the n^+ strips to ground, and applies a negative voltage to the backplane. The high voltage system utilises 6 power supply modules,[9] each controlling up to 16 sensors, which are housed in an

---

[8]Manufactured by CAEN.
[9]Manufactured by ISEG Spezialelektronik GmbH.

2008 JINST 3 S08005

uninterruptible power supply crate in the detector counting house. The output is fed via 37-core cables to a patch panel in the counting house. Long 56-core cables connect the counting house to a second patch panel located near the detector. Three-core cables then provide the high voltage, high voltage guard and ground to the repeater board of each module. The high voltage guard connection provides the voltage to a guard trace on the sensor hybrids, which surrounds the detector high voltage trace, thus reducing possibilities of shorting. The high voltage guard line can be connected to the high voltage or left floating by adjustment of jumper switches in the counting house patch panel. The high voltage system is controlled through PVSS. Voltage and current limits are also set in hardware on the power supply units. The high voltage power supplies interface to the hardware interlock system.

Grounding and power supply

The power distribution and grounding scheme partitioning of the VELO and the pile-up electronics follows the detector topology. Each silicon detector with its hybrid forms a group. The number of groups connected to the same power distribution connection is k ept to a minimum. There are in total 84 VELO and 4 pile-up hybrids with 16 FE chips each installed inside the tank. The tank is the central part of the system and is connected to the LHC machine. The LHC machine earth cables form part of the cavern network grounding. All metallic devices, such as electrical cabinets and cable trays, have ground connection to the main VELO tank support. All electrical devices forming part of the cooling and vacuum system must be grounded for safety reasons. All components connected to the main power network line are equipped with protection circuits and electrically floating devices made of conductive material are not permitted.

The analog FE electronics is potentially prone to pickup from external noise sources. The effects are minimised by keeping the signal current path as short as practicable. The reference voltage of the charge preamplifier in the FE chip is internally connected to the ground pins of the chip. The current loop for the signal generated in the sensor is closed through the sensor bias line. The bias line is AC-connected to the reference ground of the FE chip. The silicon detectors and hybrids are located close to the detector RF shield, which is connected to the ground. Potential differences between these two components give rise to the main source of noise in the detector. This is minimised by keeping the hybrid ground plane at the same potential as the RF shield. Each hybrid ground plane is tied to the module support with a silver-plated copper grounding strap.

5.1.5 Material budget

The material budget was investigated in the simulation by generating straight tracks originating from the interaction point and extrapolating them through the VELO. The radiation length seen by the track was calculated for each volume it crossed in the geometry description. The average radiation length is shown as a function of the azimuthal angle ϕ and the pseudorapidity η, with $1.6 < \eta < 4.9$ in figure 5.12. The contribution of the major components is also shown. The average radiation length of the VELO is 17.5% of a radiation length with the largest contribution coming from the RF-foil.

2008 JINST 3 S08005

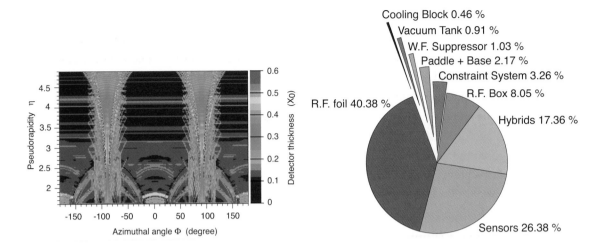

Figure 5.12: The average radiation length seen by particles passing through the VELO as a function of azimuthal angle, ϕ, and pseudorapidity, η, with $1.6 < \eta < 4.9$. For a uniform sampling over these coordinates the average contribution to the radiation length is 0.175 X_0.

5.1.6 Test Beam detector commissioning

Test Beam studies of two different configurations of fully instrumented VELO modules were carried out at the CERN H8 experimental area, using 180 GeV π beams with tuneable intensity and spot size. An external trigger was provided by a scintillator telescope that could be configured to select events including single tracks crossing the detectors without interactions, multiple track events produced by interaction in the detectors or on the entrance window of their enclosure, and, in the second data taking cycle, interactions in target modules installed in the module array. A total of 4 target planes, mounted in two modules were used. Each plane included a small Cu disk, with a thickness of 300 μm and a 2 mm diameter, centered on the beam axis, as well as 5 mm diameter Cu disks with a radial displacement of 15 mm from the beam axis. The latter targets had the purpose of investigating the vertex reconstruction capabilities of the detector in the retracted position (*open VELO*).

The first configuration included 3 fully instrumented half-disk pre-production modules built using 200 μm sensors, enclosed in a box providing accurate positioning on a table including a rotating stage that allowed data taking with the detectors oriented at an angle with respect to the beam direction. Thus the detectors were operated in air, at a typical temperature of 40–50°C. Only 1/4 of the electronics was read out, due to limitations in the available hardware. This data set provided considerable insight into the performance of the final detector modules. Figure 5.13 shows that the measured cluster multiplicity as a function of the strip number is in good agreement with the expectations based on a dedicated MonteCarlo simulation [47]. Based on Monte-Carlo simulation and the performance of the electronics a resolution of about 6 μm can be achieved at the inner radius of the sensors. This optimal resolution will be obtained by utilizing a non-linear charge-sharing algorithm that depends on the incident angle of the tracks (for the R-sensor) and the irradiation level of the sensors. All the parameters affecting the performance of the sensors and the readout electronics were explored, for example data was taken with the sensors biased with different high

2008 JINST 3 S08005

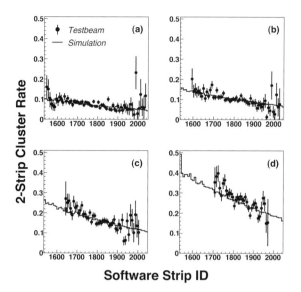

Figure 5.13: Fraction of two strip clusters in R-sensors, for different beam track angles with respect to the normal to the detector planes: a) 0°, b) 5°, c) 10° d) 15°. The horizontal axis represents the strip number, corresponding to a progressively coarser inter-strip pitch.

voltages, and the operating parameters of the Beetle chip were changed. In addition, the noise performance was studied both with random triggers, and with electronic calibration runs. These data validate in a multi-detector configuration the laboratory characterization of the individual module components. The data acquisition and monitoring infrastructure planned for the experiment were used. The system performance was excellent.

The second data set was taken using a system of 10 production modules including $300\,\mu$m thick sensors, mounted in the vacuum tank built for the final system, reading out 6 of them in different combinations, depending upon the trigger scheme chosen. Most of the data was taken in vacuum (below 10^{-3} mbar) and at a temperature of about -3°C. This test beam cycle provided valuable operating experience with the cooling system built for the experiment and with vacuum implementation and monitoring. Data were taken in air at room temperature, and it was confirmed that the module positions remained stable through the transition between air and vacuum and throughout temperature cycling.

The production detectors operated with a signal to noise ratio of between 17 and 25, depending on strip length, where signal is defined as the most probable value of the charge cluster produced by a minimum ionizing particle (MIP) and noise is the incoherent noise measured from calibration data after subtracting the coherent noise component. Their performance proved to be remarkably stable throughout the 14 days of data taking. Single track and interaction trigger data complement the first data set in assessing the hit resolution as a function of angle. In addition, target data produced reconstructed primary vertices from all the targets that help in tuning the vertex reconstruction algorithms.

2008 JINST 3 S08005

5.1.7 VELO software

Reconstruction software

The TELL1 data processing boards (see sections 5.1.4 and 8.2) perform a set of processing algorithms on the raw VELO data and identify clusters for use in the trigger and for off-line physics analysis. For use in the trigger the clusters are stored in a compressed form that is optimised for speed and provides 3-bit precision on the inter-strip position of the clusters using a simple weighted pulse height algorithm. For offline use a higher precision calculation, and an estimate of the uncertainty on this position, is provided [48]. This calculation uses the inter-strip pitch and track angle as well as the pulse-height of the strips in the cluster.

In addition to the standard output data format of the TELL1, a number of other output formats are provided for calibration and monitoring purposes and are decoded in the software framework. Notably, these include a non zero-suppressed raw data format, where the ADC values (at 8-bit precision) are provided for all strips.

A bit-perfect emulation of the full TELL1 processing algorithm is available in the software framework. Using the emulation the raw data can be processed to produce the cluster format. The performance of the TELL1 algorithms can thus be assessed at each stage of the processing. The emulation is also used to tune the optimal settings of the adjustable parameters in the TELL1, such as the signal thresholds used in the clustering algorithm.

A simulation framework for the VELO has been provided. This framework describes the material and layout of the VELO detector. The response of the silicon detectors and front-end chip pulse shape to the passage of particles is described, based on physically motivated parametrisations tuned to describe laboratory and test beam data. The resulting simulated analog signals are passed through the emulated TELL1 clustering algorithm and the output clusters are stored in the same format as for the real data [49].

Monitoring

The VELO data monitoring can be divided into two strands: the short term operational checks performed on-line; and the longer-term off-line performance monitoring.

The on-line monitoring is performed using the LHCb monitoring farm. Cluster and track monitoring, including monitoring of residuals for the alignment, is performed using the standard output data. Raw data is also produced for a subset of events at a rate of a fraction of a Hz and, through use of a special calibration trigger, read out to the monitoring farm. This rate allows the performance of individual channels to be accurately assessed on a timescale of one hour. The full information of the TELL1 processing boards is available through monitoring using the TELL1 credit-card PC. Preliminary tests of the on-line monitoring have already been performed in the VELO test beam.

A critical element of the monitoring is the determination of the beam-position. The alignment framework, reconstruction, pattern recognition, track fitting and vertex-finding algorithms are used to build up a 3 dimensional picture of the beam position. This monitoring process is used to determine the correct step-wise movements that are required to close the two halves and centre

2008 JINST 3 S08005

them around the beam at the start of an LHC fill. The beam stability is then monitored during LHC operation.

The off-line monitoring uses a range of analyses to assess the performance and to tune operational parameters including the high voltage applied to each sensor, the TELL1 hit processing parameters, and the cluster resolution model used in the tracking. The analyses include: time alignment studies for beam synchronisation; charge collection efficiency and signal-to-noise studies; resolution studies as a function of detector pitch and projected angle; cross-coupling, pedestal, noise and common-mode noise studies making particular use of the TELL1 emulation. These studies use the full range of VELO TELL1 output formats for the data and also make use of special calibration trigger and test-pulses generated in the Beetle front-end chip of the VELO modules.

Alignment

The alignment of the VELO relies on three components: the precision construction and assembly of the hardware; the metrology of the individual modules and assembled system; and the software alignment of the system using tracks.

The construction and assembly of the system is reported elsewhere in this section. The construction precision has tight mechanical tolerances, for example the silicon sensors are nominally located only 1 mm from the the aluminium RF foil. However, the driving factor for the required construction tolerance is the successful operation of the LHCb trigger. The VELO pattern recognition algorithm, used to identify high impact parameter tracks in the trigger, is performed for speed reasons initially in the rz projection. This requires that the strips on the R-sensors accurately describe circles around the beam position.

A survey of the individual modules and of the assembled halves on the module supports was performed. The relative positions of the modules and of the R- and ϕ-sensors on a single module were measured to a precison of better than 10 μm. The silicon sensors were found to have no significant curvature: 8 points were measured on the surface of the silicon sensors and the mean RMS deviation of the sensors from a plane was found to be 14 μm. The deviations of the modules from their nominal positions are shown in figure 5.14 for the two detector halves (A and C sides). The scatters give an impression of the total assembly precision. In the x coordinate the scatter is very small, and the overall offsets are fully compensated by the fact that the two halves move independently in x. In y there is a small slope seen in the C-side results, which was traced to the fact that the module support was not perfectly flat, but had a 40 μm corkscrew twist between the corners. The resulting slope was fully compensated by adjustments of the detector supports during the installation of the halves.

The precision survey is an important element of the alignment: not only does it provide the starting position for the VELO software alignment but it also constrains degrees of freedom of the system which will not be possible to accurately measure with data. For example, the overall z positions of the sensors are obtained from the metrology. The sensor alignment parameters obtained from the survey were propagated to the LHCb conditions database.

Whilst the survey was performed at room temperature and pressure, no significant deviations are expected for the final system. The module support will be maintained at a constant temperature of 20°C. The deviations of the system under vacuum have been determined from the software

2008 JINST 3 S08005

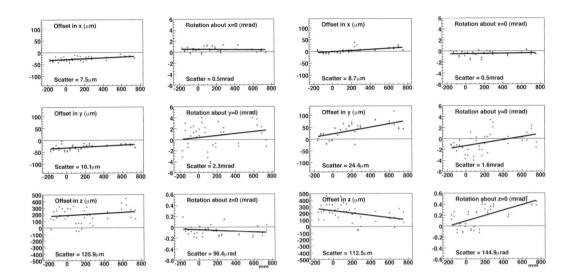

Figure 5.14: Results of the metrology of the fully mounted VELO halves vs z. The deviations from nominal are shown for every sensor. The six plots on the left show the result for the A side, and on the right for the C side. The rz tracking is sensitive to scatters and offsets in the x coordinate (between modules) and y coordinate (between modules, and between the detector halves).

alignment in a test beam using a partially assembled VELO and seen to be typically 10 μm or less, as shown in figure 5.15.

As previously stated, prior to the LHC establishing stable beams, the VELO is in a retracted position and is brought into its nominal position only after stable beam is established. The position of the two halves will be known through the motion control and position measurement system to an accuracy of 10 μm. Combining this information with the relative alignment of the modules obtained from the previous fill is expected to provide sufficient alignment accuracy for operation of the VELO trigger. However, the option to perform a software alignment at the start of each fill remains, should this prove necessary.

The software alignment procedure for the detector divides into four distinct parts:

- An alignment of the relative position of the R and Φ sensors on each module using the shape of the residual distributions across the sensors.

- An alignment of the modules within each VELO-half box using the residuals of hits on reconstructed tracks.

- A relative alignment of the two half-boxes with respect to each other principally relying on using tracks passing through the geometrical overlap between the modules in the two half-boxes.

- A global alignment of all sub-detectors relative to each other. This part is reviewed in [50].

2008 JINST 3 S08005

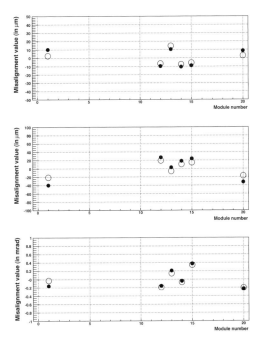

Figure 5.15: *x*-axis translation alignment constants of the VELO modules determined by software alignment from data recorded during the VELO test beam in air (open circles) and in vacuum (solid points). The modules are seen to be stable in the different conditions, including different thermal gradients across the modules.

Relative sensor alignment

The R- and ϕ-sensors bonded in an individual module have had their relative positions measured during the system metrology. To further improve and monitor their relative misalignment a method has been developed that exploits distortions observed in the residuals across the sensor. It can be shown that the relation between residuals ($\varepsilon_{R/\Phi}$) and misalignments in the sensor plane ($\Delta_x, \Delta_y, \Delta_\gamma$) is given by

$$\begin{cases} \varepsilon_R = -\Delta_x \cos\phi_{track} \quad +\Delta_y \sin\phi_{track} & \text{(R sensor)} \\ \varepsilon_\Phi = +\Delta_x \sin\phi_{track} \quad +\Delta_y \cos\phi_{track} \quad +\Delta_\gamma r_{track} & \text{(}\Phi\text{ sensor)} \end{cases}, \quad (5.1)$$

where r_{track} and ϕ_{track} are the radius and the azimuthal angle of the extrapolated track position, respectively. The misalignments Δ_x, Δ_y are determined by a fit to the shape of the residual distribution as a function of the azimuthal angle, while Δ_γ, the rotation misalignment around the *z*-axis, is determined by a fit to the shape of the residual distribution as a function of the radius. The optimal alignment can be found after three iterations of this procedure, using the previously determined alignment constants as input to the next iteration.

The method has been tested using MonteCarlo simulations and VELO test beam data. It has been shown that an alignment precision at the μm level can be achieved for Δ_x and Δ_y, while Δ_γ will be determined to higher precision by the module alignment algorithm.

2008 JINST 3 S08005

Module alignment and VELO half alignment

The module alignment and the VELO half alignment are dependent on the same approach, a non-iterative method using matrix inversion. The alignment is based upon a χ^2 function produced from the residuals between the tracks and the measured clusters. The track and alignment parameters can be obtained through minimisation of this χ^2 function.

The equations which describe the trajectories of particles are expressed as a linear combination of both the local (track-dependent) parameters and the global (alignment) parameters. All tracks are correlated since the global alignment parameters are common to each track, hence it is necessary to fit all tracks simultaneously.

The χ^2 function can be minimised by solving the set of simultaneous equations given by the derivatives of the χ^2 with respect to the local track parameters and global alignment parameters. This results in a system of equations of a final size, n_{total} given by:

$$n_{total} = n_{local} \times n_{tracks} + n_{global} \tag{5.2}$$

where n_{local} is the number of local parameters per track (four parameters for a straight line in 3D) , n_{tracks} is the number of tracks used for the alignment and n_{global} is the number of alignment constants. Whilst the direct inversion of such large matrices is not computationally practical, the alignment can be handled by inverting the matrix by partition, thus reducing the problem to a $n_{global} \times n_{global}$ matrix inversion. Inversion by partitioning is handled by the Millepede program [51].

The number of tracks required for an effective alignment is relatively modest but the alignment is improved by using a mixture of tracks from primary vertex interactions and a complementary track set from a source such as beam-halo particles. The relative alignment of the two half-boxes is primarily constrained by tracks that pass through both halves. However, when the VELO is retracted an alternative technique is required which relies upon fitting primary vertices using tracks fitted in both halves of the VELO. The CPU requirements of the alignment are also low: of order minutes on a single PC.

Tests using data from the VELO test beam and on MonteCarlo simulation have demonstrated that x and y-axis translations of the modules can be constrained at the few μm level and rotations around the z axis of order 0.1 mrad, with weaker sensitivity obtained to the other degrees of freedom. MonteCarlo simulation tests have demonstrated that x and y translations of the half-boxes can be constrained at better than 20 μm and rotations around these axes to better than 0.1 mrad. Rotations around the z-axis are constrained at the 0.2 mrad level.

5.1.8 VELO performance

The VELO layout has been optimised to minimise the amount of material in the acceptance while providing good geometrical coverage. All tracks inside the LHCb acceptance ($1.6 < \eta < 4.9$) pass through at least three modules, as shown in figure 5.16.

The individual hit resolution of the sensors has been determined in a test beam and is a strong function of the sensor pitch and projected angle (the angle perpendicular to the strip direction), as shown in figure 5.17. The best raw resolution obtained is 7 μm. As shown in figure 5.18 perfor-

2008 JINST 3 S08005

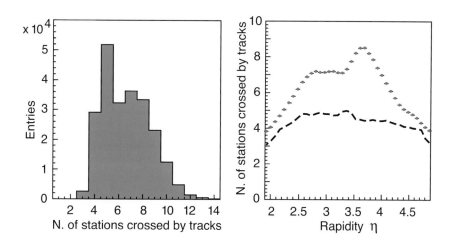

Figure 5.16: The left plot shows the number of stations hit per track in the VELO and the right plot shows the number of hits of a track in the VELO modules as a function of the pseudorapidity of the track. The dashed line indicates the limit above which 95% of the tracks lie.

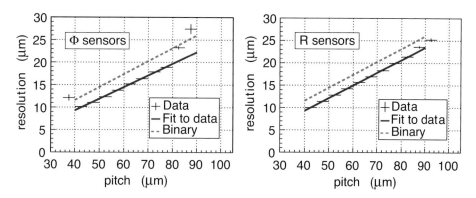

Figure 5.17: The raw hit resolution as a function of strip pitch as measured in the test beam for particles of normal incidence. The dashed line indicates the resolution expected for digital readout. The data points show the resolution as measured from the weighted centre of the charges on the strips.

mance improves for the low angle tracks when imperfections in the weighted charge distribution between two strips are taken into account [52].

In addition, crosstalk originating from inter-strip coupling, from coupling between electronic channels, and from signal feed-forward and backward in the analog transmission have not been taken into account. Once these have been fully parametrised further improvement in the resolution obtained from the system is anticipated.

2008 JINST 3 S08005

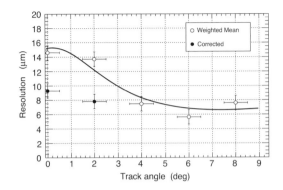

Figure 5.18: The individual hit resolution of a VELO R-sensor as a function of the projected angle for a pitch of 85 μm. The open circles show the resolution as derived from a weighted mean. The filled circles include the corrections for the imperfections in the weighted charge distribution between two strips.

5.2   Silicon Tracker

The Silicon Tracker (ST) comprises two detectors: the Tracker Turicensis[10] (TT) [2, 53] and the Inner Tracker (IT) [54]. Both TT and IT use silicon microstrip sensors with a strip pitch of about 200 μm. The TT is a 150 cm wide and 130 cm high planar tracking station that is located upstream of the LHCb dipole magnet and covers the full acceptance of the experiment. The IT covers a 120 cm wide and 40 cm high cross shaped region in the centre of the three tracking stations downstream of the magnet. Each of the four ST stations has four detection layers in an (x-u-v-x) arrangement with vertical strips in the first and the last layer and strips rotated by a stereo angle of -5° and +5° in the second and the third layer, respectively. The TT has an active area of about 8.4 m^2 with 143360 readout strips of up to 38 cm in length. The IT has an active area of 4.0 m^2 with 129024 readout strips of either 11 cm or 22 cm in length.

The main design choices for the Silicon Tracker detectors were largely driven by the following considerations:

Spatial resolution. Simulation studies have demonstrated that a single-hit resolution of about 50 μm is adequate for both the TT and the IT. The momentum resolution of the spectrometer is then dominated by multiple scattering over almost the full range of particle momenta. Readout strip pitches of about 200 μm meet this requirement and were therefore chosen for both detectors.

Hit occupancy. Charged particle densities of about 5×10^{-2} per cm^2 for minimum bias events are expected in the innermost regions of the TT. They fall off by two orders of magnitude to about 5×10^{-4} per cm^2 in the outermost regions of the detector. Different readout strip lengths were chosen for different regions of the detector to keep maximum strip occupancies at the level of a few percent while minimizing the number of readout channels. For the IT, expected charged-particle densities for minimum-bias events range from about 1.5×10^{-2} per cm^2 close to the LHC beampipe to 2×10^{-3} per cm^2 in the outer regions of the detector. Also here, the chosen strip geometries result in maximum strip occupancies that do not exceed a few percent.

---

[10]The Tracker Turicensis was formerly known as the Trigger Tracker.

2008 JINST 3 S08005

Signal shaping time. In order to avoid pile-up of events from consecutive LHC bunch crossings, fast front-end amplifiers with a shaping time of the order of the bunch crossing interval of 25 ns have to be used. The benchmark parameter is the remaining fraction of the signal amplitude at the sampling time of the subsequent bunch crossing, 25 ns after the maximum of the pulse. Simulation studies have shown that signal remainders of 50% for the TT and 30% for the IT are acceptable for the track reconstruction algorithms.

Single-hit efficiency. Each detection layer should provide full single-hit efficiency for minimum ionising particles while maintaining an acceptably low noise hit rate. The critical parameter is the signal-to-noise ratio, defined as the most probable signal amplitude for a minimum ionising particle divided by the RMS of the single strip noise distribution. Test beam studies have shown that the hit efficiency starts to decrease rapidly as the signal-to-noise ratio drops below 10:1. The detector was designed such that a signal-to-noise ratio in excess of 12:1 can be expected taking into account the expected deterioration from radiation damage corresponding to ten years of operation at nominal luminosity.

Radiation damage. For ten years of operation at nominal luminosity, expected 1 MeV neutron equivalent fluences in the innermost regions of the detectors do not exceed 5×10^{14} per cm^2 for the TT and 9×10^{12} per cm^2 for the IT. Basic design rules for radiation hard silicon sensors were followed to ensure that the detectors will survive these fluences. The detector was designed and tested to work at bias voltages of up to 500 V. The sensors need to be operated at a temperature of 5°C or lower to suppress radiation damage induced leakage currents to a level where (a) shot noise does not significantly deteriorate the signal-to-noise performance of the detector and (b) the risk of thermal runaway due to the power dissipated by the leakage currents is avoided.

Material budget. As the momentum resolution of the LHCb spectrometer is dominated by multiple scattering, the material budget of the detectors had to be kept as small as possible. The TT was designed such that front-end readout electronics and mechanical supports are located outside of the LHCb acceptance. This was not possible in the case of the IT, which is located in front of the active region of the OT detectors. Here, a significant design effort was made to keep the amount of material for mechanical supports and for the cooling of front-end electronics as small as possible.

Number of readout channels. Readout electronics are a major contribution to the overall cost of the detector. The largest readout pitches compatible with the required spatial resolution and the longest readout strips compatible with requirements on occupancy and signal-to-noise performance were chosen in order to minimize the number of readout channels.

Different constraints on the detector geometries resulted in different designs for the detector modules and station mechanics of the TT and the IT. These are described in sections 5.2.1 and 5.2.2, respectively. Common to both parts of the ST are the readout electronics, the power distribution, and the detector control and monitor systems. These are the topic of section 5.2.3. Finally, the expected detector performance, based on test beam measurements and simulation studies, is discussed in section 5.2.4.

5.2.1 Tracker Turicensis

All four detection layers of the TT are housed in one large light tight and thermally and electrically insulated detector volume, in which a temperature below 5°C is maintained [55]. The detector

2008 JINST 3 S08005

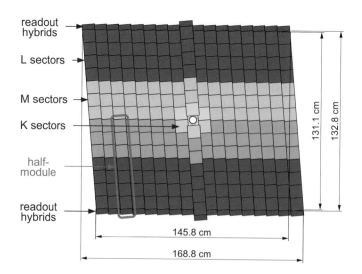

readout
hybrids

L sectors

M sectors

K sectors

half-
module

readout
hybrids

131.1 cm   132.8 cm

145.8 cm

168.8 cm

Figure 5.19: Layout of the third TT detection layer. Different readout sectors are indicated by different shadings.

volume is continuously flushed with nitrogen to avoid condensation on the cold surfaces. To aid track reconstruction algorithms, the four detection layers are arranged in two pairs, (x,u) and (v,x), that are separated by approximately 27 cm along the LHC beam axis.

The layout of one of the detection layers is illustrated in figure 5.19. Its basic building block is a half module that covers half the height of the LHCb acceptance. It consists of a row of seven silicon sensors organized into either two or three readout sectors. The readout hybrids for all readout sectors are mounted at one end of the module. The regions above and below the LHC beampipe are covered by one such half module each. The regions to the sides of the beampipe are covered by rows of seven (for the first two detection layers) or eight (for the last two detection layers) 14-sensor long full modules. These full modules cover the full height of the LHCb acceptance and are assembled from two half modules that are joined together end-to-end. Adjacent modules within a detection layer are staggered by about 1 cm in z and overlap by a few millimeters in x to avoid acceptance gaps and to facilitate the relative alignment of the modules. In the u and v detection layers, each module is individually rotated by the respective stereo angle.

A main advantage of this detector design is that all front-end hybrids and the infrastructure for cooling and module supports are located above and below the active area of the detector, outside of the acceptance of the experiment.

TT detector modules

The layout of a half module is illustrated in figure 5.20. It consists of a row of seven silicon sensors with a stack of two or three readout hybrids at one end. For half modules close to the beampipe, where the expected particle density is highest, the seven sensors are organized into three readout sectors (4-2-1 type half modules).

For the other half modules, the sensors are organized into two readout sectors (4-3 type half modules). In both cases, the first readout sector (L sector) is formed by the four sensors closest to

2008 JINST 3 S08005

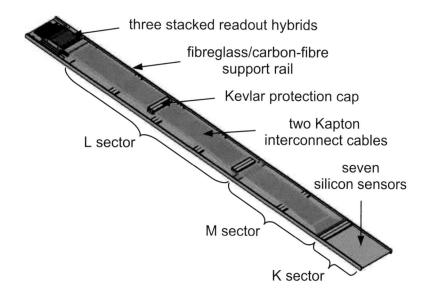

three stacked readout hybrids

fibreglass/carbon-fibre support rail

Kevlar protection cap

two Kapton interconnect cables

seven silicon sensors

L sector

M sector

K sector

Figure 5.20: View of a 4-2-1 type TT detector module.

the readout hybrids and furthest away from the beam. The strips of the four sensors are bonded together and directly connected to the lower-most readout hybrid. For 4-3 type half modules, the strips of the remaining three sensors are bonded together and form the second readout sector (M sector). They are connected via a 39 cm long Kapton flex cable (interconnect cable) to a second readout hybrid mounted on top of the L hybrid. For 4-2-1 type half modules, the three remaining sensors are subdivided into an intermediate two sensor sector (M sector) and a third sector consisting of the single sensor closest to the beam (K sector). The two readout sectors are connected via 39 cm respectively 58 cm long Kapton interconnect cables to two separate front-end hybrids that are mounted on top of the L hybrid. Bias voltage is provided to the sensor backplanes via a thin Kapton flex cable that runs along the back of the half module. The half module is mechanically held together by two thin fibreglass/carbon fibre rails that are glued along the edges of the L hybrid and the seven silicon sensors.

Silicon sensors. The silicon sensors for the TT are 500 μm thick, single sided p^+-on-n sensors.[11] They are 9.64 cm wide and 9.44 cm long and carry 512 readout strips with a strip pitch of 183 μm.

Kapton interconnect cables. The Kapton interconnect cables for the M and K readout sectors were produced using standard plasma-etching technology.[12] They carry 512 signal strips and two pairs of bias voltage and ground strips on a 100 μm thick Kapton substrate. The strips consist of 7 μm thick copper with a 1 μm thick gold plating, are 15 μm wide and have a pitch of 112 μm. A short pitch-adapter section in which the strip pitch widens to 180 μm permits to directly wire-bond the strips on the cable to the silicon sensor strips. A copper mesh backplane provides a solid ground connection and shielding against pick-up noise. The small strip width was required to keep the strip capacitance of the cable small, but led to an unacceptably low production yield for fault

---

[11]The sensors are identical in design to the OB2 sensors used in the Outer Barrel of the CMS Silicon Tracker [56] and were produced by Hamamatsu Photonics K.K., Hamamatsu City, Japan.

[12]The Kapton interconnect cables were produced by Dyconex AG, Bassersdorf, Switzerland.

2008 JINST 3 S08005

free cables of the required length. The 39 cm long cables for the M sectors therefore had to be assembled from two shorter pieces, and the 58 cm long cables for the K sectors were assembled from three pieces. The pieces were joined together end-to-end by gluing them onto a thin strip of fibreglass reinforced epoxy. An electrically conductive adhesive tape was used to provide the electrical connection between the copper mesh backplanes of the two cable pieces. The signal, bias voltage and ground strips on the strip side of the cables were joined together by wire bonds.

Kevlar caps. Small Kevlar caps protect the wire bond rows on the strip side of the Kapton interconnect cables as well as those between silicon sensors. These caps are glued onto the surface of the cable or the sensors using standard two component epoxy glue.[13]

Readout hybrids. The front-end readout hybrids [57] consist of a carrier plate, a pitch adapter, and a four layer Kapton flex circuit that carries four front-end readout chips, some passive SMD components and an 80-pin board-to-board connector.[14] Through this connector, the multiplexed analog detector signals are read out and the control signals, low voltage and bias voltage are provided to the half module. Two of the four conductive layers of the flex circuit are used for digital and analog power and ground. The other two layers carry the signal and control lines. Due to mechanical constraints, three variants of the readout hybrid are used for the three different types of readout sectors. The Kapton flex circuits for all three variants are identical except for a different overall length. The upper hybrids have to be shorter than the lower ones to make the readout connectors on all hybrids accessible when these are mounted on top of each other. The carrier plates give mechanical stability to the hybrid and act as a heat sink for the heat produced by the front-end chips. The pitch adapter matches the input pitch of the front-end chips to the pitch of the silicon sensors in case of the L hybrid and to the pitch of the Kapton interconnect cable in case of the K and M hybrids. For these, the carrier plate is made from gold plated copper and the pitch adapter is a rectangular piece of alumina (Al_2O_3) substrate with strip lines produced using standard thin film technology. The pitch adapter is glued onto the carrier plate together with the Kapton flex circuit. The carrier plate for the L hybrid is a much more complicated piece that consists of aluminium nitride substrate and combines several functionalities.[15] First of all, it carries not only the strip lines of the pitch adapter for the L sector, produced using standard thick film technology, but also additional traces and vias that serve to connect the bias voltage for all readout sectors. Next, the support rails of the detector module are glued along the sides of this carrier plate. And finally, this carrier plate provides the mechanical and thermal interface of the half module to the detector station. All these functionalities will be described in more detail below. Aluminium nitride was chosen as the material for this carrier plate because of its high thermal conductivity and its small thermal expansion coefficient that is reasonably well matched to that of the silicon sensors.

The K and M hybrids are mounted on top of the carrier plate of the L hybrid using 2.5 mm thick spacers made of copper. These ensure good thermal contact between the carrier plates of the K and M hybrids and the one of the L hybrid.

Support rails. The two half module support rails are 5.5 mm high and consist of a 1 mm thick strip of carbon fibre glued to a 1 mm thick strip of fibreglass reinforced epoxy. A small groove

---

[13] Araldite 2011 (AW106/HV953U), by Huntsman Advanced Materials, Basel, Switzerland.

[14] The flex circuits were produced by Optiprint AG, Berneck, Switzerland.

[15] The production of the pitch adapters for the K and M hybrids and of the aluminium nitride carrier plate for the L hybrids as well as the assembly and bonding of all hybrids was done by RHe Microsystems, Radeberg, Germany.

2008 JINST 3 S08005

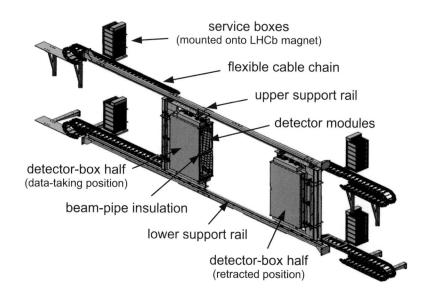

service boxes
(mounted onto LHCb magnet)

flexible cable chain

upper support rail

detector modules

detector-box half
(data-taking position)

beam-pipe insulation

lower support rail

detector-box half
(retracted position)

Figure 5.21: View of the TT station mechanics.

is milled into the flat side of the fibreglass strip which permits to slide the rail over the edges of the seven silicon sensors and the carrier plate of the L hybrid. The rail is glued to these using standard two component epoxy glue. The rôle of the fibreglass strip is to ensure the necessary electrical insulation between the strip side of the silicon sensors (which are at ground potential) and their backplanes (which carry the bias voltage of up to 500 V). The mechanical rigidity of the rail is defined mainly by the carbon fibre strip. The fibreglass strip spans the full length of the half module but the carbon fibre strip ends at the fourth silicon sensor from the hybrids. This permits to join two half modules to a 14-sensor long full module by gluing an additional carbon fibre strip to the free sections of fibreglass strip on both half modules.

Bias voltage. Bias voltage is supplied separately for each of the readout sectors on a half module via the cable that plugs into the corresponding front-end hybrid. From the hybrid it is connected to aluminium traces on the carrier plate of the L sector, using wire bonds in case of the L hybrid and thin copper wires in case of the M and K hybrids. From here, all bias voltages are brought to the back of the half module through aluminium vias that are embedded in the aluminium nitride substrate. Finally, a thin Kapton flex cable, which is glued along the back of the half module and carries one copper trace per readout sector, carries the bias voltage to the backplanes of the silicon sensors. The electrical connections between the Kapton flex cable and the sensor backplanes and between the cable and the bias voltage pads on the back of the aluminium nitride are made by wire bonding.

TT detector station

An isometric drawing of the detector station is shown in figure 5.21. It consists of two halves, one on each side of the LHC beampipe.

The half stations are mounted on rails and can be retracted horizontally for detector maintenance and bakeouts of the LHC beampipe. The main structural element of each half station is a C-shaped aluminium frame. It carries a detector box that is made of light weight aluminium clad

2008 JINST 3 S08005

foam. This box is open on the side facing the beampipe such that the two half stations in data taking position define one large volume that contains all detector modules. Mounted against the top and bottom walls of the detector box are horizontal cooling plates that provide the mechanical support for the detector modules as well as cooling of the front-end hybrids and the detector volume. The cooling plates incorporate cooling pipes through which C_6F_{14} at -15°C is circulated as a cooling agent. Additional cooling elements are mounted vertically, close to the outer side walls of the detector volume. All electrical signals (detector signals, control signals and supply voltages) are transmitted on Kapton-flex cables through specially designed feedthroughs in the top and bottom walls of the detector box.

Detector box. The C-shaped support frames are assembled from 15 mm thick aluminium plates. They rest on a lower precision rail and are guided by an upper precision rail. These two rails are aligned parallel to each other to better than $100\,\mu$m in order to avoid possible distortions of the C-frame during insertion or retraction. Mounted flat against the inner surfaces of the C-frames are stiff sandwich plates consisting of a 30 mm thick aramid honeycomb structure with 1 mm thick aluminium cladding. These sandwich plates define the outer walls of the detector box. The front and rear walls of the box are made of 40 mm thick panels of polyetherimide foam[16] that are laminated on both sides with $25\,\mu$m of aluminium for electrical insulation and $275\,\mu$m of Kevlar for mechanical protection. These panels are screwed against the outer walls of the box and can be easily removed for the installation and maintenance of detector modules. Similar plates of 40 mm thick aluminium and Kevlar clad polyetherimide foam are also mounted flat against the inner surfaces of the outer walls of the box to improve thermal insulation here. Finally, the detector volume is closed off around the LHC beampipe by two specially machined semicylindrical pieces that again consist of the same polyetherimide foam clad with aluminium and Kevlar. The wall thickness of these beampipe insulation pieces is 30 mm, except for cutouts at the locations of the detection layers. Here, the wall thickness is reduced to about 5 mm to reduce the dead space in between the beampipe and the innermost detector modules. A clearance of 5 mm between the detector box and the beampipe had to be maintained to satisfy LHC safety demands.

Cooling plates. There are a total of four cooling plates, one for each quadrant of the detector. They are mounted horizontally onto pillars made of polyacetal (POM) that are fixed against the upper or the lower walls of the detector box. A drawing of a cooling plate is shown in figure 5.22. It is a precisely machined plate of 8 mm thick aluminium that measures 897 mm in x and 348 mm in z. Machined into its outer surface are semicircular grooves into which two coiled aluminium cooling pipes with an outer diameter of 10 mm and a total length of about 3.5 m are glued. Its inner surface is machined to an overall flatness of better than $100\,\mu$m.

Cooling balconies. Mounted vertically against the flat inner surface of the cooling plate are the aluminium cooling balconies that provide the mechanical, thermal and electrical interface between cooling plate and detector modules. Precision holes and pins ensure the accurate positioning of the balconies on the cooling plate. The detector module is screwed onto the flat, vertical surface of the balcony, ensuring a large contact surface and therefore good thermal contact between the balcony and the aluminium nitride carrier plate of the half module. The correct positioning of the module is ensured by precision holes and pins in the balcony and laser cut holes in the aluminium

---

[16]Airex R82.60, by Gaugler & Lutz oHG, Aalen-Ebnat, Germany.

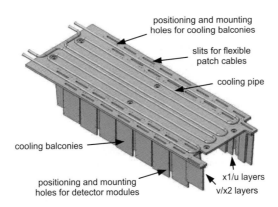

positioning and mounting
holes for cooling balconies

slits for flexible
patch cables

cooling pipe

cooling balconies

positioning and mounting
holes for detector modules

x1/u layers
v/x2 layers

Figure 5.22: View of one TT cooling plate with mounted cooling balconies.

nitride carrier plate. There are two types of balconies, one for mounting modules vertically and one for mounting modules under an angle of 5°. Detector modules in the first two detection layers are mounted onto their balconies from the upstream side of the detector, those for the last two layers from the downstream side of the detector.

Cooling elements. The vertical cooling elements that are installed at both sides of the detector volume consist of 1 mm thick copper plates onto which long, coiled cooling ducts with a rectangular cross section are soldered.

Electrical connections. Detector signals are read out and control signals, low voltage and bias voltage supplied to the detector modules via 50 cm long Kapton flex cables. These cables pass through dedicated slits in the cooling plate and through specially designed feedthroughs in the top and bottom walls of the detector box. There is a separate Kapton flex cable for each readout sector. At one end it plugs directly into the board-to-board connector on the readout hybrid, at the other end it connects to a patch panel that is mounted on the outside of the detector box. From this patch panel, shielded twisted-pair cables lead through flexible cable chains to service boxes that are mounted against the front face of the LHCb dipole magnet. Here, the signals are prepared for digital optical transmission to the counting house as described in section 5.2.3. Each quadrant of the detector has a flexible cable chain and a stack of six service boxes.

5.2.2 Inner Tracker

Each of the three IT stations consists of four individual detector boxes that are arranged around the beampipe as shown in figure 5.23.

The detector boxes are light tight and electrically and thermally insulated, and a temperature below 5°C is maintained inside them. They are continuously flushed with nitrogen to avoid condensation on the cold surfaces. Each detector box contains four detection layers and each detection layer consists of seven detector modules. Adjacent modules in a detection layer are staggered by 4 mm in z and overlap by 3 mm in x to avoid acceptance gaps and facilitate the relative alignment of the modules. Detector modules in the boxes above and below the beampipe (top and bottom boxes) consist of a single silicon sensor and a readout hybrid. Detector modules in the boxes to the left and right of the beampipe (side boxes) consist of two silicon sensors and a readout hybrid. The resulting layout and dimensions of one of the IT detection layers are illustrated in figure 5.24.

2008 JINST 3 S08005

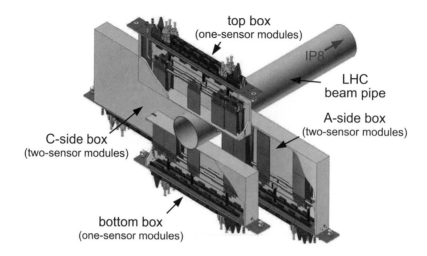

Figure 5.23: View of the four IT detector boxes arranged around the LHC beampipe.

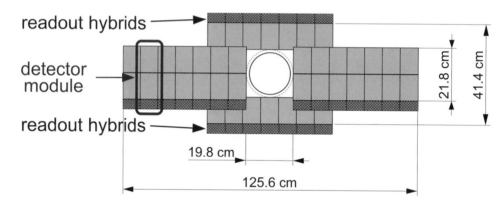

Figure 5.24: Layout of an x detection layer in the second IT station.

IT detector modules

An exploded view of a detector module is shown in figure 5.25. The module consists of either one or two silicon sensors that are connected via a pitch adapter to a front-end readout hybrid. The sensor(s) and the readout hybrid are all glued onto a flat module support plate. Bias voltage is provided to the sensor backplane from the strip side through n^+ wells that are implanted in the n-type silicon bulk. A small aluminium insert (minibalcony) that is embedded into the support plate at the location of the readout hybrid provides the mechanical and thermal interface of the module to the detector box.

Silicon sensors. Two types of silicon sensors of different thickness, but otherwise identical in design, are used in the IT.[17] They are single-sided p^+-on-n sensors, 7.6 cm wide and 11 cm long, and carry 384 readout strips with a strip pitch of 198 μm. The sensors for one-sensor modules are 320 μm thick, those for two-sensor modules are 410 μm thick. As explained in section 5.2.4 below, these thicknesses were chosen to ensure sufficiently high signal-to-noise ratios for each module type while minimising the material budget of the detector.

---

[17]The sensors were designed and produced by Hamamatsu Photonics K.K., Hamamatsu City, Japan.

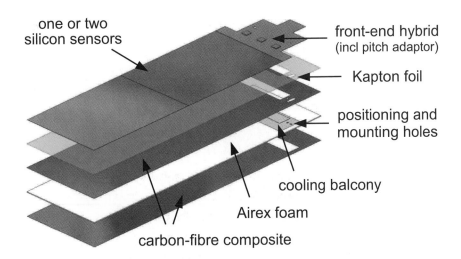

one or two silicon sensors

front-end hybrid (incl pitch adaptor)

Kapton foil

positioning and mounting holes

cooling balcony

Airex foam

carbon-fibre composite

Figure 5.25: Exploded view of a two-sensor IT module. One-sensor modules are similar except that the support plate is shorter and carries only one sensor.

Readout hybrids. The IT front-end readout hybrids consist of a four layer Kapton flex circuit that is very similar in design and routing to that of the TT hybrids, and a pitch adapter that is similar to that used for the M and K hybrids of the TT.[18] The only differences are (a) that the Kapton flex circuit for the IT carries only three front-end chips and (b) that it incorporates an 89 mm long readout tail with straight traces, at the end of which a 60-pin board-to-board connector is mounted. The pitch adapter is glued onto the Kapton flex circuit and the Kapton flex circuit is glued directly onto the module support plate.

Module support plate. The module support plate[19] consists of a 1 mm thick sheet of polyetherimide foam[20] sandwiched in between two 200 μm thick layers of carbon fibre composite. The latter are produced from two layers of thermally highly conductive carbon fibres[21] that are oriented at $\pm 10°$ with respect to the module axis. A 25 μm thick Kapton foil is laminated on top of the upper carbon fibre layer to electrically insulate it from the backplane of the silicon sensors, which carries the sensor bias voltage of up to 500 V. The support plate extends on all sides by 1 mm over the edges of the silicon sensors to protect these mechanically. The edges of the support plate are sealed with a non conductive epoxide resin to prevent loose fibres from sticking out and touching the sensor, where they might cause a short between the strip side and the backplane. At the location of the front-end readout chips, a 70 mm wide, 15 mm high and 1.5 mm thick aluminium piece called minibalcony is inserted in the support plate. It is glued to the support plate using thermally conductive glue.[22]

Minibalcony. The minibalcony defines the mechanical and thermal interface of the module to the detector box. It is machined to a flatness of better than 30 μm and contains precision holes for

---

[18]The production of flex prints and pitch adapters and the assembly of the readout hybrids took place at the same two companies as for the TT.

[19]The module support plates were produced by Composite Design, Echandens, Switzerland.

[20]Airex R82.60, by Gaugler & Lutz oHG, Aalen-Ebnat, Germany.

[21]K13D2U, by Mitsubishi Chemical Corp., Tokyo, Japan.

[22]TRA-DUCT 2902, by TRA-CON Inc., Bedford, Massachusetts, USA.

2008 JINST 3 S08005

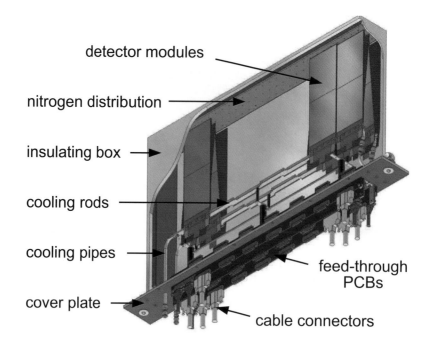

detector modules

nitrogen distribution

insulating box

cooling rods

cooling pipes

feed-through PCBs

cover plate

cable connectors

Figure 5.26: View of an IT side box. Top/bottom boxes are similar except that the box is shorter and contains one-sensor modules.

the mounting and exact positioning of the module. There are two types of minibalconies: one for modules that will be mounted vertically and another one for modules that will be mounted with the 5° stereo angle. The minibalcony provides a direct heat path from the front-end chips to the cooling rod, onto which the modules are mounted as described below. It also thermally connects the carbon fibre sheets of the module support plate to the cooling rod. Due to their good thermal conductivity along the module axis and their large surface area, the module support plates therefore contribute to the cooling of the silicon sensors and the detector volume.

The silicon sensors are glued onto the module support plate using strips of silicone glue.[23] The hybrids are glued onto the module support plate using standard two component epoxy glue. Small spots of thermally conductive glue[24] are applied at the location of the front-end readout chips in order to improve the thermal contact between the chips and the minibalcony.

IT detector boxes

An isometric view of a detector box is shown in figure 5.26. Its main structural element is a cover plate, onto which two cooling rods are mounted. These cooling rods incorporate cooling pipes through which C_6F_{14} at -15°C circulates as a cooling agent. Printed-circuit boards that are inserted vertically through the cover plate serve to transmit supply voltage and detector and control signals from and to the detector modules inside the box. The detector volume is closed by an insulating box that is assembled from flat sheets of a light but rigid aluminium clad foam.

---

[23]NEE-001-weiss by Dr. Neumann Peltier Technik, Utting, Germany; for a characterisation of this glue, see [58].
[24]EpoTek 129-4, by Epoxy Technology, Billerica, Massachusetts, USA.

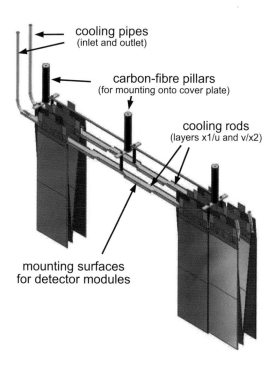

Figure 5.27: View of an IT cooling rod with a few detector modules.

Cover plate. The cover plate is made from a a 14 mm thick polymethacrylimide foam (Rohacell) sandwiched in between two layers of carbon fibre composite. Four printed-circuit boards, one for each detection layer, are inserted vertically through slits in the cover plate. They have four copper layers and serve to feed supply voltage and detector and control signals through the box. The outer layers carry the detector bias voltage and the analog and digital supply voltage, respectively. The two inners layers are used for the differential signals. Inside the detector box, the printed-circuit boards carry 60-pin board-to-board connectors into which the Kapton tails of the readout hybrids are plugged. Outside the box they are equipped with low mass connectors for signal cables and bias voltage cables. Cooling and nitrogen supply pipes also pass through the cover plate. Finally, the cover plate contains mounting holes for fixing the detector box on the IT support frames described below.

Cooling rods. An isometric view of the two cooling rods is shown in figure 5.27. They are mounted on the cover plate using pillars made out of a carbon fibre composite. Each cooling rod is machined out of a single piece of aluminium. It consists of a 3 mm thick central part and vertical mounting surfaces for each of the detector modules. An aluminium cooling pipe with an outer diameter of 6 mm and a wall thickness of 0.4 mm is glued into a semicircular groove that runs along the central part of the cooling rod. The mounting surfaces for the detector modules are 6 mm high and 70 mm wide and contain precision holes and pins to ensure the accurate positioning of the modules. Detector modules are mounted on both sides of the cooling rod, such that each cooling rod supports a pair of detection layers. The cooling pipes on the two cooling rods are connected in series using a short nitrile rubber hose.

Box enclosure. The box enclosure is assembled from 6 mm thick, flat sheets of polyisocyanurat (PIR) foam reinforced with a single, 200 μm thick carbon fibre skin and clad on both sides

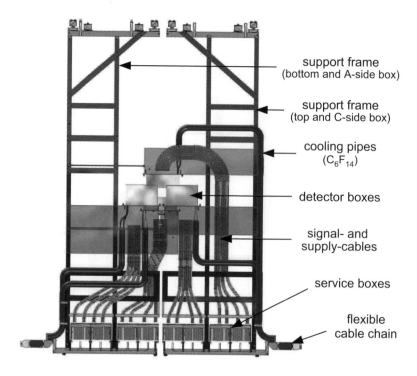

support frame
(bottom and A-side box)

support frame
(top and C-side box)

cooling pipes
(C_6F_{14})

detector boxes

signal- and
supply-cables

service boxes

flexible
cable chain

Figure 5.28: Front view of an IT detector station.

with 25 μm thick aluminium foil. For the side of the box facing the beampipe, the wall thickness is reduced to 2 mm to decrease the distance between the beam and the innermost detector modules. Mounted on the inside wall of the enclosure is a distribution channel for the nitrogen with which the box is flushed. Small inserts made of fibreglass reinforced epoxy are embedded in the upper rim of the enclosure and permit to screw it onto the cover plate.

IT detector station

A front view of a detector station is shown in figure 5.28.

The detector boxes are mounted onto two support frames that are mounted on rails and can be retracted horizontally for detector maintenance and bakeouts of the LHC beampipe. The support frames are suspended from the upper support rail, which is mounted onto the Outer Tracker bridge (see section 5.3) and are guided by the lower rail that is mounted onto the LHCb bunker. The innermost sections of both support rails are precision machined to ensure an accurate positioning of the support frames in data taking position. The support frames are assembled from rectangular rods made of fibreglass reinforced epoxy and carbon fibre composite and from flat plates of aramide honeycomb clad with skins of a carbon fibre composite. Signal and bias voltage cables and flexible supply lines for C_6F_{14} and nitrogen are routed along the support frames from the detector boxes to the lower end of the support frame. Here, the service boxes are mounted in which the detector signals are prepared for digital optical transmission to the counting house as described in section 5.2.3. Optical fibres, cables and supply tubes are further routed through a flexible cable chain that is fixed to the lower end of the support frame at one end and to the edge of the LHCb bunker at the other end.

2008 JINST 3 S08005

5.2.3 Electronics

A central position in the ST electronics is occupied by the service boxes [59] that have already been mentioned in the descriptions of the TT and IT detector stations. The service boxes are located close to the detectors but outside of the acceptance of the experiment. They are custom-made crates that hold 12 (TT) or 16 (IT) digitizer cards, a backplane for the distribution of control signals and low voltage, and a control card that provides interfaces to the LHCb Timing and Fast Control system (TFC, see section 8.3) and Experiment Control System (ECS, see section 8.4). On the digitizer cards, the analog output signals from the front-end readout chips are digitized, multiplexed and converted to optical signals. They are further transmitted via 120 m long optical fibres to the counting house, where they are received on the TELL1 board (see section 8.2).

Bias voltage for the silicon sensors and operation voltage for the readout electronics are provided by commercial voltage supplies. The grounding scheme follows LHCb grounding rules layed out in [60]. Temperature and humidity sensors are installed at various locations inside the detector boxes and on the service box backplane to monitor environmental conditions.

Readout and data transmission

Front-end chips. Both the TT and the IT make use of the Beetle front-end readout chip.[25] Four (TT) or three (IT) Beetle chips are located on a front-end readout hybrid. Each Beetle chip amplifies and shapes the detector signals of 128 readout strips, samples them at the LHC bunch crossing frequency of 40 MHz, stores the sampled data in an analog pipeline, and upon a Level-0 trigger accept transmits the analog data 32-fold multiplexed via four differential output ports.

Copper cables. All output signals from one front-end hybrid are transmitted from the detector boxes to the service boxes via a shielded 68-wire twisted-pair cable. Only 32 (TT) or 24 (IT) of the 68 wires are needed for the transmission of the detector signals. The remaining wires are used to provide timing and slow-control signals, low voltage and ground from the service box to the front-end hybrid. The twisted-pair cables are between 2.7 m (IT bottom boxes) and 8 m (TT) long. Since, in the case of the IT, they go through the acceptance of the experiment, custom-made cables with significantly reduced shielding braids are employed to minimize the material budget.

Digitizer cards. Each digitizer card processes the data from one front-end hybrid. There are two variants of the card: a TT version to process the data from the four chip hybrids of the TT and an IT version to process the data from the three chip IT hybrids. The basic functional block for the processing of the signals from a single Beetle chip is illustrated in figure 5.29. Four differential line receivers convert the signals from the four Beetle output ports from differential to single-ended and match the signal levels to the input range of the ADC chips. Four single channel 8-bit ADC chips are used to digitize the data. These ADC chips operate at 40 MHz and are phase locked to the sampling clock of the Beetle chip. The 4×8-bit wide output data from the four ADC chips is then fed into a single Gigabit Optical Link (GOL) chip [6]. The GOL multiplexes the data and encodes them to a single Gigabit Ethernet data stream with a data rate of 1.6 Gbit/s. The laser driver integrated into the GOL chip is used to drive a 850 nm wavelength VCSEL diode that feeds the digitized optical data into a single optical fibre. This functional block is repeated four times on

---

[25]The Beetle front-end chip is a common development for ST and VELO. It has already been described in section 5.1.4.

2008 JINST 3 S08005

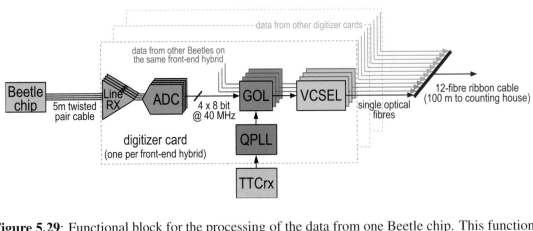

Figure 5.29: Functional block for the processing of the data from one Beetle chip. This functional block is repeated four times on a TT digitizer card and three times on an IT digitizer card.

a TT digitizer card and three times on an IT digitizer card. In addition, both variants of the card carry a central functional block for the distribution of the timing and control signals that the card receives from the service box control card.

Optical fibres. To transmit the data from the service boxes to the counting house, the outputs of twelve VCSEL diodes, corresponding to three TT digitizer cards or four IT digitizer cards, are connected to one twelve-fibre optical ribbon cable. This grouping defines a readout partitioning into groups of three readout sectors for the TT and four detector modules for the IT. The same partitioning is followed by the low voltage and bias voltage distribution and by the detector control system. A TT service box holds twelve (four groups of three), an IT service box 16 (four groups of four) digitizer cards. Both types of service boxes, therefore, feed four twelve-fibre ribbon cables.

TELL1 boards. In the counting house, two fibre ribbon cables are connected to each TELL1 board. One TELL1 board therefore receives the data from six TT readout sectors or eight IT modules. A total of 84 TELL1 boards is required to read out the 280 readout sectors of the TT and the 336 detector modules of the IT. The functionality of the TELL1 board is described in section 8.2. Pedestals are calculated and subtracted for each readout channel, common-mode noise is calculated and subtracted for each event. A cluster-finding algorithm is applied and the positions and ADC values of the clusters are transmitted to the computer farm. Non-zero-suppressed data can be transmitted for monitoring and debugging purposes.

Detector control and monitoring

Detector control and monitoring is the main task of the service box control cards [61].

TFC. The control card holds a TTCrq mezzanine [62], which collects clock, trigger and timing information from the TFC network. The TFC signals are distributed to the digitizer cards via impedance controlled differential traces on the service box backplane. All GOL chips and Beetle chips associated with the same service box receive their clock signal from the same TTCrq mezzanine. The layouts of the backplane and the digitizer cards were optimized to equalize trace lengths, resulting in signal propagation time differences that do not exceed 3 ns.

ECS. The interface to the ECS is provided by two SPECS slave mezzanines that are mounted on each control card and that provide a total of eight I^{2}C busses. Four of these busses are used

2008 JINST 3 S08005

to control the GOL chips per group of three (TT) respectively four (IT) digitizer cards. The other four are used to control the Beetle chips per group of three respectively four readout hybrids. In addition, 36 I/O control lines permit to individually switch off the low-voltage regulators that provide the power for the readout hybrids and digitizer cards (see below).

Monitoring. The SPECS mezzanines also provide a number of ADC channels that are employed to read out temperature sensors (PT1000) and humidity sensors at various locations in the detector boxes. Additional ADC chips are located on each digitizer card. They are employed to monitor over-current conditions of the Beetle chips and to read out a PT1000 temperature sensor that is located on each readout hybrid.

Power distribution and grounding scheme

Low voltage. Low voltage levels of 2.5 V, 3.3 V and 5 V are required for the Beetle, GOL and ADC chips, the line receivers, and various LVDS drivers on the digitizer cards and the service box backplane. They are derived from voltage levels of about 5.5 V and 8 V that are generated by MARATON power supplies[26] in the LHCb cavern. The MARATON supplies are connected to the service box backplanes where they drive radiation tolerant programmable linear power regulators.[27] Two of these power regulators are used to provide each readout hybrid with digital and analog power. Analog and digital power for the Beetle chips are kept separate throughout the system and are connected only on the readout hybrids. Another two power regulators provide each group of three (TT) respectively four (IT) digitizer cards with the required voltage levels, following the partitioning defined by the readout. These power regulators are located on the service box backplane and control card. They are cooled using the LHCb mixed water cooling system. The regulators for each readout hybrid and for each group of three respectively four digitizer cards can be individually switched off via the ECS.

Bias voltage. Detector bias voltage is provided by commercial high-voltage supplies[28] located in the counting house. It is connected to the detector boxes via 120 m long cables. The HV modules can provide up to 500 V and deliver a current of up to 10 mA per channel. Only the innermost readout sectors of the TT have individual HV channels to cope with the sensor leakage currents expected after several years of operation. Everywhere else, groups of three TT readout sectors and four IT detector modules are connected to one HV channel, following the same partitioning as the readout. Each readout sector and detector module, however, has a separate supply line from a HV patch panel in the counting house to the detector. The HV patch panel carries a jumper for each readout sector and detector module. This permits to manually disconnect individual readout sectors and detector modules from their HV supply.

Grounding scheme. The grounding scheme [63] of the detector boxes is illustrated in figure 5.30. The common ground for each detector box is defined by the cooling plates (TT) respectively cooling rods (IT) onto which the detector modules are mounted as described in sections 5.2.1 and 5.2.2. Thin copper wires are employed to connect ground pads on each of the Kapton flex prints

---

[26]MARATON low voltage power supply system for hazardous hostile environment, by W-IE-NE-R, Plein & Baus GmbH, Burscheid, Germany.

[27]LHC4913, developed by the CERN micro-electronics group and produced by ST Microelectronics, Geneva, Switzerland.

[28]CAEN SY1527 crates with A1511B modules, by CAEN S.p.A., Viareggio, Italy.

2008 JINST 3 S08005

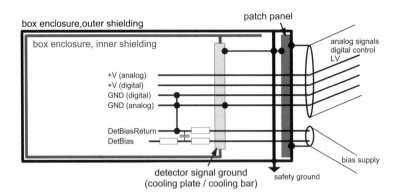

Figure 5.30: Grounding scheme of the detector boxes.

to the metallic screws with which the modules are fixed to the cooling balconies or cooling rods. The walls of the detector boxes are coated on both sides with 25 μm thick foils of aluminium. The inner shielding is connected to the common ground of the detector box and the outer shielding is connected to the LHCb safety ground. The two are connected with each other at one well defined location in the detector box. The shieldings of the signal and supply cables that connect to a detector box are connected to the outer box shielding. Both the LV and HV power supplies are kept floating and are connected to the LHCb general ground only in the detector boxes. In addition, the bias voltage for each module respectively readout sector is filtered using a passive low-pass RC filter that is implemented on the front-end readout hybrids.

5.2.4 Detector performance

An extensive R&D programme has been carried out to validate the detector concept, to optimize detector parameters and to estimate the expected performance of the detectors. It included simulation studies as well as various tests of prototype detectors in the laboratory and in test beams [64–68]. In view of the combination of the long readout strips and the fast pulse shapes employed, the signal-to-noise performance of the detectors was a major concern in these studies. The test beam measurements also confirmed that the expected spatial resolution of the detectors can be achieved. Other studies concerned the expected strip occupancies, which were estimated using events samples generated using the full GEANT 4 based simulation of the LHCb detector. A detailed analysis of the material budget of the detector was performed.

Signal-to-noise and efficiency

Various prototype detectors were built to establish the expected noise performance, charge collection efficiency and signal-to-noise performance of the final detectors. Effective readout strip lengths on these prototype detectors ranged from 108 mm up to 324 mm. Silicon sensors were employed that measured 320 μm to 500 μm in thickness, had strip pitches between 183 μm and 228 μm and ratios of strip implant width over strip pitch from 0.25 to 0.35. Some of the tested prototypes included Kapton interconnect cables of the same type and length as used in the M and K readout sectors of the TT. The performance of the prototype detectors was measured in an infrared laser

2007 JINST 3 S08005

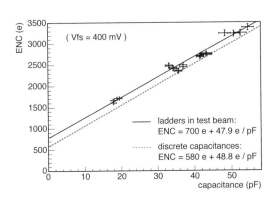

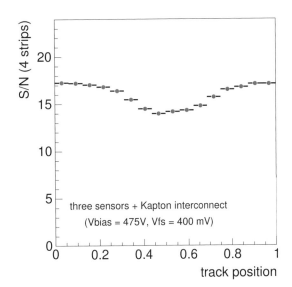

Figure 5.31: ENC obtained in test beam measurements as a function of the measured total strip capacitance of the tested prototype modules. The full line is a fit to the test beam results, the dashed line describes the results of laboratory measurements in which discrete capacitances were attached directly to the input of the Beetle chips.

Figure 5.32: Most probable signal-to-noise ratio as a function of the inter-strip position (0 = centre of left strip, 1 = centre of right strip) measured in a CERN test beam. In order to rule out a potential bias due to clustering algorithms, the signal was calculated as the sum of the charges on the four strips closest to the particle impact point given by a beam telescope.

test stand and in several test beam periods in a $120\,\text{GeV}\ \pi^-$ beam at CERN. The expected noise performance of the various detector configurations was also investigated in a SPICE simulation that included a detailed description of the Beetle front-end, and in which the readout strips of the detectors were described as an extended LCR network [69]. The results of this simulation agreed with the test beam measurements. The measured noise performance is summarized in figure 5.31. In this figure, the measured equivalent noise charge (ENC) for the different tested detector configurations is shown as a function of their total strip capacitance. A linear dependence is observed and the slope of a line fitted to the data agrees well with that obtained in test-bench measurements of the Beetle chips, in which discrete load capacitances were attached to the Beetle inputs. Both the measurements and the SPICE simulations have demonstrated that the Kapton interconnect cables behave purely as an additional load capacitance and cause no deterioration of the quality and integrity of the detector signals.

Measurements of the charge collection efficiency were performed as a function of the position on the detector. No significant dependence was found on the position along the readout strips. However, in the direction orthogonal to the strips, a significant drop of the charge collection efficiency was observed in the central region between two readout strips. The effect is illustrated in figure 5.32 for a prototype module with the same detector geometry as a three-sensor readout sector of the TT. A similar charge loss was observed for all tested detector configurations. Its size did not depend on the strip length but was found to depend on the strip geometry. It decreased

2008 JINST 3 S08005

with increasing ratio of implant width to strip pitch (w/p) and with increasing sensor thickness (d) and depended roughly linearly on the ratio $(p - w)/d$. The charge loss could not be reduced by overbiasing the detectors or by increasing the shaping time within the limits allowed by the Beetle chips. It is attributed to charge trapping at the interface between the silicon bulk and the silicon oxide in between the readout strips.

This charge loss does not affect particle detection efficiency as long as the signal-to-noise ratio in the central region in between the strips remains high enough. Full particle detection efficiency above 99.8% was measured for all detector configurations as long as the most probable signal-to-noise ratio stayed above 10:1. Below that value, the particle detection efficiency started to decrease rather quickly. With the chosen thicknesses for the silicon sensors, most probable signal-to-noise ratios in excess of 12:1 are expected over the full surface of the detectors for both types of IT modules and all four types of TT readout sectors.

Spatial resolution and alignment

The spatial resolution of the detector modules was measured in test beams and was found to be about $50\,\mu$m, consistent with the expected resolution for the chosen strip pitches. Simulation studies have shown that, for two-strip clusters, it should be possible to further improve the spatial resolution by taking into account the position-dependent charge-sharing between the strips.

In order not to compromise the spatial resolution of the detectors, the positioning of each sensitive detector element in the x coordinate should be known to better than about $25\,\mu$m. The relative positioning accuracy of the individual silicon sensors on a detector module was monitored throughout the module production and was found to be better than $10\,\mu$m R.M.S. Various surveys of module positions inside the detector boxes and of detector boxes with respect to the LHCb reference frame have been performed. The results of these measurements are foreseen to be used to provide initial values for the software alignment of the detectors that will use reconstructed tracks from the LHCb spectrometer.

Strip occupancies

The strip occupancies presented here [70] were obtained from a sample of 5000 $B_d \to J/\psi(\mu^+\mu^-)$ $K_S(\pi^+\pi^-)$ events. The simulation software includes detailed descriptions of the detector geometry and of the signal collection, amplification and digitization. The simulation of the detector response was tuned to reproduce the results of the test beam measurements described before. For the TT, average strip occupancies of up to about 3.5% are found in the K sectors close to the beampipe. They drop to about 0.35% in the outermost L sectors. For the side boxes of the first IT station, average strip occupancies drop from about 2.5% on the strips closest to the beam to about 0.5% on the outermost strips. In the top/bottom boxes, occupancies vary between 0.5% and 0.3%. In the second and the third IT station, occupancies are about 10%, respectively 20% lower than in the first. This is mainly due to the larger distance of these stations from the beampipe supports (see section 3) that are located at the exit of the LHCb magnet and are a prolific source of secondary particles.

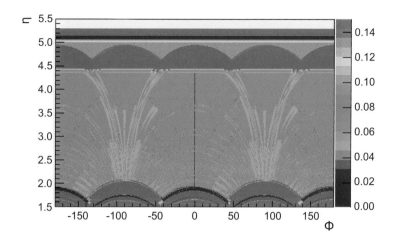

Figure 5.33: Radiation length of the TT as a function of the pseudorapidity η and the azimuthal angle ϕ.

Material budget

A careful analysis was performed of all materials that are located inside the acceptance of the experiment. Based on this analysis, a detailed description of all active detector elements and a simplified description of the passive components has been implemented [71, 72] in the XML based LHCb detector geometry description.

For the TT, where most of the dead material from detector supports, cooling etc. is located outside the acceptance, the material distribution is rather uniform. In total, it amounts to about $0.04\,X_0$, where more than $0.02\,X_0$ are due to the active material of the silicon sensors. An increase up to almost $0.13\,X_0$ is observed in the very forward region, due to the material of the insulation piece around the beampipe. The result of a material scan as a function of the azimuthal angle ϕ and the pseudorapidity η is shown in figure 5.33. The scan was performed by generating straight tracks originating from the nominal interaction point, extrapolating them through the TT station, and adding up the radiation lengths of all volumes in the geometry description that they crossed.

The material distribution for the IT is much less uniform, due to the readout hybrids, mechanical supports, cooling pipes and cables that are located inside the LHCb acceptance. In the active region of the detector, close to the beampipe, the material budget adds up to about $0.035\,X_0$ per station, out of which more than $0.015\,X_0$ are due to the active material of the silicon sensors. The material budget peaks at almost $0.30\,X_0$ in the very narrow region of the cooling rods. The result of a material scan for one IT station is shown in figure 5.34.

5.3 Outer Tracker

The LHCb Outer Tracker (OT) is a drift-time detector [73], for the tracking of charged particles and the measurement of their momentum over a large acceptance area. Excellent momentum resolution is necessary for a precise determination of the invariant mass of the reconstructed b-hadrons: a mass resolution of $10\,\mathrm{MeV/c^2}$ for the decay $B^0_s \to D^-_s \pi^+$ translates into a required momentum resolution of $\delta p/p \approx 0.4\%$. The reconstruction of high multiplicity B decays demands a high tracking

2008 JINST 3 S08005

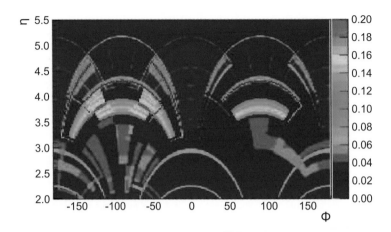

Figure 5.34: Radiation length of one IT station as a function of the pseudorapidity η and the azimuthal angle ϕ.

efficiency and at the same time a low fraction of wrongly reconstructed tracks: a track efficiency of 95% would result, for the decay $B_s^0 \to D_s^- \pi^+$, in an overall reconstruction efficiency of 80%.

5.3.1 Detector layout

The OT is designed as an array of individual, gas-tight straw-tube modules. Each module contains two staggered layers (monolayers) of drift-tubes with inner diameters of 4.9 mm. As a counting gas, a mixture of Argon (70%) and CO_2 (30%) is chosen in order to guarantee a fast drift time (below 50 ns), and a sufficient drift-coordinate resolution (200 μm). The gas purification, mixing and distribution system foresees the possibility of circulating a counting gas mixture of up to three components in a closed loop [74].

The detector modules are arranged in three stations (see figure 5.35). Each station consists of four layers, arranged in an x-u-v-x geometry: the modules in the x-layers are oriented vertically, whereas those in the u and v layers are tilted by $\pm 5^o$ with respect to the vertical, respectively. The total active area of a station is 5971×4850 mm^2. The outer boundary corresponds to an acceptance of 300 mrad in the magnet bending plane (horizontal) and 250 mrad in the non-bending plane (vertical). The inner cross-shaped boundary of the OT acceptance was determined by the requirement that occupancies should not exceed 10% at a luminosity of 2×10^{32} cm^{-2} s^{-1} (this area is covered by the IT, see section 5.2.2).

The OT assembly is shown in figure 5.35. The detector modules are supported by aluminium structures. Each station is split into two halves, retractable on both sides of the beam line. Each half consists of two independently movable units of two half layers (C-frames). The modules are positionned on the C-frames by means of precision dowel pins. The C-frames also provide routing for all detector services (gas, low and high voltage, water cooling, data fibres, slow and fast control). The OT C-frames are sustained by a stainless steel structure (OT bridge), equipped with rails allowing the independent movement of all twelve C-frames.

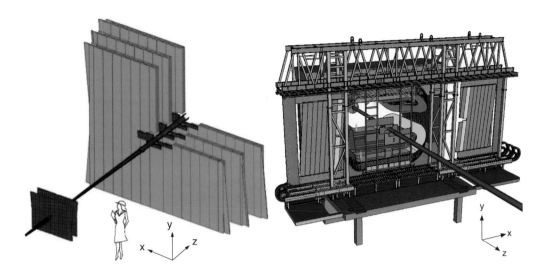

Figure 5.35: Arrangement of OT straw-tube modules in layers and stations (left) and overview of the OT bridge carrying the C-frames (right). The C-frames on both sides of the beam pipe are retracted.

5.3.2 Detector technology

Design

The design of the straw-tube module is based on the following requirements:

- Rigidity: the mechanical stability must guarantee the straw-tube position within a precision of 100 (500) μm in the x (z) direction; the anode wire has to be centered with respect to the straw tube within 50 μm over the entire straw length. The module box must be gas-tight and must withstand an overpressure of 10 mbar. The leak rate at this pressure has to be below 8×10^{-4} l/s.

- Material budget: to limit multiple scattering and the material in front of the calorimeters, the material introduced in the OT active area must not exceed few percent of a radiation length X_0 per station.

- Electrical shielding: the drift tubes must be properly shielded to avoid crosstalk and noise. Each straw must have a firm connection to the module ground. The module envelope itself must form a Faraday cage connected to the ground of the straw tubes and of the front-end electronics.

- Radiation hardness: the detector should withstand 10 years of operation at the nominal luminosity without a significant degradation of its performance. During that time the anode wires will accumulate a charge of up to 1 C/cm in the most irradiated area. As a consequence, all detector materials have to be radiation resistant and must have low outgassing.

The layout of the straw-tube modules is shown in figure 5.36. The modules are composed of two staggered layers (monolayers) of 64 drift tubes each. In the longest modules (type F) the monolayers are split longitudinally in the middle into two sections composed of individual straw

2008 JINST 3 S08005

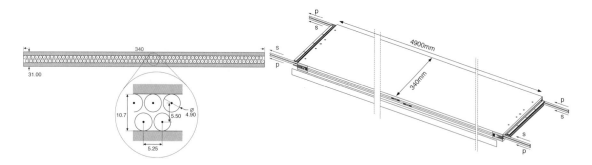

Figure 5.36: Cross section of a straw-tubes module (left) and overview of a straw-tubes module design (right).

tubes. Both sections are read out from the outer end. The splitting in two sections is done at a different position for the two monolayers to avoid insensitive regions in the middle of the module. F-modules have an active length of 4850 mm and contain a total of 256 straws. In addition to the F-type modules there exist short modules (type S) which are located above and below the beam pipe. These modules have about half the length of F-type modules, contain 128 single drift tubes, and are read out only from the outer module end. A layer half is built from 7 long and 4 short modules. The complete OT detector consists of 168 long and 96 short modules and comprises about 55000 single straw-tube channels.

Construction

The straw tubes are produced by winding together two strips of thin foils,[29] as shown in figure 5.37: the inner (cathode) foil is made of 40 μm carbon doped polyimide (Kapton-XC[30]); the outer foil (Kapton-aluminium) is a laminate[31] made of 25 μm polyimide, to enhance the straws gas tightness, and 12.5 μm aluminium, crucial to ensure fast signal transmission and good shielding.

To build a monolayer the straw-tubes were glued to panels with a cored sandwich structure consisting of a 10 mm Rohacell core and two 120 μm carbon fibre skins. High precision aluminium templates (figure 5.37) were used during the glueing to position the straw-tubes to better than 50 μm over the entire module length. After the straw-tubes were glued to the panel the wiring was started. A gold-plated tungsten wire[32] with a diameter of 25.4 μm is used for the anodes. The wire was sucked through the straw-tube. At each end the wire is guided using injection-molded Noryl endpieces. To centre the wire also along the straw-tube Noryl wire locators had been placed every 80 cm inside the straws. The wires were strung with a tension of 0.7 N and were soldered to 5 mm long pads of a printed circuit board.

Special holding-devices, shown in figure 5.38, were used to keep the support panels flat to within 100 μm during the glueing of the straws and wiring. They were also used to assemble two monolayer panels into a detector module (figure 5.38). The sides of the modules were closed by 400 μm thick carbon fibre sidewalls. Spacers at the two module ends ensure the proper separation

---

[29]Lamina Dieletrics Ltd., UK.
[30]DuPont™.
[31]GTS Flexible Materials Ltd., USA.
[32]California Fine Wire, USA.

2008 JINST 3 S08005

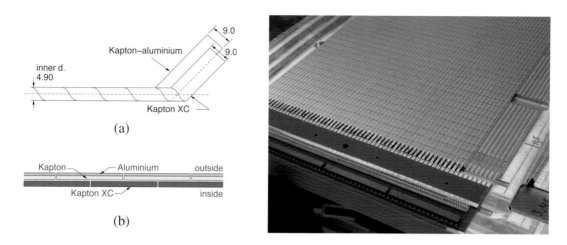

Figure 5.37: Left: (a) scheme of the straw winding using two foils; (b) Kapton-XC as inner foil and a Kapton-aluminium laminate as outer foil. Right: straws on the high precision aluminium template.

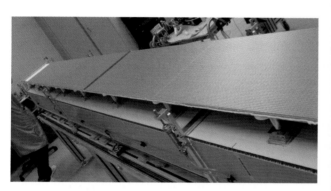

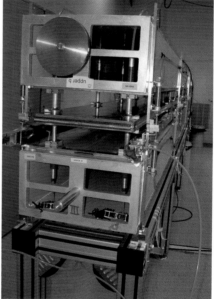

Figure 5.38: Left: straw-tube monolayer on a holding-device ready for gluing. Right: two straw-tube monolayers in a holding device while being glued to form a detector module.

of the two monolayers and provide an interface to the module gas pipes. All glueing steps were performed using Araldite AY103 in combination with the HY991 hardener. The glue viscosity was enhanced by adding silica gel.

The side walls and also the inner sides of the support panels are covered by the Kapton-aluminium laminate, which ensures the gas tightness of the module and provides a closed Faraday cage.

The construction of the detector modules was completed by three production sites in about two years. All detector parts were centrally checked and then distributed to the production sites. The production procedure and the quality monitoring steps and tools were the same in all produc-

2008 JINST 3 S08005

tion sites. Quality assurance included the check of the wire tension, pitch, and leakage current (in air) prior to the module sealing. Finished modules were tested for gas tightness. Using CO_2 as counting gas the modules were operated with a slowly increasing anode voltage to ensure that the leakage current per wire dropped below 1 nA for a voltage of 1700 V. Finally, the uniformity of the signal response of all drift cells was checked with a radioactive source.

Material budget

The forward geometry of the LHCb detector allows all detector services and supports of the OT to be located outside the detector acceptance. The OT material inside the LHCb acceptance (12 layers of modules) is estimated from the weights of the single components and the total amount of glue used (140 g per panel, 400 g to glue straw-tubes and to close the module) [75]. The total material of one station (four layers of modules, i.e. 8 monolayer panels) is on average equivalent to 3.2% of X_0. The total OT material sums up to 9.6% of X_0.

Ageing tests

In the region closest to the beam axis, the OT detector modules are foreseen to operate under particle rates per straw length of up 100 kHz/cm. Extensive ageing studies of test modules and of scaled-down prototypes showed that the detector technology is resistant to radiation doses corresponding to accumulated charges of up to 1.3 C/cm. No hints of a change of the gas amplificaton were seen in these studies which were performed with an average acceleration factor of a approximately 25.

However, irradiating mass production modules with low intensity β or γ sources with acceleration factors of O(1) produced a significant drop of the gas amplification. Most strikingly, this gain loss was not observed in the region of highest irradiation intensity (anode currents around 20 nA/cm) but at modest intensities and anode currents of 2–5 nA/cm [76]. The damage was only observed upstream (with respect to the gas flow) of the irradiating source. An analysis of the affected anode wires revealed a thin (less than 1 μm thick) insulating deposit. Although the exact mechanism is not yet understood, the glue (Araldite AY103) used to build the modules is identified as cause of the depositions. A number of preventive and remedial actions have been studied: long-term flushing of the detector modules with gas (CO_2) as well as warming-up the modules to 40°C while being flushed, significantly reduce this effect. Large anode currents deliberately provoked by increasing the high voltage above the nominal operating voltage can be used to clean the anode wires, should the insulating deposits reduce the gain beyond an acceptable level.

5.3.3 Electronics

The front-end (FE) electronics measures the drift times of the ionization clusters produced by charged particles traversing the straw-tubes with respect to the beam crossing (BX) signal [77]. The drift times are digitized for every bunch crossing (25 ns) and stored in a digital pipeline to await the Level-0 decision. On a positive L0 decision, the digitized data of up to 3 bunch crossings (to cover a time range of up to 75 ns) is transmitted via optical links to the Level-1 buffer (TELL1)

2008 JINST 3 S08005

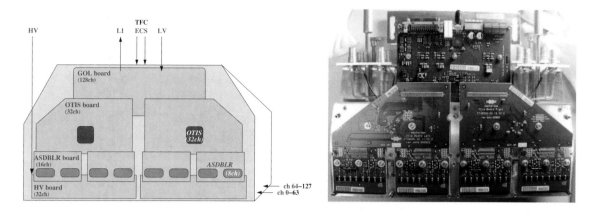

Figure 5.39: Design (left) and photograph (right) of the FE electronics mounted in a FE box. In the photograph the HV boards are not visible, because hidden by the ASDBLR boards.

boards. The radiation dose expected for the front-end electronics is only 10 kRad, well below the maximum tolerable dose of 2 Mrad.

As shown in figure 5.39, the FE electronics has a modular design, consisting of several interconnected boards housed inside a metallic box (FE box). These boxes are mounted at each end of the detector modules. A FE box is the smallest independent readout unit of the OT: the digitized data of the 128 channels of one module are sent via an optical link and received by the TELL1 board; high- and low-voltage, as well as fast- and slow-control signals are connected to each FE box individually. In total, 432 FE boxes are used to read out the OT detector.

The main components of the OT readout electronics are the High Voltage (HV) board, the ASDBLR board, the OTIS board, and the GOL auxiliary (GOL/AUX) board.

Four 32-channel HV boards plug directly into the signal feedthrough of each straw-tube module. The signal feedthrough is provided by a passive printed circuit board (PCB) built into the module end and defining the reference ground for the straw-tubes and readout electronics. The HV board has a single HV connection and is thus the smallest independent HV supply unit. Anode signals are decoupled using 300 pF capacitors[33] on the PCB.

Each ASDBLR board hosts two ASDBLR chips [78]. These are custom integrated circuits, providing the complete analog signal processing chain (amplification, shaping, baseline restoration, and discrimination) for straw sensors. The ASDBLR is implemented in bipolar technology and produced with the radiation hard DMILL process It includes eight identical channels per chip, with a peaking time of 7–8 ns, selectable shaping circuits and a three-state LVDS output. The Equivalent Noise Charge (ENC) at the ASDBLR input is about $2200\,e^- + 140\,e^-/pF$, corresponding to a global ENC of about 0.9 fC when connected to the detector.

The hit outputs of two ASDBLR boards (32 channels) are connected to an OTIS board, which hosts one OTIS chip for drift time digitization. The OTIS ASIC is a radiation hard 32-channel Time-to-Digital Converter (TDC), developed specifically for the OT and manufactured in a standard $0.25\,\mu m$ CMOS process [79, 80]. The OTIS block diagram is shown in figure 5.40. The TDC core measures the arrival time of the ASDBLR signals with respect to the LHC clock propagating through a 25 ns long Delay Locked Loop (DLL), a regulated chain of 32 double-staged

---

[33]JOHANSON 302R29W331KV4E.

2008 JINST 3 S08005

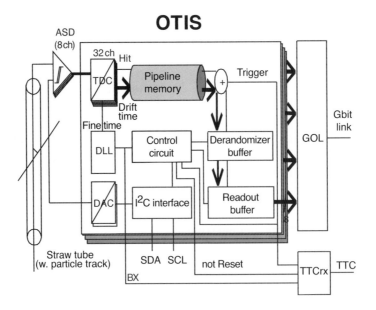

Figure 5.40: OTIS Block Diagram.

delay elements. The time digitization is done using the 64 delay-stages of the DLL (64 time bins) giving a theoretical bin size of 390 ps. The drift time data is stored in a pipeline memory with a depth of 164 events, allowing a L0 trigger latency of 160 clock cycles to compensate for trigger rate fluctuations. If a trigger occurs, the corresponding data words of up to 3 bunch crossings (the number of bunch crossings transferred is selectable) are transferred to a derandomizing buffer, able to store data from up to 16 consecutive triggers. Both, pipeline memory and derandomizing buffer are dual-ported SRAM memories. A control unit processes and reads out the data of each triggered event within 900 ns. The readout interface of the OTIS chip is 8-bit wide.

The data processing within the OTIS is clock driven. The chip operates synchronous to the 40 MHz LHC clock. A standard I^2C interface is used for setup and slow control.

The OTIS boards in a FE box are connected to one GOL/AUX board. This board [81] provides the outside connections to the FE box: the power connection, the interface to the fast-control (BX clock, triggers, resets) and the interface to the slow-control (I^2C). Three power regulators supply the different voltages (+2.5 V ±3.0 V) needed by the OTIS and the ASDBLR chips. The GOL/AUX board hosts the GOL optical serializer chip [6] connected to an optical receiver mezzanine card on the TELL1 board.

As the data volume of the OT is large compared to other sub-detectors only the optical links of the nine FE boxes belonging to a layer quadrant are connected to a single TELL1 board. To read out the 432 FE boxes of the OT 48 TELL1 boards are used.

Cooling

As the FE box is entirely closed, cooling of the electronic components inside the boxes is necessary. All electronic boards are therefore mounted on a cooling frame (see figure 5.39) which is screwed to water-cooled plates on the C-frames.

2008 JINST 3 S08005

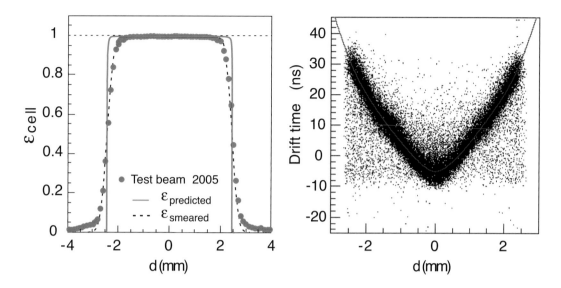

Figure 5.41: Left: hit efficiency as a function of the distance to the anode wire. Right: relation between the drift time and the calculated hit distance to the wire. Note the maximum drift time of approximately 45 ns.

High-voltage system

Each FE box has four independent HV connections, one for each 32-channels HV board. Two CAEN SY1527LC mainframes, each equipped with four 28-channels A1833BPLC supply boards, are used as HV supply. Using an 8-to-1 distribution scheme the 1680 HV connections of the detector are mapped on 210 CAEN HV channels. The distribution is realized using a patch panel wich offers the possibility to disconnect individual HV boards (32 channels) by means of an HV jumper. Both components, the HV supply as well as the patch panel are located in the counting house. Access to the HV system during data taking is therefore possible.

5.3.4 Test Beam results

To determine the performance of the detector modules in combination with the readout electronics, 4 short modules from the mass production equipped with FE boxes were tested at the 6 GeV electron beam of the DESY II facility in Hamburg [82]. Although the number of OT modules (4 modules, or 8 monolayers) was sufficient to allow full track reconstruction, a silicon strip telescope was used to provide redundant information for the determination of the coordinates at which the beam particle traverses the detector. The trigger signal (which was also used offline as a time reference) was generated by a coincidence of two scintillator counters installed downstream of the OT modules. The nominal counting gas mixture Ar/CO_2 was used.

The electron beam illuminated up to 7 straws per monolayer. In the offline analysis, the relation between the measured drift time and the distance to the wire (R-t relation, see figure 5.41) was established using the predicted distance of closest approach of the particle to the anode wire. The R-t relation was then used to convert measured drift times to coordinates. The hit finding efficiency, shown as a function of the distance to the wire in figure 5.41, is determined by verifying

2008 JINST 3 S08005

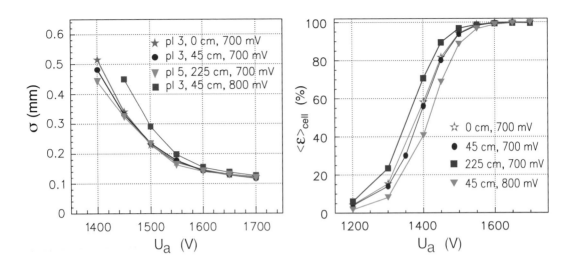

Figure 5.42: Performance of the straw-tube module: the position resolution (left) and the average efficiency (right) of a single cell are shown as a function of the HV value. The different curves correspond to different discriminator threshold voltages, and different distances between the electron beam spot and the front-end electronics.

whether the OT produced a hit at the predicted position. The position resolution is determined by comparing the measured hit coordinates to the predicted ones (residual) and by fitting a single gaussian to the distribution.

The performance of the OT straw-tube modules is determined for HV values ranging between 1200 and 1700 V, and for ASDBLR discriminator thresholds ranging from 1.5 fC to 5.5 fC. As shown in figure 5.42, efficiencies larger than 99% in the centre of the straw (dropping at the edge of the straw) and position resolutions of single cells below 200 μm can be attained for high voltage values above 1550 V. The noise level was found to be low: at a high voltage of 1550 V and a discriminator threshold voltage of 800 mV (corresponding to a signal threshold of 4 fC), the noise rate is below 1 kHz per channel. This corresponds to an average channel occupancy of $(7.5 \times 10^{-3})\%$. The probability to find a coherent hit in neighbouring channels (crosstalk) is found to be lower than 5% for high voltage values below 1600 V and discriminator threshold voltages above 800 mV (4 fC).

5.3.5 Alignment and monitoring

Errors in the mechanical alignment of the drift tubes can significantly degrade the track reconstruction. A single cell resolution of about 200 μm requires that the drift tubes be aligned within an accuracy of 100 μm (1 mm) in the x (z) coordinate. Therefore, care was taken during each step of the detector construction and installation to minimize alignment errors. The issue of the mechanical tolerances in the module production has been discussed in section 5.3.2. All detector C-frames which hold the modules were built with stringent requirements on the mechanical tolerances [83, 84]. During installation the positions of all modules were surveyed and the C-frames positions have been adjusted accordingly.

The reproducibility of the C-frames positioning after movement was checked to be better than the 200 μm precision of the optical survey.

2008 JINST 3 S08005

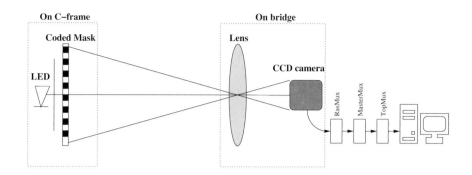

Figure 5.43: Schematic of the RASNIK alignment system.

The stability of the C-frames relative position during data taking is monitored by means of the RASNIK system [85], whose basic idea is to project the image of a detailed pattern through a lens onto a CCD camera (figure 5.43). Movements perpendicular to the optical axis are observed as change of the pattern position processed by the CCD camera, whereas movements along the axis are measured by the change in the image size. A total of 50 RASNIK lines are used for the OT monitoring. The intrinsic resolution of the system perpendicular (parallel) to the beam axis is better than 10 (150) μm respectively [86].

2008 JINST 3 S08005

Chapter 6

Particle identification

6.1 RICH

Particle identification (PID) is a fundamental requirement for LHCb. It is essential for the goals of the experiment to separate pions from kaons in selected B hadron decays. At large polar angles the momentum spectrum is softer while at small polar angles the momentum spectrum is harder; hence the particle identification system consistes of two RICH detectors to cover the full momentum range. The upstream detector, RICH 1, covers the low momentum charged particle range $\sim$1–60 GeV/c using aerogel and C_4F_{10} radiators, while the downstream detector, RICH 2, covers the high momentum range from $\sim$15 GeV/c up to and beyond 100 GeV/c using a CF_4 radiator (see figure 6.1). RICH 1 has a wide acceptance covering the full LHCb acceptance from $\pm$25 mrad to $\pm$300 mrad (horizontal) and $\pm$250 mrad (vertical) and is located upstream of the magnet to detect the low momentum particles. RICH 2 is located downstream of the magnet and has a limited angular acceptance of $\sim \pm$15 mrad to $\pm$120 mrad (horizontal) and $\pm$100 mrad (vertical) but covers the region where high momentum particles are produced. In both RICH detectors the focusing of the Cherenkov light is accomplished using a combination of spherical and flat mirrors to reflect the image out of the spectrometer acceptance. In the RICH 1 the optical layout is vertical whereas in RICH 2 is horizontal. Hybrid Photon Detectors (HPDs) are used to detect the Cherenkov photons in the wavelength range 200–600 nm. The HPDs are surrounded by external iron shields and are placed in MuMetal cylinders to permit operation in magnetic fields up to 50 mT. The RICH detector system including its electronics, monitoring, control, and the performance are described below.

6.1.1 RICH 1

The RICH 1 detector [2, 87] is located upstream of the LHCb dipole magnet, between the VELO and the Trigger Tracker, see figure 2.1. RICH 1 contains aerogel and fluorobutane (C_4F_{10}) gas radiators, providing PID from approximately $1 - -60$ GeV/c for particles inside the acceptance. A schematic, 3D model and photo of the RICH 1 detector is shown in figure 6.2. It is aligned to the LHCb coordinate axes and occupies the region $990 < z < 2165$ mm. The z-axis follows the beamline which is inclined at 3.6 mrad to the horizontal. The overall design has to respect the following constraints:

2008 JINST 3 S08005

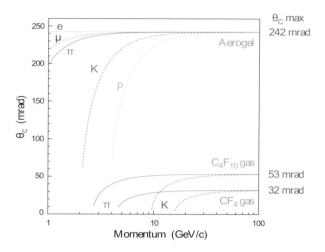

Figure 6.1: Cherenkov angle versus particle momentum for the RICH radiators.

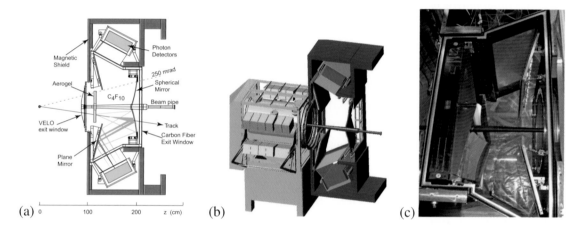

(a)   (b)   (c)

Figure 6.2: (a) Side view schematic layout of the RICH 1 detector. (b) Cut-away 3D model of the RICH 1 detector, shown attached by its gas-tight seal to the VELO tank. (c) Photo of the RICH1 gas enclosure containing the flat and spherical mirrors. Note that in (a) and (b) the interaction point is on the left, while in (c) is on the right.

- minimizing the material budget within the particle acceptance of RICH 1 calls for lightweight spherical mirrors with all other components of the optical system located outside the acceptance. The total radiation length of RICH 1, including the radiators, is $\sim 8\%\ X_0$.

- the low angle acceptance of RICH 1 is limited by the 25 mrad section of the LHCb beryllium beampipe (see figure 3.1) which passes through the detector. The installation of the beampipe and the provision of access for its bakeout have motivated several features of the RICH 1 design.

- the HPDs of the RICH detectors, described in section 6.1.5, need to be shielded from the fringe field of the LHCb dipole. Local shields of high-permeability alloy are not by themselves sufficient so large iron shield boxes are also used.

2008 JINST 3 S08005

The HPDs are located outside of the LHCb acceptance, above and below the beamline, in a region where the iron shield can be accommodated. Additional planar (flat) mirrors are required to reflect the image from the tilted spherical mirrors onto the photon detector planes.

Optical system

The parameters of the RICH 1 optical layout have been optimized with the aid of simulation. Charged particle tracks, originating from the interaction point (IP) are followed through the RICH 1 radiators. Cherenkov photons are generated uniformly along the length of each track in the aerogel and gas radiators, using the appropriate refractive indices for photons within the wavelength acceptance of the HPD photocathodes. These photons are ray-traced through the optical system and their impact points on the planes of HPDs are recorded. The Cherenkov angle at emission is then reconstructed for each photon in turn, assuming that the emission point is midway along the track trajectory through the radiator. As the true emission point is randomly distributed along the track, the tilted mirror geometry causes the reconstructed Cherenkov angle to differ from its true value and results in a smearing of the reconstructed angle. The RMS of the resulting distribution is referred to as the emission point error. The RICH 1 optical system is designed such that the emission point error is not larger than other sources of finite angular resolution, such as the HPD pixel size and the chromatic dispersion of the radiator.

In addition to the emission point error, the optical layout determines the required area of coverage of the two HPD planes. The optimization procedure required close to 100% geometrical acceptance for photons emitted by the gas radiator, while a compromise dictated by the cost, and not affecting significantly the final expected performance, reduced the acceptance for the aerogel photons to 68%. The parameters of the optics are constrained by limited space and the tilt of the spherical mirrors must ensure that the flat mirrors lie outside the acceptance of the charged particle trackers. The location of the photon detector planes is also determined by the performance of the magnetic shield boxes. To avoid loss of efficiency, the HPD planes must be in a region where the field does not exceed 3 mT and be tilted to ensure that, on average, Cherenkov photons strike the HPDs at close to normal incidence.

The parameters resulting from the optimization procedure have been adopted for the engineering design of RICH 1. The spherical mirrors have radius of curvature 2700 mm with centres of curvature at $x, y, z = 0, \pm 838, -664$ mm, which define the mirror tilt. This results in an emission point error of 0.67 mrad for the gas radiator, a value that is negligible compared with other sources of error for the aerogel. The flat mirrors are tilted at an angle 0.250 rad with respect to the y-axis, with horizontal edges lying closest to the beam line located at $y, z = \pm 350, 1310$ mm. The two HPD planes are centered at $x, y, z = 0, \pm 1187, 1502$ mm and tilted at an angle 1.091 rad with respect to the y-axis. They are each covered with 7 rows of 14 HPDs, hexagonally close packed, with centres separated by 89.5 mm. This results in two detector planes of 1302 mm $\times$ 555 mm each.

Spherical mirrors

The spherical mirrors are located within the LHCb acceptance and are traversed by charged particles and photons. Glass mirrors and their associated supports would contribute about 8% X_0, so a carbon fibre reinforced polymer (CFRP) substrate, with the mirror support outside the acceptance,

2008 JINST 3 S08005

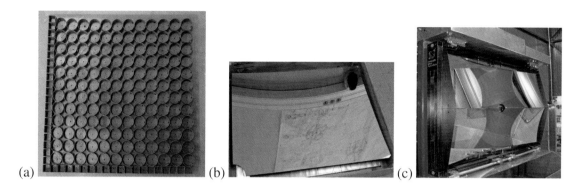

(a)   (b)   (c)

Figure 6.3: Photo of (a) the internal structure of the RICH 1 carbon fibre (CFRP) mirror; (b) a CFRP mirror; (c) the spherical mirror array viewed from the front, mounted onto its CFRP support frame.

is adopted to keep the material budget below $2\%\,X_0$. The two tilted spherical mirror surfaces, one above the beryllium beampipe, the other below, are each composed of two CFRP mirrors, making four mirror quadrants in total [88]. Each mirror has dimensions $830\,\text{mm} \times 630\,\text{mm}$ when projected onto the $x - y$ plane. The mirror construction is from two CFRP[1] sheets, moulded over a polished glass mandrel to a spherical surface of $2700\,\text{mm}$ radius and separated by a reinforcing matrix of CFRP cylinders, configured as shown in figure 6.3a. The box elements at the two outer edges provide stiffness for the three-point mounting brackets that attach the mirror to a CFRP frame (see figure 6.3c). Each mirror has a circular cut-out of radius $62.5\,\text{mm}$ to provide a nominal $10\,\text{mm}$ clearance from the beampipe (see figure 6.3b). The overall structure has an areal density of $6\,\text{kg}\,\text{m}^{-2}$, thus contributing about $1.5\%\,X_0$ to the material budget of RICH 1.

The geometrical quality of a spherical mirror is characterized by the variation in the mean radius R of each mirror and the parameter D_0, the diameter of the image in which is contained 95% of the light from a point source placed at the centre of curvature. Provided $D_0 < 2.5\,\text{mm}$ and $\Delta R/R < 1\%$, the geometry of the mirrors provides a negligible contribution to the reconstructed Cherenkov angle precision. The manufacturing and subsequent quality assurance ensures that the mirrors satisfy these specifications.

The mirror assembly is made from two CFRP half frames. Each carries an upper and a lower quadrant. The half frames are divided in this way to allow insertion into the RICH 1 gas enclosure (described further on in this section) from either side of the beampipe, following which the frames are clamped to form a rigid structure around the periphery. The CFRP frame is mounted on rails and supported by an optical alignment rig. Upper and lower mirror pairs are aligned to a common centre of curvature and the CFRP frame is surveyed. This frame is then installed in the gas enclosure using an identical rail system, where the frame can again be surveyed and adjusted if necessary. Simulations [89] have shown that provided all mirror segments are aligned to a precision of about 1 mrad, the alignment can be further corrected using data from reconstructed Cherenkov ring images.

The mirrors are coated using a deposition of Al(80nm)+MgF$_2$(160nm). The reflectivity that can be achieved on the CFRP substrate is the same as that on a glass support, as shown by curve V in figure 6.6 and described in section 6.1.4.

---

[1]Fibres: Toray M46J; Matrix: Bryte Technologies, EX-1515 cyanate ester resin; Manufacturer: Composite Mirror Applications Inc.,Tucson, USA.

2008 JINST 3 S08005

Flat mirrors

The flat mirrors are assembled into two planes, one above and one below the beamline. They are located outside of the acceptance, so glass substrates can be used. Each plane comprises eight rectangular mirrors with dimensions 380 mm × 347.5 mm, fabricated using 6.5 mm thick Simax[2] glass. As for the spherical mirrors, the flat mirror geometry is characterized through the parameters R and D_0. All mirrors have $|R| > 600$ m and $D_0 < 2.5$ mm. Assuming the deviations from surface sphericity are randomly distributed, this value of D_0 contributes < 0.2 mrad to the single photon Cherenkov angle precision. The mirrors are coated using the same ($Al+SiO_2+HfO_2$) process used for the RICH 2 mirrors (section 6.1.2). Each of the eight mirror segments is connected to a three-point adjustment system via a polycarbonate flange, described in section 6.1.2. The adjustment mechanism is bolted to a rigid plate that is suspended from rails. The eight mirror segments are adjusted in angle to form a single plane, then the angle of this plane is set using the optical alignment rig. Following alignment and survey, the plate is mounted on an identical rail system attached to the upstream wall of the RICH 1 gas enclosure, where the angle can again be surveyed and adjusted if necessary.

RICH 1 structure

The total weight of the RICH 1 detector is about 16 tons, mainly due to the magnetic shielding boxes. The lower box is fixed to the LHCb cavern floor and supports the gas enclosure and the lower photon detector assembly. The upper box is fixed to the cavern wall and supports the upper photon detector assembly.

Gas enclosure

The functions of the gas enclosure are to contain the C_4F_{10} gas radiator and to provide a light-tight and mechanically stable platform for all optical components. The gas enclosure must sustain a ±300 Pa pressure differential between the C_4F_{10} gas and the outside atmospheric environment. It is essentially a six-sided box machined from 30 mm thick aluminium alloy tooling plate[3] that is welded at the edges to form a 600 kg structure with a total volume of about 3.5 m³ (see figure 6.2c). All six faces have apertures. The boundaries of the upstream and downstream apertures are clear of the RICH 1 acceptance region. The upstream face attaches to a 300 μm thick stainless steel bellows that provides a gas-tight, mechanically compliant (axial stiffness 37 Nmm⁻¹) seal to the downstream face of the VELO vacuum tank. The downstream face is closed by a low-mass exit window that is sealed to a flange on the beryllium beampipe using a 1 mm thick opaque moulded silicone[4] diaphragm. The exit window is manufactured from a sandwich of two 0.5 mm thick CFRP skins separated by 16 mm thick polymethacrylimid foam. Its radiation length corresponds to 0.6% X_0. The choice of material thickness for the exit window is a compromise between material budget and the deflection (±4 mm) due to the ±300 Pa pressure differential that will be maintained by the C_4F_{10} gas system.

---

[2]3.3 borosilicate glass by SKLÁRNY KAVALIER, a.s. COMPAS, Kinskeho 703, CZ-51101 Turnov.
[3]C250, cast using type 5083 alloy.
[4]Dow Corning Sylgard 186, with 5% black pigment added.

2008 JINST 3 S08005

The side faces of the gas enclosure are fully open to maximize access for installation of the optical components and to the beampipe. They are closed by 10 mm thick aluminium door panels. With the doors bolted in place the maximum displacement of any part (except the exit window) of the gas enclosure due to variations of gas pressure is less than 150 μm. Apertures above and below the beamline are sealed using windows that allow Cherenkov light to reach the HPDs. These windows are 8 mm thick quartz[5] with dimensions 1360 mm $\times$ 574 mm, fabricated from two equal-size panes, glued together along one edge. The quartz windows are coated with MgF_2 to reduce surface reflection losses from 8% to 4%.

Magnetic shield boxes

The HPDs are located in the upstream fringe field of the LHCb dipole of about 60 mT. They operate at full efficiency at a B-field up to a maximum of 3 mT. So the shield boxes need to attenuate the external field by a factor of at least 20, they need to be large enough to accommodate the HPDs and their associated readout, and they must not obstruct Cherenkov light falling on the HPD photocathodes. In addition, the bending of charged particles in the region between the VELO and the TT station provides a momentum measurement that is important for the trigger. Therefore, in designing the magnetic shields, due consideration was given to maintaining the field integral in this region.

A schematic of the shielding structure is shown in figure 6.2. The magnetic design was optimized using the OPERA/TOSCA[6] finite element modelling software. It is assembled from 50 and 100 mm thick high purity ARMCO[7] plates. Measurements made with the shields in place and the LHCb dipole at full field indicate that the maximum B-field at the HPD plane is 2.4 mT, while the field integral between the IP ($z = 0$) and the TT ($z = 2500$ mm) is 0.12 Tm. Further details of the modelling and measurements are reported in reference [90]. The overall dimensions (x, y, z) of the shield are 1950 mm $\times$ 4000 mm $\times$ 1175 mm. The weight of each box is about 75 kN and the magnetic forces at full field are about 50 kN. The rigidity of the shielding structure and mounting ensures that any displacement of the HPD assembly is less than 0.5 mm when the LHCb magnet current is switched on.

6.1.2   RICH 2

The RICH 2 detector [91, 92] is located between the last tracking station and the first muon station, see figure 2.1. It contains a CF_4 gas radiator, providing PID from approximately 15 to ≥ 100 GeV/c for particles within the reduced polar angle acceptance of ± 120 mrad (horizontal) and ± 100 mrad (vertical). Two schematics and a photograph of the RICH 2 detector are shown in figure 6.4. It is aligned vertically, with its front face positioned at 9500 mm from the interaction point and with a depth of 2332 mm. The overall design had to comply with the following constraints:

- the supporting structures and the photon detectors need to be placed outside the acceptance of the spectrometer and the HPDs are located left and right of the beamline where the iron

---

[5]HERAEUS Suprasil 2B.
[6]Vector Fields plc, Oxford, UK.
[7]ARMCO - Stabilized iron; C$\leq$ 0.01%, S= 0.01%, Mn$\leq$ 0.06%, Si: traces, P= 0.01%.

2008 JINST 3 S08005

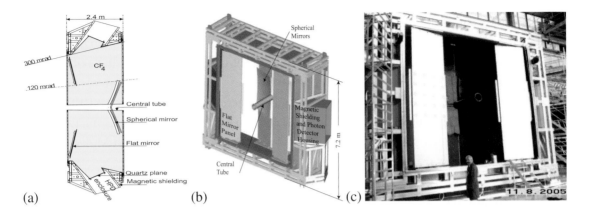

(a) (b) (c)

Figure 6.4: (a) Top view schematic of the RICH 2 detector. (b) A schematic layout of the RICH 2 detector. (c) A photograph of RICH 2 with the entrance window removed.

shielding is accommodated. To shorten the overall length of the detector, the reflected images from tilted spherical mirrors are reflected by flat secondary mirrors onto the detector planes. The requirement that the photon detectors are situated outside the full LHCb acceptance defines the lateral dimensions of the detector. The total radiation length of RICH 2, including the gas radiator, is about 0.15 X_0.

- the lower angular acceptance of the RICH 2 detector, 15 mrad, is limited by the necessary clearance of 45 mm around the beampipe. This distance is required to accommodate the heating jacket and thermal insulation which is required for the bakeout of the vacuum chamber (chapter 3). To gain mechanical stability of RICH 2 and minimize the material in the acceptance of the spectrometer, the detector does not split in two halves along the $x = 0$ plane.

- as for RICH 1, the HPDs are located in large iron boxes in order to be shielded from the fringe field of the LHCb dipole.

Optical system

The final adjustment of the optical layout of RICH 2 has been performed with the aid of simulation, in a similar way to that described in section 6.1.1. This involves defining the position and radius of curvature of the two spherical mirror planes, the position of the two flat mirror planes, and the position of the two photon detector planes. The smearing of the reconstructed Cherenkov angle distribution provides a measure of the quality of the focusing. The RMS of the emission-point error should be small compared to the other contributions to the Cherenkov angle resolution such as the pixelization of the photon detectors and the chromatic dispersion of the radiator. The latter effect is the limiting factor for the resolution in RICH 2, and corresponds to an uncertainty of 0.42 mrad on the Cherenkov angle per photon [91]. The optical elements of RICH 2 must therefore be set such that the emission-point error is small compared to this value.

The parameters resulting from the optimization procedure have been adopted for the engineering design of RICH 2. The spherical mirrors have radius of curvature 8600 mm with centres of

2008 JINST 3 S08005

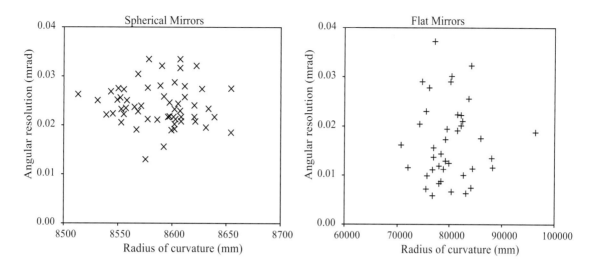

Figure 6.5: Angular precision as a function of radius of curvature for the spherical and the flat mirrors in RICH 2. The angular precision of a mirror is defined as the RMS angular deviation of the normal to the mirror surface at the given point from the radius of curvature R, and is related to D_0 by the expression $D_0/8R$, under the assumption that the light distribution of the spot is gaussian.

curvature at $x, y, z = \pm 3270, 0, 3291$ mm which defines the mirror tilt. The flat mirrors are tilted at an angle 0.185 rad with respect to the x-axis, with vertical edges lying closest to the beam line located at $x, z = \pm 1234, 9880$ mm. The two HPD planes are centered at $x, y, z = \pm 3892, 0, 10761$ mm and tilted at an angle 1.065 rad with respect to the x-axis. They are each covered with 9 rows of 16 HPDs, hexagonally close packed, with centres separated by 89.5 mm. This results in two detector planes of 710 mm× 1477 mm each.

Spherical and flat mirrors

There are two spherical mirror surfaces and two planes of flat mirrors, assembled either side of the beamline. The mirror substrates are made from 6 mm thick Simax glass; the development of these mirrors is described elsewhere [93–96]. The spherical mirrors are composed of hexagonal mirror elements with a circumscribed diameter of 510 mm, and there are 26 mirrors (or half-mirrors) in each plane. The flat mirror surfaces are formed from 20 rectangular mirror segments in each plane, each 410×380 mm² in area. The greatest challenge for the manufacturers was the stability of the thin flat mirror substrates, leading to highly astigmatic or edge deformations. We have therefore chosen to use as flat mirrors, substrates with a finite but large radius of curvature, of about 80 m. The measured properties of the mirrors are shown in figure 6.5. The impact on the resolution is discussed in section 6.1.8.

Mirror support and alignment

The mirror supports are the crucial elements that will allow the construction of a near perfect reflective surface from the individual mirror segments; the initial alignments of the mirrors must be better than 1 mrad to have a negligible effect on the Cherenkov ring reconstruction [89]. Each

2008 JINST 3 S08005

mirror substrate is connected to a three-point adjustment system via polycarbonate flanges and rods [92]. The adjustment mechanism is attached to large aluminium *sandwich* panels which are fastened to the top and the bottom of the superstructure. These panels are made from two 1 mm thick aluminium skins separated by 28 mm aluminium honeycomb,[8] corresponding to $\sim 4\%$ X_0. This choice of material is again a trade-off between a long-term stability requirement, reduction of the radiation length and fluorocarbon compatibility. The mirror-support system has been tested in the laboratory for more than one year and, after an initial relaxation period, it is stable to within 100 μrad [94, 96]. The fluctuations are mainly governed by temperature variations.

The mirrors have been installed and aligned in a three-step process [97]. First, all of the spherical mirror segments were aligned to within 50 μrad of their common focal point. Then a few flat mirrors were aligned together with the coupled spherical mirrors. The final step was to align the rest of the flat mirrors with respect to these. The total error on the alignment is of the order of 100 μrad. Even though the fully equipped RICH 2 detector was transported by road from the laboratory to the experimental area, no change of the alignment larger than 300 μrad of any mirror has been observed.

RICH 2 structure

The total weight of the RICH 2 detector is about 30 tons, a large fraction of which, ~ 12 tons, is the overall magnetic shielding structure. The superstructure provides the mechanically stable environment for the optical system, the overall magnetic shielding containing the photon detectors, and a lightweight configuration for the radiator gas enclosure. It is a rectangular box-shaped structure made from welded aluminium alloy rectangular hollow box sections. The deflection of the top of the structure is measured to be < 100 μm under the influence of the magnetic load. The RICH 2 detector is placed and surveyed into position as one unit on the beam line and, after this, the beampipe is installed.

Gas enclosure

The total volume of the gas enclosure is about 95 m^3, defined by the superstructure, the entrance and the exit windows. The entrance window, constituting a radiation length of 1.0% X_0, is a low mass composite panel made from two 1 mm thick carbon fibre reinforced epoxy skins, separated by 28 mm thick polymethacrylimide (PMI) foam. The exit window, constituting a radiation length of 2.5% X_0, is similarly made from two 1 mm thick aluminium skins separated by 30 mm PMI foam. The choice of core thicknesses and skin materials is a compromise between radiation length and deflection due to hydrostatic pressure exerted by the Cherenkov gas. The latter will be controlled to within $^{+200}_{-100}$ Pa at the top of the detector. The two windows are clamped and sealed onto the superstructure and are connected to each other by a castellated central tube running coaxial to the vacuum chamber; the tube is made from 2 mm thick carbon fibre epoxy composite. The diameter of the tube at the entrance window is 284.5 mm and 350.5 mm at the exit.

The two planes of photon detectors are separated from the Cherenkov gas by quartz windows on each side. Each window is made from three quartz panes glued together. Each quartz pane

---

[8]Euro-Composites S.A, Zone Industrielle - B.P. 24, 6401 Echternach.

2008 JINST 3 S08005

is 740 mm by 1480 mm and 5 mm thick, with the light opening being 720 mm by 1460 mm. The quartz plates have the same antireflective coating as for RICH 1 (section 6.1.1).

Magnetic shielding structure

The RICH 2 detector is positioned almost halfway between the 1600 ton iron yoke of the dipole and the massive ferromagnetic structure of the hadron calorimeter, shown in figure 2.1. The maximum stray field in the region where the photon detectors are located is more than 15 mT and is rapidly varying in all directions [98]. The magnetic shield boxes, which are bolted onto both sides of the RICH 2 structure, must provide a mechanically stable and light tight environment for the photon detectors and attenuate the magnetic stray field by a factor of ≥ 15. The shielding, shown in figure 6.4, is a trapezoidal structure made from 60 mm thick ARMCO iron plates. The residual magnetic field measured at the position of the photon detector plane is between 0.2 and 0.6 mT, to be compared to the simulated value of ≤ 0.4 mT.

6.1.3 Radiators

Aerogel is the ideal radiator to cover the very difficult range of refractive indices between gas and liquid. Silica aerogel is a colloidal form of quartz, solid but with an extremely low density. Its refractive index is tuneable in the range 1.01–1.10, and is ideal for the identification of particles with momentum of a few GeV/c. Aerogel has a long-established use in threshold Cherenkov counters. The development of high quality very clear samples [99] has allowed its use in RICH detectors. The dominant cause of photon loss within aerogel is Rayleigh scattering; this leads to the transmission of light with wavelength λ through a block of thickness L being proportional to e^{-CL/λ^4}, where the clarity coefficient, C, characterizes the transparency of the sample. Large hygroscopic silica aerogel [99] tiles of dimension $20.0 \times 20.0 \times 5.1$ cm^3 have been produced and tested for the LHCb experiment [100]. The refractive index is 1.030 at λ=400 nm and the clarity is below $C = 0.0054$ μm^4/cm. The effect of scattering in the aerogel dominates at high energy, so a thin (0.30 mm) window of glass is placed after the aerogel to absorb the photons with $E_\gamma > 3.5$ eV. This serves to reduce the chromatic aberration.

For a track passing through 5 cm of aerogel with $n = 1.03$, the resulting number of detected photoelectrons in a saturated ring (β=1) is expected to be ~ 6.5, calculated by MonteCarlo considering the detailed geometrical setup of the optics of RICH 1 and the wavelength response of the photon detectors. The MonteCarlo was found to describe reasonably well the number of photoelectrons measured in a test beam [100]. Tests have shown [101] that the optical properties will not degrade significantly over the timescale of the LHCb experiment. The aerogel is stable against intense irradiation and shows no significant change in transparency once tested after an accumulated fluence of up to 5.5 x 10^{13}/cm^2 of neutrons or protons, nor after a γ dose of 2.5×10^5 Gy. It is sensitive to water vapour absorption, but its transparency can be restored after a bakeout of the tiles. The volume of aerogel required is modest, ~ 30 ℓ, so its replacement, if required, would be relatively straightforward. The refractive index is fairly uniform across a tile, despite the large transverse dimension and thickness. The spread has been measured [102] to be $\sigma_{n-1}/(n-1) \sim 0.76\%$. In RICH 1 the aerogel sits in the C$_4$F$_{10}$ gas radiator. Tests have shown that C$_4$F$_{10}$ does not significantly degrade the aerogel performance [103].

2008 JINST 3 S08005

The fluorocarbon gases C_4F_{10} (RICH 1) and CF_4 (RICH 2) were chosen because their refractive indices are well matched to the momentum spectrum of particles from B decays at LHCb and because they have a low chromatic dispersion. The refractive indices at $0°C$ and 101325 Pa are parameterized by:

$$C_4F_{10} : (n-1) \times 10^6 = 0.25324/(73.7^{-2} - \lambda^{-2})$$

and

$$CF_4 : (n-1) \times 10^6 = 0.12489/(61.8^{-2} - \lambda^{-2})$$

where the photon wavelength λ is in nm [104]. For C_4F_{10}, n=1.0014 and for CF_4, n=1.0005 at $\lambda = 400$ nm. The effective radiator lengths are about 95 cm in C_4F_{10} and 180 cm in CF_4. The estimated photoelectron yield is ~30 and ~22 respectively for charged $\beta \approx 1$ particles.

The gas radiators are operated slightly above atmospheric pressure $\lesssim 50$ Pa (measured at the top of the gas vessel) and at ambient temperature. Pressure and temperature are recorded in order to compensate variations in the refractive index (section 6.1.7). These fluorocarbons are transparent well below 150 nm; CO_2 is used as a pressure balancing gas which itself is transparent down to 180 nm [105]. Since the quantum efficiency of the HPDs is zero below 190 nm (section 6.1.5), air contamination does not significantly affect the photon yield. O_2 and H_2O contamination are however kept low at about 100 ppm, mainly due to possible radiation-induced formation of HF. The CO_2 fraction is kept constant at ~1%.

6.1.4 Mirror reflectivity studies

Several reflectivity coatings are available for RICH mirrors; the choice depends on the Cherenkov photon spectrum, the mean angle of incidence, the long term stability and compatibility to fluorocarbons. Seven different coatings have been tested [93, 106] and the reflectivity measured with a spectrophotometer at an incidence angle of 30°, close to the average angle with which the photons will impinge on the RICH 2 mirrors. The results are shown in figure 6.6. The reflectivity coatings for the RICH 1 mirrors have been optimized for the the different mean angles of incidence, i.e. 25° for the spherical mirrors and 45° for the flat mirrors.

Simulation studies have been performed by convoluting the reflectivity data with the quantum efficiency of the photon detectors, the Cherenkov photon energy spectra and the transmittance of the CF_4 radiator in RICH 2. The results of the simulation, in terms of the relative number of detected photons, are summarised in table 6.1.

The reflectivity of the two coatings with a layer of hafnium oxide (HfO_2) is very high in the near UV (curve I and II in figure 6.6), where the quantum efficiency of the photon detector is peaked. The simulation shows that good matching, taking into account the two reflections on spherical and flat mirrors, leads to a detected photon yield 5% higher for this coating compared to other UV extended coatings with magnesium fluoride (MgF_2) as the surface layer. Magnesium fluoride coatings have been successfully used in RICH detectors with C_4F_{10} and C_5F_{12} gas radiators in the DELPHI [107] and COMPASS [108] experiments, and hafnium oxide coatings have been successfully tested in C_6F_{14} vapour. Hafnium oxide also provides a very hard and chemically inert protective layer for the mirrors. For these reasons the Al + SiO_2 + HfO_2 coating was chosen for all RICH 1 and RICH 2 glass mirrors. SiO_2 is used for the middle layer of the multi-layer coating, and not MgF_2, for technical reasons.

2008 JINST 3 S08005

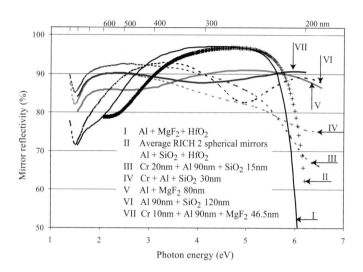

Figure 6.6: Reflectivity of several mirror coatings on glass as a function of the photon energy. The angle of incidence is 30°.

Table 6.1: Relative number of detected photons simulated in RICH 2 for different mirror coatings. The values are normalised to the highest photoelectron yield, set to 1.

Coating	Photoelectron yield
$Cr + Al + SiO_2$ (30 nm)	0.865
$Al + SiO_2$	0.945
$Cr + Al + MgF_2$	0.947
$Al + MgF_2$	0.960
$Cr + Al + SiO_2$ (15 nm)	0.960
$Al + SiO_2 + HfO_2$	1
$Al + MgF_2 + HfO_2$	1.00

6.1.5 Photon Detectors

Pixel Hybrid Photon Detector

The RICH detectors utilize Hybrid Photon Detectors (HPDs) to measure the spatial positions of emitted Cherenkov photons. The HPD is a vacuum photon detector in which a photoelectron, released from the conversion in a photocathode of an incident photon, is accelerated by an applied high voltage of typically 10 to 20 kV onto a reverse-biased silicon detector. During the photoelectron energy dissipation process in silicon, electron-hole pairs are created at an average yield of one for every 3.6 eV of deposited energy. Carefully-designed readout electronics and interconnects to the silicon detector result in very high efficiency at detecting single photoelectrons.

A dedicated pixel-HPD has been developed by LHCb, in close collaboration with industry [109]. The specific RICH requirements are a large area coverage ($\sim$3.5 m^2) with high active-to-total area ratio after close-packing (64%), high granularity (2.5$\times$2.5 mm^2 at the photocathode) and high speed (25 ns timing resolution). The pixel-HPD is shown in figure 6.7. It is

2008 JINST 3 S08005

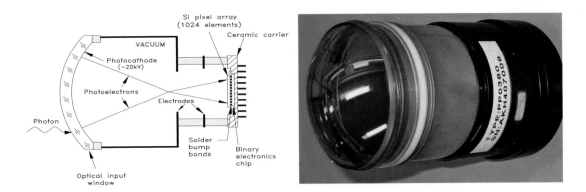

Figure 6.7: Left: a schematic and right: a photograph of the pixel-HPD.

based on an electrostatically focussed tube design with a tetrode structure, de-magnifying by a factor of ~5 the photocathode image onto a small silicon detector array. The silicon detector is segmented into 1024 pixels, each 500 μm×500 μm in size and arranged as a matrix of 32 rows and 32 columns. This leads to the required pixel size at the HPD entrance window of 2.5×2.5 mm^2. The nominal operating voltage of the HPD is -20 kV, corresponding to ~5000 electron-hole pairs released in the silicon.

The silicon pixel detector array is bump-bonded to a binary readout chip (section 6.1.6). This flip-chip assembly is mounted and wire-bonded onto a Pin Grid Array (PGA) ceramic carrier, forming the HPD anode. Since all anode parts are encapsulated in vacuum, they must be compatible with the vacuum tube technologies, and must stand high (300°C) bakeout temperatures. In particular, a specific fine-pitch bump-bonding process has been developed for this application.[9] The HPD entrance window is fabricated from quartz and forms a spherical surface, with 7 mm thickness and 55 mm inner radius of curvature. The photocathode is of the *thin-S20* multi-alkali type, deposited on the quartz inner surface. Normally-incident Cherenkov photons to the HPD plane can be detected over an active diameter of 75 mm and, since the overall tube diameter is 83 mm, the intrinsic tube active area fraction is (75/83)^2=0.817. A total of 484 tubes (196 for RICH1 and 288 for RICH2) are required to cover the four RICH photon detection surfaces.

The demagnification by 5 of the photoelectron image is achieved by biasing the photocathode at -20 kV, the first electrode at -19.7 kV and the second electrode at -16.4 kV. The RMS values for the point spread function (PSF) at the pixel array are constant over the tube radius and equal to 80 μm for red light and 180 μm for blue-near UV light, in the absence of magnetic field.

HPD test results

The HPDs have been fabricated in industry[10] and were then qualified at two test facilities to determine their efficiency and optimum working parameters, before installation at CERN. Each HPD in turn was placed in a light-tight box, illuminated with an LED of wavelength 470 nm, and read out by custom electronics. A selection of test results is presented below. Measurements of the quantum efficiencies (QEs) were carried out after manufacture at Photonis-DEP. Measurements were then

---

[9]VTT, Finland.
[10]Photonis-DEP, Roden, Netherlands.

2008 JINST 3 S08005

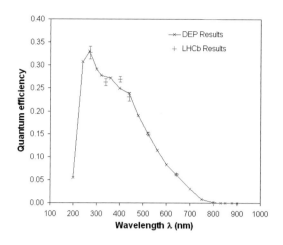

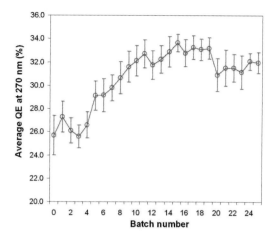

Figure 6.8: QE measurement for one of the best HPD.

Figure 6.9: The average QE(%) at 270 nm versus the HPD batch number.

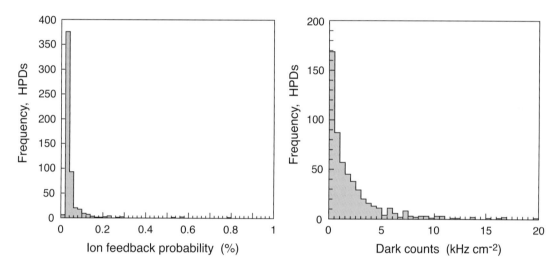

Figure 6.10: Distributions of the ion-feedback rate (left) and of the dark-count rates (right).

repeated at the test facilities for a subsample of 10% of the HPDs, using a calibrated photodiode and a quartz-tungsten halogen lamp. The QE curve for one of the best tubes is shown in figure 6.8. The average QE value per HPD batch number and the running average QE value are shown in figure 6.9 for all HPDs (484 tubes plus 66 spares). The QE curves show an average maximum of 31% at 270 nm, considerably above the specification minimum of 20%.

The vacuum quality in the HPD tube is determined by measuring ion feedback. During the acceleration process, photoelectrons may hit residual gas atoms, producing ions. These drift to the photocathode, releasing 10–40 electrons which are detected 200–300 ns after the primary photon signal. Figure 6.10 shows that the ion feedback rate is well below the specification maximum of 1%, indicating that the vacuum quality is excellent.

An important quality factor of an HPD is low dark-count rate, the main sources being thermionic electron emission at the photocathode, electrostatic field emission and any resulting

2008 JINST 3 S08005

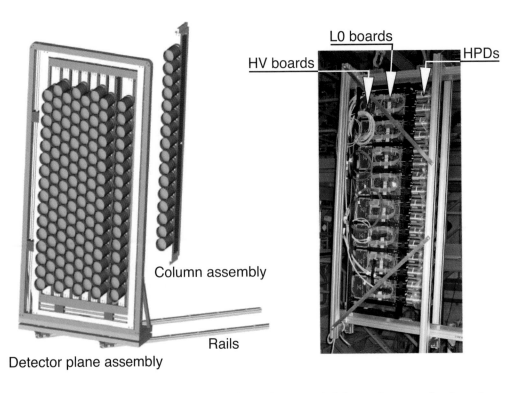

Figure 6.11: Left: the RICH 2 column mounting scheme and right: a photograph of a column.

ion feedback. Figure 6.10 shows the measured dark-count rates in the sample of HPDs in a run with the LEDs off. Dark-count rates are typically below the specification value, 5 kHz/cm^2 with respect to the photocathode area, which in turn is $\sim10^3$ less than the maximum occupancy expected in the RICH detectors.

HPD testing was carried out at a rate of 30–40 HPDs per month. A total of 97% have been found to meet or exceed the design criteria in key areas.

Photon Detector integration

The HPDs are grouped in four detection planes (two for RICH1 and two for RICH2) and positioned on a hexagonal lattice. The hexagonal close-packing factor is 0.907. Each tube is completely surrounded by a 1 mm thick cylindrical magnetic shield which protects against stray external B-fields up to 5 mT (the maximum field value within the RICH 1 magnetic shielding has been measured to be 2.4 mT, see section 6.1.1). A tube-to-tube pitch of 89.5 mm in both RICH detectors has been chosen, resulting in a packing factor of $(75/89.5)^2 \times 0.907 = 0.64$. The HPDs are mounted on columns which are installed in the magnetic shielding boxes of the two RICH detectors. There are 2×7 columns of HPDs in RICH 1 with 14 HPDs per column and 2×9 columns in RICH 2 with 16 HPDs per column. Figure 6.11 illustrates the column mounting scheme for RICH 2. The column also contains front-end electronics boards (one per pair of HPDs), power supply distribution, cabling and active cooling, all within one mechanical module. The electronics boards and power distribution are described in section 6.1.6.

2008 JINST 3 S08005

6.1.6 Electronics

The RICH electronics system reads out data from the HPDs (about 5×10^5 channels) and conforms to the general electronics architecture of LHCb (see section 2.2). The electronics system is divided into so-called Level-0 (L0) and Level-1 (L1) regions. The L0 electronics are all located on-detector where they will be exposed to radiation and must therefore contain only radiation-qualified components. The L1 electronics modules are housed in the counting house behind the radiation-shield wall and hence are not required to be radiation tolerant.

Level-0 electronics

The L0 electronics comprises the pixel chip, ZIFs/kaptons, L0 board and LV/HV distribution, and is described below.

Pixel Readout Chip: At the beginning of the electronics readout chain is the LHCBPIX1 pixel chip [110] that forms part of the anode assembly of the HPD (section 6.1.5). The chip has been designed in a commercial 0.25 μm CMOS process using special layout techniques to enhance its resistance to radiation. The chip is connected to a silicon pixel sensor by an array of solder bump-bonds, one per channel. Each pixel measures 62.5 μm by 500 μm and 8192 pixels are arranged as a matrix of 32 columns by 256 rows. Circuitry on the chip logically ORes eight adjacent pixels, thus transforming the matrix into 1024 channels of 32 by 32, each of size 500 μm by 500 μm. Signals from the silicon sensor are amplified, shaped and then compared with a global threshold. Hits are buffered for the duration of the Level-0 trigger latency and triggered events are then read out by way of a 16-deep multi-event FIFO buffer. The 32 columns are read out in parallel. The analog behaviour of the chip is crucial for a good photodetection efficiency, in particular low noise and uniform threshold. Measured values are well within the HPD specifications, with typically 160 electrons noise, compared to a signal of 5000 electrons, and a mean threshold of 1200 electrons with RMS spread of 100 electrons.

ZIFs and Kaptons: Signals to and from the HPD pass through the pins of the ceramic pin-grid-array carrier. This is plugged into a 321-pin Zero-Insertion-Force (ZIF) connector mounted on a small circuit board. The board also contains passive components for filtering and line-termination. Signals are then transmitted on two Kapton cables which also carry the low-voltage power to the HPD. These Kaptons allow mechanical flexibility between the mounting of the HPDs and the other Level-0 components.

L0 Board: The L0 board [111] acts as an interface between the HPDs and the ECS (Experiment Control System), TFC (Timing and Fast Control) and data transmission systems. This interfacing is implemented in the Pixel Interface (PINT). The antifuse gate array, ACTEL AX1000, was chosen for its tolerance to single event effects (single event latch-up and single event upset). Its main tasks are to receive data from two HPDs, add headers containing event information and data-integrity checks, and transfer events to the data transmission system. A total of 242 L0 boards are used in the RICH detectors. A photograph of a single board is shown in figure 6.12. The tolerance of the PINT to single event effects was verified by irradiation tests to simulate the expected dose in the LHCb environment. The measured rate of single event upset (SEU) was negligible, no cases of latch-up were observed and chips survived many times the expected dose of ionising radi-

2008 JINST 3 S08005

Figure 6.12: A photograph of the L0 board. The optical receiver and transmitters are visible at the top. The PINT gate array is in the centre of the board.

ation. All other components on the L0 board have been designed in radiation-hardened or tolerant technologies already qualified to levels far in excess of the RICH environment.

The optical data transmission consists of Gigabit Optical Link (GOL) chips [112] and Vertical Cavity Surface Emitting Lasers (VCSEL). The GOLs serialise the data into a 1.6 Gbit/s bit stream using 8 b/10 b encoding and the VCSELs convert this into an optical signal of 850 nm wavelength. Two output fibres, one per HPD, transmit the data from each L0 board. At a 1MHz trigger rate, the aggregate output data rate from the RICH photon detectors is in the region of 500 Gbit/s distributed over 484 optical fibres. Also on the board is a TTCrx [113] which generates the 40 MHz clock and trigger and calibration signals. The input to the TTCrx arrives on fibres connected to the global TFC system. Finally, a chip known as the Analog-Pilot generates reference voltages required by the HPDs and digitizes monitoring signals such as the temperature of the board as measured by PT1000 sensors.

LV/HV Distribution: The low voltages required by the HPDs and the L0 boards are provided by the LV distribution system. These voltages are generated locally using radiation-tolerant linear voltage regulators mounted on the LV boards. Each LV board can power two L0 boards independently, and four LV boards are daisy-chained together in an HPD column. The top-most contains a SPECS slave module [41] which provides the interface for the configuration of the HPDs and L0 boards in that column. The SPECS interface is also used for switching on and off the voltage regulators, thus allowing careful control of the powering of the column.

The high voltages for the HPDs are provided by the HV distribution system [114]. As shown in figure 6.13b, the three voltages are derived from a 20 kV input by means of a resistive divider, one per half-column, and short circuit protection is provided by 1 Gohm resistors in series with each HPD voltage line. Various measures have been taken to minimise the risk of discharge or breakdown. The bare PCB of the HV cards is machined to introduce cuts around critical points which are then filled with dielectric gel to improve insulation. After component mounting and cabling, the entire assembly is encapsulated in silicone rubber. A photograph of a completed board is shown in figure 6.13. A total of 242 boards are used to equip the RICH detectors.

Figure 6.14 shows a photograph of all front-end electronics components mounted on a RICH HPD column. On the left are the Kapton cables shown plugged into the L0 boards, then comes a

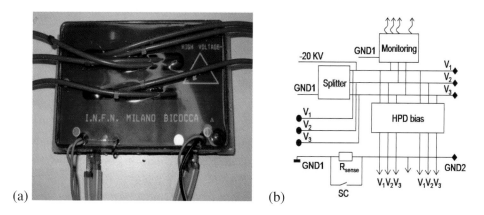

(a)   (b)

Figure 6.13: A photograph (a) and the scheme (b) of an HV board. Around the board is the silicone coating.

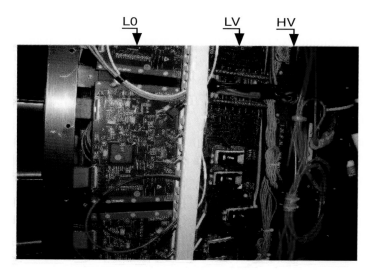

Figure 6.14: A photograph of L0, LV and HV boards mounted on a RICH HPD column.

cable tray to carry the optical fibres. Next comes the LV board which has heat sinks mounted on the surface of the voltage regulators. At the far right are the HV boards.

Level-1 electronics

The RICH L1 electronics, located off-detector in the counting room, has been designed to implement data compression and also to serve as the interface between the custom data transmission protocol of the L0 electronics and the industry-standard Gbit Ethernet protocol used by the DAQ network. The off-detector electronics also performs the important function of isolating the DAQ network from errors induced in the L0 data due to radiation induced SEU.

Each incoming serial data channel is first converted from optical to electrical using Agilent HFBR-782 optical receivers. The serial electrical data are then AC coupled to dedicated I/O pins of Virtex2Pro FPGAs, where they are deserialised using integrated Gbit transceivers that are compatible with the data encoding used by the GOL serialisers in the L0 electronics. All further data processing is done in the FPGA programmable logic.

The L1 electronics modules are controlled by signals broadcast synchronously to all subdetectors by the readout supervisor. These signals are used to control the generation of the data packets sent by the L1 to the DAQ network (see section 8.3). The data content of these packets is extracted from the incoming L0 data frames. The generation of the data packets operates autonomously to the arrival of the L0 data and therefore cannot be disrupted by incoming erroneous data. In order to predict the time of arrival of the L0 data frames so that they can be correctly inserted into the generated data packets, the operation of the L0 electronics is emulated in the off-detector modules using the TFC broadcast signals.

Once the incoming data frames have been received, the zero-suppression algorithm (L1 module copies only the non-zero bytes into the zero-suppressed buffer) is applied in parallel to all streams. The fully pipelined algorithm operates at the 1 MHz input event rate and therefore does not introduce dead-time. Zero-suppressed data are buffered in internal memory in the four ingress FPGAs before being multiplexed into multi-HPD event packets. These packets are then forwarded to the egress FPGA which further multiplexes the data into multi-event packets and transmits them using Gbit Ethernet protocol to the DAQ network using the LHCb quad Gbit Ethernet interface.

The L1 module is configured and monitored via an LHCb Credit Card PC (CCPC) [115] interface. The L1 modules are in 9U format and each can receive data from a maximum of 36 HPDs. The input links are distributed across three 12-channel optical receivers and four Virtex2Pro ingress FPGAs. For 1 MHz operation, the data throughput is expected to be limited by the capacity of the four 1 Gbit/s DAQ links at higher luminosity. Static load balancing is done by physically distributing the input fibre-optic cables across the modules. The bandwidth is distributed across 21 L1 boards to avoid bottlenecks and problems associated with inhomogeneous occupancies in the different parts of the RICH detectors.

6.1.7 Monitoring and control

The RICH Detector Control System (DCS) [116] monitors the working conditions of both RICH 1 and RICH 2, controls the operating conditions and ensures the integration of RICHes in the LHCb detector control system. It is composed of several parts:

- Power supply control and monitoring (low voltage, silicon detector bias and very high voltage);

- Environment monitoring (temperature, pressure, humidity);

- Gas quality monitoring (gas purity);

- Magnetic distortion monitoring (and correction);

- Laser alignment monitoring system.

Power supplies

Low voltage (5 V) for the front-end electronic boards is provided by commercial off-the-shelf devices, the Wiener MARATON power supply. It is radiation and magnetic field tolerant, and can be remotely monitored via a network using standard software interfaces provided by the manufacturer (OPC server). Other lower voltages (e.g. 3.3 V) required by the electronics components are generated, regulated and monitored on each front-end LV board. In addition, to improve reliability, temperature sensors placed near hot spots and critical points allow a quick check of the integrity of the electronics. A similar solution has been adopted for biasing the HPD internal silicon pixel detectors: a standard CAEN SY1527 mainframe power supply with plug-in modules. For the very high voltage of the HPDs (20 kV), no satisfactory commercial solution was found so the system was designed in-house. The system is built around a commercial HV module (ISEG CPn–200 504 24 10) controlled and monitored by a pair of DACs and ADCs connected via an I2C bus interface to a CCPC running the software to regulate the voltage and to connect to the network. The CCPC, using a *bare-bones* version of Linux, runs the control program which, in an endless loop, checks all voltages and currents, and via a DIM protocol [117] reports measurements to the high level control system. In the unlikely case of a loss of the network connection, the CCPC can still check the working conditions and cut power to the HPDs to avoid damage to personnel and HPDs.

Environment

Environmental monitoring (temperature, pressure, humidity of the radiator gas and HPD planes) is achieved using standard commercial sensors, namely platinum resistors for temperature, diaphragm sensors for pressure and HMX2000-HT sensors (by Hygrometrix) for humidity. All these devices are mounted in the harsh radiation environment hence they must be read by radiation tolerant electronics i.e. the *Embedded Local Monitor Board* (ELMB) [118].

Gas quality

The purity of the gas radiator is critical to obtain good photon transparency and for this reason a quick analysis tool to spot any contamination is employed. The stability of the gas composition is checked by periodically monitoring the speed of sound of the gas in the vessel. The speed of sound is given by $v_s = \sqrt{\frac{\gamma R T}{M}}$ where $\gamma = \frac{C_p}{C_v}$ is the ratio of specific heats of the gas, R is the universal gas constant, T the absolute temperature and M the average molecular mass. The speed is monitored by measuring the time that a sound pulse takes to propagate from an electrostatic transducer to the end of a cylindrical vessel and then, reflected by the end wall, back to the same transducer, working now as a microphonic sensor. For RICH 1 this vessel is 0.5 m long and the measured time interval is of the order of 10 ms in C_4F_{10}. For RICH 2 the vessel is approximately 0.3 m long and the relative propagation time is of the order of 3.8 ms in CF_4. The whole system is built around a timer/counter provided by a National Instrument acquisition board. The internal counter, running at 20 MHz, provides 50 ns time resolution, more than adequate to detect a 1% CO_2 contamination (which will give a 50 μs change in C_4F_{10} and 30 μs change in CF_4 for the total transit time). There are two such systems for each RICH detector, one placed on the inlet pipe and the second on the outlet of the fluid system. A typical measurement is shown in figure 6.15 which shows the change in the propagation time when the percentage of CO_2 changes from 0 to 5%.

2008 JINST 3 S08005

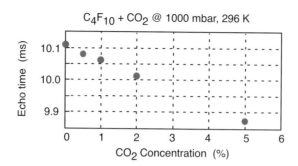

Figure 6.15: Typical sound propagation time as a function of the CO_2 percentage in C_4F_{10}.

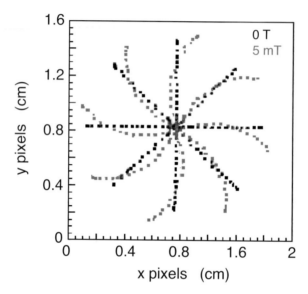

Figure 6.16: Image of a star pattern recorded on an HPD with and without a B-field of 5 mT applied parallel to the HPD axis.

Magnetic distortions

The fringe field of the LHCb dipole magnet distorts the photoelectron trajectories within the hybrid photon detectors, hence distorting the image recorded by the pixel chip. The HPDs are individually shielded by MuMetal cylinders and the arrays are completely surrounded by iron shields, however residual stray fields (up to an expected maximum of 2.4 mT in RICH 1) are sufficient to severely degrade the required precision. This effect can be clearly seen in figure 6.16, which shows how a star pattern recorded without B-field is badly distorted with a 5 mT field applied parallel to the HPD axis. Hence individual correction factors are required for each HPD and the effect of the B-field must be monitored periodically. For RICH 1 an LED system mounted in the *photon funnel* region between the HPDs and the quartz window is used. For RICH 2 a commercial light projection system projecting a fixed pattern of dots from outside the RICH vessel will monitor the magnetic distortions. In both cases the data will be acquired during dedicated calibration runs and the magnetic corrections applied off-line.

2008 JINST 3 S08005

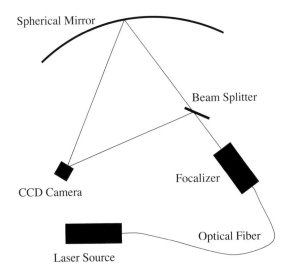

Spherical Mirror

Beam Splitter

Focalizer

CCD Camera

Optical Fiber

Laser Source

Figure 6.17: Schematic of the mirror alignment monitoring system.

Mirror alignment

Mechanical stability of the mirrors is of paramount importance to achieve the required Cherenkov angular resolution. This stability is challenging due to the size of the mirrors and the difficulty of securing them without introducing mechanical distortions to the reflecting surface. An alignment system which uses a CCD camera monitors mirror movements. On the focal plane of a given mirror, the images of two light spots are formed: the first comes directly from a laser source and the second is reflected back from the monitored mirror. Any change in the relative position of the two spots is an indication of mirror mechanical misalignment and the information is used to make an off-line correction. A schematic of the system is shown in figure 6.17. The laser light source feeds a bundle of optical fibers which generate all the required light paths (eight mirrors will be monitored in RICH 1, 16 in RICH 2). The beams are then directed to the beam splitters which guide the reference beams directly to the CCDs and the secondary beams to the mirrors.

It can be demonstrated that there is a linear transformation law between a change in the mirror tilt $(\Delta\Theta_x, \Delta\Theta_y)$ and the relative movement of the reflected spot on the CCD (Δ_x, Δ_y):

$$\begin{aligned} \Delta\Theta_x &= A\Delta_x + B\Delta_y \\ \Delta\Theta_y &= C\Delta_x + D\Delta_y, \end{aligned}$$

where the parameters A to D are fixed constants which depend on the geometry of the system. The mirror tilts can then be determined by inverting this transformation after observing the spot movement. The system tracks the displacement between the two beam spots, even if the spots move together, with an accuracy of better than 0.01 mrad.

6.1.8 RICH performance

Test Beam studies

An extensive test beam programme has allowed the RICH photodetectors, readout electronics and radiators to be evaluated with Cherenkov radiation in a realistic environment. Of particular impor-

2008 JINST 3 S08005

Table 6.2: Comparison of the measured and expected photon yields for the individual HPDs in the RICH test beam run. The first column indicates the label of each HPD.

HPD	$\mu_{meas.}$	μ_{exp}	$\mu_{meas.}/\mu_{exp}$
L0	8.1 ±0.10	11.4 ±0.73	0.71 ±0.07
L1	10.2 ±0.16	10.0 ±0.66	1.02 ±0.07
C1	11.5 ±0.33	11.2 ±0.78	1.02 ±0.07
R0	8.7 ±0.24	8.9 ±0.73	0.98 ±0.09
R1	10.1 ±0.03	10.7 ±0.83	0.95 ±0.08

tance has been the comparison of the expected and observed photoelectron yields and Cherenkov angle resolutions. Because the predictions of these quantities for test beam operation are made using a simulation with identical assumptions to those of the full LHCb MonteCarlo, agreement between prediction and observation is an important indicator that the RICH system will perform to specification.

A demonstrator RICH detector was operated in a test beam utilizing pre-production photon detectors and realistic prototypes of the associated RICH electronics [119]. The tests were performed at the CERN-PS in the T9 facility using 10 GeV/c pions together with an N$_2$ gas radiator to generate Cherenkov light. The HPDs were arranged in columns with the close-packing arrangement that will be used in the experiment and were read out at the LHC frequency of 40 MHz. In this configuration, the Cherenkov rings from the N_2 gas radiator were fully contained within a single HPD. Having included corrections for the asynchronous nature of the test beam set-up, the photoelectron yields were found to be in good agreement with those expected from the MonteCarlo simulation, as shown in table 6.2. A distribution of the number of pixel hits observed per event on a single HPD is shown in figure 6.18. Uncertainties in the corrections for the asynchronous beam structure explain the residual differences between the data and simulated distributions.

The distribution of reconstructed Cherenkov angles was also found to be in good agreement with the simulation (see figure 6.19). The Cherenkov angle resolution was determined to be 1.66 ± 0.03 mrad, to be compared with the simulation expectation of 1.64 mrad. The dominant contributions to the Cherenkov angle resolution came from the uncertainty in the beam direction, the HPD point-spread function and the HPD pixelisation. The relative contributions of the latter two effects were significant owing to the test beam geometry but are not expected to be dominant in the final LHCb experiment.

Detector simulation

The LHCb RICH system is modelled as part of the LHCb Simulation program based on the GEANT4 simulation toolkit (see chapter 10). All important aspects of the geometry and the material description are fully simulated. A database is setup with all this information which is then input into the simulation and the reconstruction programs.

The Cherenkov light generation is performed inside GEANT4, and the photons propagated with full knowledge of the expected reflectivities, transmissions and refraction effects at the various optical elements. The Rayleigh scattering in aerogel and absorption in the various media are also

2008 JINST 3 S08005

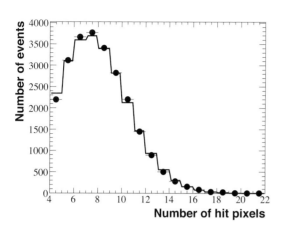

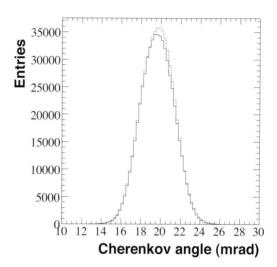

Figure 6.18: Number of pixel hits per event for data (points) and simulation (histogram) for a single HPD used in the RICH test beam run.

Figure 6.19: Reconstructed Cherenkov angle for data (solid histogram) and simulation (dotted line) on one of the HPDs used in the 2004 RICH test beam run.

included. Inside the HPDs, using the measured quantum efficiencies and cross-focussing relations, the photoelectrons created from the photocathode are mapped down onto the silicon detectors (hits location and energy). From these hits, the charge sharing in the pixels and the response of front-end readout are modelled in a separate package, which creates the digitized hits in the same format which will be output from the operational detector. All known sources of background are simulated. The most important components come from Rayleigh scattered photons in the aerogel, rings from secondary particles without associated reconstructed tracks and Cherenkov light generation in the HPD windows from traversing charged particles. More information on the LHCb RICH simulation may be found in [120]. Figure 6.20 shows a simulated event display in RICH 1.

For a given pixel-track association, the apparent Cherenkov angle is reconstructed through knowledge of the track direction, the hit pixel location, and the geometry of the RICH optics. This reconstruction assumes that the Cherenkov photon was emitted at the midpoint of the radiator. In simulation the resolution on the Cherenkov angle per photoelectron, and the mean number of photoelectrons detected per $\beta \approx 1$ track can be determined by using truth information to ensure that the hit pixel-track association is correct. The mean number of photoelectrons is found to be 6.7 for aerogel, 30.3 for C_4F_{10} and 21.9 for CF_4. The resolution results are shown in table 6.3, where both the total resolutions and the individual contributions are listed. The single photoelectron resolution is largest for the aerogel, at 2.6 mrad, and smallest for the CF_4, at 0.7 mrad. These resolutions receive contributions from the uncertainty associated with the photon emission point, the chromatic dispersion of the radiator, the finite pixel size and the point spread function (together listed as 'HPD' in the table). For the aerogel it is the chromatic dispersion error which dominates, whereas for the other two radiators the contributions are well matched. An additional uncertainty comes from the reconstruction of the track direction.

The resulting particle identification performance of the RICH system will be discussed in section 10.

2008 JINST 3 S08005

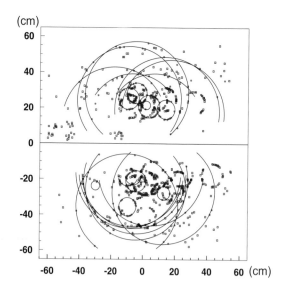

Figure 6.20: Display of a typical LHCb event in RICH 1.

Table 6.3: Single photoelectron resolutions for the three RICH radiators. All numbers are in mrad. Individual contributions from each source are given, together with the total.

	Aerogel	C_4F_{10}	CF_4
Emission	0.4	0.8	0.2
Chromatic	2.1	0.9	0.5
HPD	0.5	0.6	0.2
Track	0.4	0.4	0.4
Total	2.6	1.5	0.7

6.2 Calorimeters

The calorimeter system performs several functions. It selects transverse energy hadron, electron and photon candidates for the first trigger level (L0), which makes a decision 4μs after the interaction. It provides the identification of electrons, photons and hadrons as well as the measurement of their energies and positions. The reconstruction with good accuracy of π^0 and prompt photons is essential for flavour tagging and for the study of B-meson decays and therefore is important for the physics program.

The set of constraints resulting from these functionalities defines the general structure and the main characteristics of the calorimeter system and its associated electronics [1, 121]. The ultimate performance for hadron and electron identification will be obtained at the offline analysis level. The requirement of a good background rejection and reasonable efficiency for B decays adds demanding conditions on the detector performance in terms of resolution and shower separation.

2008 JINST 3 S08005

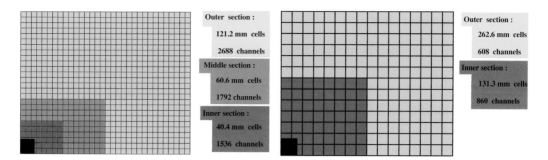

Figure 6.21: Lateral segmentation of the SPD/PS and ECAL (left) and the HCAL (right). One quarter of the detector front face is shown. In the left figure the cell dimensions are given for the ECAL.

6.2.1 General detector structure

A classical structure of an electromagnetic calorimeter (ECAL) followed by a hadron calorimeter (HCAL) has been adopted. The most demanding identification is that of electrons. Within the bandwidth allocated to the electron trigger (cf. section 7.1.2) the electron Level 0 trigger is required to reject 99% of the inelastic pp interactions while providing an enrichment factor of at least 15 in b events. This is accomplished through the selection of electrons of large transverse energy E_T. The rejection of a high background of charged pions requires longitudinal segmentation of the electromagnetic shower detection, i.e. a preshower detector (PS) followed by the main section of the ECAL. The choice of the lead thickness results from a compromise between trigger performance and ultimate energy resolution [122]. The electron trigger must also reject a background of π^0's with high E_T. Such rejection is provided by the introduction, in front of the PS, of a scintillator pad detector (SPD) plane used to select charged particles. A thin lead converter is placed between SPD and PS detectors. At Level 0, the background to the electron trigger will then be dominated by photon conversions in the upstream spectrometer material, which cannot be identified at this stage. Optimal energy resolution requires the full containment of the showers from high energy photons. For this reason, the thickness of ECAL was chosen to be 25 radiation lengths [123]. On the other hand, the trigger requirements on the HCAL resolution do not impose a stringent hadronic shower containment condition. Its thickness is therefore set to 5.6 interaction lengths [124] due to space limitations.

The PS/SPD, ECAL and HCAL adopt a variable lateral segmentation (shown in figure 6.21) since the hit density varies by two orders of magnitude over the calorimeter surface. A segmentation into three different sections has been chosen for the ECAL and projectively for the SPD/PS. Given the dimensions of the hadronic showers, the HCAL is segmented into two zones with larger cell sizes.

All calorimeters follow the same basic principle: scintillation light is transmitted to a Photo-Multiplier (PMT) by wavelength-shifting (WLS) fibres. The single fibres for the SPD/PS cells are read out using multianode photomultiplier tubes (MAPMT), while the fibre bunches in the ECAL and HCAL modules require individual phototubes. In order to have a constant E_T scale the gain in the ECAL and HCAL phototubes is set in proportion to their distance from the beampipe. Since the light yield delivered by the HCAL module is a factor 30 less than that of the ECAL, the HCAL tubes operate at higher gain.

2008 JINST 3 S08005

6.2.2 Electronics overview

The basic structure is dictated by the need to handle the data for the Level 0 trigger as fast as possible. The front-end electronics and the PS/SPD photomultipliers are located at the detector periphery. The HCAL and ECAL phototubes are housed directly on the detector modules. The signals are shaped directly on the back of the photomultiplier for the PS/SPD or after 12 m and 16 m long cables for ECAL and HCAL respectively. They are then digitized in crates positioned on top of the detectors and the trigger circuits, hosted in the same crates, perform the clustering operations required by the trigger [125]. For each channel, the data, sampled at the bunch crossing rate of 40 MHz, are stored in a digital pipeline until the Level-0 trigger decision. In order to exploit the intrinsic calorimeter resolution over the full dynamic range, ECAL and HCAL signals are digitized by a 12-bit flash ADC [126]. Ten bits are enough for the preshower, and the SPD information is only one bit, a simple discriminator recording whether a cell has been hit or not [127, 128]. An additional requirement is to reduce the tails of signals associated to the bunch crossing preceding the one being sampled. For ECAL and HCAL, this goal can be achieved at the percent level by suitable signal treatment within 25 ns. In the case of the PS and SPD, the signal shape fluctuations require the longest possible signal integration time. They therefore use a different front-end design for the integrator, as described in section 6.2.7. Finally, in order not to degrade the resolution, the electronic noise must remain at the least significant bit level [129]. At the short shaping times being used, this requires careful design of the very front-end part.

6.2.3 The pad/preshower detector

The pad/preshower (SPD/PS) detector uses scintillator pad readout by WLS fibres that are coupled to MAPMT via clear plastic fibres. The choice of a 64 channel MAPMT allowed the design of a fast, multi-channel pad detector with an affordable cost per channel.

The SPD/PS detector consists of a 15 mm lead converter 2.5 X_0 thick, that is sandwiched between two almost identical planes of rectangular scintillator pads of high granularity with a total of 12032 detection channels (figure 6.22 left). The sensitive area of the detector is 7.6 m wide and 6.2 m high. Due to the projectivity requirements, all dimensions of the SPD plane are smaller than those of the PS by $\sim 0.45\%$. The detector planes are divided vertically into two halves. Each can slide independently on horizontal rails to the left and right side in order to allow service and maintenance work. The distance along the beam axis between the centres of the PS and the SPD scintillator planes is 56 mm. In order to achieve a one-to-one projective correspondence with the ECAL segmentation (described in section 6.2.4), each PS and SPD plane is subdivided into inner (3072 cells), middle (3584 cells) and outer (5376 cells) sections with approximately 4×4, 6×6 and $12 \times 12\,\text{cm}^2$ cell dimensions.

The cells are packed in $\sim 48 \times 48\,\text{cm}^2$ boxes (detector units) that are grouped into supermodules. Each supermodule has a width of ≈ 96 cm, a height of ≈ 7.7 m and consists of detector units that form 2 rows and 13 columns. The space available for the SPD/PS detector between the first muon chamber and the electromagnetic calorimeter is only 180 mm. Figure 6.22 (right) shows an individual scintillator pad with the WLS fibre layout. The diameter of the WLS fibre groove is a few mm smaller than the tile size; exact parameters of the tile geometry can be found in [130]. The basic plastic component is polystyrene to which primary and secondary WLS dopants, parater-

2008 JINST 3 S08005

 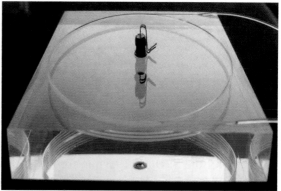

Figure 6.22: Front view of one half of the SPD/PS installed in the LHCb experimental hall (left). Individual scintillator pad with the WLS fibre layout and the LED housing in the middle (right).

phenyl (PTP), 1.5% and POPOP, 0.04%, are added.[11] The square structure of a pad is cut out from a 15 mm thick scintillator plate, and the scintillator surface is polished to reach the necessary optical quality. In order to maximize the light collection efficiency, WLS fibres are coiled and placed into a ring groove that is milled in the body of the cell. The rectangular cross section of the groove is 4.1 mm deep and 1.1 mm wide. The groove contains 3.5 loops of WLS fibre. The number of loops was chosen to achieve an overall optimization of the light collection efficiency [131] and the signal formation [132]. Two additional grooves are milled in the scintillator allowing both ends of the WLS fibre to exit the plate. The fibre is glued inside the groove[12] using a dedicated semi-automatic device that provides the winding of the fibre and a uniform glue filling along the groove. A 1.0 mm diameter Y11(250) MS70 multi-cladding S-type WLS fibre[13] was chosen as a reasonable compromise between light output and durability. The pad is wrapped with 0.15 mm thick TYVEK[14] paper in order to improve the light reflection and to minimize the dead space between adjacent pads. Light produced by an ionizing particle in the scintillator is guided by the WLS fibre to the exit of the detector box. At this point optical connectors (described in [130]) join the WLS fibres to long clear fibres. The two clear fibres connected to the two ends of the WLS fibre of a given pad are viewed by a single MAPMT pixel [130]. The length of clear fibres varies from 0.7 to 3.5 m but all the fibres connected to a particular PMT have the same length in accordance with the front-end electronics specification [127, 128]. The clear fibre allows the transport of the scintillator light from the SPD/PS planes over a few metres to the multi-anode PMT without significant attenuation.

The scintillator cells are grouped into self-supporting detector units that are packed inside square boxes with dimension 476 mm × 476 mm (SPD) and 478 mm × 478 mm (PS) boxes, yield-

---

[11]produced at SSI *Institute for Single Crystals* NAS of Ukraine, 60 Lenin Ave, Kharkov, 61001, Ukraine.

[12]with BICRON BC-600 glue, BICRON Corp., 12345 Kinsman Rd. Newbury OH 440 USA.

[13]KURARAY Corp., 3-10, Nihonbashi, 2 chome, Chuo-ku, Tokyo, Japan.

[14]TYVEK of type 1057D used, product of E.I. du Pont de Nemours and Company.

2008 JINST 3 S08005

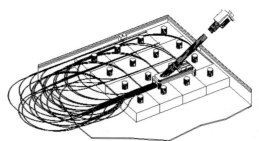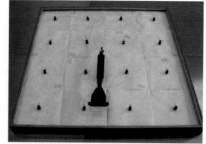

Figure 6.23: Fibre routing for the inner (left) and outer (right) module boxes.

ing a total of 26 boxes per supermodule. Since there are three sections with different cell sizes for the SPD/PS planes, the boxes are filled with a different number of pads with sizes that add up to 119 mm for the SPD to 119.5 mm for the PS planes. A dedicated fibreglass technology of box manufacturing was developed in order to obtain stiff boxes with a minimum amount of material between the adjacent cells of neighbouring boxes. The lateral walls of the monolithic box frame are manufactured using Fibreglass Reinforced Plastic (FGRP) with a wall thickness of 0.3 mm. This fabrication method consists of a one cycle polymerization process with predefined curing parameters. To ensure light tightness a layer of black paper was incorporated in addition to the FGRP layer. The top and bottom layers of the box are made of 2 mm thick Al plate and G10 plastic. The bottom cover is glued to the FGRP frame by epoxy and the top one is fixed by screws. On the top cover there are output plastic ports, made of relatively cheap pressure die casting technology, disposed to allow exit of fibre bundles out of the box. The module assembly procedure is as follows. All cells in a detector unit are grouped in matrices of 4×4 cells. The scintillator pads with glued WLS fibres are placed into the box after quality control tests. The fibre ends are grouped by 32, fit into a light-tight flexible tube and glued into an optical connector, before being cut and polished. The routing of fibres inside a box from one matrix is shown in figure 6.23. The bending diameter always exceeds 100 mm. Depending on the number of scintillator cells inside a unit, the boxes are equipped with one (outer region), four (middle region) or nine (inner region) output port(s) and light connector(s).

The detector units are designed to be mounted on a supermodule support plate. All supermodules of the SPD/PS planes have identical design. Each consists of 26 detector units mounted on a long aluminium strip in two columns. The photomultiplier tubes are located on both the top and bottom ends of the supermodule support outside the detector acceptance. The detector units are optically connected to the PMTs by bundles of 32 clear fibres, enclosed in a light-tight plastic tube, by means of a photo-tube coupler. The PMT is a (8-stage) R5900-M64 manufactured by Hamamatsu[15][133, 134] and has a bialkali photocatode segmented into 64 pixels of 2×2 mm^2. The HV is provided by a Cockroft-Walton voltage multiplier.

The quality of the phototubes has been extensively studied using measurements of the nonuniformities of anode response within one MAPMT, the linearity over the required dynamic range of the PS, the absolute gain of the MAPMT channels and the electronic crosstalk. The nonuniformity

---

[15]HAMAMATSU Photonics KK, Electron Tube Center, 314-5, Shimokanzo, Toyooka-village, Iwata-gun, Shizuoka-ken, 438-01 Japan.

of response within one MAPMT was found to be in a ratio of 1 to 2 (minimum to maximum) for most of the installed tubes. A special care has been brought to the selection of the best tubes for the PS in order to limit the digital correction to at most a factor of 2 at the level of the front-end (FE) electronics. While the crosstalk between the PMT electronics channels has been measured to be negligible, a large number of tubes showed large crosstalk produced at the level of the focussing grid, immediately behind the MAPMT photocathode. This was one of the major cause for rejection. The response linearity was found to be well within specification for all the tested phototubes [135].

Specific measurements of the MAPMT behaviour in the magnetic field were carried out as well. It has been discovered that these phototubes, initially thought to be robust in a magnetic field were significantly sensitive to fields as weak as 1 mT. A dedicated magnetic shielding has been designed. A MuMetal cylinder (6 cm long with a 4 cm diameter) is used along the tube axis and the MAPMT (together with the very front-end (VFE) electronics) are housed in a box made of soft iron. Special attention was given to evaluate the long term behaviour of the phototubes subject to the conditions of the largest illumination of the PS (DC currents for the SPD are much smaller than for the PS [136]). The PMT gain is set to 10^4, which gives stable conditions of operation. Prior to the installation all the SPD and PS modules were tested using a cosmic ray facility. Using a reference LED the average number of photoelectrons per Minimum Ionizing Particle (MIP) was measured to be 26, 28 and 21 for the PS and SPD cells of the inner, middle and outer regions correspondingly. During the production phase the light yield was measured for all tiles using a gamma radiation source. The tiles with similar light yield were grouped within the same matrix. The uniformity of matrices, also affected by the uniformity of the optical cables, was measured in a cosmic test of the detector supermodules. The uniformity of response within matrices was found to be within 6% RMS.

Performance of the SPD/PS modules

The e/π separation performance of the PS prototype was measured in the X7 test beam at the CERN SPS with electrons and pions between 10 and 50 GeV/c momentum. The energy deposited in the PS for 50 GeV/c electrons and pions is shown in figure 6.24.

The measurements show that with a threshold of 4 MIPs (about 100 ADC channels), pion rejection factors of 99.6%, 99.6% and 99.7% with electron retentions of 91%, 92% and 97% are achieved for 10, 20 and 50 GeV/c particle momentum, respectively. From measurements with 20 GeV electrons in the combined PS and ECAL test, it is confirmed that the energy resolution of the ECAL does not deteriorate if one corrects for the energy absorbed in the PS lead converter using the energy measured in the PS scintillator [131]. In order to separate photons and electrons at Level 0 of the ECAL trigger, the information from the SPD positioned in front of the lead absorber is used. Charged particles deposit energy in the scintillator material, while neutrals particles do not interact. However, several processes can lead to an energy deposit in the scintillator and result in the misidentification of photons. The dominant one is the photon conversion in the detector material before the SPD (see sections 10.2.3 and 10.2.4). Two other sources are interactions in the SPD that produce charged particles inside the SPD, and backwards moving charged particles, *back splash*, that are generated in the lead absorber or in the electromagnetic calorimeter. The latter two

2008 JINST 3 S08005

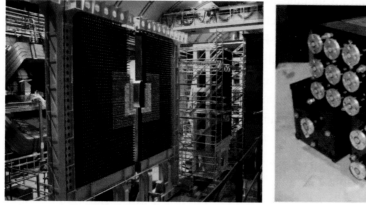

Figure 6.24: Energy deposition of (a) 50 GeV electrons and (b) pions in the PS.

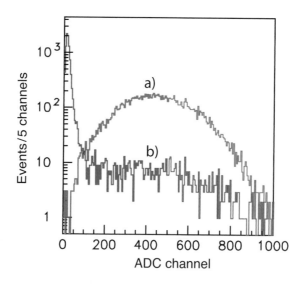

Figure 6.25: Downstream view of the ECAL installed (but not completely closed) with the exception of some detector elements above the beam line. Outer, middle and inner type ECAL modules (right).

effects have been studied with the prototype in both a tagged photon beam and beams of electrons and pions of different energies, in the CERN X7 test beam area. The results were compared with simulation. The measurements for photon energies between 20 and 50 GeV show [137] that the probability of photon misidentification due to interactions in the SPD scintillator is $(0.8\pm0.3)\%$, when applying a threshold of 0.7 MIPs. The probability to pass this threshold due to backward moving charged particles was measured to be $(0.9\pm0.6)\%$ and $(1.4\pm0.6)\%$ for 20 and 50 GeV photons, respectively. All these numbers are in very good agreement with MonteCarlo simulation study. More details on backsplash study can be found in [137].

2008 JINST 3 S08005

Table 6.4: Main parameters of the LHCb electromagnetic calorimeter. (*) Only 1536 channels are active, instead of 1584, due to the clearance around the beam.

	Inner section	Middle section	Outer section
Inner dimension, $x \times y$, cm^2	65×65	194×145	388×242
Outer dimension, $x \times y$, cm^2	194×145	388×242	776×630
Cell size, cm^2	4.04×4.04	6.06×6.06	12.12×12.12
# of modules	176	448	2688
# of channels	1536*	1792	2688
# of cells per module	9	4	1
# of fibres per module	144	144	64
Fibre density, cm^{-2}	0.98	0.98	0.44

6.2.4 The electromagnetic calorimeter

The shashlik calorimeter technology, i.e. a sampling scintillator/lead structure readout by plastic WLS fibres, has been chosen for the electromagnetic calorimeter not only by LHCb but by a number of other experiments [138, 139]. This decision was made taking into account modest energy resolution, fast time response, acceptable radiation resistance and reliability of the shashlik technology, as well as the experience accumulated by other experiments [140–142]. Specific features of the LHCb shashlik ECAL are an improved uniformity and an advanced monitoring system. The design energy resolution of $\sigma_E/E = 10\%/\sqrt{E} \oplus 1\%$ (E in GeV) results in a B mass resolution of 65 MeV/c^2 for the $B \to K^*\gamma$ penguin decay with a high-E_T photon and of 75 MeV/c^2 for $B \to \rho\pi$ decay with the π^0 mass resolution of ~ 8 MeV/c^2.

The electromagnetic calorimeter, shown in figure 6.25 (left), is placed at 12.5 m from the interaction point. The outer dimensions of the ECAL match projectively those of the tracking system, $\theta_x < 300$ mrad and $\theta_y < 250$ mrad; the inner acceptance is mainly limited by $\theta_{x,y} > 25$ mrad around the beampipe due to the substantial radiation dose level. The hit density is a steep function of the distance from the beampipe, and varies over the active calorimeter surface by two orders of magnitude. The calorimeter is therefore subdivided into inner, middle and outer sections (table 6.4) with appropriate cell size, as shown in figure 6.25 (right).

A module is built from alternating layers of 2 mm thick lead, 120 μm thick, white, reflecting TYVEK[16] paper and 4 mm thick scintillator tiles. In depth, the 66 Pb and scintillator layers form a 42 cm stack corresponding to 25 X_0. The Moliere radius of the stack is 3.5 cm. The stack is wrapped with black paper, to ensure light tightness, pressed and fixed from the sides by the welding of 100 μm steel foil.

The scintillator tiles are produced from polystyrene[17] with 2.5% PTP[18] and 0.01% POPOP[19] admixtures. The scintillator tile production employs a high pressure injection moulding technique. Tile edges are chemically treated to provide diffusive reflection and consequently improved light

---

[16]TYVEK of type 1025D used, product of E.I. du Pont de Nemours and Company.

[17]Polystherene in pellets, Polystyrol 165H, [Cn Hn], product of BASF AG, Badische Anilin- & Soda Fabrik Aktiengesellschaft, Carl-Bosch-Strasse 38, D-67056 Ludwigshafen, Germany, mailto:global.info@basf.com.

[18]PTP, p-Terphenyl, 1,4-Diphenylbenzene, [C6 H5 C6 H4 C6 H5], product of FLUKA(TM), Sigma-Aldrich Chemie GmbH, CH-9470, Buchs, Switzerland, mailto:fluka@sial.com.

[19]POPOP, 1,4-Bis(5-phenyl-2-oxazolyl)benzene, [C24 H16 N2 O2], product of FLUKA(TM), Sigma-Aldrich Chemie GmbH, CH-9470, Buchs, Switzerland, mailto:fluka@sial.com.

2008 JINST 3 S08005

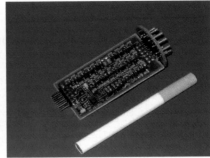

Figure 6.26: Hamamatsu R7899-20 phototube, light mixer and MuMetal magnetic shielding screen (left). Cockcroft-Walton voltage multiplier (right).

collection efficiency and prevent tile-to-tile light crosstalk for the inner and middle modules. The tile-to-tile light yield fluctuation has an RMS smaller than 2.5%. The Pb plates are produced using sheet-metal stamping. In order to ease handling of the lead plates during module assembly the plates are covered with a 3μm thick layer of tin. Both the scintillator tiles and lead plates incorporate a pattern of precisely positioned holes that are needed for the traversing fibres. The demanding tolerances are ensured by injection moulding for the scintillator tiles and a punching technique for the lead plates.

The light from the scintillator tiles is absorbed, re-emitted and transported by 1.2 mm diameter WLS Kuraray Y-11(250)MSJ fibres, traversing the entire module. In order to improve light collection efficiency the fibres are looped such that each traverses the module twice, the looped part remaining in a housing outside the front of the module. Fibre bending under uniformly distributed dry heat made it possible to produce fibre loops with radii as small as 10 mm, where the light loss is determined by the geometrical optics of reflection down the loop. When measured after the fibre loop, the light yield varies from loop to loop with an RMS of the spread of 1.6%. The fibres belonging to each cell are bundled at the rear end of the module and polished.

The light is read out with Hamamatsu R7899-20 phototubes where the high voltage is provided by a Cockcroft-Walton (CW) base (figure 6.26).

Before installation all ECAL modules underwent detailed quality control at various stages of production. The final control was made with cosmic rays [143]. The standard deviations of the mean energy deposition by a MIP in the ECAL module was measured to be 7.4%, 4.4% and 6.0% for the outer, middle and inner sections respectively. The number of photoelectrons recorded for a MIP and for electrons in the test beam was calculated using the measurements of the amplitude and width of the LED signal. This method gives for the inner modules about 3100 photoelectrons per GeV of deposited energy, 3500 for the middle and 2600 for the outer modules. The differences are due to the differing WLS fibre density in the inner, middle and outer modules and to the cell size differences which influence the probability of photon absorption in the scintillating tiles.

Performance of the ECAL modules

The energy resolution and, in particular, the uniformity in response of the ECAL were studied at the test beam [144]. Only a few percent of the scintillation light is registered by the phototubes

2008 JINST 3 S08005

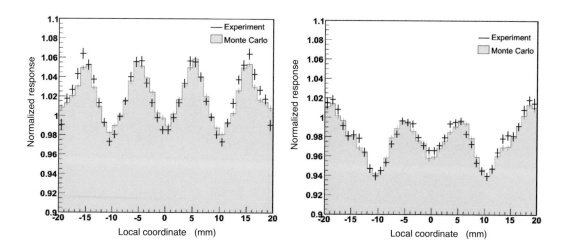

Figure 6.27: Uniformity of response to $100 \, \text{GeV/c}^2$ muons of the inner module. The scan was made in 1 mm wide slices through the fibre positions (left) and in between two fibre rows (right).

after capture and re-emission in the WLS fibres; about half of this light is delivered by the WLS fibres close to the light's origin. Some lateral nonuniformity in the light collection efficiency was expected from two sources: imperfect reflection from tile edges (the so-called global nonuniformity effect), and a dependence on the emission point of the scintillating light with respect to the fibres (local or inter-fibre nonuniformity). The global nonuniformity depends on the mean light path, which is a function of tile transparency, edge reflection quality and fibre density. In addition the module response at the edge is further degraded due to the presence of the stainless steel foils between the active volumes of two adjacent modules. The local nonuniformity is affected by the inter-fibre distance and the diameter of the fibre.

The light collection efficiency was studied using test beam data and a dedicated MonteCarlo simulation of the light propagation and absorption in the plastic tiles which takes into account the transparency of the scintillator as a function of wavelength, the tile-edge and TYVEK reflection properties and the WLS fibre absorption spectrum. The modules of the inner, middle and outer sections were scanned using 100 GeV/c muons with a 1 mm transverse step. As shown in figure 6.27, the measured inner module response is well described by MonteCarlo simulation. Shown are two different scans for the inner module, one using 1 mm wide slices through the WLS fibre positions (left plot), and the other between two fibre rows (right plot). In the outer modules the inter-fibre nonuniformity is slightly higher due to a factor of 1.5 larger fibre-to-fibre distance (15 mm instead of 10 mm for the inner and middle modules). The global nonuniformity of response was measured to be negligible for all module types. A slight increase of response in the vicinity of the module edges is explained by diffuse reflection from the boundary layer introduced by the dedicated chemical treatment of the tile edges. The effect of signal loss in the dead material between the modules is overcompensated by 8% at -20 and 20 mm, as visible in figure 6.27 (right). Electromagnetic showers of electrons and photons considerably reduce the inter-fibre nonuniformity of response compared to that measured for MIPs. The results of a lateral scan with 50 GeV/c electrons is shown in figure 6.28 for the inner and outer ECAL modules. The module response is

2008 JINST 3 S08005

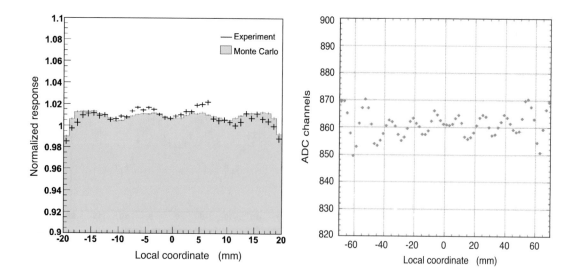

Figure 6.28: Uniformity of response to 50 GeV/c electrons of the inner (left) and outer (right) modules. The scan was made in 1 mm wide slices through the fibre positions.

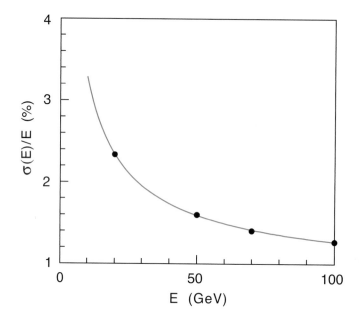

Figure 6.29: The energy resolution as measured with electrons over a surface of ($\pm$ 15 mm , $\pm$ 30 mm) in an outer module.

uniform within 0.8%. The energy resolution of the ECAL modules has been determined at the test beam. The parametrization $\sigma_E/E = a/\sqrt{E} \oplus b \oplus c/E$ (E in GeV) is used, where a, b and c stand for the stochastic, constant and noise terms respectively. Depending on the type of module and test beam conditions the stochastic and constant terms were measured to be 8.5% < a < 9.5% and b ~0.8% (see figure 6.29).

2008 JINST 3 S08005

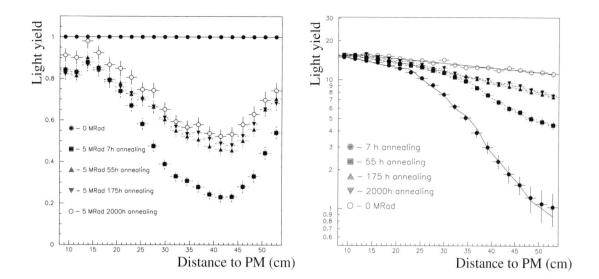

Figure 6.30: Scintillator (left) and WLS fibre (right) degradation and annealing effect after irradiation at LIL. The light yield (scintillator) and PMT current (fibres) are shown vs. the distance to the PMT (the shower maximum position corresponds to a distance from the PMT of 42 cm).

Radiation resistance of the ECAL modules

Detailed measurements and simulation studies were performed to determine the degradation of the ECAL resolution due to radiation damage of the optical components. The expected annual radiation dose at the shower maximum for the ECAL modules closest to the beampipe is 0.25 MRad assuming a luminosity of $2 \times 10^{32} \text{cm}^{-2}\text{s}^{-1}$ and 10^7 s per nominal year. The optical components of the ECAL modules, namely the $40 \times 40 \text{mm}^2$ scintillating tiles and WLS fibres, were irradiated at the LEP Injector Linac (LIL) at CERN with electrons of 500 MeV energy. The total irradiation dose was as large as 5 MRad at a dose delivery rate of 10 Rad/s; that is 200 times higher than the rate expected at LHCb. Figure 6.30 shows the degradation in light yield and transparency, and the subsequent annealing of the irradiated components as a function of the distance to the phototube. In order to determine the degradation of the energy resolution due to irradiation, the energy response of the ECAL module was simulated using the expected longitudinal dose profile and the measured degradation of the scintillating tiles and WLS fibres in accordance with figure 6.30. The effects induced by irradiation of 2.2 MRad leads to an increase of the constant term from 0.8% up to 1.5%. Such a degradation in the ECAL resolution is expected after about eight years of operation under nominal conditions and is acceptable. However, taking into account simulation uncertainties on the expected radiation doses at the LHC, the ECAL detector was designed such that the modules closest to the beampipe could be replaced if this should become necessary.

6.2.5 The hadron calorimeter

The LHCb hadron calorimeter (HCAL) [1, 121] is a sampling device made from iron and scintillating tiles, as absorber and active material respectively. The special feature of this sampling structure is the orientation of the scintillating tiles that run parallel to the beam axis. In the lateral direction

2008 JINST 3 S08005

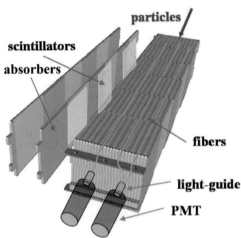

Figure 6.31: View from upstream of the HCAL detector installed behind the two retracted ECAL halves in the LHCb cavern (left). A schematic of the internal cell structure (right). The exploded view of two *scintillator-absorber* layers illustrates the elementary periodic structure of a HCAL module.

tiles are interspersed with 1 cm of iron, whereas in the longitudinal direction the length of tiles and iron spacers corresponds to the hadron interaction length λ_I in steel. The light in this structure is collected by WLS fibres running along the detector towards the back side where photomultiplier tubes (PMTs) are housed. As shown in figure 6.31, three scintillator tiles arranged in depth are in optical contact with 1.2 mm diameter Kuraray[20] Y-11(250)MSJ fibre [145] that run along the tile edges. The total weight of the HCAL is about 500 tons.

The HCAL is segmented transeversely [146] into square cells of size 131.3 mm (inner section) and 262.6 mm (outer section). Readout cells of different sizes are defined by grouping together different sets of fibres onto one photomultiplier tube that is fixed to the rear of the sampling structure. The lateral dimensions of the two sections are ±2101 mm and ±4202 mm in x and ±1838 mm and ±3414 mm in y for the inner and outer section, respectively. The optics is designed such that the two different cell sizes can be realized with an absorber structure that is identical over the whole HCAL. The overall HCAL structure is built as a wall, positioned at a distance from the interaction point of z=13.33 m with dimensions of 8.4 m in height, 6.8 m in width and 1.65 m in depth. The structure is divided vertically into two symmetric parts that are positioned on movable platforms, to allow access to the detector. Each half is built from 26 modules piled on top of each other in the final installation phase. The assembled HCAL is shown in figure 6.31(left). The absorber structure, shown in figure 6.31 (right), is made from laminated steel plates of only six different dimensions that are glued together. Identical periods of 20 mm thickness are repeated 216 times in the module. One period consists of two 6 mm thick master plates with a length of 1283 mm and a height of 260 mm that are glued in two layers to several 4 mm thick spacers of 256.5 mm in height and variable length. The space is filled with 3 mm scintillator.

---

[20]KURARAY Corp., 3-10, Nihonbashi, 2 chome, Chuo-ku, Tokyo, Japan.

The periodic structure of the system is designed to be self supporting and uniformly instrumented with no dead zones. To facilitate the construction of modules, each module is subdivided into eight sub-modules that have a manageable size for assembly from the individual absorber plates. A total of 416 submodules have been produced to form 52 modules needed to build up the two halves of the HCAL structure. The mechanical structure is reinforced by welded cross members and is completely independent from the optical instrumentation.

The optics of the tile calorimeter consists of three components: the scintillating tile, the WLS fibre and a small square light mixer just in front of the photo-multiplier entrance window. The scintillating light propagates through the 3 mm thick tile to its edges where it is collected by 1.2 mm diameter WLS fibres.

In total more than 86000 tiles of two different dimensions have been produced by the cost effective casting technology using polystyrene as a base and two dopants: paraterphenyl (PTP, 1.75%) and POPOP (0.05%). Each tile of 197×256 mm^2 or 197×127 mm^2 is wrapped in a 120–150 micron thick TYVEK envelope.[21]

The edges of a tile are wrapped in such a way that the fibre running along the edge can be easily inserted between the envelope and the tile edge during the module optics assembly. This reflective envelope avoids light crosstalk between adjacent edges of the small tiles, enhances the light collection in the wavelength shifting fibre and in addition protects the optical reflective surface of the tiles. Each fibre collects light from three scintillator tiles arranged along the shower development direction. There are a total of 50k fibres in the HCAL with an identical length of 1.6 m. In order to increase the light collection efficiency both fibre ends were cut with a diamond mill, and opposite to the photomultiplier end coated with a layer of reflective aluminum deposited in vacuum. The reflectivity of all fibres was checked on a measuring stand specially designed for that purpose. All fibres were measured to have a mirror reflectivity in the range of $(85 \pm 10)\%$. The light propagates along the fibre by total reflection but tiles located further from the PMT yield less light due to attenuation in the WLS fibre. To compensate for this effect, the tile-fibre optical contact was progressively reduced for the different tile layers in depth. The last tile layer closest to the PMT has an optical contact reduced by 22% as compared to the first layer at the entry of the HCAL. This precaution minimizes the difference in response between tiles, providing light to the same PMT with a uniformity at a level of a few percent.

Each cell is read out by one photomultiplier tube that is attached to the rear mechanical structure of the module. The optical connection between the fibre bundle and the photomultiplier is ensured by a 35 mm long light mixer of square shape. To shield the photomultiplier tube from the stray magnetic field the tube, including the light mixer, is housed inside a 3 mm thick iron tube and MuMetal foil. The influence of the magnetic field on a PMTs performance was studied during the LHCb magnet measurement. A field of approximately 2 mT along z, but negligible in x and y, is expected in the region of the HCAL PMTs [23]. No variation of the monitoring LED signal has been observed within about 0.1% measurement error while switching on and off the magnet full power and when changing its polarity.

In order to monitor the HCAL stability an embedded self-calibrating scheme with ^{137}Cs gamma source has been implemented [147]. A capsule of 10 mCi activity can be transported

---

[21]TYVEK of type 1057D used, product of E.I. du Pont de Nemours and Company.

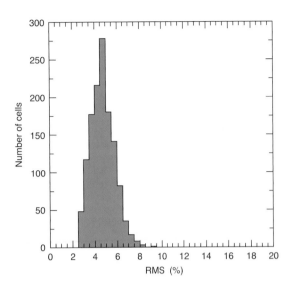
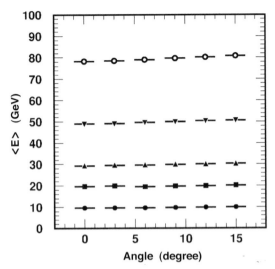

Figure 6.32: The distribution of RMS light yield for tiles read out by the same PMT.

Figure 6.33: The angular dependence of the HCAL prototype response at different energies.

through a stainless steel pipe fed through all tiles. The source is encapsulated in a 2 mm diameter, 4 mm long stainless steel tube that is welded at both ends. The hydraulic driving system filled with distilled water includes a garage to store the source, and computer controlled pump and valves that allow reversal of the water flow direction. A separate readout circuit measures the integrated anode current every 5 ms resulting from the scan of a half detector when the source propagates sequentially through 26 HCAL modules with an average velocity of about 20–40 cm/s. This procedure takes less than one hour. The method was widely used both during construction and in the final test of modules before installation in the cavern. Furthermore this system is used for the absolute calibration of the HCAL in-situ.

Beam tests performed with several HCAL modules allow the correspondence between the anode current induced by the radioactive source and the measured beam particle energy to be determined. Being absolutely calibrated the HCAL provides a unique possibility to cross-check the calibration of the upstream detectors (e.g. electromagnetic calorimeter) by comparison of the average energy deposition of the hadronic shower in the corresponding cells of two detectors. The energy sharing function varies slowly over the calorimeter surface and can be extracted from the MonteCarlo simulation.

The tile response during optics assembly was monitored using the radioactive source system. A maximum deviation of 20% from the average anode current for tiles grouped to the same PMT was accepted. The tiles and fibres not satisfying this requirement have been replaced. A distribution of the RMS of tile responses within the groups coupled to the same PMT is shown in figure 6.32. The mean value of this distribution is 4.7%.

2008 JINST 3 S08005

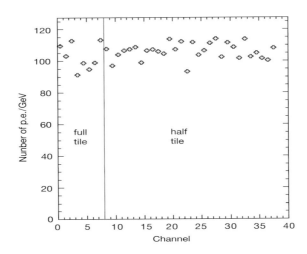

Figure 6.34: The light yield for the HCAL module measured in the test beam. The left part of the plot corresponds to 8 big cells of $26 \times 26 \, \text{cm}^2$. The other 32 cells comprise half-size cells of $13 \times 13 \, \text{cm}^2$.

Performance of the HCAL modules

The performance of the HCAL has been studied with prototypes [148] and continuously checked during module assembly using the CERN SPS test beam [149]. The dependence of the HCAL response on the angle of the incoming particle has been studied by rotating the detector between $0°$ and $15°$ around a vertical axis that traverses the HCAL close to the average shower maximum. Figure 6.33 shows the response of the 5.6 λ_I long prototype for pion energies between 10 GeV and 80 GeV. From a lateral scan of the particle beam across the prototype front surface the uniformity in response is measured to be well within $\pm3\%$.

During the assembly process [150] tiles with similar properties were grouped into the same cell to minimize nonuniformities. The light yield of all cells from one typical module is shown in figure 6.34. In total five modules (out of 52) were tested in the beam with an average light yield of 105 p.e./GeV.

The moderate requirements for the HCAL energy resolution allow the ratio of the active to passive material in the detector to be as low as 0.18. Furthermore, owing to the limited space available, the length of the HCAL has been chosen at 5.6 λ_I. The upstream ECAL adds a further 1.2 λ_I. Beam-test measurements were compared in detail with results using different software packages for the simulation of the hadronic shower development. The energy response to 50 GeV pions is shown by the hatched histogram in the left-hand plot of figure 6.35. The tail towards low energies due to leakage of the shower is easily seen. However, this tail is not a concern for the hadron trigger performance since it only introduces some minor inefficiency for high E_T signal events but does not affect the rejection of low E_T minimum-bias events. The black dots show the result of a MonteCarlo simulation that is in good agreement with the data, when using the GEANT (MICAP+FLUKA) interface. The energy resolution has been determined by fitting the energy spectrum with a gaussian distribution bounded by $\pm2.5\sigma$. The resolution extracted from a fit to the data at several energies is $\sigma_E/E = (69 \pm 5)\%/\sqrt{E} \oplus (9 \pm 2)\%$ (E in GeV) as shown in the right-hand plot of figure 6.35.

2008 JINST 3 S08005

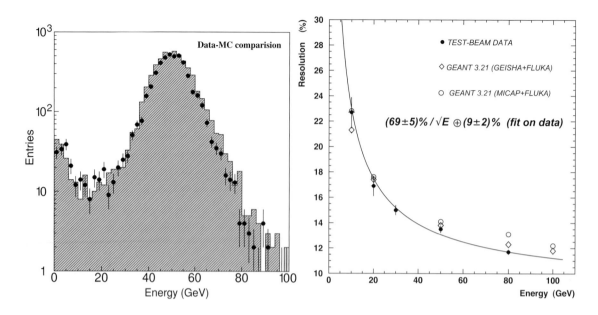

Figure 6.35: Left: energy response for 50 GeV pions from test-beam data (hatched) and from simulation (dots). Right: HCAL energy resolution, both for data and for simulation with three different hadronic simulation codes. The curve is a fit to the data.

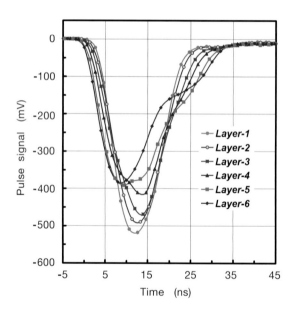

Figure 6.36: The average signal pulse shape of 30 GeV electrons in tile layers at different depths.

Another important feature of the HCAL is its signal timing properties. A precise signal shape measurement has been done with an electron beam of 30 GeV hitting layers of tiles at different depths. For this purpose the HCAL modules have been rotated by 90° and moved transversely with respect to beam line. Average pulse shapes of the detected signals are shown in figure 6.36. The

2008 JINST 3 S08005

variation of the shape is due to light reflection from the mirror at the end of the fibre opposite to the PMT. For layer 1, for example, the direct and reflected light reach the PMTs simultaneously, but for layer 6, closest to the PMT, the direct light reaches the photocathode earlier than the reflected one by the propagation delay in the 1.2 m long WLS fibre.

Radiation resistance of the HCAL modules

A comprehensive study of the degradation under irradiation has been performed for all optical components of the HCAL [151]. Scintillating tiles and WLS fibres have been irradiated at the IHEP 70 GeV proton synchrotron near the internal target area to get realistic environmental conditions as expected during the LHC operation. The transparency of tiles degrades by 25% after 250 kRad irradiation, but then steadily decreases by a further 20% with irradiation up to 1.4 MRad. The relative light yield after irradiation shows almost the same behaviour. Another important effect is the radiation degradation of the WLS fibres which introduces a longitudinal nonuniformity of the calorimeter response [152]. For example, the attenuation length in the WLS fibre degrades by 30% after irradiation with a dose of about 0.5 MRad, which corresponds to 10 years of operation for the most central cells of the HCAL at nominal luminosity of $2 \times 10^{32} \mathrm{cm}^{-2}\mathrm{s}^{-1}$. As a result of the same amount of irradiation, the constant term of the HCAL resolution degrades by 20%. To monitor the fibres radiation damage we intend to use the embedded calibration system with the radioactive source, that allows measurement of the response from each tile along the detector depth with a few percent accuracy.

6.2.6 Electronics of ECAL/HCAL

Because of the similarity of input signals and functionalities, it has been decided to use a common electronic system for the ECAL and HCAL. This system is based on a deadtimeless and low pedestal integrator system using delay lines, followed by ADCs and pipeline buffers. Each card is connected to 32 channels of the ECAL or the HCAL. After digitization in the front-end card the data is processed further and sent to a trigger validation card. The data is also pipelined and stored on the front-end card, and then sent through the back plane to a calorimeter readout card (CROC).

Pulse shaping and front-end chip

In order to take advantage of the inherent speed of the scintillator and WLS based calorimeter system the electronic system is capable of measuring every bunch crossing independently of signals from associated neighboring bunch crossings (pileup). The PMT pulses therefore are shaped to eliminate the small tail of pulses extending beyond 25 ns. A schematic of the PMT signal shaping and of the front-end chip is shown in figure 6.37 for HCAL. The PMT pulse is shortened by a clipping line which is a cable for the HCAL and a delay chip for the ECAL due to lack of space. The length of the line is typically one metre, giving a FWHM of about 10 ns. The resistor load at the end of the line is adjusted to obtain a return to a 0 Volt level after clipping. Due to fluctuations in the number of photoelectrons as a function of time, a fluctuation is also present in the shaped pulse. However the effect is small, especially for the ECAL where about 3000 photoelectrons produced per GeV. The pulses are then sent along 10 m of coaxial cables to the front-end cards which reside in

2008 JINST 3 S08005

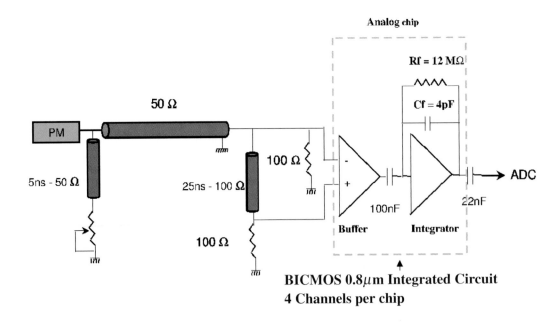

Figure 6.37: Schematic of the PM signal shaping and of the front-end chip.

crates above the calorimeters. The pulse-shape distortion produced by the cable is compensated to first order by a pole-zero circuit placed after the integrator. The first element of the pole-zero card is a front-end chip which contains a buffer amplifier and an integrator. To discharge the integrator the same pulse is subtracted in a buffer amplifier after a 25 ns delay obtained by a lumped-element delay line. Simulated input and output pulses using a 10 ns rectangular pulse are shown in figure 6.38, as well as an average 80 GeV PM HCAL pulse (averaged over 1000 measurements on a digital scope) and the resulting integrated pulse.

The schematic of the analog chip is given in figure 6.39. The circuit has been realized in AMS 0.8 μm BICMOS technology. A typical noise of 150 μV has been obtained after a 25 ns integration, which should correspond to a total noise of less than one ADC count. As measured with prototypes, the tail of the pulse integral in the next sampling is about 2% with an additional fluctuation of 1%. The impact of the amplifier noise on the physics performance is found to be negligible compared to the energy resolution of the ECAL.

The ECAL/HCAL front-end board

Figure 6.40 shows the block diagram of the 32 channel front-end board. It is a 9U board using VME mechanics with a specialized serial bus used for Experiment Control System purposes (see section 8.4). The pulses from the front-end chip, described above, are sent to 12-bit ADCs. The pulses after integration are flat (within 1%) over ± 2 ns around the maximum. To strobe at the maximum of the pulse, the different delays in the photomultipliers have to be compensated. This is achieved by adjusting the clock of each ADC by a delay chip to an accuracy of 1 ns. The digitized output of the ADCs are then resynchronized to a common clock (per card) in a register at the input of the next chip. The pulses at the integrator output can be subject to baseline shift and to the

2008 JINST 3 S08005

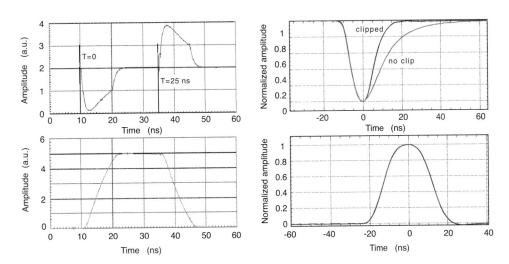

Figure 6.38: Left: simulated input pulse of a 10 ns rectangular pulse and the corresponding output pulse of the integrator: buffer output current before integration (top) and output integrated signal (bottom). Right: 80 GeV HCAL signals. The upper figure shows the PM signal with and without clipping, the lower one shows the same clipped signal at the output of the integrator.

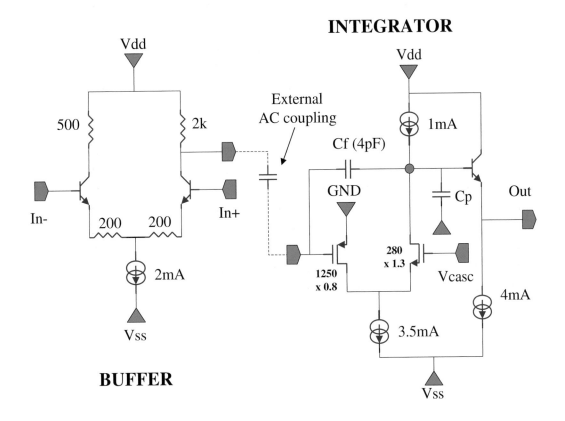

Figure 6.39: Schematic of the analog chip.

influence of low frequency pickup noise which would cause slow variation of the ADC pedestal. These variations are cancelled through a *digital differentiation* by subtracting the digitization in a

2008 JINST 3 S08005

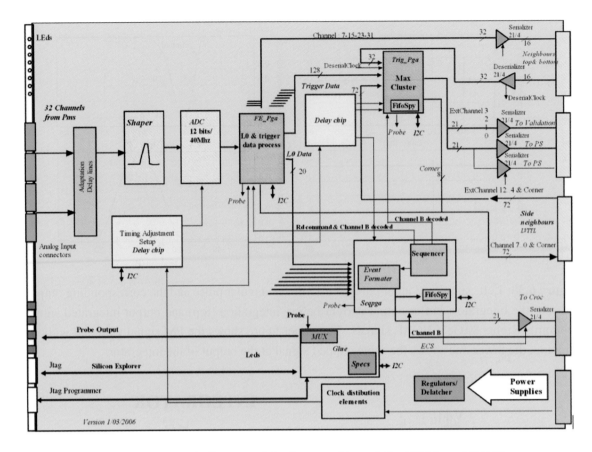

Figure 6.40: Block diagram of the front-end board, for ECAL and HCAL.

preceding sample (25 ns before). This subtraction also defines the effective integration time of the amplifier and therefore limits the integrated thermal noise from the buffer amplifier. To decrease the possibility of subtracting a signal present in the same channel, the quantity subtracted is actually the smallest of the two preceding measurements. Even at the highest occupancy, about 5%, the probability of subtracting a significant signal is therefore reduced to less than 0.25%. Simulations have shown that this procedure introduces negligible deterioration of energy and position measurements [129]. However the procedure introduces a pedestal shift of about 40% of the 40 MHz noise (i.e less then one ADC count) and an increase of the 40 MHz noise by 16%. The subtraction of the smallest of the two preceding samples is performed in 8 dedicated anti-fuse based FPGAs (cf. section 7.1.3) [22] called FE-PGAs, each of these being used to process four ADC channels [153]. Actually each FE-PGA has, for each ADC channel, four functional blocks. The first one processes the input ADC data, as described above. The second block produces the trigger data, converting the 12 bits of the ADC to 8 bits by a simplified multiplier with an adjustable 8 bits calibration constant. The third block is in charge of storing the data (12 ADC bits and 8 trigger bits per ADC, 80 bits per FE-PGA), during the L0 latency, and upon L0-Yes store again the data in a derandomizer and send them as four successive groups of 20 bits to the SEQ-PGA. The last block of the FE-PGA permits injecting test values at the input, in place of the ADC values, in order to check the proper behaviour of the card.

---

[22] AX250 anti-fuse PGA from ACTEL.

To adjust the timing of the clock signals used to strobe the ADCs and to synchronize the PGAs, delay-chip modules are used. These delay chips are custom made ASICs which shift the 40 MHz clock sent by the crate controller, the CROC. The delay-chips' clock shifts have a 25 ns range and steps of 1 ns.

Three other PGAs are used on the board for specific functions: The Trig-PGA is used to process the 8 bits trigger data from each of the 32 channels of a board together with the 8 side-neighbours channels from adjacent boards 4 top neighbours and one corner neighbour from other crates. The Trig-PGA computes the total transverse energy of the board and the information on the 2X2 cluster of cells with the highest transverse energy. This information is then passed to further boards involved in the trigger decision (the PS/SPD FE Board and the Trigger Validation Board). The Trig-PGA is implemented in an anti-fuse AX500 from ACTEL. The SEQ-PGA, mentioned above, serializes the 32 channels of the front-end board and sends them to the readout controller, the CROC. It also dispatches the L0 trigger signals and control signals linked to the trigger, the so-called *channel B*, to the FE-PGAs. The Glue-PGA is an interface between the Experiment Control System (based on the SPECS system) and the other PGAs of the board. It allows to load and read back *constant* parameters which adjust the delay chip values, calibration constants in FE-PGAs and so on. The SEQ and Glue PGAs are implemented in reprogrammable flash-based PGAs from ACTEL the APA300 and APA150.

The calorimeter readout card (CROC)

The CROC (for a conceptual design see [129]) is the board, which gathers the front-end L0 data of a calorimeter crate and sends them through optical fibres to the LHCb DAQ system (the TELL1 boards). Each of the 26 crates housing up to 16 ECAL, HCAL or PS/SPD front-end boards, are equipped with one single CROC, plugged into the central slot. The CROC also provides the clock, trigger signal, broadcast (channel B) and slow control command for all boards of a crate. In the DAQ path the data from front-end boards, which has been serialized at a 280 Mbits/s rate and sent through the backplane, are first deserialized and then captured and resynchronized in 4 FE-PGAs. These FE-PGAs (APA300) detect the presence of data (header detection) and add to the 21 bits of data coming from front-end boards 11 bits providing the data type and the board and crate identification numbers. The data are then sent to 2 GOL mezzanines each equipped with 8 fibres. In the absence of data the FE-PGAs send a special signal used to periodically synchronize the fibres drivers and receivers in the TELL1 boards. A spy functionality is also implemented in the FE-PGAs where data for up to 15 L0 events can be copied into RAMs. The data are then collected by a dedicated Spy-PGA based on an APA450. These dcalorimeter system is inherently fast, it has been decided to ata can be read at a slow rate using a slave mezzanine of the SPECS ECS system, which is mounted on the CROC board. The SPECS mezzanine also loads and reads control data onto the board, and also sends through the backplane, ECS data to the Glue-PGAs of each front-end board which are programmed to act as SPECS slaves. Finally a TTCrx mezzanine mounted on the CROC board receives by a fiber the 40 MHz clock, the L0 trigger signal and the channel B signals which have been generated in the readout supervisor boards in the electronic barracks. These signals are buffered and sent through the backplane to each other board in the crate. For debugging purposes the CROC can work as a stand alone system locally generating the clock L0 and channel B signals.

2008 JINST 3 S08005

Calorimeter specific TELL1 features

The TELL1 boards of LHCb are described in section 8.2. The specifications of the calorimeters are described in [154].

A preprocessor FPGA (PP-FPGA) collects and treats the incoming data from front-end boards sent by the CROC to the TELL1 board through an optical receiver mezzanine card (O-Rx card) which ensures the optical to electrical conversion and data synchronization. The PP-FPGA treats the event according to the detector identification (ECAL/HCAL or PS/SPD). Inside each PP-FPGA, a zero suppression is performed on the events during physics runs for PS/SPD data and a data compression without loss of information for ECAL and HCAL data [155]. The output data of each PP-FPGA are collected by the SyncLink-FPGA which then packs them in a Multiple Event Packet (MEP). For each event, the SyncLink-FPGA gives the trigger type of the run (physics or calibration) to the PP-FPGA. The MEPs are sent to the DAQ through a Gigabit-Ethernet (GBE) card. The output bandwidth of the GBE limits the use of one among the two O-Rx cards for ECAL and HCAL and thus two PP-FPGAs among the four. The two O-Rx cards are used for PS/SPD. In case of no data and/or synchronization error from the optical input links in the O-Rx card, an error bank is optionally generated (it is suppressed by default due to bandwidth limit). In order to keep track of these errors, a minimal information is kept in each event header.

The LED monitoring system is described in section 6.2.8. During calibration runs the LED data are not affected by the zero suppression, and only non-zero values are kept for PS/SPD. During physics runs, the data coming from the PIN boards (FE boards devoted to the PIN diode signals of ECAL/HCAL) are ignored.

6.2.7 Electronics of PS and SPD detectors

The signal of the PS and SPD has about the same duration as the ECAL and HCAL pulses; on average 85% of the charge is obtained in 25 ns. However, since the average number of photoelectrons is only about 25 per MIP, there are very large fluctuations in the signal pulse shape [156]. It was therefore considered unreasonable to try to implement the delay-line pulse shaping used for the ECAL/HCAL. On the other hand, since the useful dynamic range of the PS is typically only from 1 MIP to 100 MIP, an ADC with only 10-bits can be used and pedestal stability is not as important as for the ECAL/HCAL electronics, although it is important to integrate the signal over a time as long as possible within the 25 ns limitations. The phototube chosen to detect the light from the PS and SPD fibres is a 64 channel multi-anode PM. The HV is common to all 64 channels and there is a nonadjustable gain dispersion among these channels of a factor of 3, which however is constant in time. For this reason it was decided to introduce a Very Front End (VFE) stage of integration on the back of the phototubes in order to compensate the gain variation using a digital correction of a factor up to 2 in the front-end electronics.

The PS very front-end design

The solution adopted for the PS is to alternate every 25 ns between two integrators and to reset one integrator when the other one is active. The signal is sampled by track-and-hold circuits and the output of the active integrator is chosen by a multiplexer, followed by a twisted-pair cable driver.

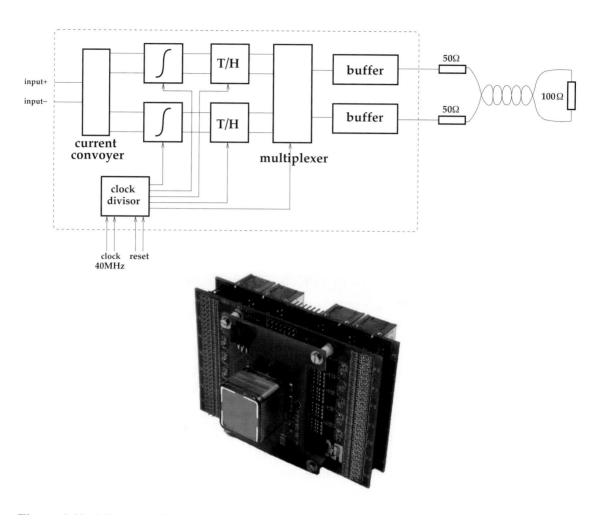

Figure 6.41: Schematic of the PS *Very Front-End* integrator (top) and a photograph of the integrator card mounted behind the MAPMT (bottom).

All circuit elements are functioning in differential mode to improve stability and pickup-noise rejection. The circuit design is shown in figure 6.41 and its detailed description is given in [157]. The phasing of the clock with respect to the signal determines the start of the integration. Since the length of the 64 fibres connected to a given PM are identical and the delay inside the PM is identical within a fraction of 1 ns, it is sufficient to have one clock adjustment (in steps of 1 ns) per phototube. The amplifier integrator circuit is realized in monolithic AMS 0.8 μm BICMOS technology with 4 channels implemented per chip. The dynamic range is 1 Volt with a noise of 1 mV. Sixteen chips are grouped in a card on each phototube. The outputs of each chip (4 channels) are sent through 27 m long ethernet cables[23] with RJ45 connectors to the ADC located on the FE board. Two clock and two reset signals delivered by the corresponding FE board are received by the VFE board through a cable of the same type as those used for the signal.

---

[23]from Kerpen company, Geramny.

2008 JINST 3 S08005

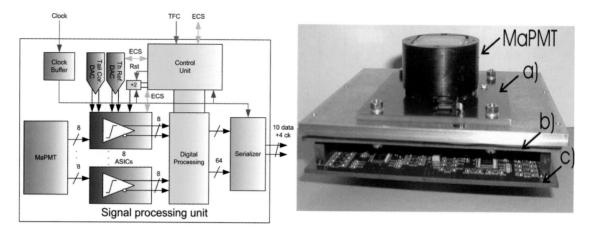

Figure 6.42: Left: block diagram of the SPD VFE card. Right: picture of the VFE assembly where the components are a) PMT base board, b) ASICs board and c) FPGA board.

The SPD very front-end and control board design

The SPD function is to discriminate between charged particles and neutrals in a detector which matches the preshower and ECAL cell size. The SPD signals are obtained, as in the case of the PS, from 64 channel multianode photomultipliers. The main difference of specification is that there is no compelling reason to perform pulseheight analysis on SPD signals. It was therefore decided to use a simpler solution with a simple discriminator output and a threshold set at 0.5 MIP thus obtaining 98% efficiency on charged particles [131, 137]. The principle of the design is shown in figure 6.42 and described in [127]. Although the functional architecture of a signal processing channel is similar to that of the PS, the circuits have been designed for the SPD specifically [158, 159]. The main architectural difference is the inclusion of an on chip pile-up compensation system and a comparator. The pile-up compensation system takes a tunable fraction of the integrator output at the current period and stores it on a track and hold circuit. This cancels on average the charge delivered by a pulse in the time interval between 25 and 50 ns after its start. The reference threshold value is set by a 7-bit DAC. The integration of each channel uses an independent DAC to compensate the offsets and the gain nonuniformity of the PMT. The circuit is realized in the AMS BICMOS 0.8 μm technology with 8 channels per chip. There are two external (not on-chip) DAC, with I2C interface to set some analogue references for the signal processing part. The control unit, the digital processing and clock divider used to obtain the 20 MHz clock that controls the ASICs are implemented in a reprogrammable FPGA, the ProASIC Plus ACTEL APA300. Triple voting registers (TVRs) are used to minimize signal event upset (SEU) errors. The digital processing consists of mapping PMT channels to given serializer channels to match the PS and SPD detector cell and injecting arbitrary patterns to test the detector data flow. The 64 channels and the 20 MHz clock are sent via standard shielded twisted pair (SSTP) LAN cables to the PS/SPD FE board, by means of 4 serializer chips (DS90CR215) with 3 data pairs and 1 clock pair each, requiring a serializing factor of 7. Control boards provide the VFE cards with links to the ECS and the timing and fast control (TFC) system. The boards are located in the FE crates. Two boards are needed for each of the 8 crates corresponding to the PS/SPD subsystem.

2008 JINST 3 S08005

The PS/SPD front-end board

The PS/SPD front-end boards implement functions similar to the HCAL/ECAL boards i.e an ADC for the preshower signal, pedestal correction and gain calibration, preparation of the trigger information, pipeline storage and selection of data for readout upon reception of trigger signals. The PS/SPD board handles 64 PS data channels for raw data readout and trigger purposes, and 64 SPD single bit trigger channels. The PS raw data dynamic range corresponds to 10 bits, coding energy from 0.1 MIP(1 ADC count) to 100 MIPs. A general overview of the board is given in figure 6.43 for the PS. An identical board is used for the SPD. Its general architecture is similar to the ECAL/HCAL boards with five major components:

- An analog block receiving the 64 analog PS channels from the VFE part and digitizing them. Each channel is composed of a fully differential operational amplifier followed by a 10-bit 40 MHz differential ADC. A synchronization signal (clock and reset) is sent to the VFE.

- A processing block made of 8 identical FE PGAs. Each of them is in charge of processing 8 PS channels. After applying corrections for pedestal subtraction, gain adjustment and pile-up, the 10-bit data are coded into an 8-bit floating format. A trigger bit is produced for each channel by applying a threshold on the corrected data. Eight SPD channels are also received. Two PS and SPD channels are packed together, stored and retrieved after L0. Two blocks of memory per two channels are used in each FE PGA for the L0 pipeline and derandomizer. The processing block is very resource consuming. Since the VFE comprises two interleaved integrators working in alternance, the gain and offset corrections have to be applied differently for two consecutive events leading to two effective subchannels per physical channel. Also the data inputs, 8 SPD channels of 1-bit and 8 PS channels of 10 bits are important. Consequently, the FE PGA chosen was the AX1000 of the ACTEL anti-fuse technology.

- A trigger block made of one Trig-PGA. It handles the processing for the production of the L0 information. The block receives the address of each cell and its local maximum of transverse energy from the ECAL Front End Board (FEB). As the ECAL electronics is organized into 32 channel boards, each 64 channel PS/SPD FEB is seen by the system as two 32 channel half boards, each receiving its own request address. The Trig-PGA is an APA450 of the ACTEL ProASIC plus Flash based FPGA family.

- A SEQ PGA builds the data block after a L0-Yes signal, and sends it to the CROC. It also issues control and synchronization signals for the other 8 FE PGAs and the Trig-PGA.

- A SPECS slave called GLUE PGA handling all the I2C communication of the board. The last two blocks, SEQ PGA and GLUE PGA, are identical to the ones of the ECAL/HCAL FE electronics and are described in reference [128].

All registers holding permanent information are radiation protected in static mode by triple voting and, during data transfers, by Hamming code.

2008 JINST 3 S08005

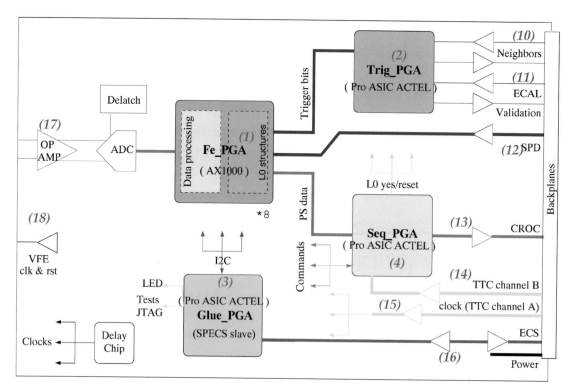

Figure 6.43: Schematic of the front-end board for the PS.

6.2.8 Monitoring and high voltage system

The calorimeter High Voltage (HV) and LED light intensity control systems share a common control board, the HV-LED-DAC board, that interfaces them to the Experiment Control System (ECS).

The High Voltage system

All calorimeter subdetectors are equipped with Hamamatsu photomultipliers. Eight thousand R7899-20 tubes are used for ECAL and HCAL and two hundred 64 channels multi-anode R7600-00-M64 for the SPD/PS detectors. All PMTs passed quality checks on dedicated test benches before installation on the detectors. The quality requirements included a better than 5% linearity and better than 3% gain stability as a function of rate, a low dark current and, for the SPD/PS PMTs, pixel-to-pixel uniformity of better than 1 to 3 (minimum to maximum) and crosstalk of less than 2%.

The HV system for the PMTs (figure 6.44) is based on a Cockroft-Walton (CW) voltage converter located on the base of each PMT and controlled by HV-LED-DAC control boards located in a few boxes distributed over the detector periphery and connected to the (ECS) by a SPECS [160] serial bus. For the SPD and PS the CWs and control boards are located in a VME crate on top of the ECAL and the HV is distributed to the PMTs with cables. The maximum HV is 1500 V for ECAL and HCAL and 800 V for SPD and PS. The CW base [161] is a reoptimized and radiation hard version of the one used in the HERA-B experiment [162]. It is implemented on a 25 mm x 60 mm CW board and consists of 22 multiplication stages, a control operational amplifier, an

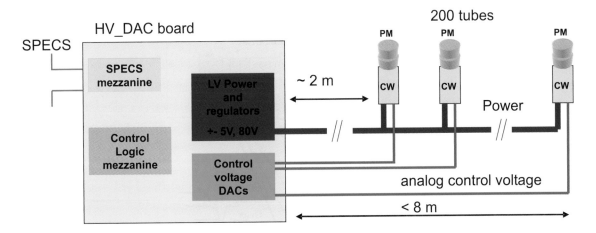

Figure 6.44: An overview of the High Voltage system of the calorimeter.

oscillator of 50 kHz and fast transistor switches. It features individual and precise gain adjustment of each PMT, effective operation at high background anode current, low power dissipation and only low voltage ($\pm$ 6V) power supplies. It requires, in addition, 100 V which is converted locally to a high voltage in the 100–2000 V range selectable through a 0 to 5V control voltage supplied by the control board. This conversion, being made locally for ECAL and HCAL, minimizes the number of high voltage cables and connectors. The characteristics of the CW are a gain drop of less than 2% for anode currents as high as 12 μA, a voltage ripple of less than 200 mV, a spread of output voltages of about 1% and a power consumption of less than 130 mW. Each HV-LED-DAC board can control 200 CWs and consists of a mother board and four mezzanine cards. A SPECS slave mezzanine is used for interconnection to the ECS system. The 200 PMTs are controlled by five 40-channel HV control signal generating cards using 12-bit DAC integrated circuits. A control logic board equipped with a radiation tolerant FPGA ACTEL APA075 provides an interface between the ECS and the 200 DAC signal generating integrated circuits. This board also allows automated monitoring and ramp-up of the high voltage. The fourth mezzanine card generates a 16 channel LED intensity control signal.

The LED monitoring system

The energy calibration of each cell of the ECAL calorimeter is obtained during data-taking by a variety of methods, such as monitoring their response to electrons, π^0's and minimum ionizing particles. ECAL and HCAL stability is monitored using LEDs, in order to obtain the best energy resolution essential for both triggering and reconstruction issues. The concept of the sytem is outlined in figure 6.45. Each cell of the four subdetectors is illuminated by an LED. They are triggered by LED drivers (labeled LED in figure 6.45) and their intensity controlled by the HV-LED-DAC boards. Multichannel LED Trigger Signal Boards (LEDTSB) perform the overall control and adjust the timing. For SPD and PS an individual LED is located on each tile and illuminates the PMT through the scintillator. Groups of 16 LEDs are controlled by 770 LED drivers located on the supermodules which are fired by 100 trigger channels.

On ECAL, LEDs are located in light-tight boxes situated above and below the calorimeter.

2008 JINST 3 S08005

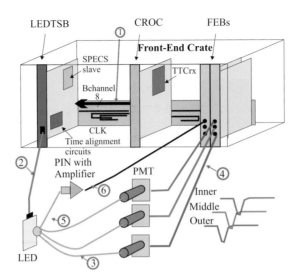

Figure 6.45: A sketch of the LED monitoring of the calorimeter.1: FE crate backplane over which the monitoring trigger request is transmitted, 2: LED trigger pulse cable, 3: Clear fibre to cell, 4: PMT signal cable, 5: Clear fibre to PIN diode, 6: PIN signal cable.

Each LED illuminates 9 or 16 cells via clear fibres routing the light to a connector at the front of each cell, and from there via a second clear fibre traversing the module and conducting the light directly through the light mixer to the PMT. Each LED also illuminates a PIN diode for monitoring the stability of the LED light output. There are 456 LEDs, each controlled by the LED driver, and 124 PIN diodes so that the LEDs sharing a PIN can be fired at different times.

Each HCAL module is equipped with two LEDs each illuminating every cell in the module. Since the PMTs in a module have different gains, which depend on the average momentum of the particles they are detecting, the light output of the two LEDs is set in the ratio of 1:4. Clear fibres bring the light of both LEDs to each PMT via its light mixer. One PIN diode monitors the stability of each LED. The 2 LEDs in each of the 52 modules illuminate 16 or 40 cells and are controlled by 104 LED drivers.

A LED monitoring sequence is initiated by the Readout Supervisor (RS) upon request and transmitted to the LEDTSBs via the CROCs and the FE crate backplane. The LEDTSBs are located in the front-end crates on the calorimeter platforms and each controls 64 LED drivers. A total of 686 LED drivers in the system therefore require 12 LEDTSBs. A correspondence between LEDs or groups of LEDs fired by each LEDTSB is preprogrammed in the LEDTSB FPGA. This allows a different pattern of the 64 drivers to be fired in each of 64 consecutive triggering sequences, thus providing maximum flexibility. The LED firing time is adjusted in the LEDTSB in steps of 1 ns so as to arrive at the first cell of the readout pipeline, 16 clock cycles (400 ns) after the RS pulse. It emerges 4 μs later from the pipeline in time for the calorimeter trigger.

The LED trigger boards are decoupled with air transformer, are edge triggered, and use fast on board pulse shapers. They provide a pulse of less than 25 ns to fit within an LHC bucket and with a shape compatible with that generated by a particle.

The light intensity of the LEDs is controlled via ECS by the HV-LED-DAC boards which are located in areas of low radiation. A wide range of intensities is implemented to monitor the linearity of the PMTs.

2008 JINST 3 S08005

For each LED monitoring sequence a subset of each of the subdetectors is illuminated. A given group of channels is fired at a rate of 20–30 Hz, resulting in an overall monitoring rate of 1 kHz. For each trigger 3–5% of the channels contain data.

These data are read out and transferred to a monitoring farm, consisting of a dedicated node of the processing farm where they are analyzed to check the stability of the calorimeters. Should any channel be observed to be drifting in gain an alarm is generated. Depending on the type of alarm, the run is paused or a suitable correction to the HV computed and applied via the ECS system.

The LED system is also used to detect malfunctioning cells and bad cable connections. It also allows a first relative timing of the cells.

6.3 Muon System

Muon triggering and offline muon identification are fundamental requirements of the LHCb experiment. Muons are present in the final states of many CP-sensitive B decays, in particular the two *gold-plated* decays, $B_d^0 \rightarrow J/\psi\,(\mu^+\mu^-)K_S^0$ and $B_s^0 \rightarrow J/\psi\,(\mu^+\mu^-)\phi$ [2]. They play a major role in CP asymmetry and oscillation measurements, since muons from semi-leptonic b decays provide a tag of the initial state flavor of the accompanying neutral B mesons. In addition, the study of rare B decays such as the flavour-changing neutral current decay, $B_s^0 \rightarrow \mu^+\mu^-$, may reveal new physics beyond the Standard Model [163].

The muon system provides fast information for the high-p_T muon trigger at the earliest level (Level-0) and muon identification for the high-level trigger (HLT) and offline analysis.

6.3.1 Overview

The muon system [164–166], shown in figure 6.46, is composed of five stations (M1-M5) of rectangular shape, placed along the beam axis. The full system comprises 1380 chambers and covers a total area of 435 m^2. The inner and outer angular acceptances of the muon system are 20 (16) mrad and 306 (258) mrad in the bending (non-bending) plane respectively. This results in an acceptance of about 20% for muons from inclusive b semileptonic decays.

Stations M2 to M5 are placed downstream the calorimeters and are interleaved with iron absorbers 80 cm thick to select penetrating muons. The minimum momentum of a muon to cross the five stations is approximately 6 GeV/c since the total absorber thickness, including the calorimeters, is approximately 20 interaction lengths. Station M1 is placed in front of the calorimeters and is used to improve the p_T measurement in the trigger. The geometry of the five stations is projective, meaning that all their transverse dimensions scale with the distance from the interaction point.

The detectors provide space point measurements of the tracks, providing binary (yes/no) information to the trigger processor (see section 7.1) and to the DAQ. The information is obtained by partitioning the detector into rectangular *logical pads* whose dimensions define the x, y resolution.

The muon trigger is based on stand-alone muon track reconstruction and p_T measurement and requires aligned hits in all five stations. Stations M1–M3 have a high spatial resolution along the x coordinate (bending plane). They are used to define the track direction and to calculate the p_T of the candidate muon with a resolution of 20%. Stations M4 and M5 have a limited spatial resolution, their main purpose being the identification of penetrating particles.

2008 JINST 3 S08005

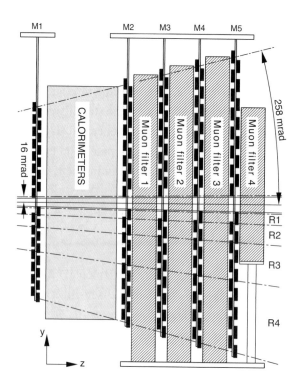

Figure 6.46: Side view of the muon system.

Appropriate programming of the L0 processing unit (see section 7.1.2) allows the muon trigger to operate in the absence of one station (M1, M4 or M5) or with missing chamber parts, although with degraded performance (worse p_T resolution).

The layout of the muon stations is shown in figure 6.47. Each Muon Station is divided into four regions, R1 to R4 with increasing distance from the beam axis. The linear dimensions of the regions R1, R2, R3, R4, and their segmentations scale in the ratio 1:2:4:8. With this geometry, the particle flux and channel occupancy are expected to be roughly the same over the four regions of a given station. The (x, y) spatial resolution worsens far from the beam axis, where it is in any case limited by the increase of multiple scattering at large angles. The right part of figure 6.47 shows schematically the partitioning of the station M1 into logical pads and the (x, y) granularity. Table 6.5 gives detailed information on the geometry of the muon stations.

Simulation

A complete simulation of the muon system was performed using GEANT4. Starting from the energy deposits of charged particles in the sensitive volumes, the detector signals were created and digitized taking into account detector effects such as efficiency, cross-talk, and dead time as well as effects arising from pile-up and spill-over of events occurring in previous bunch crossings [167].

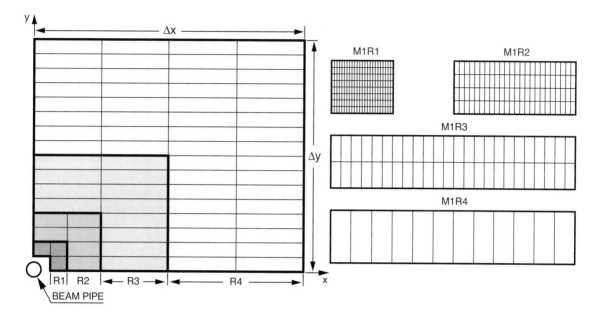

Figure 6.47: Left: front view of a quadrant of a muon station. Each rectangle represents one chamber. Each station contains 276 chambers. Right: division into logical pads of four chambers belonging to the four regions of station M1. In each region of stations M2-M3 (M4-M5) the number of pad columns per chamber is double (half) the number in the corresponding region of station M1, while the number of pad rows per chamber is the same (see table 6.5).

A realistic simulation of the detector occupancy requires the detailed description of the cavern geometry and of the beam line elements and the use of very low energy thresholds in GEANT4. The CPU time needed for such a simulation would be prohibitive for the stations M2–M5 interleaved with iron filters. The strategy chosen to overcome this problem was therefore to generate once for all a high statistics run of minimum bias events with low thresholds. The distributions of hit multiplicities obtained were parametrized and then used to statistically add hits to the standard LHCb simulated events. The latter were obtained by running GEANT4 at higher thresholds and with a simplified geometry of the cavern and the beam line [168]. Simulated events have been extensively used to evaluate the rates in the various detector regions in order to establish the required rate capabilities and ageing properties of the chambers and to evaluate the data flow through the DAQ system [169]. At a luminosity of 2×10^{32} cm^{-2} s^{-1} the highest rates expected in the inner regions of M1 and M2 are respectively 80 kHz/cm^2 and 13 kHz/cm^2 per detector plane. In the detector design studies, a safety factor of 2 was applied to the M1 hit multiplicity and the low energy background in stations M2-M5 has been conservatively multiplied by a factor of 5 to account for uncertainties in the simulation.

Detector technology

The LHC bunch crossing rate of 40 MHz and the intense flux of particles in the muon system [169] impose stringent requirements on the efficiency, time resolution, rate capability and ageing characteristics of the detectors, as well as on the speed and radiation resistance of the electronics.

2008 JINST 3 S08005

Table 6.5: Basic information for the five stations M1–M5 and the four regions R1–R4. All dimensions in cm. z: distance of the stations from the IP; Δx and Δy: dimensions of a quadrant in each station (see figure 6.47). Rows R1-R4: granularity of the different regions of the muon detector as seen by trigger and DAQ. Number of logical pads per chamber (in brackets) and size of the logical pads, along x and y. In parentheses: size of the logical pads projected onto station M1.

	M1	M2	M3	M4	M5
z	1210	1527	1647	1767	1887
Δx	384	480	518	556	594
Δy	320	400	432	464	495
R1	$[24 \times 8]$ 1×2.5	$[48 \times 8]$ 0.63×3.1 (0.5×2.5)	$[48 \times 8]$ 0.67×3.4 (0.5×2.5)	$[12 \times 8]$ 2.9×3.6 (2×2.5)	$[12 \times 8]$ 3.1×3.9 (2×2.5)
R2	$[24 \times 4]$ 2×5	$[48 \times 4]$ 1.25×6.3 (1×5)	$[48 \times 4]$ 1.35×6.8 (1×5)	$[12 \times 4]$ 5.8×7.3 (4×5)	$[12 \times 4]$ 6.2×7.7 (4×5)
R3	$[24 \times 2]$ 4×10	$[48 \times 2]$ 2.5×12.5 (2×10)	$[48 \times 2]$ 2.7×13.5 (2×10)	$[12 \times 2]$ 11.6×14.5 (8×10)	$[12 \times 2]$ 12.4×15.5 (8×10)
R4	$[12 \times 1]$ 8×20	$[24 \times 1]$ 5×25 (4×20)	$[24 \times 1]$ 5.4×27 (4×20)	$[6 \times 1]$ 23.1×29 (16×20)	$[6 \times 1]$ 24.8×30.9 (16×20)

Multi-wire proportional chambers (MWPC) are used for all regions except the inner region of station M1 where the expected particle rate exceeds safety limits for ageing. In this region triple-GEM detectors are used [166].

The trigger algorithm requires a five-fold coincidence between all the stations, therefore the efficiency of each station must be high enough to obtain a trigger efficiency of at least 95%, within a time window smaller than 25 ns in order to unambiguously identify the bunch crossing.[24] The necessary time resolution is ensured by a fast gas mixture and an optimized charge-collection geometry both for the MWPC and the GEM detectors. Moreover, the chambers are composed of four or two OR-ed *gas gaps* depending on station. In stations M2–M5 the MWPCs are composed of four gas gaps arranged in two sensitive layers with independent readout. In station M1 the chambers have only two gas gaps to minimize the material in front of the electromagnetic calorimeter. In region M1R1 two superimposed GEM chambers connected in OR are used.

To simplify the synchronization procedure and improve time alignment, the readout electronics is equipped with a 4-bit TDC which allows a fine time measurement of the signals with respect to the 25 ns machine clock. The fine time tuning is perfomed by selecting the hits belonging to penetrating tracks.

In addition, the use of two layers with independent HV supplies and the flexibility of the readout provide a high degree of redundancy built into the system.

---

[24]In the following, the system has been characterized assuming a conservative 20 ns window.

2008 JINST 3 S08005

Table 6.6: Readout methods used in the muon chambers.

Readout type	Region
MWPC	
Wire pads	R4
Mixed wire-cathode pads	R1-R2 in M2-M3
Cathode pads	everywhere else
GEM	
Anode pads	M1R1

Readout

To satisfy the requirements of spatial resolution and rate capability that vary strongly over the detectors, different technical solutions are employed for the MWPC in different stations and regions.

All the chambers are segmented into *physical pads*: anode wire pads or cathode pads in the MWPCs and anode pads in the GEM chambers. Each physical pad is read out by one front-end (FE) electronics channel. The FE electronics is based on custom radiation-hard chips especially developed for the muon system. The input stage can be wired to handle either signal polarity: negative for anode pads, positive for cathode pads.

The electronics includes flexible logical units performing the OR of a variable number of FE channels following the requirements of the readout. The readout methods used in different detector regions are summarized in table 6.6.

The R4 regions contain most of the chambers and the spatial resolution required there is relatively modest. Therefore the simplest and safest technology was adopted: the physical pads are a group of adjacent wires connected together to the same FE channel. The length of the anode wires defines the spatial y resolution, all the wires being aligned vertically. The requirement on the resolution limits the vertical size of the chambers to $20 - -30$ cm, and results in a large number of chambers.

Cathode pads (anode pads for GEM) are obtained by etching the desired pattern in the cathode (anode) planes. As can be seen from figure 6.47 all pads in R3 chambers can be accessed directly from the upper and lower sides. On the other hand, the chambers belonging to R1 and R2 have a chessboard pad structure so that a multilayer printed circuit board is used to bring the signals outside.

To keep the noise and the dead-time of the FE channels to an acceptable level, the rate of a given pad and its electrical capacitance must be limited. This implies that in most chambers the size of the physical pads (either wire or cathode pads) must be smaller than required by spatial resolution. In these cases up to four adjacent physical pads are OR-ed by the FE electronics to build a logical pad. However, in regions R1-R2 of stations M2-M3 the required spatial resolution in x imposes logical pads which are too small to be practically built. For those chambers a mixed readout has been adopted: a narrow wire-strip to define the x resolution, and a larger cathode pad to define the y resolution, together defining are the logical channels seen by the trigger and DAQ. Logical pads are then obtained as an AND between wire and cathode pads (figure 6.48).

2008 JINST 3 S08005

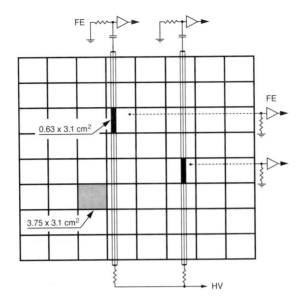

Figure 6.48: Scheme of the mixed wire-cathode pads readout in one M2R1 chamber. Two wire-pad and two cathode-pad readout channels are shown. The coincidence between crossing vertical wire-pads and the cathode physical pads defines the logical pads, shown in black.

In the M1 station, where the foreseen channel occupancy is high, the signals from the logical pads are sent directly to the trigger and DAQ. In most of the other regions, in order to reduce the number of output optical fibres, several contiguous logical pads are further OR-ed to build larger *logical channels* in the form of vertical and horizontal strips. The logical pads are then reconstructed by the coincidence of two crossing strips. This operation is performed in the Level-0 Trigger Processor (see 7.1) and in the DAQ TELL1 boards (see 8.2).

Figure 6.49 shows the partitioning of a quadrant of stations M2 and M3 into *sectors* containing the crossing strips. The sector size is adapted to the trigger processing elements that work on a fixed number of logical pads belonging to a projective tower over the five stations.

The full muon system comprises 122112 physical channels ORed into 25920 logical channels which are transmitted via optical links to the Level-0 trigger and DAQ electronics. Appropriate combinations of logical channels in the Level-0 and High-Level Trigger provide the 55296 logical pads used for the muon tracking.

The specifications of the MWPCs and GEMs and their performance are summarised in the following sections.

6.3.2 Wire chambers

Design

The LHCb muon system comprises 1368 Multi Wire Proportional Chambers. Prototype studies [170–176] showed that a time resolution of about 5 ns can be achieved in a gas gap with a wire plane of 2 mm spacing, symmetrically placed in a 5 mm gas gap, using fast, non-flammable, gas mixtures of $Ar/CO_2/CF_4$ with 40% Ar and variable concentrations of CO_2/CF_4. Finally the

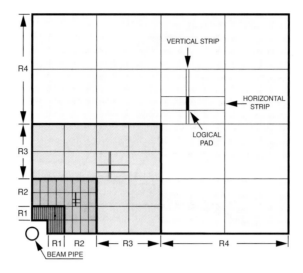

Figure 6.49: Front view of one quadrant of stations M2 and M3 showing the partitioning into sectors. In one sector of each region a horizontal and a vertical strip are shown. The intersection of a horizontal and a vertical strip defines a logical pad (see text). A Sector of region R1 (R2, R3, R4) contains 8 (4, 4, 4) horizontal strips and 6 (12, 24, 24) vertical strips.

Table 6.7: Main MWPC parameters.

Parameter	Design value
No. of gaps	4 (2 in M1)
Gas gap thickness	5 mm
Anode-cathode spacing	2.5 mm
Wire	Gold-plated Tungsten 30 μm diameter
Wire spacing	2.0 mm
Wire length	250 to 310 mm
Wire mechanical tension	0.7 N
Total no. of wires	$\approx 3 \cdot 10^6$
Operating voltage	2.5–2.8 kV
Gas mixture	Ar / CO_2 / CF_4 (40:55:5)
Primary ionisation	$\simeq 70\,e^-$/cm
Gas Gain	$\simeq 10^5$ @ 2.65 kV
Gain uniformity	$\pm 20\%$ typical
Charge/MIP (one gap)	$\simeq 0.6\,$pC @ 2.65 kV

mixture $Ar/CO_2/CF_4(40:55:5)$ was adopted. By OR-ing the signals from two adjacent gas gaps the resulting *double gap* has an efficiency better than 95% in a 20 ns window at a gas gain of $G \simeq 10^5$. This gain is achieved at a voltage of 2600–2700 V [177]. Prototype tests with intense beams (100 kHz/cm^2) confirmed the prediction that space-charge effects are negligible at the rates expected for the experiment [178].

The main parameters of the MWPC detectors are summarized in table 6.7. Detailed simulations [179] based on GARFIELD [180] were performed to optimize the design and to establish

2008 JINST 3 S08005

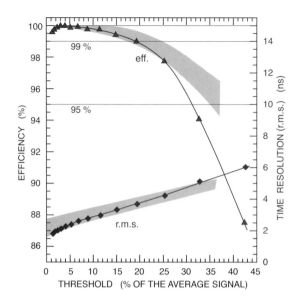

Figure 6.50: MWPC double-gap efficiency and time resolution vs. discriminator threshold for a prototype chamber. Solid lines: experimental results. The MonteCarlo simulation is shown in grey; the band accounts for different track angles.

the geometrical tolerances for the chamber construction. The primary ionisation was simulated by HEED [181] and drift and diffusion by MAGBOLTZ [182]. The design of the pad readout was optimized with SPICE [69] in order to keep the cross-talk between pads below 5%. The maximal deviations of the construction parameters was established under the assumption of a maximum variation of gas gain of ±20%.

Figure 6.50 shows the good agreement of a MonteCarlo simulation for double-gap efficiency and time resolution versus FE threshold and the values measured on for a chamber prototype.

In stations M2–M5 a chamber is made of four equal gas gaps superimposed and rigidly stacked together with the gas flowing serially through all the gaps. Two contiguous gas gaps have their corresponding readout electrodes (either wire or cathode pads) hard-wired together in OR to form a double gap layer. The readout electrodes of the resulting layer are in turn connected to separate FE channels. As already mentioned, the M1 chambers contain only two gas gaps. These two gaps form the two layers which are readout independently. In order to maximize operation flexibility each gap has its own HV line and can be powered or switched off independently of the others.

Figure 6.51 shows an exploded schematic view of a chamber. The structural elements of the chamber are the panels, 9 mm thick, made of an insulating core sandwiched between two conducting planes. The conducting planes inside the chamber form the cathodes while the two external planes are grounded and act as an electrical shield. The panels are stacked using 2.5 mm thick PCB bars glued to the panels and superimposed to create the 5 mm gas gap. The wires are soldered and glued to the wire fixation bars while other bars seal the gap along the periphery. The 5 mm gap is ensured by several precision dowels inserted in the bars.

A cross section of a chamber is shown in figure 6.52. A U-shaped brass channel running around the chamber edges is soldered to the outer conductive planes to complete the chamber Faraday cage. The front-end boards, the LV voltage regulators and the HV filters are mounted

2008 JINST 3 S08005

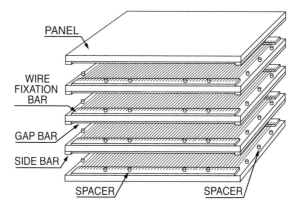

Figure 6.51: Exploded schematic view of a chamber showing the various elements.

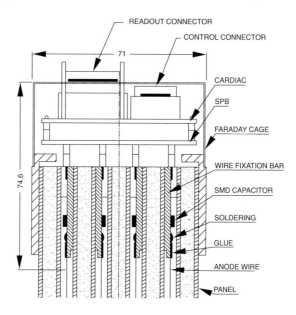

Figure 6.52: Cross section of a wire chamber showing the four gas gaps and the connection to the readout electronics. SPB: Spark Protection Board; CARDIAC: FE Electronics Board. In this case the hardwired OR forming the two Double Gaps (see text) is achieved in the SPB.

inside the Faraday cage to minimize electrical pickup. The HV is brought in through a custom-made multipin connector and multiconductor cable. LVDS shielded cables are used for signal transmission and control.

The general design and construction is the same for all chambers and is discussed in detail in [183].

Chamber construction

Given the large number of chambers, the production was distributed among six production sites. A great effort went into ensuring that all those sites had equivalent facilities and tooling, albeit with some flexibility. The same stringent quality criteria and test protocols were adopted throughout to ensure a constant quality of the produced chambers.

2008 JINST 3 S08005

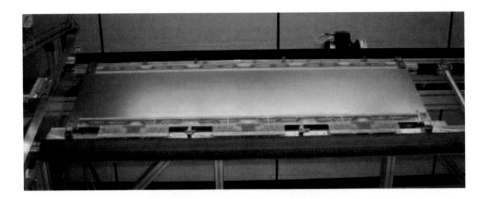

Figure 6.53: Panels mounted onto the winding machine frame ready to start wiring. The two combs which guide the wire are also visible. Below the panel in the foreground there is a second one attached to the underside of the frame. The two panels are wound simultaneously.

Panels The panels are the basis of the chamber mechanical structure. A panel consists of two copper clad fire-resistant fibreglass epoxy laminates (FR4), interleaved with a structural core. The panels are individually wired and then assembled to form the complete chamber.

The panel precision and its planarity define the gap quality. Therefore it is very important to achieve tight tolerances and stability in time, coupled with adequate robustness. In addition the panels must be light and stiff and easily adapted to mass production. The choice for the structural core was a polyurethane foam core for stations M2–M5 and a light honeycomb core for station M1 where a lower material budget is mandatory.

The panels were produced industrially. For the M2–M5 chambers precision machined molds were used to inject the polyurethane foam into the FR4 sandwich. Three molds of different sizes produced all the panels. For M1 chambers the core was made from a light NOMEX® sheet purchased with precise tolerance on thickness, and glued between the two FR4 foils. The pressure during gluing was assured by a vacuum bag. So the planarity of the panels is due to the quality of the honeycomb core and of the flatness of the assembly table.

The wire fixation bars (figure 6.51) were glued to the panels before the wiring process using an epoxy adhesive.[25] The gluing was performed on a special table which ensured the exact height of the bars above the panel itself.

Wiring Specially built automatic winding machines were used in all the production sites to rapidly perform panel wiring. The machines could wind one or two panels simultaneously in about one hour for the largest chambers. The panels were fixed to a rigid frame, and grooved dowels (combs) were installed parallel to the panels long sides (figure 6.53). To achieve the required precision on wire pitch, the wire spacing was determined by the combs while the wire height with respect to the cathode-plane was adjusted by precision bars mounted to the frame. The winding machines were equipped with brake motors or electronic devices to keep the mechanical wire tension constant.

Once the winding was completed, the wires were glued and soldered. The wires were glued to the wire fixation bars using epoxy adhesive before soldering. This procedure guarantees that the

---

[25] Adekit A140 epoxy, Axon Technologies, USA.

2008 JINST 3 S08005

Figure 6.54: A M1R4 chamber completely assembled before the installation of the Faraday cage. The three honeycomb panels are visible. On the corners of the panels there are plastic inserts with internal channels for gas circulation. The gas nipples are inserted in the top and bottom panels. Decoupling HV capacitors, resistors and connectors for the FE boards are mounted on the printed cicuit boards on the right.

wires are kept in place with a fixed height with respect to the cathode plane. The gluing also keeps the wire tension to its nominal value.

Due to the large number of solder joints in the construction of the chambers, the use of an automated and reliable method was desirable. Automatic soldering stations [183] both with conventional soldering heads and with laser heads were employed.

Final assembly In the final assembly of the chamber the panels were superimposed and glued together using cylindrical precision spacers for alignment (see figure 6.51). The glue[26] ensures the chamber gas tightness. In the chambers of region R1 in stations M2–M3 and of region R2 in stations M1–M3, no glue was used and gas tightness was ensured by O-rings made of natural rubber. This allows to open the chambers easily if needed. Screws were used to keep together the panels. Finally the brass channels forming the Faraday cage were soldered to the outer copper cladding of the panels. Figure 6.54 shows an assembled M1R4 without Faraday cage.

Quality control and testing

Uniform quality of the chambers produced in the various sites was ensured by stringent quality tests of the individual chamber components and of the assembled chambers [184–186]. All the panels were individully measured at production and then shipped to the production sites where they were checked once more before assembly. Despite the tight tolerances the yield of good panels was 90%.

Once the panels were produced, the pitch and the mechanical tension were measured for all wires. The wire pitch was determined with an automated device based on two digital cameras [186]. The distribution of the measured wire pitch has an r.m.s. of $16\,\mu$m. Only a very small number of wires with pitch value outside tolerance (±0.1 mm) had to be replaced.

---

[26]Adekit A145 and Araldite 2011 epoxy, Huntsman Advanced Materials, Switzerland.

2008 JINST 3 S08005

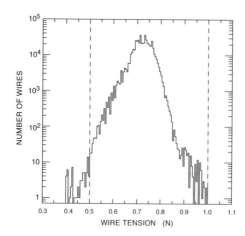

Figure 6.55: Distribution of the mechanical tensions of the wires as deduced from a measurement of the wire mechanical resonant frequency. The mean value of the tension is 0.73 N with an r.m.s. of 0.091 N. The wires having a tension outside the interval 0.5–1 N (dashed lines) were replaced.

To determine the wire mechanical tension automated systems were developed [187, 188] which measures the mechanical resonant frequency of each wire. The distribution of the wire tension measured on the above mentioned sample is reported in figure 6.55.

The checks on the assembled chambers consisted of a gas leak test and a HV test at 2800–2900 V using the standard gas mixture. The chamber gas leakage was determined by monitoring the decrease in time of an initial overpressure of 5 mbar. The method [186] had a sensitivity of about 0.01 mbar/hour well below the maximum gas leakage rate accepted of 2 mbar/hour.

The uniformity of the gas gain in the gaps was systematically checked using radioactive sources mounted on automated tables which performed an (x, y) scan over the complete chamber surface [185, 186, 189]. Figure 6.56 shows the gain measurement on a sample of 184 chambers.

All the above checks were performed without the readout electronics installed.

Finally all chambers, fully equipped with the front-end electronics, underwent a final test with cosmic rays prior to installation and the electronic noise was checked once more when the chambers were mounted in the experiment. The maximum accepted noise rate was 1 kHz per FE channel, a value which has no impact on the trigger system.

In addition, all the chambers for the regions exposed to the largest particle flux, were conditioned at the CERN Gamma Irradiation Facility (GIF) [190] to ensure their stable functionality under high radiation.

Important information about the individual components and the final chamber was stored in a database. This allows to retrieve at any time the results of all quality control measurements and will aid in understanding possible problems.

Aging properties

Extensive aging tests were performed on prototypes at the CERN GIF and at the Calliope[27] facility. The goal of the tests was to prove that the performance of these chambers is not deteriorated by

---

[27]ENEA-Casaccia Research Centre, Rome.

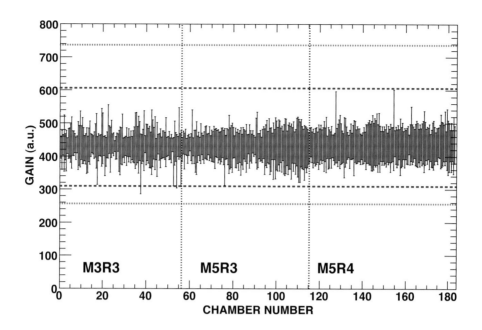

Figure 6.56: Gain uniformity measured for a sample of 184 chambers. The bars are proportional to the total gain spread of a double gap. The horizontal lines indicate the allowed acceptance intervals for good (in blue) and spare (in red) chambers.

the large radiation dose expected in the experiment in ten years of operation (10^8 s) at the nominal luminosity of 2×10^{32} cm^{-2} s^{-1} . In these tests the gain loss was measured against a non-irradiated reference chamber or gas gap.

In the test performed at the GIF facility at CERN, a four gap MWPC was irradiated for six months, accumulating a charge of 0.25 C/cm without detecting any gain loss [191].

In an accelerated test during 30 days of irradiation at the ^{60}Co source of Calliope, we monitored the currents in five four-gap MWPCs: four test chambers and a reference one [176, 192]. The chambers were operated at a voltage of 2.75 kV, corresponding to a gas gain of $1.8 \cdot 10^5$ [177], twice the value that will be adopted in the experiment. The largest integrated charge collected on a chamber wire was 0.44 C/cm. This corresponds [169] to about 7 years (10^7 s/year) of operation of the most irradiated chamber (in M1R2) at a luminosity of 2×10^{32} cm^{-2} s^{-1} , assuming a safety factor of 2. No gain loss or other significant effect was detected.

6.3.3 GEM chambers

In the innermost region R1 of the station M1, the most stringent requirements for the detector is a rate capability of up to 500 kHz/cm^2 of charged particles. Due to the large particle flux in this region the chambers must also be especially radiation hard such that no ageing effects will be visible in 10 years of LHCb operation. This is difficult to achieve in wire chambers unless the gain is decreased, at the price of a worse signal-to-noise ratio.

After an extensive R&D program triple-GEM chambers with active area of 20×24 cm^2 were selected for M1R1. Each of the 12 chambers consists of two triple-GEM detectors superimposed and forming the two sensitive layers, which are then logically OR-ed.

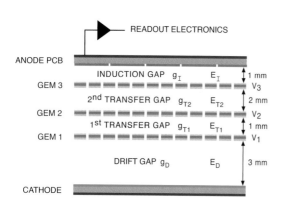

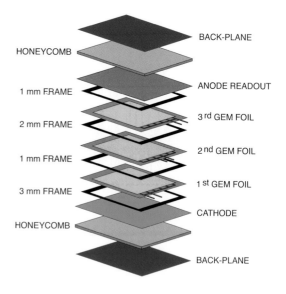

Figure 6.57: Schematic cross section of a triple-GEM detector showing the most relevant elements and dimensions (see text).

Figure 6.58: Exploded view of a triple-GEM detector.

Design

The triple-GEM detector, which consists of three gas electron multiplier (GEM) [193–195] foils sandwiched between anode and cathode planes, can effectively be used as tracking detector with good time and position resolution. A cross section of the detector, showing the different elements and their physical dimensions, is shown in figure 6.57. An exploded view is presented in figure 6.58.

The ionisation electrons, produced in the drift gap between the cathode and the first GEM foil, are attracted by electric fields through the three GEM foils where they are multiplied. Once they cross the last GEM foil they drift to the anode in the induction gap, giving rise to an induced current signal on the pads.

Prototype tests have shown that the fast $Ar/CO_2/CF_4(45:15:40)$ gas mixture allowed to achieve a time resolution better than 3 ns, to be compared with the time resolution of $\sim$10 ns obtained with the standard Ar/CO_2 (70:30) gas mixture [196].

Another improvement in time performance has been obtained by optimizing the detector geometry. Mechanical considerations indicate that a minimum distance of 1 mm should be kept between GEM foils. The size of the drift gap g_D is large enough to guarantee full efficiency for charged tracks. The first transfer gap g_{T1} is kept as small as possible to avoid that primary electrons produced in the same gap give rise to a signal over threshold. The second transfer gap g_{T2} is larger than the first one to let the diffusion spread the charge over more holes and then lower the discharge probability. The induction gap g_I is kept as small as possible to maximize the signal fraction integrated by the amplifier.

The best values of the gap fields and of the voltage across the GEM foils were determined experimentally by optimizing time resolution versus discharge probability and are typically $E_D = 3.5$ kV/cm, $E_T = 3.5$ kV/cm and $E_I = 5$ kV/cm and $V_1 = 440$ V, $V_2 = 430$ V, $V_3 = 410$ V. The anode pad printed circuit board is such that the pad to pad distance is 0.6 mm and the pads are surrounded by a ground grid of 0.2 mm thickness to suppress cross-talk.

2008 JINST 3 S08005

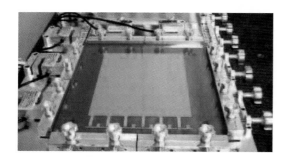

Figure 6.59: Stretching of a GEM foil.

Figure 6.60: GEM chamber fully assembled with the 24 FE electronics boards. The cutouts in the Faraday cage allow the insertion of the cable connectors.

Measurements on prototype chambers made of two detectors in OR showed an efficiency better than 96% in a 20 ns window at a gain of $6 \cdot 10^3$. The pad cluster size upper limit of 1.2 and the discharge studies suggested a maximum working gain of about $2 \cdot 10^4$ [195].

Chamber construction

All the critical steps in chamber assembly were carried out in class 1000 clean rooms or under class 1000 huts, with controlled temperature and humidity conditions. The huts were used for all operations involving GEM foils.

The GEM foils, 50 μm thick Kapton with two-sided Cu cladding of 5 μm, have an active area of 202×242 mm^2 and were manufactured by the CERN-EST-DEM workshop. The holes have a bi-conical structure with external (internal) diameter of 70 (50) μm and a pitch of 140 μm. In order to limit the damage in case of discharge, one side of the GEM foil is divided into six sectors, of about 33 mm $\times$ 240 mm. The separation between sectors is 200 μm. Each individual foil was visually inspected for defects and for leakage current. Then the foils were stretched with a mechanical tension of about 1 kg/cm with a special device visible in figure 6.59.

After the GEM stretching, a fibreglass frame was glued on the GEM foil using a Ciba 2012 epoxy. Both cathode and readout pad electrodes, realized on standard 1.0 mm thick printed circuit board, were respectively coupled with a 1.0 mm fibreglass foil by means of an 8 mm thick honeycomb structure, The back-panel with a 12 μm copper layer deposition on its external side is used as a Faraday cage for the detector. The stiff cathode and pad panels act as support plates for the whole detector. These panels house two gas inlets and two gas outlets, made with machined Stesalit inserts.

All fibreglass parts that are in contact with the sensitive volume of the detector, were visually inspected in order to eliminate any residual spikes or broken fibres. They were then cleaned in an ultrasonic bath with de-mineralized water and dried in an oven at a temperature of 80°C during one night.

2008 JINST 3 S08005

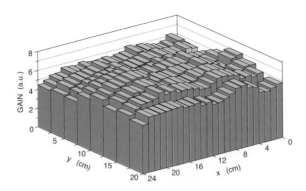

Figure 6.61: Response uniformity of a GEM chamber measured with an X-ray gun. The RMS gain variation over the 24×8 pads is typically less than 10%.

The detectors were built on a high-precision reference plane by piling up and gluing together the component parts in the following order (see figure 6.58): cathode panel; the first GEM foil (GEM1) glued on a 3 mm thick fibreglass frame; the second GEM foil (GEM2) glued on a 1 mm thick frame; the third GEM foil (GEM3) glued on a 2 mm thick frame and then the last 1 mm thick frame followed by the pad panel. All the gluing operations were performed using Araldite AY103 epoxy and HY991 hardener. The aging properties of both glues have been studied during irradiation tests [197, 198]. A complete chamber is shown in figure 6.60.

Quality control and testing

Several quality checks were performed on individual detector components before chamber assembly. Since the cathode and anode panels are the main mechanical structure of the detector, they were checked for planarity. Measurements over the whole panels showed that the deviation from the average plane was of the order of $50\,\mu$m (r.m.s).

The quality of GEM foils was checked by performing various tests. A preliminary optical inspection was performed with a microscope to check for photolithographic imperfections. If the GEM foil passed the visual inspection, a high voltage test was performed. Such a test was done in a gas tight box, flushed with nitrogen too keep the relative humidity at $\sim$25% level. The foil was accepted if the leakage current was less than 1 nA at 500 V.

After construction, the detector gas leak rate was measured. This measurement was performed by inflating the detector to an overpressure of $\sim$10 mbar together with another gas-tight chamber used as reference, and recording the overpressure decay. The typical gas leak rate of a detector is of the order of few mbar/day. At the gas flow forseen in the experiment (80 cm^3/min) this leakage rate will result in an acceptable humidity level lower than 100 ppm.

A gain uniformity test, performed with an X-ray gun, checked both the mechanical tolerance and the response uniformity of single detectors. A typical result is presented in figure 6.61. The current signals induced on each of the 192 pads of each detector were corrected for temperature and pressure variations. The current deviations from the average were all below 20% with a typical RMS $<$ 10%. Finally, a cosmic ray test was performed on all chambers fully equipped with front-end electronics.

2008 JINST 3 S08005

Discharge and aging properties

The use of the non-standard $Ar/CO_2/CF_4(45:15:40)$ gas mixture required the demonstration of high robusteness of the GEM to discharges and ageing effects. In fact the choice of the electric field in the detector gaps and the unbalanced configuration of the voltages applied to the GEM foils ($V_1 > V_2 > V_3$, see figure 6.57) are the result of a minimization of discharges produced by alpha particles. More than 5000 discharges were integrated with neither breakdown nor performance losses using alpha particles and a high intensity low momentum pion/proton beam. These measurements demonstrated that GEMs in M1R1 can operate safely. The large fraction of CF_4 in the gas required that a global irradiation test of the final chamber be performed to check the compatibility between the construction materials and the gas mixture. For this reason a test was performed at the Calliope facility with an intense gamma ray flux from a ^{60}Co source. In this test, a charge of 2.2 C/cm^2 on the anode pads and GEM3 foil was integrated. This is the charge foreseen for more than 10 years running if the GEMs are operated with a gain of ~ 6000 and a safety factor of 2 is applied. The performance of these chambers was measured in a test beam before and after irradiation and no damage or performance losses were detected [197, 198].

6.3.4 Muon System mechanics

All muon stations, including the iron filters, are separated into two halves which can move on rails away from the beampipe for maintenance and installation. The chambers, mounted on support walls, can also move with respect to the iron filters which are normally located close to the beampipe. Iron plugs minimize the free space between the beampipe and the iron filters to reduce small-angle background.

For M2–M5 two large support structures built from iron beams accomodate the suspensions for the four chamber support walls and have platforms for the electronics racks and gas systems. Cable chains are used to connect the cables, fibers, gas pipes and water cooling pipes with the outside. Station M1 has independent support structure and the related racks are located on the floor of the cavern. Cable chains are used in M1 to carry the 1200 cables to the racks.

The walls are designed to support the weight of the half-stations with minimal thickess and are built of aluminium sandwich plates. M1 wall is thinner to minimize material in front of the electromagnetic calorimeter. This is possible since the weight of M1 chambers is reduced thanks to the use of only two gaps and honeycomb panels. The material budget of the M1 station is 0.26 X_0 on average with the chambers and the FE electronics contributing 0.16 X_0 and the mechanics, cables and gas pipes contributing the rest.

Alignment

The position of the chambers must be adjusted in order to minimize chamber overlaps which would introduce ambiguities. Moreover, since the muon trigger relies on the projectivity of the stations, a precise relative space alignment has to be performed, in particular in the inner region where an accuracy of about 1 mm is required.

The chambers are mounted with screws on angle brackets fixed to the supporting walls. The walls were first precisely aligned by adjusting the overhead suspensions, then each chamber was

2008 JINST 3 S08005

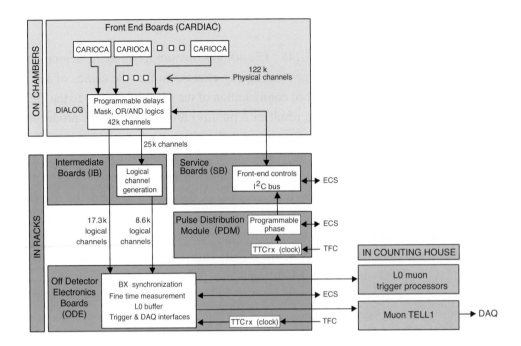

Figure 6.62: Simplified scheme of the Muon electronics architecture.

aligned relative to the wall. The position was adjusted vertically using spacers and horizontally via the slotted holes in the brackets. For horizontal and vertical alignment, the reference points were the support wall edge close to the beampipe and the top edge, respectively. Finally, the equipped walls were precisely aligned together using as reference each half-station, the centre of the beampipe. The reproducibility of the measurements is $\mathcal{O}(1)$ mm and the reproducibility of the position after moving the walls is of the same order.

6.3.5 Electronics

Figure 6.62 shows schematically the architecture of the Muon readout electronics. The task of the electronics is twofold: prepare the information needed by the Level-0 muon trigger and send the data to the DAQ system. The main steps are:

i. the front-end CARDIAC boards perform the amplification, shaping and discrimination of the ≈ 120 k chamber signals. The time alignment to within 1.6 ns of the different channels needed to correct for different cable lengths and different chamber behaviour is also done in this step. This is mandatory since the Muon Trigger is fully synchronous with is also done in this step, the LHC cycle.

ii. The ≈ 26k logical-channel signals are generated by suitable logical ORs of the physical channels. This step is performed on the FE boards and on special Intermediate Boards (IB), when the logical channel spans more than one FE board.

iii. The Off Detector Electronics (ODE) boards receive the signals from the logical channels. They are tagged with the number of the bunch crossing (BX identifier) and routed to the trigger processors via optical links without zero suppression.

2008 JINST 3 S08005

iv. The fine time information, measured by the TDC on the ODE boards, is added and the data are transmitted via optical links to the TELL1 board and from the TELL1 to the DAQ system.

As far as possible, step ii. is performed on the chambers front-end boards in order to minimize the number of LVDS links exiting the detector. The other steps are performed on dedicated electronics boards mounted on racks on the left and right sides of the muon stations M2–M5 which also accomodate the LV and HV power supplies. Since the racks are installed on the same structure which supports the stations, cable chains for the chambers could be avoided. For station M1 the electronics racks are placed under the RICH and, as mentioned above, are connected via cable chains to the chamber walls.

Radiation issues

The Muon electronics must operate reliably for more than 10 years in a hostile environment. The FE boards in the regions close to the beampipe are exposed to very high radiation doses: in M1 the maximum total ionising dose (TID) foreseen in 10 years is 5000 Gy. This decreases by only a factor 3 for M2. The maximum neutron and hadron fluences are in the range of $10^{13}/\mathrm{cm}^2$. Therefore, all the ASICs used in the FE Electronics were produced using radiation-hard technology.

The radiation dose is considerably less on the detector periphery where the electronics racks are located. TID values of up to 10 Gy in 10 years are expected in the electronics racks.[28] These doses nevertheless dictate the use of radiation tolerant components or a proper qualification of commercial components.

For complex logic design, two kinds of FPGA both from the ACTEL family are used. The A54SX family was chosen first for good radiation immunity and was used in the Intermediate Boards (IB). A more advanced type of FPGA from the flash-based ProASICPLUS APA family, was chosen in the design of ODE, PDM and SB boards. Based on ACTEL flash technology, ProASICPLUS devices offer reprogrammability and nonvolatility in a high density programmable logic product. The ProASICPLUS is also suitable in a high radiation environment thanks to the radiation hardness of its flash cells.

Commercial off-the-shelf electronics (COTS) was used for glue logic and signal conversion. All chip were validated with respect to the radiation environment.

Dedicated ASICs

The large number of channels in the muon system, the flexibility necessary to adapt the readout scheme to the different regions, the necessity to synchronize all the channels in a 20 ns window, the high radiation expected in M1 and in the inner regions led us to develop three dedicated rad-hard ASICs (CARIOCA, DIALOG and SYNC) using IBM 0.25 micron technology. All chips provide and accept logical LVDS data.

Front-end board

The chamber readout is performed via front-end boards (CARDIAC) [199] plugged directly onto the chambers. Each CARDIAC has 16 inputs and 8 outputs, and is equipped with two CARIOCA

---

[28]this value includes a safety factor of 2.

2008 JINST 3 S08005

Figure 6.63: Top and bottom views of the CARDIAC board, showing the two CARIOCA chips and the DIALOG chip.

chips and one DIALOG chip, as shown in figure 6.63. A special diode circuit protects the front-end amplifiers from sparks and is mounted on a separated board.

The CARIOCA [200–202] is a front-end amplifier-shaper-discriminator chip with eight channels whose input polarity is selectable. The front-end current preamplifier can handle well the large spread in detector capacitances encountered in the muon chambers (from 20 pF for the M1R1 to 220 pF for the M5R4 chambers). The peaking time is ~10 ns at the lowest detector capacitance. The input impedance is 50 Ohm which is important to reduce internal pad-pad cross-talk. The chip includes tail cancellation and baseline restoring. The dead time of a fired channel, almost independent of the pulse height, is in the range 50–60 ns.

The CARIOCA has separate thresholds for all the channels in order to overcome the problem of channel-to-channel uniformity in the internal discriminators. Equivalent noise is about 2000 electrons at 0 capacitance, and increases as (42–45) e/pF. Power consumption is about 45 mW/ch.

The DIALOG [203, 204] chip has 16 inputs to receive the outputs from two CARIOCA chips, and performs the logical OR of corresponding pads in the two layers of a chamber to form logical channels. The DIALOG is equipped with adjustable delays for every input allowing the various input signals to be aligned with a step of 1.6 ns. In addition, the DIALOG also allows setting the CARIOCA thresholds and can mask individual channels. It also contains features useful for system set-up, monitoring and debugging. Triple-voting and auto-corrected registers are used to increase single event upset immunity.

The CARDIAC boards are enclosed inside the chamber Faraday cage, together with radiation-tolerant voltage regulators (LH4913) which supply the necessary 2.5 V to the boards. The R4 chambers use only three CARDIAC boards and one regulator each, while the M1R2 chambers require 24 CARDIAC boards and six regulators each.

Given the large number of readout channels the muon system comprises nearly 8000 CARDIACs. All the boards were tested after assembly, and had to pass successfully a thermal cycle to be accepted. Once mounted on the chamber the characteristics of each board, in particular with respect to noise, were measured again.

A special version of the CARIOCA chip, with lower threshold and longer shaping time because of the lower gas gain, CARIOCAGEM [202], has been produced for use on the GEMs. The tail cancellation is suppressed considering the purely electron signal in the GEM case. A more compact CARDIAC card has also been designed, given the tight space available in the R1 region.

2008 JINST 3 S08005

SB and PDM boards

The front-end boards are managed by the Service Boards (SB) [205] that handle the setting of the thresholds in the CARIOCA chip, as well as the adjustable delays, the channel masking and the setting of the AND/OR logics in the DIALOG chip. Each SB houses four ELMB [206] modules based on an 8-bit microcontroller (Atmel ATMega128) whose firmware was customized to permit I^2C communication with the CARDIACs via twelve serial links. Each SB can control up to 192 CARDIAC boards. The full system comprises 156 SBs, managing the approximately 8000 CARDIAC boards of the muon system. Most of the calibration and test procedures of the front-end are implemented in the ELMB firmware and are performed directly by the SBs.

A Pulse Distribution Module (PDM) resides in each of the 10 crates containing the service boards. The PDM is based on an ELMB and houses one TTCrx chip which generates low-jitter pulses in a chosen phase relation with the LHC machine clock. The pulses are then distributed to the service boards by means of a custom back plane. This facility is crucial for the time alignment of the muon system.

IB board

Whenever the generation of the logical channels is not possible at the DIALOG level, an additional logical layer is needed. This happens in regions R2, R3 and R4 of stations M2 to M5. The needed layer, the Intermediate Board (IB), implements the necessary logic on three ACTEL A54SX16A anti-fuse FPGAs. Anti-fuse technology offers good tolerance against high radiation doses. The IB has been tested successfully with up to 68.5 Gy without failures. The system comprises 168 IB boards which are installed in the electronics racks.

ODE board

The ODE board [207] contains the Level-0 pipelines and DAQ interface. It synchronizes signals and dispatches them to the Level-0 trigger. Each ODE receives synchronous TFC signals by way of a TTCrx chip [113]. On-board clock de-jittering and distribution is managed by a QPLL chip [208]. A total of 152 ODE installed on the same racks as the IBs, are used.

Each board receives up to 192 logical channels and outputs data to the Level-0 muon trigger and to the DAQ system. The incoming signals are assigned the appropriate BX identifier and are sent to the Level-0 muon trigger directly via twelve 1.6 Gb/s optical links, each served by one GOL chip [209]. In parallel, the data are sent to the Level-0 pipelines, where they reside for $4\,\mu$s before receiving the *L0-accept* signal. Upon reception of a trigger, data are written into the L0 derandomizer, a FIFO programmable to a maximum depth of 16 data words. The derandomizer allows the data to be read out at a regular rate of 1.1 MHz with a safe margin with respect to the L0 average trigger rate of 1 MHz. Its programmable depth allows it to cope with instantaneous bursts of up to 16 consecutive triggers. Finally the data are formatted and sent to the TELL1 boards. The LVDS receivers, the Level-0 pipelines, the Level-0 derandomizer and the 4-bit TDC for fine time alignment are integrated into a single component, the SYNC chip [204]. The chip incorporates a number of error-detection features, allowing remote control and diagnosis of possible malfunctions on the boards. The other main board components (board controller, Level-0 buffer and DAQ interfaces)

2008 JINST 3 S08005

are based on one FPGA.[29] Each ODE board also contains a CAN node, based on one Embedded Local Monitor Board (ELMB) [206], for board control via the ECS.

Channel mapping to the Level-0 trigger is organized by grouping the logical channels in three different ways. This is accomplished placing the SYNC chips on daughter-boards of three different sizes, containing 2, 4 or 6 chips, while the ODE mother board is always the same. In the three cases 12, 8 or 6 links respectively are active on the daughter board. The design of the ODE board has been very challenging because it must cope with several, and sometime contradictory, requirements. Due to the limited space available, the board has a high channel density (192 differential inputs into a 6U card), and should provide a good level of flexibility and at the same time match the different trigger sector topologies. High signal integrity is also mandatory to guarantee high quality optical transmission. For radiation tolerance, a triple modular redundancy technique has been used whenever possible to increase single event upset immunity.

Muon TELL1 features

Upon reception of a trigger, the data from the detector logical channels are transmitted from the ODE to the TELL1 and from the TELL1 to the DAQ system. The description of the TELL1 board is given in section 8.2. The muon-specific TELL1 board, performs standard control of event synchronization, as well as zero suppression and is also programmed to reconstruct the logical pads as the intersection of two crossing logical channels of the stations M2 to M5. This information is added to the event data to speed up the muon identification algorithm used in the HLT trigger. The muon system requires 14 TELL1 boards (four in the M1 and M2 stations and 2 in the M3, M4, and M5 stations). These numbers are determined by data flow and connectivity requirements as well as the required ECS partitioning.

6.3.6 LV and HV systems

The Low Voltage and High Voltage systems are based on radiation-tolerant power supplies. They are installed in the pit on racks on both sides of the muon stations M2–M5 and in the radiation safe area under the RICH. Eight LV power supplies[30] are used for the CARDIAC boards and ten for the off-detector electronics boards.

The HV cabling for the wire chambers is designed to supply independently all the gaps, i.e. potentially about 5000 channels. Two distinct power supply systems are used. The first system, developed by PNPI and the University of Florida for CMS, is based on 36-channel modules and powers the R4 and R3 chambers in M2-M5. Some of the gaps of R4 chambers are connected in parallel in groups of four via patch panels. In this way the number of independent HV channels is reduced from 3840 to 1920. The gaps connected in parallel always belong to different chambers to minimize the loss of efficiency in case, e.g., one gap should become shorted. The second system is a commercial one based on 32-channel modules.[31] It powers the chambers more exposed to

---

[29] ACTEL flash ProASICPLUS FPGA (APA450PQG208).

[30] MARATON low voltage power supply system for hazardous hostile environment; W-IE-NE-R, Plein & Baus GmbH, Burscheid, Germany.

[31] CAEN Easy 3000 and A3535P.

radiation and drawing larger currents, and for this reason all the 1152 channels can be individually controlled and monitored.

Both HV systems have been tested for radiation resistance (hadrons, total dose and neutrons) and are apt to satisfy LHCb requirements for 10-year operation with a 10-fold safety factor.

The GEM detectors require several voltages to operate. To achieve maximum flexibility and safety a customized system [210] was designed, which allows independent settings for all of the GEM electrodes for a total of 168 channels. This system is entirely installed in the counting house.

6.3.7 Experiment control system

The control of the muon detectors is carried out with a distributed system where the processing capacity is shared among the system nodes. CANBus was chosen because of its features of multi-master protocol with real-time capability, error correction, long distance communication and low noise. CAN nodes based on ELMBs are present in the ODE, SB and PDM boards. The implementation of calibration and test procedures in the ELMB firmware, as is the case for the SBs, maximizes the parallelism of the system and minimizes the traffic on the CANBus which is only used to communicate the results of the procedures.

All the physical channels which cannot be accessed via DAQ can be monitored via ECS while running the experiment to measure noise level and detecting dead channels. More complex procedures such as noise measurements at several thresholds to detect faulty FE channels will be performed offline, The pulse system (PDM) will allow for checks of the time alignment of the full detector.

The ECS software (see section 8.4) was developed in PVSS following the general experiment guidelines and exploiting the tools provided by the LHCb PVSS framework. The muon ECS is partitioned in two independent left-right halves and is organized in hierarchycal topological structures. Each device of the muon system, like SBs, ODE Boards, HV and LV power supplies, is seen as a Finite State Machine with well defined states and interactions with other machines.

Ten PCs running PVSS programs are used to manage all the CARDIAC, ODE and SB boards. Six are used to control the HV and LV power supplies and one to monitor the environment pressure and temperature. The entire hierarchy is controlled by two PCs, one for the left and one for the right side of the muon system.

6.3.8 Gas system

The gas system has been designed in collaboration with the CERN Gas Group. Due to the rather large gas volume of the MWPCs (8.3 m^3), a recirculation system is used with a planned regeneration rate of about 90%. A pump in the return line allows the gas to be compressed before entering the gas building at the surface, where the mixing and purifying units are located. The purifier in the recirculation circuit contains two cleaning agents: a molecular sieve to keep the water contamination below the level of 100 ppm, and activated copper as a reducing agent for oxygen impurities, which should be kept below the 50 ppm level. A humidity and an oxygen meter allow for measurement of the impurity concentration before or after the purifier. Due to the small gas volume of only 10 litres, a vented system is used for the GEM chambers.

2008 JINST 3 S08005

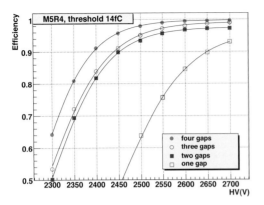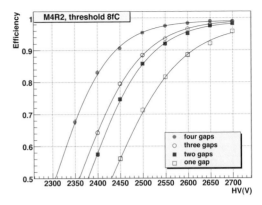

Figure 6.64: Plateau curves showing the efficiency in a 20 ns window for an anode-readout chamber (left) and a cathode-readout chamber (right). The four curves refer to different number of gaps being operated (see text). The threshold values in fC are also indicated, a lower value being used for cathode readout.

The flow rate varies across the detector surface from one volume exchange per hour, for the regions exposed to the largest irradiation (inner regions of station M1), to two volume exchanges per day for the outer regions of stations M4 and M5. Six distribution circuits are used: two for M1, two for M2–M3 and two for M4–M5. They are equipped with gas flow meters for the inputs and outputs of each supply line.

While the 12 GEM chambers have individual supply lines, only 180 supply lines are used for the 1368 MWPCs. To maintain still a parallel gas supply for each chamber, which is required to ensure an optimal performance of each individual chamber, several distributors serving 5–8 chambers have been installed on the support walls. In order to equalize the gas flow through the chambers connected to each distributor, capillaries with an impedance of about 1 mbar are introduced at the input of each chamber.

6.3.9 Performance

MWPC

Extensive tests were performed on prototypes and final MWPCs both in test beams and with cosmic rays at the production sites to measure the chamber performance. All measurements were conservatively done using a 20 ns time window.

Whereas MWPCs are expected to operate normally with four gaps in OR (two in case of M1 chambers), it is possible that a chamber will be operated with fewer gaps. Figure 6.64 shows the efficiency as a function of the applied voltage for the largest chamber with anode readout (M5R4) and for one chamber with cathode readout (M4R2). The curves are given for the standard four-gap OR configuration, but also for three-gap configuration (one double-gap fully working and the second with one gap shut off), for two gaps read by the same front-end and finally for the single-gap case. The curves show clearly the large improvement obtained by adding gaps, but also that,

2008 JINST 3 S08005

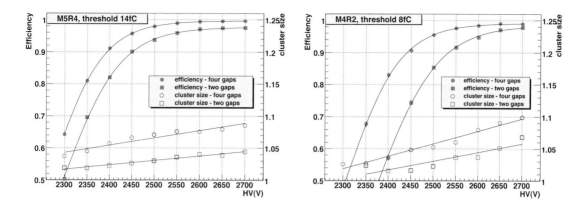

Figure 6.65: Efficiency and cluster size in a 20 ns window for the four-gap and double-gap configurations vs. HV. Anode readout-type chamber (left) and cathode readout-type chamber (right).

in case one gap should be shut off during the data taking, the redundancy built into the chambers will make the loss in performance negligible.

Another important parameter is the cluster size, i.e. the average number of pads fired by a crossing particle. The cluster size affects directly the space resolution and the p_T measurement in the Level-0 trigger since the yes-no readout does not allow an interpolation between adjacent pads. A non-negligible contribution to the cluster size comes simply from the geometry given the fact that inclined tracks can cross two adjacent pads belonging to different gaps. Another contribution comes from the chamber itself: inductive and capacitive cross-talk in the chamber and in the electronics. The design criteria requires that the intrinsic cluster size should be less than 1.2. This is well satisfied as can be seen in figure 6.65 which shows the cluster size distribution for the M5R4 and M2R4 chambers measured with perpendicular tracks [211]. Cosmic rays have also been used to check the gas gain uniformity on final chambers [212].

The rate capability of the MWPCs was studied at the CERN GIF [213] test beam. The detection efficiency of the chamber exposed to the intense gamma flux was measured with a 100 GeV muon beam. The chamber performance was studied for several detector gap configurations and different values of the background rate from the source.

No effect was detected at the maximum gamma rate allowed at the GIF where a current density of 28 nA/cm^2 was measured at a high voltage of 2.75 kV. This value is about the one expected in the chamber with the highest occupancy in the nominal conditions of running. This is in agreement with the results of the simulations [179] which show that space charge effects due to accumulation of ions are expected only at much higher currents.

GEM chambers

Triple-GEM detectors with the final FE electronics were tested both in a dedicated 40 MHz test beam and with cosmics in the lab.

Efficiency and cluster size in a 20 ns window, as a function of gain, are shown in figure 6.66 for a chamber composed of two triple-GEM detectors. Thanks to the longer shaping time of the CARIOCAGEM with respect to the standard CARIOCA chip the beginning of the efficiency plateau

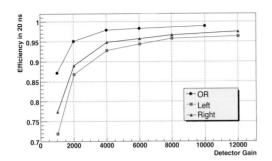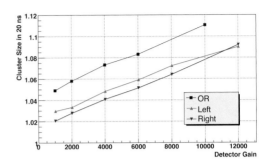

Figure 6.66: Efficiency and cluster size in a 20 ns window vs. gain for a chamber composed of two triple-GEM detectors. The curves show the data for the single detectors and for the OR of the two.

has moved from a detector gain of 6000 to 4000. This allows to operate the chambers with an integrated charge decreased by 30% and in safer conditions with respect to discharges.

2008 JINST 3 S08005

Chapter 7

Trigger

The LHCb experiment plans to operate at an average luminosity of 2×10^{32} cm^{-2} s^{-1}, much lower than the maximum design luminosity of the LHC, reducing the radiation damage to the detectors and electronics. Futhermore, the number of interactions per bunch crossing is dominated by single interactions, which facilitates the triggering and reconstruction by assuring low channel occupancy. Due to the LHC bunch structure and low luminosity, the crossing frequency with interactions visible[1] by the spectrometer is about 10 MHz, which has to be reduced by the trigger to about 2 kHz, at which rate the events are written to storage for further offline analysis. This reduction is achieved in two trigger levels [214] as shown in figure 7.1: Level-0 (L0) and the High Level Trigger (HLT). The L0 trigger is implemented using custom made electronics, operating synchronously with the 40 MHz bunch crossing frequency, while the HLT is executed asynchronously on a processor farm, using commercially available equipment. At a luminosity of 2×10^{32} cm^{-2} s^{-1} the bunch crossings with visible pp interactions are expected to contain a rate of about 100 kHz of b$\bar{\text{b}}$-pairs. However, only about 15% of these events will include at least one B meson with all its decay products contained in the spectrometer acceptance. Furthermore the branching ratios of interesting B meson decays used to study for instance CP violation are typically less than 10^{-3}. The offline analysis uses event selections based on the masses of the B mesons, their lifetimes and other stringent cuts to enhance the signal over background. For the best overall performance the trigger was therefore optimised to achieve the highest efficiency for the events selected in the offline analysis, while rejecting uninteresting background events as strongly as possible.

The purpose of the L0 trigger is to reduce the LHC beam crossing rate of 40 MHz to the rate of 1 MHz with which the entire detector can be read out. Due to their large mass, B mesons decays often produce particles with large transverse momentum (p_T) and energy (E_T) respectively. The Level-0 trigger attempts to reconstruct:

- the highest E_T hadron, electron and photon clusters in the calorimeters,

- the two highest p_T muons in the muon chambers.

In addition, a pile-up system in the VELO estimates the number of primary pp interactions in each bunch crossing. The calorimeters calculate the total observed energy and an estimate for the num-

---

[1] An interaction is defined to be visible if it produces at least two charged particles with sufficient hits in the VELO and T1–T3 to allow them to be reconstructible.

2008 JINST 3 S08005

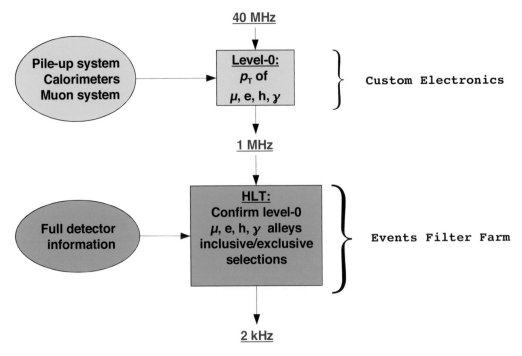

Figure 7.1: Scheme of the LHCb trigger.

ber of tracks, based on the number of hits in the SPD. With the help of these global quantities events may be rejected, which would otherwise be triggered due to large combinatorics, and would occupy a disproportionate fraction of the data-flow bandwidth or available processing power in the HLT.

A Level-0 Decision Unit (DU) collects all the information and derives the final Level-0 trigger decision for each bunch crossing. It allows for overlapping of several trigger conditions and for prescaling.

The L0 trigger system is fully synchronous with the 40 MHz bunch crossing signal of the LHC. The latencies are fixed and depend neither on the occupancy nor on the bunch crossing history. All Level-0 electronics is implemented in fully custom-designed boards which make use of parallelism and pipelining to do the necessary calculations with sufficient speed.

In order to be able to reduce the event rate from 1 MHz down to 2 kHz, the HLT makes use of the full event data. The generic HLT algorithms refine candidates found by the Level-0 trigger and divide them into independent *alleys* (see section 7.2). The alleys to be followed are selected from the Level-0 decision. The alley selections are based on the principle of confirming a previous trigger stage by requiring the candidate tracks to be reconstructed in the VELO and/or the T-stations. Requiring candidate tracks with a combination of high p_T and/or large impact parameter reduces the rate to about 30 kHz. At this rate interesting final states are selected using inclusive and exclusive criteria.

Generally speaking, selection cuts are relaxed compared to the offline analysis, in order to be able to study the sensitivity of the selections and to profit from refinements due to improved calibration constants. A large fraction of the output bandwidth is devoted to calibration and monitoring. In order to monitor trigger efficiencies and systematic uncertainties both trigger levels can be emulated fully on stored data.

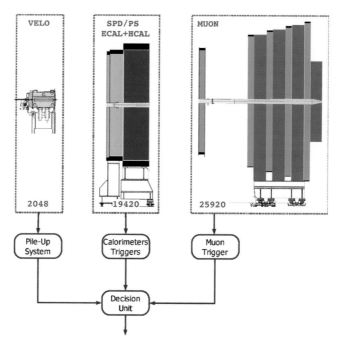

Figure 7.2: Overview of the Level-0 trigger. Every 25 ns the pile-up system receives 2048 channels from the pile-up detector, the Level-0 calorimeters 19420 channels from the scintillating pad detector, preshower, electromagnetic and hadronic calorimeters while the Level-0 muon handles 25920 logical channels from the muon detector.

7.1 Level 0 trigger

7.1.1 Overview

As shown in figure 7.2, the Level-0 trigger is subdivided into three components: the pile-up system, the Level-0 calorimeter trigger and the Level-0 muon trigger. Each component is connected to one detector and to the Level-0 DU which collects all information calculated by the trigger systems to evaluate the final decision.

The pile-up system aims at distinguishing between crossings with single and multiple visible interactions. It uses four silicon sensors of the same type as those used in the VELO to measure the radial position of tracks. The pile-up system provides the position of the primary vertices candidates along the beam-line and a measure of the total backward charged track multiplicity.

The Calorimeter Trigger system looks for high E_T particles: electrons, γ's, π^0's or hadrons. It forms clusters by adding the E_T of $2{\times}2$ cells and selecting the clusters with the largest E_T. Clusters are identified as electron, γ or hadron based on the information from the SPD, PS, ECAL and HCAL Calorimeter. The E_T of all HCAL cells is summed to reject crossings without visible interactions and to reject triggers on muon from the halo. The total number of SPD cells with a hit are counted to provide a measure of the charged track multiplicity in the crossing.

The muon chambers allow stand-alone muon reconstruction with a p_T resolution of $\sim 20\%$. Track finding is performed by processing elements which combine the strip and pad data from the five muon stations to form towers pointing towards the interaction region. The Level-0 muon trigger selects the two muons with the highest p_T for each quadrant of the muon detector.

2008 JINST 3 S08005

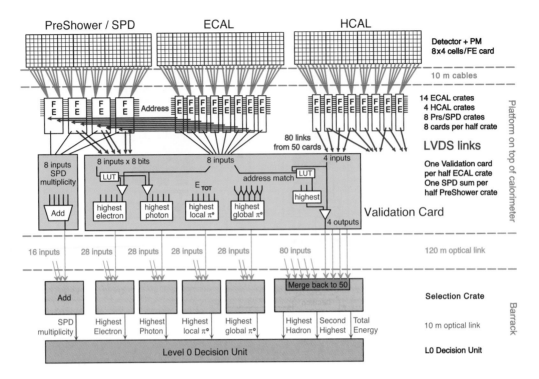

Figure 7.3: Overview of the Level-0 calorimeter trigger architecture.

The Level-0 DU collects all information from Level-0 components to form the Level-0 trigger. It is able to perform simple logic to combine all signatures into one decision per crossing. This decision is passed to the Readout Supervisor (see section 8.3) which transmits it to the front-end electronics.

The latency of Level-0, i.e. the time elapsed between a pp interaction and the arrival of the Level-0 trigger decision at the front-end electronics, is fixed to $4\,\mu$s. This time which includes the time-of-flight of the particles, cable delays and all delays in the front-end electronics, leaves $2\,\mu$s for the processing of the data in the Level-0 trigger to derive a decision.

7.1.2 Architecture

Calorimeter trigger

A zone of 2 by 2 cells is used, since it is large enough to contain most of the energy, and small enough to avoid overlap of various particles. Ultimately, only the particle with the highest E_T enters into the trigger decision. Therefore, to minimize the number of candidates to be processed, only the highest E_T candidate is kept at this stage.

These candidates are provided by a three step selection system as shown in figure 7.3:

- a first selection of high E_T deposits is performed on the Front-End card, which is the same for ECAL and HCAL. Each card handles 32 cells, and the highest E_T sum over the 32 sums of 2×2 cells is selected. To compute these 32 sums, access to cells in other cards is an important issue.

- the Validation Card merges the ECAL with the PS and SPD information prepared by the preshower front-end card. It identifies the type of electromagnetic candidate, electron, γ or π^0. Only the highest E_T candidate per type is selected and sent to the next stage. The same card also adds the energy deposited in ECAL to the corresponding hadron candidates. Similar cards in the PreShower crates compute the SPD multiplicity.

- the Selection Crate selects the candidate with the highest E_T for each type, and also produces a measure of the total E_T in HCAL and the total SPD multiplicity.

The first two steps are performed on the calorimeter platform, at a location where the radiation dose is expected to be below 50 Gy over the whole lifetime of the experiment, and where single event upsets are expected to occur. Each component has been tested for radiation tolerance and robustness against single event upsets. Anti-fuse FPGAs are used, as well as *triple-voting* techniques.

The trigger interface is housed in one anti-fuse FPGA from ACTEL for ECAL/HCAL front-end cards and in one flash EEPROM based FPGA for PS/SPD front-end boards. There is a large data flow between these components at a frequency of 40 MHZ, through a dedicated backplane, where interconnections are realized by point-to-point links running a multiplexed LVDS signals at 280 MHz. The same backplane is used for PreShower, ECAL and HCAL crates.

The validation card is a 9U board with 16 layers. Clusters, PS and SPD hit maps arrive through the backplane via 20 LVDS links running at 280 MHz. The cluster identification is performed by two ProAsic FPGAs from ACTEL. Electron, γ, hadron and π^0 candidates are transmitted to the selection crate via an 8-channel optical mezzanine which serializes data at 1.6 Gbps and drives a ribbon of 12 fibres. The control of the validation and calorimeter front-end cards are performed by a SPECS interface.

The selection crate is located in the counting house in a radiation free environment. It is a modular system containing eight 16-layer 9U VME selection boards. The design of the selection boards is unique and adapted to perform both the electromagnetic and the hadron clusters selection. The electromagnetic cluster selection is performed on one board for each cluster type (electron, γ, π^0) while the hadron selection requires three boards. The results of the two first boards are transmitted to the third one where the final selection is performed. Finally, one board is used to sum the SPD multiplicity. Inputs arrive via 28 optical links grouped into three ribbons of 12 fibres. High-speed serial signals are deserialized by 28 TLK2501 chips.[2] The selection of the highest E_T candidate of each type is performed by six FPGAs from the Xilink Virtex II family. The selected candidates are sent to the Level-0 DU via a mezzanine with 1-channel high speed optical link. Inputs and outputs of the Selection Boards are sent to the data acquisition system via two high speed optical links connected to the TELL1 board. The Selection Boards are controlled by a credit card PC.

The types and total numbers of boards for the Level-0 Calorimeters Trigger are summarized in table 7.1.

2008 JINST 3 S08005

Table 7.1: Boards of the Level-0 calorimeters trigger.

Boards	Number
ECAL/HCAL front-end	246
PS/SPD front-end	100
8-channels optical mezzanine	80
1-channels optical mezzanine	40
Validation card	28
SPD Control board	16
Selection Board	8

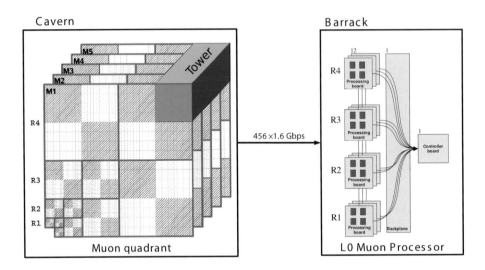

Figure 7.4: Overview of the Level-0 muon architecture.

Muon trigger

An overview of the Level-0 muon architecture is given in figure 7.4 and a detailed description in [215]. Each quadrant of the muon detector is connected to a Level-0 muon processor via 456 optical links grouped in 38 ribbons containing 12 optical fibres each. An optical fibre transmits serialized data at 1.6 Gbps over a distance of approximately 100 meters. The 4 Level-0 muon processors are located in the counting house, a place immune to radiation effects.

A L0 muon processor looks for the two muon tracks with the largest and second largest p_T. The track finding is performed on the logical pads. It searches for hits defining a straight line through the five muon stations and pointing towards the interaction point. The position of a track in the first two stations allows the determination of its p_T. The final algorithm is very close to the one reported in the Technical Proposal [1] and in the Muon Technical Design Report [164].

Seeds of the track finding algorithm are hits in M3. For each logical pad hit in M3, an extrapolated position is set in M2, M4 and M5 along a straight line passing through the hit and the interaction point. Hits are looked for in these stations in search windows termed Field Of Interest (FOI) which are approximately centred on the extrapolated positions. FOIs are opened along the x-

---

[2]from Texas Instrument, USA.

axis for all stations and along the *y*-axis only for stations M4 and M5. The size of the FOI depends on the station being considered, the level of background and the minimum-bias retention allowed. When at least one hit is found inside the FOI for each station M2, M4 and M5, a muon track is flagged and the pad hit in M2 closest to the extrapolation from M3 is selected for a subsequent use.

The track position in station M1 is determined by making a straight-line extrapolation from M3 and M2, and identifying, in the M1 FOI, the pad hit closest to the extrapolation point.

Since the logical layout is projective, there is a one-to-one mapping from pads in M3 to pads in M2, M4 and M5. There is also a one-to one mapping from pairs of pads in M2 and M3 to pads in M1. This allows the track finding algorithm to be implemented using only logical operations.

To simplify the processing and to hide the complex layout of the stations, the muon detector is subdivided into 192 towers (48 per quadrant) pointing towards the interaction point. All towers have the same layout with 288 logical pads[3] each. Therefore, the same algorithm can be executed in each tower. Each tower is connected to a processing element, the basic component of the Level-0 Muon processor.

To collect data coming from a tower spread over five stations and to send them to the processing element, a patch panel close to the muon processor is used.

Processing elements have to exchange a large number[4] of logical channels with each other to avoid inefficiencies on borders of towers. The topology of the data exchange depends strongly on the location of the tower.

A processing element runs 96 tracking algorithms in parallel, one per M3 seed, on logical channels from a tower. It is implemented in a FPGA named Processing Unit (PU). A processing board contains four PUs and an additional FPGA to select the two muons with the highest transverse momentum within the board. A Level-0 Muon processor consists of a crate housing 12 Processing Boards, a custom backplane and a controller board. The custom backplane is mandatory to exchange logical channels between PUs. The controller board collects candidates found by the 12 Processing Boards and selects the two with the highest p_T. It also distributes signals coming from the TTC.

The Level-0 Muon implementation relies on the massive use of multigigabit serial links deserialized inside FPGAs. Processors are interfaced to the outside world via optical links while processing elements are interconnected with high speed copper serial links.

The Processing Board contains five FPGAs from the Altera Stratix GX family and 92 high speed serial links with serialiazers and deserializers embedded in FPGAs. The board sends data to the data acquisition system via two high speed optical links. The processing board is remotely controlled via Ethernet by a credit card PC running Linux. The size of the printed circuit is 366.7×220 mm and is composed of 18 layers and a total of 1512 components. The power consumption is less than 60 W.

The Controller Board contains two FPGAs from the Stratix GX family. The board shares many common functionalities with the Processing Board: the same credit card PC, the same mechanism to send information to the data acquisition system. The printed circuit measues

---

[3] 48 pads from M1, 2×96 pads from M2 and M3, 2×24 pads from M4 and M5.

[4] A processing element handles 288 logical pads. It sends a maximum of 224 and receives a maximum of 214 logical channels from neighbouring elements.

2008 JINST 3 S08005

Table 7.2: Boards of the Level-0 muon trigger.

Boards	Number
Processing Board	48
Controller Board	4
Backplane	4

366.7×220 mm and is composed of 14 layers with 948 mounted components. The power consumption is less than 50 W.

The backplane contains 15 slots: 12 for the Processing Boards, one for the Controller Board and two for test. It distributes power supplies, signals coming from the TTC, and assures the connectivity between the processing elements via 288 single-ended links (40 MHz) and 110 differential high speed serial links (1.6 Gbps). The size of the 18-layer printed circuit board is $395,4 \times 426,72$ mm.

The types and total numbers of boards for the Level-0 Muon Trigger are summarized in table 7.2.

Pile-Up system

The pile-up system consists of two planes (*A* and *B*) perpendicular to the beam-line and located upstream of the VELO (see figure 5.1). Each $300\,\mu$m thick silicon plane consists of two overlapping VELO R-sensors which have strips at constant radii, and each strip covers $45°$. In both planes the radii of track hits, r_a and r_b, are measured. The hits belonging to tracks from the same origin have the simple relation $k = r_b/r_a$, giving:

$$z_v = \frac{kz_a - z_b}{k - 1} \tag{7.1}$$

where z_b, z_a are the detector positions and z_v is the position of the track origin on the beam axis, *i.e.* the vertex. The equation is exact for tracks originating from the beam-line. All hits in the same octant of both planes are combined according to equation 7.1 and the resulting values of z_v are entered into an appropriately binned histogram, in which a peak search is performed, as shown in figure 7.5. The resolution of z_v is limited to around 3 mm by multiple scattering and the hit resolution of the radial measurements. All hits contributing to the highest peak in this histogram are masked, after which a second peak is searched for. The height of this second peak is a measure of the number of tracks coming from a second vertex. A cut is applied on this number to detect multiple interactions. If multiple interactions are found, the crossing is vetoed.

The architecture of the pile-up system is shown in figure 7.6. It uses the signals of the integrated comparators of the Beetle chips located on the four hybrids. The outputs of neighbouring comparators are OR-ed in groups of four, resulting in 256 LVDS links running at 80 Mbit/s per hybrid, which send the Level-0 signals to eight Optical Transmission Boards. Two Optical Transmission Boards cover one quadrant. They time align and multiplex input hit maps to four Vertex Processing Boards. Hit maps of one bunch crossing are sent to one of the four Vertex Processing Board (VEPROB) in four consecutive clock cycles, while hit maps of the following bunch crossing

2008 JINST 3 S08005

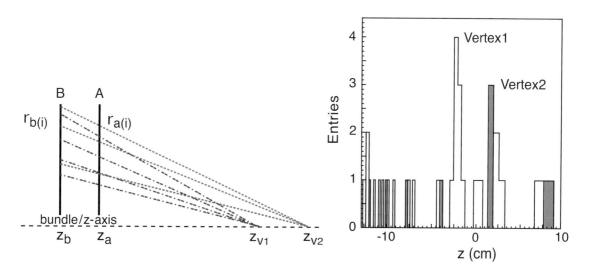

Figure 7.5: The basic principle of detecting vertices in an event. The hits of plane A and B are combined in a coincidence matrix. All combinations are projected onto a z_v-histogram. The peaks indicated correspond to the two interaction vertices in this particular MonteCarlo event. After the first vertex finding iteration, the hits corresponding to the two highest bins are masked, resulting in the hatched histogram.

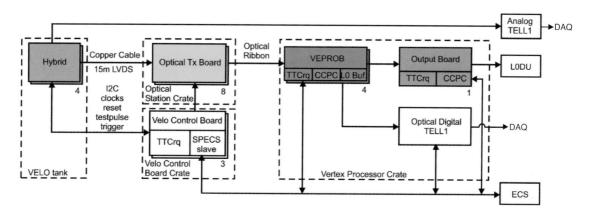

Figure 7.6: Overview of the Level-0 pile-up Architecture.

are sent to the second VEPROB in four consecutive clock cycles. Bunch-crossings are distributed over the four Vertex Processing Boards in a round-robin fashion. The Optical transmision board is a 9U board controlled by a SPEC interface via the VELO control board.

Vertex Processing boards are 9U boards located in the radiation-free electronics barracks. They are connected to the Optical Transmission boards via 24 high speed optical links. The vertex processing board is the key component of the pile-up system. It houses a large FPGA from Xilinx Virtex II family which runs the pile-up algorithm. A board handles one of four events and sends its trigger decision to the output board via a high speed copper link (1.6 Gbps). The VEPROB is controlled by a credit card PC and sends the inputs and outputs of the vertex finding algorithm to the DAQ system via two high speed optical links.

The output board is a simple 9U board multiplexing the inputs from the vertex processing

2008 JINST 3 S08005

Table 7.3: Boards of the pile-up system.

Boards	Number
Hybrids	4
Optical Transmition Board	8
Vertex Processing Board	4
Output Board	1

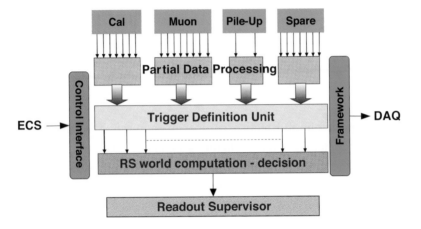

Figure 7.7: Level-0 DU architecture.

board and sends the number of primary pp interactions for each bunch crossing to the Level-0 DU. In addition, the output boards make histograms of trigger decisions made by the pile-up system. These histograms are accessible via the ECS interface.

The types total numbers of boards for the pile-up system are summarized in table 7.3.

Decision Unit

The Level-0 DU receives information from the calorimeter, muon and pile-up sub-triggers at 40 MHz, which arrive at different fixed times. The computation of the decision can start with a sub-set of information coming from a Level-0 sub-trigger, after which the sub-trigger information is time aligned. An algorithm is executed to determine the trigger decision. The decision is sent to the Readout Supervisor, which makes the ultimate decision about whether to accept an event or not. The Readout Supervisor is able to generate and time-in all types of self-triggers (random triggers, calibration, etc.) and to control the trigger rate by taking into account the status of the different components in order to prevent buffer overflows and to enable/disable the triggers at appropriate times during resets.

The architecture of the Level-0 DU is shown in figure 7.7. For each data source, a Partial Data Processing system performs a specific part of the algorithm and the synchronisation between the various data sources. Then a trigger definition unit combines the information from the above systems to form a set of trigger conditions based on multi-source information.

The trigger conditions are logically OR-ed to obtain the Level-0 decision after they have been individually downscaled if necessary.

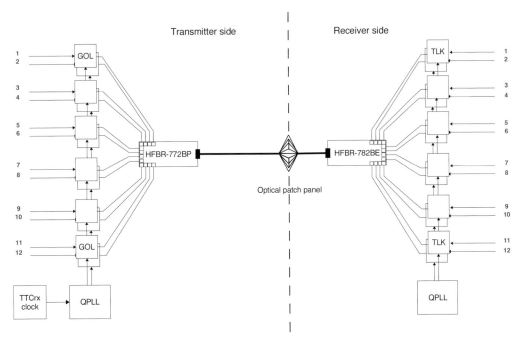

Figure 7.8: Overview of ribbon optical link.

The Level-0 DU is based on the TELL1 board with optical cards replaced by a single mezzanine in which Level-0 DU hardware is implemented. Inputs are received on two ribbons of 12 high speed optical links. Serial signals are deserialized by a 24 TLK2501 chip.[5] and sent to two large FPGAs from the Stratix Family. Electron, γ, π^0, hadron and muon candidates as well as intermediate and final decisions are sent to the DAQ via the TELL1 mother boards. This information can be used later on by the HLT to confirm the Level-0 candidates using more refined algorithms.

7.1.3 Technology

The implementation of the Level-0 trigger relies on the massive use of large FPGAs, high speed serial links and common techniques which simplify debugging and commissioning.

High speed links

The transport of information from the front-end electronics to Level-0 trigger boards located in the barrack is based on three concepts:

- serialization of the detector data;

- use of optical links as transport media;

- use of high density devices.

High speed serial transmission reduces the number of signal lines required to transmit data from one point to another. It also offers a high level of integration with many advantages: high reliability

---

[5]from Texas Instrument, USA.

for data transfer over 100 meters; complete electrical isolation avoids ground loops and common mode problems. In addition, the integration of several high speed optical links in a single device increases data rate while keeping a manageable component count and a reasonable cost.

Ribbon optical links integrate twelve optical transmitters (fibres, receivers) in one module. The important benefit of ribbon optical links is based on low-cost array integration of electronic and opto-electronic components. It also results a low power consumption and a high level of integration.

An overview of the ribbon optical link developed for the Level-0 trigger is shown in figure 7.8. The emitter stage relies on twelve serializer chips connected to one optical transmitter. The serializer is the GOL, a radiation hard chip designed by the CERN microelectronic group, which every 25 ns, transforms a 32-bit word into a serial signal with a frequency of 1.6 GHz using a 8B/10B encoding. High frequency signals are converted into optical signals by the 12-channel optical transmitter from Agilent HFBR-772BE. The module is designed to operate multimode fibres at a nominal wavelength of 850 nm.

Initially the LHC clock distribution was not intended to be used for optical data transmission and hence, does not fulfill the severe jitter constraints required by high speed serializers. The GOL requires a maximum jitter of 100 ps peak to peak to operate correctly whereas the LHC clock jitter is as large as 400 or 500 ps. To reduce the jitter, a radiation hard chip, the QPLL, designed by the CERN microelectronics group is used. It filters out the jitter up to an acceptable value with the help of a reference quartz crystal associated to a phase locked loop.

The emitter side is close to the detector in a place where the radiation dose is below 50 Gy over 10 years where single event upsets (SEU) are expected to occur. The GOL and QPLL chips are radiation hard chips immune to SEU. However, the optical transceiver is a commercial component designed to work in an environment free of radiation. An irradiation campaign took place at the Paul Scherrer Institute in December 2003. The component was found to work within its specifications up to a total dose of 150 Gy. The cross-section for single event upsets is equal to $(4.1 \pm 0.1) \times 10^{-10}$ cm^2 per single optical link. The expected SEU rate is 1 every 220 minutes for the Level-0 muon trigger. When this happens, a single optical link emitter is not synchronized with its receiver anymore. All emitter/receiver pairs are resynchronized automatically at the end of each LHC cycle. Therefore, the link will not transmit data during a maximum of one LHC cycle or 89 μs. The corresponding inefficiency is negligible.

The physical media between the front-end electronic boards and the Level-0 trigger board consist of ribbons of twelve fibres with MPO connectors on both sides ($\sim$ 10 m.), MPO-MPO patch panels, long cables containing eight ribbons with MPO connectors ($\sim$ 80 m.), fanout panels (MPO-MPO or MPO-SC), short ribbons of twelve fibres ($\sim$ 3 m) with MPO connector on one side and a MPO or 12 SC connectors on the other side.

The receiving side is the mirror of the emitting side. Optical signals are converted into 1.6 Gbps serial electrical signals by the 12-channel optical receiver HFBR-782BE. The twelve high-frequency signals are deserialized into 16-bit words at 80 MHz by twelve TLK2501 chips. The receiving side is located in the counting room. Therefore standard components can be used. In the muon processing board, where the density of input signal is high, TLK2501 chips are replaced by serializers and deserializers embedded in the Stratix GX FPGA.

2008 JINST 3 S08005

The routing of the differential high speed traces between serializer/deserializer and the optical transceiver requires considerable care since the geometry of the tracks must be totally controlled to guarantee good impedance matching and to minimize electromagnetic emissions to the environment as well as sensitivity to electromagnetic perturbations from the environment.

The performance of the optical link has been measured with several setups in different ways. The bit error ratio measured with Lecroy SDA11000 Serial Data Analyser is below 10^{-16} for a single fibre of 100 m long.

Field Programmable Gate Arrays

Three FPGA technologies are used in the Level-0 trigger. They are characterized by the way they are configured:

- Anti-fuse based FPGAs (ACTEL AX family), that can be programmed only once;

- Flash-EEPROM based FPGAs (ACTEL pro-ASIC family), that can be erased and reprogrammed;

- RAM based FPGAs (Altera Acex, Flex, Stratix and Stratix GX families or Xilinx Virtex family) that can be reprogrammed an unlimited number of times.

Anti-fuse and flash FPGAs are used in the front-end boards close to the detector and are therefore exposed to significant radiation doses. These components have been tested in heavy ion beams and have shown very low sensitivity to single event upsets and single event latch-up. Special mechanisms such as triple-voting or horizontal and vertical parity are implemented to increase the protection of registers containing critical data. Dose effects begin to appear in Flash based FPGAs for doses an order of magnitude above the total dose received during 10 years by the trigger front-end electronics.

RAM-based FPGAs are known to be very sensitive to single event upsets. For this reason their use is restricted to boards located in the barracks which is a radiation free area.

All the FPGAs used in the trigger provide for good visibility of internal node behavior during the debug phase by providing embedded logic analyzer features (Silicon Explorer for ACTEL, SignalTap for the largest components of the Altera family and Chipscope for the Xilinx family).

Debugging and monitoring tools

Each Level-0 trigger board includes either a credit card PC or a SPECS component interfaced to the embedded FPGAs by a custom 16-bit bus. By this means the operation of any of the FPGAs is controlled and error detection mechanisms, such as error counters, spy and snooping mechanisms are implemented.

To test a complete sub-trigger in stand-alone mode, a data injection buffer to substitute input data is implemented. Results of the processing can be read back via the credit card PC at the output of dedicated SPY memories

The level-0 trigger is a very complex system. Any malfunctions can therefore be difficult to understand and interpret. At each stage the input and results of the processing are logged. In

2008 JINST 3 S08005

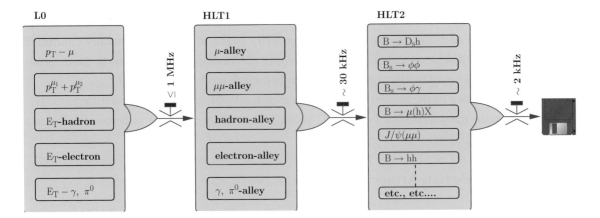

Figure 7.9: Flow-diagram of the different trigger sequences.

addition, a software emulator was developped which reproduces the behaviour of the hardware at the bit level. By comparing results computed by the hardware with those of the emulator run on the same input data, any faulty components can quickly be located.

7.2 High Level Trigger

The High Level Trigger (HLT) consists of a C++ application which runs on every CPU of the Event Filter Farm (EFF). The EFF contains up to 2000 computing nodes and is described in section 8. Each HLT application has access to all data in one event, and thus, in principle, could execute the off-line selection algorithms. However, given the 1 MHz output rate of the Level-0 trigger and CPU power limitations, the HLT aims to reject the bulk of the uninteresting events by using only part of the full event data. In this section, the algorithm flow is described which, according to MonteCarlo simulation studies, is thought to give the optimal performance within the allowed time budget. However, it should be kept in mind that since the HLT is fully implemented in software, it is very flexible and will evolve with the knowledge of the first real data and the physics priorities of the experiment. In addition the HLT is subject to developments and adjustments following the evolution of the event reconstruction and selection software.

A schematic of the overall trigger flow is shown in figure 7.9. Level-0 triggers on having at least one cluster in the HCAL with $E_T^{\text{hadron}} > 3.5\,\text{GeV}$, or the ECAL with $E_T^{e,\ \gamma,\ \pi^0} > 2.5\,\text{GeV}$, or a muon candidate in the muon chambers with $p_T^{\mu} > 1.2\,\text{GeV}$, or $p_T^{\mu_1} + p_T^{\mu_2} > 1.\,\text{GeV}$, where μ_1 and μ_2 are the two muons with the largest p_T. The above thresholds are typical for running at a luminosity of $2 \times 10^{32}\ \text{cm}^{-2}\text{s}^{-1}$, but depend on luminosity and the relative bandwidth division between the different Level-0 triggers. All Level-0 calorimeter clusters and muon tracks above threshold are passed to the HLT as part of the Level-0 trigger information as described in section 7.1.2, and will be referred to as Level-0 objects henceforward.

The HLT is subdivided in two stages, HLT1 and HLT2. The purpose of HLT1 is to reconstruct particles in the VELO and T-stations corresponding to the Level-0 objects, or in the case of Level-0 γ and π^0 candidates to confirm the absence of a charged particle which could be associated to these objects. This is called Level-0 confirmation, and the details of how this is achieved within the

2008 JINST 3 S08005

CPU time budget is explained below. HLT1 should reduce the rate to a sufficiently low level to allow for full pattern recognition on the remaining events, which corresponds to a rate of about 30 kHz. At this rate HLT2 performs a combination of inclusive trigger algorithms where the B decay is reconstructed only partially, and exclusive trigger algorithms which aim to fully reconstruct B-hadron final states.

7.3   HLT1

HLT1 starts with so-called *alleys*, where each alley addresses one of the trigger types of the Level-0 trigger. About $\sim 15\%$ of the Level-0 events are selected by multiple triggers, and will consequently pass by more than one alley. To confirm the Level-0 objects each alley makes use of the following algorithms:

L0→T: The Level-0 objects are assumed to originate from the interaction region, which defines the whole trajectory of the candidate in the spectrometer. So-called T-seeds are reconstructed in the T-stations, decoding only the hits in a window around the trajectory, or in case of the calorimeter clusters the two trajectories corresponding to the two charge hypothesis. The seeds are required to match the Level-0 object in both space and momentum.

L0→VELO: VELO-seeds are reconstructed in two stages. First the information from the R-sensors are used to reconstruct 2D-tracks. The χ^2 is calculated for the matching of a 2D track with the Level-0 object, and only candidates with a sufficiently low χ^2 are used to reconstruct a VELO-seed using the ϕ-sensor information. These VELO-seeds in turn are required to match the Level-0 object with a sufficiently small χ^2. In addition the 2D-tracks are used to reconstruct the primary vertexes in the event [216].

VELO→T: The VELO-seeds above define a trajectory in the T-stations, around which a T-seed is reconstructed completely analogue to the L0→T algorithm described above.

T→VELO: this algorithm finds the VELO-seeds which match a T-seed, using an algorithm analogue to the L0→VELO algorithm, but now starting from a T-seed, rather than a Level-0 object.

Each HLT1 alley uses a sequence of the above algorithms to reduce the rate. An algorithm common to all alleys is used for computing the primary vertex with the 2D tracks reconstructed in the VELO. While the alleys are operating independently, care has been taken to avoid having to reconstruct the same track or primary vertex twice to avoid wasting precious CPU power.

While the bandwidth division between the alleys has not been defined, the performance of the alleys will be illustrated with two typical alleys, the muon and hadron alleys running at a luminosity of 2×10^{32} cm^{-2}s^{-1}.

The HLT1 μ-alley input rate will be $\sim$230 kHz, and contain 1.2 L0$^{\mu}$ objects per event. L0$^{\mu}$ →T reduces the rate to 120 kHz, while the number of candidates increases to 1.8 T-seeds per event. T→VELO reduces the rate to 80 kHz. Requiring the remaining candidates to have an impact parameter to any primary vertex larger than 0.1 mm reduces the rate to 10 kHz. The HLT1 hadron-alley input rate will be $\sim$600 kHz, and contain 1.3 L0^{hadron} objects per event. L0^{hadron} →VELO, requiring a 0.1 mm impact parameter of the VELO-seeds to any primary vertex reduces the rate to 300 kHz which contain 2.2 VELO-seeds per event. VELO→T reduces this rate to 30 kHz with 1.2 candidates per event. Since this rate is still too large for the HLT2 stage, a further reduction is obtained by requiring a VELO-track with a distance of closest approach to the confirmed Level-0

2008 JINST 3 S08005

track of less than 0.2 mm, and a p_T of at least 1 GeV. This reduces the rate to 11 kHz with 3.2 candidate secondary vertices per event. The other HLT1 alleys employ similar strategies.

7.4 HLT2

The combined output rate of events accepted by the HLT1 alleys is sufficiently low to allow an off-line track reconstruction as described in section 10.1. The HLT-tracks differ from the off-line in not having been fitted with a Kalman filter to obtain a full covariance matrix since this is too CPU intensive. Prior to the final selection, a set of tracks is selected with very loose cuts on their momentum and impact parameter. These tracks are used to form composite particles, such as $K^* \rightarrow K^+ \pi^-$, $\phi \rightarrow K^+ K^-$, $D^0 \rightarrow hh$, $D_s \rightarrow K^+ K^- \pi^-$ and $J/\psi \rightarrow \mu^+ \mu^-$, which are subsequently used for all selections to avoid duplication in the creation of final states.

The HLT2 stage uses therefore cuts either on invariant mass, or on pointing of the B momentum towards the primary vertex. The resulting inclusive and exclusive selections aim to reduce the rate to about 2 kHz, the rate at which the data is written to storage for further analysis. The exclusive triggers are sensitive to tracking performance, while the inclusive triggers select partial B decays to ϕX, $J/\psi X$, $D^* X$, $\mu^{\pm} X$, $\mu^{\pm} hX$ and $\mu^+ \mu^- X$ and therefore are less dependent on the on-line reconstruction. However, the exclusive selection of these channels produces a smaller rate, thus allowing for a more relaxed set of cuts. The final trigger is the logical OR of the inclusive and exclusive selections.

7.5 HLT monitoring

Each HLT1 alley and HLT2 selection produces summary information which is written to storage for the accepted events. This summary contains the information of all tracks and vertexes which triggered the event. It is foreseen to reserve a significant fraction of the output bandwidth for triggers on semi-leptonic B-decays, hence a sample in which the trigger did not bias the decay of the accompanying B-hadron. The summary information is used to check if an event would have triggered, even if the B decay of interest would not have participated in the trigger. It therefore allows to study the trigger performance. The summary information also guarantees that during the analysis the trigger source of an individual event is known.

To assure that during off-line analysis the trigger conditions are known, the combination of trigger algorithms with their selection parameters will be assigned a unique key, the Trigger Configuration Key (TCK). All trigger configurations with their associated TCK are pre-loaded in the EFF before a fill. To change from one trigger configuration to another one, for example to follow the decaying luminosity in a fill, a new TCK must be selected. This TCK is attached by the Time and Fast Control system (TFC, see section 8.3) to each event, and it steers the configuration of the algorithms on the EFF and allows full traceability of the used configuration.

2008 JINST 3 S08005

Chapter 8

Online System

The task of the Online system is to ensure the transfer of data from the front-end electronics to permanent storage under known and controlled conditions. This includes not only the movement of the data themselves, but also the configuration of all operational parameters and the monitoring of these, as well as environmental parameters, such as temperatures or pressures. The online system also must ensure that all detector channels are properly synchronized with the LHC clock. The LHCb Online system is described in detail in [214, 217, 218]

8.1 System decomposition and architecture

The LHCb Online system consists of three components:

- the Data Acquisition (DAQ) system,

- the Timing and Fast Control (TFC) system,

- the Experiment Control System (ECS).

The general architecture of the LHCb online system is shown in figure 8.1.

8.2 Data Acquisition System

The purpose of the Data Acquisition (DAQ) system is the transport of the data belonging to a given bunch crossing,and identified by the trigger, from the detector front-end electronics to permanent storage. The design principles for the DAQ architecture (figure 8.1) are:

- Simplicity: simple protocols and a small number of components with simple functionalities

- Scalability: ability to react to changing system parameters, such as event sizes, trigger rates or the CPU needs of trigger algorithms.

- Only point-to-point links: components are connected through point-to-point links only. No buses are used (outside monolithical boards). This leads to a more robust system.

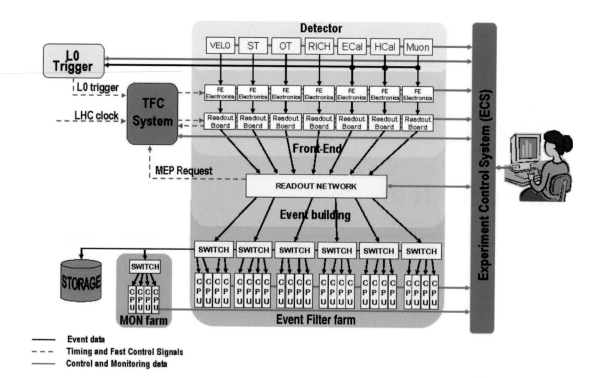

Figure 8.1: General architecture of the LHCb Online system with its three major components: Timing and Fast Controls, Data Acquisition and Experiment Control System. A blow-up of the the TFC box is shown in figure 8.3.

- Use of Commercial off-the-shelf (COTS) products and, wherever possible, commodity components and protocols.

These principles allowed to construct a reliable and robust system with enough flexibility to cope with possible new requirements, motivated by experience with real data.

Data from the on/near-detector electronics (front-end electronics) are collected in LHCb-wide standardized readout boards (TELL1).[1] Figure 8.2 shows a simplified block diagram of the TELL1 board. A detailed description can be found in [10].

Data are received from the detector electronics either by optical or analogue receiver cards and processed in four pre-processing FPGAs,[2] where common-mode processing, zero-suppression or data compression is performed depending on the needs of individual detectors. The resulting data fragments are collected by a fifth FPGA (SyncLink) and formatted into a raw IP-packet that is subsequently sent to the DAQ system via the 4-channel GbEthernet mezzanine card. The board interfaces to the Experiment Control System (ECS) by means of a credit-card sized PC mounted on the board. Clock and synchronization signals (e.g. triggers) are transmitted through the on-board Trigger, Timing and Control (TTC) interface [219]. Flow control to the TFC system is performed through the throttle signal driven by the SyncLink FPGA.

---

[1]The RICH detectors use a specific board (c.f. 6.1) which is, from the data readout point of view, functionally identical to the TELL1.

[2]Altera Stratix 1S25.

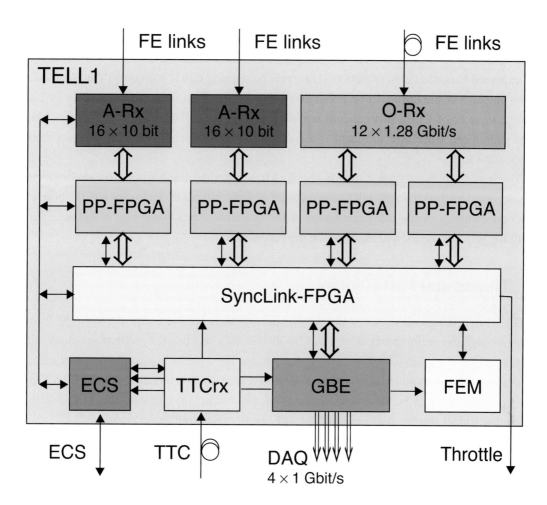

Figure 8.2: Simplified block diagram of the common readout board TELL1. The FEM (Front-End Multiplexer) allows to merge event fragments from several input links to form one output fragment.

In the CPU farm, the HLT algorithm selects interesting interactions; upon a positive decision, the data are subsequently sent to permanent storage. The HLT (see 7.2) is expected to reduce the overall rate from the original trigger rate of 1 MHz to ~2 kHz, hence by a factor of 500. The storage system is expected to have a capacity of ~40 TB, which should offer sufficient buffer space to cope with possible interruptions of the transfer to permanent storage at CERN. Gigabit-Ethernet was chosen as link technology, mainly because of its wide, almost monopoly-like, acceptance in the LAN market and its low price. The very wide range of speed from 10 Mb/s to 10 Gb/s, and the availability of very big switches (>1200 ports per chassis) are also important assets.

The TELL1 board offers 4 Gb Ethernet ports as output stages. Some of these are fed into a large switching network providing the connectivity between the TELL1 boards and the individual Farm nodes. To overcome the significant overhead per frame of Ethernet, the concept of Multi-Event Packets has been devised, in which the data of several triggers (~10) are collected in one IP packet and transferred subsequently through the network. The size of the CPU farm running the HLT trigger algorithms is determined by the average execution time of the HLT algorithm per event but also possibly by the maximum bandwidth into an individual processing node: if the execution time were to be very low, the input bandwidth might constitute the limiting factor and the number of *boxes* would have to be increased. The HLT algorithms are executed on a sizeable farm of CPUs. It's is expected to consist of 1000–2000 1U servers containing CPUs with multi-core technologies. The starting size of the farm will be about 200 servers. The maximum available space is 2200 U. The large number of CPUs is organized into 50 sub-farms of 20–40 CPUs each. The scalability is then guaranteed since one sub-farm is a functional unit and there is no cross-communication between sub-farms.

The quality of the acquired data is checked in a separate monitoring farm that will receive events accepted by the HLT and will house user-defined algorithms to determine e.g. the efficiencies of detector channels or the mass resolution of the detector. Also, some rate of L0 accepted and random triggers will be used to monitor the trigger itself.

8.3   Timing and Fast Control

The TFC system drives all stages of the data readout of the LHCb detector between the front-end electronics and the online processing farm by distributing the beam-synchronous clock, the L0 trigger, synchronous resets and fast control commands. The system is a combination of electronic components common to all LHC experiments and LHCb custom electronics. The TFC architecture shown in figure 8.3 can be described in terms of three main ingredients, the TFC distribution network, the trigger throttle network, and the TFC master (Readout Supervisor).

The TFC optical distribution network with transmitters and receivers is based on the LHC-wide TTC system developed at CERN [219]. In addition to transmitting the beam synchronous clock, the protocol features a low-latency trigger channel and a second channel with framed user data used to encode the control commands. A switch has been developed and introduced into the distribution network to allow a dynamic partitioning of the LHCb detector to support independent and concurrent sub-detector activities such as commissioning, calibration and testing.

The optical throttle network is used to transmit back-pressure, that is a trigger inhibit, from the asynchronous parts of the readout system to the Readout Supervisor in case of congestion of the data path. The network incorporates a Throttle Switch to support the requirement that the readout system is partitionable, and to allow modules to perform an *OR* of the throttle signals of each sub-system locally.

The heart of the system, the Readout Supervisor, implements the interface between the LHCb trigger system and the readout chain. The Readout Supervisor synchronizes trigger decisions and beam-synchronous commands to the LHC clock and orbit signal provided by the LHC. It is also capable of producing a variety of auto-triggers for sub-detector calibration and tests, and performs the trigger control as a function of the load on the readout system. In order to perform dynamic load balancing among the nodes in the online processing farm, the Readout Supervisor also selects and broadcasts the destination for the next set of events to the Readout Boards based on a credit scheme in which the farm nodes send data requests directly to the Readout Supervisor.

For each trigger the Readout Supervisor transmits a data bank over the readout network which is appended to the event data and which contains the identifier of the event, the time and the source of the trigger.

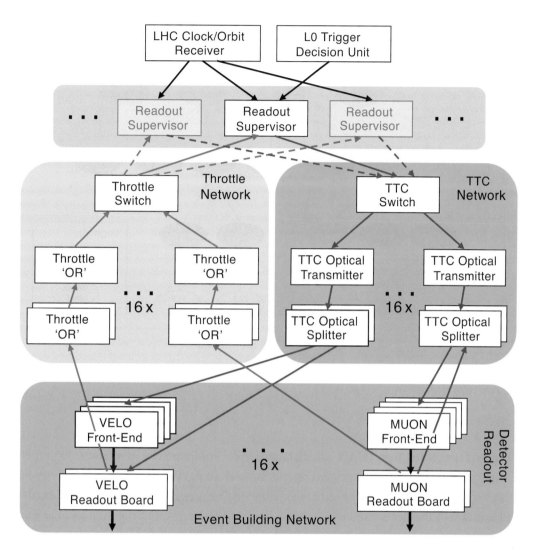

Figure 8.3: Schematic diagram of the TFC architecture. For a given partition there is only one RS, but several partitions can operate at the same time.

8.4 Experiment Control System

The Experiment Control System (ECS) ensures the control and monitoring of the operational state of the entire LHCb detector. This encompasses not only the traditional detector control domains, such as high and low voltages, temperatures, gas flows, or pressures, but also the control and monitoring of the Trigger, TFC, and DAQ systems. The hardware components of the ECS are somewhat diverse, mainly as a consequence of the variety of the equipment to be controlled, ranging from standard crates and power supplies to individual electronics boards. In LHCb, a large effort was made to minimize the number of different types of interfaces and connecting busses. The field busses have been restricted to:

- SPECS, Serial Protocol for ECS, a serial bus providing high-speed, 10Mb/s, control access to front-end electronics [41],

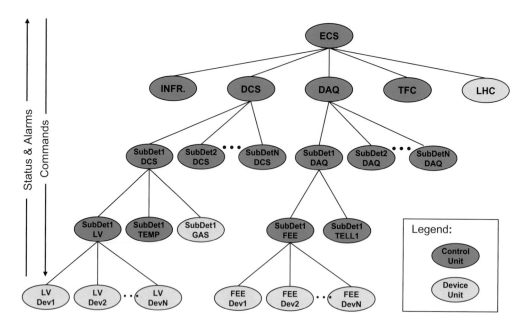

Figure 8.4: ECS architecture.

- CAN (Controller Area Network[3]),

- (fast)Ethernet.

The first two, SPECS and CAN, are mainly used for equipment residing in the high radiation area close to the detector. The associated interfaces tolerate modest levels of radioactivity but are not radiation hard. Ethernet is only used in the radiation free areas, such as the electronics barracks or on the surface. Ethernet is used to control individual PCs, as well as the individual electronics boards usedfor the readout through Credit-Card sized PCs mounted directly on each board. This choice allows the use of normal PCs over their standard Ethernet interfaces for controlling the readout electronics.

The ECS software is based on PVSS II, a commercial SCADA (Supervisory Control And Data Acquisition) system. This toolkit provides the infrastructure needed for building the ECS system, such as a configuration database and communication between distributed components, graphical libraries to build operations panels, and an alarm system as well as components, such as OPC clients. Based on PVSS, a hierarchical and distributed system was designed as depicted in figure 8.4.

Device Units, in figure 8.4, denote low-level access components which model the physical device and typically communicate directly with the hardware. In general they only implement a very simple state machine which is exclusively driven by the controlling Control Unit. Examples of Device Units are power supplies, and software processes, such as the HLT processes.

Control Units implement high-level states and transitions and also local logic to support recovery from errors of subordinate Device Units. Typical examples of Control Units are a HV subsystem, or the component that controls the ensemble of crates of a sub-detector or an entire

---

[3]*ISO Standard 11898*, see e.g. www.iso.org.

2008 JINST 3 S08005

sub-farm of the Event Filter Farm. Control Units can be controlled by other Control Units, to allow the building of a hierarchy of arbitrary depth. State sequencing in the ECS system is achieved using a Finite State Machine package, based on SMI++ that allows creating complex logic needed, for example, for implementing elaborate sequencing or automatic error recovery.

The distributed components of the ECS system are connected with a large Ethernet network consisting of several hundred Gigabit and Fast Ethernet links.

2008 JINST 3 S08005

Chapter 9

Computing and Resources

This section describes the dataflow of the LHCb computing model for all stages in the processing of the real and simulated LHCb events [22]. The roles of the various Tier centres are discussed and the distribution of the processing load and storage are outlined.

There are several phases in the processing of event data. The various stages normally follow each other in a sequential manner, but some stages may be repeated a number of times. The workflow presented here reflects the present understanding of how to process the data. A schematic of the logical dataflow is shown in figure 9.1 and is described in more detail below.

The raw data from the detector is produced via the Event Filter farm of the online system. The first step is to collect data, triggering on events of interest. The raw data are transferred to the CERN Tier 0 centre for further processing and archiving. The raw data, whether real or simulated, must then be reconstructed to form physical quantities such as the calorimeter clusters needed to provide the energy of electromagnetic and hadronic showers, tracker hits to be associated to tracks whose position and momentum are to be determined. Information about particle identification (electron, photon, π^0, charged hadrons, muon) is also reconstructed from the appropriate sub-systems. The

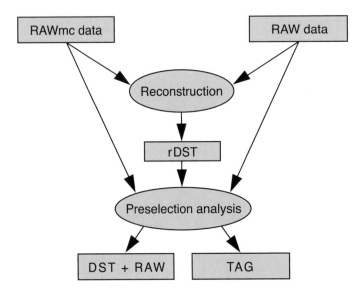

Figure 9.1: The LHCb computing logical dataflow model.

event reconstruction results in the generation of new data, the *Data Summary Tape* (DST). Only enough data will be stored in the DST to allow the physics pre-selection algorithms to be run at the next stage: this is known as a reduced DST (rDST). The first pass of the reconstruction will happen in quasi-real time. It is planned to reprocess the data of a given year once, after the end of data taking for that year, and then periodically as required. This is to accommodate improvements in the reconstruction algorithms and to make use of improved determinations of the calibration and alignment of the detector in order to generate new improved rDST information.

The rDST is analysed in a production-type mode in order to produce streams of selected events for further individual analysis. This activity is known as *stripping*. The rDST information is used to determine the four-momentum vectors corresponding to the measured particles, to locate primary and secondary vertices and reconstruct composite particles such as B candidates. A pre-selection algorithm will be provided for each channel of interest. Since these algorithms use tools that are common to many different physics analyses they are run in production-mode as a first step in the analysis process. The events that pass the selection criteria will be fully re-reconstructed, recreating the full information associated with each event. The output of the stripping stage will be referred to as the (full) DST and contains more information than the rDST. Before being stored, the events that pass the selection criteria will have their raw data added in order to have as detailed event information as needed for the analysis. An event tag collection will also be created for faster reference to selected events. The tag contains a brief summary of each event's characteristics as well as the results of the pre-selection algorithms and a reference to the actual DST record. The event tags are stored in files independent of the actual DST files. It is planned to run this production-analysis phase 4 times per year: once with the original data reconstruction; once with the re-processing of the raw data, and twice more, as the selection cuts and analysis algorithms evolve.

The baseline LHCb computing model is based on a distributed multi-tier regional centre model. It attempts to build in flexibility that will allow effective analysis of the data whether the Grid middleware meets expectations or not. A schematic of the LHCb computing model is given in figure 9.2.

CERN is the central production centre and will be responsible for distributing the raw data in quasi-real time to the Tier-1 centres. CERN will also take on the role of a Tier-1 centre. Six additional Tier-1 centres have been identified: CNAF (Italy), FZK (Germany), IN2P3 (France), NIKHEF (The Netherlands), PIC (Spain) and RAL (United Kingdom): there is also a number of Tier-2 computing centres. CERN and the Tier-1 centres will be responsible for all the production-processing phases associated with the real data. The raw data will be stored in its entirety at CERN, with another copy distributed across the other 6 Tier-1 centres. The second pass of the full reconstruction of the raw data will also use the resources of the LHCb online farm. As the production of the stripped DSTs will occur at these computing centres, it is envisaged that the majority of the distributed analyses will be performed at CERN and at the Tier-1 centres. The current year's stripped DST will be distributed to all centres to ensure load balancing. It should be noted that although no user analysis is envisaged at the Tier-2 centres in the baseline model presented, it should not be proscribed, particularly for the larger Tier-2 centres.

It is expected that the reconstruction and the first stripping of data at CERN and at the Tier-1 centres will follow the production in quasi real-time, with a maximum delay of a few days. The DST output of the stripping will remain on disk for analysis and be distributed to all other Tier-1 centres and CERN, whilst the raw and rDST will be migrated to the mass storage system, MSS.

2008 JINST 3 S08005

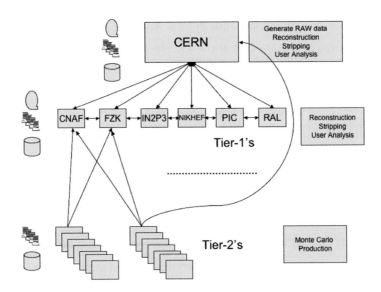

Figure 9.2: Schematic of the LHCb Computing Model.

Table 9.1: Projected resource usage in 2008 at CERN, the Tier-1 and Tier-2 centres. A 1 GHz PIII processor is equivalent to 400 KSI2k.

Site	CPU (MSI2k.years)	Disk (TB)	Tape (TB)
CERN	0.36	350	631
Tier-1	1.77	1025	860
Tier-2	4.55	-	-

The re-processing of the data will occur over a two-month period. During this process the raw data will need to be accessed from the MSS both at CERN and the Tier-1 centres. The CPU resources available at the pit allow a significant fraction of the total re-processing and perhaps the subsequent stripping to be performed there. Hence at CERN there is an additional complication that the raw data will also have to be transferred to the pit; similarly, the produced rDST will have to be transferred back to the CERN computing centre. To enable later stripping, it is necessary to distribute a fraction of the rDST produced at CERN during this re-processing to the Tier-1 centres; this is a consequence of the large contribution from the online farm.

The (two) stripping productions outside of the reconstruction or of the re-processing of the data will be performed over a one-month period. Both the raw and the rDST will need to be accessed from the MSS to perform this production. The produced stripped DSTs will be distributed to all production centres.

The Tier-2 centres will be primarily MonteCarlo production centres, with both CERN and the Tier-1 centres acting as the central repositories for the simulated data. The MonteCarlo production is expected to be an ongoing activity throughout the year and is the mainstay of the Tier-2 centres. The whole of the current year's MonteCarlo production DST will be available on disk at CERN and another 3 copies, on disk, distributed amongst the other 6 Tier-1 centres.

The 2008 resource requirements needed for the LHCb computing model at CERN and integrated across the Tier-1 centres and the Tier-2 centres are given in table 9.1.

Chapter 10

Performance

The data used to study the performance of the LHCb detector has been obtained from detailed MonteCarlo simulation, which produces a raw data format identical to real data. The proton-proton collisions are simulated with the PYTHIA program [220]. The generated particles are tracked through the detector and the surrounding material using the GEANT package [221]. The geometry and material composition of the LHCb detector are described in detail. The detector response, resolution, noise, crosstalk, etc. have been tuned to comply with test beam results. Details about this can be found in [2].

The performance quoted in this chapter is only qualitative, for two main reasons: 1) the MonteCarlo estimations are being constantly refined due to better and more detailed description of the detector, its material, the response of the electronics, more realistic source of noise, and also due to improvements in GEANT, and 2) more importantly, the real performance will be established and understood only using the first collected data as LHC will collide beams.

In the following, a description of the procedures for the main LHCb detector tasks, i.e. tracking, vertex reconstruction, particle identification, mass reconstruction, is given.

10.1 Track reconstruction

In the track reconstruction software the hits in the VELO, the TT, the IT and the OT detectors are combined to form particle trajectories from the VELO to the calorimeters. The reconstruction algorithm aims to find all tracks in the event which leave sufficient detector hits, and not only those from b-hadron decay.

Depending on their trajectories inside the spectrometer the following classes of tracks are defined, illustrated in figure 10.1:

- **Long tracks,** traversing the full tracking set-up from the VELO to the T stations. These have the most precise momentum determination and therefore are the most important set of tracks for b-hadron decay reconstruction.

- **Upstream tracks,** traversing only the VELO and TT stations. These are in general lower momentum tracks that are bent out of the detector acceptance by the magnetic field. However, they pass through the RICH 1 detector and may generate Cherenkov photons if they have

2008 JINST 3 S08005

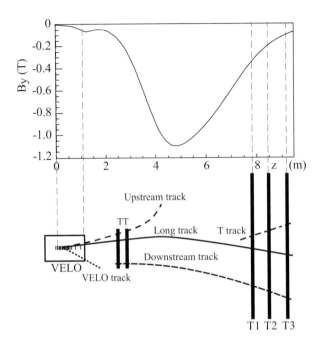

Figure 10.1: A schematic illustration of the various track types: long, upstream, downstream, VELO and T tracks. For reference the main B-field component (B_y) is plotted above as a function of the z coordinate.

velocities above threshold. They are therefore used to understand backgrounds in the RICH particle identification algorithm. They may also be used for b-hadron decay reconstruction or flavour tagging, although their momentum resolution is rather poor.

- **Downstream tracks,** traversing only the TT and T stations. The most relevant cases are the decay products of K_S^0 and Λ that decay outside the VELO acceptance.

- **VELO tracks,** measured in the VELO only and are typically large angle or backward tracks, useful for the primary vertex reconstruction.

- **T tracks:** are only measured in the T stations. They are typically produced in secondary interactions, but are useful for the global pattern recognition in RICH 2.

The track reconstruction starts with a search for track *seeds*, the initial track candidates [222], in the VELO region and the T stations where the magnetic field is low. After tracks have been found, their trajectories are refitted with a Kalman filter [223] which accounts for multiple scattering and corrects for dE/dx energy loss. The quality of the reconstructed tracks is monitored by the χ^2 of the fit and the *pull* distribution of the track parameters.

The pattern recognition performance is evaluated in terms of efficiencies and ghost rates. The efficiencies are normalized to the reconstructible track samples. To be considered reconstructible, a track must have a minimum number of hits in the relevant subdetectors. To be considered as *successfully reconstructed*, a track must have at least 70% of its associated hits originating from a single MonteCarlo particle. The reconstruction efficiency is defined as the fraction of reconstructible tracks that are successfully reconstructed, and the ghost rate is defined as the fraction of

2008 JINST 3 S08005

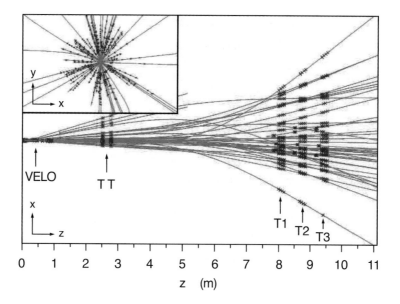

Figure 10.2: Display of the reconstructed tracks and assigned hits in an event. The insert shows a zoom in the plane (x,y) into the VELO region.

reconstructed tracks that are not matched to a true MonteCarlo particle. The results quoted in this section are obtained from a sample of $B^0 \rightarrow J/\psi K_S^0$ events.

An example of a reconstructed event is displayed in figure 10.2. The average number of successfully reconstructed tracks in fully simulated $b\bar{b}$ events is about 72, which are distributed among the track types as follows: 26 long tracks, 11 upstream tracks, 4 downstream tracks, 26 VELO tracks and 5 T tracks. The track finding performance is summarized in the following for the most important cases: the long tracks, the low momentum (upstream) tracks and K_S^0 decay (downstream) tracks.

The efficiency to find as a long track the trajectory of a particle with momentum larger than 10 GeV/c is on average $\sim$94%. The corresponding average ghost fraction is about 9%, but most ghost tracks have a low reconstructed p_T.

The momentum and impact parameter resolutions of the reconstructed long tracks are shown in figure 10.3. The momentum resolution is plotted as a function of the track momentum and is seen to be increasing from $\delta p/p = 0.35\%$ for low momentum tracks to $\delta p/p = 0.55\%$ for tracks at the high end of the spectrum. In the same figure the momentum spectrum for B decay tracks is also illustrated. The impact parameter resolution is plotted as function of $1/p_T$ of the track. The linear dependence can be parametrized as $\sigma_{IP} = 14\,\mu m + 35\,\mu m/p_T$ with p_T in GeV/c. For comparison the $1/p_T$ spectrum of B decay particles in the detector acceptance is plotted in the same figure.

The efficiency of the upstream track finding for particles with $p > 1$ GeV/c is approximately 75% with a corresponding ghost rate of 15%. The momentum resolution is only $\delta p/p \sim 15\%$, due to the small value of the total magnetic field integral in the considered region.

The efficiency for finding downstream tracks above 5 GeV/c is about 80%. Since the downstream tracks traverse most of the magnetic field, the momentum resolution is relatively good with an average of $\delta p/p = 0.43\%$ for pions originating from K_S^0 decays in $B^0 \rightarrow J/\psi K_S^0$ events. In order

2008 JINST 3 S08005

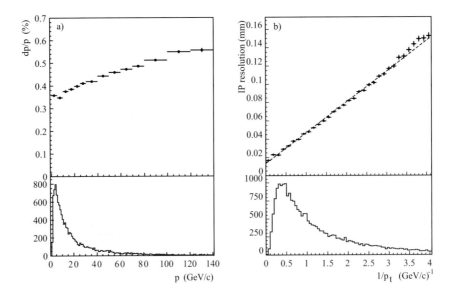

Figure 10.3: Resolution on the reconstructed track parameters at the production vertex of the track: (a) momentum resolution as a function of track momentum, (b) impact parameter resolution, calculated as the sum of the errors in the three projections added in quadrature, as a function of $1/p_T$. For comparison, the $1/p_T$ spectra of B decay particles are shown in the lower part of the plots.

to maintain high efficiency, the reconstruction allows for typically two or three track candidates in the TT to be linked to a single track seed in the T stations.

K_S^0 candidates are reconstructed through their decay to $\pi^+\pi^-$. For K_S^0 from $B^0 \to J/\psi K_S^0$ decays, about 25% decay inside the active region of the VELO, 50% decay outside the active region of the VELO but upstream of TT, and the rest decay after TT, and will therefore be difficult to reconstruct. The K_S^0 that decay outside the active region of the VELO but before TT are reconstructed using pairs of oppositely charged downstream tracks. The pions from K_S^0 that decay within the VELO acceptance give either a long track or an upstream track. The corresponding mass plots are shown in figure 10.4. As can be seen, there exists some combinatorial background from other tracks in the signal events, particularly for the long-upstream category, but this background can be removed by the additional requirements that are imposed when reconstructing the B meson.

10.2 Particle identification

The information from the two RICH detectors, the calorimeters and the muon system is combined for optimal identification of charged particle types (e, μ, π, K, p). Photons and neutral pions (γ, π^0) are identified using the electromagnetic calorimeter, where the $\pi^0 \to \gamma\gamma$ decay may be detected as two separate electromagnetic clusters or as a merged cluster.

2008 JINST 3 S08005

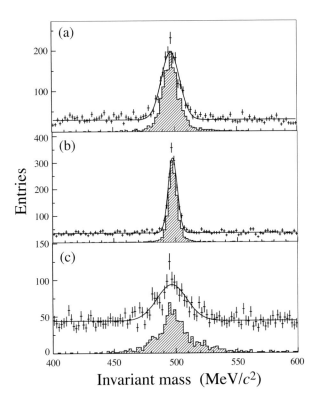

Figure 10.4: Reconstruction of $K_S^0 \rightarrow \pi^+\pi^-$. The $\pi^+\pi^-$ invariant mass is shown in $B^0 \rightarrow J/\psi K_S^0$ signal events, using different categories of tracks for the pion candidates: (a) downstream-downstream, (b) long-long, (c) long-upstream. Combinations coming from true K_S^0 are indicated by the shaded histograms.

10.2.1 Hadron identification

Particle identification with the RICH system is performed as follows. The baseline algorithm is based on a log-likelihood approach which matches the observed pattern of hit pixels in the RICH photodetectors to that expected from the reconstructed tracks under a given set of particle hypotheses [224]. In constructing this likelihood it is necessary to calculate the effective emission angle for all pixel-track combinations which could physically be associated through Cherenkov radiation. The likelihood is maximised by varying the particle hypotheses of each track in turn, through electron, muon, pion, kaon and proton. As the likelihood considers all found tracks in the event, and all three radiators simultaneously, the method is referred to as the *global pattern-recognition*.

The output of the global pattern-recognition is a best hypothesis for each track, and the decrease in log-likelihood when changing from this solution to another hypothesis.

The RICH system provides good particle identification over the entire momentum range. The average efficiency for kaon identification for momenta between 2 and $100\,\mathrm{GeV}/c$ is $\varepsilon(K \rightarrow K) \sim 95\%$, with a corresponding average pion misidentification rate $\varepsilon(\pi \rightarrow K) \sim 5\%$. Around $30\,\mathrm{GeV}/c$ the identification probability is $\sim 97\%$ and the misidentification probability $\sim 5\%$.

Other methods have been investigated to find the Cherenkov rings in the absence of tracking information. These include Markov chain MonteCarlo and Hough Transform techniques [225].

2008 JINST 3 S08005

Such approaches may be particularly useful in the early stages of data taking, when it may be necessary to study the performance of the RICH detector independently of spectrometer information.

For physics analyses and detector diagnostics it will be very important to understand the performance of the RICH particle identification independently of simulation studies. The dominant $D^{*\pm} \to D^0(K^-\pi^-)\pi^\pm$ decay mode will provide a very high statistics unbiased sample of pions and kaons which may be used to measure the RICH performance directly. Studies indicate that with kinematic cuts alone purities of $> 95\%$ can be achieved.

10.2.2 Muon identification

Muons are identified by extrapolating well reconstructed tracks with $p > 3\,\text{GeV}/c$ into the muon stations (particles with $p < 3\,\text{GeV}/c$ do not reach the muon system). Hits are searched within fields of interest (FOI) around the extrapolation point of the track in each muon station, parameterized as a function of momenta for each station and region. A track is considered as a muon candidate when a minimum number of stations (2–4 depending on momentum) have hits in their corresponding FOI. This number optimizes the resulting efficiency [226].

Using a sample of $B^0 \to J/\psi\,K_S^0$ the muon identification efficiency was measured to be $\varepsilon(\mu \to \mu) \sim 94\%$ with a corresponding misidentification $\varepsilon(\pi \to \mu) \sim 3\%$. The efficiency is a flat function of the momentum above $10\,\text{GeV}/c$.

Discriminating variables helping to improve the muon selection purity are constructed from the comparison of slopes in the muon system and the main tracker, and from the average track-hit distance of all hits in FOI associated to the track. For each track the difference in log-likelihood between the muon hypothesis and pion hypothesis is determined, and summed with the values from the RICH and calorimeter systems (if available). By doing this the pion misidentification rate can be reduced to $\sim 1\%$, whilst maintaining a muon efficiency of $\sim 93\%$ for muons above $3\,\text{GeV}/c$.

The high purity that can be achieved with such cuts is illustrated in figure 10.5 where the $\mu^+\mu^-$ mass plot is shown at the first step in the analysis of $B_s^0 \to J/\psi\,\phi$ events, taking all oppositely charged pairs of tracks from signal events that pass the muon identification requirements. The J/ψ mass peak is reconstructed with a resolution of about $13\,\text{MeV}/c^2$.

10.2.3 Electron identification

The electron identification [227] is mainly based on the balance of track momentum and energy of the charged cluster in the ECAL (figure 10.6), and the matching between the corrected barycenter position of the cluster with the extrapolated track impact point.

A second estimator is related to the bremsstrahlung photons emitted by electrons before the magnet. As there is little material within the magnet, such neutral clusters are expected in a well defined position given by the electron track extrapolation from before the magnet, as illustrated in figure 10.7: if an electron radiates photons when passing through material before the magnet, a cluster with energy E_1 is seen in the ECAL. If it radiates after the magnet, the bremsstrahlung photon will not lead to a separate cluster. For electron identification the corresponding cluster energy E_2 will be compared to the track momentum $E_2 = p$, while the energy of the electron at the origin is $E_0 = E_1 + E_2$.

2008 JINST 3 S08005

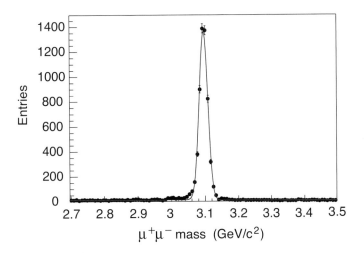

Figure 10.5: Invariant mass plots for the reconstruction of $J/\psi \to \mu^+\mu^-$ decays in $B_s^0 \to J/\psi\,\phi$ signal events.

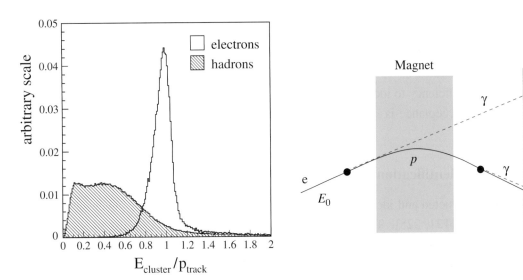

Figure 10.6: The ratio of uncorrected energy of the charged cluster in ECAL to the momentum of reconstructed tracks for electrons (open histogram) and hadrons (shaded histogram).

Figure 10.7: Schematic illustration of bremsstrahlung correction.

Further improvement in electron identification is obtained by using the track energy deposition in the preshower detector and the deposition of the energy along the extrapolated particle trajectory in the hadronic calorimeter HCAL.

For particle identification, the calorimeter information is combined with that from the RICH and muon detectors.

To illustrate the performance of electron reconstruction, the J/ψ mass plot for the decay $J/\psi \to e^+e^-$ is shown as open points in figure 10.8. The signal is fitted with a function plus a radiative tail, to account for the imperfect correction of bremsstrahlung. The background tracks are

2008 JINST 3 S08005

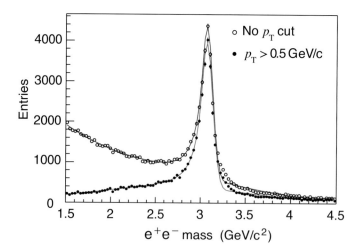

Figure 10.8: Invariant mass plots for the reconstruction of $J/\psi \to e^+e^-$ decays in $B_s^0 \to J/\psi\,\phi$ signal events, where the open points are before any p_T cut, and the solid points are after requiring $p_T > 0.5\,\mathrm{GeV/c}$ for the $e^\pm$ candidates.

dominantly of low p_T, and can be efficiently rejected by applying the requirement $p_T > 0.5\,\mathrm{GeV/c}$ for the electron candidates, as shown by the solid points in figure 10.8.

The average efficiency to identify electrons from $J/\psi \to e^+e^-$ decays in $B^0 \to J/\psi\,K_S^0$ events in the calorimeter acceptance is $\sim 95\%$. The pion misidentification fraction for the same events is 0.7%.

10.2.4 Photon identification

Photons are reconstructed and identified with the electromagnetic calorimeter, as clusters without an associated track [121, 228]. The reconstructed tracks are extrapolated to the ECAL face and a cluster-to-track position matching estimator, χ_γ^2, is calculated. Photon candidates correspond to $\chi_\gamma^2 > 4$, and are clearly separated from charged particles which form a peak at a small value of χ_γ^2.

The identification of photons converted in the passive material of the apparatus after passing the magnet, e.g. in RICH 2 or in M1, is based on whether there is a hit in the SPD cell that lies in front of central cell of the ECAL cluster. Reconstructed photons from $B^0 \to K^*\gamma$ decays reach the ECAL unconverted in 69% of cases, while 31% are converted before the calorimeter. A cut on the energy deposition in the preshower detector can improve the purity of selected samples both for converted and unconverted photons [229].

10.2.5 π^0 reconstruction

The neutral pion reconstruction reported in this section is based on the study of $B^0 \to \pi^+\pi^-\pi^0$ decay channel for which the mean transverse momentum of the π^0 is about $3\,\mathrm{GeV/c}$. Below this value the π^0 decays are mostly reconstructed as a resolved pair of well separated photons, while for higher p_T a large fraction of the pairs of photons cannot be resolved as a pair of clusters within the ECAL granularity. About 30% of the reconstructible π^0 from $B^0 \to \pi^+\pi^-\pi^0$ lead to a single cluster, referred to as a merged π^0.

2008 JINST 3 S08005

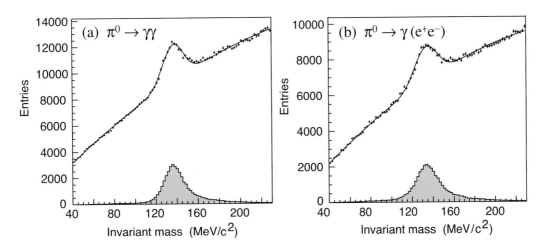

Figure 10.9: π^0 mass distributions, where (a) neither photon has converted, (b) one γ converted before the calorimeter. The conversions are identified using the SPD information. The contributions of true π^0 are indicated by the shaded histograms.

Figure 10.9 shows the mass distributions obtained in the case where both photon candidates with $p_T > 200\,\mathrm{MeV}/c$ reach the calorimeter (a), and for the case that one photon converted before the calorimeter (b), where the identification of the conversion relies on the SPD signal. The distributions are fitted with the sum of a gaussian and a polynomial function to describe the combinatorial background. The fit results in both cases in a mass resolution for the π^0 of $\sim 10\,\mathrm{MeV}/c^2$.

An algorithm has been developed to disentangle a potential pair of photons merged into a single cluster. The energy of each cell of the cluster is shared between two virtual sub-clusters according to an iterative procedure based on the expected transverse shape of photon showers. Each of the two sub-clusters is then reconstructed as coming from a photon, as for isolated photons.

The reconstruction efficiency for π^0 that give photons inside the geometrical acceptance is summarized in figure 10.10 for the resolved and merged case.

10.2.6 Expected global performance

Given the reconstruction performance described above, the global performance for the reconstruction of B decays in the LHCb detector is expected to be: a primary vertex resolution of $\sim 10\,\mu\mathrm{m}$ transverse to the beam axis and $\sim 60\,\mu\mathrm{m}$ along the beam axis; an invariant mass resolution typically in the range between $12\,\mathrm{MeV}/c$ and $25\,\mathrm{MeV}/c$; and a proper lifetime resolution of $\sim 40\,\mathrm{fs}$, with a dependence on the decay channel studied.

2008 JINST 3 S08005

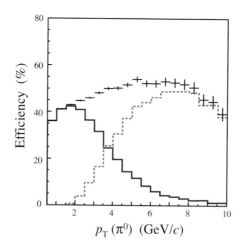

Figure 10.10: The reconstruction efficiency for π^0 decaying into photons inside the geometrical acceptance with $p_T > 200\,\text{MeV/c}$, versus the π^0 transverse momentum. The contributions from resolved and merged π^0 reconstruction are indicated by the solid and dashed histograms, respectively.

Chapter 11

Summary

The LHCb experiment has been described as it will be operational at the start up of the LHC, including the detector, its interface to the machine, the hardware-based first level and software-based high level triggers, and the online system. The intrinsic performance of all detector components, as studied in the laboratory and with test-beam measurements, corresponds to expectations. The overall performance for event reconstruction has also been presented, including tracking, vertexing and particle identification, as determined through detailed simulation.

The LHCb experiment will be operational at the time of the very first collisions of the LHC. The first data will be used to measure the real performance of the detector, the trigger behaviour, the reconstruction capabilities and the event selections, and to ensure that the design resolutions have been achieved. This will permit interesting results to be produced in the domain of heavy flavour physics, even with the first period of stable beams in the LHC. The experiment and its associated computing tools will allow a search to be made for the effects of new physics, through high precision measurements of CP violation and rare decays in the b- and c-physics sectors.

2008 JINST 3 S08005

Acknowledgements

We are greatly indebted to all CERN departments, without whose support, assistance and active contribution, the preparation of the experimental site, its infrastructure and installation of the LHCb detector would not have been possible.

We are deeply grateful to our colleagues from the LHC machine for the collaborative relationship and friendly cooperation which enabled running both projects smoothly and effective close to each other.

We acknowledge all the funding agencies which supported the construction and the commissioning of the LHCb detector and also provided the computing infrastructure:

Brazil: CNPq, FINEP and FAPERJ

China: the National Natural Science Foundation of China under contract Nos. 10225522, 10421140657, 10620130426, and the Key Laboratory of Particle and Imaging (Tsinghua University), Ministry of Education of the People's Republic of China

France: CNRS-Institut National de Physique Nucléaire et de Physique des Particules (IN2P3)

Germany: Bundesministerium für Bildung und Forschung and Deutsche Forschungsgemeinschaft

Italy: Istituto Nazionale di Fisica Nucleare (INFN)

The Netherlands: Foundation of Fundamental Research of Matter (FOM)

Poland: Ministry of Science and Higher Education

Romania: Ministry of Education and Research

Russia: the Ministry of Science and Technology for the Russian Federation and the Russian Federal Agency for Atomic Energy

Spain: the Spanish MEC (projects FPA2005-06889, FPA2005-06441, FPA2005-07761-C02-01, FPA2005-07761-C02-02, and project CPAN CSD2007-00042 of the Programme Consolider-Ingenio 2010), the "Generalitat de Catalunya" (AGAUR 2005SGR00385) and by the "Xunta de Galicia" (PGIDIT 06PXIC206066PN)

Switzerland: the State Secretariat for Education and Research, the Swiss National Science Foundation and the Ecole Polytechnique Fédérale de Lausanne; the cantons of Vaud and Zuerich

Ukraine: Academy of Sciences of Ukraine

United Kingdom: the Science and Technology Facilities Council (previously PPARC), the Royal Society

United States of America: the U. S. National Science Foundation.

We also acknowledge the European Community support through the projects: HELEN, INTAS, Marie Curie, RII3-CT-2004506078; the regional support from the Region Auvergne (France).

The construction of the detector would not have been possible without the technical support in each of the participating laboratories: we wish to thank A. Iacoangeli of Università Roma La Sapienza; R. Lunadei and C. Piscitelli of INFN-Roma1; W. Lau, J. Tacon, M. Tacon and S. Yang of Oxford.

Bibliography

[1] LHCb collaboration, *A Large Hadron Collider beauty experiment*, Technical Proposal, CERN-LHCC-98-004, http://cdsweb.cern.ch/record/622031.

[2] LHCb collaboration, R. Antunes-Nobrega et al., *LHCb reoptimized detector design and performance*, CERN-LHCC-2003-030, http://cdsweb.cern.ch/record/630827.

[3] M. Needham and T. Ruf, *Estimation of the material budget of the LHCb detector*, Note LHCb-2007-025, http://cdsweb.cern.ch/record/1023537.

[4] J. Christiansen, *Requirements to the L0 front-end electronics*, Note LHCb-2001-014, http://cdsweb.cern.ch/record/691647.

[5] J. Christiansen, *Requirements to the L1 front-end electronics*, EDMS document https://edms.cern.ch/document/715154.

[6] P. Moreira et al., *G-Link and gigabit ethernet compliant serializer for LHC data transmission*, *IEEE Nucl. Sci. Symp. Conf. Rec.* **2** (2000) 9/6; *A radiation tolerant gigabit serializer for LHC data transmission*, http://edms.cern.ch/file/906036/1/.

[7] J. Christiansen, *Test, time alignment, calibration and monitoring in the LHCb front-end electronics*, EDMS document https://edms.cern.ch/document/692583.

[8] B. Taylor, *Timing distribution at the LHC*, *Proceedings of the LECC 2002 Workshop*, Colmar France (2002), http://cdsweb.cern.ch/record/592719.

[9] *Embedded Local Monitor Board home page*, http://elmb.web.cern.ch/ELMB/ELMBhome.html.

[10] G. Haefeli et al., *The LHCb DAQ interface board TELL1*, *Nucl. Instrum. Meth.* **A 560** (2006) 494.

[11] *Radiation hardness assurance*, http://lhcb-elec.web.cern.ch/lhcb-elec/html/radiation_hardness.htm.

[12] G. Corti and G. von Holtey, *Study of beampipe induced background in the LHCb detector for the optimization of the vacuum chamber design*, Note LHCb-2003-085.

2008 JINST 3 S08005

[13] J.R. Knaster, *The vacuum chamber in the interaction region of particle colliders: a historical study and developments implemented in the LHCb experiment at CERN*, Ph.D. Thesis, CERN-ETSII, Geneva Switzerland (2004).

[14] CERN Safety Instruction IS nr 25, http://safety-commission.web.cern.ch/safety-commission/SC-site/sc_pages/documents/instructions.html

[15] R. Veness et al., *Study of minimised UHV flanges for LHC experiments*, CERN Vacuum tech. Note EDMS document https://edms.cern.ch/document/350384.

[16] D. Ramos, *Design of the fixed beampipe supports inside the acceptance region of the LHCb experiment*, CERN Vacuum Tech. Note, EDMS document https://edms.cern.ch/document/882924.

[17] C. Benvenuti et al., *Vacuum properties of TiZrV non-evaporable getter films*, Vacuum **60** (2001) 57.

[18] O. Grobner, *Overview of the LHC vacuum system*, Vacuum **60** (2001) 25.

[19] L. Fernandez-Herando et al., *The radiation monitoring system for the LHC experimental areas*, TS-Note-2004-006, http://cdsweb.cern.ch/record/740728.

[20] B. Todd et al., *The architecture, design and realisation of the LHC beam interlock system*, in *Proceedings of the 10th ICALEPCS International Conference on Accelerator & Large Experimental Physics Control System*, Geneva Switzerland (2005).

[21] E. Effinger et al., *Single gain radiation tolerant LHC beam loss acquisition card*, in *Proceedings of the 8th European Workshop on Beam Diagnostics and Instrumentation for Particle Accelerators*, Venice Italy (2007), http://cdsweb.cern.ch/record/1045244.

[22] LHCb collaboration, R. Antunes-Nobrega et al., *LHCb computing technical design report*, CERN-LHCC-2005-019, http://cdsweb.cern.ch/record/835156.

[23] LHCb collaboration, S. Amato et al., *LHCb magnet technical design report*, CERN-LHCC-2000-007, http://cdsweb.cern.ch/record/424338.

[24] J. André et al., *Status of the LHCb magnet system*, IEEE Trans. Appl. Supercond. **12** (2002) 366.

[25] J. André, et al., *Status of the LHCb dipole magnet*, IEEE Trans. Appl. Supercond. **14** (2004) 509.

[26] M. Patel, M. Losasso and T. Gys., *Magnetic shielding studies of the LHCb rich photon detectors*, Nucl. Instrum. Meth. **A 553** (2005) 114.

[27] F. Bersgma, *Calibration of Hall sensors in three dimensions*, in *Proceedings of the 13th International Magnetic Measurement Workshop (IMMW13)*, SLAC Stanford, California U.S.A. (2003), http://cdsweb.cern.ch/record/1072471.

[28] LHCb collaboration, P.R. Barbosa-Marinho et al., *Vertex locator technical design report*, CERN-LHCC-2001-011, http://cdsweb.cern.ch/record/504321.

[29] P. Koppenburg, *Simulation of the vertex trigger preprocessor:effects of noise on L1 performance*, Note LHCb-1999-003, http://cdsweb.cern.ch/record/691699.

[30] P. Koppenburg, *Effect of pulse overspill on the level 1 trigger*, Note LHCb-2001-078, http://cdsweb.cern.ch/record/684442.

[31] D. Petrie, C. Parkes and S. Viret, *Study of the impact of VELO misalignments on the LHCb tracking and L1 trigger performance*, Note LHCb-2005-056, http://cdsweb.cern.ch/record/899299.

[32] M. Ferro-Luzzi et al., *A first study of wake fields in the LHCb detector*, Note LHCb-99-041, http://cdsweb.cern.ch/record/684454; *Wake fields in the LHCb vertex detector*, Note LHCb-99-043, http://cdsweb.cern.ch/record/691632;
N. Van Bakel et al., *Wake fields in the LHCb vertex detector: alternative design for the wake fields suppressor*, Note LHCb-99-044, http://cdsweb.cern.ch/record/691599.

[33] LHCb VELO GROUP collaboration, *Review of the planned replacement of n-on-n with n-on-p detectors for LHCb-Velo*, EDMS document https://edms.cern.ch/document/883223.

[34] S. Löchner and M. Schmelling, *The Beetle Reference Manual*, Note LHCb-2005-105, http://cdsweb.cern.ch/record/1000429.

[35] R. Mountain et al., *VELO module transport box document and operational guide*, Syracuse University note, SU-LHCb-2006-02-03.

[36] A. Bates et. al., *A facility for long term evaluation and quality assurance of LHCb vertex detector modules*, Note LHCb-2007-102, http://cdsweb.cern.ch/record/1061056.

[37] M. Schmelling, *Specification of the front-end electronics for the LHCb vertex locator*, Note LHCb-2001-048, http://cdsweb.cern.ch/record/691610.

[38] A. Bates et. al., *VELO module characterisation: results from the Glasgow LHCb VELO module burn-in*, Note LHCb-2007-103, http://cdsweb.cern.ch/record/1046811.

[39] L. Eklund et. al., *Radiation tests of the VELO ECS and Analogue Repeater Mezzanines*, Note LHCb-2006-001, http://cdsweb.cern.ch/record/926372.

[40] L. Eklund, *Control and monitoring of VELO and pile-up level 0 electronics*, EDMS document https://edms.cern.ch/document/596194.

[41] D. Breton and D. Charlet, *SPECS: the Serial Protocol for the Experiment Control System of LHCb*, Note LHCb-2003-004, http://cdsweb.cern.ch/record/681284.

[42] S. Kersten and P. Kind, *Technical description of the interlock circuit and system of the ATLAS pixel detector*, ATL-IP-ES-0041.

[43] G. Haefeli, *Contribution to the development of the acquisition electronics for the LHCb experiment*, LPHE Master thesis, Lausanne Switzerland (2004).

[44] LHCb ST and VELO GROUP collaborations, G. Haefeli and A. Gong, *LHCb VELO and ST clusterization on TELL1* EDMS document https://edms.cern.ch/document/690585.

[45] LHCb VELO GROUP, D. Eckstein, *VELO raw data format and strip numbering*, EDMS document https://edms.cern.ch/document/637676.

[46] LHCb VELO GROUP collaboration, M. Ferro-Luzzi, *VELO hardware interlocks*, EDMS document https://edms.cern.ch/document/706629.

[47] M. Artuso and J.C. Wang, *Study of the spatial resolution achievable with the BTeV pixel sensors*, *Nucl. Instrum. Meth.* **A 465** (2000) 115 [hep-ex/0007054].

[48] C. Parkes and T. Szumlak, *VELO event model*, Note LHCb-2006-054, http://cdsweb.cern.ch/record/989093.

[49] C. Parkes, T. Ruf and T. Szumlak, *Reconstruction of cluster positions in the LHCb VELO*, Note LHCb-2007-151, http://cdsweb.cern.ch/record/1074928.

[50] W. Baldini et al., *LHCb alignment strategy*, Note LHCb-2006-035, http://cdsweb.cern.ch/record/964804.

[51] V. Blobel and C. Kleinwort, *A new method for the high-precision alignment of track detectors*, *Contribution to the Conference on Advanced Statistical Techniques in Particle Physics PHYSTAT2002*, Durham U.K., hep-ex/0208021.

[52] T.W. Versloot, *Position reconstruction and charge distribution in LHCb VELO silicon sensors*, Note LHCb-2007-119, http://cdsweb.cern.ch/record/1073483.

[53] J. Gassner, M. Needham and O. Steinkamp, *Layout and expected performance of the LHCb TT station*, Note LHCb-2003-140, http://cdsweb.cern.ch/record/728548.

[54] LHCb collaboration, P.R. Barbosa-Marinho et al., *LHCb inner tracker technical design report*, CERN-LHCC-2002-029, http://cdsweb.cern.ch/record/582793.

[55] J. Gassner, F. Lehner and S. Steiner, *The mechanical design of the LHCb silicon trigger tracker*, Note LHCb-2004-110, http://cdsweb.cern.ch/record/858499.

[56] J.-L. Agram et al., *The silicon sensors for the Compact Muon Solenoid tracker — design and qualification procedure*, Note CMS-2003-015, http://cdsweb.cern.ch/record/687875.

[57] A. Bay et al., *Hybrid design, procurement and testing for the LHCb silicon tracker*, Note LHCb-2005-061, http://cdsweb.cern.ch/record/885752.

[58] I. Abt et al., *Gluing silicon with silicone*, *Nucl. Instrum. Meth.* **A 411** (1998) 191.

[59] A. Vollhardt, *A radiation tolerant fiber-optic readout system for the LHCb silicon tracker*, Note LHCb-2005-032, http://cdsweb.cern.ch/record/872267.

2008 JINST 3 S08005

[60] V. Bobillier, J. Christiansen and R. Frei, *Grounding, shielding and power distribution in LHCb*, Note LHCb-2004-039, http://cdsweb.cern.ch/record/738180.

[61] D. Esperante and A. Vollhardt, *Design and development of the control board for the LHCb silicon tracker*, Note LHCb-2007-153, http://cdsweb.cern.ch/record/1082457.

[62] *TTCrq*, http://proj-qpll.web.cern.ch/proj-qpll/ttcrq.htm.

[63] C. Bauer et al., *Grounding, shielding and power distribution for the LHCb silicon tracking*, Note LHCb-2004-101, http://cdsweb.cern.ch/record/836185.

[64] M. Agari et al., *Test beam results of multi-geometry prototype sensors for the LHCb inner tracker*, Note LHCb-2002-058, http://cdsweb.cern.ch/record/684437.

[65] R. Bernhard et al., *Measurements of prototype ladders for the silicon tracker with laser*, Note LHCb-2003-075, http://cdsweb.cern.ch/record/684488.

[66] M. Agari et al., *Test-beam measurements on prototype ladders for the LHCb TT station and Inner Tracker*, Note LHCb-2003-082, http://cdsweb.cern.ch/record/722699.

[67] J. Gassner et al., *Measurements of prototype ladders for the TT station with a laser*, Note LHCb-2004-102, http://cdsweb.cern.ch/record/818585.

[68] M. Agari et al., *Measurements of a prototype ladder for the TT station in a* $120\,GeV/c\ \pi^-$ *beam*, Note LHCb-2004-103, http://cdsweb.cern.ch/record/811085.

[69] S. Köstner and U. Straumann, *Noise considerations for the beetle amplifier used with long silicon strip detectors*, Note LHCb-2005-029, http://cdsweb.cern.ch/record/837194.

[70] M. Needham, *Silicon tracker occupancies and clustering*, Note LHCb-2007-024, http://cdsweb.cern.ch/record/1023456.

[71] M. Needham and D. Volyanskyy, *Updated geometry description for the LHCb trigger tracker*, Note LHCb-2006-032, http://cdsweb.cern.ch/record/961216.

[72] A. Perrin and K. Vervink, *The inner tracker detector description and its implementation in the XML database*, Note LHCb-2006-018, http://cdsweb.cern.ch/record/962061.

[73] LHCb collaboration, P.R. Barbosa-Marinho et al., *Outer tracker technical design report*, CERN-LHCC-2001-024, http://cdsweb.cern.ch/record/519146.

[74] S. Bachmann, *Specifications for the drift gas quality of the outer tracking system*, Note LHCb-2002-031; *Proposal for the gas distribution in the outer tracking system*, Note LHCb-2003-054.

[75] J. Nardulli and N. Tuning, *A study of the material in an outer tracker module*, Note LHCb-2004-114, http://cdsweb.cern.ch/record/815493.

[76] T. Haas, *Aging phenomena in the LHCb outer tracker*, *Nucl. Instrum. Meth.* **A 581** (2007) 164.

[77] A. Berkien et al., *The LHCb outer tracker front-end electronics*, Note LHCb-2005-025, http://cdsweb.cern.ch/record/1089278;
Y. Guz et al., *Study of the global performance of an LHCb OT front-end electronics prototype*, Note LHCb-2004-120.

[78] N. Dressnandt et al., *Implementation of the ASDBLR and DTMROC ASICS for the ATLAS TRT in DMILL technology*, *Proceedings of the* 6th *Workshop on Electronics for LHC Experiments*, Cracow Poland (2000), http://cdsweb.cern.ch/record/478863;
R. Bevensee et al., *An amplifier-shaper-discriminator with baseline restoration for the ATLAS transition radiation tracker*, *IEEE Trans. Nucl. Sci.* **43** (1996) 1725.

[79] H. Deppe, et al., *The OTIS reference manual*, Note LHCb-2008-010, http://cdsweb.cern.ch/record/1089277.

[80] U. Stange, *Development and characterization of a rad hard readout chip for the LHCb outer tracker detector*, PhD Thesis, Heidelberg Germany (2005).

[81] U. Uwer et al., *Specifications for the IF13-2 prototype of the auxiliary board for the outer tracker*, Note LHCb-2005-039.

[82] G.W. van Apeldoorn et al., *Beam tests of final modules and electronics of the LHCb outer tracker in* 2005, Note LHCb-2005-076, http://cdsweb.cern.ch/record/896901.

[83] T. Bauer, J. Nardulli and N. Tuning, *Flatness of an outer tracker module*, Note LHCb-2005-009.

[84] N. Tuning and A. Pellegrino, *Flatness of an outer tracker layer in a prototype C-frame*, Note LHCb-2008-003.

[85] H. Dekker et al., *The RASNIK/CCD 3-dimensional alignment system*, in *Proceedings of the* 3rd *International Workshop On Accelerator Alignment (IWAA* 93), Annecy France (1993).

[86] M. Adamus, A. Nawrot and M. Szczekowski, *Alignment system for the outer tracker detector in LHCb experiment*, Note LHCb-2001-006, http://cdsweb.cern.ch/record/691623;
M. Adamus et al., *First results from a prototype of the RASNIK alignment system for the outer tracker detector in LHCb experiment*, Note LHCb-2002-016.

[87] LHCb RICH GROUP collaboration, N. Brook et al., *LHCb RICH* 1 *engineering design review report*, Note LHCb-2004-121, http://cdsweb.cern.ch/record/897981.

[88] F. Metlica, *Development of light-weight spherical mirrors for RICH detectors*, NIMA 48462, http://dx.doi.org/10.1016/j.nima.2008.07.026.

[89] A. Papanestis, *Limits of software compensation for mirror misalignment of the RICH detectors*, Note LHCb-2001-141.

[90] R. Plackett, *Photon detectors for the Ring Imaging Cherenkov detectors of the LHCb experiment*, PhD Thesis, University of London, London U.K. (2006).

[91] LHCb collaboration, S. Amato et al., *LHCb RICH technical design report*, CERN-LHCC-2000-037, http://cdsweb.cern.ch/record/494263.

[92] LHCb RICH GROUP collaboration, M. Adinolfi et al., *LHCb RICH 2 engineering design review report*, Note LHCb-2002-009, http://cdsweb.cern.ch/record/691478.

[93] T. Bellunato, *Development of ring imaging Cherenkov detectors for LHCb*, PhD Thesis, Università degli Studi di Milano, Milano Italy (2001).

[94] M. Laub, *Development of opto-mechanical tools and procedures for a new generation of RICH-detectors at CERN*, PhD Thesis, Ceské vysoké ucení technické v Praze, Prague Czech Republic (2001).

[95] L. Fernández Hernando, *New automatic techniques to test optical components of the next generation of RICH detectors at CERN*, PhD Thesis, Universitat Politècnica de Catalunya, Barcelona Spain (2001).

[96] G. Aglieri-Rinella, *Development of the photon detection, acquisition and optical systems of modern ring imaging Cherenkov detectors*, PhD Thesis, Università degli Studi di Palermo, Palermo Italy (2006).

[97] C. D'Ambrosio et al., *The optical systems of LHCb RICHes: a study on the mirror walls and mirrors specifications*, Note LHCb-2000-071, http://cdsweb.cern.ch/record/691486.

[98] T. Gys, *Magnetic field simulations for the LHCb-RICH 2 detector*, Note LHCb-2002-029;
M. Patel et al., *Magnetic shielding studies of the RICH photon detectors*, Note LHCb-2005-055, http://cdsweb.cern.ch/record/920381;
M. Alemi, *Passive magnetic shielding calculation for the photodetectors of RICH2*, Note LHCb-1998-017, http://cdsweb.cern.ch/record/691679.

[99] M.Y. Barnykov et al., *Development of aerogel Cherenkov counters with wavelength shifters and phototubes*, Nucl. Instrum. Meth. **A 419** (1998) 584.

[100] T. Bellunato et al., *Performance of aerogel as Cherenkov radiator*, Nucl. Instrum. Meth. **A 519** (2004) 493.

[101] T. Bellunato et al., *Study of ageing effects in aerogel*, Nucl. Instrum. Meth. **A 527** (2004) 319.

[102] T. Bellunato et al., *Refractive index inhomogeneity within an aerogel block*, Nucl. Instrum. Meth. **A 556** (2006) 140.

[103] D. Perego, *Ageing tests and recovery procedures of silica aerogel*, Note LHCb-2008-004.

[104] O. Ullaland, *Fluid systems for RICH detectors*, Nucl. Instrum. Meth. **A 553** (2005) 107.

[105] M. Bosteels et al., *LHCb RICH gas system proposal*, LHCb-2000-079, http://cdsweb.cern.ch/record/684687.

[106] A. Braem et al., *Metal multi-dielectric mirror coatings for Cherenkov detectors*, *Nucl. Instrum. Meth.* **A 553** (2005) 182.

[107] E. Albrecht et al., *Operation, optimisation and performance of the DELPHI RICH detectors*, *Nucl. Instrum. Meth.* **A 433** (1999) 47.

[108] E. Albrecht et al., *The mirror system of COMPASS RICH* 1, *Nucl. Instrum. Meth.* **A 502** (2003) 236;
P. Fauland, *The COMPASS experiment and the RICH-1 detector*, PhD Thesis, Universität Bielefeld, Mannheim Germany (2004).

[109] M. Alemi et al., *First operation of a hybrid photon detector prototype with electrostatic cross-focussing and integrated silicon pixel readout*, *Nucl. Instrum. Meth.* **A 449** (2000) 48.

[110] K. Wyllie et al., *Silicon detectors and electronics for pixel hybrid photon detectors*, *Nucl. Instrum. Meth.* **A 530** (2004) 82.

[111] M. Adinolfi, *System test of a three-column LHCb RICH* 2 *prototype detector*, *Nucl. Instrum. Meth.* **A 553** (2005) 328.

[112] P. Moreira et al., *A radiation tolerant gigabit serializer for LHC data transmission*, *Proceedings of the Seventh Workshop on Electronics for LHC Experiments*, CERN-LHCC-2001-034, http://cdsweb.cern.ch/record/588665.

[113] J. Christiansen et al., *Receiver ASIC for timing, trigger and control distribution in LHC experiments*, *IEEE Trans. Nucl. Sci* **43** (1996) 1773;
TTCrx reference manual V. 3.10, http://ttc.web.cern.ch/TTC/TTCrx_manual3.10.pdf, (2005).

[114] C. Arnaboldi et al., *The high voltage distribution system for the hybrid photodetector arrays of RICH* 1 *and RICH* 2 *at LHCb*, *IEEE Nucl. Sci. Symp. Conf. Rec.* **1** (2005) 413.

[115] C. Gaspar et al, *The use of credit card-sized PCs for interfacing electronics boards to the LHCb ECS*, Note LHCb-2001-147.

[116] C. D'Ambrosio et al., *The LHCb RICH detector control system*, Note LHCb-2004-071, http://cdsweb.cern.ch/record/793159.

[117] C. Gaspar and M. Dönszelmann, *DIM: a distributed information management system for the DELPHI experiment at CERN*, presented at *IEEE Conference REAL TIME* '93, Vancouver Canada (1993), http://cdsweb.cern.ch/record/254799.

[118] B. Hallgren et al., *The Embedded Local Monitor Board (ELMB) in the LHC front-end I/O control system*, presented at the 7th *Workshop on Electronics for LHC Experiments*, Stockholm Sweden (2001), http://cdsweb.cern.ch/record/530675.

[119] M. Adinolfi et al., *Performance of the LHCb RICH photodetectors in a charged particle beam*, *Nucl. Instrum. Meth.* **A 574** (2007) 39.

[120] S. Easo et al., *Simulation of LHCb RICH detectors using GEANT4*, *IEEE Trans. Nucl. Sci.* **52** (2005) 1665.

[121] LHCb collaboration, S. Amato et al., *LHCb calorimeters technical design report*, CERN-LHCC-2000-036, http://cdsweb.cern.ch/record/494264.

[122] E. Guschin and S.V. Laptev, *Monte-Carlo study of LHCb preshower*, Note LHCb-2000-030, http://cdsweb.cern.ch/record/691547.

[123] S. Barsuk et al., *Design and construction of the electromagnetic calorimeter for the LHCb experiment*, Note LHCb-2000-043, http://cdsweb.cern.ch/record/691508.

[124] R. Djeliadine, O. Iouchtchenko and V.F. Obraztsov, *LHCb hadron trigger and HCAL cell size and length optimisation*, Note LHCb-1999-035, http://cdsweb.cern.ch/record/691688.

[125] C. Beigbeder-Beau et al., *A joint proposal for the level 0 calorimetric triggers*, Note LHCb-99-017, http://cdsweb.cern.ch/record/691582.

[126] C. Beigbeder-Beau et al., *The front-end electronics for LHCb calorimeters*, Note LHCb-2000-028, http://cdsweb.cern.ch/record/691705.

[127] S. Bota et al., *Scintillator pad detector front-end electronics*, Note LHCb-2000-027, http://cdsweb.cern.ch/record/691544.

[128] G. Böhner et al., *Front-end electronics for the LHCb preshower detector*, Note LHCb-2000-048, http://cdsweb.cern.ch/record/691511.

[129] B. Delcourt, J. Lefrançois, *Investigation of widening of the π^0 mass peak with electronic defects*, Note LHCb-2000-029, http://cdsweb.cern.ch/record/691719.

[130] S.N. Filippov et al., *Design and construction of the LHCb scintillator-pad/preshower detector*, Note LHCb-2000-042, http://cdsweb.cern.ch/record/691521.

[131] S.N. Filippov et al., *Experimental performance of PS/SPD prototypes*, Note LHCb-2000-031, http://cdsweb.cern.ch/record/691545.

[132] G. Böhner et al., *Very front-end electronics for LHCb preshower*, Note LHCb-2000-047, http://cdsweb.cern.ch/record/691512.

[133] Z. Ajaltouni et al., *Study of multianode photomultipliers for the electromagnetic calorimeter preshower read out of the LHCb experiment*, *Nucl. Instrum. Meth.* **A 504** (2003) 9; *Photomultiplier pulse read out system for the preshower detector of the LHCb experiment*, *Nucl. Instrum. Meth.* **A 504** (2003) 250.

[134] E. Aguiló et al., *Test of multi-anode photomultiplier tubes for the LHCb scintillator pad detector*, *Nucl. Instrum. Meth.* **A 538** (2005) 255.

[135] E. Graugés et al., *Mass characterization of MaPMT tubes for the LHCb scintillator pad detector*, *Nucl. Instrum. Meth.* **A 572** (2007) 427.

[136] S. Monteil, *Photodetector performance for the LHCb pre-shower detector*, in *Proceedings of the* 11th *International Conference on Calorimetry in High-Energy Physics, CALOR 2004*, Perugia Italy (2004).

[137] L. Garrido et al., *Results of tagged photon test beam for the scintillator pad detector*, Note LHCb-2000-032, http://cdsweb.cern.ch/record/691546;
E. Aguiló et al., *Backsplash testbeam results for the SPD subdetector of LHCb*, *Nucl. Instrum. Meth.* **A 546** (2005) 438.

[138] HERA-B collaboration, *HERA-B: an experiment to study CP violation in the B system using an internal target at the HERA proton ring. Proposal*, DESY-PRC-94-002; *HERA-B: an experiment to study CP violation in the B system using an internal target at the HERA proton ring. Design report*, DESY-PRC-95-01.

[139] PHENIX collaboration, *PHENIX: preliminary conceptual design report*, BNL-PROPOSAL-R2.

[140] HERA-B collaboration, E. Tarkovsky, *The HERA-B electromagnetic calorimeter*, *Nucl. Instrum. Meth.* **A 379** (1996) 515.

[141] A. Bazilevsky et al., *Performance of the PHENIX EM calorimeter*, *IEEE Trans. Nucl. Sci.* **43** (1996) 1491.

[142] J. Badier et al., *Shashlik calorimeter beam-test results*, *Nucl. Instrum. Meth.* **A 348** (1994) 74.

[143] A. Arefiev et al., *Design, construction, quality control and performance study with cosmic rays of modules for the LHCb electromagnetic calorimeter*, Note LHCb-2007-148, http://cdsweb.cern.ch/record/1080559.

[144] A. Arefiev et al., *Beam test results of the LHCb electromagnetic calorimeter*, Note LHCb-2007-149, http://cdsweb.cern.ch/record/1103500.

[145] V. Brekhovskikh et al., *The WLS fiber time properties study*, Note LHCb-2000-039, http://cdsweb.cern.ch/record/691514.

[146] R.I. Dzhelyadin, *The LHCb hadron calorimeter*, *Nucl. Instrum. Meth.* **A 494** (2002) 332, also in *Proceedings of the* 8th *International Conference on Instrumentation for Colliding Beam Physics*, Novosibirsk Russia (2002).

[147] L.G. Afanasieva et al., *The hadron calorimeter design and construction*, Note LHCb-2000-045, http://cdsweb.cern.ch/record/691506.

[148] M. Bonnet et al., *The hadron calorimeter prototype design and construction*, Note LHCb-2000-035, http://cdsweb.cern.ch/record/691513.

[149] C. Coca et al., *The hadron calorimeter prototype beam-test results*, Note LHCb-2000-036, http://cdsweb.cern.ch/record/691519.

[150] R.I. Dzhelyadin et al., *The hadron calorimeter module-0 construction*, Note LHCb-2001-122.

[151] G.I. Britvich et al., *The HCAL optics radiation damage study*, Note LHCb-2000-037, http://cdsweb.cern.ch/record/691516.

[152] I. Korolko, J. Ocariz and A. Schopper, *HCAL performance with irradiated sub-components*, Note LHCb-2000-038, http://cdsweb.cern.ch/record/691524.

[153] C. Beigbeder-Beau et al., *The readout of the LHCb calorimeters*, Note LHCb-2000-046, http://cdsweb.cern.ch/record/691493.

[154] N. Dumont-Dayot, *The preprocessor FPGA for the ECAL/HCAL and PS/SPD detectors*, LAPP EDMS I-008689 https://edms.in2p3.fr/file/I-008689/1/pp-fpga-firmware.pdf.

[155] D. Boget et al., *The readout of the LHCb calorimeters*, EDMS 527942 http://edms.cern.ch/document/527942.

[156] G. Böhner, *LHCb preshower signal characteristics*, Note LHCb-2000-026, http://cdsweb.cern.ch/record/691597.

[157] D. Gascón et al, *The front-end electronics of the scintillator pad detector of LHCb calorimeter*, in *Proceedings of the 12th LECC Workshop*, Valencia Spain (2006), http://cdsweb.cern.ch/record/1027429.

[158] D. Gascón et al., *A BICMOS synchronous pulse discriminator for the LHCb calorimeter system*, in *Proceedings of the 8th LECC Workshop*, Colmar France (2002), http://cdsweb.cern.ch/record/619291.

[159] S. Luengo et al., *SPD very front end electronics*, *Nucl. Instrum. Meth.* **A 567** (2006) 310.

[160] D. Breton and D. Charlet, *Using the SPECS in LHCb*, Note LHCb-2003-005.

[161] A. Arefiev et al., *Design of PMT base for the LHCb electromagnetic calorimeter*, Note LHCb-2003-150.

[162] G. Avoni et al., *The HERA-B ECAL electronics and monitoring*, in *Proceedings of International Conference on Calorimetry in Particle Physics, CALOR* 2000, Annecy France (2000).

[163] S. Amato et al., *Analysis of the $B_s^0 \to \mu^+\mu^-$ decay with the reoptimized LHCb detector*, Note LHCb-2003-165, http://cdsweb.cern.ch/record/726431.

[164] LHCb collaboration, *LHCb muon system technical design report*, CERN-LHCC-2001-010, http://cdsweb.cern.ch/record/504326.

[165] LHCb collaboration, *LHCb addendum to the muon system technical design report*, CERN-LHCC-2003-002, http://cdsweb.cern.ch/record/600536.

[166] LHCb collaboration, *LHCb second addendum to the muon system technical design report*, CERN-LHCC-2005-012, http://cdsweb.cern.ch/record/831955.

[167] G. Martellotti, R. Santacesaria and A. Satta, *Muon system digitization*, Note LHCb-2004-063, http://cdsweb.cern.ch/record/784561.

[168] R. Santacesaria and A. Satta, *A new calculation of the low energy background in the muon system*, Note LHCb-2003-057, http://cdsweb.cern.ch/record/684464.

[169] G. Martellotti, R. Santacesaria and A. Satta, *Particle rates in the LHCb muon detector*, Note LHCb-2005-075, http://cdsweb.cern.ch/record/896904.

[170] B. Bochin et al., *Wire pad chamber for LHCb muon system*, Note LHCb-2000-003, http://cdsweb.cern.ch/record/681334.

[171] B. Bochin et al., *Beam tests of WPC-7 prototype of wire pad chambers for the LHCb muon system*, Note LHCb-2000-102, http://cdsweb.cern.ch/record/691718.

[172] D. Hutchcroft et al., *Results obtained with the first four gap MWPC prototype chamber*, Note LHCb-2001-024, http://cdsweb.cern.ch/record/691631.

[173] B. Bochin et al., *Test results of a full size prototype of the muon chambers for region M2/R4 of the LHCb muon system*, Note LHCb-2002-025, http://cdsweb.cern.ch/record/681216.

[174] B. Maréchal et al., *Construction and test of the prototype chamber for region 1 of the LHCb muon station 2*, Note LHCb-2002-034, http://cdsweb.cern.ch/record/691482.

[175] M. Anelli et al., *Test of MWPC prototypes for R3 of the LHCb muon system*, Note LHCb-2004-074, http://cdsweb.cern.ch/record/793160.

[176] G. Lanfranchi, *Time resolution and aging properties of the MWPCs for the LHCb muon system*, Nucl. Instrum. Meth. **A 535** (2004) 221.

[177] E. Danè et al., *Detailed study of the gain of the MWPCs for the LHCb muon system*, Nucl. Instrum. Meth. **A 572** (2007) 682.

[178] A. Kachtchouk et al., *Performance study of a MWPC prototype for the LHCb muon system with the ASDQ chip*, Note LHCb-2000-062, http://cdsweb.cern.ch/record/681340.

[179] W. Riegler, *Detector physics and performance: simulation of the MWPCs for the full LHCb muon system*, Note LHCb-2000-060, http://cdsweb.cern.ch/record/681186.

[180] R. Veenhof, *Garfield — simulation of gaseous detectors*, http://consult.cern.ch/writeup/garfield/.

[181] I. Smirnov, *Heed: interactions of particles with gases*, http://consult.cern.ch/writeup/heed/.

[182] S. Biagi, *Magboltz: transport of electrons in gas mixtures*, http://consult.cern.ch/writeup/magboltz/.

[183] A. Kachtchouk et al., *Design and construction of the wire chambers for the LHCb muon system*, Note LHCb-2001-026, http://cdsweb.cern.ch/record/684460.

[184] M. Anelli et al., *Quality tests of the LHCb muon chambers at the LNF production site*, *IEEE Trans. Nucl. Sci.* **53** (2006) 330.

[185] A.F. Barbosa et al., *Production and quality control of MWPC for the LHCb muon system at CERN*, *IEEE Trans. Nucl. Sci.* **53** (2006) 336.

[186] E. Dané, D. Pinci and A. Sarti, *Results of the quality controls of the four-gap MWPCs produced at LNF for LHCb*, *IEEE Trans. Nucl. Sci.* **54** (2007) 354.

[187] P. Ciambrone et al., *Automated wire tension measurement system for LHCb muon chambers*, *Nucl. Instrum. Meth.* **A 545** (2005) 156.

[188] W. Baldini et al., *A laser based instrument for MWPC wire tension measurement*, Note LHCb-2007-120, http://cdsweb.cern.ch/record/1055333.

[189] A. Alves et al., *Results of the MWPC gas gain uniformity test performed at CERN*, Note LHCb-2007-115, http://cdsweb.cern.ch/record/1054084.

[190] S. Agosteo et al., *A facility for the test of large-area muon chambers at high rates*, *Nucl. Instrum. Meth.* **A 452** (2000) 94.

[191] V. Souvorov et al., *First results of an aging test of a full scale MWPC prototype for the LHCb muon system*, *Nucl. Instrum. Meth.* **A 515** (2003) 220.

[192] M. Anelli et al., *Extensive ageing test of two prototypes of four-gap MWPC for the LHCb muon system*, Note LHCb-2004-029, http://cdsweb.cern.ch/record/733605.

[193] F. Sauli, *GEM: a new concept for electron amplification in gas detectors*, *Nucl. Instrum. Meth.* **A 386** (1997) 531.

[194] G. Bencivenni et al., *Advances in triple-GEM detector operation for high-rate particle triggering*, *Nucl. Instrum. Meth.* **A 513** (2003) 264.

[195] M. Alfonsi et al., *Advances in fast multi-GEM-based detector operation for high-rate charged-particle triggering*, *IEEE Trans. Nucl. Sci.* **51** (2004) 2135.

[196] A. Bressan et al., *Beam tests of the gas electron multiplier*, *Nucl. Instrum. Meth.* **A 425** (1999) 262.

[197] M. Alfonsi et al., *Studies of etching effects on triple-GEM detectors operated with CF/sub 4/-based gas mixtures*, *IEEE Trans. Nucl. Sci.* **52** (2005) 2872.

[198] M. Alfonsi et al., *Aging measurements on triple-GEM detectors operated with CF_4 based gas mixtures*, *Nucl. Phys.* **B 150** *(Proc. Suppl.)* (2006) 159.

[199] W. Bonivento, D. Marras and G. Auriemma, *Production of the front-end boards of the LHCb muon system*, Note LHCb-2007-150, http://cdsweb.cern.ch/record/1079951.

[200] D. Moraes et al., *CARIOCA 0.25 μm CMOS fast binary front-end for sensor interface using a novel current-mode feedback technique, , IEEE Proc. Int. Symp. Circuits Syst.* **1** (2001) 360.

[201] W. Bonivento et al., *Status of the CARIOCA project*, in *Proceedings of the 7th workshop on electronics for LHC experiments*, Stockholm Sweden (2001), http://lhc-electronics-workshop.web.cern.ch/LHC-electronics-workshop/2001/muon/moraesboniv.pdf.

[202] W. Bonivento, *Design and performance of the front-end electronics of the LHCb muon detector*, in *Proceedings of the 11th workshop on electronics for LHC and future experiments*, Heidelberg Germany (2005), http://www.lecc2005.uni-hd.de/.

[203] S. Cadeddu, C. Deplano and A. Lai, *The DIALOG chip in the front-end electronics of the LHCb muon detector, IEEE Trans. Nucl. Sci.* **52** (2005) 2726.

[204] S. Cadeddu et al., *DIALOG and SYNC: a VLSI chip set for timing of the LHCb muon detector, IEEE Trans. Nucl. Sci.* **51** (2004) 1961.

[205] V. Bocci et al., *The services boards system for the LHCb muon detector (equalization, timing and monitoring of the 120k front end channels in the LHCb muon detector), IEEE Nucl. Sci. Symp. Conf. Rec.* **3** (2007) 2134.

[206] Technical documentation on the ELMB can be found at *Embedded Local Monitor Board home page*, http://elmb.web.cern.ch/ELMB/ELMBhome.html.

[207] G. Felici et al., *The L0 Off Detector Electronics (ODE) for the LHCb muon spectrometer*, in *Proceedings of the 10th Workshop on Electronics for LHC and future experiments*, Boston U.S.A. (2004), http://lhc-workshop-2004.web.cern.ch/lhc-workshop-2004/.

[208] P. Moreira, *QPLL manual v. 1.1*, http://proj-qpll.web.cern.ch/proj-qpll/images/qpllManual.pdf, (2005).

[209] P. Moreira et al., *A radiation tolerant gigabit serializer for LHC data transmission*, in *Proceedings of the 7th Workshop on Electronics for LHC Experiments*, Stockholm Sweden (2001), http://lhc-electronics-workshop.web.cern.ch/LHC-electronics-workshop/2001/opto/Moreira.pdf.

[210] G. Corradi et al., *A novel high-voltage system for a triple GEM detector, Nucl. Instrum. Meth.* **A 572** (2007) 96.

[211] G. Sabatino et al., *Cluster size measurements for the LHCb muon system M5R4 MWPCs using cosmic rays*, Note LHCb-2006-011, http://cdsweb.cern.ch/record/939097.

[212] S. de Capua et al., *Study of gas gain uniformity for the LHCb muon system MWPCs using cosmic rays*, Note LHCb-2006-010, http://cdsweb.cern.ch/record/939085.

[213] M. Anelli et al., *Test of a MPWC for the LHCb muon system at the GIF at CERN*, Note LHCb-2005-003, http://cdsweb.cern.ch/record/815058.

2008 JINST 3 S08005

[214] LHCb collaboration, R. Antunes-Nobrega et al., *LHCb trigger system technical design report*, CERN-LHCC-2003-031, http://cdsweb.cern.ch/record/630828.

[215] E. Aslanides et al., *The level-0 muon trigger for the LHCb experiment*, *Nucl. Instrum. Meth.* **A 579** (2007) 989.

[216] M. Krasowski et al., *Primary vertex reconstruction*, Note LHCb-2007-011, http://cdsweb.cern.ch/record/1057577.

[217] LHCb collaboration, P.R. Barbosa-Marinho et al., *LHCb online system technical design report*, CERN-LHCC-2001-040, http://cdsweb.cern.ch/record/545306.

[218] LHCb collaboration, *Addendum to the LHCb online system technical design report*, CERN-LHCC-2005-039, http://cdsweb.cern.ch/record/903611.

[219] RD12 collaboration, *Timing, Trigger and Control (TTC) systems for the LHC*, http://ttc.web.cern.ch/TTC/ and links therein.

[220] T. Sjöstrand et al., *High-energy physics event generation with PYTHIA 6.1*, *Comput. Phys. Commun.* **135** (2001) 238 [hep-ph/0010017].

[221] *GEANT detector description and simulation tool*, CERN Program Library long writeup W5013 (1994).

[222] J. van Tilburg, *Matching VELO tracks with seeding tracks*, Note LHCb-2001-103, http://cdsweb.cern.ch/record/691686;
R. Forty, *Track seeding*, Note LHCb-2001-109, http://cdsweb.cern.ch/record/691473;
R. Hierck, *Track following in LHCb*, Note LHCb-2001-112, http://cdsweb.cern.ch/record/691752;
M. Benayoun and O. Callot, *The forward tracking, an optical model method*, Note LHCb-2002-008, http://cdsweb.cern.ch/record/684710;
Y. Xie, *Short track reconstruction with VELO and TT*, Note LHCb-2003-100, http://cdsweb.cern.ch/record/684462;
O. Callot, M. Kucharczyk and M. Witek, *VELO-TT track reconstruction*, Note LHCb-2007-010, http://cdsweb.cern.ch/record/1027834;
D. Hutchcroft et al., *VELO pattern recognition*, Note LHCb-2007-013, http://cdsweb.cern.ch/record/1023540;
O. Callot and S. Hansmann-Menzemer, *Performance of the forward tracking*, Note LHCb-2007-015, http://cdsweb.cern.ch/record/1033584;
R. Forty and M. Needham, *Updated performance of the T-seeding*, Note LHCb-2007-023, http://cdsweb.cern.ch/record/1023581;
O. Callot, *Downstream pattern recognition*, Note LHCb-2007-026, http://cdsweb.cern.ch/record/1025827;
M. Needham, *Performance of the track matching*, Note LHCb-2007-129, http://cdsweb.cern.ch/record/1060807; *Performance of the LHCb track reconstruction software*, Note LHCb-2007-144, http://cdsweb.cern.ch/record/1080556.

2008 JINST 3 S08005

[223] R. Hierck et al., *Performance of the LHCb OO track-fitting software*, Note LHCb-2000-086, http://cdsweb.cern.ch/record/684697;
E. Rodrigues, *The LHCb track Kalman fit*, Note LHCb-2007-014;
E. Bos et al., *The trajectory model for track fitting and alignment*, Note LHCb-2007-008, http://cdsweb.cern.ch/record/1025826.

[224] R. Forty and O. Schneider, *RICH pattern recognition*, Note LHCb-98-040, http://cdsweb.cern.ch/record/684714.

[225] R. Muresan, *Cherenkov ring reconstruction methods*, Note LHCb-2007-121, http://cdsweb.cern.ch/record/1057872.

[226] J.R.T. de Mello Neto and M. Gandelman, *Muon ID performance with the reoptimized LHCb detector*, Note LHCb-2003-089, http://cdsweb.cern.ch/record/691744;
M. Gandelman and E. Polycarpo, *The performance of the LHCb muon identification procedure*, Note LHCb-2007-145, http://cdsweb.cern.ch/record/1093941.

[227] H. Terrier and I. Belyaev, *Particle identification with LHCb calorimeters*, Note LHCb-2003-092, http://cdsweb.cern.ch/record/691743.

[228] V. Breton, N. Brun and P. Perret, *A clustering algorithm for the LHCb electromagnetic calorimeter using cellular automaton*, Note LHCb-2001-123, http://cdsweb.cern.ch/record/681262.

[229] O. Deschamps et al., *Photon and neutral pion reconstruction*, Note LHCb-2003-091, http://cdsweb.cern.ch/record/691634.

2008 JINST 3 S08005

PUBLISHED BY INSTITUTE OF PHYSICS PUBLISHING AND SISSA

RECEIVED: *April 11, 2008*
ACCEPTED: *July 10, 2008*
PUBLISHED: *August 14, 2008*

THE CERN LARGE HADRON COLLIDER: ACCELERATOR AND EXPERIMENTS

The LHCf detector at the CERN Large Hadron Collider

The LHCf Collaboration

ABSTRACT: LHCf is an experiment dedicated to the measurement of neutral particles emitted in the very forward region of LHC collisions. The physics goal is to provide data for calibrating the hadron interaction models that are used in the study of Extremely High-Energy Cosmic-Rays. This is possible since the laboratory equivalent collision energy of LHC is 10^{17} eV. Two LHCf detectors, consisting of imaging calorimeters made of tungsten plates, plastic scintillator and position sensitive sensors, are installed at zero degree collision angle ± 140 m from an interaction point (IP). Although the lateral dimensions of these calorimeters are very compact, ranging from $20\,\text{mm} \times 20\,\text{mm}$ to $40\,\text{mm} \times 40\,\text{mm}$, the energy resolution is expected to be better than 6% and the position resolution better than 0.2 mm for γ-rays with energy from 100 GeV to 7 TeV. This has been confirmed by test beam results at the CERN SPS. These calorimeters can measure particles emitted in the pseudo rapidity range $\eta > 8.4$. Detectors, data acquisition and electronics are optimized to operate during the early phase of the LHC commissioning with luminosity below $10^{30}\,\text{cm}^{-2}\text{s}^{-1}$. LHCf is expected to obtain data to compare with the major hadron interaction models within a week or so of operation at luminosity $\sim 10^{29}\,\text{cm}^{-2}\text{s}^{-1}$. After ~ 10 days of operation at luminosity $\sim 10^{29}\,\text{cm}^{-2}\text{s}^{-1}$, the light output of the plastic scintillators is expected to degrade by $\sim 10\%$ due to radiation damage. This degradation will be monitored and corrected for using calibration pulses from a laser.

KEYWORDS: Photon detectors for UV, visible and IR photons; Scintillators, scintillation and light emission processes; Solid state detectors; Calorimeters; Gamma detectors; Particle identification methods; Particle tracking detectors; Photon detectors for UV, visible and IR photons; Gamma detectors; Particle detectors; Radiation damage to detector materials; Data acquisition concepts; Detector control systems; Front-end electronics for detector readout; Trigger concepts and systems; Analysis and statistical methods; Pattern recognition, cluster finding, calibration and fitting methods; Simulation methods and programs; Scintillators and scintillating fibers and light guides; Detector alignment and calibration methods; Overall mechanics design.

2008 JINST 3 S08006

The LHCf Collaboration

O. Adriani,[a] L. Bonechi,[a] M. Bongi,[b] G. Castellini,[c] R. D'Alessandro,[a] D.A. Faus,[d] K. Fukui,[e]
M. Grandi,[b] M. Haguenauer,[f] Y. Itow,[e] K. Kasahara,[g] D. Macina,[h] T. Mase,[e] K. Masuda,[e]
Y. Matsubara,[e] H. Menjo,[e] M. Mizuishi,[g] Y. Muraki,[i] P. Papini,[b] A.L. Perrot,[h] S. Ricciarini,[b]
T. Sako,[e] Y. Shimizu,[g] K. Taki,[e] T. Tamura,[j] S. Torii,[g] A. Tricomi,[k] W.C. Turner,[l] J. Velasco,[d]
A. Viciani,[b] H. Watanabe[e] and K. Yoshida[m]

[a]Università degli Studi di Firenze and INFN Sezione di Firenze, Firenze, Italy
[b]INFN Sezione di Firenze, Firenze, Italy
[c]IFAC CNR and INFN Sezione di Firenze, Firenze, Italy
[d]IFIC, Centro Mixto CSIC-UVEG, Valencia, Spain
[e]Solar-Terrestrial Environment laboratory, Nagoya University, Nagoya, Japan
[f]Ecole-Polytechnique, Paris, France
[g]Research Institute for Science and Engineering, Waseda University, Tokyo, Japan
[h]CERN, Geneva, Switzerland
[i]Konan University, Kobe, Japan
[j]Kanagawa University, Yokohama, Japan
[k]Università degli Studi di Catania and INFN Sezione di Catania, Catania, Italy
[l]LBNL, Berkeley, California, USA
[m]Shibaura Institute of Technology, Saitama, Japan

Corresponding authors:
Daniela Macina (Daniela.Macina@cern.ch) and Yoshitaka Itow (itow@stelab.nagoya-u.ac.jp)

2008 JINST 3 S08006

Contents

2008 JINST 3 S08006

Chapter 1

Introduction

1.1 Physics of the LHCf experiment

Research on the highest energy cosmic-rays (energy above 10^{19} eV) has great scientific interest since their origin, propagation and interactions are unknown and may yield information about new physics. To give an idea of the type of information available we briefly summarize the situations with the spectrum and composition of the highest energy cosmic rays and then describe how the LHCf experiment can make a contribution to this field.

Ten years have passed since the air shower experiment AGASA reported that the cosmic ray spectrum at the highest energy may extend beyond 10^{20} eV and the GZK cut-off might not exist [1]. If this were true, the origin of the highest energy cosmic-rays would need an exotic explanation like the decay of cosmic strings or Z_0 bursts [2] and so on. However another result obtained by the HiRes experiment was consistent with the existence of the GZK cut-off [3]. The AGASA experiment used a large array of surface detectors whereas the HiRes experiment employed a novel calorimetric technique utilizing observation of atmospheric fluorescence. Recently new results have been published by the Auger collaboration at the international cosmic-ray conference ICRC07 [4]. Auger employs a combination of surface detectors and atmospheric fluorescence telescopes and the new results support the existence of the GZK cut-off. The results of these three experiments are shown in figure 1.1. If the energy scale of the AGASA results were reduced by 45% then their results would be in agreement with the others.

Measurement of the chemical composition of the highest energy cosmic rays can also give important information about where they are produced. Several astronomical candidates for the production of the highest energy cosmic rays have been discussed in the literature and the maximum energy obtained depends on the composition to be accelerated. The highest energy cosmic-rays can travel through nearby inter-galactic space almost without deviation by magnetic fields. Auger has reported that the arrival direction of the highest energy events is correlated with the distribution of active galactic nuclei (AGN) [5]. This naturally suggests that the primaries are most likely protons. However composition measurements reported by Auger indicate that the primary composition is a mixture of protons and heavy nuclei (Fe) up to the highest energy where they so far have sufficient statistics for composition analysis - 4×10^{19} eV [6].

2008 JINST 3 S08006

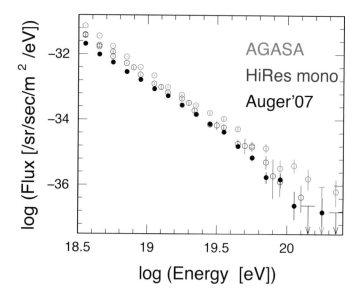

Figure 1.1: Energy spectra of primary cosmic-rays obtained by three large experiments. The red, blue and black points represent the result of AGASA, HiRes and Auger, respectively.

If it turns out that the highest energy primaries have significant Fe composition then the "GZK-cut off"-like feature could perhaps be interpreted as photo-dissociation by cosmic microwave background (CMB) photons. Further investigations are needed for a consistent understanding of all measurements.

It is well known that understanding the results of cosmic ray experiments depends strongly on the use of Monte Carlo codes. However the hadronic interaction models used in these codes have not been verified experimentally near the GZK energy region 10^{20} eV which is 6 orders of magnitude higher than the laboratory equivalent energy of the $Sp\bar{p}S$ or Tevatron. The perturbative QCD models used for simulation of air shower experiments are essentially phenomenological models calibrated with experimental data where they are available. So far only data from the UA7 experiment taken at the $Sp\bar{p}S$ have been available for calibration of the forward neutral pion production spectrum at 10^{14} eV [9]. The 14 TeV center of momentum energy of the Large Hadron Collider (LHC) will push the laboratory equivalent collision energy up to 10^{17} eV.

There are two key quantities at the primary interaction vertices which determine the development of air showers; the total inelastic cross section and the particle production energy spectra at very forward angles. The former will be measured at LHC with roman pot detectors such as employed by the TOTEM [7] or ATLAS collaborations [8]. Therefore a new measurement on forward production spectra in LHC is strongly desired to calibrate the models at 10^{17} eV. LHCf is an experiment to perform a measurement of the very forward production cross sections and energy spectra of neutral pions and neutrons. Measurement will be done in a short period during the early phase of the LHC commissioning before the luminosity reaches 10^{30} cm^{-2}s^{-1}. In this paper, an overview of the LHCf instrumentation is given. Previous study of the prototype detectors is found elsewhere [10]. After providing an outline of the LHCf experiment in section 1.2, the details of the detectors and the data acquisition system will be described in section 2 and section 3, respectively. In section 4, simulation studies of the expected performance during the LHC operation and the first results from beam tests performed in 2007 at the CERN SPS are reported.

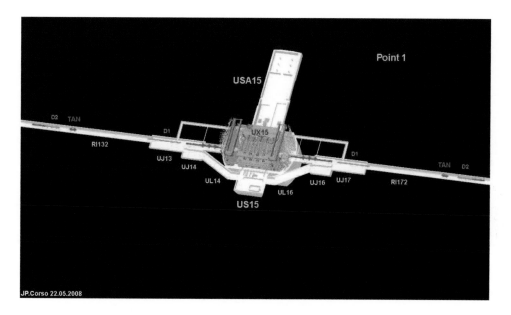

Figure 1.2: Geometry of the IP1 area of LHC. The structure seen in the center represents the ATLAS detector surrounding the interaction point. The straight line from top-left to bottom-right indicates the long straight section of the LHC tunnel and the LHCf detectors are installed at the places marked 'TAN' at both sides of IP1.

1.2 Experimental overview

The LHC has massive zero degree neutral absorbers (Target Neutral Absorber; TAN) located ± 140 m from interaction points (IP) 1 and 5 in order to protect the outer superconducting beam separation dipoles (D2) from neutral particle debris from the IP (figure 1.2, figure 1.3). Charged particles from the IP are swept aside by the inner beam separation dipole D1 before reaching the TAN. Inside TAN the beam vacuum chamber makes a Y shaped transition from a single common beam tube facing the IP to two separate beam tubes joining to the arcs of LHC. The Y-chamber has been carefully machined to have a uniform one radiation length projected thickness over a $100\,\text{mm} \times 100\,\text{mm}$ square centered on the zero degree crossing angle beamline. In the crotch of this "Y-chamber", just behind the $100\,\text{mm} \times 100\,\text{mm}$ square there is an instrumentation slot of $96\,\text{mm}^w \times 607\,\text{mm}^h \times 1000\,\text{mm}^l$ extending from 67 mm below the beam height to the top of the TAN. The aperture for the LHCf measurements is limited by the width of the slot and by the vertical aperture of the beam pipe in the D1 dipole projected to the TAN. The cross sections of the D1 beam pipe projected to the detector plane and of the instrumentation slot of the TAN are drawn in figure 1.4. This unique location covers the pseudo-rapidity range from 8.4 to infinity.

The LHCf detectors are two independent shower calorimeters inserted in the TAN instrumentation slots on both sides of IP1. Each occupies a 300 mm length in the most upstream position of the instrumentation slots followed by BRAN luminosity monitors 100 mm in length [12] and finally the ATLAS ZDCs [11]. Both the LHCf detectors consist of a pair of small sampling and imaging calorimeters made of plastic scintillators interleaved with tungsten converters. Position sensitive layers are inserted in order to provide incident shower positions. The two detectors are similar, but use different techniques and geometry for the purposes of redundancy and consistency checks of

2008 JINST 3 S08006

Figure 1.3: Photo of the TAN absorber located 140 m from the IP. Left: TAN fully assembled in the LHC tunnel seen from the IP side. Right: TAN during assembly at CERN seen from the top facing the IP. The 96 mm gap between the two beam pipes allows space for installation of detectors.

the measurements. In addition, coincidence between these detectors may be useful for rejection of background due to beam-gas interactions and for application to diffractive physics. The calorimeters are designed to have energy and position resolutions better than 5% and 0.2 mm, respectively. With such properties, the experiment will be able to discriminate between the major interaction models used in cosmic-ray studies, or to construct new models. In this paper, the detector installed in LSS1L (Arm 1; IP8 side) is referred as detector 1 and the detector installed in LSS1R (Arm 2; IP2 side) is referred as detector 2. Standing inside the LHC ring and looking at IP1, detector 1 is on the left and detector 2 is on the right.

Both detectors are supported by manipulators mounted to the top surface of the TAN in order to have the capability of remotely moving the detectors vertically by a 120 mm stroke. Figure 1.4 shows the geometrical configuration of each detector viewed from IP1. In default setting, the center of the smaller calorimeters is placed on the horizontal midplane. Using the manipulators to move the detectors vertically from their default positions increases the range of P_T that can be measured. The P_T range would be further increased by operation with a non-zero beam crossing angle of 140 μrad, because the center of neutral particle flux moves downward. The geometry of detector 2 is designed to maximize the P_T coverage without scanning and/or employing a finite crossing angle. In front of each detector, a Front Counter (FC) made of plastic scintillators is inserted. They provide useful trigger information by covering a larger aperture than the calorimeters.

With these detectors we will be able to identify γ-rays, measure the γ-ray energy spectrum (>100 GeV) with a few per cent energy resolution, measure the γ-ray incident position and reconstruct the γ-ray pair invariant mass distribution that shows a clear peak at the neutral pion mass. Hadron showers of high energy neutrons at zero degrees can be also measured, however, with decreased energy resolution of about 30%.

LHCf is not designed to be a radiation hard detector and so will be removed when the LHC luminosity exceeds 10^{30} cm^{-2}s^{-1}. Owing to the limitations imposed by radiation and the configuration of the DAQ, data taking of LHCf is planed for the 43 bunch operation and 10^{10} protons per

2008 JINST 3 S08006

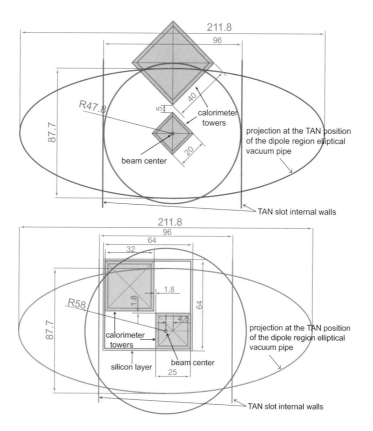

Figure 1.4: Cross sections of detector 1 (top) and detector 2 (bottom). Grey squares indicate the calorimeters in the detectors while a green square shows the coverage of the silicon strip sensor. Vertical and elliptical blue lines indicate the physical aperture limited by the walls of the TAN and the beam pipe, respectively.

bunch which are foreseen at the very beginning of LHC commissioning. At this low intensity and luminosity (10^{29} cm^{-2}s^{-1}) a few minutes of data taking can provide enough statistics to discriminate between hadron interaction models. After a week or so of operation it is anticipated that the LHCf detector will be removed from TAN during a brief machine stop. In the absence of LHCf three Cu bars (each 94 mm^w × 605 mm^h ×99 mm^l) will occupy the region in front of the BRAN. The purpose of the Cu bars is to generate showers for detection by the BRAN as well as to provide shielding for the downstream D2 magnets. The LHCf calorimeters and the Cu bars have nearly the same length in nuclear interaction lengths so the BRAN signals will be very similar for operation with LHCf and with the Cu bars.

2008 JINST 3 S08006

Chapter 2

The detectors

2.1 Detector overview

Both LHCf detectors employ two imaging shower calorimeters. While the structure of the calorimeters is similar (except for their sizes and orientation), the position sensitive sensors are quite different. Detector 1 uses scintillating fibers (SciFi) and Multi-anode PMTs (MAPMTs), while detector 2 uses silicon strip sensors. Four X-Y pairs of the position sensors are installed at 6, 10, 30 and 42 X_0 for detector 1 and 6, 12, 30 and 42 X_0 for detector 2. The first two pairs are optimized to detect the shower maximum of gamma-ray induced showers and the other two are for hadronic showers developed deep in the calorimeters. These position sensitive sensors are necessary not only to obtain the transverse momentum of the incident primary but also to correct for the effect of leakage from the edges of the calorimeters. Because the fraction of shower leakage with respect to the total energy is only a function of the position and independent of the energy, we can correct for this effect by measuring the position of the shower. Details of the shower leakage correction are found elsewhere [10].

Calorimeter components (scintillator, tungsten and PMT), position sensors and their front-end electronics are packed in a $92\,\text{mm}^w \times 620\,\text{mm}^h \times 280\,\text{mm}^l$ aluminum box for each detector as shown in figure 2.1, 2.2, 2.3. The size is designed to fit the narrow instrumentation slot in the TAN. One wall of the box for detector 2 is made of copper to better dissipate the heat generated by the front-end circuitry for the silicon strips. The detectors in their boxes are attached to and supported by the manipulators. In front of each detector (facing the IP), a counter composed of thin plastic scintillators called the Front Counter (FC) is installed.

2.2 Calorimeter

The longitudinal (along the beam direction) structure of the calorimeter is shown in figure 2.4. Each calorimeter consists of 16 layers of tungsten plates interleaved with 3 mm thick plastic scintillators (Eljen Technology EJ-260) for measuring the deposited energy. The thickness of the tungsten plates is 7 mm for the first 11 layers and 14 mm for the rest. Including the position sensors the total length is 220 mm. In units of radiation and hadron interaction lengths the total length of a calorimeter is 44 X_0 and 1.7 λ, respectively. Most of the tungsten layers are attached to holders made of G10

2008 JINST 3 S08006

Figure 2.1: Photo of detector 1 (left) and detector 2 (right).

while the holders near the silicon layers are made of Delrin. All the layers are stacked together and pinned in position with two G10 rods. The transverse sizes of the calorimeters are 20 mm×20 mm and 40 mm×40 mm for detector 1 and 25 mm×25 mm and 32 mm×32 mm for detector 2. The cross sections of two detectors are shown in figure 1.4. Because of the small Moliere radius of tungsten (9 mm), electro-magnetic showers are well contained even for such small calorimeters. In addition the incident position provided by the position sensitive layers is used to correct for shower-leakage.

Each plastic scintillator is viewed by an acrylic light guide and then read out by a PMT (HAMAMATSU R7400U) through 1 mm diameter optical fibers. The signals from the PMTs are amplified by pre-amplifiers installed on the top of the TAN (amplification factor = 4.8) and sent to the counting room (USA15) through 200 m coaxial cables. Because of the light guide geometry, scintillation light is not collected uniformly over the area of a scintillator. The position dependence of light yield has been measured for each scintillator light-guide combination before detector assembly. The light yield from the scintillators was measured on a 4 mm×4 mm grid with a ^{90}Sr β-ray source through a 2 mm diameter collimator. An example of the measured non-uniformity of light yield is shown in figure 2.5. The correction of this non-uniformity was also checked with muons in a test beam at the SPS. Typical non-uniformity is about ±10%, and is corrected in further analysis as described in section 4.2.1.

The coaxial cable of 50 Ω impedance (C-50-3-1) has a delay of 4.23 ns/m and attenuates the pulse height from the amplifiers by a factor of 5 but transfers 90% of the total charge. To obtain linearity over a wide dynamic range, the combination of scintillator and PMT have been carefully chosen. The scintillator has a long decay time (9.4 nsec) to reduce the peak current in the PMT. Also the bias resistor network of the PMT was optimized to assure a good linear response over a wide dynamic range.

2008 JINST 3 S08006

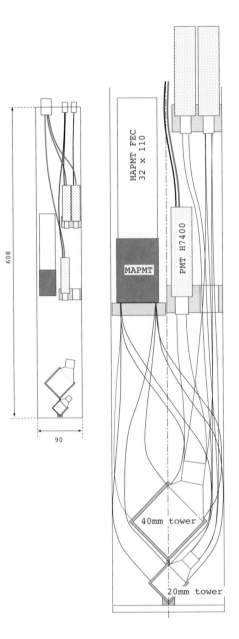

Figure 2.2: Front cut-away view of detector 1 showing the structure of the calorimeters, flexible light guide fibers, PMTs, MAPMTs front-end circuit box and inner cabling. The right figure is an enlarged view of the left one.

The linearity of the system is measured using a fast nitrogen laser (USHO KEN-1020; emission wavelength at 337 nm). Because the nitrogen laser directly excites the wavelength shifter in the scintillator with a 0.3 nsec pulse, the time profile of the scintillation light is nearly the same as that excited by a charged particle. Figure 2.6 shows the typical linearity of the PMT response with different bias HV. The modified PMT shows good linearity with a typical HV of 400 V while a single minimum ionizing particle (MIP) can be detected with about 1000 V HV.

These linearity curves have been measured for all PMT's for various values of bias HV. At typical operating HV, the linearity was checked for all the PMT's by changing the intensity of the

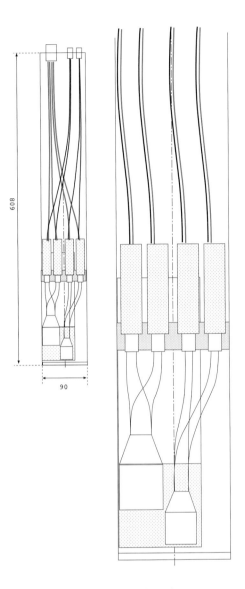

Figure 2.3: Front cut-away view of detector 2 showing the structure of the calorimeters, flexible light guide fibers, PMTs, silicon layers, their front-end circuit boards and inner cabling. The right figure is an enlarged view of the left one.

fast nitrogen laser precisely with a variety of neutral density (ND) filters. Figure 2.7 shows an example of the linearity of the PMT response. Here the horizontal axis indicates the nitrogen laser intensity in units of the equivalent number of shower particles (MIPs) detected at a layer. The vertical axis is the output of the PMT. Thus all the PMTs were checked to assure good linearity (<5% deviation) for incident light intensity varying from that corresponding to 1 MIP up to the 10^5 MIPs expected at the shower maximum of a 10 TeV γ-ray.

In order to monitor and correct for time variation of gain or radiation damage to the scintillators, a fast nitrogen laser will be installed in USA15 for periodically illuminating each scintillator through 200 m bundles of quartz fibers. Pulse to pulse variation of laser intensity is about 20% and will be monitored during the run by two dedicated PMTs at USA15.

2008 JINST 3 S08006

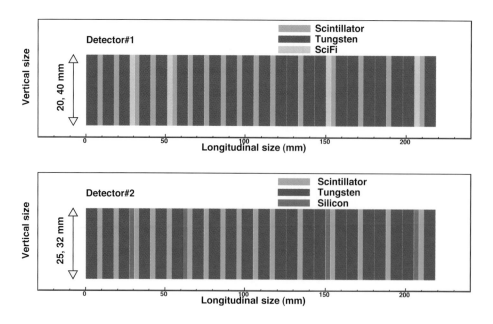

Figure 2.4: Longitudinal structure of detector 1 (top) and detector 2 (bottom); grey, light blue, orange and red indicate the layers of tungsten, plastic scintillator, SciFi and silicon strip sensor, respectively.

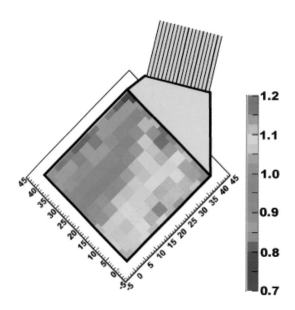

Figure 2.5: Position dependence of the light yield in a plastic scintillator. Color scale indicates relative signal intensity generated by β-rays.

2.3 SciFi and MAPMT

The position sensor of detector 1 is composed of 4 X-Y pairs of SciFi belts (KURARAY SCSF-38). A SciFi belt consists of 20 (40) SciFi's in a single hodoscope plane for the 20 mm (40 mm)

2008 JINST 3 S08006

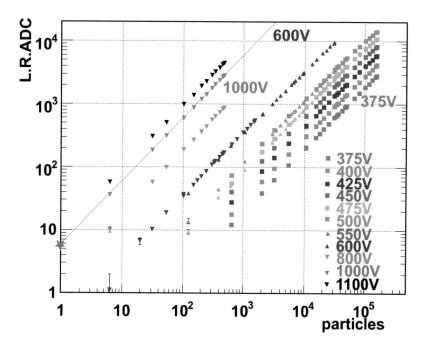

Figure 2.6: Linearity of scintillator and PMT excited by a nitrogen laser. Horizontal axis is the incident laser intensity in units of equivalent MIPs and vertical axis is AD count of the PMT output (1 AD count corresponds to 0.025 pC). Results are given for PMT HV bias from 375V to 1100V.

calorimeter. Each SciFi has 1 mm square cross-section. The SciFi belts are painted with white acrylic water paint to improve light collection efficiency, to reduce cross talk between SciFi's, and to fix the SciFi's in a plane. Because fixing the SciFi's with paint is not very strong, both surfaces of a SciFi belt are covered with kapton tape. Hodoscope planes of the 20 mm and 40 mm calorimeters that are inserted in the same layer are glued on the acrylic frame (figure 2.8) and pinned together with the scintillator and tungsten layers with G10 rods. The total number of SciFi channels is 480. Each SciFi is connected channel by channel with optical cement to a clear round fiber of 1 mm diameter. The clear fiber is attached as a light guide to one of 64 anodes of a MAPMT (HAMAMATSU H7546). The SciFi photon yield of a single MIP corresponds to more than 5 photo electrons. We need 8 MAPMTs to read out 480 channels of SciFi's, so the total number of channels of the 8 MAPMTs (512) exceeds that of the SciFi's.

2.4 Silicon strip detector

The position sensor of detector 2 is composed of 4 planes of microstrip silicon sensors. Each plane consists of 2 single-sided sensors, identical to those used by the ATLAS experiment for the barrel part of the Semi-Conductor Tracker (SCT) [13] , which are used for the measurement of two orthogonal coordinates. These silicon sensors have 64 mm × 64 mm total surface area, which is enough to cover the entire cross section of the calorimeter, and are produced on a 285 μm thick n-type wafer. A sequence of 768 p+ microstrips with 80 μm pitch is implanted on the junction side. The PACE3 chip, a 32 ch device designed to work with the LHC 40 MHz clock and produced for the

2008 JINST 3 S08006

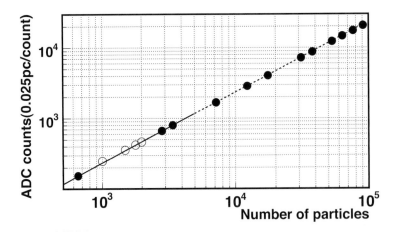

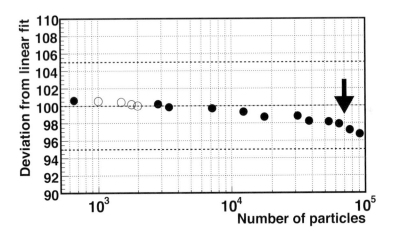

Figure 2.7: Linearity and dynamic range for one of the PMTs at nominal HV. The filled circles show the result of the laser calibration while the open circles show the result of the beam test at SPS. Horizontal axis shows relative intensity of the laser light in units of the equivalent number of MIPs determined from the beam test. The mean number of shower particles at the 7 TeV γ-ray shower maximum is indicated by an arrow.

CMS Silicon Preshower Detector [14], has been chosen for the front-end read-out. With a properly adjusted working point, the chips have a high dynamic range (up to 600 MIPs with a maximum deviation from linearity of 6%). Due to the limited space inside the TAN and the small Moliere radius in tungsten, we decided to read out every other strip; the read-out pitch is hence 160 μm. In this way we have a total of 384 channels for each silicon sensor (12 PACE3 chips, housed on two printed circuit boards). The silicon sensor is glued on a thin fiberglass fan-out circuit that is also used to provide bias to the sensor through its backplane by means of a conducting glue [15]. Microstrips on the silicon sensors have been wire-bonded to the fan-out lines in the clean room of INFN-Florence. The front-end electronics are glued to dedicated kapton fan-out circuits, that in turn are wire-bonded to the boards and to the fiberglass circuit, as shown in figure 2.9. Each tracking layer is then glued on a 0.5 mm thick aluminum layer (used for mechanical support) and

Figure 2.8: Photo of the SciFi hodoscope glued on the acrylic frame. Left and right parts are single hodoscope planes of 40 mm and 20 mm calorimeters, respectively.

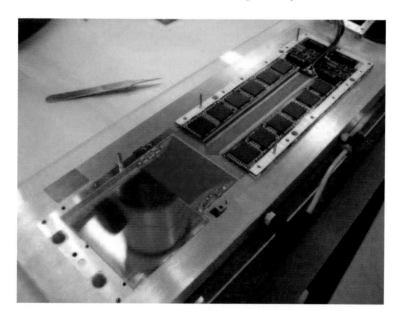

Figure 2.9: Photograph of a silicon layer during the assembly phase.

covered by a black Delrin frame on the silicon and by a 8.5 mm thick aluminum frame on the circuitry part. This metal frame is also used to extract the heat produced by the chips (silicon front-end circuits dissipate approximately 60 W in total) by means of a good thermal contact with the thick copper wall used in the detector package of detector 2.

2008 JINST 3 S08006

2.5 Manipulator

The manipulators move the detectors in the vertical direction in order to increase the range of P_T coverage as well as to retract the detectors from the beam line to avoid unnecessary radiation damage when data is not being taken. The manipulators can be operated remotely. Considering the limited access to the TAN area and its high radiation environment, the manipulators were designed to be as robust as possible to avoid any mechanical trouble during LHC operation. A DC motor is driven by DC power supplied from the control room. The movement direction is determined by the polarity of the power supply that is also switched in the control room. Two mechanical switches are installed at the top and bottom to limit the stroke.

The absolute position of the detector is measured by two methods. One is to use a linear optical encoder (Mutoh DS-25) with a precision of 25 μm. When the motor is driven with 15 V DC nominal voltage, the detector moves with a speed of 10 mm/min. During movement the encoder sends out two sequences of pulses with different phases. A counter installed in the counting room receives these pulses and gives the position of the detector. However, generally, optical encoders are known to be susceptible to radiation damage. Consequently a potentiometer has been prepared for a backup. The potentiometer (Mutoh RECTI P12) is simply a variable resistance with the sliding point moving with the detector. By measuring two variable resistances (R_1 and R_2) and calculating $P_{\text{pot}} = \frac{R_1}{R_1 + R_2}$, one can obtain a good position resolution. The use of a resistance ratio compensates for the possible effect of temperature change. To determine the resolution we compared the optical encoder value and P_{pot} measured at the same time for various positions. The rms deviation of the residual from a linear fit was 70 μm. This same result was obtained several times at intervals of one week.

2.6 Front counters

The FCs have a thickness of 8 mm and are inserted in front of detector 1 and detector 2. Two pairs of thin plastic scintillators (40 mm $\times$ 80 mm $\times$ 2.0 mm; Saint-Gobain Crystals BC404) are aligned in the vertical and horizontal directions to compose a double layer counter as shown in figure 2.10. Between the two layers, a copper plate of 0.5 mm thickness is inserted. Scintillation light outputs are sent through an acrylic light guide and optical fibers to four PMTs (HAMAMATSU H3164-10) placed outside of the TAN instrumentation slot. The PMT signals are sent to the counting room and recorded by ADCs. The signals are also sent to discriminators and may be used for an additional trigger information. The FC can be used to tag IP interactions with particles produced in both Arms with as wide an acceptance as possible for reducing background events produced by beam-gas interactions and beam-halo interactions with the beam pipe upstream of the TAN. The FC can also be used in anti-coincidence mode to ensure that neutral particles are being detected by the calorimeters and not charged particle background produced by beam-gas and beam-halo interactions. Using the segmented structure of the FC, we also expect a certain level of position measurement of incident particles.

2008 JINST 3 S08006

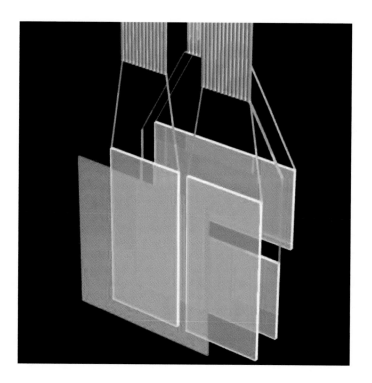

Figure 2.10: A schematic view of a front counter (FC). Two pairs of plastic scintillators segmented in vertical and horizontal directions are indicated by light blue rectangles. A copper plate of 0.5 mm thickness is inserted between the pairs. The scintillator light outputs are fed to PMTs via an acrylic light guide and optical fibers.

2008 JINST 3 S08006

Chapter 3

Trigger and DAQ electronics

3.1 Global flow of trigger and DAQ

Data acquisition is carried out in the ATLAS counting room (USA15). All the sequences are optimized for 43 bunch operation. A timing diagram of trigger and data acquisition is shown in figure 3.1. Signals from the detectors reach the electronics in the counting room though 200 m cables. A first level trigger is generated when a bunch crossing (BX) occurs that can be identified using two BPTX signals generated by two Beam Position Monitors (BPMs) installed 175 m away from the interaction point. At every first level trigger, a 500 nsec gate signal is sent to the ADC for the plastic scintillators (CAEN V965). The particle flight time from the interaction point to our detectors is 466 nsec and the signal propagation time between the detector and USA15 is 860 nsec. The signals from plastic scintillators arriving at USA15 are split into ADCs and discriminators (CAEN V814B) by custom made NIM FANOUT modules with amplification factors of 1 and 4, respectively. The outputs of the discriminators are sent to VME FPGA boards (GND GPIO GN-

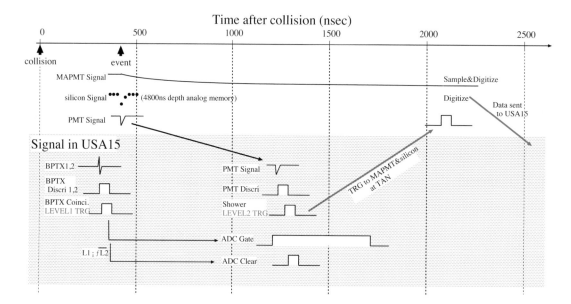

Figure 3.1: The timing chart for trigger and DAQ.

0324-3). Then the second level trigger is issued when more than 3 successive layers detect more than 300 particles corresponding to the energy threshold of about 100 GeV. Details of the trigger logic and energy threshold will be further optimized considering the actual beam conditions at the time of LHC operation. If the second level trigger is not generated within 1 μsec after the first level trigger, the ADC is cleared. At the second level trigger, if the acquisition PC is enabled to read data, a final signal to collect all the data is issued. For the SciFi in detector 1, the second level trigger is sent to the FECs to sample and digitize the MAPMT signal as described in section 3.2. For the silicon tracker in detector 2, the signal stored in the analog memory at the proper timing is digitized as described in section 3.3. Then digitized pulse height data is sent to the counting room and recorded together with the calorimeter data.

The data acquisition is carried out independently for the two arms. However in case of a high background counting rate, which can be expected if the residual gas in the beam pipe is far worse than expected, we can use a coincidence between the two arms to suppress this background. The FC with large acceptance coverage are expected to supply coincidence signals with the detector on the opposite side.

The data acquisition is carried out using the MIDAS package (Maximum Integration Data Acquisition System, [16]). One MIDAS server PC controls two front end PCs for detector 1 and detector 2. The raw data sizes of a single event for two arms are 1.2 kbytes and 14 kbytes in the MIDAS format. The MIDAS server PC also performs a RAID1 storage and can store up to 1.5 Tbytes of data, corresponding to about 10^8 events from both arms. Two other PCs, one for each arm, also communicate with the MIDAS server for a fast analysis during the run. The MIDAS format can be converted to the ROOT format by which fast on-line analysis will be made with the standard ROOT analysis tools [17]. Some basic results of the fast analysis (counting rate, event position, etc.) are distributed in the CERN network every second through the Data Interchange Protocol (DIP). Slow control data (electronics temperature, HV, LV values, manipulator position, etc) are also recorded. Some important machine conditions (luminosity, crossing angle, etc.) are also received through the DIP and recorded in our data base.

In order to synchronize with ATLAS events in possible further analysis, we count the number of the ATLAS level-1 (L1A) triggers and 40 MHz clock (Bunch Clock or BC) counts. These counts are reset roughly every second by the Event Counter Reset (ECR) signal that is also issued from ATLAS. These counts are latched and stored in FIFO when a L1A signal arrives and readout when a LHCf trigger is generated. Time synchronization of the acquisition PC with the CERN time server with one second accuracy can enable us to correlate LHCf and ATLAS events. The combination of the PC clock and the BC count gives the absolute time of each event with a precision of 25 nsec. Because the interval between bunch crossings will be 2 μsec during LHCf operation, we can easily identify the correlated events. These methods will also be used to identify the coincident events of detector 1 and detector 2.

3.2 Electronics and DAQ for the SciFi detector

The MAPMT signals are read out with the Front End Circuits (FECs) packed in the detector on which analog ASICs (VA32HDR14), ADCs and sequencers are mounted. Two VA32HDR14 chips, each of which contains 32 sets of preamplifier, shaping amplifier, sample and hold circuits,

2008 JINST 3 S08006

and one analog multiplexer, are used to read out the 64 channels for one MAPMT. Peaking time of the shaping amplifier is 1.9 μs. The peak voltages recorded by the sample and hold circuits are read out through an analog multiplexer. One ADC coupled to one VA32HDR14 performs the digital conversion of 32 channels in 64 μs. The digital data are transferred in a serial line from the detector via LVDS to an interface board installed on the VME bus. The processes after sampling are carried out when a trigger signal arrives at the FEC according to the level-2 trigger described in section 3.1. The trigger signal arriving 1.9 μs after the shower matches with the peaking time of the shaping amplifier.

3.3 Electronics and DAQ for the silicon tracking detector .

The DAQ used for the silicon part of detector 2 is mainly based on the fast electronics developed for the large LHC experiments, inserted in custom made boards and produced taking into account the LHCf requirements.

The analog preamplifier (PACE3) outputs are digitized by custom made ADC boards with 12 bit resolution. These boards are mounted, piggy-back, on a mother board which also takes care of the optical link communications and clock, level-2 trigger and slow control distribution to the PACE3 chips. Two silicon detectors are serviced by one mother board in such a way that a total of 4 mother boards are installed in the TAN area. The digitized data, along with other status information, are sent via optical fiber links to a VME receiver board in the Atlas USA15 counting room. The receiver board formats the data in an appropriate way for the common detector 2 DAQ to digest. The PACE3 chips receive the LHC 40 MHz clock and level-2 trigger through the TTCrx system developed at CERN for LHC [18]. The signals are coded through a Front End Controller (FEC) module (developed for the CMS experiment [19]) which also takes care of the I2C commands needed to properly set the PACE3 internal registers. From the FEC these fast control signals are sent through optical links down to the experiment in the tunnel. A custom receiver board then decodes the signals and sends them via an electrical token ring to the Clock and Control Unit Modules(CCUM) on the mother boards. These CCUM [19], developed for the CMS tracker, decode both clock, trigger and I2C commands for the PACE3 chips.

2008 JINST 3 S08006

Chapter 4

Performance of the LHCf detectors

4.1 Expected performance of the LHCf detectors

Here we present the results of Monte Carlo studies for evaluating the performance of the LHCf detectors described in section 2. Detector performance was also checked by beam tests described later in section 4.2 In these studies, EPICS [20], which is widely used in air shower experiments, was used for detector simulation. EPICS simulates all electromagnetic and hadronic processes which have been well benchmarked by results from EGS4 or CERN test beam experiments. The primary hadronic interaction model used in this section is DPMJET3 [21] which is also commonly used in air shower simulations.

Energy resolution

The LHCf detectors consist of tungsten sampling shower calorimeters ($44 X_0$ and 1.7λ) with compact apertures which results in shower particle leakage from the edges of the calorimeters.

The number of shower particles contained in calorimeter is plotted in figure 4.1 as a function of the distance between the shower center and the nearest edge. Though the leakage fraction is not negligible, we have found that it does not depend on the energy of the incident primary particle. Using the shower position measured by the position sensitive layers together with the leakage function in figure 4.1, the measured shower energy can be corrected for shower leakage.

The expected energy resolution of the $20 \, \text{mm} \times 20 \, \text{mm}$ calorimeter after shower leakage correction is plotted in figure 4.2 as a function of incident γ-ray energy. Here the γ-ray energy is reconstructed from the energy deposited by shower particles after the 3rd tungsten layer (at $6 X_0$) in order to prevent contamination due to background of low energy γ-rays. Selecting events with shower axis 2 mm or more from the nearest edge of the calorimeter and applying the leakage correction, the expected energy resolution is 6.3% for 100 GeV and 2.8% for 1 TeV γ-rays.

While the total length of the calorimeters expressed in nuclear interaction lengths is small (1.7λ), the detector still can be used as a hadron shower calorimeter. To minimize longitudinal shower leakage, events are selected which start their shower development near the front of the detector. Selecting events for which the shower axis is 2 mm or more from the closest edge, and requiring that the energy deposited in the first radiation length exceeds that deposited by 20 MIPs,

2008 JINST 3 S08006

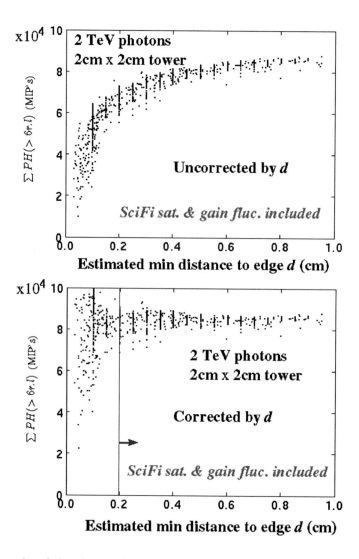

Figure 4.1: Example of the shower leakage function for $2\,\text{TeV}$ γ-rays for the $20\,\text{mm}\times20\,\text{mm}$ calorimeter. The upper plot shows the number of shower particles after $6\,X_0$ as a function of distance of the incident position from the nearest edge. The lower plot shows the same data after correction by the leakage function. The blue arrow shows the fiducial area where the incident shower positions are $2\,\text{mm}$ or more from the nearest edge.

then a 30% energy resolution is expected for $6\,\text{TeV}$ neutrons. The detection efficiency after applying the cuts discussed above is about 4%.

Position determination

The simulated position resolution of the SciFi layers for detector 1 is shown in figure 4.3. The incident shower position is estimated from the fiber with the peak signal and the adjacent 2 fibers weighted by their ADC counts. The resolution is better than $0.2\,\text{mm}$ over the energy range of $100\,\text{GeV}$ to $7\,\text{TeV}$ though it worsens at higher energy due to saturation. The position resolution of the silicon layers of detector 2 was also simulated and it is $15\,\mu\text{m}$ for $1\,\text{TeV}$ γ-rays. The effect of saturation is almost negligible at this energy.

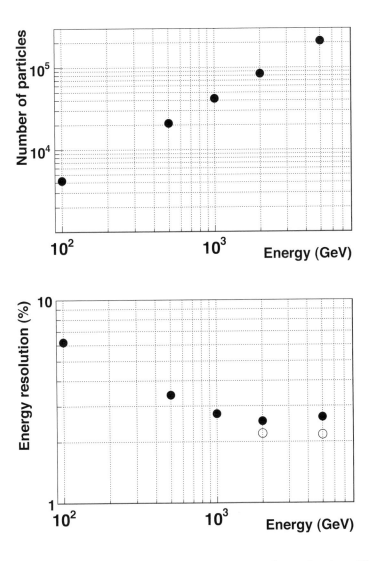

Figure 4.2: The linearity and resolution in the γ-ray energy determination. The upper plot shows number of shower particles after 6 X_0 and after the shower leakage correction. The lower plot shows energy resolution up to 7 TeV. Here the open circles are the data before and the filled circles after the saturation effect of the SciFi has been taken into account.

Detector geometry and acceptance

The LHCf detectors are installed between two beam pipes embedded in the TAN absorbers ±140 m from the IP. At this location, the inner beam separation dipole has swept away all the charged secondary particles so that only neutral particles such as γ-rays from π^0 decays, neutrons or neutral kaons reach the detector. In the case of 7 + 7 TeV collisions, their flux is mostly concentrated within a few cm around the center of the neutral particle flux arriving from the IP, which is the direction of the proton beam at collision projected to the detector plane.

Figure 4.4 shows the geometrical acceptances for single γ-ray events. Here the acceptance is drawn as a function of the distance between the center of the neutral particle flux and the impact point of a particle on LHCf. Without beam crossing angle, detector 1 will locate the center of

2008 JINST 3 S08006

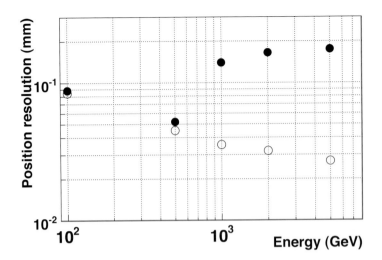

Figure 4.3: Position resolution of SciFi up to 7 TeV. The effect of saturation of the SciFi is taken into account in the filled circles but not in the open circles.

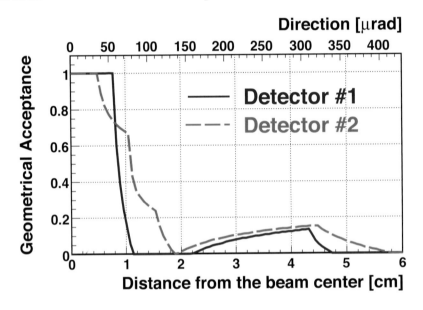

Figure 4.4: Geometrical acceptance of detector 1 (solid blue) and detector 2 (dotted red) for single γ-ray events as function of the distance from the beam axis.

20 mm×20 mm calorimeter at the center of beam-pipe where center of the flux of neutral particles exists. In this case, about half of the 40 mm×40 mm calorimeter will be cut off by the beam-pipe aperture of ±43.8 mm at the D1 magnet location. With a beam crossing angle of 140 μrad, the center of neutral particle flux moves downward by 2 cm. In this case the center of 20 mm×20 mm calorimeter will be adjusted downward by 2 cm and the P_T region covered by the detector will be enhanced.

Figure 4.5 shows the E_γ-$P_{T\gamma}$ correlation plot of photons for 7 + 7 TeV proton collisions. The curve shows the P_T acceptance of detector 1 defined by the vertical aperture of the beam pipe in the D1 magnet. The upper and the lower curves correspond to the beam crossing angles of 140 μrad

2008 JINST 3 S08006

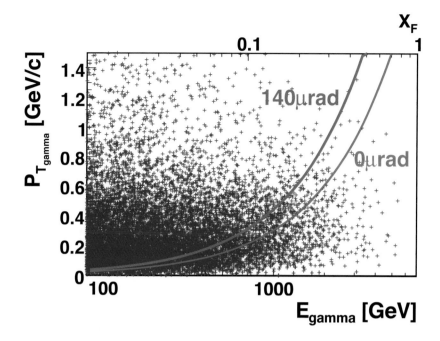

Figure 4.5: The E_γ-$P_{T\gamma}$ correlation plot. High energy photons with small P_{T_γ} can be recorded by the LHCf shower counter. The curves show geometrical cuts for our shower calorimeter arising from the configuration of the beam pipe and magnets. The upper curve (magenta) and the lower curve (red) correspond to beam crossing angles of 140 μrad. and 0 μrad, respectively.

and 0 μrad,respectively. The photons that fall in the area under the curves will be detected by LHCf. From these curves it can be seen that almost all γ-rays with energies higher than 2 TeV can be detected by LHCf.

π^0 reconstruction

The π^0 mass can be reconstructed in the invariant mass distribution of two γ-rays, one each hitting the two tower calorimeters of detector 1 or detector 2. The expected mass resolution is about 5% after taking into account 5% energy resolution and 0.2 mm position resolution.

The π^0 mass peak can be used for the absolute calibration of the energy scale. It also helps for rejection of beam-gas interactions by giving a constraint for location of the neutral pion production vertex. The acceptance of detector 1 and detector 2 for π^0 detection are shown in figure 4.6 for 1, 2 and 5 TeV. In these estimations, the crossing angle is zero and the small calorimeters are located on the horizontal midplane as shown in figure 1.4. The lower horizontal axis gives the distance between the impact point defined by extrapolation of the π^0 trajectory at production to the detector and the center of the neutral particle flux from the IP. The top horizontal axis expresses this distance as the π^0 production angle.

2008 JINST 3 S08006

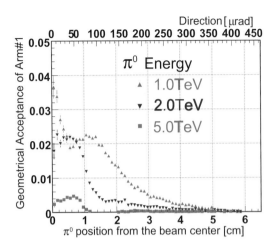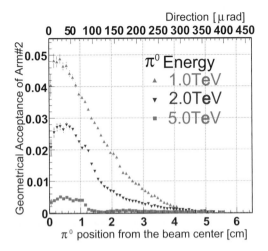

Figure 4.6: Geometrical acceptance for π^0's. Left and right plots show the acceptances for detector 1 and detector 2, respectively. Acceptances for three different π^0 energies are plotted as functions of the distance between the center of the neutral particle flux and the impact point defined by extrapolating the π^0 trajectory at production to the plane of the detector.

4.2 Results of SPS beam tests

The assembly of the detectors was finished in April 2007 and their performance was tested at the CERN SPS North Area H4 beamline from 24 August to 11 September 2007. Both detectors were exposed to electron, hadron and muon beams. Electron beams with energies of 50, 100, 150, 180 and 200 GeV, hadron beams with energies of 150 and 350 GeV and a muon beam with an energy of 150 GeV were used.

The beam test setup is illustrated in figure 4.7. One of the detectors was placed on a movable table in the beam area. Data from the calorimeters and position sensors was recorded when triggered by scintillators placed in front of the detector. At the same time, data from an external silicon strip detector (ADAMO) [22] installed between the detector and the trigger scintillators were also recorded. These data are used to precisely determine the incident position of the beam particle for comparison with the internal position sensitive layers.

In this article we briefly report preliminary results for detector 1 from the SPS2007 beam test. A detailed report on the analysis as well as results for detector 2 is in preparation.

4.2.1 Results for the calorimeters

In the beam test, the PMTs were operated at several different gains. Low gain is a default mode, in which PMTs were operated with a gain of 1 000. With this gain, the dynamic range of the calorimeters is optimized to cover 100 GeV to 7 TeV electromagnetic showers. Some higher gain modes ranging from 3 000 to 10 000 are optimized for measurements below 1 TeV with improved resolution and possibly overcoming unexpected noise in the DAQ electronics. For the muon runs, which are only available in the SPS test beam, the PMTs were operated at the highest gain of about

2008 JINST 3 S08006

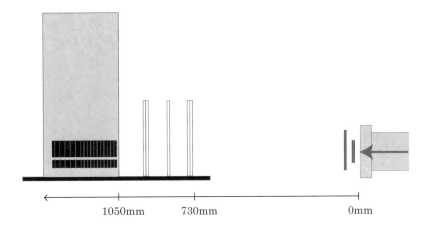

Figure 4.7: Setup of the SPS experiment. Beam enters from right along the red arrow. Two plastic scintillators indicated by blue rectangles were used to trigger beam particles. Five open rectangles show the silicon tracker, ADAMO, placed in front of the LHCf detector that is drawn as a big grey rectangle. The two black-blue structures shown in the detector are the calorimeters. The detector and ADAMO were placed on a movable stage.

10^5 to measure a single MIP. The relative gains of the different modes were measured during the pre-assembly calibration for each PMT as described in section 2.2.

The position of the shower axis was determined by the SciFi layers by finding the peak of the lateral shower shape. Gain calibration was carried out for all of the scintillating fibers in each SciFi layer. Position resolution was checked with ADAMO. The measured shower axis was used to correct for the position dependence of light yield from plastic scintillators and the shower leakage effect by referring to the previously measured non-uniformity maps and shower leakage studies.

The gain calibration of each plastic scintillator layer was carried out by using the electromagnetic showers produced by electron beams. Figure 4.8 shows an ADC distribution at the 4th layer for a 100 GeV/c electron beam. The energy that is expected from MC simulations of the shower particles is also shown. By comparing the two distributions a conversion factor from ADC to energy deposited by shower particles is determined for each layer. Conversion factors for different beam energies were obtained and are compared with each other in figure 4.10. We found these factors are consistent at the 2% level for 50 - 200 GeV electrons. To check consistency with the energy deposited by a single MIP, the muon data was analyzed as shown in figure 4.9. In this comparison, the relative PMT gain difference for the different HV settings for the electron and the muon runs was taken into account. The pedestal fluctuations of 8 AD counts (rms) due to electrical noise was also taken into account in the MC calculations. We can observe good agreement between the two distributions.

Summing up the signal in all the layers except the first, the energy resolution is defined as root-mean-square of the distribution. Here showers for which the incident particle position is reconstructed to lie >2 mm from the nearest edge of the calorimeter are used. The energy resolutions obtained in the beam test and in MC simulation are plotted in figure 4.11 for high gain and low gain operation. Resolution was worst for 50 GeV with low gain (450V HV) due to the electrical noise level during the SPS beam test. The electrical noise was negligible for the high gain mode

2008 JINST 3 S08006

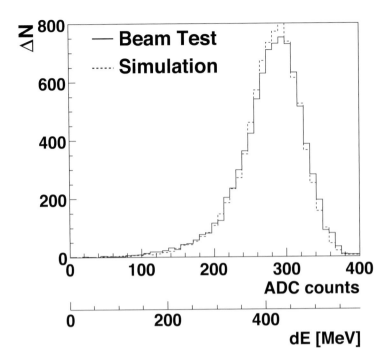

Figure 4.8: The ADC distribution at the 4th scintillation layer for 100 GeV electron showers (solid). The distribution of deposited energy expected from MC calculations (dashed) is also shown.

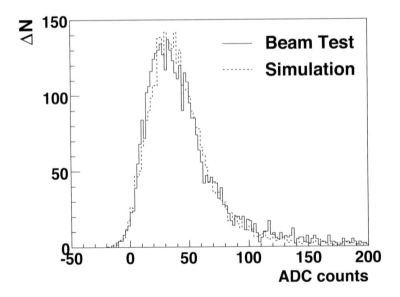

Figure 4.9: The ADC distribution at the 4-th scintillation layer for 150 GeV muon tracks (solid). The energy distribution expected from MC calculations (dashed) is also shown.

(600V HV). In any case, we have obtained excellent agreement between the data and the MC simulations showing the energy resolution is satisfactory for the experiment.

2008 JINST 3 S08006

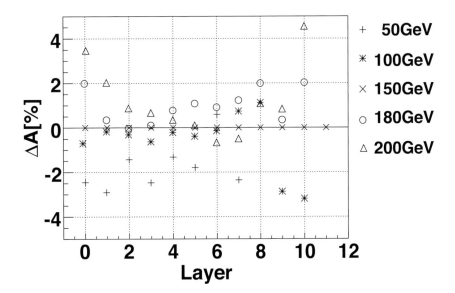

Figure 4.10: Comparison of gain conversion factors obtained from electron showers of different energy. Here the relative differences from the 150 GeV beam are shown for each layer.

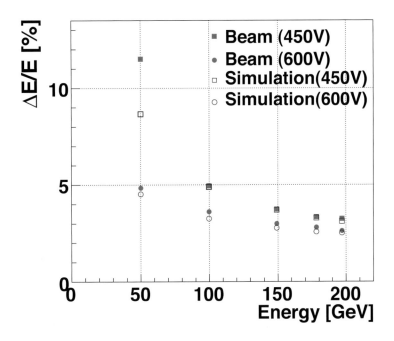

Figure 4.11: Energy resolution for electrons with two different bias HV values are given. The results of MC simulation are also plotted with blue circles.

4.2.2 Position resolution of the SciFi

The position resolution of the SciFi hodoscope used in detector 1 has been studied by using the lateral spread of electron showers at $6\,X_0$ inside the calorimeter. The position of each SciFi is calibrated beforehand by detecting a muon track which is also detected by ADAMO placed in front of the detector [22]. The center of the shower is determined from the peak signal and the signals in

2008 JINST 3 S08006

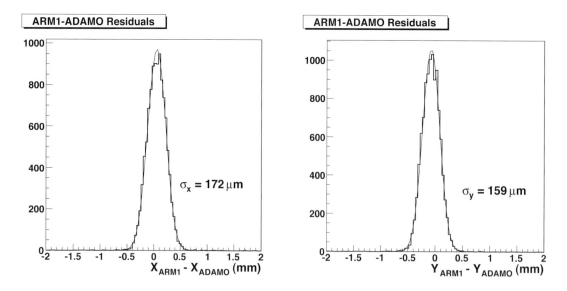

Figure 4.12: Position resolution of the SciFi in detector 1. Distributions of the difference between the shower center and incident particle position determined by SciFi and ADAMO, respectively, are plotted. The results for X and Y directions are shown in the left and right plots, respectively.

the two adjacent fibers weighted by their AD counts. The center determined by the SciFi hodoscope is compared with the incident particle position estimated by ADAMO. The distributions of the differences between these measurements in the X and Y directions are presented in figure 4.12 for 200 GeV electrons observed by the 20 mm×20 mm tower. The electron beams were uniformly scanned over the surface of the calorimeter, and the events >2 mm from the nearest edge were selected for this analysis. The distributions can be fit by Gaussian distributions with a standard deviation of σ_x=170 μm and σ_y=160 μm. The same analysis has been carried out for electron beams of 50, 100, 150 and 180 GeV. The resolution becomes slightly better with increasing energy from 200 μm to 170 μm in the X direction and from 210 μm to 160 μm in the Y direction. The analysis for the 40 mm×40 mm tower was done at an electron beam energy of 100 GeV, and the resolution obtained was 170 μm in the X direction and 230 μm in the Y direction. The results are very close to the 0.2 mm desired position resolution for energy above 100 GeV. Mis-alignment information between the LHCf detector and ADAMO has not yet been taken into account, hence an improvement in resolution is expected.

4.2.3   Position resolution of the silicon tracker

The silicon based tracker of detector 2 allows for a very good reconstruction of the γ-ray impact point on the calorimeter, that improves with increasing the γ-ray energy. From a MC simulation of the system, we calculated an expected impact point reconstruction resolution better than 100 μm for photon energy greater than 100 GeV.

A very preliminary data analysis has been done to give an estimate of the spatial resolution for the silicon based system of detector 2. This analysis was done using ADAMO for the reconstruction of the trajectory of each particle hitting the calorimeter. ADAMO was designed measuring the trajectories of single minimum ionizing particles.

2008 JINST 3 S08006

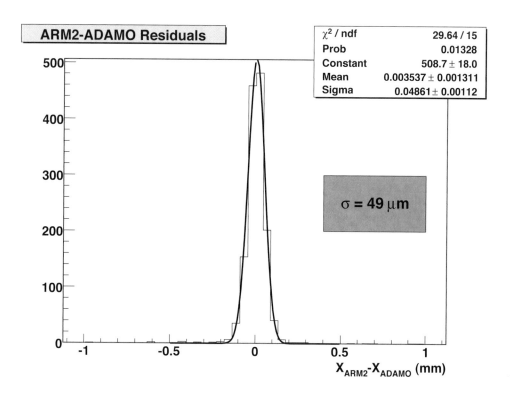

Figure 4.13: Position resolution of the silicon strip sensor in detector 2. Distribution of the differences between the measured positions of the shower centers of 200 GeV electrons at $6\,X_0$ inside the calorimeter and the impact points extrapolated at the same depth by using the ADAMO tracker.

Figure 4.13 shows the distribution of the differences between the measured positions of the shower centers on the LHCf silicon layer located at $6\,X_0$ inside the calorimeter and the impact points extrapolated at the same depth by using the ADAMO tracker. A data set of 200 GeV electrons events has been used for this analysis. Because the ADAMO system has an intrinsic spatial resolution of a few μm for minimum ionizing particles, the width of this distribution is dominated in good approximation by the LHCf silicon spatial resolution. These first results show therefore that the center of a 200 GeV e.m. shower can be reconstructed on the silicon layer located at $6\,X_0$ inside the calorimeter with a spatial resolution of about 50 μm.

4.2.4 Demonstration of π^0 mass reconstruction capability

To demonstrate the capability of the LHCf detectors for π^0 mass reconstruction, an experiment was performed at the SPS H4 test beam with detector 1. To produce π^0's, a carbon target of 60 mm thickness was placed 10 m in front of the detector and the target was exposed to a 350 GeV proton beam. With this geometry and energy, we can expect typically 20 GeV γ-ray pairs entering in the calorimeters. The PMTs were operated at 800 V. With this voltage the gain is 40 times higher than the gain at the nominal voltage of 450 V. To trigger on gamma-ray pairs, the trigger logic was set so that both calorimeters were required to have signals corresponding to more than 40–80 MIPS in

2008 JINST 3 S08006

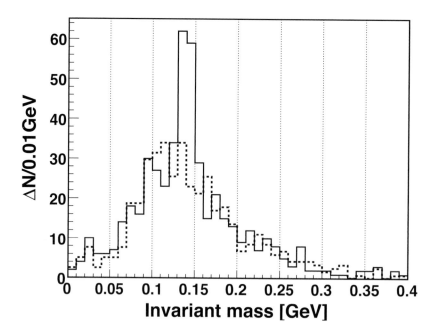

Figure 4.14: Invariant mass distribution calculated from the γ-ray pairs observed in the SPS test beam. A clear peak at the mass of π^0 (135 MeV) implies the calibration and analysis procedure were working correctly. The background shown in the dashed histogram was calculated by using uncorrelated γ-ray pairs.

any of the layers from 2 to 5. At the same time, to reduce the large proton background, we required that none of the last two scintillation layers in both calorimeters have a signal exceeding 20 MIPs.

After 6×10^7 protons entered the carbon target, 300 000 events generated the trigger and were recorded. Data reduction was carried out based on the processes described in the previous sections, i.e., position determination based on the SciFi data, 2 mm edge cut, correction for non-uniform light collection, leakage correction, and conversion from measured signals to energy deposited. The difference between the PMT gain in the nominal beam tests and in this special run was also accounted for based on the laser calibration data. Clear γ-ray pairs, each having energy more than 20 GeV, are identified in 0.6% of these recorded events. From the energies and the transverse positions of the pair, the invariant mass was calculated. The invariant mass distribution is shown in figure 4.14. A clear peak at the mass of the π^0 (135 MeV) implies the calibration and analysis procedure are working correctly. The background is caused by uncorrelated pairs those accidentally hit the two calorimeters simultaneously. The background distribution was evaluated by shifting the events in the two calorimeters so that any correlated pairs disappear. The result is also shown in figure 4.14 by dashed line and confirms the peak is really produced by π^0's. Here we note that the energy range of γ-rays in this test (20–50 GeV) was below the range that will be investigated in LHCf (>100 GeV).

2008 JINST 3 S08006

4.3 Results of radiation damage tests

The LHCf detectors will be exposed to a considerable amount of ionizing radiation. Mokhov et al. (2003) calculated the absorbed dose distribution around the TAN [23]. Their result showed that the LHCf detector would receive a maximum radiation dose of 10 Gy/day at a nominal luminosity of 10^{29} cm^{-2}s^{-1}. We have tested the tolerances of our plastic scintillators and clear-fiber light-guides to ionizing radiation. The test experiments were carried out with a heavy ion beam from a synchrotron at HIMAC of NIRS (National Institute of Radiological Science, Japan) and with γ-rays at the ^{60}Co Radiation Facility of Nagoya University. Effects of irradiation such as a change in the light output from the plastic scintillators and change in transparency of the light guides for the scintillation photons and also the recovery from radiation damage with time were measured.

For the heavy ion test, two kinds of plastic scintillator (EJ-260 and BC-404) and a clear-fiber light-guide (CLEARPSM, Kuraray) were irradiated with 290 MeV/n ^{12}C ion beams. Absorbed radiation dose was measured by an air ionization chamber coupled with measurements by plastic scintillators. The final integrated dose was 30 kGy with a beam intensity of 10^8 particles s^{-1}cm^{-2}. The degradation of scintillator light outputs were evaluated by measuring the signal for the weak ^{12}C beam itself and for UV light (350 nm) from a filtered Xe flash lamp (Hamamatsu L4633-01). Different irradiation rates (3×10^4 Gy/h, 8×10^4 Gy/h and increasing rate from 2×10^0 to 8×10^4 Gy/h) were compared. For γ-ray tests, similar materials were irradiated by a 100 TBq ^{60}Co source. The absorbed dose was calculated from the geometry of the source and target materials. Two dose rates (22 Gy/h and 250 Gy/h) were used by changing the distance between the source and the irradiated materials. The evaluation of the light output was done by using UV light from the Xe flash lamp. The short-term recovery of damage was also measured just after irradiation by both heavy ions and γ-rays. The long-term recovery was measured by using a radioactive beta-ray source (^{90}Sr) for several days or more. Figure 4.15 shows the variation of the scintillator and light guide light outputs for irradiation by heavy ions and γ-rays. The scintillator light outputs are almost constant up to ten Gy of absorbed dose and then decrease to 90% of the pre-irradiation value at 100 Gy or more. Most samples show a decrease of light output to 40% of the pre-irradiation value at the maximum absorbed dose of 30 kGy. There was no significant difference in the effects of irradiation measured by UV light or by the ^{12}C beam. Irradiation of the fiber light-guide showed a small decrease of light transmission for the wavelength of 490 nm because of the decrease in transparency due to irradiation. The measurement for irradiation by γ-rays showed a decrease of light output similar to that for heavy ions. The light output decreases to 90% of the initial value around 100 Gy and to 80% at 500 Gy. The damaged scintillators showed a tendency to recover within a few hours after finishing the irradiation, but the extent of recovery was very small. After one day or more, a clear recovery was observed and the light output increased from ~40% to ~60% of the initial light output before irradiation.

In conclusion, the plastic scintillators can be damaged by irradiation with heavy ions and γ-rays but the decrease of the light output is not large for doses of interest for LHCf. No significant dependence of radiation damage on the type of scintillator, the type of radiation, the irradiation rate, and so on were observed. Partial recovery of decreased light output is observed over several days after irradiation. Normally, the LHCf detectors will receive a dose of several tens of Gy during one week oepration. This is enough to complete the measurements unless background event rates

2008 JINST 3 S08006

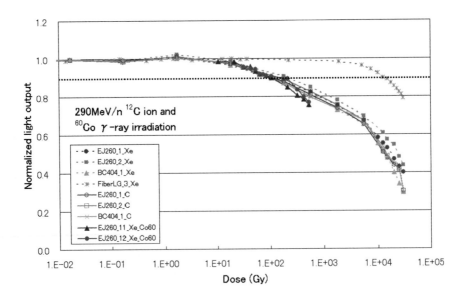

Figure 4.15: The variation of the scintillator light outputs (EJ260 and BC404) and light guide transmission for irradiation by heavy ions and γ-rays.

are very high and the run must be extended. A small decrease of light output can be corrected for by the laser calibration system and the accuracy of energy measurement will not be affected.

2008 JINST 3 S08006

Chapter 5

Summary

The LHCf is an experiment to measure very forward neutral particles emitted in LHC collisions in order to calibrate the hadron interaction models used in simulation of Extremely High Energy Cosmic-Rays at a laboratory equivalent energy of 10^{17} eV. In this paper, we have given an experimental overview, a description of details of the instrumentation and data acquisition system, simulation of performance of the detectors during LHC operation and reported preliminary results of SPS test beam experiments.

Two LHCf detectors are installed at ± 140 m from IP1 where the neutral particle absorbers (TAN) are located. Each of the two detectors is composed of two independent sampling calorimeters made of tungsten plates, plastic scintillators and position sensitive layers. The position sensitive layers are scintillation fibers and multi-anode photomultipliers for detector 1 and silicon strip detectors for detector 2. Because of the limited space for installation, these calorimeters are very compact, but are still capable of measuring energy and position of the incident particles with sufficient resolutions. Simulations predict that the energy resolution is better than 5% and the position resolution as good as 0.2 mm at 100 GeV; these predictions have been confirmed by measurements in SPS test beams at CERN. The use of front scintillation counters is expected to help reduce background events generated by beam-gas interactions during early LHC operation when vacuum conditions may not be as good as anticipated. The detectors are equipped with vertical manipulators to increase the P_T range that can be measured and to remove the detectors from unnecessary radiation damage when they are not in use. The experiment covers a pseudo rapidity range from 8.4 to infinity. Data acquisition during LHC operation will be carried out in the ATLAS counting room, USA15. An event tagging scheme based on the time stamp of the LHC clock has been developed to correlate LHCf and ATLAS events for possible further analysis. Detectors, data acquisition and electronics are optimized to operate during the early phases of LHC commissioning with luminosity below 10^{30} cm^{-2}s^{-1}. The event rates are expected to be high enough that LHCf can get all of its data in one week of LHC operation at the luminosity of 10^{29} cm^{-2}s^{-1}. After a week of operation under these conditions, the output of the plastic scintillators will be degraded by $\sim$10% due to radiation damage. Radiation damage will be monitored and corrected for with a pulsed laser calibration system. The LHCf detectors will be removed once the luminosity exceeds 10^{30} cm^{-2}s^{-1}.

2008 JINST 3 S08006

Acknowledgments

This work is partly supported by Grant-in-Aid for Scientific Research (B:16403003), Grant-in-Aid for Scientific Research on Priority Areas (Highest Cosmic Rays: 15077205, 1733004, 19012003) and Grant-in-Aid for Young Scientists (B:18740141), by the Ministry of Education, Culture, Sports, Science and Technology (MEXT) of Japan. This work is also partially supported by the Mitsubishi Foundation in Japan and by Istituto Nazionale di Fisica Nucleare (INFN) in Italy. The receipt of a Japan Society for the Promotion of Science (JSPS) Research Fellowship (H.M.) is also acknowledged. The authors would like to thank CERN for the support shown to our experiment.

Bibliography

[1] M. Takeda et al., *Extension of the cosmic ray energy spectrum beyond the predicted Greisen-Zatsepin-Kuz'min cutoff*, Phys. Rev. Lett. **81** (1998) 1163.

[2] S. Yoshida et al., *Extremely high-energy neutrinos and their detection. Astrophys. J.* **479** (1997) 547.

[3] R.U. Abbasi et al., *Measurement of the Flux of Ultrahigh Energy Cosmic Rays from Monocular Observations by the High Resolution Fly's Eye Experiment*, Phys. Rev. Lett. **92** (2004) 151101.

[4] T. Yamamoto et al., *The UHECR spectrum measured at the Pierre Auger Observatory and its astrophysical implications*, Proc. of 30th Intl. Cosmic Ray Conference, Merida Mexico (2007).

[5] The Pierre Auger Collaboration, *Correlation of the Highest-Energy Cosmic Rays with Nearby Extragalactic Objects*, Science **318** (2007) 938.

[6] M. Unger et al., *Study of the Cosmic Ray Composition above 0.4 EeV using the Longitudinal Profiles of Showers observed at the Pierre Auger Observatory*, Proc. of 30th Intl. Cosmic Ray Conference, Merida Mexico (2007).

[7] The TOTEM collaboration, *The TOTEM Experiment at the CERN Large Hadron Collider*, 2008 *JINST* **3** S08007.

[8] The ATLAS collaboration, *ATLAS Forward Detectors for Measurement of Elastic Scattering and Luminosity*, CERN-LHCC-2008-004, http://cdsweb.cern.ch/record/1095847.

[9] E. Paré et al., *Inclusive production of π^0's in the fragmentation region at the SppS collider*, Phys. Lett. **B 242** (1990) 531.

[10] T. Sako et al., *Performance of the prototype detector for the LHCf experiment*, Nucl. Instrum. Meth. **A 578** (2007) 146.

[11] The ATLAS collaboration, *Zero Degree Calorimeters for ATLAS*, CERN-LHCC-2007-001, http://cdsweb.cern.ch/record/1009649.

[12] P. Datte et al., *Initial test results of an ionization chamber shower detector for a LHC luminosity monitor*, IEEE Trans. Nucl. Sci. **50** (2003) 258.

2008 JINST 3 S08006

[13] http://atlas.web.cern.ch/Atlas/GROUPS/INNER_DETECTOR/SCT/, following the link for the barrel module.

[14] P. Aspell et al., *PACE3: a large dynamic range analog memory front-end ASIC assembly for the charge readout of silicon sensors*, *IEEE Nucl. Sci. Symp. Conf. Rec.* **2** (2005) 904.

[15] L. Bonechi et al., *Production and test of the LHCf microstrip silicon system*, *Presented at the RD07 Conference*, Florence Italy, June 27–29 2007.

[16] MIDAS Homepage, https://midas.psi.ch/

[17] ROOT Homepage, http://root.cern.ch/

[18] J. Varela eds., *CMS L1 Trigger Control System*, CMS-NOTE-2002-033, http://cdsweb.cern.ch/record/687458.

[19] CMS collaboration, V. Karimäki, *CMS Tracker Technical Design Report*, CERN-LHCC-98-006, CMS-TDR-005, http://cdsweb.cern.ch/record/368412.

[20] K. Kasahara, EPICS Homepage, http://cosmos.n.kanagawa-u.ac.jp/.

[21] J. Ranft, *Dual parton model at cosmic ray energies*, *Phys. Rev.* **D 51** (1995) 64.

[22] L. Bonechi et al., *Development of the ADAMO detector: test with cosmic rays at different zenith angles*, *Proc. of 29th Intl. Cosmic Ray Conference*, Pune India, **9** (2005) 283, http://icrc2005.tifr.res.in/htm/Vol-Web/Volume9_index.html.

[23] N.V. Mokhov et al., *Protecting LHC IP1/IP5 Components Against Radiation Resulting from Colliding Beam Interactions*, LHC-Project-Report-633 (2003), http://cdsweb.cern.ch/record/613167.

2008 JINST 3 S08006

PUBLISHED BY INSTITUTE OF PHYSICS PUBLISHING AND SISSA

RECEIVED: *December 28, 2007*
REVISED: *May 28, 2008*
ACCEPTED: *June 14, 2008*
PUBLISHED: *August 14, 2008*

THE CERN LARGE HADRON COLLIDER: ACCELERATOR AND EXPERIMENTS

The TOTEM Experiment at the CERN Large Hadron Collider

The TOTEM Collaboration

ABSTRACT: The TOTEM Experiment will measure the total pp cross-section with the luminosity-independent method and study elastic and diffractive scattering at the LHC. To achieve optimum forward coverage for charged particles emitted by the pp collisions in the interaction point IP5, two tracking telescopes, T1 and T2, will be installed on each side in the pseudorapidity region $3.1 \leq |\eta| \leq 6.5$, and Roman Pot stations will be placed at distances of ± 147 m and ± 220 m from IP5. Being an independent experiment but technically integrated into CMS, TOTEM will first operate in standalone mode to pursue its own physics programme and at a later stage together with CMS for a common physics programme. This article gives a description of the TOTEM apparatus and its performance.

Keywords: Gaseous detectors; Solid state detectors; Particle tracking detectors; Analogue electronic circuits; Data acquisition circuits; Data acquisition concepts; Detector control systems; Digital electronic circuits; Electronic detector readout concepts; Electronic detector readout concepts; Front-end electronics for detector readout; Modular electronics; Optical detector readout concepts; Trigger concepts and systems; VLSI circuits; Detector cooling and thermo-stabilization; Detector design and construction; Overall mechanics design.

2008 JINST 3 S08007

The TOTEM Collaboration

G. Anelli,[1] G. Antchev,[1] P. Aspell,[1] V. Avati,[1,9] M.G. Bagliesi,[5] V. Berardi,[4] M. Berretti,[5]
V. Boccone,[2] U. Bottigli,[5] M. Bozzo,[2] E. Brücken,[6] A. Buzzo,[2] F. Cafagna,[4] M. Calicchio,[4]
F. Capurro,[2] M.G. Catanesi,[4] P.L. Catastini,[5] R. Cecchi,[5] S. Cerchi,[2] R. Cereseto,[2]
M.A. Ciocci,[5] S. Cuneo,[2] C. Da Già,[11] E. David,[1] M. Deile,[1] E. Dimovasili,[1,9] M. Doubrava,[10]
K. Eggert,[1] V. Eremin,[12] F. Ferro,[2] A. Foussat,[1] M. Galuška,[10] F. Garcia,[6] F. Gherarducci,[5]
S. Giani,[1] V. Greco,[5] J. Hasi,[11] F. Haug,[1] J. Heino,[6] T. Hilden,[6] P. Jarron,[1] C. Joram,[1]
J. Kalliopuska,[6] J. Kaplon,[1] J. Kašpar,[1,7] V. Kundrát,[7] K. Kurvinen,[6] J.M. Lacroix,[1]
S. Lami,[5] G. Latino,[5] R. Lauhakangas,[6] E. Lippmaa,[8] M. Lokajíček,[7] M. Lo Vetere,[2]
F. Lucas Rodriguez,[1] D. Macina,[1] M. Macrí,[2] C. Magazzù,[5] G. Magazzù,[5] A. Magri,[2]
G. Maire,[1] A. Manco,[2] M. Meucci,[5] S. Minutoli,[2] A. Morelli,[2] P. Musico,[2] M. Negri,[2]
H. Niewiadomski,[1,9] E. Noschis,[1] G. Notarnicola,[4] E. Oliveri,[5] F. Oljemark,[6] R. Orava,[6]
M. Oriunno,[1] A.-L. Perrot,[1] K. Österberg,[6] R. Paoletti,[5] E. Pedreschi,[5] J. Petäjäjärvi,[6]
P. Pollovio,[2] M. Quinto,[4] E. Radermacher,[1] E. Radicioni,[4] S. Rangod,[1] F. Ravotti,[1] G. Rella,[4]
E. Robutti,[2] L. Ropelewski,[1] G. Ruggiero,[1] A. Rummel,[8] H. Saarikko,[6] G. Sanguinetti,[5]
A. Santroni,[2] A. Scribano,[5] G. Sette,[2] W. Snoeys,[1] F. Spinella,[5] P. Squillacioti,[5] A. Ster,[13]
C. Taylor,[3] A. Tazzioli,[5] D. Torazza,[2] A. Trovato,[2] A. Trummal,[8] N. Turini,[5] V. Vacek,[1,10]
N. Van Remortel,[6] V. Vinš,[10] S. Watts,[11] J. Whitmore,[9] and J. Wu[1]

[1]CERN, Genève, Switzerland
[2]Università di Genova and Sezione INFN, Genova, Italy
[3]Case Western Reserve University, Dept. of Physics, Cleveland, OH, U.S.A.
[4]INFN Sezione di Bari and Politecnico di Bari, Bari, Italy
[5]INFN Sezione di Pisa and Università di Siena, Italy
[6]Helsinki Institute of Physics and Department of Physical Sciences, University of Helsinki, Finland
[7]Institute of Physics of the Academy of Sciences of the Czech Republic, Praha, Czech Republic
[8]National Institute of Chemical Physics and Biophysics NICPB, Tallinn, Estonia
[9]Penn State University, Dept. of Physics, University Park, PA, U.S.A.
[10]On leave from Czech Technical University, Prague, Czech Republic
[11]Brunel University, Uxbridge, UK; now at the University of Manchester, U.K.
[12]On leave from Ioffe Physico-Technical Institute,
  Polytechnicheskaya Str. 26, 194021 St-Petersburg, Russian Federation
[13]Individual participant from MTA KFKI RMKI, Budapest, Hungary

Corresponding author: Mario Deile (Mario.Deile@cern.ch)

2008 JINST 3 S08007

Contents

2008 JINST 3 S08007

2008 JINST 3 S08007

Chapter 1

Introduction

The TOTEM experiment [1] — small in size compared to the others at the LHC — is dedicated to the measurement of the total proton-proton cross-section with the luminosity-independent method based on the Optical Theorem, which requires a detailed study of the elastic scattering cross-section down to a squared four-momentum transfer of $|t| \sim 10^{-3}\,\mathrm{GeV}^2$ and the measurement of the total inelastic rate. Furthermore, TOTEM's physics programme aims at a deeper understanding of the proton structure by studying elastic scattering with large momentum transfers, and via a comprehensive menu of diffractive processes — partly in cooperation with CMS [2], located at the same interaction point, IP5. Hence the TOTEM collaboration focusses on physics complementary to the programmes of the general-purpose experiments at the LHC, and therefore had to invest heavily in the design of detectors that will be capable of meeting the challenge of triggering and recording events in the very forward region. To perform these measurements, TOTEM requires a good acceptance for particles produced at very small angles with respect to the beam. TOTEM's coverage in the pseudo-rapidity range of $3.1 \le |\eta| \le 6.5$ ($\eta = -\ln\tan\frac{\theta}{2}$) on both sides of the interaction point is accomplished by two telescopes for inelastically produced charged particles (figure 1.1), and complemented by detectors in special movable beam-pipe insertions — so-called Roman Pots ("RP") — placed at about 147 m and 220 m from the interaction point, designed to detect leading protons at merely a few mm from the beam centre (figure 1.2).

The telescope closest to the interaction point (T1, centered at $z = 9$ m) consists of Cathode Strip Chambers CSC (section 5.2), while the second one (T2, centered at 13.5 m) exploits Gas Electron Multipliers GEM (section 5.3). The proton detectors in the Roman Pots (chapter 4) are silicon devices designed by TOTEM with the specific objective of reducing the insensitive area at the edge facing the beam to only a few tens of microns. High efficiency up to the physical detector border is an essential feature in view of maximising the experiment's acceptance for protons scattered elastically or diffractively at polar angles down to a few microradians at the IP. To measure protons at the lowest possible emission angles, special beam optics have been conceived to optimise proton detection in terms of acceptance and resolution (chapter 3).

The read-out of all TOTEM subsystems is based on the custom-developed digital VFAT chip with trigger capability (chapter 7). The data acquisition system (chapter 9) is designed to be compatible with the CMS DAQ to make common data taking possible at a later stage.

2008 JINST 3 S08007

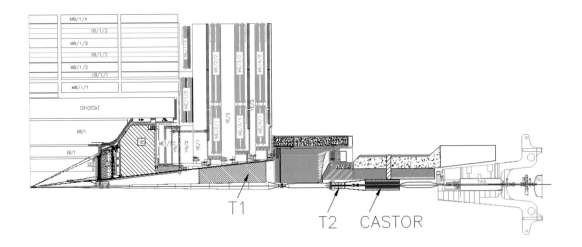

Figure 1.1: The TOTEM forward trackers T1 and T2 embedded in the CMS detector together with the planned CMS forward calorimeter CASTOR.

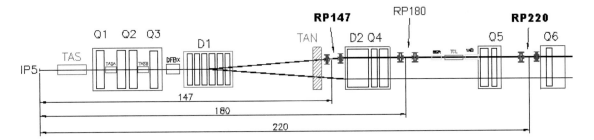

Figure 1.2: The LHC beam line on one side of interaction point IP5 and the TOTEM Roman Pots at distances of about 147 m (RP147) and 220 m (RP220). RP180 at 180 m is another possible location but presently not equipped.

2008 JINST 3 S08007

Chapter 2

Physics objectives

The TOTEM apparatus with its unique coverage for charged particles at high rapidities (figure 2.1, left) is the ideal tool for studying forward phenomena, including elastic and diffractive scattering. Furthermore, energy flow and particle multiplicity of inelastic events peak in the forward region (figure 2.1 right; $\eta = 3$ corresponds to a polar angle $\theta = 100\,\mathrm{mrad}$.). About 99.5% of all non-diffractive minimum bias events and 84% of all diffractive events have charged particles within the acceptance of T1 or T2 and are thus triggerable with these detectors.

An important application is the luminosity-independent measurement of the total cross-section based on the Optical Theorem.

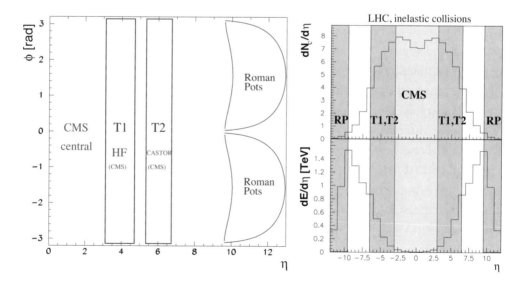

Figure 2.1: Left: coverage of different detectors in the pseudorapidity (η) - azimuthal angle (ϕ) plane. Right: charged particle multiplicity and energy flow as a function of pseudorapidity for inelastic events at $\sqrt{s} = 14\,\mathrm{TeV}$.

2008 JINST 3 S08007

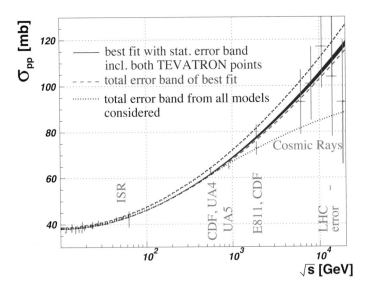

Figure 2.2: Fits from the COMPETE collaboration [5] to all available pp and $p\bar{p}$ scattering data with statistical (blue solid) and total (green dashed) error bands, the latter taking into account the discrepancy of the two Tevatron measurements. The outermost curves (dotted) give the total error band from all parameterisations considered.

2.1 Total pp cross-section

A precise measurement of the total pp cross-section σ_{tot} and of the elastic scattering over a large range in the squared four-momentum transfer t (section 2.2) is of primary importance for distinguishing between different models of soft proton interactions.

Figure 2.2 summarises the existing measurements of σ_{tot} from low energies up to collider and cosmic-ray energies. Unfortunately the large uncertainties of the cosmic-ray data and the 2.6 standard-deviations discrepancy between the two final results from the Tevatron [3, 4] make an extrapolation to higher energies uncertain, leaving a wide range for the expected value of the total cross-section at the LHC energy of $\sqrt{s} = 14\,\text{TeV}$, typically from 90 to 130 mb, depending on the model used for the extrapolation.

TOTEM will measure σ_{tot} and the luminosity $\mathcal{L}$ simultaneously by taking advantage of the Optical Theorem:

$$\mathcal{L}\,\sigma_{\text{tot}}^2 = \frac{16\pi}{1+\rho^2} \cdot \frac{dN_{\text{el}}}{dt}\bigg|_{t=0}. \tag{2.1}$$

With the additional relation

$$\mathcal{L}\,\sigma_{\text{tot}} = N_{\text{el}} + N_{\text{inel}} \tag{2.2}$$

one obtains a system of 2 equations which can be solved for σ_{tot} or $\mathcal{L}$. The parameter

$$\rho = \frac{\mathscr{R}[f_{\text{el}}(0)]}{\mathscr{I}[f_{\text{el}}(0)]}, \tag{2.3}$$

2008 JINST 3 S08007

where $f_{\text{el}}(0)$ is the forward nuclear elastic amplitude, has to be taken from external theoretical predictions, e.g. [5]. Since $\rho \sim 0.14$ enters only in a $1 + \rho^2$ term, its impact is small (see estimate in section 6.3.3).

Hence the quantities to be measured are the following:

- The inelastic rate N_{inel} consisting of non-diffractive minimum bias events ($\sim$65 mb at LHC) and diffractive events ($\sim$18 mb at LHC) which will be measured by T1 and T2.

- The total nuclear elastic rate N_{el} measured by the Roman Pot system.

- $dN_{\text{el}}/dt|_{t=0}$: The nuclear part of the elastic cross-section extrapolated to $t = 0$ (see section 2.2). The expected uncertainty of the extrapolation depends on the acceptance for elastically scattered protons at small $|t|$-values and hence on the beam optics.

For the rate measurements it is important that all TOTEM detector systems have trigger capability.

At an early stage with non-optimal beams, TOTEM will measure the total cross-section and the luminosity with a precision of about 5%. After having understood the initial measurements and with improved beams at $\beta^* = 1540$ m (cf. chapter 3), a precision around 1% should be achievable.

Even later, a measurement of ρ via the interference between Coulomb and hadronic contributions to the elastic scattering cross-section might be attempted at a reduced centre-of-mass energy of about 8 TeV [6]. The main interest of ρ lies in its predictive power for σ_{tot} at higher energies via the dispersion relation

$$\rho(s) = \frac{\pi}{2\sigma_{\text{tot}}(s)} \frac{d\sigma_{\text{tot}}}{d\ln s}.$$

(2.4)

2.2 Elastic pp scattering

Much of the interest in large-impact-parameter collisions centres on elastic scattering and soft inelastic diffraction. High-energy elastic nucleon scattering represents one of the collision processes in which very precise data over a large energy range have been gathered. The differential cross-section of elastic pp interactions at 14 TeV, as predicted by different models [7], is given in figures 2.3 and 2.4.

The dashed graphs show the cross-section of pure nuclear scattering, i.e. neglecting the influence of the Coulomb component, which would be justified for $|t| > 10^{-3}$ GeV^2 assuming the validity of the West and Yennie description [8] of the Coulomb-nuclear interference. However, it has been shown that this formula requires $\rho(t)$ to be t independent which is not fulfilled experimentally and theoretically inconsistent [9]. Hence a second set of graphs (continuous lines) is shown taking into account the Coulomb component with a formulation of the total amplitude based on the eikonal approach. This model also describes the influence of Coulomb scattering at higher values of $|t|$, which is visible in figure 2.4 above 0.25 GeV^2.

Increasing $|t|$ means looking deeper into the proton at smaller distances. Several t-regions with different behaviour can be distinguished:

- $|t| < 6.5 \times 10^{-4}$ GeV^2 (at $\sqrt{s}$=14 TeV): The Coulomb region where elastic scattering is dominated by photon exchange: $d\sigma/dt \sim 1/t^2$.

2008 JINST 3 S08007

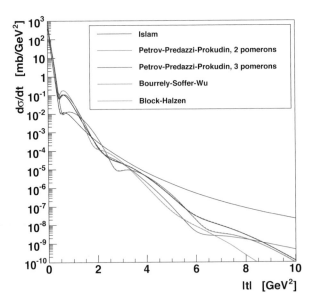

Figure 2.3: Differential cross-section of elastic scattering at $\sqrt{s} = 14\,\mathrm{TeV}$ as predicted by various models [7]. On this scale, the cross-sections with and without the Coulomb component (continuous and dashed lines respectively) cannot be distinguished.

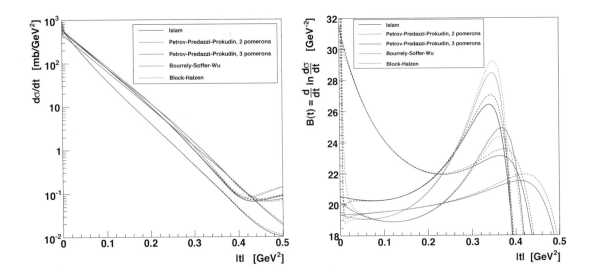

Figure 2.4: Left: differential cross-section of elastic scattering at $14\,\mathrm{TeV}$ as predicted by various models [7], focussing on the quasi-exponential domain at low $|t|$. Right: exponential slope of the differential cross-section. The deviations from a constant slope show how the cross-sections differ from a pure exponential shape. Continuous (dashed) lines: with (without) Coulomb interaction.

- $10^{-3}\,\mathrm{GeV}^2 < |t| < 0.5\,\mathrm{GeV}^2$: The nuclear region described in a simplified way by "single-Pomeron exchange"[1] with an approximately exponential cross-section $d\sigma/dt \sim \mathrm{e}^{-B|t|}$ (figure 2.4, left). This quasi-exponential domain is important for the extrapolation of the differential counting-rate dN_{el}/dt to $t = 0$, needed for the measurement of σ_{tot}. The t-dependence of the exponential slope $B(t) = \frac{d}{dt}\ln\frac{d\sigma}{dt}$ reveals slight model-dependent deviations from the exponential shape (figure 2.4, right). This theoretical uncertainty contributes to the systematic error of the total cross-section measurement (section 6.3.2).

- Between the above two regions, the nuclear and Coulomb scattering interfere, complicating the extrapolation of the nuclear cross-section to $t = 0$.

- $0.5\,\mathrm{GeV}^2 < |t| < 1\,\mathrm{GeV}^2$: A region exhibiting the diffractive structure of the proton.

- $|t| > 1\,\mathrm{GeV}^2$: The domain of central elastic collisions at high $|t|$, described by perturbative QCD, e.g. in terms of triple-gluon exchange with a predicted cross-section proportional to $|t|^{-8}$. The model dependence of the predictions being very pronounced in this region, measurements will be able to test the validity of the different models.

With different beam optics and running conditions (chapter 3), TOTEM will cover the $|t|$-range from $2 \times 10^{-3}\,\mathrm{GeV}^2$ to about $10\,\mathrm{GeV}^2$.

2.3 Diffraction

Diffractive scattering comprises Single Diffraction, Double Diffraction, Central Diffraction (a.k.a. "Double Pomeron Exchange"), and higher order ("Multi Pomeron") processes. Together with the elastic scattering these processes represent about 50% of the total cross-section. Many details of these processes with close ties to proton structure and low-energy QCD are still poorly understood. The majority of diffractive events (figure 2.5) exhibits intact ("leading") protons in the final state, characterised by their t and by their fractional momentum loss $\xi \equiv \Delta p/p$. Depending on the beam optics (chapter 3) most of these protons can be detected in Roman Pot detectors far away from the interaction point. Already at an early stage, TOTEM will be able to measure ξ-, t- and mass-distributions in soft Double Pomeron and Single Diffractive events. The full structure of diffractive events with one or more sizeable rapidity gaps in the particle distributions (figure 2.5) will be optimally accessible when the detectors of CMS and TOTEM will be combined for common data taking with an unprecedented rapidity coverage, as discussed in [2].

---

[1]Nuclear elastic and diffractive scattering are characterised by the exchange of hadronic colour singlets, for which the Pomeron is one model.

2008 JINST 3 S08007

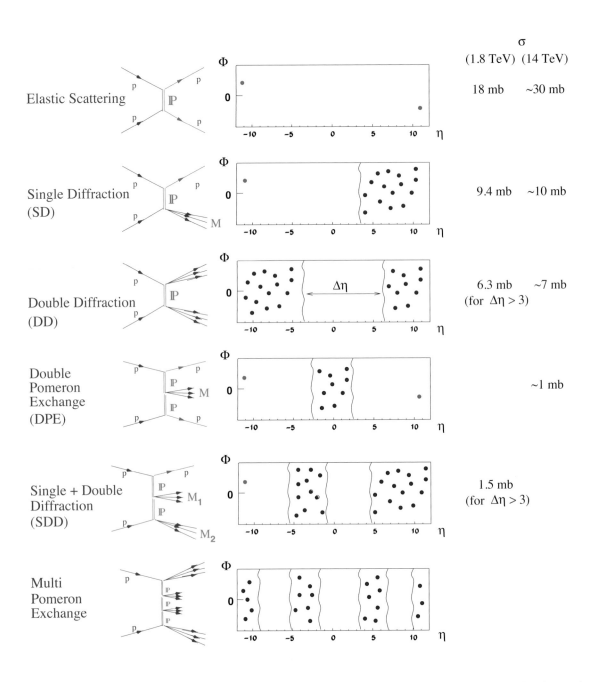

Figure 2.5: Diffractive process classes and their cross-sections measured at Tevatron and estimated for the LHC.

Chapter 3

Beam optics and running conditions

2008 JINST 3 S08007

For the luminosity independent total cross-section measurement TOTEM has to reach the lowest possible values of the squared four momentum transfer $-t \sim p^2 \Theta^2$ in elastic pp scattering.

Scattered particles close to the beam can be detected downstream on either side of the Interaction Point (IP) if the displacement at the detector location is large enough (at least $10\sigma_{\text{beam}}$ away from the beam center) and if the beam divergence ($\sim 1/\sqrt{\beta^*}$) at the IP is small compared to the scattering angle. In order to achieve these conditions special high beta optics are required: the larger the β^*, the smaller the beam divergence will be.

Two optics have been proposed: the ultimate one with $\beta^* = 1540$ m, probably foreseen at a later stage, and another one with $\beta^* = 90$ m. The latter uses the standard injection optics and the beam conditions typical for early LHC running: zero degree crossing-angle and consequently at most 156 bunches together with a low number of protons per bunch.

3.1 Properties of the high-β^* Optics

The properties of the optics can be expressed by the two optical functions L (effective length) and v (magnification) which, at a distance s from the IP, are defined by the betatron function $\beta(s)$ and the phase advance $\Delta\mu(s)$:

$$
\begin{aligned}
v(s) &= \sqrt{\frac{\beta(s)}{\beta^*}} \cos \Delta\mu(s) \\
L(s) &= \sqrt{\beta(s)\beta^*} \sin \Delta\mu(s) \\
\text{with} \quad \Delta\mu(s) &= \int_0^s \frac{1}{\beta(s')} ds'
\end{aligned}
\tag{3.1}
$$

The transverse displacement $(x(s), y(s))$ of a proton at a distance s from the IP is related to its transverse origin (x^*, y^*) and its momentum vector (expressed by the horizontal and vertical scattering angles Θ_x^* and Θ_y^* and by $\xi = \Delta p/p$) at the IP via the above optical functions and the dispersion $D(s)$ of the machine:

$$
\begin{aligned}
y(s) &= v_y(s) \cdot y^* + L_y(s) \cdot \Theta_y^* \\
x(s) &= v_x(s) \cdot x^* + L_x(s) \cdot \Theta_x^* + \xi \cdot D(s)
\end{aligned}
\tag{3.2}
$$

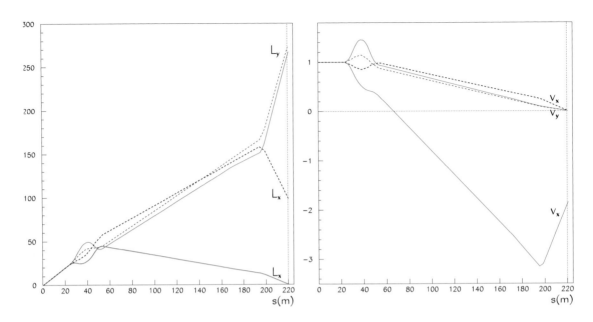

Figure 3.1: The optical functions for β^*=90 m (solid) and 1540 m (dashed) as function of the distance s to IP5: effective length L [in m] (left) and magnification v (right).

As a consequence of the high β^*, the beam size at the IP is large ($\sigma^*_{\text{beam}} \propto \sqrt{\beta^*}$). To eliminate the dependence on the transverse position of the proton at the collision point, the magnification has to be chosen close to zero (parallel-to-point focussing, $\Delta\mu = \pi/2$). At the same time, a large effective length ensures a sizeable displacement from the beam centre.

Having in mind the above optimisation for the position of the RP station RP220, two scenarios have been studied. Their optical functions are compared in figure 3.1. For $\beta^* = 1540$ m, the parallel-to-point focussing is achieved in both projections whereas for $\beta^* = 90$ m only in the vertical one. In both cases, the large L_y pushes the protons vertically into the acceptance of the RP detectors.

The minimum distance of a detector from the beam is proportional to the beam size:

$$y_{\text{min}} = K \sigma_y^{\text{beam}} = K \sqrt{\varepsilon \beta_y(s)}, \tag{3.3}$$

where ε is the transverse beam emittance and K is around 10–15. Assuming perfect parallel-to-point focussing, the smallest detectable angle is:

$$\Theta^*_{y\ min} = K \sqrt{\frac{\varepsilon}{\beta^*_y}}. \tag{3.4}$$

The parallel-to-point focussing condition allows the measurement of both t components (t_x, t_y) for elastically scattered protons at $\beta^* = 1540$ m but only the vertical component at $\beta^* = 90$ m.

Both optics also offer the possibility of detecting diffractive protons almost independent of their momentum loss. To be able to measure the momentum loss ξ with an acceptable resolution, L_x has to vanish to eliminate the dependence on the horizontal scattering angle Θ^*_x (cf. eq. (3.2)). This condition can only be achieved with the $\beta^* = 90$ m optics (figure 3.1).

2008 JINST 3 S08007

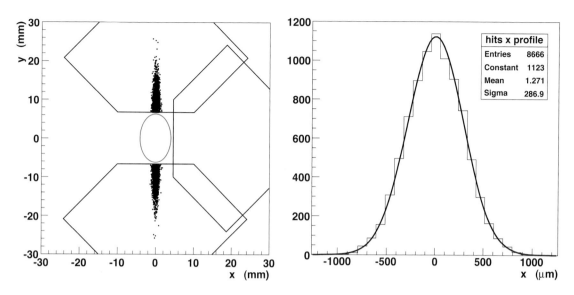

Figure 3.2: Left: hit distribution for elastic-scattering events in the detectors of RP220 with the $\beta^* = 90$ m optics; the $10\,\sigma_{beam}$ beam envelope is also shown. Right: hit distribution in the horizontal projection (x) at RP220.

3.2 Beam diagnostics

In addition to the luminosity measurement via the Optical Theorem, TOTEM can contribute more information to beam diagnostics, in particular with the $\beta^* = 90$ m optics. There, the horizontal hit positions of elastically scattered protons in the RP 220 m station depend only on the vertex position and not on the horizontal scattering angle. Thus the narrow hit distribution (figure 3.2) reflects well the horizontal beam position at the Roman Pot which can be used for an absolute calibration of the Beam Position Monitors on the micrometre level. Furthermore, this hit distribution gives access to the horizontal vertex distribution which can furthermore — assuming round beams — be exploited for an independent luminosity measurement based on beam parameters.

3.3 Running scenarios

The versatile physics programme of TOTEM requires different running scenarios that have to be adapted to the LHC commissioning and operation in the first years. A flexible trigger can be provided by the Roman Pot detectors and the T1 and T2 telescopes as discussed in chapter 8. TOTEM will take data under all optics conditions, adjusting the trigger schemes to the luminosity. The DAQ will allow trigger rates up to a few kHz without involving a higher level trigger.

The high-β^* runs (table 3.1) with 156 bunches, zero degree crossing-angle and maximum luminosity between 10^{29} and $10^{30}\,\mathrm{cm}^{-2}\mathrm{s}^{-1}$, will concentrate on low-$|t|$ elastic scattering, total cross-section, minimum bias physics and soft diffraction. A large fraction of forward protons will be detected even at the lowest ξ values.

Low-β^* runs (table 3.2) with more bunches and higher luminosity ($10^{32} - 10^{33}\,\mathrm{cm}^{-2}\mathrm{s}^{-1}$) will be used for large-$|t|$ elastic scattering and diffractive studies for $\xi > 0.02$. Hard diffractive events come within reach.

2008 JINST 3 S08007

Table 3.1: Running Scenarios for high β^* (k: number of bunches, N: number of protons per bunch). The t ranges given correspond to the $\geq 50\%$ acceptance intervals.

β^* [m]	k	$N/10^{11}$	$\mathscr{L}$ [cm^{-2}s^{-1}]	$\lvert t \rvert$-range [GeV^2] @ $\xi = 0$	ξ-range
1540	$43 \div 156$	$0.6 \div 1.15$	$10^{28} \div 2 \times 10^{29}$	$0.002 \div 1.5$	< 0.2
90	156	$0.1 \div 1.15$	$2 \times 10^{28} \div 3 \times 10^{30}$	$0.03 \div 10$	<0.2

Table 3.2: Running Scenarios for low β^* (k: number of bunches, N: number of protons per bunch)

β^* [m]	k	$N/10^{11}$	$\mathscr{L}$ [cm^{-2}s^{-1}]	$\lvert t \rvert$-range [GeV^2] @ $\xi = 0$	ξ-range
11	$936 \div 2808$	1.15	3×10^{32}	$0.6 \div 8$	$0.02 \div 0.2$
$0.5 \div 2$	$936 \div 2808$	1.15	10^{33}	$1 \div 10$	$0.02 \div 0.2$

2008 JINST 3 S08007

Chapter 4

The Roman Pot system

4.1 System strategy and overview

The detection of very forward protons in movable beam insertions — called Roman Pots (RP) — is an experimental technique introduced at the ISR [10]. It has been successfully employed in other colliders like the S$\bar{p}$pS, TEVATRON, RHIC and HERA. Detectors are placed inside a secondary vacuum vessel, called a pot, and moved into the primary vacuum of the machine through vacuum bellows. In this way, the detectors are physically separated from the primary vacuum which is thus preserved against an uncontrolled out-gassing of the detector's materials.

The challenging constraints of the LHC, such as the thin high-intensity beam, the Ultra High Vacuum and the high radiation fluxes have required the development of new Roman Pots. The main differences to RPs designed for earlier machines lie in the window technology of the pots, which have to be placed much closer to the beam, and in the driving mechanism, which must have high precision and radiation hardness.

Being symmetric with respect to IP5, TOTEM's RP system allows the reconstruction of protons on both sides of the interaction point. On each side, two stations of Roman Pots will be mounted on the beam pipe of the outgoing beam. Their positions have been defined in an interplay with the development of the special optics used by TOTEM, with constraints given by the space available between the LHC machine components. The centre of the first station ('RP147') is placed at 149.6 m from IP5, and the second ('RP220') at 217.3 m. Between the two stations, the dipole magnet D2 provides a dispersion difference which helps in proton momentum reconstruction. To have a lever arm for local track reconstruction and trigger selections by track angle, each RP station is composed of two units separated by a distance limited by integration constraints with the other beam elements (figure 4.1). The stations RP147 and RP220 span distances of 1.2 m and 5 m respectively. Each RP unit consists of 3 pots, 2 approaching the beam vertically and 1 horizontally. A schematic drawing of the beam-pipe of a RP unit with its insertions is shown in figure 4.2 (left). In summary, a total of 8 identical Roman Pot units or 24 individual pots are installed in the LHC.

The single horizontal pot in each unit, placed on the radially outer side of the LHC ring, serves two purposes. Firstly, it completes the acceptance for diffractively scattered protons whose momentum loss deviates them towards this pot. On the radially inner side of the LHC ring no detector is needed since only background protons arrive in that position. Secondly, the detectors in

2008 JINST 3 S08007

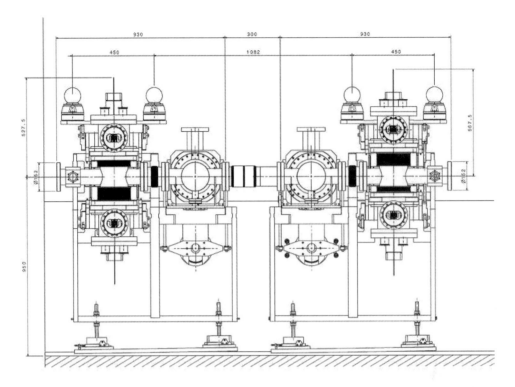

Figure 4.1: Design drawing of the station RP147, i.e. an assembly of two RP units. The other station, RP220, is identical apart from the bigger distance between the two units.

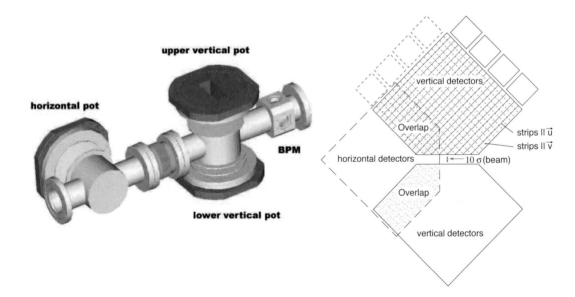

Figure 4.2: Left: the vacuum chambers of a RP unit accomodating the horizontal and the vertical pots and the Beam Position Monitor. Right: the overlap between the horizontal and vertical detectors.

2008 JINST 3 S08007

Figure 4.3: A unit of the first RP220 station installed in the LHC.

the horizontal pots overlap with the ones in the vertical pots, which correlates their positions via common particle tracks (see figure 4.2, right). This feature is used for the relative alignment of the three pots in a unit. For the absolute alignment, i.e. with respect to the beam, a Beam Position Monitor (BPM), based on a button feed-through technology, is integrated in the vacuum chamber of the vertical RP. A pre-calibration of the BPM relative to the pots is done in a metrology laboratory.

Each pot is equipped with a stack of 10 planes of novel "edgeless" silicon strip detectors (section 4.3). Half of them will have their strips oriented at an angle of $+45°$ with respect to the edge facing the beam, and the other half at an angle of $-45°$, measuring the coordinates u and v respectively. This configuration has the advantage that the hit profiles in the two projections are equivalent. The measurement of each track projection in five planes is advantageous for the reduction of uncorrelated background via programmable coincidences, requiring e.g. collinear hits in a majority of the planes.

Figure 4.3 shows a unit of an RP220 station after installation in the LHC.

2008 JINST 3 S08007

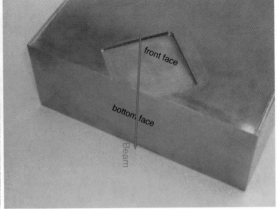

Figure 4.4: Left: the pot with the thin window and the Ferrite collar (black) needed to reduce the beam coupling impedance. Right: detailed view of the thin window; the front face is 0.5 mm thick, while the bottom face (towards the beam) is 0.15 mm thick.

4.2 Mechanical design of the Roman Pot

4.2.1 The vacuum chamber

Like all the 'warm' (i.e. non-cryogenic) vacuum equipment of the LHC, the RP vacuum chambers had to be baked out at 150°C. The supports of the two Roman pot vacuum chambers have been designed to allow a free dilatation during the bake out. Such a feature relieves the stress on the components and prevents permanent deformation. In addition, an interconnection bellow between the two vacuum chambers decouples the thermal deformations.

4.2.2 The pot and its thin window

The pot (figure 4.4) provides a volume with a secondary vacuum where the detectors and the services are enclosed. It has the shape of a 50 mm × 124 mm × 105 mm rectangular box, with 2 mm wall thickness, made of stainless steel (316LN). A support flange is attached to the box by electron beam welding. One side of the flange is connected to a bellow to close the machine vacuum volume (figure 4.5). The opposite side is connected to a second flange equipped with the detectors, which closes the secondary vacuum volume.

The RP window is composed of three parts: one facing the beam ("bottom face") and two orthogonal to the beam ("front and rear faces"). All faces have to be as thin as possible:

- The bottom face is a part of the insensitive space between the point of closest physical RP-to-beam approach and the efficient detector region. This insensitive space has to be kept small.

- The front and rear faces are traversed perpendicularly by the protons to be measured and by beam halo. To minimise signal proton deflections and showers, the window has to be kept thin.

2008 JINST 3 S08007

Figure 4.5: Detail of the RP220 station: the vertical pots attached to the vacuum tube by bellows.

Hence the window material, design and manufacturing technique have been optimised in view of achieving a minimum thickness and a flatness better than $50\,\mu$m, while maintaining UHV leak tightness and minimising deformations under pressure differences up to a safety-imposed limit of 1.5 bar. Comparative studies have shown that for the bottom face a thickness of 0.15 mm in stainless steel represents an optimum, while for the front and rear faces a thickness of 0.5 mm was chosen.

Several assembly procedures, like brazing, TIG and EB welding, have been investigated at CERN by the Assembly Technique group. The most satisfactory results have been obtained by brazing. The first step consists in brazing a thin window of stainless steel 316L on the bottom part of the pot. Successively the milling of the lateral sides is done, obtaining a 0.5 mm window. An excellent planarity down to $30\,\mu$m has been obtained on the prototypes.

Pressure cycles in the range ±1 bar were applied, followed by vacuum leak tests. The maximum deformation was 0.4 mm at 1 bar, while no leaks were detected with a threshold of 2×10^{-12} mbar l/s. An ultimate hydraulic pressure test was done on two prototypes. One was loaded with a fast pressure rise, and it broke at 50 bar. The second was loaded more slowly, and the test was stopped at 80 bars without rupture (figure 4.6). For both cases, the pressure levels are many times higher than the 1.5 bar required for safety.

The pot together with the bellow creates a resonant RF cavity for the beam running along the axis of the Roman Pot. Measurements of the beam coupling impedance have been performed in the lab where a metallic wire was strung through the RP [11]. A vector network analyser generated current pulses to simulate the beam and measured the complex transmission coefficient. The bare RP (without any ferrites mounted) shows several resonances in its longitudinal beam-coupling impedance Z_L. The dominant line at 740 MHz has an impedance of $1.2\,$kΩ corresponding to a broad-band value $Z/n = 18\,$mΩ with $n = f_{\text{resonance}}/f_{\text{LHC}} = 740\,$MHz $/ 11\,$kHz. This value was still well below but uncomfortably close to the LHC limit of $Z/n = 0.1\,\Omega$. However, a 2 mm thin collar of ferrites fixed on the external wall of the pot insertion (figure 4.4, left) removes all the resonances within the frequency domain relevant for the LHC, i.e. $0 - 1.5\,$GHz.

2008 JINST 3 S08007

Figure 4.6: Deformation of the thin window after the ultimate pressure test, stopped at 80 bar.

4.2.3 The movements

Each pot is independently moved by micro-stepping motors with angular steps of $(0.90 \pm 0.03)°$ per step, corresponding to 400 steps per turn. The transformation from the motor's rotational movement to the pot's translation movement is done by roller screws which provide high precision and zero backlashes.

A mechanical compensation system (figure 4.7) balances the atmospheric pressure load on the pot. The system relieves the stress on the driving mechanism, improving the movement accuracy and the safety of the operations. It is based on a separate vacuum system connected to the primary vacuum of the machine through a by-pass. The atmospheric pressure load on the pot-bellow system is $\sim$3000 N. With such a compensation system the stepper motor works only against the weight of the pot assembly ($\sim$100 N), leaving the possibility to achieve a better accuracy of the motor drive mechanism. With bellows on the compensation system larger than the pot bellows, a constant pulling load on the pots is guaranteed, and since the roller screws are a reversible mechanism, this feature is exploited to provide auto-retraction of the pots in case of a motor power cut.

The nominal mechanical pot-positioning resolution of the driving mechanism is 5 μm, but the final precision depends on the assembly of the motors and the roller screws. The stepper motors are equipped with angular resolvers which give the absolute position of each pot with respect to the nominal beam axis. Additional displacement inductive sensors (LVDT) provide the absolute position of each pot.

The driver units and the power supplies are placed in the counting room at up to 300 m cable distance, in a radiation protected area, where access is always possible, even with circulating beams.

4.3 "Edgeless" silicon detectors with current terminating structure

Due to their high energy, the LHC beams are very thin ($10\sigma \approx 0.8$ mm at RP220 for $\beta^* = 1540$ m). It is therefore mandatory that the silicon detectors, housed in the RPs, approach the beam centre

2008 JINST 3 S08007

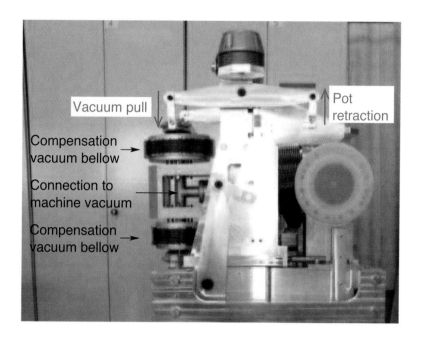

Vacuum pull

Pot retraction

Compensation vacuum bellow

Connection to machine vacuum

Compensation vacuum bellow

Figure 4.7: The vacuum compensation system.

to a distance as small as 1 mm. Consequently the detectors have to be fully efficient up to their mechanical edge.

Silicon detectors fabricated with standard planar technology require terminating structures to reduce electric field maxima at the detector periphery to prevent the surface irregularities on the chip cut from affecting the device performance, and to reduce the breakdown probability. They are generally a sequence of floating guardrings surrounding the sensitive part of the device and adding an external dead volume. This ring structure, called "voltage terminating structure", controls the potential distribution between the detector's sensitive area and the cut edge to have a vanishing potential drop at the chip cut. The insensitive margin increases with the number of rings, and for high voltage applications, as is the case for silicon detectors used in harsh radiation environments, it can be more than 1 mm wide. For the TOTEM experiment the reduction of this dead space is vital.

These requirements first led to tests with silicon detectors operated at cryogenic temperatures ($\sim 110\,\mathrm{K}$, [12]) and finally triggered the development of a new terminating structure that allows detectors fabricated with standard planar technology to reach full sensitivity within less than $100\,\mu\mathrm{m}$ from the cut edge and to operate with high bias at room temperature [13].

4.3.1 The concept of current terminating structures

For segmented devices with this new so-called "Current Terminating Structure (CTS)", the potential applied to bias the device has to be applied also across the cut edges via a guardring running along the die cut and surrounding the whole sample. This external guardring, also called "Current Terminating Ring (CTR)" collects the current generated in the highly damaged region at the cut edge, avoiding its diffusion into the sensitive volume, and is separated from the biasing electrode (BE). In this manner the sensitive volume can start at less than $50\,\mu\mathrm{m}$ from the cut edge. To prevent

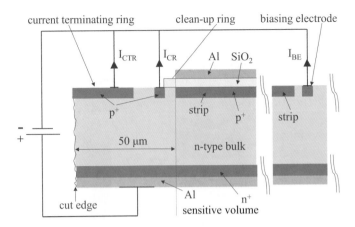

Figure 4.8: Cross-section of a silicon detector with CTS in the plane parallel to the strips and its biasing scheme.

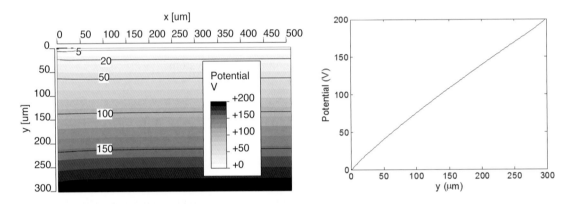

Figure 4.9: Left: potential distribution at the edge of a $300\,\mu$m thick silicon pad detector with CTS for a bias voltage of 200 V. The calculation extended up to $500\,\mu$m into the detector from the cut edge. Right: electric potential at the cut edge with an almost linear behaviour.

any further diffusion of this edge current into the sensitive volume, another implanted ring — the Clean-up Ring (CR) — can be placed between the CTR and the sensitive volume. The CTS and its biasing scheme are shown in figure 4.8.

For devices with this type of CTS, the leakage current in the sensitive volume (I_{BE}) which contributes to noise is not affected by the edge current ($I_{CTR} + I_{CR}$). The leakage current and the edge current have been shown to be completely decoupled. Moreover, for such devices, the charge collection efficiency has been shown to rise steeply from the edge of the sensitive volume reaching full efficiency within a few tens of micrometers (see section 4.6.1.1).

The electric potential distribution at the edge of a device with CTS has been modelled taking into account the highly damaged surface at the chip cut, where the irregularities within the first atomic layers could be assimilated to amorphous silicon. The results of this modelling have shown good consistency with the experimental results [14]. The potential distribution calculated with ISE TCAD [15] is shown in figure 4.9.

2008 JINST 3 S08007

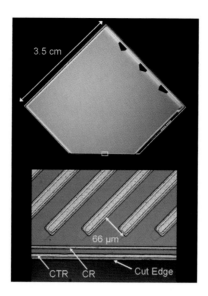

Figure 4.10: Picture of a Planar Edgeless Detector with CTS (top). The magnification of a portion of the chip cut region (bottom) shows the details of the CTS.

4.3.2 The silicon detector for the TOTEM Roman Pots

The advantages offered by the CTS have led TOTEM to choose this technology for the RP detectors. Geometry and granularity have been adapted to the specific requirements on surface coverage and spatial resolution.

The detectors have been developed and produced in a joint effort of the TOTEM group at CERN and Megaimpulse, a spin-off company from the Ioffe Physico-Technical Institute in St. Petersburg (Russia). These devices are single-sided AC p^+-n microstrip detectors with 512 strips and a pitch of 66 μm processed on very high resistivity n-type silicon wafers ($> 10\,\mathrm{k\Omega\,cm}$), 300 μm thick. All of them have the CTS as described in section 4.3 on one edge, i.e. the edge facing the beam. At one end of the strips an integrated pitch adapter reduces the inter-strip distance from 66 μm to 44 μm, producing four separated groups of 128 channels. This allows direct wire bonding to the readout chip VFAT. A picture of the planar edgeless Silicon detector for the TOTEM Roman Pots and a detail of the CTS are shown in figure 4.10. In these sensors the biasing is made via "punch-through" from a biasing electrode placed inside the CR. On all the sides where the sensitivity at the edge is not required, the CTS is integrated into a standard voltage terminating structure. The strips on the detector are at an angle of $45°$ with respect to the edge facing the beam.

4.3.3 Electrical characterisation

For the detector polarised according to the biasing scheme shown above, the typical values of currents measured at the CTR and the CR, $I_{\mathrm{CTR}} + I_{\mathrm{CR}}$, are compared to the current measured at the biasing electrode, I_{BE}, and shown in figures 4.11 and 4.12. There is a difference of four orders of magnitude between the current at the biasing electrode flowing through the sensitive volume of the detector and the one flowing through CR and CTR. This evidences that virtually all the leakage

2008 JINST 3 S08007

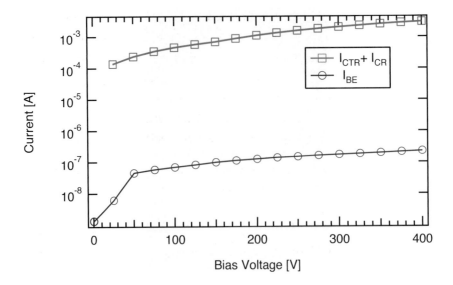

Figure 4.11: Current vs. voltage characteristics through the biasing electrode (I_{BE}) and across a detector edge ($I_{CTR} + I_{CR}$), measured at room temperature.

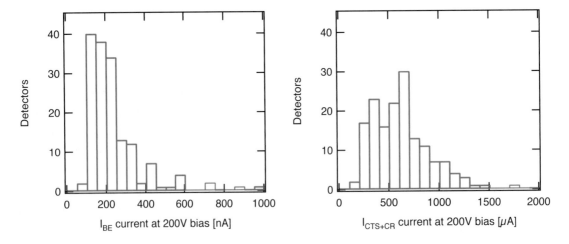

Figure 4.12: Distributions of the bulk current I_{BE} (left) and the edge current $I_{CTR} + I_{CR}$ (right) for a sample of 158 detectors at a bias voltage of 200 V.

current generated at the edge surface is collected by the CTR and the CR and does not flow through the sensitive volume where it would make detector operation impossible. The low current flowing into the biasing electrode confirms the validity of the current termination approach.

2008 JINST 3 S08007

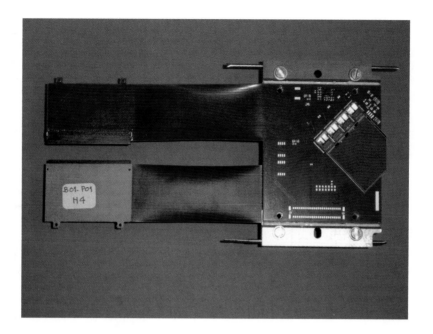

Figure 4.13: Two RP hybrids mounted back-to-back. Each hybrid carries the silicon detector and four VFAT readout chips.

4.4 On-detector electronics

The generalised electronics are described in more detail in chapter 7. Only the electronic boards that are relevant to the mechanical construction and the detector monitoring are discussed here. The silicon detector hybrid (figure 4.13) carries the detector with 512 strips wire-bonded to the input channels of 4 readout chips "VFAT" (section 7.1), and a Detector Control Unit (DCU) chip. Each VFAT provides tracking and trigger generation signals from 128 strips. The DCU chip is used to monitor detector leakage currents, power supply voltages and temperature. Via an 80 pin connector each VFAT will send the trigger outputs and the serialised tracking data from all strips to the motherboard, together with clock and trigger input signals, HV and LV power, and connections for a heater and a PT100 resistance thermometer for temperature control.

Due to the ±45° orientation of the detector strips, flipping the detector hybrid and mounting it face to face with the next one results in mutually orthogonal strips giving the u and v coordinate information. To avoid losing space in between two hybrids, all electrical components are mounted on one side such that they do not overlap for the two cards mounted face to face and that they can be separated by only one component height.

In such way 10 detector hybrids closely arranged in 5 pairs, can be connected to one motherboard feeding all electrical connections through the flange between the pot's secondary vacuum and the outside world at atmospheric pressure.

The motherboard (figure 4.14) hosts clock and trigger distribution circuitry, Gigabit Optical Hybrids (GOH) — three for data and two for trigger bit transfer, two Coincidence Chip mezzanines, LVDS-to-CMOS converters, Trigger VFAT mezzanine, Control Unit mezzanine CCUM, Radiation Monitor circuitry and temperature sensors. The binary tracking data are stored in a digital memory

2008 JINST 3 S08007

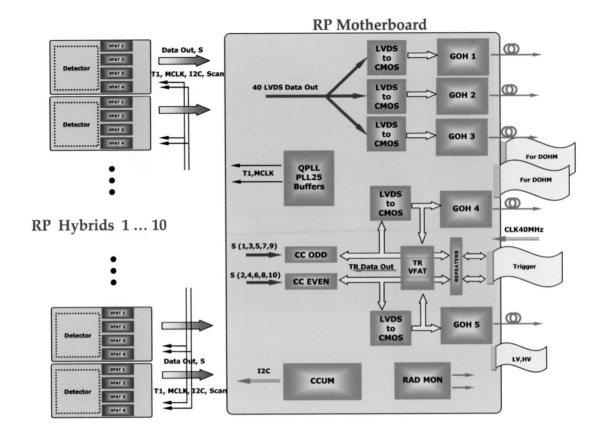

Figure 4.14: Block diagram of the RP motherboard with the connections to the hybrids.

and read out upon application of a readout trigger. A front panel with connectors for low and high voltage, control, data and trigger bit transfer to facilitates the connection to the central patch panel of the RP station.

To transmit the trigger bits to the counting room two options are implemented: the preferred choice — optical fibers — is used for the 150 m RP station and in TOTEM standalone runs also for the 220 m station. Common runs with CMS on the other hand are subject to CMS's limited trigger latency time, imposing trigger bit transmission with LVDS signals through fast electrical cables. The electrical transmission over such a long distance requires care to preserve signal integrity. This can only be achieved by restoring the LVDS signals to full levels at regular intervals over the transmission distance. A special integrated circuit was designed for this purpose: the LVDS repeater chip can treat 16 LVDS channels in parallel and was designed in special layout to guarantee radiation tolerance. This chip will be mounted on a small repeater board. At regular intervals of about 70 m a repeater station is introduced which consists of several repeater boards with cable connectors. Power for the repeaters is supplied along the cable as well, and filtered on board.

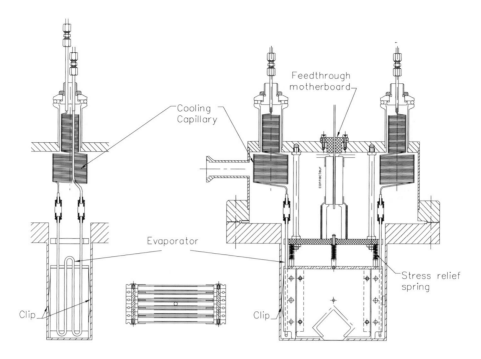

Figure 4.15: Conceptual design of the silicon detector package in the pot. In both views the clips for the alignment of the assembly are shown. The capillaries and evaporators are parts of the cooling system.

4.5 Detector integration and cooling in the Roman Pot

4.5.1 Integration of detector stacks in the pot

Each pot houses a compact stack of 10 detector planes with their hybrid boards and cooling pipes (figures 4.15, 4.16).

To keep the total width of the inefficient zone between the outer RP window surface and the active detector area below 0.5 mm, the distance between the thin window and the physical detector edge must not exceed $200\,\mu$m. The targeted alignment precision of $30\,\mu$m has to hold both at the mounting time and at the operation time. Since the detector modules will be mounted and operated at different temperatures, thermal contractions and expansions have to be taken into account.

The hybrid board is made of a processed Kapton film laminated on a high thermal conductivity substrate with a thickness of 0.5 mm. The material of the substrate is an Al-Si 70%–30% alloy (CE07), which has the advantage of a high thermal conductivity and a thermal expansion closely matching the one of the silicon sensor. The connectivity between the hybrid and the vacuum feedthrough card (motherboard) is based on a kapton 'pigtail' with end connector. Both the silicon sensor and the four VFAT chips are glued with thermally conductive thermoplastic film to the hybrid. The chips are aligned on the hybrid using precision markers. After bonding the outputs of the chips to the hybrid the proper functioning of the complete hybrid is tested. In a second step, the sensor is aligned such that the bond pads of chips and sensor are best matched, and the input side of the chips is then bonded to the sensor. No special tools, except a bonding jig are required up to this point. Ten completed hybrids are then assembled by means of precision dowels and micrometre

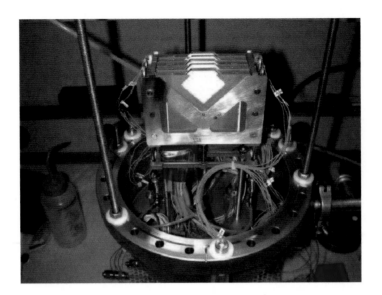

Figure 4.16: The detector package prototype mounted on the vacuum chamber.

stages to form the detector package. Survey with a 3D Coordinate Measuring Machine (CMM) is performed to determine the edge locations of all ten silicon sensors.

The assembly is fixed by means of a slightly flexible fixation on the support plate which is rigidly attached to the detector vacuum flange. The fixation is spring loaded. Once the detector is inserted in the Roman Pot, it exerts a small force on the bottom plate of the Pot ensuring the positioning of the assembly relative to the bottom plate. A flexible clip on the side of the assembly maintains the assembly with a slight force aligned to one side wall of the pot. A second similar clip will ensure the alignment of the assembly with respect to the front and back walls. The entire structure is conceived such that it can be dismantled and reassembled.

4.5.2 The cooling system

The cooling system integrated in the RP insertion will have to remove the thermal load from the sensors and the electronics. Moreover, to allow operation after high irradiation the RP silicon detectors will be operated at about -10°C to reduce the radiation induced thermally generated bulk current and to control the reverse annealing after high irradiation. Nevertheless given the geometry of the package it will be difficult to keep all modules at the same temperature. A spread of less than 10°C between the ten plates can be tolerated and does not represent a strong constraint. The major contribution to the thermal load of the whole system is given by the readout chips (VFATs). The total load per pot is about 20 W.

Because of the high radiation environment of the LHC tunnel, the main part of the refrigeration system is not installed near the RP but in the underground service area USC55 at IP5, a protected and always accessible place.

An evaporative fluorocarbon cooling strategy [16] has been adopted since it can transport fluid at ambient temperature over long distances (from USC55 near IP5 to the RP stations at 147 m and 220 m) without heat losses but only pressure drops which are still low and can be balanced by the compressors. The throttling of the fluid is done in the pot and is based on metal capillary

2008 JINST 3 S08007

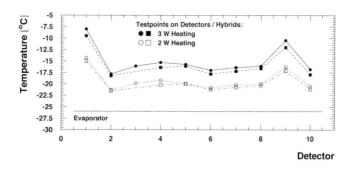

Figure 4.17: Temperature distribution measured on testpoints on the detectors (circular markers) and on the hybrids (square markers) for a heating power of 2 W and 3 W (open and solid markers respectively), compared with the evaporator temperature.

tubes. The C_3F_8 fluorocarbon dielectric fluid has been selected because it is non-flammable, non-conductive and radiation resistant. The heat transfer process is very effective because of the two phase flow regime.

The evaporative cooling system has been designed to guarantee a total cooling capacity of 1.2 kW and supply a global mass flow rate of 40 g/s to be uniformly shared between the 24 TOTEM Roman Pots. The fluid is supplied in liquid phase and at high pressure at the RP circuit inlet. The system is completely oil free and the process fluid adequately filtered to avoid any mechanical particle obstructing the lamination capillaries' inner section under irradiation.

Inside the Roman Pot the fluid medium flows through thin-walled copper-nickel pipes of 2.5 mm outer diameter. Two independent pipe evaporators supply fluid to the right and left side of the detector package. The evaporators are mechanically decoupled from the detector assembly at the inputs and outputs either by a bellow or by a spiral section. They are shaped in a double-S configuration and are squeezed in between the frame structure which foresees precisely machined grooves for this purpose. The evaporators are fed by capillary tubes that provide the throttling of the fluid. The coolant in gas phase is exhausted via larger diameter pipes. Both the capillaries and the exhausting pipes enter and leave the pot through two vacuum feed-throughs.

4.5.3 Tests on the thermo-mechanical prototype

A thermo-mechanical prototype has been assembled to characterise the conceptual design, the choice of the materials and the fluido-dynamic parameters of the cooling system. The VFAT chips on the hybrids were replaced with heaters with equivalent power density. The prototype was fixed to a vacuum chamber flange and inserted in an experimental vacuum chamber. All the connections of the pressure and temperatures sensors were read out through the vacuum feed-through. A capillary tube with an inner diameter of 0.55 mm was used.

The measurements showed that for the expected heating power of 2 W the temperature spread on a single hybrid card is within 3°C, and the maximum temperature difference between detectors is less than 10°C (figure 4.17).

The final length of the capillary, 1.5 m, is the result of an optimisation in view of obtaining a suitable pressure drop. The capillary will be coiled up in the pot to minimise the heat loss and the need of additional insulation.

2008 JINST 3 S08007

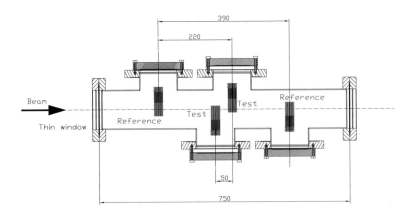

Figure 4.18: Arrangement of the test detectors and reference detectors with respect to the beam axis (dashed line) inside a test vacuum tube.

4.6 Detector performance

4.6.1 Detector tests with analog readout

4.6.1.1 Testbeam measurement of CTS detector performance

Edgeless silicon detectors have been tested in autumn 2004 with a muon beam in the SPS X5 area at CERN [13, 17]. The sensors had the final size and strip pitch of $66\,\mu$m. They were assembled into 4 packages each consisting of 8 detectors. The majority was read out with CMS's analogue APV25 chips [18] while a few were equipped with prototypes of TOTEM's own front-end chip, the VFAT, to test its trigger functionality. The packages formed a telescope placed inside a vacuum tube (see figure 4.18).

The outermost assemblies were used as reference to define tracks while the inner ones served as devices under test. The detector positions were measured with a precision of a few tens of microns. In the data analysis, the detector alignment was further refined with a global χ^2 minimisation algorithm to the precision of the order of $1\,\mu$m.

The detector setup was used to determine the resolution and the behaviour of the efficiency at the active edge of the test detectors. For these studies the detectors were operated at a temperature of around -10°C.

The CTS detectors in the test setup were biased at of 50 V, enough to overdeplete them and allow the full charge collection within the integration time of the readout electronics. Since more than 80% of hit clusters in these detectors consisted of one strip, the resolution of the detectors was close to the theoretical result when charge sharing is negligible, which is given by $d/\sqrt{12} = 19\,\mu$m, where $d = 66\,\mu$m is the strip pitch. A typical residual distribution is shown in figure 4.19 (left).

The efficiencies of the test detectors with respect to their geometrical coordinates were computed as fractions of accepted tracks. A track was considered as accepted when the test detector registered a hit within $\pm100\,\mu$m from the track. The combined reconstruction and alignment information was used to determine the position of the cut detector edges. The observed 10%–90% efficiency rise interval at the active edge was for all detectors smaller than $50\,\mu$m, and the re-

2008 JINST 3 S08007

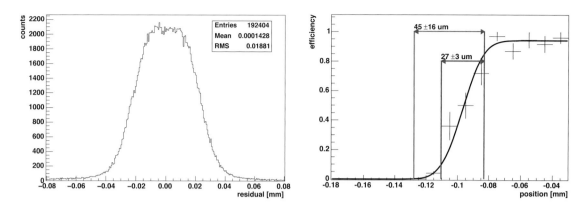

Figure 4.19: Left: residual distribution of a CTS test detector. The observed resolution was about $19\,\mu$m for all the test detectors, as expected from theory. Right: the efficiency of a CTS detector at the sensitive edge. The left-most vertical line indicates the reconstructed position of the physical edge, the other two vertical lines indicate the 10%–90% efficiency rise interval. The fit was performed with a Gaussian error function.

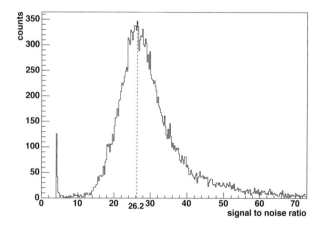

Figure 4.20: Signal-to-noise ratio distributions of a CTS test detector operated at a bias voltage of 100 V and at -11°C. The value of the most probable signal-to-noise ratio equals 26.2.

constructed distance between the cut edge and the position where 90% efficiency is reached was smaller than $60\,\mu$m. Figure 4.19 (right) shows the behaviour of the efficiency of one of the test detectors along the direction perpendicular to the cut edge.

Depending on the bias voltage and the detector thickness, the most probable value of signal-to-noise ratio was between 20 and 30. Figure 4.20 presents an example signal-to-noise distribution of the over-depleted test detector, operated at the bias voltage of 100 V.

2008 JINST 3 S08007

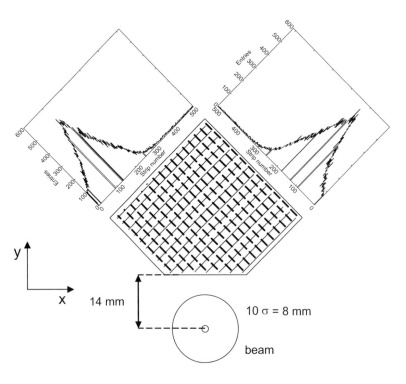

Figure 4.21: Profile of the SPS beam halo as seen by two orthogonal CTS detector planes at a distance of 14 mm from the beam centre. The data were taken with the bottom pot and the picture has been rotated by 180° around the beam axis for more convenience.

4.6.1.2 Full RP operation test in the SPS accelerator

The full operation of a Roman Pot unit prototype, consisting of a vacuum chamber equipped with two vertical insertions, was tested in a coasting beam experiment in the beamline of the SPS accelerator at CERN [11]. Each of the two insertions hosted four pairs of edgeless silicon detectors mounted back to back. In this early test, three pairs in each pot were used for tracking and were read out with the analogue APV25 chips. One pair was read out with a first prototype version of the digital VFAT chips delivering the fast-OR signal of all 512 strips used for triggering the data acquisition system in coincidence with the sum signal of the four pick-up electrodes of a beam position monitor located close to the detectors. Three different bunch structures were tested in the SPS accelerator: 1 single bunch in the accelerator ring, 4 bunches equally spaced, and 4 equally spaced trains of 4 bunches of 8×10^{10} 270 GeV protons with a revolution period of 23 μs. Detector data were taken with the two pots moving independently between 6 mm and 14 mm ($\sigma_{\text{beam}} = 0.8$ mm) from the beam pipe centre. Beam halo protons were detected at typical rates of 3 kHz. Figure 4.21 shows the halo profiles measured by two orthogonal detector planes of this pot. There were a few noisy channels on both detectors which have been removed from the profiles.

2008 JINST 3 S08007

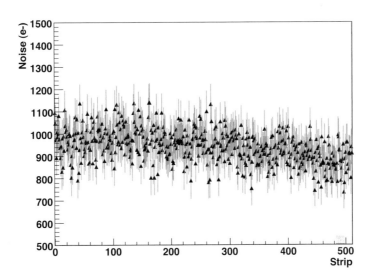

Figure 4.22: Noise at the different VFAT channels bonded to the edgeless detector biased with 150 V.

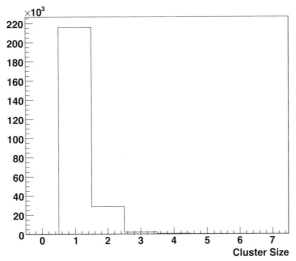

Figure 4.23: Cluster size in number of strips for particles perpendicular to the detector plane (detector bias: 150 V).

4.6.2 Operation of CTS detectors with VFAT chip

During 2007, the silicon detectors with CTS were tested in the H8 beam with the final electronics. Each detector was mounted on a final hybrid as described in section 4.4. Figure 4.22 shows the noise per strip, expressed in electrons, for all strips of one detector. The average noise and the rms are about 1000 and 100 electrons respectively. No outstandingly noisy channels were observed.

Tracks were defined in the H8 beam with a small size scintillator hodoscope, adjusted to the beam size. The cluster size for tracks, perpendicular to the test detector plane, is plotted in figure 4.23. In 90% of the cases, the cluster contains only 1 strip. This is a typical scenario for the forward protons in the TOTEM experiment since they are parallel to the beams and hence perpendicular to the detector planes within better than 1 mrad.

2008 JINST 3 S08007

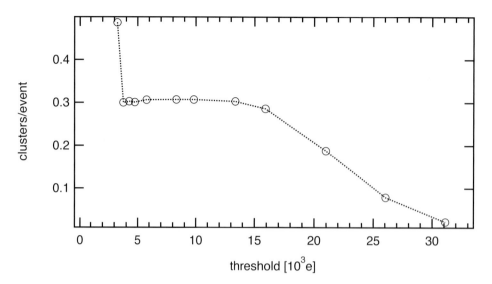

Figure 4.24: Threshold scan for one of the four VFAT chips of the Roman Pot Hybrid performed with a pion beam from the SPS. The number of clusters per triggered event is plotted versus the discriminator threshold expressed in electrons (detector bias: 150 V). The trigger was given by two scintillators in coincidence whose overlap covered slightly less than the whole CTS detector, about 3 times the area read out by the VFAT considered here, which explains the plateau level of $\sim 30\%$.

In order to demonstrate the detector response, several threshold scans were performed with a pion beam. In figure 4.24 the number of clusters per triggered event is plotted versus the discriminator threshold expressed in electrons. The noise starts to become visible at a threshold of 3000 electrons (three times above the average noise, see figure 4.22), at an occupancy level of 0.2% per strip. The wide plateau extends over a range of 10000 electrons. The maximum of the pulse height distribution can be estimated from the falling edge of the threshold curve. It corresponds to an efficiency loss of about 1/3 at a threshold of 21000 electrons, resulting in a signal-to-noise ratio in the range of 20 to 25.

4.6.3 Irradiation studies for CTS detectors

It is important to evaluate the radiation hardness of the edgeless Silicon detectors. However, there are no indications to believe that the performance of the edgeless devices with CTS after high radiation would degrade faster than the ones with standard voltage terminating structures provided that the edge current ($I_{CTR} + I_{CR}$) and the sensitive volume current (I_{BE}) whose dominant component is the bulk current, remain decoupled also after high radiation. To prove this assumption, edgeless silicon detectors have been irradiated at the neutron reactor TRIGA in Ljubljana at different fluxes up to 10^{14} 1 MeV n/cm². The edge current stays constant, independent of the radiation dose (figure 4.25, left). The bulk current I_{BE} increases proportional to the fluence Φ (figure 4.25, right). The damage factor α, defined as

$$\alpha = \frac{I_{BE}}{\mathcal{V}\Phi},$$

(4.1)

where $\mathcal{V}$ is the detector volume, amounts to about 5×10^{-17} A/cm [19], which is in agreement with earlier measurements on devices using standard voltage terminating structures [20].

2008 JINST 3 S08007

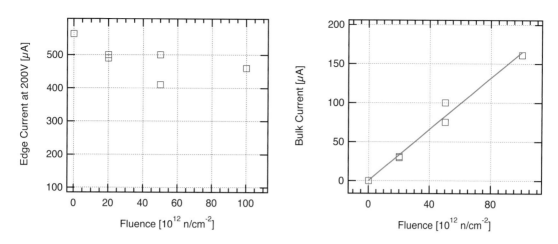

Figure 4.25: Left: edge current of CTS detectors biased at 200 V after different neutron fluences. Right: bulk current at full depletion voltage as a function of the fluence fitted with a linear function.

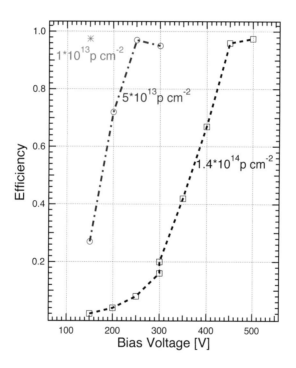

Figure 4.26: Efficiency of irradiated Edgeless Detectors with CTS at the working temperature of -18°C. The efficiency has been calculated by comparing the hits in the irradiated detector with the hits in a non-irradiated detector placed in front, along the beam axis.

More detectors have been irradiated with 24 GeV protons at CERN. The efficiency of these detectors as measured in the H8 test beam is given in figure 4.26 as a function of the bias voltage. Whilst a radiation up to 10^{13} p/cm^2 does not change the detector behaviour, stronger irradiated detectors (1.4×10^{14} p/cm^2) need a much higher bias voltage up to 450 V to be fully efficient. Presently, a radiation of 10^{14} p/cm^2 is considered as an upper limit for a functioning detector.

2008 JINST 3 S08007

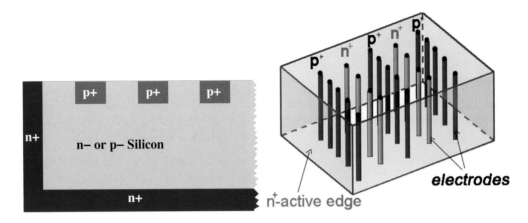

Figure 4.27: Left: sketch of a planar-3D detector. The edge (dark region) on the left hand side of the sketch, is an extension of the backside n^+ electrode and allows full control of the electric field lines at the edge. Right: sketch of a full 3D detector where the p^+ and n^+ electrodes are processed inside the silicon bulk. The edges constitute another n^+ electrode surrounding the 3D volume.

The above detectors were homogenously irradiated whereas in the experiment, due to diffractive protons, only a tiny area of a few mm^2 close to the sensitive edge is exposed to high proton fluence. Therefore, a non-irradiated detector was tested with bias voltages up to 500 V. Performance problems at this large bias voltage were not observed. However, a few strips showed a higher noise occupancy than at lower voltages.

Calculations of the diffractive proton flux hitting the detectors indicate that the present detectors will probably be alive up to an integrated luminosity of about 1 fb^{-1}. To cope with higher luminosities, TOTEM has initiated an INTAS project [21] to develop radiation harder edgeless detectors.

4.7 Alternative detector technologies: planar-3D and full 3D silicon

In addition to the planar silicon detectors with CTS, TOTEM is considering to equip some RPs partly with another novel type of "edgeless" silicon detectors: the planar-3D detectors [22], i.e. devices with a conventional planar microstrip interior and active edges as introduced with the full 3D detector technology [23]. In this configuration, the free edges of a planar detector are deep etched and n^+ dopant diffused in. Then the sensor is removed from the wafer again by etching, avoiding in this way the typical surface defects produced by saw cuts. In this way the edges of the sensor become an extension of the back-side n^+ electrode to the front side, as shown schematically in figure 4.27 (left). This enclosing n^+ electrode — the "active edge" — completely defines the electric field lines when a reverse bias voltage is applied. Also with this technology, the dead area which would be needed for guard rings in conventional planar detectors is reduced to no more than a few tens of microns.

Prototypes of planar-3D detectors have been tested in the 2004 testbeam together with the CTS detectors. Both the efficiency rise at the edge and the spatial resolution of the planar-3D detectors were measured to be very similar to those of the CTS detectors. However, these early

2008 JINST 3 S08007

sensor prototypes had only a thickness of 235 μm and — due to a production problem — could only be biassed with voltages up to 30 V where they are not yet fully depleted. Both facts led to a most probable signal-to-noise ratio of only 11.5. Studies on more advanced samples of this detector technology are being continued.

On the quest for edgeless radiation-hard detector technologies, TOTEM has also conducted the first beamtest with small prototypes of full 3D active-edge detectors, as sketched in figure 4.27 (right) and described in [23]. The test results were very encouraging [24]. In particular, the 10-to-90% efficiency rise at the edge happens over a distance of only 18 μm, and the measured sensitive width of the detector is equal to the physical width within 10 μm. While the production of large-area sensors is still difficult at present, this intrinsically radiation-hard technology [25] is a promising upgrade option for future operation at highest luminosities.

2008 JINST 3 S08007

Chapter 5

The forward telescopes

5.1 System strategy

The measurement of the inelastic rate, which is necessary for the total cross-section determination, is performed by identifying all beam-beam events with detectors capable to trigger and to reconstruct the interaction vertex. Monte Carlo studies have shown that a good detector coverage in the forward region is necessary for a complete measurement of the inelastic rate. The main requirements of these detectors are:

- to provide a fully inclusive trigger for minimum bias and diffractive events, with minimal losses at a level of a few percent of the inelastic rate;

- to enable the reconstruction of the primary vertex of an event, in order to disentangle beam-beam events from the background via a partial event reconstruction (mainly the tracks coming from the primary vertex);

- a detector arrangement which is left-right symmetric with respect to the IP, in order to have a better control of the systematic uncertainties.

The requirements for such detectors are somewhat different from those for detectors that must guarantee detection and reconstruction of each particle in the event, which has influenced the choice of the technology for T1 and T2.

The TOTEM forward telescopes cover a rapidity range of about 4 units and are installed symmetrically in the forward regions of CMS (figure 1.1) on both sides ("arms") of the IP:

- T1 ($3.1 \leq |\eta| \leq 4.7$) is made of 5 planes per arm, each consisting of 6 trapezoidal Cathode Strip Chambers (CSC), and will be installed in the CMS End Caps between the vacuum chamber and the iron of the magnet, at a distance of 7.5 to 10.5 m from the IP.

- T2 ($5.3 \leq |\eta| \leq 6.5$) is made of 20 half circular sectors of GEM (Gas Electron Multiplier) detectors per arm and will be installed between the vacuum chamber and the inner shielding of the HF calorimeter at an average distance of 13.5 m from the IP.

In addition to the measurement of the total inelastic rate, T1 and T2 will be key detectors for the study of inelastic processes either by TOTEM or by the joint CMS/TOTEM experiments [2]. At low luminosities ($\mathscr{L} < 10^{31}\,\mathrm{cm}^{-2}\mathrm{s}^{-1}$):

- The integrated inclusive Single Diffractive (SD) and Double Pomeron Exchange (DPE) cross-sections can be measured, as well as their t and M_X dependence (where M_X is the mass of the diffractive system). SD and DPE events have a clean signature in TOTEM and can be triggered requiring at least one track in T1 or T2 in coincidence with the proton(s) detected in the Roman Pots.

- T1 and T2 contribute to the detection and measurement of the rapidity gaps in diffractive events, which may provide a complementary measurement of the fractional momentum loss of the surviving proton(s), as well as shed new light on the problem of the rapidity gap survival probability.

- The telescopes' coverage and granularity allow the measurement of the charged multiplicity in the forward region, providing important information for the cosmic ray physics community (mainly to tune their event generators). More details can be found in [26].

At higher luminosity, in the range $10^{31} < \mathscr{L} < 10^{33}\,\mathrm{cm}^{-2}\mathrm{s}^{-1}$, T2 can be used in the joint CMS/ TOTEM experiment for hard diffraction and forward physics studies. It can be used as a rapidity gap trigger in order to reduce QCD background in exclusive particle production in DPE events, as well as to help in very forward lepton identification in Drell-Yan pair production. The possibility of exploiting T2 track information in the study of rare processes such as single-diffractive proton dissociation into three very forward jets is still under investigation.

5.2   T1 telescope

5.2.1   Requirements and choice of detector technology

The T1 telescope, installed in two cone-shaped regions in the endcaps of CMS, detects charged particles in the pseudo-rapidity range $3.1 \leq |\eta| \leq 4.7$.

At $\mathscr{L} = 10^{28}\mathrm{cm}^{-2}\mathrm{s}^{-1}$ with a reduced number of bunches, the expected number of interactions per bunch crossing is expected to be 2.5×10^{-3} which translates to an inelastic interaction rate of about 1 kHz. The average number of charged particles per event in T1 is expected to be ~ 40.

The inelastic trigger plays an important role in the measurement of the total cross-section: one needs a minimum bias trigger with a very high and measured efficiency. Systematics in the measurement of the trigger efficiency will be studied using different trigger combinations and cross-checks of their stability during the measurement. The basic trigger elements (primitives) are arranged in a roughly pointing arrangement to perform, if necessary, a first level background suppression, and will be useful also to define the different sub triggers. To discriminate good beam-beam events from the background, which includes beam-gas interactions (pointing to different regions in z inside the beam pipe) and other machine backgrounds such as the muon halo (approximately parallel to the beam), TOTEM needs to reconstruct only a number of tracks sufficient to reconstruct the position of the interaction vertex and check that it is compatible with the interaction point.

A detector with a well-known technology to meet these general requirements is the multi-wire proportional chamber with segmented cathode read-out: the Cathode Strip Chamber (CSC).

2008 JINST 3 S08007

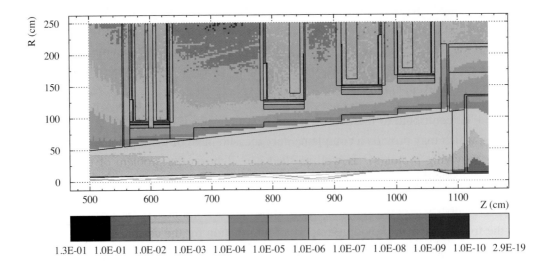

Figure 5.1: Expected accumulated dose, in Gy, from a simulation for 1 s at $10^{34}\,\mathrm{cm^{-2}s^{-1}}$ luminosity, in the region occupied by T1.

These detectors, in which a single gas gap with segmented cathode planes allows a two-dimensional measurement of the particle position, are well understood (see for example [27]). Gas detectors of this kind are slow, but the response time for a CSC with a 10.0 mm gas gap is still compatible with the expected hit rates for TOTEM. Moreover, TOTEM's CSCs can be built in shapes suitable to cover the required area of the T1 telescope. They have small material densities which is important because they are positioned in front of forward calorimeters.

Another delicate parameter to consider is the behaviour in a high-radiation environment. Detailed simulations [28] estimate the flux of charged and neutral particles and the accumulated dose in the T1 region (figure 5.1).

The ageing properties of the TOTEM CSCs have been tested at the Gamma Irradiation Facility at CERN: two chambers have been irradiated, integrating a total charge on the anode wires of 0.065 C/cm, without showing any loss of performance, in agreement with tests performed by CMS [29]. This accumulated dose is equivalent to about 5 years of running at luminosities of $10^{30}\mathrm{cm^{-2}s^{-1}}$. In the outer region of T1, where the cathode read-out electronics will be installed, the expected dose is lower by about two orders of magnitude.

5.2.2 Detector and telescope design

5.2.2.1 Detector geometry

The two *arms* of the T1 telescope, one on either side of the IP5, fit in the space between two conical surfaces, the beam pipe and the inner envelope of the flux return yoke of the CMS end-cap, at a distance between 7.5 m and 10.5 m from the interaction point. The telescopes will be the last to be inserted when closing and the first to be removed when opening the CMS detector.

Each telescope consists of five planes of CSCs, equally spaced in *z*, numbered as 1 to 5 from the closest (smallest) to the farthest (largest) from the interaction point. The vacuum chamber is

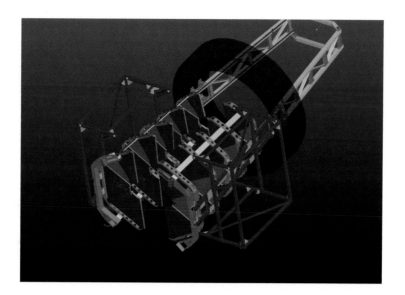

Figure 5.2: The two halves of one T1 telescope arm before insertion in CMS.

in place and aligned when the installation of T1 takes place: for this reason each telescope arm is built in two vertically divided halves (*half arms*) as depicted in figure 5.2.

A detector plane is composed of six CSC wire chambers covering roughly a region of 60° in ϕ and, as mentioned above, is split in two halves and mounted on different supports. Overlap is provided between adjacent detectors (also for the ones on different supports) to cover with continuous efficiency the approximately circular region of each telescope plane. In addition, the detector sextants in each plane are slightly rotated with respect to each other by angles varying from $-6°$ to $+6°$ in steps of 3°, the "reference" orientation being that of layer 5. This arrangement is useful for pattern recognition and helps to reduce the localised concentration of material in front of the CMS HF (Hadronic Forward) Calorimeter.

The conical volume reserved for the telescope contains also the mechanical support structure for installation inside the CMS end cap, which implies the construction of CSC detectors of 10 different dimensions (2 different types in each plane identified by the codes nG, nP). Figure 5.3 shows the layout of the 30 detectors of one arm.

5.2.2.2 Description of the T1 detectors

CSCs have been studied in detail in RD5 [27], and CSCs of very large dimensions have been built for ATLAS [30], CMS [31] and LHCb [32]. The TOTEM CSCs use basically the same technology developed for the other larger experiments, which we want to acknowledge here, tailoring specific parameters to the TOTEM requirements.

An exploded view of the different components making up a chamber assembly is shown in figure 5.4.

Two stiff panels of trapezoidal shape determine the flat surfaces of the cathode planes. A thin continuous frame is inserted between the two panels to keep with a good precision the two cathode planes parallel with a gap of 10.0 mm. The frame also has the function of defining a tight volume in which high purity gas will be flushed with a slight overpressure of a few g/cm^2.

2008 JINST 3 S08007

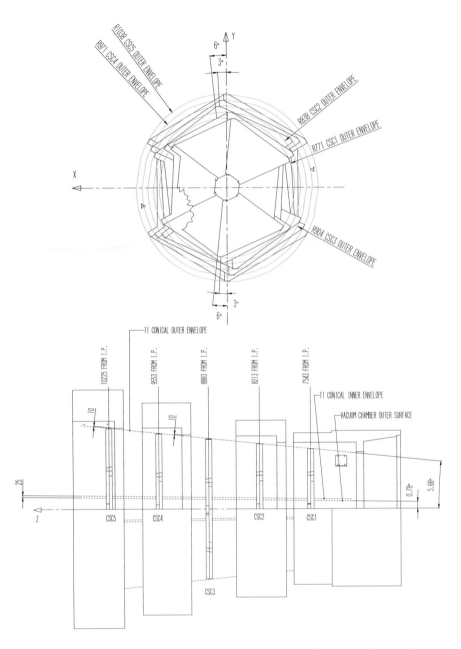

Figure 5.3: Layout of one T1 detector arm. The front view (left) shows the small rotations of the different planes.

The cathode panels are composite structures, sandwich panels of standard glass-epoxy laminates with a core of honeycomb, and provide the necessary stiffness. A study and tests were performed to optimise the thickness of both skins and of the core in the sandwich panel, in order to meet the stability requirements under load and minimise the material of the detector. The two panels are made with a 15 mm thick Nomex hexagonal honeycomb, enclosed between two 0.8 mm thick "skins" of fiberglass/epoxy laminate. Both skins are covered by a 35 μm thick copper layer. Cathode strips are etched and gold-plated with standard PCB technology on one of the two skins of a panel before its manufacture. The correct width of the gas gap is ensured by a G-10 frame glued

2008 JINST 3 S08007

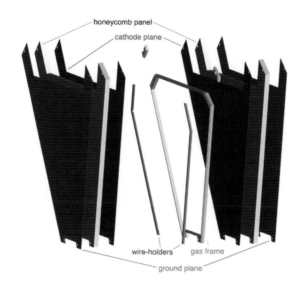

Figure 5.4: Exploded view of a TOTEM CSC detector.

to one of the two panels ("gas frame"). Besides acting as spacer, the frame guarantees gas tightness to the detector and gas distribution. The gas input and output lines enter the detector in the large side of the trapezoid and continue through a narrow duct machined through the full length of the sides: uniform gas distribution to the sensitive volume of the detector is achieved on each side via six equally spaced holes of 1.0 mm diameter.

The anode of the detector is composed of gold-plated (gold content of 6–8%) tungsten wires with 30 μm diameter, produced by Luma Metall;[1] the wires are strung parallel to the base of the trapezoid with a tension of 0.7 N at a pitch of 3.0 mm. The support for the wires ("wire holder" in figure 5.5) is provided by two printed circuit bars precisely machined to a thickness of 5.0 mm glued on the wire panel along the oblique sides of the detector and inside the gas volume. The wires are soldered and glued to pads on top of the bars; the pads are in turn electrically connected to tracks on the external region of the cathode plane. The first and the last anode wire, close to the inner and the outer edge of the detector, are field-shaping electrodes and have a larger diameter (100 μm). High voltage is applied on one side; on the opposite side the front-end card is directly soldered to pads connected to each single anode wire.

The cathode electrodes are parallel strips obtained as gold-plated tracks oriented at $\pm 60°$ with respect to the direction of the wires and have 5.0 mm pitch (4.5 mm width and 0.5 mm separation). Each strip is connected to high-density connectors mounted outside the gas volume as shown in figure 5.5.

The orientations of the cathode strips and of the anode wires allow for three measurements in the plane of the position of the avalanche thus providing three measured coordinates for each particle track, which significantly helps to reduce the number of fake hits from random combinations ("ghosts").

The geometrical parameters of all 10 types of chambers are summarised in table 5.1; the numbers of anode and cathode read-out channels are listed in table 5.2.

---

[1]LUMA METALL AB, S-39127 Kalmar Sweden.

2008 JINST 3 S08007

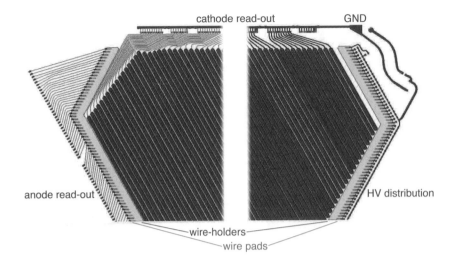

Figure 5.5: Cathode strips and wire-holder printed circuit boards.

Table 5.1: CSC geometrical parameters.

detector type	1G	1P	2G	2P	3G	3P	4G	4P	5G	5P
major base width [mm]	766	641	833	717	894	751	967	840	1016	957
minor base width [mm]	233	233	244	244	255	255	267	267	260	290
height [mm]	498	385	546	453	591	477	642	543	681	615
gas gap	10 mm									
anode wire spacing	3 mm									
anode wire diameter	$30\,\mu\text{m}$									
cathode strip pitch	5 mm									
cathode strip width	4.5 mm									

Table 5.2: T1 read-out channels.

chamber type	1G	1P	2G	2P	3G	3P	4G	4P	5G	5P
wires per anode plane	165	127	181	150	196	158	213	180	226	204
strips per cathode plane	118	97	129	108	137	114	150	127	164	150
total anode channels	11124									
total cathode channels	15936									

5.2.2.3 T1 detector production

Immediately after assembly, the T1 CSC are submitted to a set of acceptance tests. The gas gain uniformity is measured by displacing a point-like ^{90}Sr radioactive source on the surface of a CSC operated at a high voltage of 3.6 kV, flushed with an Ar/CO_2 (50/50) mixture and measuring the current drawn by the power supply (figure 5.6).

2008 JINST 3 S08007

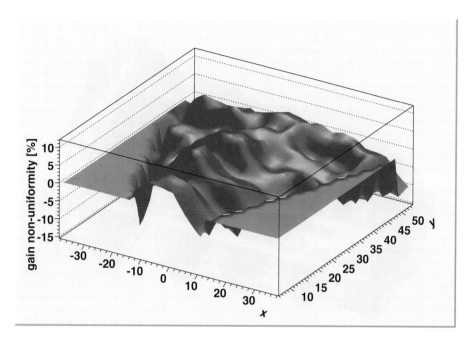

Figure 5.6: Gas gain uniformity deviations over a TOTEM CSC.

Figure 5.7: Completed CSC chambers for T1 in a test area at CERN.

After arriving at CERN, the detectors are submitted to further tests; figure 5.7 shows completed CSC chambers in the assembly laboratory.

The detectors that compose a half-plane are then secured to an aluminium frame with an overlap of the sensitive areas between them of few centimeters. Each of the five detector planes of one half telescope, plus a sixth frame that supports patch panels for the connections of the "services" (readout lines, trigger lines, high voltage, low voltage and gas and cooling lines), is fixed

2008 JINST 3 S08007

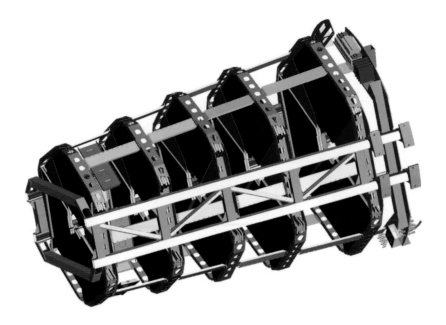

Figure 5.8: T1 assembly (one arm) with support structure. Some of the spacers between the detector planes and one support bar for the cathode read-out electronics are visible. On the right-hand side, the service support frame and the fixation plates securing the whole assembly to the internal surface of the CMS flux return yoke can be seen.

separately to the rails. The relative positions of the planes are defined by a series of appropriately positioned aluminium spacers. One telescope arm (two halves) in its final position on the truss is shown in figure 5.8.

5.2.2.4 Support structure and installation in CMS

The installation of the T1 telescope inside the CMS end-cap is delicate due to the tight geometrical constraints. Firstly, the zone is only accessible through the front circular opening and the installation can only be made when the end-caps are in place. Secondly, the beam pipe is also in place and the detector must be "closed" very carefully around it, avoiding contact with the two vertical rods supporting the pipe. Thirdly, the path of several CMS alignment laser beams traverse the volume of T1 and must be kept free.

Each of the two telescopes is therefore vertically divided in two halves, with independent support structures and services.

Two steel trusses are bolted to the third sector (YE3) of the CMS end cap, the same that supports the vacuum pipe, thus minimising any possible movement of T1 relative to the vacuum pipe as a result of the end cap deformation when the magnet is switched on. To guarantee the minimum acceptable deformation under load and at the same time minimise the cross-section of the structure, the trusses are joined together at the other end by two transverse bars. At installation T1 slides in position on rails mounted on each truss.

2008 JINST 3 S08007

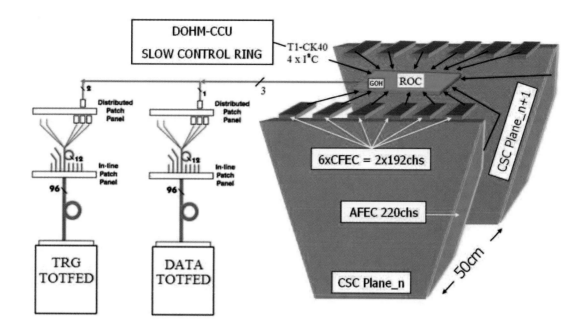

Figure 5.9: Overview of the T1 electronics system.

The half telescope is assembled and prepared for installation inside a specific structure with two rails similar to the truss ones. The half planes of T1 are mounted on this temporary structure, equipped with read out electronics, connected and tested. The structure also serves as support for the service racks of T1. For installation the structure is positioned on top of the HF calorimeter, the rails on the end cap and on the structure are aligned and the two telescope halves are slid into position inside the CMS end-cap. After this operation the CMS HF calorimeter can be raised to its final position, with the T1 external support structure still on its top.

5.2.3 T1 electronics system

The CSC anode and cathode signals are collected by custom-designed Anode Front-End Cards (AFEC) and Cathode Front-End Cards (CFEC), and conditioned by dedicated VLSI devices [33]. The serial digital data stream and the trigger signals coming out from the AFEC and CFEC are collected by the custom-designed Read-Out Card (ROC [33]) where they are serialised and optically transmitted to the DAQ system through a dedicated CMS Gigabit Optical Hybrid (GOH) [34]. The configuration and monitoring of the system is performed by the I^2C standard protocol distributed through the optical CMS Slow Control Ring SCR (DOHM [35] + CCUM [36]).

The T1 electronic front-end system globally involves 60 AFEC, 252 CFEC, 36 ROC, 96 GOH, 4 DOHM, 36 CCUM, while the T1 DAQ structure is based on a TOTEM custom board that can perform data (data FED) and trigger (trigger FED) signal analysis (section 7.2.2). An overview of the system is shown in figure 5.9.

2008 JINST 3 S08007

5.2.3.1 AFEC

The AFEC is the board that collects and groups the anode wires of the CSC detector. Due to the conic structure of the telescope, ten different types of AFECs have been adapted to the chambers, for a total of 60 boards installed. The AFECs are soldered directly on the edges of the chambers, and the dimensions vary between 60 cm and 100 cm. The AFEC contains for every channel a double-stage high-pass filter isolating the high voltage on the wire from the readout, and adapting impedance and signal shape. The readout of up to 256 wires per chamber is carried out by two VFAT chips (section 7.1), each mounted on a VFAT hybrid (section 5.3.4) connected to the AFEC through a compact 130 pin connector.

Trigger information, permitting both individual TOTEM and CMS-integrated runs, is generated on the VFAT by grouping anode wire signals into 16 groups to form primitive hits for road reconstruction.

The connection of the AFEC to the ROC board, that represents the superior level of the DAQ chain, is realised by two high-density halogen free 50-wire cables.

5.2.3.2 CFEC

The CFEC is the board that collects and groups the cathode strip signals of the CSC detector. Each board processes 128 input signals with a passive network and delivers the outputs to a VFAT chip on a VFAT hybrid connected to the CFEC through a compact 130 pin connector. Due to the different sizes of the detectors, for each layer of the telescope a different number of CFEC boards are needed.

In order to improve the position resolution, a second version of the board has been designed and tested. In the new board the analog signal processing is performed by the BUCKEYE and LCT-COMP devices [37], developed for the CMS Muon project. The BUCKEYE chip includes a 5th order preamplifier, shaper and tail cancellation stages, while the LCT-COMP performs the discrimination of the BUCKEYE analog outputs. Each comparator output is serially coded on three bits (TRIADE) that contain the information about the side (right or left) of the strip where the charge is distributed.

The serial decoding of the discriminator outputs and the management of the slow-control features of the CFEC, like threshold settings, channel masking and calibration, are accomplished by an ACTEL Antifuse FPGA (A54SX32A)[2] device.

5.2.3.3 ROC

The ROC board represents the data, trigger and low voltage junction point of the T1 detector front-end boards and performs a similar function for the CSCs as the motherboard for the RPs. Each card is able to acquire data and trigger bits from two CSC detectors.

The board receives data from 16 VFAT hybrids hosted on the AFEC and CFEC cards, for a total of 2048 CSC signals.

The serial data stream received from the front-end is converted from LVDS to CMOS level, connected to the GOH mezzanine and optically transmitted to the DAQ system through the custom data FED board in the counting-room (section 7.2.2 and Ref. [38]).

---

[2]SX-A Family FPGAs, Actel Corp., February 2007.

Each detector has allocated up to 8 front-end connections, divided in two for the anodes and six for the cathodes. Only the AFECs produce trigger information. For each detector a total of 16 trigger bits are generated and transmitted to the TOTEM trigger system (trigger FED board) via a dedicated GOH optical link. The trigger information can also be merged with the data using a spare Gigabit Optical Link data channel and a special VFAT trigger hybrid.

For slow control, the CMS tracker and ECAL token ring system was adopted: similar to the RP system, a CCUM mezzanine mounted on the ROC forms a node in the slow control token ring. This system contains a skip fault architecture for additional redundancy based on doubling signal paths and bypassing of interconnection lines between CCUMs. Each CCUM controls the reset signal, three 8-bit general-purpose I/O ports and up to 16 I^2C serial line connections.

The 40 MHz master clock and the LHC fast commands are extracted in the ROC also from the token ring, and regenerated by CMS PLL devices (PLL25 [39] and QPLL). The distribution of the clock and the LHC fast commands to the front-end boards is implemented adopting a tree structure in order to minimise the skew and the delay time between different front-end receiver circuits.

In order to avoid missing data in case of failure of the master VFAT that enables the GOH serial data transmission, redundancy logic has been foreseen in the design of the ROC. The swapping of the master VFAT can be done via the general purpose I/O bits available through the SCR. As for the data, also the trigger bit transmission is modifiable changing the functionality of the logic with the SCR I/O connections.

A spy test port is foreseen on the ROC board, all the front-end connections are routed to dedicated connectors in order to plug a piggy-back mezzanine where a dedicated Xilinx FPGA (XC3S1500FG456)[3] and USB 2.0 logic can emulate the DAQ system chain.

5.2.3.4 High and low voltage supplies

The high and low voltage distribution for the CSC detectors is organised per half telescope arm (15 detectors). The high voltage system is based on the 24 channel A1550P board [40] (5 kV, 1 mA) and the CAEN SY1527 controller [41] placed in the counting-room.

The low voltage has to be applied locally, and thus the Wiener Marathon system [42] was chosen for its robustness against radiation and magnetic fields. One crate with 12 channels (2-8 V, 55 A) provides digital and analog power separately for half a telescope arm.

5.3 T2 telescope

5.3.1 Requirements and Choice of Detector Technology

The T2 telescopes, located at ± 13.5 m on both sides of IP5 (figure 1.1), detect charged particles in the pseudorapidity range of $5.3 \leq |\eta| \leq 6.5$. Generic requirements for the T2 (like for T1) include a fully inclusive trigger for diffractive events, hit pattern reconstruction for vertex finding to be used in discriminating against possible beam-gas background and for left-right symmetric alignment of telescopes for better control of the systematic effects.

The T2 telescope has been designed for good coverage of forward physics processes with varying beam conditions both at low luminosities (total cross-section and soft diffractive scattering)

---

[3]Xilinx Inc., *Spartan-3 FPGA family — v. DS099*, 25 May 2007.

2008 JINST 3 S08007

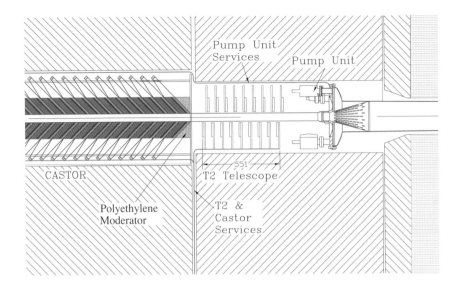

Figure 5.10: The location of the TOTEM T2 telescope within the shielding of CMS.

and at moderate luminosities (semi-hard diffractive scattering, low-x physics). Moreover, the T2 telescope is expected to operate up to luminosities of the order of $10^{33}\,\mathrm{cm}^{-2}\mathrm{s}^{-1}$ [1] where hard diffraction, heavy particle searches and physics beyond the standard model could be probed.

Due to the shape of the LHC vacuum chamber at the T2 location, an increased rate of particle-wall interactions is expected and had to be carefully considered. As a result, a compact detector array with a resolution in polar angle, $\Delta\theta/\theta$, matching the corresponding T1 resolution was adopted as a design criterium.

The gaseous electron multipliers (GEM) were selected for detectors of the T2 telescope thanks to their high rate capability, good spatial resolution, robust mechanical structure and excellent ageing characteristics. Invented a decade ago by Fabio Sauli [43] and studied by numerous research groups in experimental high energy physics, the GEM technology may be considered as a mature technology for the LHC environment. Excellent results of the COMPASS experiment [44], obtained during running periods extending over several years in high-rate environment, support also the choice of the GEM technology. Consequently, the COMPASS GEM design was adopted as a guideline for the GEMs of the TOTEM T2 telescope.

5.3.2 Detector Layout

5.3.2.1 The Telescope

The T2 telescopes are installed in the forward shielding of CMS between the vacuum chamber and the inner shielding of the HF calorimeter. There is a vacuum pump unit in front of T2 and the CMS CASTOR calorimeters behind it (figure 5.10). To reduce the neutron flux at T2 and HF, an additional polyethylene moderator will be installed between T2 and CASTOR. According the CMS simulations performed with the FLUKA Monte-Carlo package, the expected fluence of charged particles is around $10^6\,\mathrm{cm}^{-2}\mathrm{s}^{-1}$ with the moderator installed [1].

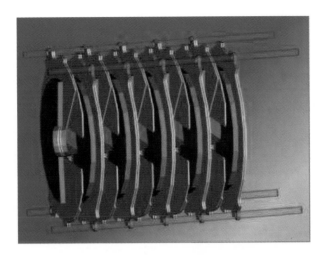

Figure 5.11: A CAD drawing depicting the arrangement of the 20 consecutive half-planes of Gaseous Electron Multiplier (GEM) detectors into one of the two T2 telescopes. In each detector layer, two GEM half-planes are slid together for maximal azimuthal angle coverage. With the ten double detector layers both high efficiency for detecting the primary tracks from the interaction point and efficient rejection of interactions with the LHC vacuum chamber is achieved.

In each T2 arm, 20 semi-circular GEM planes – with overlapping regions – are interleaved on both sides of the beam vacuum chamber to form ten detector planes of full azimuthal coverage (figure 5.11). The GEMs are installed as pairs with a back-to-back configuration. This arrangement of active detector planes allows both track coordinates and local trigger – based on hit multiplicities and track routes pointing to the interaction region – to be obtained. The material budget of T2 telescopes is minimised by using low-Z construction materials and honeycomb structures in manufacturing the GEM support mechanics.

5.3.2.2 T2 GEM Detectors

The shape of the GEM detector used in T2 telescope is semi-circular with an active area covering an azimuthal angle of 192° and extending from 43 mm up to 144 mm in radius from the beam axis (figure 5.12).

The design of the T2 GEM detector is based on utilisation of the standard GEM foils manufactured by the CERN-TS-DEM workshop. The foil consists of 50 μm polyimide foil (Apical) with 5 μm copper cladding on both sides. Due to the bidirectional wet etching process used by the workshop the shapes of the holes are double conical. The diameters of the holes in the middle of the foil and on the surface are 65 and 80 μm, respectively.

Three GEM foils are used as a cascade in one detector (figure 5.13) to reduce the discharge probability below 10^{-12} [45]. For the same reason the voltage divider supplying the voltages for the foils is designed such that the potential difference is gradually decreasing from the uppermost foil to the lowest one (nearest to the readout board). Moreover, the high voltage side of each foil is divided into four concentric segments for limiting the energy available for sparks (figure 5.14).

2008 JINST 3 S08007

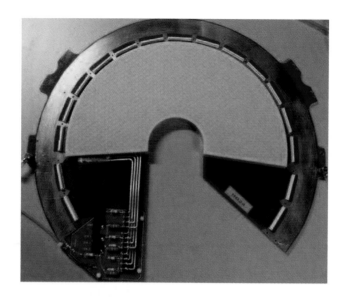

Figure 5.12: The TOTEM T2 GEM detector without front-end electronics and cooling pipes.

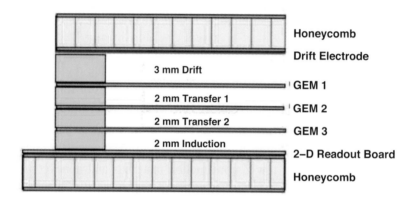

Figure 5.13: A side view of the T2 GEM detector structure: Three Gaseous Electron Multiplier (GEM) amplification stages are realised by three perforated and Cu-clad polyimide foils supported by honeycomb plates. A 3 mm drift space is followed by two 2 mm deep charge transfer regions (Transfer 1 and Transfer 2) and a 2 mm charge induction space. The large signal charges are collected, in two dimensions, by a read-out board underneath of the induction layer. The lightweight construction and support materials are chosen for low-Z material budget and mechanical robustness.

The segments are biassed separately through high voltage resistors, enabling switching off the innermost segment if required. The ground sides of the foils are continuous.

At the design value of the operating voltage, the gas amplification over all the three foils will be roughly 8000, a value selected by the COMPASS experiment too. Consequently, the average amplification over a single foil is typically 20. The thickness of the drift space is 3 mm, whereas the transfer 1 and 2 and the induction gaps are all 2 mm (see figure 5.13). The corresponding electric fields over the gaps are approximately 2.4 kV/cm and 3.6 kV/cm, respectively.

2008 JINST 3 S08007

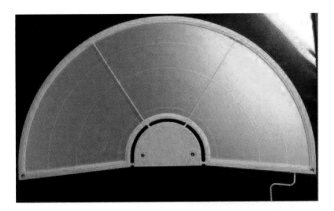

Figure 5.14: The T2 GEM foil glued to the support frame. The division of the electrode into four ring segments to minimise the energy available for discharges is visible.

The GEM foils are stretched and glued over supporting frames, which are manufactured by Computer Numerical Control (CNC) machining from fiberglass reinforced epoxy plates (Permaglas) with thicknesses of 2 mm. Two additional supporting spacers of thickness 0.5 mm are designed in the middle of the frames (see figure 5.14). Their position is slightly asymmetric to minimise dead areas. The drift frame is similar, except that the thickness is 3 mm and that no thin spacers in the middle of the frame are used.

An outgassing analysis of the frame material revealed emission of several organic compounds. Most of them were solvent-like remnants from the manufacturing process. One of these was toluene, which is known to cause ageing in ordinary wire chambers [46]. To remove the solvents from the material, all the frames were baked in a vacuum oven for several hours at a temperature of 80°C.

A polyimide foil with a copper cladding (5 μm) on a single side with thickness of 50 μm is used as a drift electrode which is glued to the front plate. The front and back plates are honeycomb structures, in which a honeycomb sheet of thickness 3 mm (Nomex) is sandwiched between two thin FR4 sheets of thickness 125 μm and enclosed inside a supporting frame made of the same material as the frames of the foils. The readout board is glued to the back plate.

A printed circuit board covered by polyimide foil with a pattern of strips and pads is used as a two-dimensional readout board. The rather complicated structure is manufactured partly by a commercial company and partly by a CERN workshop (TS-DEM group). The readout board contains 2×256 concentric strips for the radial coordinates and a matrix of 1560 pads for azimuthal coordinates and for the T2 local trigger (figure 5.15).

The strips lie on top of the pads and are isolated from the pads by a thin layer of polyimide, which is removed between the strips by wet etching (figure 5.16). The width and spacing of the strips are 80 and 400 μm respectively. To reduce the occupancy, the strips are divided into two parts, each covering 96° in azimuthal angle. The readout of the strips is located on both ends of the chamber.

The pads are divided into 65 radial sectors each containing 24 pads with sizes ranging from $2 \times 2 \, \text{mm}^2$ close to the vacuum chamber wall to $7 \times 7 \, \text{mm}^2$ at the outer edge of the semi-circular planes. The charge collected by the pads is read, with help of vias and strips on the backside of the board, at the outer edge of the readout board.

2008 JINST 3 S08007

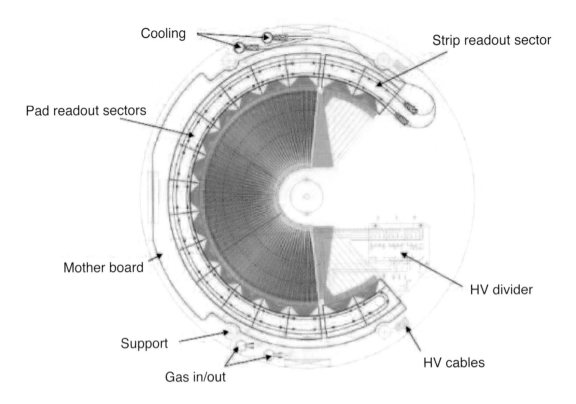

Figure 5.15: The design drawing of the TOTEM T2 GEM detector.

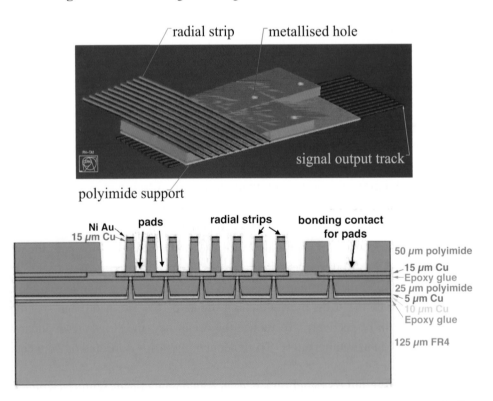

Figure 5.16: Detailed views of the strip/pad structure of the T2 GEM readout. Top: 3-dimensional view, bottom: cross-section.

2008 JINST 3 S08007

Unlike in the COMPASS experiment, the readout electronics are connected to the readout board by connectors. No wire bonding on the readout board is required. SMD-connectors of 130 pins with 0.5 mm pitch are soldered directly on the board. Four connectors are required for the strip readout (128 strips per connector) and 13 for the pad readout. The pad connectors are hence used to read five sectors of 24 pads (120 pads), the other pins in the connectors are grounded.

The gas connectors are also installed on the readout board. The fill gas of the GEM (Ar/CO_2 70/30 mixture) is supplied through channels engraved in the fiberglass frame beneath the polyimide foil. The frames of the GEM foils contain also holes in two corners for a uniform distribution of the gas to the drift, transfer and induction gaps.

5.3.3 Detector Manufacture

The production of the required 50 individual GEM detectors (2×20 detector planes for the left and right T2 telescopes, 10 in reserve) was initiated in summer 2006 in Helsinki. Due to the harsh operating environment in the forward region, special care has been taken in devising efficient quality control processes both for the GEM components and their overall performance criteria.

The GEMs are almost exclusively manufactured in clean rooms of the Detector Laboratory where a dedicated assembly line for the large GEM detectors was set up. Although the production process is mostly based on manual assembly phases, some of the quality-control related tasks are made automatic. These include leakage current measurements of the GEM foils, optical inspection of the foils and search for broken or short-circuited strips/pads on the readout board.

An automatic leakage current measurement system for the GEM foils was devised and consists of a programmable electrometer, a special arrangement for electric contacts and a LabView based software package. The GEM foils are considered acceptable when the leakage current stays over half an hour below 0.5 nA at a test voltage of 500 V over the foil in dry atmosphere.

In addition to the leakage current measurement, the quality control of the GEM foils contains visual inspection of the foils and optical scanning of the whole foil surfaces. The aim of the scanning is to record the known defects of the foils for later use. A commercial flatbed scanner and an external background lighting setup are combined for automatic GEM foil scanning. The foils are scanned from each side with a resolution of 2400 dpi. Background light is utilised for spotting the holes in which the polyimide layer was incompletely etched or when the hole was entirely absent on the other side of the foil. In addition to finding defects on the surface of the foil, the system is also used for measuring the variation of hole sizes across the foil area.

Broken strips and short circuits between strips and pads may cause data corruption and additional noise in GEMs. These defects are easily seen in capacitance values of the strips and the pads. Due to the large number of channels (1560 pads and 512 strips), a special automated capacitance measurement system for the strips and pads of the GEM readout boards was developed. The system consists of a computer controlled x-y table, a programmable LCR-meter and a custom-made test board. The pad geometry, with pads growing larger when moving from inside out in radial direction from the beam vacuum chamber wall, is clearly seen in the resulting graphs. The measured variation of strip capacitances is relatively small.

In the finishing stage of the manufacturing process the basic characteristics of the GEMs filled with a gas mixture of Ar/CO_2 (70/30) are measured in the laboratory with the help of standard ^{55}Fe

2008 JINST 3 S08007

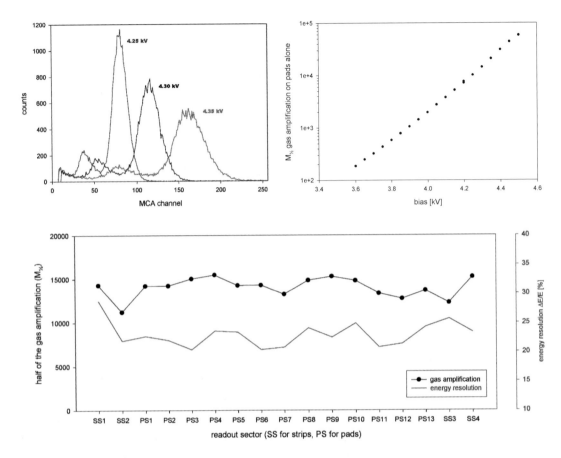

Figure 5.17: Examples of operational tests of the T2 GEMs with gas mixture Ar/CO_2 (70/30) done after the detector assembly: a) ^{55}Fe X-ray spectra at different bias voltages, b) a gas amplification vs. bias voltage, c) variation of the gas gain and the energy resolution over the readout sectors.

X-ray sources (5.9 keV). These consist of gas amplification and energy resolution measurement at different bias voltages and in different readout sectors (figure 5.17). All the GEMs are tested with a gas amplification up to 10^5, which corresponds to a gain one order of magnitude higher than the design value. Moreover, the characteristics of the GEMS and their readout electronics are tested in several beam tests during the years 2006-2007.

5.3.4 On-detector electronics

The T2 detector consists of 40 GEM detectors arranged in 4 quarters of 10 detectors. Each detector is read out by 17 VFATs 13 for the pads (120 pads per VFAT) and 4 for the strips (128 strips per VFAT). Each VFAT is mounted on its own VFAT hybrid (figure 5.18). All 17 VFAT hybrids of one GEM detector are mounted on a "horseshoe card" named after its physical shape (figure 5.19) The horseshoe cards of the 10 detectors of one T2 telescope half arm are connected to the so-called "11th card" which provides the interface to the outside world. A schematic view of the entire system is shown in Figure 5.20.

2008 JINST 3 S08007

Figure 5.18: The TOTEM gas detector hybrid carrying one VFAT readout chip (under the cover).

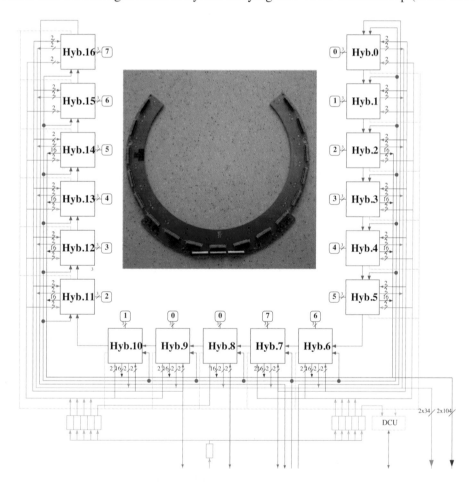

Figure 5.19: Architecture of the Horse-Shoe card (red for I^{2}C lines, cyan for clock and trigger lines and LVDS buffers, pink for DCU and monitoring lines, blue for trigger hybrid outputs, green for data and data valid hybrid outputs, magenta for scan test lines, dark green for pad VFAT hybrids, dark brown for strip VFAT hybrids).

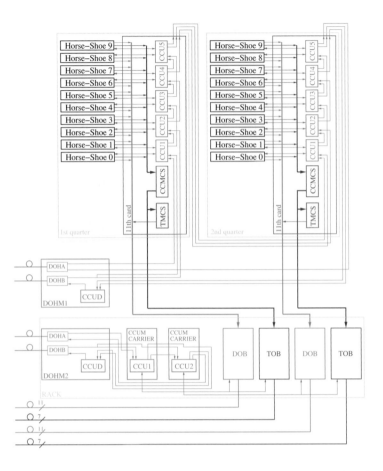

Figure 5.20: Architecture of the readout electronics of half of the detector (black for Horse-Shoe cards, magenta for 11th cards, red for CCUMs, DOHMs and control, clock and trigger lines, blue for trigger hybrid outputs, CCMCs and Trigger Opto-Boards, green for data outputs and Data Opto-Boards, dark green for TMCs and TMC outputs to Data Opto-Boards.)

The VFAT hybrids are linked to their horseshoe card by a 50-pin connector transmitting:

- precision data and trigger data from the VFATs to the horseshoe card, and

- clock, trigger and control signals, HV and LV power from the horseshoe card to the VFAT hybrids.

5.3.4.1 Data Path

The precision data (green lines in figure 5.20) and the tracking data (blue lines) originating from all hybrids of a T2 half arm (or quarter of the full telescope) are transmitted via the 10 horseshoe cards to the 11th card (magenta boxes in the figure) which performs coincidence analysis on the grouped trigger data coming from the VFAT fast-or logic. For the latter purpose, the 11th card houses 13 mezzanine cards equipped with a coincidence chip (CCMCs, blue boxes).

Both full-precision data as well as results of the trigger coincidence logic are sent from the 11th card to Opto-Boards equipped with GOHs (Gigabit Optical Hybrids) for optical transmission

2008 JINST 3 S08007

to the counting-room. The extreme radiation levels in the T2 station preclude the use of optohybrids on the 11th card, which therefore had to be placed in a rack on the GEM platform just outside the shielding of the detector. Data transmission to the optohybrids is carried out electrically using LVDS signals over about 6 metres.

Since one GOH can handle up to 16 data lines, the $10 \times 17 = 170$ precision data lines from a T2 half arm are regrouped in the 11th card and sent to 11 GOHs mounted on one Opto-Board ("Data Opto-Board", green boxes "DOB" in the figure).

The $13 \times 8 = 104$ trigger outputs of the CCMCs are also regrouped and sent to 7 GOHs mounted on a second Opto-Board ("Trigger Opto-Board", blue boxes "TOB" in the figure).

In order to include trigger information into the data stream, a second branch of the 104 trigger signal lines is regrouped into two sets of 64 and 40 signals respectively and sent to 2 Trigger Mezzanine Cards (TMCs, dark green boxes in the figure) equipped with a VFAT chip. Each TMC generates a data stream containing trigger information that is sent to the Data Opto-Board together with the output data from the VFAT hybrids.

For the whole T2 system 8 optoboards are foreseen, 4 on either side, 2 for each half arm, one for tracking data and one for trigger data.

5.3.4.2 Controls

A Detector Control Unit (DCU) on the horseshoe card monitors temperature, analog and digital power supply voltages, and the output voltages and currents generated in the DAC integrated in the VFAT chips. The DCUs are controlled via I^{2}C links by Communication and Control Units (CCUs), each of them mounted on a CCU mezzanine card (CCUMs) on the 11th card. With 1 CCU per 2 horseshoe cards, each 11th card is equipped with 5 CCUs. The 2×5 CCUs on the two 11th cards of each T2 arm communicate with the control token ring via 1 Digital Opto Hybrid Module (DOHM). See also section 7.2.1.

The controls for the Opto-Boards are generated by two additional CCUMs mounted on CCUM carriers in the rack on the GEM platform outside the detector shielding. These CCUMs are connected to a second DOHM for communication with the control token ring.

The clock signals and trigger commands for the Horseshoe cards, the TMCs, the CCMCs and the Opto-Boards are distributed by the CCUMs after extraction from the control token ring.

5.3.4.3 Power Supplies

Two 11th cards and the 20 connected horseshoe cards are powered by a 12-channel Wiener Power Supply. Eight channels are used for analogue and digital power supply voltages of odd and even Horse-Shoe cards connected to the two 11th cards. Two other channels are used to power the first DOHM and the CCUMs in the 11th cards and the second DOHM, the CCUM in the CCUM carriers in the rack and the Opto-Boards respectively. Two channels are used as spares.

5.3.5 Detector Performance

Some of the TOTEM GEM detectors underwent several tests in a laboratory setup as well as in an SPS testbeam. The aim of these tests was to verify the performance and quality of the GEM detectors, the optimisation of the noise level measured with the TOTEM VFAT readout chip.

2008 JINST 3 S08007

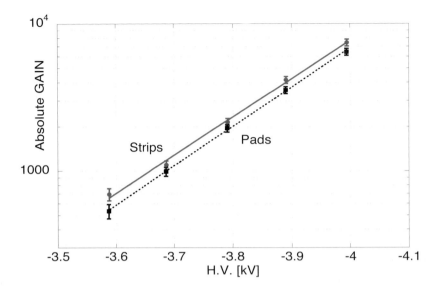

Figure 5.21: Absolute Gain calibration as a function of the applied High Voltage for strips (solid) and pads (dashed). This calibration curve was obtained with a Cu X-ray tube source, by measuring the X-ray interaction rate in the gas and the current collected by strips and pads.

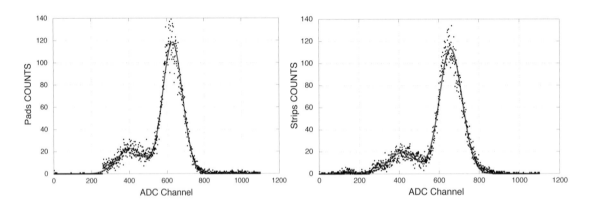

Figure 5.22: Cu X-ray spectrum as measured with a group of 48 pads (left) and with a group of 16 strips (right) on a GEM with a high voltage of -4 kV.

The absolute gain calibration curve for strips and pads irradiated by a Cu X-ray tube is shown in figure 5.21 as a function of the High Voltage applied. The comparison of the results of this test for different positions on the sensitive area of each detector and between different chambers, is in agreement with the expectations.

Figure 5.22 shows typical spectra obtained with a Cu X-ray tube, from which we can extract information about energy resolution (figure 5.23, left) and charge sharing between strips and pads (figure 5.23, right). These spectra were obtained with a 142IH ORTEC charge preamplifier and an ORTEC 450 research amplifier while the detector was powered with a HV of -4 kV.

Tests of GEMs equipped with the final TOTEM readout chip VFAT have been done to study the combined performance. Figure 5.24 shows the noise level for some strips (left-hand and mid-

2008 JINST 3 S08007

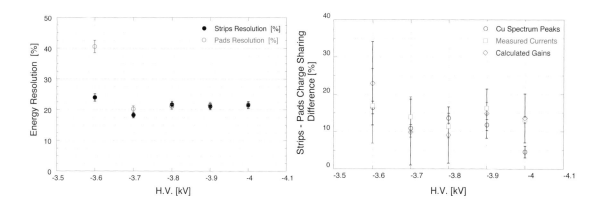

Figure 5.23: Left: energy resolution for strips and pads measured on the Cu Kα (and Kβ) emission peaks as a function of the applied HV. Right: charge sharing between strips and pads (open circles), as obtained by the relative difference between the positions of the Cu $K\alpha$ peak of strips and pads obtained from spectra analogous to the ones in figure 5.22. Also shown are the relative differences between the currents collected from strips and pads (open squares), and between the gains (open diamonds).

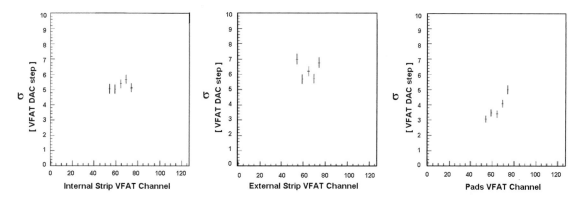

Figure 5.24: GEM read out by VFAT: noise σ of a group of internal strips with radii in the range 42.5 mm $\lesssim r \lesssim$ 93.3 mm (left), external strips with 93.7 mm $\lesssim r \lesssim$ 144.5 mm (middle), and a sector of pads (right), obtained with the calibration pulse scan available for the VFAT testing procedure. One VFAT DAC step corresponds to about 600 electrons.

dle plot) and pads (right-hand plot) obtained by varying the VFAT calibration pulse amplitude controlled by a Digital-to-Analog Converter (DAC), while keeping the threshold constant (see section 7.1, figure 7.6). An rms noise of $\sigma_{\text{noise}} \approx 5$ DAC units corresponds to about 3000 electrons. The pad noise clearly increases with the pad capacitance given in figure 5.25.

The CERN SPS beam test was important for understanding the response of the electronic readout chain to the typical signals of the GEM.

Events were triggered with two aligned scintillation counters of 5×5 cm^2 size, positioned up- and downstream of the GEM chambers under test.

2008 JINST 3 S08007

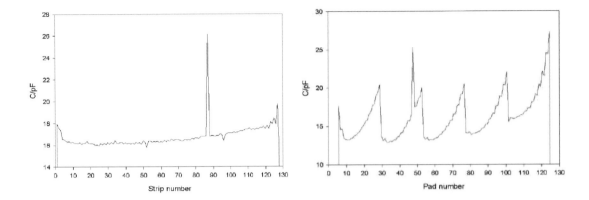

Figure 5.25: Capacitance measurement for strips (left) and pads (right). The spikes are caused by shorts between strips and pads.

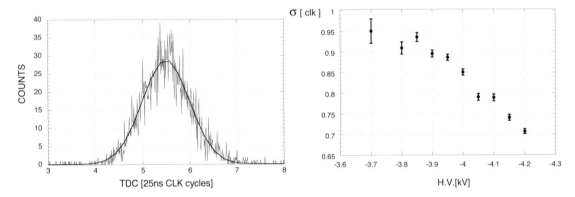

Figure 5.26: Left: distribution of the GEM VFAT trigger time with respect to the scintillator trigger time, measured with a TDC. Right: width σ, expressed in clock cycles, of the previous time distribution as a function of the high voltage.

Figure 5.26 (left) shows a measurement of the time difference between the GEM trigger signal and the scintillator trigger (asynchronous to the 25 ns clock), obtained with a TDC unit. The spread of this distribution, defining the time resolution of the GEMs, is shown in the right-hand plot as a function of the high voltage. As expected, increasing the voltage leads to a higher electric field and hence a shorter signal rise time with less time walk and a better time resolution.

The trigger time distribution extends over several clock cycles of 25 ns. Therefore, upon receiving a trigger, the readout has to accept signals within a time window covering several clock cycles, in order to avoid missing hits. The VFAT can accomplish this task by storing each hit in a programmable number of subsequent 25 ns bins of its memory (cf. section 7.1). An alternative approach for ensuring full efficiency is the reduction of the signal rise time by either increasing the electric field in the GEM or by adding CF_4 to the gas mixture.

Figure 5.27 shows the cluster size distribution for strips and pads at the typical HV of -4 kV. In figure 5.28 the mean cluster size is shown as a function of the high voltage and the VFAT threshold. The cluster sizes found are compatible with the results obtained by simulation.

2008 JINST 3 S08007

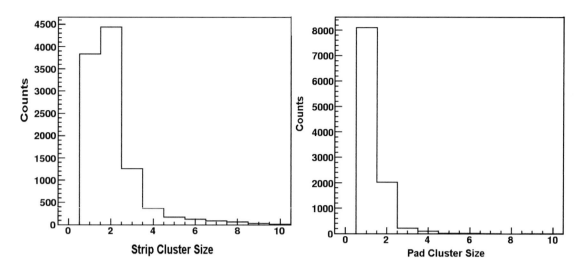

Figure 5.27: Strip and pad cluster size at HV ≈ -4.0 kV, with a threshold of 40 DAC steps (or 24000 electrons) and a signal sampling time window of 2 clock cycles in the VFAT.

The cluster size distribution has an impact on the spatial resolution of the detector. For the operating parameters chosen for the tests underlying figure 5.27, pad clusters consist predominantly of only one pad, which leads to a resolution of $p/\sqrt{12}$ (where p is the pad width), ranging from $2\,\text{mm}/\sqrt{12} \approx 580\,\mu\text{m}$ to $7\,\text{mm}/\sqrt{12} \approx 2\,\text{mm}$. The strip clusters on the other hand contain mainly one or two strips, with approximately equal probability. Since tracks passing near the centre of a strip produce preferrably 1-strip clusters whereas tracks passing between two strips will rather give 2-strip clusters, the resolution will be better than for a pure 1-strip cluster population. While the precise value of the resolution depends on details of the charge sharing mechanism, one can expect it to lie in the range from $0.5\,d/\sqrt{12} \approx 58\,\mu\text{m}$ to $d/\sqrt{12} \approx 115\,\mu\text{m}$, where $d = 400\,\mu\text{m}$ is the strip pitch. In the testbeam setup at hand, no external reference detector was available, which excludes a direct measurement of the resolution. However, with the hit measurements in two GEM planes and an approximate knowledge of the beam parallelism, a very rough consistency check is possible. Figure 5.29 shows the distribution of the radial distance between the strip cluster centres belonging to projective track hits in the two GEM planes with a distance $\Delta Z_{\text{GEM}} = 395\,\text{mm}$ along the beam. The observed standard deviation, $\sigma_{\text{obs}} \approx 235\,\mu\text{m}$, of this distribution can be decomposed according to the relationship

$$\sigma_{\text{obs}}^2 = 2\sigma_{\text{GEM}}^2 + \Delta Z_{\text{GEM}}^2 \sigma^2(\theta_{\text{beam}}). \tag{5.1}$$

Solving (5.1) for the angular spread of the beam, $\sigma(\theta_{\text{beam}})$, yields a value between 0.43 and 0.56 mrad which is well consistent with expectations for this beam.

2008 JINST 3 S08007

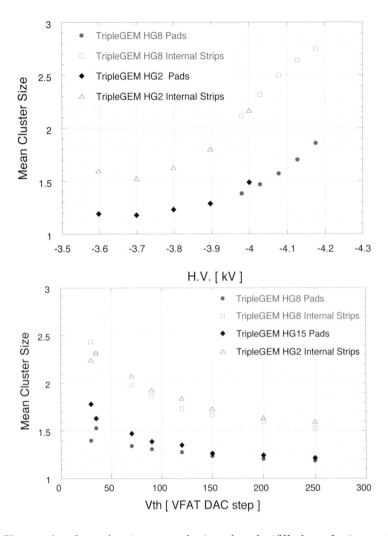

Figure 5.28: Cluster size for strips (open marker) and pads (filled marker) as a function of the high voltage for a threshold of 35 DAC steps (top), and as a function of the VFAT threshold for $HV = -4.1\,kV$ (bottom) for different GEM planes (HG8, HG2, HG15). 1 DAC step corresponds to about 600 electrons. In all cases, the signal sampling time window in the VFAT was 2 clock cycles wide.

2008 JINST 3 S08007

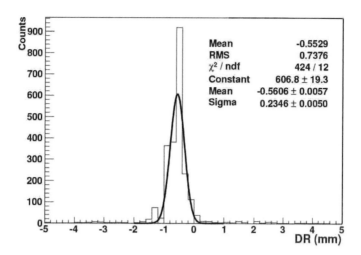

Figure 5.29: Radial distance of strip cluster centres belonging to aligned hits in two different T2 planes.

2008 JINST 3 S08007

Chapter 6

Physics performance

6.1 Principle of proton reconstruction

Protons emerging from elastic and diffractive scattering at LHC are emitted at very small angles (10 to 150 μrad) and undergo no or small ($10^{-7} \div 0.1$) fractional momentum loss ($\xi = |\Delta p|/p$, respectively. Hence they are very close to the beam and can only be detected in the RP detectors downstream symmetrically on either side of the interaction point (IP) if their displacement at the detector location is large enough.

The transverse displacement $(x(s), y(s))$ of an elastically or diffractively scattered proton at a distance s from the IP is related to its origin $(x^*, y^*, 0)$, scattering angles $\Theta_{x,y}^*$ and ξ value at the IP via the optical functions L, v, D as described in chapter 3. The optical functions (L, v, D) determining the explicit path of the particle through the magnetic elements, depend mainly on the position along the beam line (i.e. on all the magnetic elements traversed before reaching that position and their settings which is optics dependent) but also on the particle parameters at the IP (3.2).

The proton tracking through the accelerator lattice is based on the parametrization of the optical functions (extracted for each configuration from the program MAD-X [47]); their slight dependency on the kinematic variables, $\Theta_{x,y}^*$ and ξ, is also taken into account [48].

The transverse vertex position and the scattering angle at the IP are smeared assuming Gaussian distributions with widths given by the transverse beam size and the beam divergence, both determined by β^* and by the (normalised) emittance ε_n. Table 6.1 summarises the beam parameters at the IP for the different optics settings. In addition an energy spread of 10^{-4} is always assumed. The minimum distance of a RP station to the beam on one hand and constraints imposed by the beam pipe or beam screen size [49] on the other hand will determine the proton acceptance of a RP station. The minimum distance of a RP to the beam is proportional to the beam size $((10-15) \times \sigma_{x(y)}(s))$.

6.1.1 Acceptance

The acceptance of the RP system for elastically or diffractively scattered protons depends on the optics configuration. The complementarity of the acceptance of different optics configurations is shown in figure 6.1. As discussed in chapter 3, the TOTEM-specific optics with $\beta^* = 1540$ m was

2008 JINST 3 S08007

Table 6.1: Parameters of the different optics settings at nominal emittance ε_n=3.75 μm·rad (ε_n = 1 μm · rad for β^*=1540 m).

β^* [m]	crossing angle [μrad]	IP offset in x [μm]	IP beam size [μm]	IP beam divergence [μrad]
1540	0	0	450	0.3
90	0	0	213	2.3
2	92	322	32	16

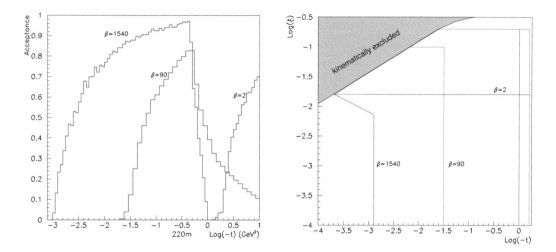

Figure 6.1: Left: acceptance in $\log_{10}|t|$ for elastically scattered protons at the Roman Pot station at 220 m for different optics settings. Right: acceptance in $\log_{10}|t|$ and $\log_{10}\xi$ for diffractively scattered protons at the same RP station for different optics settings. The contour lines represent the 10% level.

particularly optimised for accepting protons down to very low $|t|$-values and — in the diffractive case — with all kinematically allowed values of ξ (blue graphs in figure 6.1, left and right, respectively). With the $\beta^* = 90$ m optics, diffractive scattered protons are still accepted independently from their ξ-value, but the t-acceptance is reduced compared to $\beta^* = 1540$ m optics (red graphs in figure 6.1, right and left, respectively). With high luminosity optics ($\beta^* = 0.5$ m $\div$ 2 m) on the other hand, the diffractive protons are within the acceptance of the RP detectors because of their ξ value almost independently of their t value (magenta graph in figure 6.1, right). In addition, elastically scattered protons can be detected at very large t (see magenta graph in figure 6.1, left).

The complementarity of the different optics configurations in the measurement of elastic and central diffraction cross-section is shown in figure 6.2. In elastic events (figure 6.2, left), the full t-range from 0.002 up to 10 GeV^2 will be covered by combining data from runs at several optics configurations. With typical running times of 10^5 s (i.e. a bit more than a day), enough statistics can be accumulated for each interval (see table 6.2). The statistics is also sufficient for the physics alignment of the RP detectors. The overlapping regions between the acceptances of the different optics configurations will allow for cross-checks of the measurements.

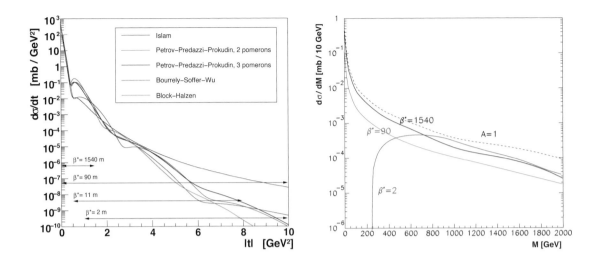

Figure 6.2: Left: differential cross-section of elastic scattering at $\sqrt{s} = 14\,\text{TeV}$ as predicted by various models together with the t-acceptance ranges of different optics settings. Right: predicted differential cross-section of central diffraction at $\sqrt{s} = 14\,\text{TeV}$ with (solid) and without (dashed) taking the proton acceptance into account for different optics settings.

Figure 6.2 (right) shows the predicted central diffractive mass distribution together with the acceptance corrected distributions for three different optics settings. With the high and intermediate β^* optics, all diffractive masses, down to the lowest values are observable. For low-β^* optics on the other hand, the acceptance starts at around 250 GeV but has the advantage of better statistics for high masses due to the higher luminosity. By combining data from runs at low-β^* optics with data from high or intermediate optics runs, the differential cross-section as function of the central diffractive mass can be measured with good precision over the full mass range.

6.1.2   Reconstruction of diffractive proton kinematics

The reconstruction procedure for diffractively scattered protons aims at a determination of the kinematics parameters $\Theta_{x,y}$ and ξ of the proton. For elastic scattering, i.e. when $\xi = 0$, the reconstruction is simpler and will be discussed more in detail in section 6.1.3. In the following, the reconstruction procedure and its performance for diffractive protons with the $\beta^* = 90\,\text{m}$ optics will be discussed in detail. The reconstruction performance for other optics will only be briefly summarised.

6.1.2.1   Diffractive proton reconstruction with the $\beta^* = 90\,\text{m}$ optics

The transverse coordinates of the proton at the IP $(x^*, y^*$, see eq. (3.2)) are considered as additional free variables since their uncertainty contribute significantly to the reconstruction uncertainty, especially for the high β^* optics characterised by large beam sizes at the IP. To reconstruct the full set of kinematic variables, $(\Theta_x, \Theta_y, x^*, y^*, \xi)$, the proton transport equations (3.2) are inverted by χ^2 minimisation procedure [48, 50].

2008 JINST 3 S08007

Table 6.2: Expected number of collected elastic scattering events in different t-intervals for the BSW model in runs lasting 10^5 s (i.e. slightly more than a day) with different optics settings.

$|t|$-range [GeV^2]	β^* [m]	typical $\mathcal{L}$ [cm^{-2}s^{-1}]	Events / 10^5 s	
$0.0012 \div 0.03$	1540	10^{28}	1×10^7	or $20 \times 10^3 / 10^{-3}$ GeV^2
$0.03 \div 0.5$	1540	10^{28}	1.4×10^7	or $28 \times 10^3 / 10^{-3}$ GeV^2
	90	10^{30}	7.5×10^8	or $1.5 \times 10^6 / 10^{-3}$ GeV^2
$0.5 \div 2$	90	10^{30}	5×10^5	or $300 / 10^{-3}$ GeV^2
	11	10^{32}	8×10^7	or $48 \times 10^3 / 10^{-3}$ GeV^2
	2	10^{33}	1×10^7	or $6 \times 10^3 / 10^{-3}$ GeV^2
$2 \div 3$	90	10^{30}	1.4×10^3	or $1.4 / 10^{-3}$ GeV^2
	11	10^{32}	1.4×10^5	or $140 / 10^{-3}$ GeV^2
	2	10^{33}	1.1×10^6	or $1100 / 10^{-3}$ GeV^2
$3 \div 6$	90	10^{30}	170	or 56/GeV^2
	11	10^{32}	17×10^3	or 5600/GeV^2
	2	10^{33}	430×10^3	or 143×10^3/GeV^2
$6 \div 10$	2	10^{33}	500	or 125/GeV^2

The resolution in ξ of diffractively scattered protons using only information from the RP station at 220 m is shown in figure 6.3 (left). The ξ-resolution is about 6×10^{-3}, except for large $|t|$ (> 1 GeV^2), where it worsens, and large ξ (> 0.01) where it improves. If the scattering vertex can be determined to a precision of $30\,\mu$m with the central CMS detector during common data taking, the ξ-resolution improves to about 1.6×10^{-3} [2]. The corresponding t-resolution is almost independent of ξ and ranges from 3×10^{-3} GeV^2 at $t = -1 \times 10^{-2}$ GeV^2 to 1 GeV^2 at $t = -10$ GeV^2 [48]. The ξ and the t determination will e.g. be used for measuring the diffractive mass ($\approx \sqrt{s\xi}$) and t distribution for single diffractive events.

Further studies showed that including the information from a RP station at 147 m improves the performance only slightly and only for large $|t|$ due to large contributions to the uncertainty from multiple scattering in the detectors and window material of the RP station at 147 m.

In the case of central diffraction, the two protons originate from a common scattering vertex position which slightly improves the reconstruction resolution. The resolution in the diffractive mass, reconstructed purely from the proton information according to

$$M^2 = \xi_1 \xi_2 s, \tag{6.1}$$

where $\sqrt{s} = 14$ TeV, is shown in figure 6.3 (right). The mass resolution ranges from 40 GeV for symmetric events, i.e. those with $\xi_1 \approx \xi_2$, to 180 GeV for the very asymmetric events, where one of the ξ values is three orders of magnitude larger than the ξ value of the other. If the scattering vertex can be determined to a precision of $30\,\mu$m with the central CMS detector during common running, the mass resolution improves by approximatively a factor three [2].

2008 JINST 3 S08007

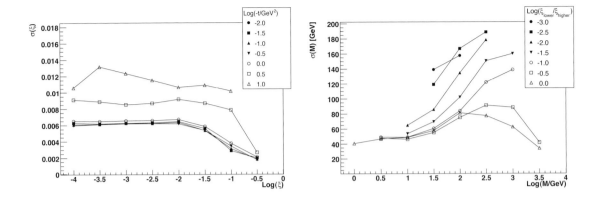

Figure 6.3: Left: resolution for the ξ reconstruction of a single diffractive proton based only on the information from the RP station at 220 m at $\beta^* = 90$ m optics. The different markers corresponds to the resolution at different $\log_{10}(-t)$ values. Right: resolution on the reconstruction of the central mass based on the measurement of the two scattered protons in central diffractive events for $\beta^* = 90$ m optics. Both protons are reconstructed with the RP stations at 220 m. The different markers corresponds to different values of the $\xi_{\text{lower}}/\xi_{\text{higher}}$ ratio, where ξ_{lower} (ξ_{higher}) is the ξ-value of the proton that lost less (more) momentum.

6.1.2.2   Diffractive proton reconstruction performance with other optics

At low β optics only protons with a ξ above 0.02 are detected with a RP station at 220 m. The ξ resolution ranges from 1×10^{-3} at $\xi = 0.02$ to 2×10^{-3} at $\xi = 0.2$ with only a small t dependence. If both protons are detected at the 220 m location, the accepted mass of the central system in central diffractive events is larger than 250 GeV and the mass resolution ranges from 5 GeV for a central mass of 250 GeV to 20 GeV for a central mass of 2.5 TeV. All accepted events are more or less symmetric, i.e. $\xi_1 \approx \xi_2$, due to the limited ξ acceptance. For further details see ref. [2].

With $\beta^* = 1540$ m optics, protons are detected independently of their ξ but the large beam size at the IP and large L_x value complicates the disentangling of the x^*, Θ_x^* and ξ contributions to the horizontal displacement of the proton at the RP station. To constrain the parameters, information from both the RP station at 147 and 220 m are used for the reconstruction. The ξ resolution of this method ranges between 5 to 10×10^{-3} with dependencies on the azimuthal angle and the size of t. The accepted mass of the central system in central diffractive events spans the whole mass range for this optics. The resolution on the central mass ranges in the best case, for symmetric events, from 50 GeV for a mass of 50 GeV, to 80 GeV for a mass of 2 TeV. A more detailed description of the reconstruction method and the performance can be found in ref. [2, 50].

6.1.3   Reconstruction of elastic protons

Here the algorithm for the reconstruction of elastic events is briefly described. The detailed description can be found in ref. [51]. The algorithm consists in the following three steps:

- Selection of elastic proton candidates: RP detector hits belonging to the particle tracks of elastic protons (in both arms) are selected.

2008 JINST 3 S08007

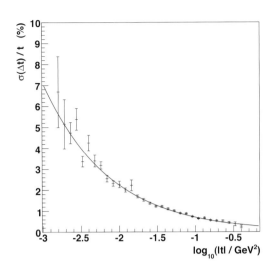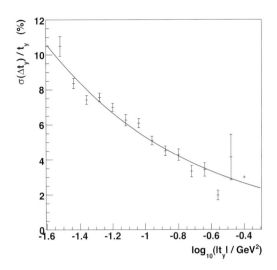

Figure 6.4: Relative resolution on t (left) and t_y (right) from the elastic event reconstruction based on the RP stations at 220 m with $\beta^* = 1540$ m and $\beta^* = 90$ m optics respectively. The solid line in the left (right) plot shows the expected $1/\sqrt{|t|}$ ($1/\sqrt{|t_y|}$) dependence.

- Fitting of the proton kinematics. Three fits made: one for the right arm fit, one for the left arm and a global one. The fits are made using a linear model approach based on the proton transport equations (3.2).

- Final selection. Fits for the left and right arm are compared. The differences in the reconstructed scattering angles Θ_x^*, Θ_y^* and vertex positions x^*, y^* are required to be within the expected uncertainties. For events passing all selections, the global fit is taken as the result.

With $\beta^* = 1540$ m, both effective lengths, L_x and L_y, are large and both magnifications, v_x and v_y, small at the RP station of 220 m enabling the measurement of both projections of the scattering angle and hence the unambiguous reconstruction of $t = t_x + t_y$, where $t_x \equiv t \cos^2 \varphi \approx (p\,\Theta_x^*)^2$ and $t_y \equiv t \sin^2 \varphi \approx (p\,\Theta_y^*)^2$. The relative precision of the t measurement with $\beta^* = 1540$ m optics is shown in figure 6.4 (left) and follows the expected $1/\sqrt{|t|}$ dependence.

With $\beta^* = 90$ m on the other hand, $L_x(220\,\text{m})$ at the RP station at 220 m is zero. Hence in this station only the y-component of the scattering angle is measured and only the t_y component reconstructed. The relative precision of the t measurement with $\beta^* = 90$ m optics is shown in figure 6.4 (right) and follows the expected $1/\sqrt{|t_y|}$ dependence.

6.2 Measurement of inelastic events

6.2.1 Track and vertex reconstruction

T1 and T2 have been designed with the goal of detecting primary particles to reconstruct the primary vertex with a precision sufficient to discriminate beam-beam events from the background (mainly beam-gas events and halo muons). Due to the very low angle with respect to the beam of

2008 JINST 3 S08007

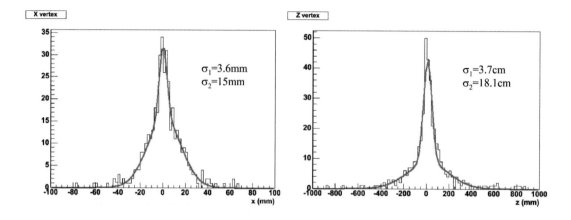

Figure 6.5: Simulated vertex reconstruction capability for T1 in the transverse plane (left) and longitudinally (right).

the charged tracks detected in the telescopes, a good spatial resolution is needed: T1 provides an average single hit resolution of ~ 0.8 mm while T2 provides a radial resolution of $\sim 100\,\mu$m. Simulations show that in presence of the CMS magnetic field, the primary vertex can be reconstructed with a precision of ~ 1.5 cm in the radial direction and ~ 20 cm in the beam direction (figure 6.5). Resolutions one order of magnitude better can be achieved running with the CMS magnetic field switched off.

The main background in the cross-section measurement comes from beam-gas events, which can be largely rejected with the obtained accuracy on the primary vertex reconstruction. Simulation studies show that only $\sim 3\%$ of the beam-gas events are misidentified as beam-beam, corresponding to a rate below 1 Hz ([1], p. 191) for a running scenario with $k = 156$ bunches à 1.15×10^{11} protons.

6.2.2 Trigger acceptance

The L1 trigger in T1 is generated combining the digital signals coming from different groups of anode wires, to maximise the signal generation speed, while in T2 the L1 trigger is generated combining the signals coming from arrays of pads from different planes. An efficient trigger is a key point in avoiding biases in the measurement of the total or diffractive cross-section. With a double-arm trigger more than 99% of non-diffractive events can be detected, while with a single arm trigger one can detect the events escaping the double-arm trigger and most of the diffractive interactions that have all visible tracks in only one arm.

Dedicated studies show that single and double diffractive events are responsible for the major loss in the inelastic rate; with a single-arm trigger, a fraction of these events, corresponding to ~ 2.8 mb, escapes detection. The lost events are mainly those with a very low mass (below $\sim 10\,\text{GeV}/c^2$), since all their particles are produced at pseudo-rapidities beyond the T2 acceptance and escape therefore the detection. To obtain the total inelastic rate, the fraction of events lost be-

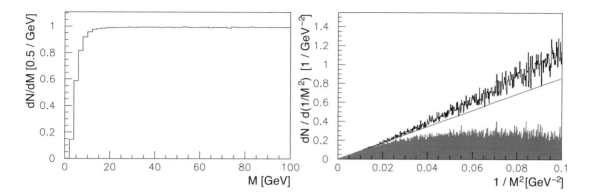

Figure 6.6: Left: ratio of detected Single Diffractive events as a function of the diffractive mass, M. Right: simulation (unshaded) and acceptance corrected (shaded) Single Diffractive distribution as function of $1/M^2$. The line shows a linear fit based on the acceptance corrected events in the mass region above $10\,\mathrm{GeV}/c^2$.

cause of the incomplete angular coverage can be estimated by extrapolation. In the case of single diffraction, the reconstructed $1/M^2$ distribution has been linearly fitted for $M > 10\,\mathrm{GeV}/c^2$, and the extrapolation to low masses has then be compared with simulation. For Single Diffraction, the extrapolated number of events differs from the simulation expectations by 4%, corresponding to a 0.6 mb uncertainty on the total cross-section (figure 6.6). The same estimation for the Double Diffraction and Double Pomeron Exchange gives a 0.1 mb and 0.2 mb uncertainty, respectively.

In the study of diffraction, the telescopes can be used to trigger and/or measure rapidity gaps. Best result are expected in combined running of the TOTEM and CMS detectors; nevertheless studies show that using only T1 and T2 telescopes, the rapidity gaps in DPE events can be measured with a precision $\lesssim 1$ unit of rapidity. Moreover, the comparison of results from SD and DPE events open the possibility of estimate the rapidity gap survival probability at LHC energies.

6.3 Total cross-section measurement

The total pp cross-section, σ_{tot}, will be measured first in runs with the $\beta^* = 90\,\mathrm{m}$ optics and later — with better precision — with the $\beta^* = 1540\,\mathrm{m}$ optics (chapter 3). The method based on the Optical Theorem and the quantities to be measured have been explained in section 2.1. The total uncertainty of σ_{tot} has the following contributions.

6.3.1 Inelastic rate

The uncertainty on the inelastic rate is dominated by the inelastic trigger losses $\delta(N_{\mathrm{inel}})/N_{\mathrm{inel}} \approx 1\%$ as discussed in section 6.2.2. The second component — trigger contamination by beam-gas background — is much smaller. This estimate is almost independent from the beam optics, exceptions being SD and DPE where for some trigger strategies leading protons are parts of the signature.

2008 JINST 3 S08007

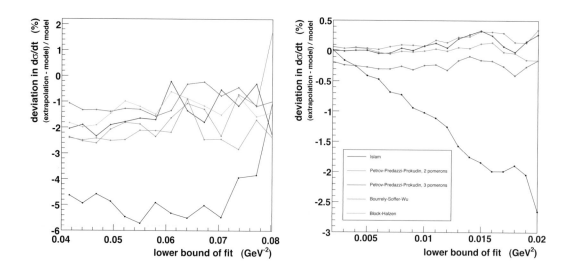

Figure 6.7: Relative deviation of the extrapolation results based on a simulation (not including an error on L_x). Left: $\beta^* = 90$ m, right: $\beta^* = 1540$ m. The t_y- and t-distributions were fitted from the indicated lower bound (abscissa) to $0.25\,\text{GeV}^2$ and $0.04\,\text{GeV}^2$, respectively. The different solid lines corresponds to different models.

6.3.2 Elastic rate and extrapolation of the cross-section to t = 0

The determination of σ_{tot} requires two aspects of elastic scattering to be measured: the total elastic rate and the extrapolation of the differential cross-section $d\sigma/dt$ to the Optical Point $t = 0$. Obviously, to be complete, the measured elastic rate has to be complemented by the extrapolated part, so that this extrapolation enters twice in the procedure.

At $\beta^* = 90$ m, protons with $|t| > 0.03\,\text{GeV}^2$ are observed in the RP detector at 220 m (chapter 3). The starting point of the acceptance lies well above the region where the delicate effects from the interference between nuclear and Coulomb scattering play a role. Hence for the early running optics no such perturbation needs to be included in the extrapolation procedure, in contrast to the extrapolation at the $\beta^* = 1540$ m optics with $|t|_{\text{min}} = 10^{-3}\,\text{GeV}^2$.

As shown in section 2.2 (figure 2.4), most theoretical models [7] predict an almost exponential behaviour of the cross-section up to $|t| \approx 0.25\,\text{GeV}^2$. For all the models considered — except for the one by Islam et al. — the deviations are small. In the t-range mentioned, the slope $B(t)$ (figure 2.4, right) can be well described by a parabola, which is therefore used for the fitting function and the extrapolation. Since this quadratic behaviour of the slope characterises all the models, the extrapolation method is valid in a model-independent way.

As explained in section 6.1.3, the extrapolation of the elastic cross-section to $t = 0$ will be based on the measurement of the $d\sigma/dt$ ($d\sigma/dt_y$) distribution for the $\beta^* = 1540$ m ($\beta^* = 90$ m) optics. For the $\beta^* = 90$ m optics, the azimuthal symmetry of the elastic scattering process, i.e. the equality of the distributions of t_y and t_x, is used to infer the distribution $d\sigma/dt$ from the $d\sigma/dt_y$ distribution.

2008 JINST 3 S08007

The accuracy of the extrapolation to $t = 0$ is shown in figure 6.7. The key contributions are the following:

- Smearing effects of the t-measurement: For $\beta^* = 90$, they are dominated by the beam divergence ($\sigma(\theta_{\text{beam}}) = 2.3 \, \mu$rad) and lead to a shift of -2% in the extrapolation result (figure 6.7 left). For $\beta^* = 1540$ m with $\sigma(\theta_{\text{beam}}) = 0.29 \, \mu$rad, this contribution is less than 0.1% (figure 6.7 right).

- The statistical error of the extrapolation with the $\beta^* = 90$ m optics for an integrated luminosity of $2 \, \text{nb}^{-1}$, i.e. about 5 hours running at a luminosity of $10^{29} \, \text{cm}^{-2} \text{s}^{-1}$, ranges between 0.6% and 4% depending on the fit interval for the extrapolation. For the $\beta^* = 1540$ m optics, this contribution is less than 0.1% for an integrated luminosity of of $0.36 \, \text{nb}^{-1}$, i.e. about 10 hours of running at a luminosity of $10^{28} \, \text{cm}^{-2} \text{s}^{-1}$.

- Systematic uncertainty of the t-measurement: the dominant contribution comes from the uncertainty of the effective length L_x. The currently expected precision of 2% would translate into an offset of the extrapolation of about 4%. Detector alignment and beam position accuracy are much more crucial for the $\beta^* = 1540$ m optics with its small beam size (the vertical beam size $\sigma_{y_{\text{beam}}} = 80 \, \mu$m at the 220 m RP station) than for $\beta^* = 90$ m, where $\sigma_{y_{\text{beam}}} = 625 \, \mu$m at the 220 m RP station.

- Model-dependent deviations of the nuclear elastic pp cross-section from an exponential shape lead to a bias in the extrapolation. Besides the Islam et al. model [7], which can be excluded or confirmed by the measured t-distribution at large $|t|$-values, the models are within $\pm 1\%$ ($\beta^* = 90$ m) or $\pm 0.2\%$ ($\beta^* = 1540$ m).

6.3.3 The ρ parameter

The ρ parameter, estimated to be about 0.14 by extrapolating measurements at lower energies [5], enters σ_{tot} in the factor $1/(1 + \rho^2) \sim 0.98$, and hence gives only a relative contribution of about 2%. Assuming a relative uncertainty of at most 33% on ρ, determined by the error of the measurements at TEVATRON [4] and the extrapolation to LHC energies, we expect an relative uncertainty contribution of less than $\delta(1 + \rho^2)/(1 + \rho^2) = 1.3\%$.

6.3.4 Combined uncertainty on total cross-section and luminosity

Combining all the above uncertainties by error propagation for the expressions

$$\sigma_{\text{tot}} = \frac{16\pi}{1 + \rho^2} \cdot \frac{dN_{\text{el}}/dt|_{t=0}}{N_{\text{el}} + N_{\text{inel}}} \quad \text{and} \tag{6.2}$$

$$\mathscr{L} = \frac{1 + \rho^2}{16\pi} \cdot \frac{(N_{\text{el}} + N_{\text{inel}})^2}{dN_{\text{el}}/dt|_{t=0}}, \tag{6.3}$$

and taking into account the correlations, yields a relative error of 4% on σ_{tot} and a relative uncertainty of 7% on $\mathscr{L}$ with $\beta^* = 90$ m. With $\beta^* = 1540$ m the expected precision is at the 1% level but this requires an improved knowledge of the optical functions and an alignment precision of the RP station better than $50 \, \mu$m.

2008 JINST 3 S08007

Chapter 7

The TOTEM electronics system

TOTEM has 3 separate and distinct detector technologies used within the three detector systems; RP, T1 and T2. Each detector system has it's own physically separate electronics system however each system is made following one common system architecture. This has the obvious benefits of reducing design effort by using common electronic components, data formats and DAQ software.

The initial requirements for the electronics system are to be able to readout the charge of the three different detectors on one side and offer full compatibility with CMS on the other.

Table 7.1 gives an overview of the three detectors with their main properties and the number of front-end chips (VFAT) needed. The gas detectors generate more signal charge, distributed over several electrodes. The silicon strips generate positive charge, T2 negative, and T1 both polarities (anodes and cathodes). The T1 and T2 detectors have a large occupancy particularly in the regions close to the beam pipe. This is due to inelastic events with a large number of particles interacting in the beam pipe and thus creating particle showers at the detector edges.

The signal properties vary considerably between detectors. However, it was decided at an early stage to design one common front-end ASIC that would be capable to provide the charge readout for all detectors. This front-end ASIC is called VFAT and is key to providing a common data format and common control and readout needs in the electronic system for all 3 detectors.

Table 7.1: Overview of electronics requirements from the different detectors.

	RP	T1	T2
No. and type of detectors	240 Si strip detectors	60 Cathode Strip Chambers	40 Gas Electron Multipliers
No. of channels	122880	11124 anodes 15936 cathodes	62400 pads 20480 strips
No. of VFATs	960	480	680
Typical input charge	∼4 fC	∼50 fC	∼50 fC
Occupancy	<1%	anodes: <10% cathodes: <20%	pads: <5% strips: <30%
Radiation Dose	<10 Mrad	<50 krad	<50 Mrad

2008 JINST 3 S08007

Figure 7.1: Photograph of the VFAT chip.

7.1 VFAT

The VFAT [52] (strictly "VFAT2", being the second version) is a trigger and tracking front-end ASIC, designed specifically for the readout of sensors in the TOTEM experiment at the LHC. The VFAT chip (shown in figure 7.1) has been designed in quarter micron CMOS technology and measures 9.43 mm by 7.58 mm.

It has two main functions; the first (Tracking) is to provide precise spatial hit information for a given triggered event. The second function (Trigger) is to provide programmable "fast OR" information based on the region of the sensor hit. This can be used for the creation of a level-1 trigger.

Figure 7.2 shows the block diagram for the signal path through the VFAT. It has 128 analog input channels each of which are equipped with a very low noise pre-amplifier and a 22 ns shaping stage plus comparator. A calibration unit allows delivery of controlled test pulses to any channel for calibration purposes. Signal discrimination on a programmable threshold provides binary hit information which passes through a synchronisation and monostable stage before being stored within SRAMs until a trigger is received. The monostable has a variable length from 1 to 8 clock periods. This has the effect of recording the hit in more than one clock period (useful for gas detectors which have an uncertainty on the signal charge rise time). The SRAM storage capacity enables trigger latencies of up to 6.4 μs and the simultaneous storage of data for up to 128 triggered events. Dead time free operation with up to 100 kHz Poisson distributed trigger rates is ensured. Time and event tags are added to the triggered data which are then formatted and read from the chip in the form of digitized data packets at 40 Mbps. The data packet format is defined as in figure 7.3.

VFAT has many programmable functions controlled through an I^{2}C interface. These include: internal biasing of analog blocks via 8 bit DACs, individual channel calibration via an internal test pulse with 8 bit programmable amplitude, calibration test pulse phase control, operate with positive

2008 JINST 3 S08007

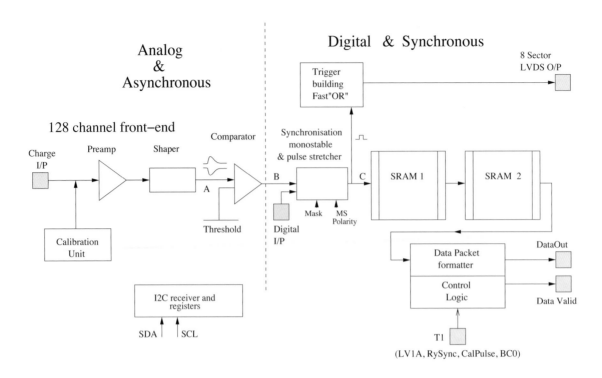

Figure 7.2: Block diagram of the signal path through the VFAT.

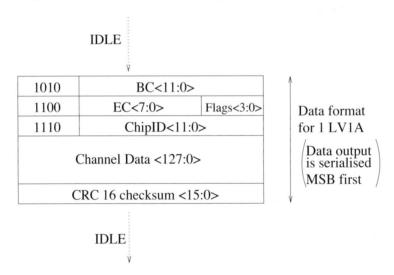

Figure 7.3: VFAT data packet format.

or negative detector charge, 8 bit global threshold plus a 5 bit trim DAC threshold adjust on each channel, multiple possibilities for channel grouping for the "Fast OR" outputs, variable latency, various test modes plus an automatic self test of the digital memories. Chip status information including occupancy and SEU rates can be read via I^2C.

Fast synchronous commands are applied via an encoded LVDS signal (T1) which is then decoded to 4 synchronous commands via an internal command decoder.

2008 JINST 3 S08007

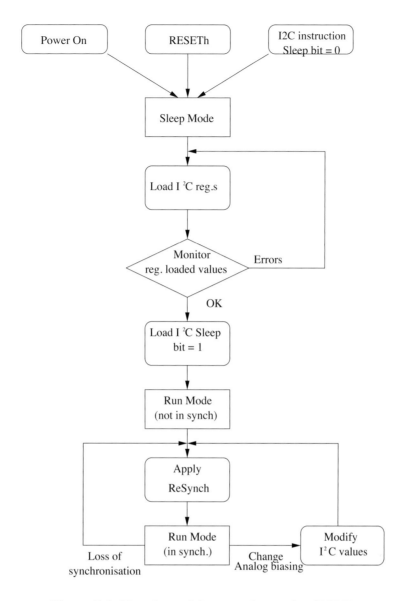

Figure 7.4: Flowchart of the operation cycle of VFAT.

For robustness against single event upsets (SEU), the digital parts of VFAT have been de-signed with hamming encoding for the SRAMs and triplication logic for the I²C interface and control logic. All analog circuitry employs layout techniques that reduce threshold voltage shifts under ionising radiation.

The operation flow of VFAT is shown in the flowchart of figure 7.4. On applying power to the chip VFAT performs an automatic power-on reset and goes directly into "Sleep Mode". Sleep Mode sets all DACs to default values providing stable but minimum power consuming conditions to the entire chip. In Sleep Mode only the I²C is active and can respond to commands. The internal registers can then be loaded with data. This data can be read back to check if loading was successful. The values loaded are not applied to the active circuits until VFAT is put into Run Mode. When VFAT is put into Run Mode, biases are applied to the analog circuits and digital circuits come out of a reset condition bringing the power consumption up to the normal level. Since

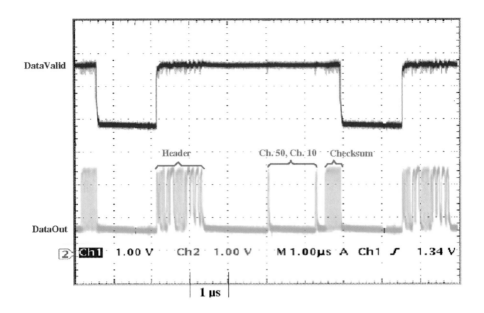

Figure 7.5: Oscilloscope view of the data packet and DataValid signal.

the I^2C is a non-synchronous slow command VFAT still requires a synchronising signal. This is applied via a ReSync signal encoded within the T1 signal. VFAT is now in a synchronous Run mode and ready for taking data. Initial functional measurements showed all functions of VFAT to be fully operational.

Measurements of the Calibration units internal test pulse generator reveal a linear charge delivery range of -2 fC to 18.5 fC with LSB of 0.08 fC.

When triggered, Data packets appear on the DataOut output as shown in figure 7.5 together with a DataValid signal which goes high for the duration of a Data Packet. The figure shows two "hit" channels, these channels received a charge pulse from the Calibration unit.

Noise measurements have been made by choosing a random threshold and then ramping the magnitude of the signal charge using the internal test pulse generator controlled via DAC (digital-to-analog converter). The range is chosen such that the test pulse amplitude VCal passes through the threshold from 0% hits to 100%. The result is an S-curve as shown in figure 7.6. The mean of an error function fit to the S-curve gives the threshold and the sigma gives the noise expressed in ENC (Equivalent Noise Charge).

S-curves have been generated for all channels. The second and third plots of figure 7.6 show histograms of the extracted thresholds and noise of 128 channels. The results show for a mean threshold of 5952 electrons there is a threshold spread (before fine adjustment with the Trim DACs) of 335 electrons rms. The mean ENC is 539 electrons with a spread of 67 electrons rms.

A major design challenge was to integrate the multitude of digital functions without having a significant impact on the analog performance. Stringent design techniques to "deafen the listener" and "silence the talker" have been employed to all analog and digital modules.

Measurements from the chip show all modules to be 100 percent functionally correct. The expected front-end noise performance of approximately $600\,e + 50\,e/pF$ of detector capacitance is maintained. The total power consumption is 572 mW.

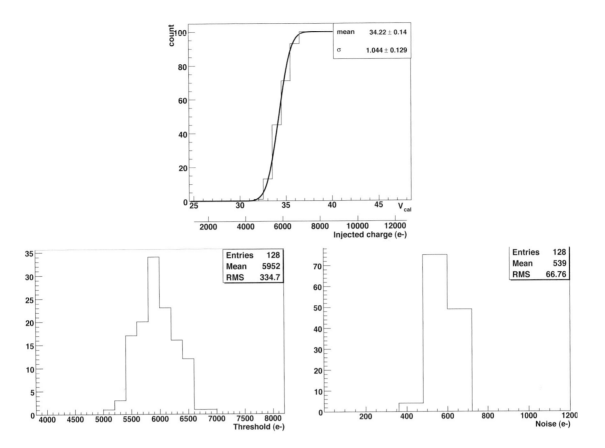

Figure 7.6: Top: S-curve (number of hits as a function of the test pulse amplitude for a fixed threshold) for one VFAT channel with a Gaussian error function fit superimposed. Bottom left: distribution of the mean thresholds (V_{cal} at 50% level of the Gaussian error function) of all 128 VFAT channels. Bottom right: distribution of the noise, i.e. the width of the fitted Gaussian error function, for all 128 channels.

VFAT has successfully integrated complex analog and digital functions into a single ASIC without compromising noise performance.

7.2   The TOTEM electronics control and readout system

The architecture of the TOTEM control and readout system is common to all 3 detector systems. This section describes the common electronics architecture and the components used.

Figure 7.7 shows a basic block diagram of the functional components used in the system. It is sub divided into physically separated regions and also data flow. The "On Detector regions" have the VFAT front-end ASIC located as close to the detector as physically possible. The "Local Detector regions" are for readout boards in the vicinity of the detector used for grouping and distributing control signals.

2008 JINST 3 S08007

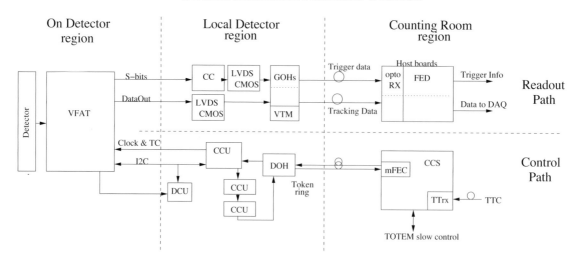

Figure 7.7: Functional block diagram of the TOTEM electronics system architecture.

7.2.1 The VFAT control path

The VFAT control path starts in the counting room with the arrival of Timing, Trigger and Control (TTC) signals [53] to the TTC receiver (TTCrx) on the Clock and Control System (CCS). The TTC signals are composed of the LHC machine clock and trigger commands (TC).

The CCS is equipped with Front End Controller (FEC) modules. TOTEM slow control instructions and TTC signals are transmitted onto a token ring via the FEC modules. The token ring starts with 40 Mb/s optical links from the FECs to the subsystems in the local detector regions. The optical signals of the token ring are converted to electrical signals in the local detector regions by a module known as the Digital Opto Hybrid Module (DOHM [54]). Communication and Control Units (CCU) sit in the token ring and are used to extract and distribute fast clock/TC signals and slow control information to and from the VFATs. The fast clock/TC signals are delivered to the VFATs via Low Voltage Differential Signals (LVDS). Slow control is achieved using the I²C protocol to be able to provide write/read access to registers inside the VFATs. The Detector Control Unit (DCU) contains analog to digital converters (ADCs) which are used to measure currents and voltages within VFAT and read back these values via I²C. The DCU is used during calibration of the VFATs.

The concept of the token ring and the design of the token ring ASICs ie. FEC, CCU, DCU plus associated PLLs [39] were designed by the CERN microelectronics group for use within CMS. The CMS tracker and Preshower use this concept for their control systems.

7.2.2 The VFAT readout path

VFAT produces both trigger and tracking data. These two types of data have very different timing requirements hence are treated separately.

Trigger data is used to aid the generation of the first level trigger hence has to be read out as fast as possible. The Sector outputs (S-bits) of the VFAT give the result of internal fast OR

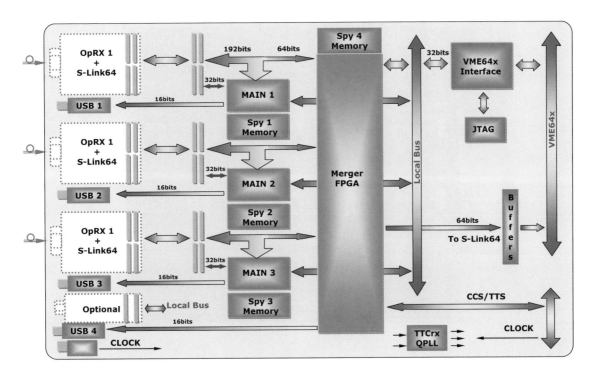

Figure 7.8: Block diagram of the TOTEM FED Host board.

operations within 1 clock cycle. These S-bits are in LVDS format. A Coincidence chip (CC, see section 8.2.1) then performs coincidence operations between VFAT sector outputs. The outputs from the CC chip (still in LVDS format) are then converted to CMOS levels by dedicated LVDS-to-CMOS converters. The trigger data are then serialised and transmitted by optical links at 800 Mb/s to the counting room. The module that performs the serialisation and optical transmission is called the Gigabit Optical Hybrid (GOH [34]).

Tracking data are data corresponding to triggered events and are buffered within VFAT for high trigger rates. Data packets are transmitted in serial LVDS form from the VFAT DataOut outputs at a bit rate of 40 Mb/s. Once again the LVDS to CMOS conversion is performed and the GOH serialises the data for transmission to the counting room via optical links. Up to 16 VFAT DataOut signals are multiplexed by one GOH into a serial stream for optical transmission. All VFATs operate synchronously, a VFAT Trigger Mezzanine (VTM) is used to control the timing of the GOH and maintain synchronisation.

Once in the counting room the optical fibres are connected to the 9U VME64x Host boards (developed by TOTEM) which contain the Front-End Drivers (FEDs [55]) used for trigger and event building. There are separate Host boards for the treatment of trigger data and tracking data. TOTEM uses 6 Host boards for the Trigger system and 8 Host Boards for the tracking data. A block diagram and photograph of the Host Board are shown in figures 7.8 and 7.9 respectively.

The incoming optical fibres (grouped in 3 bundles of 12 fibres) connect to optical receiver modules called optoRx-12. The OptoRx-12 is a plug-in module developed by the CMS preshower. It is based on a 12-channel optical receiver and a Field Programmable Gate Array (FPGA) Stratix^{TM} GX from ALTERA. The FPGA has multiple gigabit blocks, each with four full duplex channels.

2008 JINST 3 S08007

Figure 7.9: Photo of the TOTEM FED Host board.

Using clock data recovery technology, these channels can serialise or de-serialise data for transmission rates up to 3.125 Gbps. The module is compatible with the VME mechanical specification [56].

The first stage of FED data management is performed on the optoRX-12 with the de-serialisation of 32 input data streams per FPGA using the embedded high-speed deserialisers.

The second stage of data management is performed on the Host board. There are 3 Altera FPGAs Stratix^{TM} labelled "Main-1", "Main-2" and "Main-3". Each Main controller bridge receives raw data from its associated OptoRX-12 module, stores it into its corresponding memory and transfers it to the VME64x bus or to the USB for slow spy readout.

For certain FED applications the de-serialised data are processed inside the OptoRX-12 module in order to reduce their volume. Then a forth FPGA (also a Stratix^{TM}), labelled "Merger", collects the reduced data through three associated 64-bit buses in order to build the event.

In the Trigger Host boards the incoming trigger data is sent to the FPGAs where coincidence logic functions and more complex algorithms can be performed in order to prepare trigger primitives for the global L1 TOTEM trigger. There are 2 Host Boards per detector used for the trigger.

Since the TOTEM Host boards are also used for data readout, all necessary hardware is available to include the trigger data into the data stream for monitoring purposes.

In the Tracking Host boards the incoming tracking data has a format defined by the data packets of VFAT. The format is defined in figure 7.3.

The data length is organised in 16 bit words consisting of: BC$\langle 11{:}0 \rangle$ (bunch counter), EC$\langle 7{:}0 \rangle$ (event counter), Flags$\langle 3{:}0 \rangle$, Chip ID$\langle 11{:}0 \rangle$, Data$\langle 127{:}0 \rangle$, CRC 16 checksum$\langle 15{:}0 \rangle$ and four control bits for the beginning of the frame. For multiple triggers the frames for each event follow one after another.

2008 JINST 3 S08007

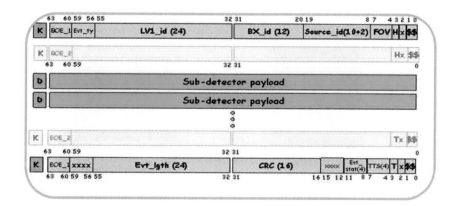

Figure 7.10: CMS FED data format.

When an event fragment is ready to be transmitted to the DAQ, the FED event builder encapsulates the data according to the common CMS FED data format [57] shown in figure 7.10.

The CMS format includes, in addition to the actual sub-detector payload, information such as event type ('Evt_ty'), event number ('LV1_id'), bunch crossing number ('BX_id'), event length ('Evt_lgth'), data source identifier ('Source_id') and CRC information.

There are 3 different possibilities implemented for sending data to the DAQ:

- VME interface: used for TOTEM operation;

- USB interface: alternative for TOTEM operation;

- S-Link64 [58] module: connection to the CMS Front-end Readout Links (FRLs) for common data taking, ensuring full compatibility with the CMS DAQ.

7.2.3 The low and high voltage power supplies

The on-detector electronics are electrically isolated from the counting room through the systematic use of floating power supplies and optical signal transmission or electrical transmission with optocouplers. The low-voltage power supplies are located as close as possible to the detectors. The high-voltage power supplies are located in the counting-room.

7.3 Specific TOTEM detector electronics

Every effort has been made to standardise the use of components across all three detector systems. However, different geometries and segmentation have inevitably led to different board designs for the "on detector" regions and "local detector" regions.

This section aims to highlight the electronic boards used in the construction of the different detector systems.

2008 JINST 3 S08007

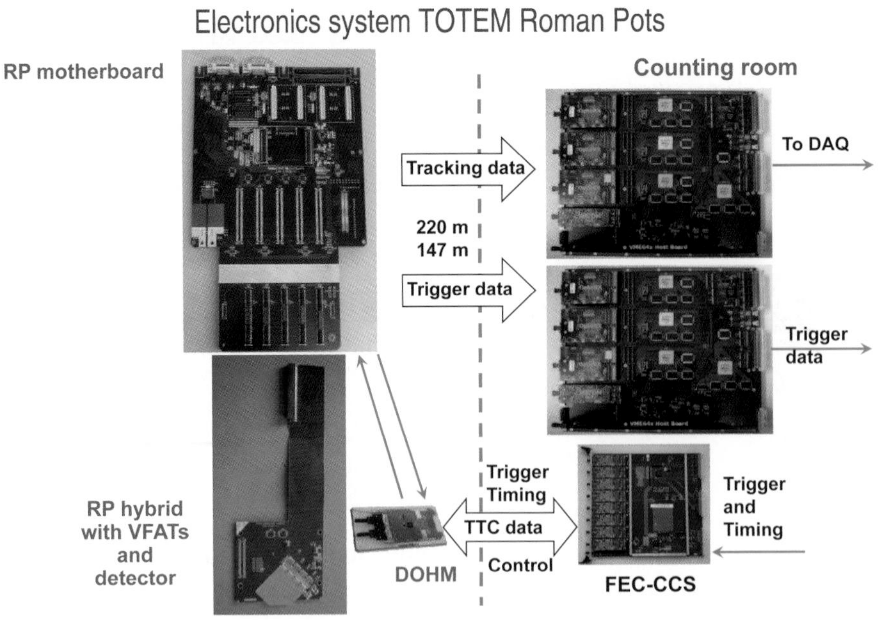

Electronics system TOTEM Roman Pots

Figure 7.11: Overview of the RP electronics system.

7.3.1 TOTEM electronics boards for the Roman Pots

Figure 7.11 gives an overview of the electronics boards used for the Roman Pot system.

The Roman Pot hybrids contain one silicon detector sub-divided into 512 strips. Four VFATs are bonded directly to each strip with 128 channels per chip. There is one clock and LVDS bus on the hybrid to which each VFAT connects in parallel. In addition the clock is fed to the DCU chip which is also located on the hybrid. A single I^2C bus is delivered to the hybrid which is connected to each VFAT and the DCU.

The RP hybrids (located in the "on detector region") plug directly into the RP mother board (located in the "near detector region"). The RP mother board contains the components necessary for the token ring in the control path and the Trigger and Tracking data transmission components in the readout path. These components were described in section 7.2.

The low voltage power supplies are located approximately 70 m from the pots in the nearest alcove in the tunnel.

7.3.2 TOTEM electronics boards for T1

An overview of the electronic boards used in T1 is shown in figure 7.12.

The VFAT used for the gas detectors is a slightly different version than that used for the Roman Pots. The difference is that the VFAT inputs have internal overload protection circuits that help avoid destructive breakdown of the chip in the case of sparks (uncontrolled charge discharges) from the detector [59]. In all other respects however the VFATs are identical. T1 and T2 use also the same hybrid. This hybrid contains one VFAT chip.

2008 JINST 3 S08007

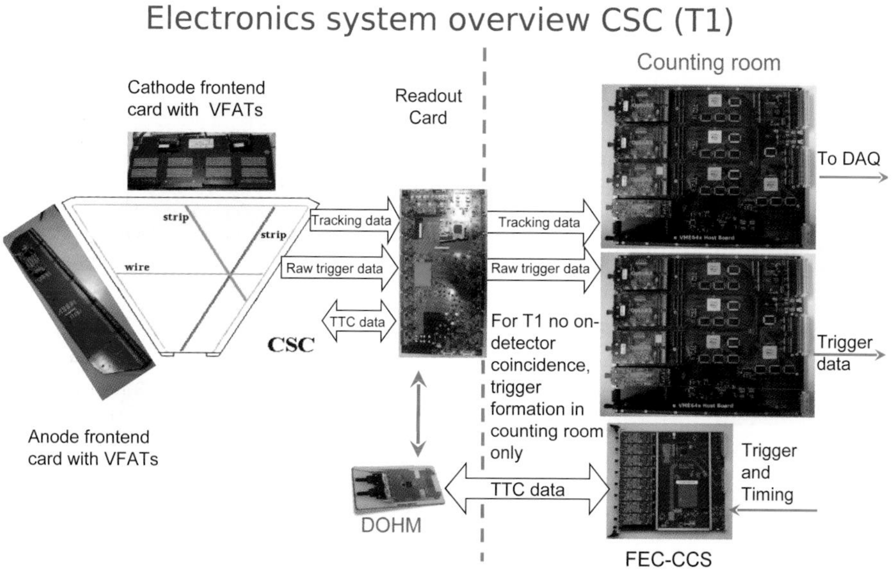

Figure 7.12: Overview of the T1 electronics system.

The connection to the T1 detector is made by plugging the hybrids into one of two readout cards adapted to the geometry of the T1 detector. One for the readout of the anodes (AFEC) and the other for the readout of cathodes (CFEC).

The "on detector region" is connected to the "local detector region" by cables. A T1 Read-Out Card (ROC) contains the components and functions shown in figure 7.7 for the local region with the exception of the CC chip. T1 will instead readout all VFAT S-bits without making any logical operations with respect to other VFATs in the system. One ROC can handle the readout of two cathode strip chambers, and can therefore be connected to up to two AFECs and up to 14 CFECs.

7.3.3 TOTEM electronics boards for T2

The electronics boards developed for the T2 system are shown in figure 7.13.

Similar to T1, the T2 detector also uses the VFATs designed for gas detectors which include the input protection circuits. The hybrids are also the same as the ones used for T1. The connection to the detector is made by plugging the hybrids into the horse-shoe card (so called because of its geometrical shape) which in turn is connected to the GEM strips and pads. The VFAT control and readout paths connect by a cable to a board known as the "11th Card". The 11th card receives data from 10 Horse-shoe cards and also contains a CC chip for the coincidence logic function of the trigger path S-bits.

T2 has the most severe ionising radiation environment of the 3 detectors of up to 50 Mrads (see table 7.1). Whilst VFAT and the CC chip are expected to survive these radiation levels the optical links will not. Hence the electronics of the "near detector region" will be placed in a rack near the detectors but behind a radiation shield.

2008 JINST 3 S08007

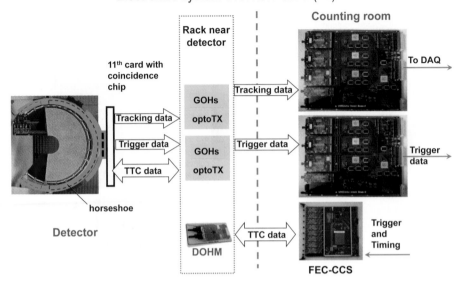

Figure 7.13: Overview of the T2 electronics system.

2008 JINST 3 S08007

Chapter 8

Trigger

8.1 Strategy

The final triggers are constructed out of all TOTEM detectors and will critically depend on the luminosity, the running and background conditions as well as on the targeted physics. Coincidences between the different detectors on both sides of the intersection point will help to reduce the background but might introduce certain biases. As an example, the total cross-section measurement requires triggers, as unbiased as possible, on all inelastic event topologies. Particularly difficult are triggers on low mass single diffractive events where the very forward particles escape detection, but where the proton on the other side can become visible, e.g. in large β^* runs. Such a single proton trigger will not be background free, mainly due to halo protons and beam-gas collisions. The calibration of all these minimum bias triggers can be foreseen with the help of real bias-free triggers on bunch-crossings. The acceptance for elastically scattered protons is predominantly determined by the β^* (being as large as possible) at the intersection point (figure 6.1). The coincidence between the two protons and their collinearity enable a clean trigger, but overlaps with Double-Pomeron events will occur at larger momentum transfers due to the less steep differential cross-section $d\sigma/dt$ of the latter process. The triggers on Double Pomeron events depend on the machine dispersion and on the optics used. Probably more background will be present in such a trigger. In general, the triggers and backgrounds have to be studied in the various running scenarios and to be understood with the help of Monte-Carlo simulations. How the triggers are performed in the TOTEM sub-detectors with standardised electronics is described below.

It is an essential feature of the three charged particle detectors that they are actively creating the first level trigger. To minimise the development effort, the read-out and trigger strategy is common to all detectors. The trigger bits are generated by the front-end chip (VFAT) itself, which provides 8 fast outputs that are programmable in a limited number of different configurations adapted to the three sub-detectors. These trigger bits are made available within the next clock cycle (25 ns) after the detection of a hit on one of the channels. The trigger is then based either on a crude track reconstruction or on hit activities in the detectors. Coincidences between the chamber planes (for RP and T2) are performed in the "Coincidence Chip" (CC, see also next section), thus reducing the number of trigger bits by an order of magnitude before they are transmitted to the counting-room. Pseudorapidity cuts for the two telescopes, already applicable on the first level

2008 JINST 3 S08007

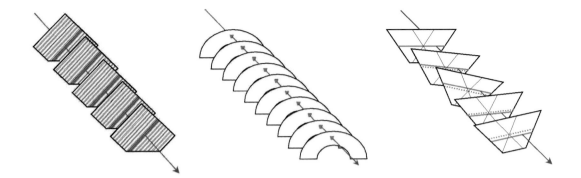

Figure 8.1: Left: RP trigger coincidence in one projection (*u* or *v*). Middle: T2 trigger coincidence in one pad. Right: due to the 3° rotation between different planes in T1 (angle exaggerated in the picture), the coincidence definition is more complicated and hence performed in the counting-room.

trigger, open the possibility to mask noisy regions, as e.g. close to the beam pipe. Cuts on hit multiplicities over larger detector areas might improve the trigger cleanliness or create a simplified trigger.

The trigger formation strategy can be explained with the aid of the principal chamber arrangements in figure 8.1.

The silicon detectors in the Roman Pots close to the beam have to trigger on protons with almost the same momentum as the beam. Consequently there is only one track that is parallel to the beam within less than 1 mrad. Altogether, 10 planes (5 planes per each strip orientation *u* and *v*), define the proton trigger in one Roman Pot station. Each detector plane is divided into 16 groups of 32 strips, defining a track road of about 2 mm per strip orientation. In a first step, the coincidence chip (CC) requires a coincidence of at least 3 out of 5 planes with hits on the same track road resulting in 32 trigger bits per pot (16 in *u* and 16 in *v*). With this loose requirement, tracks crossing the boundary of neighbour track roads are still included. Coincidences between track segments in the *u* and *v* oriented planes will further reduce the trigger rate. In the counting-room, coincidences between the two RP units with a distance of a few meters will select tracks that are parallel to the beam, and multiplicity cuts will reduce the background originating from beam-gas interactions.

For the T2 GEM chambers, the trigger is based on pads that are grouped by a fast-OR logic of 3 × 5 pads into 104 super-pads per half plane. To trigger on a straight track, the super-pads from the 10 detector planes are put into an adjustable coincidence (at least 5 out of 10). This loose coincidence again solves the problem of tracks crossing the superpad boundaries. 104 trigger bits per half arm of the T2 detector are sent to the counting-room for further trigger treatments.

For T1, the trigger is formed by the anodes which are read by two VFATs per plane. However, the more complex detector geometry (for acceptance reasons the chambers are rotated by 3° with respect to each other) makes it difficult to have on-detector coincidences. The 16 trigger outputs of the two VFATs per plane are therefore sent directly to the counting-room where the coincidences between the five planes will be performed in hardware. Simpler triggers based on hit activities in the chambers may lead to a less biased trigger at the expense of larger trigger rates.

This procedure results in 960 trigger bits for T1, 416 for T2 and 768 bits for the RPs.

2008 JINST 3 S08007

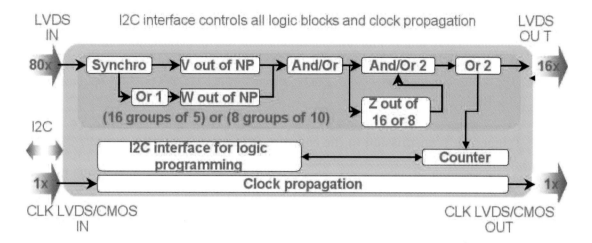

Figure 8.2: Schematic overview of the Coincindence Chip (CC).

8.2 Implementation

8.2.1 The Coincidence Chip (CC)

The Coincidence Chip provides on-detector coincidences to reduce the trigger data sent to the counting room. It is used by the RP and T2 systems, but not by T1 where the more complex geometry made its use too difficult. Figure 8.2 shows a block diagram. The chip has 80 LVDS inputs which can be grouped in two ways:

- 16 groups of 5 inputs, for 5 detector planes (RP case).

- 8 groups of 10 inputs, for 10 detector planes (T2 case).

These groups correspond to detector sectors in a similar transverse position on different detector planes.

A synchronisation block is included to synchronise the pulses to the clock and to stretch the pulses over different clock cycles for detectors with an inherent timing spread larger than a single clock cycle. Asynchronous operation is also possible. For TOTEM only synchronised operation has been adopted.

Two types of coincidences can be performed:

- A coincidence on just one group: V hits on one track road through NP detector planes.

- A coincidence which takes into account a programmable number of neighbouring groups: W hits out of NP detector planes including X neighbouring groups.

The result of these coincidences can be logically combined in a programmable way (AND/OR with possible inversion). The possibility to include neighbouring sectors or not allows a certain programmable selectivity on the direction of incoming particles.

The total number of positive coincidence results is checked (Z out of 8 or 16) and can be logically combined with the coincidence results (AND/OR2). This can be used to impose certain occupancy limits, for instance to prevent the generation of a trigger if a detector is completely filled with artificial hits, e.g. due to noise or particle showers. Finally, signals can be grouped into a smaller number (OR2) to reduce overall signal count.

2008 JINST 3 S08007

The parameters of the blocks on the Coincidence Chip can be fully configured through its I^2C interface. The VFAT chip also includes counters on the fast trigger outputs to monitor hit rates. This is achieved by a 24 bit counter which records the number of sector hits within a given time window. The duration of the time window can be selected from a list of 4 possible options (6.4 μs, 1.6 ms, 0.4 s, 107 s).

8.2.2 Trigger bit transmission to the counting-room

The trigger signals from all subdetectors are optically transmitted to the counting-room using the GOH optohybrid in the same way as the tracking data. However, the Roman Pot station RP220 is so far away from the counting-room that optically transmitted trigger data would not arrive within the latency allowed by the trigger of CMS. Therefore, in addition to optical transmission for TOTEM runs, electrical transmission with LVDS signals was implemented for commons runs with CMS. To maintain the electrical isolation between detector and counting room, optocouplers will be used to receive these electrically transmitted signals. At regular intervals of about 70 m along the total cable length of 270 m, repeaters based on a custom-designed LVDS repeater chip are inserted to preserve the electrical signal quality.

8.2.3 Trigger signal synchronisation

The large distances between the subdetectors — with RPs at up to 220 m from the interaction point — requires special attention to the synchronisation of the trigger information.

Since the trigger output from the RP220 station has the longest signal transmission time, the trigger signals from that station are the last to arrive in the counting-room. In order to minimise the latency of the combined trigger, the data from the trigger FEDs of the other subdetectors are transmitted via the VME back-plane to the trigger FED of the RP220 station where all the trigger information is merged. Thus the RP220 trigger FED acts as the master of the TOTEM trigger system, generating the global TOTEM L1 trigger decision and is also capable of sending 16 trigger bits to the CMS global trigger system [60] for common data taking with CMS in the future.

The synchronisation of the trigger generating bits is based on the BC0 signal (Beam Crossing Zero). This signal — related to the first bunch of a LHC beam revolution cycle — is issued every 3564 bunch crossings and broadcast by the TTC system. On the detector side, it is received via the control token ring and decoded by a VFAT Trigger Mezzanine (VTM) as shown in figure 7.7. It is then superimposed onto the trigger data stream transmitted to the counting-room. The trigger FEDs also receive the TTC signal including the BC0 signal. The trigger generating bits are then temporally aligned to the BCO signal. This scheme is also used for the 16 trigger bits sent to the CMS global trigger system.

Care also has to be taken in the synchronisation with respect to the transmission of the TOTEM first level trigger signal down to the "Local" and "On Detector" regions.

The level-1 trigger is transmitted to the detectors using the TTC system and the FEC card. The FEC card can adjust the phase of the fast commands and the clock. The latency of the VFAT can be adjusted to account for the differences in delay due to the spatial spread of the subdetectors and obtain synchronisation.

2008 JINST 3 S08007

Chapter 9

DAQ

9.1 Requirements

The Data Acquisition of the TOTEM experiment will perform different tasks depending on the running conditions:

- Initialisation and calibration of the front-end hardware

- TOTEM stand-alone data taking at a rate $\approx 1\,\mathrm{kHz}$;

- Data and Trigger quality monitoring;

- Data taking integrated in the CMS DAQ/Trigger system at a later stage.

9.1.1 Trigger and data rates

We consider that the upper limit of the total event size is $\approx 50\,\mathrm{kB}$. This data size is fixed since no zero-suppression is applied to the data. This choice greatly simplifies the task of evaluating the data rates and the resources needed to cope with them.

The data rate is easily computed as $50\,\mathrm{kB/event \cdot TriggerRate} = 50\,\mathrm{MB/s \cdot (TriggerRate/kHz)}$. We consider here that the standard trigger rate is $1\,\mathrm{kHz}$, with an upper limit (on redundant resources) of 2 to 3 kHz.

Two operational conditions can be envisaged:

- Calibration and Setup. The VFAT chips and related front-devices need to be initialised and calibrated before a normal run can start. The parameter space of the VFAT chip is particularly large, and its calibration procedure delicate; many different parameters need to be scanned in order to compute the optimal setting in terms of threshold and latency adjustments, taking into account the specific properties of each detector in terms of signal shape and timing. In these operating conditions the rates are typically much lower than in standard running mode, the limiting factor being the time needed to re-configure all the VFAT chips at every step of the parameter scan. We assume that a typical trigger rate in this running mode will be $\approx 100\,\mathrm{Hz}$, corresponding to $\approx 5\,\mathrm{MB/s}$

2008 JINST 3 S08007

- Once the system is properly calibrated and initialized with the computed parameters, the standard running mode can be started, and the data rate will solely be tuned by the trigger rate.

In both cases the data produced by the VFATs will flow through an infrastucture based on VME [56] and/or USB-2 (Universal Serial Bus) [61] links, independently from the one of the CMS experiment.

Irrespectively of the running mode (*standalone* or *CMS*) this *local DAQ* will always be used for setup and calibration.

9.1.2 CMS compatibility

In the special *CMS compatible* running mode, the raw data will flow through the CMS standard S-Link64 [58] lines, FRL boards and Myrinet infrastructure. The TOTEM FED boards (section 7.2.2) have been designed (as described in the relevant sections) to respect the CMS standard data format and control protocols when connected to the main CMS DAQ.

In this running mode, the *local* readout infrastructure will act as a parallel path, used for front-end initialization during the start-of-run procedures, and for data quality monitoring.

The TOTEM DAQ software is based on the same building blocks as the one of CMS. This will simplify the task of operating the TOTEM Run Control (and its end- and start-of-run procedures) system within the CMS one.

9.2 Implementation: readout chain and infrastructure

9.2.1 Readout link options

The TOTEM FED boards offer a large range of readout options.

- VME: We assume that the aggregated maximum data rate per VME crate is $\approx 40\,\mathrm{MB/s}$. Readout load splitting over > 1 VME crates is possible.
  VME is the standard communication link for hardware initialization. We decided to use a minimum 3 crates dedicated to readout FEDs to ease standalone operations of the 3 detectors during setting-up periods. One additional crate hosts the trigger FEDs. In these conditions, the minimal requirement of 1 kHz trigger is already largely satisfied.

- USB-2: Every FED carries 3 USB-2 links. If we assume the USB-2 standard to be capable of $10\,\mathrm{MB/s}$, the maximum aggregated data rate over the 20 available raw-data links amounts to $200\,\mathrm{MB/s}$, corresponding to a theoretical 4 to 5 kHz trigger rate. These numbers are challenging (although not impossible) at several levels of the DAQ system, from data transmission over the Ethernet network, to stress (and cost) of the storage system, to data mirroring in the Central Data Recording facilities. Full exploitation of these capabilities is out of the scope of the present activities, and therefore not foreseen for the moment. Suffice here to say that the TOTEM DAQ has abundant spare resources to accomodate the foreseen trigger rates.

2008 JINST 3 S08007

- S-Link: This can be considered either an electrical connection to a front-end PC (useful for laboratory testing) or the entry point into the main CMS DAQ data transport via FRL boards and the Myrinet infrastructure. It is the default option for the integration of TOTEM into the CMS DAQ and Trigger system.

9.2.2   PC cluster and local data storage

The TOTEM DAQ cluster will consist of a set of a few PCs (presently 5) for raw data readout over VME (or optionally USB), and a set of event-building and storage nodes sized to the needed storage rate and capacity.

The mimimum requirements for data storage is the ability to write data at the trigger rate of 1 to 2 kHz and the capacity to store data during one full day even in case of failure of data transfer to a central data recording system.

At the rate of 2 kHz, TOTEM will produce $\approx 360\,\text{GB}\,/\,\text{h}$, corresponding to $\approx 8.6\,\text{TB}$ of data per day of running. These capacities and rates can be easily accomodated in present medium-level storage systems based on Fiber-Channel [62] or iSCSI [63] technology. To ensure that the required rate is attained and to provide redundancy, the data load will be shared between ≥ 2 storage systems.

2008 JINST 3 S08007

Chapter 10

Detector Control System

10.1 Objectives

The Detector Control Systems (DCS) for LHC experiments are the evolution of slow control systems of the LEP era. Their aim is to permit the physicist on shift to operate and control various detector subsystems such as high and low voltage power supplies, gas circulation systems, cooling and so on, and monitor their performance as well as various relevant environmental parameters, for example temperature and radiation levels. All DCS systems of LHC experiments are built using the industrial PVSS control supervisory software running on networks of PCs (Windows and/or Linux), augmented with modules developed at CERN for typical HEP control functions and equipment, the JCOP framework. "Big.brother", the TOTEM DCS system, also uses the same guidelines, technology, tools and components.

10.2 Constraints

The TOTEM detector is located at the CMS intersection of the CERN LHC accelerator, and CMS and TOTEM also have a common physics program, so that TOTEM must be able to operate independently, but also take data together with CMS. For this reason TOTEM adopted a number of technological and organisational solutions that will permit interoperability at the level of electronics, DAQ, run control, offline data processing and so on. In the same fashion, the TOTEM detector control system is developed in the framework of the CMS DCS. This implies following the CMS DCS integration rules [64], liaising with CMS central controls, through participation in the CMS DCS coordination board, and adopting the same model of rack-mounted PCs.

10.3 Equipment under control

The three TOTEM subdetectors, Roman Pot silicon detectors, T1 and T2, require the monitoring and control of the usual equipment found around particle physics experiments. All three use CAEN HV power supplies, Wiener Maraton LV units, Wiener VME crates, and environmental sensors connected to ELMBs or read from the DAQ through the DCU technology. T1 and T2 are cooled with cold water loops derived from CMS rack cooling, while the Roman Pot Si detectors use a

2008 JINST 3 S08007

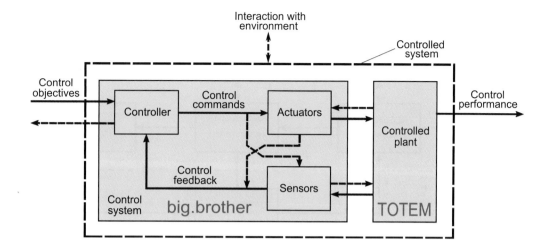

Figure 10.1: Generic control structure (adapted from [67], figure 1).

more sophisticated cooling plant. The T1 and T2 gas systems are subcontracted, including a PC running PVSS control software compliant with the GCS standard LHC gas control system [65].

The Roman Pot motor system is derived from the one of the LHC collimators, and so is the corresponding control system [66]. The front-end is based on National Instruments hardware and the Labview RealTime software, adapted to the selected sensors, and is subcontracted to PH/DT1. The high level control is also subcontracted, being derived from the Collimator Supervisory System, is integrated with the Central Collimation Application in the main control room, and sends status data and other relevant information to big.brother.

10.4 Engineering

Dealing with control, the system conforms to the standard control model of sensors, actuators and controllers depicted in figure 10.1.

The system consists of HW and SW components, therefore it requires comprehensive system engineering. As with any control system, the development process of big.brother is iterative vertically between system engineering and lower assembly engineering, and iterative horizontally between requirements engineering, design-configuration, verification-validation, and analysis (figure 10.2).

A number of HW and SW technologies have been defined already before the project started: sensors, front-end systems, the supervisory level based on PVSS and the JCOP Framework, the model of the PCs and their operating system.

The CMS DCS development model is federal, with independent subdetectors following their own engineering and project organisation, so far that as they use the agreed technology and obey the mandatory integration rules, dealing also with the definition and nesting of Finite States Machines (FSM) describing the state of the system. The situation is very different in ALICE, where the development model is centralised, and a number of engineering representations and software components have been developed centrally to be used by all subdetectors [68]. Big.brother has

2008 JINST 3 S08007

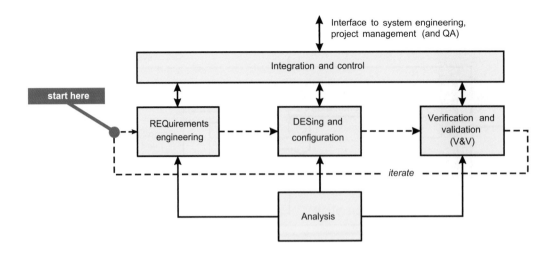

Figure 10.2: Horizontal development iteration.

adopted from ALICE DCS the requirements template, the format of the HW overview diagrams, and is considering to use some of the existing components, also for the user interface which is standardised across the three TOTEM subdetectors.

10.5 The Radiation Monitoring system —
an example of environmental monitoring

The Roman Pot silicon detectors, T1 and T2 together with their related readout electronics, are located in LHC areas where high radiation levels are expected (see for example figure 5.1 and ref. [69]). For this reason, the Total Ionising Dose (TID) and the 1-MeV neutron equivalent particle fluence (Φ_{eq}) will be monitored during operation in various locations of the TOTEM experiment, and they will be available on-line in the TOTEM DCS [70].

Measurements of TID and Φ_{eq} are needed to understand the radiation-induced changes on the detector performances, to survey the radiation damage on electronic components, to verify the TOTEM radiation field simulated with Monte Carlo codes and to survey anomalous increases of radiation levels that may arise from accidental radiation burst such as beam losses or unstable beams. This set of information can finally be used to better plan the detector operation scenario.

The basic unit of the TOTEM Radiation Monitoring (RADMON) system is the Integrated Sensor Carrier (ISC) that hosts radiation sensors connected to the electronics via readout cables. TID measurements are performed with different types of Radiation-sensing Field Effect Transistors (RadFETs), while Φ_{eq} measurements are performed with forward biased *p-i-n* diodes [71]. In both cases the dosimetric parameter (voltage) is measured upon constant current injection through the sensors. Selection of sensors, assembly of the ISC, as well as calibration constants are provided by the TS-LEA and PH-DT2 groups at CERN [72]. In the case of TOTEM each ISC will host four radiation sensors and a temperature probe, leading to a total of five channels to be read out per monitoring location.

2008 JINST 3 S08007

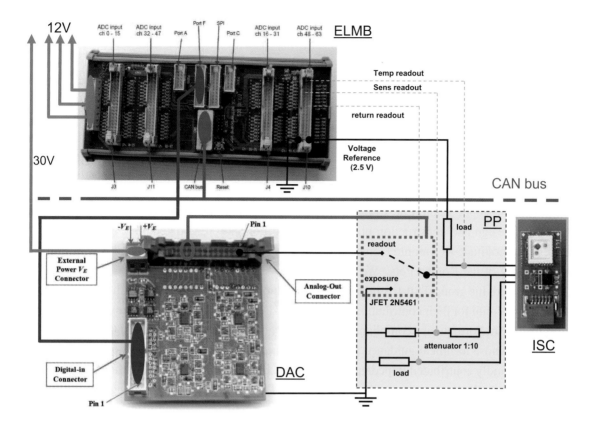

Figure 10.3: Schematic of the ELMB RADMON readout system used in TOTEM and based on the standard ATLAS electronics. This example of readout is referred to one ISC hosting 1 RADMON sensor and 1 temperature probe. On the right-hand side of the picture the ISC is visible. The readout current injected through each sensor is also monitored by measuring the voltage drop on a small resistor placed on the return line.

The design of the RADMON readout electronics in TOTEM follows the one developed by the ATLAS experiment where the sensor readout is based on Embedded Local Monitor Boards (ELMBs) [73]. As shown in figure 10.3, the readout of the ISC is based on an ELMB board, which communicate over the CAN bus with a PC running SCADA software (PVSSII) that is linked to the DCS. To drive currents through the sensors on the ISC during the readout sequence, ELMB-DAC boards are needed. The 16 channel, 12-bit DAC-module connects directly to the digital output of the ELMB motherboard. The ELMB and the ELMB-DAC finally interface with the ISC via patch panel (PP) boards. The PP host a series of JFET switches to short the sensor terminals to ground during radiation exposure and enable them for the readout. On the PP, voltage attenuators and loads to monitor the readout current sent to the radiation sensors are also present. One full readout chain consisting of 1 ELMB, 2 ELMB-DAC and 2 PP boards allows the readout of 6 ISCs in the TOTEM configuration. A total of 36 ISCs will be installed in the TOTEM experiment: one ISC will be integrated on each of the 24 RP motherboards, while 8 ISCs will be installed around T1 and 4 around T2 respectively.

2008 JINST 3 S08007

Acknowledgements

We thank Christophe Bault, Luc-Joseph Kottelat and Miranda Van Stenis for their invaluable help during the design and construction phases of Roman Pot and GEM detectors. We would like to express our gratitude to Antonio Goncalves Martins de Oliveira, Jerome Noel and Xavier Pons for the assembly of the Roman Pots. We appreciate the help of the section AT/VAC and Emmanuel Tsesmelis with his group TS/LEA during the installation phase. The help of Michele Battistin and Paolo Guglielmini for their contribution to the Roman Pot cooling system is warmly acknowledged.

Our RP radiofrequency compliance tests fully relied on the expertise of Fritz Caspers and Tom Kroyer for whose technical guidance and theoretical explanations we are very grateful. Federico Roncarolo kindly contributed impedance simulations, helping in understanding the measurements.

We thank all the members of the INTAS TOSTER Project (INTAS ref. no. 05-103-7533) for their help in the study of the edgeless CTS detector and for looking at new possibilities for radiation hard edgeless silicon detectors.

We are grateful to Ian Bohm, Didier Ferrere, Thierry Gys and Michael Moll for having made their test setup available and for interesting discussions.

We thank Maurice Glaser for all the irradiation works done for us at the CERN PS; and Marko Zavratanik, Igor Mandic and Gregor Kranberger for the irradiations at Triga (Ljubljana) and the support in the development of the radiation monitors.

We thank Chris Kenney and Sherwood Parker for providing the planar-3D and full-3D silicon detectors, studied in testbeams for the first time.

We acknowledge the excellent and careful work of the Petersburg Institute for Nuclear Physics who manufactured the cathode strip chambers for the T1 telescopes; in particular we would like to thank A. Vorobyev, A. Krivshich, V. Andreev and A. Fetysov for their leading and coordination effort.

We thank the Département de la Haute Savoie for funding the collaboration of CERN with C4i, Archamps, on the design of the VFAT chip, and the TS-DEM group for their contribution to the design and manufacturing of the electronics cards. In particular, we acknowledge the work performed by Rui de Oliveira, Betty Magnin, Manuel Sanchez Suarez, Pascal Vulliez, William Buillereau, Norbert Lopez, Jean-Marc Combe, Nicole Wauquier, Stephane Excoffier, Regine Couitti, Stephanie Kaznarek, Ercan Budun, Benilde Martins, Jean-Michel Baida and Sarah Pamelard. We also would like to thank Francoise Cossey Puget, Ian McGill, Antoine Guipet from the bonding lab for their efforts, and Francois Vasey, Karl Gill, Jan Troska, Robert Grabit and Alexander Singovski for their help on the optical components.

We thank Ferdinand Hahn and Herminio Rama-Regueiro for their contributions to the T1/T2 gas system.

2008 JINST 3 S08007

Paolo Palazzi's essential work on the Detector Control System is gratefully acknowledged.

Our testbeam experiments would not have been possible without the strong support from Christoph Rembser, Ilias Efthymiopoulos, Edda Gschwendtner and Christian Becquet.

Funding for the TOTEM experiment is provided by the following agencies:

- CERN;

- Academy of Sciences of the Czech Republic, Committee for Collaboration of the Czech Republic with CERN;

- Institute of Physics, Academy of Sciences of the Czech Republic;

- Estonian Academy of Sciences;

- Helsinki Institute of Physics (HIP), Finland;

- Istituto Nazionale di Fisica Naturale (INFN), Italy;

- National Science Foundation (NSF), USA.

- Case Western Reserve University, USA.

2008 JINST 3 S08007

TOTEM acronym list

AFEC	Anode Front-End Card of T1
BC0	Bunch Crossing Zero
BPM	Beam Position Monitor
CC	Coincidence Chip
CCMC	Coincidence Chip Mezzanine Card
CCU	Communication and Control Unit
CCUM	Communication and Control Unit Module
CFEC	Cathode Front-End Card of T1
CMM	Coordinate Measuring Machine
CNC	Computer Numerical Control
CSC	Cathode Strip Chamber
CTR	Current Terminating Ring
CTS	Current Terminating Structure
DAC	Digital-to-Analog Converter
DCS	Detector Control System
DCU	Detector Control Unit
DD	Double Diffraction
DOH	Digital Opto-Hybrid
DOHM	Digital Opto-Hybrid Module
DPE	Double Pomeron Exchange or central diffraction
ELMB	Embedded Local Monitor Board
ENC	Equivalent Noise Charge
FEC	Front-End Controller
FED	Front-End Driver
FRL	Front-End Readout Link
FPGA	Field-Programmable Gate Array
GEM	Gas Electron Multiplier
GOH	Gigabit Optical Hybrid
I^{2}C	Inter-Integrated Circuit (multi-master serial computer bus used to attach low-speed peripherals to a motherboard)
IP	Interaction Point
LVDS	Low-Voltage Differential Signalling
PCB	Printed Circuit Board

2008 JINST 3 S08007

PT100	Platinum (Pt) resistance thermometer with a resistance of $100\,\Omega$ at $0°C$
ROC	Read-Out Card
RP	Roman Pot
RP Unit	Ensemble of 2 vertical and 1 horizontal RP
RP Station	Ensemble of 2 RP Units
SCR	Slow Control Ring
SD	Single Diffraction
SEU	Single Event Upset
TDC	Time-to-Digital Converter
TTC	Timing, Trigger and Control
VFAT	Historical name inherited from the predecessor chip: Very Forward ATLAS and TOTEM chip
VTM	VFAT Trigger Mezzanine

Bibliography

[1] TOTEM collaboration, V. Berardi et al., *Total cross-section, elastic scattering and diffraction dissociation at the Large Hadron Collider at CERN: TOTEM technical design report*, CERN-LHCC-2004-002, http://cdsweb.cern.ch/record/704349; *Addendum* CERN-LHCC-2004-020, http://cdsweb.cern.ch/record/743753.

[2] THE CMS AND TOTEM DIFFRACTIVE AND FORWARD PHYSICS WORKING GROUP, M. Albrow et al., *Prospects for diffractive and forward physics at the LHC*, CERN-LHCC-2006-039, http://cdsweb.cern.ch/record/1005180.

[3] CDF collaboration, F. Abe et al., *Measurement of the antiproton-proton total cross section at $\sqrt{s} = 546$ and $1800\,GeV$, Phys. Rev.* **D 50** (1994) 5550.

[4] E710 collaboration, N.A. Amos et al., *Measurement of the $\bar{p}p$ total cross section at $\sqrt{s} = 1.8\,TeV$, Phys. Rev. Lett.* **63** (1989) 2784;
E710 collaboration, N.A. Amos et al., *A luminosity independent measurement of the $\bar{p}p$ total cross-section at $\sqrt{s} = 1.8\,TeV$, Phys. Lett.* **B 243** (1990) 158;
E811 collaboration, C. Avila et al., *A measurement of the proton-antiproton total cross-section at $\sqrt{s} = 1.8\,TeV$, Phys. Lett.* **B 445** (1999) 419;
E 811 collaboration, C. Avila et al., *The ratio, ρ, of the real to the imaginary part of the $\bar{p}p$ forward elastic scattering amplitude at $\sqrt{s} = 1.8\,TeV$, Phys. Lett.* **B 537** (2002) 41.

[5] J.R. Cudell et al., *Benchmarks for the forward observables at RHIC, the Tevatron-Run II, and the LHC, Phys. Rev. Lett.* **89** (2002) 201801.

[6] TOTEM collaboration, K. Eggert et al., *TOTEM Physics, Proceedings of 17th rencontre de Blois: 11th International Conference on Elastic and Diffractive Scattering*, Château de Blois France (2005), `hep-ex/0602025`.

[7] M.M. Islam, R.J. Luddy and A.V. Prokudin, *Near forward pp elastic scattering at LHC and nucleon structure, Int. J. Mod. Phys.* **A 21** (2006) 1;
C. Bourrely, J. Soffer and T.-T. Wu, *Impact-picture phenomenology for $\pi^{\pm}p, K^{\pm}p$ and $pp, \bar{p}p$ elastic scattering at high energies, Eur. Phys. J.* **C 28** (2003) 97;
V.A. Petrov, E. Predazzi and A. Prokudinl, *Coulomb interference in high-energy pp and $\bar{p}p$ scattering, Eur. Phys. J.* **C 28** (2003) 525;
M.M. Block, E.M. Gregores, F. Halzen and G. Pancheri, *Photon proton and photon photon scattering from nucleon nucleon forward amplitudes, Phys. Rev.* **D 60** (1999) 054024.

2008 JINST 3 S08007

[8] G.B. West and D. Yennie, *Coulomb interference in high-energy scattering*, *Phys. Rev.* **172** (1968) 1413.

[9] V. Kundrát, J. Kašpar and M. Lokajíček, *To the theory of high-energy elastic nucleon collisions*, *Proceedings of the Blois'07/EDS07 Workshop on Elastic and Diffractive Scattering*, Hamburg Germany (2007), arXiv:0712.1503.

[10] U. Amaldi et al., *The energy dependence of the proton proton total cross-section for center-of-mass energies between* 23 *and* 53 *GeV*, *Phys. Lett.* **B 44** (1973) 112.

[11] TOTEM collaboration, M. Deile et al., *Tests of a Roman Pot prototype for the TOTEM experiment*, *Proceedings of the* 2005 *Particle Accelerator Conference*, Knoxville, Tennessee U.S.A. (2005), arXiv:physics/0507080v1 [physics.ins-det];
M. Deile et al., *Beam Coupling Impedance Measurement and Mitigation for a TOTEM Roman Pot*, Proceedings of the *11th European Particle Accelerator Conference (EPAC08)*, Genova, Italy (2008), arXiv:0806.4974v1 [physics.ins-det].

[12] V. Avati et al., *First test of cold edgeless silicon microstrip detectors*, *Nucl. Instrum. Meth.* **A 518** (2004) 264.

[13] G. Ruggiero et al., *Planar edgeless silicon detectors for the TOTEM experiment*, *IEEE Trans. Nucl. Sci.* **52** (2005) 1899.

[14] E. Noschis, V. Eremin and G. Ruggiero, *Simulations of planar edgeless silicon detectors with a current terminating structure*, *Nucl. Instrum. Meth.* **A 574** (2007) 420.

[15] ISE Integrated Systems Engineering AG release 6, online at www.ise.ch.

[16] V. Vacek, G. Hallewell, S. Ilie and S. Lindsay, *Perfluorocarbons and their use in cooling systems for semiconductor particle detectors*, *Fluid Phase Equilibr.* **174** (2000) 191.

[17] E. Noschis et al., *Final size planar edgeless silicon detectors for the TOTEM experiment*, *Nucl. Instrum. Meth.* **A 563** (2006) 41.

[18] L. Jones, *APV25-S1 user guide version* 2.2,
http://www.ins.clrc.ac.uk/INS/Electronic_Systems/
Microelectronics_Design/Projects/High_Energy_Physics/CMS/APV25-S1/index.html.

[19] G. Ruggiero et al., *Planar edgeless silicon detectors for the TOTEM experiment*, *Nucl. Instrum. Meth.* **A 582** (2007) 854.

[20] H.W. Kraner, Z. Li and K.U. Posnecker, *Fast neutron damage in silicon detectors*, *Nucl. Instrum. Meth.* **A 279** (1989) 266.

[21] TOSTER project, *INTAS collaborative call with CERN 2005*, INTAS Ref. Nr. 05-103-7533.

[22] C. Kenney et al., *Active-edge planar radiation sensors*, *Nucl. Instrum. Meth.* **A 565** (2006) 272.

[23] S.I. Parker, C.J. Kenney and J. Segal, *3D — A proposed new architecture for solid state radiation detectors*, *Nucl. Instr. Meth.* **A 395** (1997) 328;
C.J. Kenney, S.I. Parker, J. Segal and C. Storment, *Silicon detectors with 3D electrode arrays fabrication and initial test results*, *IEEE Trans. Nucl. Sci.* **46** (1999) 1224;
C.J. Kenney, S.I. Parker and E. Walckiers, *Results from 3D silicon sensors with wall electrodes: near-cell-edge sensitivity measurements as a preview of active-edge sensors*, *IEEE Trans. Nucl. Sci.* **48** (2001) 2405.

[24] C. Da Già et. al, *3D active edge silicon detector tests with* $120\,GeV$ *muons*, submitted to *IEEE Trans. Nucl. Sci.*.

[25] S. Parker and C. Kenney, *Performance of 3-D architecture silicon sensors after intense proton irradiation*, *IEEE Trans. Nucl. Sci.* **48** (2001) 1629;
C. Da Già and S. Watts, *Can silicon detectors survive beyond* 10^{15} *neutrons* cm^{-2}?, *Nucl. Instrum. Meth.* **A 501** (2003) 138;
C. Da Già et al., *Advances in silicon detectors for particle tracking in extreme radiation environments*, *Nucl. Instrum. Meth.* **A 509** (2003) 86;
C. Da Già et al., *Radiation hardness properties of full-3D active edge silicon sensors*, *Nucl. Instrum. Meth.* **A 587** (2008) 243.

[26] *NEEDS Workshop Discussion* in *Very High Energy Cosmic Ray Interactions*:
L.W. Jones, *Introduction to the discussion of the "NEEDS" workshop*, Nucl. Phys. B (Proc. Suppl.)**122** (2003) 433;
R. Engel, *Extensive air showers and accelerator data — the NEEDS workshop*, Nucl. Phys. B (Proc. Suppl.)**122** (2003) 437;
K. Eggert, *The TOTEM/CMS forward experiment at the LHC*, Nucl. Phys. B (Proc. Suppl.)**122** (2003) 447;
D. Heck, *Importance of forward interactions for cosmic ray air shower simulations*, Nucl. Phys. B (Proc. Suppl.)**122** (2003) 451;
R. Jörg and R. Hörandel, *Test of high-energy hadronic interaction models with KASCADE — Particle physics with air shower detectors*, Nucl. Phys. B (Proc. Suppl.)**122** (2003) 455;
G. Schatz, *Summary of the NEEDS workshop*, Nucl. Phys. B (Proc. Suppl.) **122** (2003) 462;
Proceedings of 12th International Symposium on Very High-Energy Cosmic Ray Interactions (ISVHECRI 2002), Geneva, Switzerland, 15-20 July (2002), [NEEDS workshop: http://www-ik.fzk.de/~needs].

[27] G. Bencze et al., *Position and timing resolution of interpolating cathode strip chambers in a test beam*, *Nucl. Instrum. Meth.* **A 357** (1995) 40.

[28] M. Huhtinen, *Radiation levels at detector*, *Presentation at TOTEM T1 CSC engineering design review*, 7 March 2006, CERN, Switzerland, http://indico.cern.ch/conferenceDisplay.py?confId=a061338.

[29] D. Acosta et al., *Aging tests of full-scale CMS muon cathode strip chambers*, *Nucl. Instrum. Meth.* **A 515** (2003) 226, Fermilab-Conf-03-307, http://cdsweb.cern.ch/record/808006.

2008 JINST 3 S08007

[30] ATLAS collaboration, *ATLAS muon spectrometer: Technical Design Report*, CERN-LHCC-97-022 chapter 6, http://cdsweb.cern.ch/record/331068.

[31] CMS collaboration, *The CMS muon project: Technical Design Report*, CERN-LHCC-97-032, http://cdsweb.cern.ch/record/343814.

[32] LHCB collaboration, P.R. Barbosa-Marinho et al., *LHCb technical design report* 4, CERN-LHCC-2001-010, http://cdsweb.cern.ch/record/504326.

[33] S. Minutoli, *TOTEM T1 electronics system, Presented at the TOTEM T1 CSC engineering design review*, 7 March 2006, CERN, Switzerland, http://indico.cern.ch/conferenceDisplay.py?confId=a061338.

[34] P. Moreira et al., *A Radiation Tolerant Gigabit Serializer for LHC data Transmission*, 7th *Workshop on Electronics for LHC Experiments*, Stockholm Sweden (2001), http://cdsweb.cern.ch/record/588665; J. Grahl, *GOL Opto-Hybrid Manufacturing Specifications*, v. 3.30, CERN-CMS ECAL (2003).

[35] CMS TRACKER collaboration, *CMS Tracker control link specification. Part 2: front-end digital optohybrid*, CERN EP/CME, CERN EDMS document archive CMS-TK-ES-0019, version 2.2.

[36] C. Paillard et al., *The CCU25: a network oriented communication and control unit integrated circuit in a 0.25μm CMOS technology*, 8th *Workshop on Electronics for LHC Experiments*, Colmar France (2002), http://cdsweb.cern.ch/record/593914.

[37] L.S. Durkin, *CMS muon endcap cathode FE board — Electronic system review*, CERN, Switzerland, 18 September 2000.

[38] G. Antchev et al., *A data readout module for the TOTEM experiment, Proceedings of NEC2005*, Varna, Bulgaria (2005), http://cdsweb.cern.ch/record/1069893.

[39] A. Marchioro et al., *A PLL-delay ASIC for clock recovery and trigger distribution in the CMS tracker*, 3rd *Workshop on Electronics for LHC Experiments*, London U.K. (1997). P. Moreira et al., *CMS Tracker PLL Reference Manual - v. 2.1*, CERN - EP/MIC, July 2000, http://cdsweb.cern.ch/record/1069705.

[40] CAEN s.p.a., *MOD. A1550: 24 channel 5kV/1mA common floating RTN board, technical information manual - rev 0*, 6 July 2007.

[41] CAEN s.p.a., *MOD. SY1527: Universal Multichannel Power Supply System, User Manual-rev.13*, 6 October 2005.

[42] WIENER GmbH, *MARATHON Power Supply System, Technical Manual — v. 00691.A0*, 20 June 2006.

[43] F. Sauli, *GEM: A new concept for electron amplification in gas detectors*, Nucl. Instrum. Meth. **A 386** (1997) 531.

[44] C. Altunbas et al., *Construction, test and commissioning of the triple-GEM tracking detector for compass*, *Nucl. Instrum. Meth.* **A 490** (2002) 177;
B. Ketzer et al., *Performance of triple GEM tracking detectors in the COMPASS experiment*, *Nucl. Instrum. Meth.* **A 535** (2004) 314.

[45] M. Alfonsi et al., *High-rate particle triggering with triple-GEM detector*, *Nucl. Instrum. Meth.* **A518** (2004) 106.

[46] H. Andersson et al., *Analysis of compounds released from various detector materials and their impact on aging characteristics of proportional counters*, *IEEE Trans. Nucl. Sci.* **51** (2004) 2110.

[47] The MAD-X program, Methodical Accelerator Design, http://www.cern.ch/mad.

[48] H. Niewiadomski, *Reconstruction of proton tracks in the TOTEM Roman Pot detectors at the LHC*, PhD Thesis, University of Manchester, U.K. (2008).

[49] LHC Layout, http://www.cern.ch/lhclayout/.

[50] M. Deile, *Algebraic determination of Roman Pot acceptance and resolution for the $\beta^* = 1540\,m$ optics*, TOTEM Note 2006-002.

[51] J. Kašpar, *Reconstruction of elastic events*, TOTEM Note 2007-007.

[52] P. Aspell et al., *VFAT2: a front-end system on chip providing fast trigger information, digitized data storage and formatting for the charge sensitive readout of multi-channel silicon and gas particle detectors*, *Proceedings of TWEPP-07, Topical Workshop on Electronics for Particle Physics*, Prague Czech Republic (2007), http://cdsweb.cern.ch/record/1069906.

[53] http://www.cern.ch/TTC/intro.html;
J. Troska et al., *Implementation of the timing, trigger and control system of the CMS experiment*, *IEEE Trans. Nucl. Sci.* **53** (2006) 834.

[54] F. Drouhin et al., *The control system for the CMS tracker front-end*, *IEEE Trans. Nucl. Sci.* **49** (2002) 846.

[55] G. Antchev et al., *The TOTEM front end driver, its components and applications in the TOTEM experiment*, *Proceedings of TWEPP-07, topical workshop on electronics for particle physics*, Prague Czech Republic (2007), http://cdsweb.cern.ch/record/1069713.

[56] ITA, *VME technology specifications*, VME64x 9U × 400 mm Format, ANSI/VITA 1.3-1997 (R2003), http://www.vita.com/specifications.html.

[57] CMS collaboration, *The TriDAS project: Technical Design Report. Volume 2: data-acquisition and high-level trigger*, CERN-LHCC-2002-026, http://cdsweb.cern.ch/record/578006.

2008 JINST 3 S08007

[58] A. Racz et al., *The S-LINK 64 bit extension specification: S-LINK64*, CERN-EP-2003, http://cmsdoc.cern.ch/cms/TRIDAS/horizontal/docs/slink64.pdf.

[59] E. Noschis et al., *Protection circuit for the T2 readout electronics of the TOTEM experiment*, *Nucl. Instrum. Meth.* **A 572** (2007) 378.

[60] CMS collaboration, *CMS TriDAS project: Technical Design Report. Volume 1: the trigger systems*, CERN-LHCC-2000-038, http://cdsweb.cern.ch/record/706847.

[61] USB 2.0 specifications, http://www.usb.org/developers/docs/.

[62] Fiber Channel Tutorial, http://www.iol.unh.edu/services/testing/fc/training/tutorials/fc_tutorial.php.

[63] The iSCSI specification, http://tools.ietf.org/html/rfc3720.

[64] F. Glege, R. Gómez-Reino and J. Varela, *CMS DCS integration guidelines* 3.0, http://cmsdoc.cern.ch/cms/TRIDAS/DCS/central_dcs/guidelines.

[65] R. Barillère, *LHC gas control systems: a common approach for the control of the LHC experiments gas systems*, CERN-JCOP-2002-14, http://cdsweb.cern.ch/record/1070768; see also http://itcofe.web.cern.ch/itcofe/Projects/LHC-GCS.

[66] S. Redaelli, *Application software for the LHC collimators and movable elements*, CERN LHC-TCT-ES-0001, EDMS 826861, http://cdsweb.cern.ch/record/1070288.

[67] The European Cooperation for Space Standardisation, Space engineering - Control engineering, ECSS-E-60A ESA Publications (2004), http://www.ecss.nl.

[68] A. Augustinus, *ALICE DCS User Requirements Document*, http://alicedcs.web.cern.ch/AliceDCS/URD.

[69] N.V. Mokhov, I.L. Rakhno, J.S. Kerby and J.B. Strait, *Protecting LHC IP1/IP5 components against radiation resulting form colliding beam interactions*, LHC Project Report 633, http://citeseer.ist.psu.edu/609257.html.

[70] F. Ravotti et al., *Conception of an integrated sensor for the radiation monitoring of the CMS experiment at the large hadron collider*, *IEEE Trans. Nucl. Sci.* **51** (2004) 3642.

[71] F. Ravotti et al., *Radiation monitoring in mixed environments at CERN, from the IRRAD6 facility to the LHC experiments*, *IEEE Trans. Nucl. Sci.* **54** (2007) 1170.

[72] F. Ravotti, M. Glaser and M. Moll, *Sensor catalogue data compilation of solid-state sensors for radiation monitoring*, CERN-TS-NOTE-2005-002, http://cdsweb.cern.ch/record/835408.

[73] F. Ravotti, F. Lucas-Rodriguez and E. Dimovasili, *Technical and functional specification of the TOTEM on-line radiation monitoring system*, CERN EDMS 874945 https://edms.cern.ch/document/874945

2008 JINST 3 S08007